From an original Portrait in the Senate Chamber of Massachusetts.

Jo: Winthrop:

GOVERNOR OF MASSACHUSETTS.

THE

HISTORY OF NEW ENGLAND

FROM

1630 TO 1649.

BY

JOHN WINTHROP, ESQ.

FIRST GOVERNOUR OF THE COLONY OF THE MASSACHUSETTS BAY.

FROM

HIS ORIGINAL MANUSCRIPTS.

WITH NOTES

TO ILLUSTRATE

THE CIVIL AND ECCLESIASTICAL CONCERNS, THE GEOGRAPHY, SETTLEMENT, AND INSTITUTIONS OF THE COUNTRY, AND THE LIVES AND MANNERS OF THE PRINCIPAL PLANTERS.

BY JAMES SAVAGE,

PRESIDENT OF THE MASSACHUSETTS HISTORICAL SOCIETY.

A NEW EDITION,

WITH ADDITIONS AND CORRECTIONS BY THE FORMER EDITOR.

VOL. I.

Sæpe audivi, Q. Maximum, P. Scipionem, præterea civitatis nostræ præclaros viros, solitos ita dicere, cum majorum imagines intuerentur, vehementissime sibi animum ad virtutem accendi.

Sallust, Bell. Jugurth. c. iv.

BOSTON:

LITTLE, BROWN AND COMPANY.

MDCCCLIII.

CAMBRIDGE:
ALLEN AND FARNHAM, PRINTERS.

PREFACE

TO THIS EDITION.

For nearly six years Winthrop's History of New England has been out of print. Moved by the steadily increasing interest of liberal minds in studying the original materials of our country's story, I acknowledge the duty of supplying some addition and some correction to the results of my research, bestowed with so high delight on the former edition. Most of the corrections are, indeed, too slight to be set forth here, and may be passed, as they are generally introduced, in silence. Of some it may be better to speak. A change will be observed in the order of several of the family epistles, the most attractive part of the Appendix; and this may be approved, or not, as the judgment of the reader decides on the chronological arrangement, that depended on conjecture in a few cases, to which this change relates. Citation of authorities, in works of this character, is of prime importance; and how the references will be verified, should determine the manner in which they are to be presented. It seemed to me most respectful to students of these pages, who might prefer to search for themselves, to assume that such inquiries would be prosecuted in some public library, where the best editions of the authors to be consulted are to be found; and therefore my special citations from the Magnalia are to be sought in the original London folio, of MDCCII. Whatever value be set on that work of Mather, the learned author may justly claim, that his own division into seven books, with chapters and sections numbered, shall be obeyed, instead of quoting the page of volume I. or II. of a modern 8vo. which, in decency, must preserve the same books, chapter and sections, but otherwise may vary with every caprice. So too my respect for the History of Hutchinson, the great authority for the early annals of Massachusetts, led me to follow the pages of the London edition, though formerly I had cited one of the Boston editions, in which the enumeration is quite diverse from the other.

Enlargement of the notes, both in number and substance, needs no specification. Some benefit hasfollowed from one or another in the preceding impression. To have been the means of correcting no trifling error in such widely respected authors, as honest Anthony Wood, the generous tory, and honest Andrew Marvell, the uncompromising republican, is some reason for rejoicing; but in charging, Vol. II. 241, the noble editor of Pepys's Memoirs with mistake in the affiliation of Downing, I am taught, by my own lapse, to rejoice with trembling. Emanuel is expressly called, by Hutchinson, Vol. II. 2, "father of Sir George Downing." More than a quarter of a century has been enjoyed the satisfaction of uniting my name, in however humble degree, with that of the ever honored first Governour of the colony of Massachusetts Bay; and I have not slighted the opportunities for enlarging our acquaintance with his early family relations, as they occurred in this country or in England.

Want of knowledge about two of the Governour's sons, was especially regretted by his readers. That Mather, our first resort, commonly, for instruction as to the founders of New England, should give no light upon Forth, or the younger sons of the Governour, is less observable than his errors about the eldest, whom he particularly desired to honor, in his biography of the first Governour of the United Colony of Connecticut.

His blunder as to "a liberal education at the University, first of Cambridge in England, and then of Dublin in Ireland," that misled Belknap, and others of our most assiduous inquirers, may have an apology, since he seldom touched any thing that he did not confound, in his melting into one the education of Forth and of John. Never was the latter, probably, at Cambridge, unless for an hour or two to visit his younger brother; and he was only sixteen, when he went to Dublin. By the Registrar of the University, who examined the records, at my request, in June, 1850, it was certified, that Forth "was matriculated a Pensioner of Emanuel College on the 4th of July, 1626, having been admitted on the boards of that college in the preceding April;" and he added, "I do not find that any other of the Winthrop family were ever members of this University in the 17th century." How little reverence is by the Magnalia given to exact chronology, the best element of truth in history, appears a few lines later, in telling of this son's election, as a magistrate, "though not above twenty three years of age;" whilst only four sentences back he had given the *true* date of his birth, and, in the same line with his heedless assertion, had proved that he was more than twenty-five years and eight months old on first landing in the country. In fact, when chosen, he wanted but three days of the age of twenty-six years and three months.

The difficult question of the relationship between this Governor of Connecticut and Hugh Peters has obtained solution just as the later sheets of this work were passing under the press. That Peters was an undergraduate, not sixteen years old, at Cambridge, when the second wife of the younger Winthrop was baptized, rendered certain our denial, that she was his daughter; but my friend, Charles Deane, Esquire, of Cambridge, who corroborated my opinion by strong statement of facts, after long fruitless search, acquired the probable explication of the words of Williams and others on this subject. His first wife, the "*gentlewoman*," of whom Peters, in his Legacy to an only child, refers, was "one Mistress Read, a widow woman, dwelling near unto him," when he taught a free school at Maldon in Essex, or its vicinity, who befriended him in his poverty, "had children, and an estate of two or three hundred pounds yearly." I suppose she was some years older than this new husband, bore him no offspring, and died, perhaps, before coming to this country; at least Felt, in his list of members of the church in the time of Peters, does not show her name. This approach to explanation is gained from "the Life and Death of Hugh Peters, by William Yonge, Dr. Med. London, 1663," a very curious, and more scarce tract. The wife of Winthrop was Eliz. daughter of Col. Read of Essex.

Necessity of re-examining the question of authority of Wheelwright's deed from the Indians led to some more light on a clear case; and it may seem to some that to this, as well as the subject of claim to the title of first Governour of Massachusetts in Captain Endicott or Roger Conant, too large room is given. Exposure of the infirmity of unhappy Thomas Welde, in his Short Story of the Rise, Reign, and Ruin of Antinomianism, will compensate, I think, the curious hunter in bibliography.

June, 1853.

PREFACE

TO THE SECOND EDITION.

Early in the spring of 1816 was discovered, in the tower of the Old South Church in Boston, the third volume of the History of New England, in the original MS. of the author, John Winthrop, first governour of the Massachusetts Bay. When the precious book was presented to the Massachusetts Historical Society, at their next meeting, 25 April, the difficulty of transcribing it for the press seemed to appall several of the most competent members, whose engagement in more important duties afforded also a sufficient excuse for leaving such labor to be undertaken by any one, at any time, who could devote to it many weeks of leisure. The task appeared inviting to me. On the same evening the MS. was taken, and the study of its chirography was begun, the next day, by the aid of one of the former MSS. collated with the printed volume, usually called Winthrop's Journal. Of all the three MSS. and of the published Journal, a sufficient account may be seen in 2 Hist. Coll. IV. 200.

Before the collation of the former MS. with the volume printed in 1790 had proceeded through many pages, the discovery of numerous important errors seemed to make a new edition of the earlier part of the History very desirable; and when a transcript of the new-found volume was completed, my resolution was fixed, that it should not be printed without a perfect revision of the Journal. Notes, explanatory, in some instances, of the text, illustrating, in some degree, the biography of many persons named in it, and referring to better accounts of others than I could furnish, were thought necessary. Several hundred notes were prepared, and a careful collation of the whole printed volume, for the second time, with the original volumes of MS. was finished on 2 June, 1819. Being then required to visit a foreign country, all my preparations were suspended until I returned. Care, however, was taken to leave the corrected copy of the printed volume, with my copy of the third part, to be kept safely. Again called abroad in 1822, I so carefully disposed of my copy of the third volume, as to leave it in a forgotten place, which afforded me the gratification of making a new one, begun 8 December, 1823, and finished 30 March, 1824. This circumstance admonished me of the propriety of adopting early measures for guarding against farther accidents of that kind. Application was made, at the next session of the General Court of this commonwealth, by the Historical Society, for encouragement of the publication. In consequence of the liberal aid of the Legislature, the volume comes thus early before the public.

To the account of the three MSS. above referred to, may be added, that the whole had been in possession of Hubbard, the reverend historian of Ipswich, who made the basis, and much the most valuable part of his work, out of Winthrop's materials, using them commonly without other labor than literal copying, and disposing them in a different order. See page 297 of this volume, for an estimate of the value of that work. Nor can I forgive the slight use of these invaluable documents, which is evinced by Mather, the unhappy author of Magnalia Christi Americana, who, in the hurry of composing that endless work, seems to have preferred useless quotations of worthless books, two or three centuries older, or popular and corrupt traditions, to the full matter and precise statement of facts, dates, principles, and motives, furnished by authentic history. That he possessed these MSS. is plain enough from his citations of several passages in his Life of our author, book II. cap. 4. Perhaps he grudged the time, which must have been consumed by a devoted study of the volumes; for no other excuse can I imagine for his clumsy abbreviation of that excellent speech in § 9, that will appear in our next volume. From this mutilated transcript of Mather, we may presume, the authors of the Modern Universal History condensed and adorned, in vol. XXXIX. 291, 2, their report, as if delivered in St. Stephen's chapel, of "the following speech, which is equal to any thing of antiquity, whether we consider it as coming from a philosopher or a magistrate." It may be seen, also, in the valuable Summary History of New England by Hannah Adams, 79, 80. Agreeable as this commendation of the London compilers is, the original address from Winthrop's own pen is far superior to their copy, and its simplicity is injured by their decorations. One would as soon exchange a portrait of full size from the life for an engraving in duodecimo, as receive the version of the oration in the Universal History for our author's report of his "little speech."

These venerable MSS. afterwards were in the hands of Prince, who used part of the first in compiling his Annals, II. Hutchinson, we know, did not enjoy the use of them.

Of the title of this work, it may be desirable for the reader to understand, that it is the exact language of the author. In the first volume of MS., indeed, it is not used, nor is any other designation given to the book. But Prince labels it "History of New England, by John Winthrop, governour of the Massachusetts," and both the other MS. volumes begin, in the writer's own hand, "A Continuation of the History of New England." Perhaps it would be more gratifying, could we determine, whether Winthrop designed by this term the colony of Massachusetts only, or all the country, before 1628 and since 1660, usually called New England. It is plain enough, that, in the early part of his work, his regards are confined to Massachusetts proper, exclusive of Maine, New Hampshire, and Plimouth; nor is there, in later parts, so liberal a narrative of those colonies, or of Rhode Island and Connecticut, as we should be happy to receive from one so well acquainted with the history of all. Johnson certainly means, by New England, Massachusetts alone; and the omission of regular notices, by our author, of the annual elections, and, indeed, of all other incidents in each of the other colonies, except those incidents had close connexion with our colony, leaves it beyond question, that the name must have the same interpretation. Letters from private persons on the other side of the ocean were frequently addressed to John Winthrop, governour of New England. Sir William Berkley, the royal governour of Virginia, employs the same style; and the king and council usually designate *this* colony New England. Perhaps the great confederation of the four colonies in 1643, extended the name to them, or rather deprived Massachusetts of its improper appropriation. The next year the patent for Providence Plantations in New England was obtained, which name would certainly not have been allowed by their neighbors without authority of parliament.

My duty has called for a very scrupulous attention to the exact phraseology of the original MS. and the reader may confidently receive this text of Winthrop for a correct one, verified by collation of his autograph at three several periods in different years. The integrity of the text has, indeed, been as great an object of my labor, as the preparation of notes. Yet mistakes may have occurred; for, at different times, the same word has sometimes been variously read by me. The venerable authorities will remain in the archives of the Historical

Society for my correction by any one, who doubts of the faithfulness of a single passage.

Perhaps some of my readers will be pleased with an explanation of the style, or supputation, of the year. Before 1752, the year was, by the legal method of computation, held to begin on 25 March, Lady Day, or Annunciation, so called from the notion entertained by the church, that the event recorded in the gospel of Luke, i. 26—38, occurred on that day. The general practice of England had, indeed, several years earlier, conformed to that of the rest of Christendom, in making the first of January new year's day; and the law, at last, followed the popular wisdom, as usual, in the correction. But, in our author's time, the custom coincided with the law. It is of more importance, however, to remark, that, in reckoning the months, March was called the first, February the twelfth, September, October, November, and December, then having, consistent with their Latin etymology, the numerical rank, which is now lost. Yet it is still more important to be noticed, that a very dangerous diversity existed in styling the year by its old numeral until 25 March, or giving it the new designation from the beginning of that month. In the Appendix, A. 37, 38, 39, 40, our author dates the old year, and such course is generally followed through the History, though sometimes he varied. I have preferred uniformity with his general custom. In the Appendix G., Davenport and Gov. Eaton use 1638, where Winthrop would have written 1637. Numerous errors from this source are observable in all the writers on our early history; and even the most careful sometimes fall into them. The accurate Hutchinson, I. 16, 17, mentions the purchase by our company from the Plimouth council, 19 March, 1627, and the charter from the king, confirming the same, 4 March, 1628, in which we might suppose he followed the old style. But the first election of officers, pursuant to the charter, on the last

Wednesday in Easter term, he makes 13 May, 1628, by which we see his mistake. It was 1629.

An apology may be expected by the public for my references to the edition of Morton's Memorial by Judge Davis, when that work is not published. It is easily made. The work had been several years nearly finished, when I began my labor in 1816; and the liberal editor, — liberal in every thing but withholding from the community the fruit of so many years acquisition, — allowed me freely to peruse his notes. His friends might reasonably expect, that the volume would be soon issued of which nineteen-twentieths had so long been printed. My good fortune, however, permits the present publication to appear without the peril of a comparison with one, by which it must be so greatly overshadowed. If that long-desired work is to be postponed during the life of the editor, the community will gladly prolong their eager expectation.

For assistance received in the progress of my work, no other acknowledgments than will be seen in the notes is required by the living or the dead. But Hutchinson, Eliot, Bradford, Prince, Hazard, and other deceased writers, — Holmes, Davis, Allen, and other living ones, — are common property. The freedom used by me in correcting their errors will, I hope, entitle my humble notes to the same regard.

Hanc veniam petimusque damusque vicissim.

It would be thought only a childish affectation to give here the names of all, who lent their aid in rendering this book minutely accurate; yet, after all my obligation to them, it is expedient, for greater benefits than all their kindness bestowed, to refer to the free and unexhausted field, the soil of which is only partially turned up to the day, that lies for the cultivation of any, in our Colony, County, Town, and Church Records, whence the information derived will be equally abundant and authentic. There is, however, one gentleman, to whom my readers will feel so much indebted, that to withhold his name would be greater affectation than to publish it. My friend, James Bowdoin, Esq., procured for me most of the articles in the Appendix, especially the family letters, received from his cousin, Francis B. Winthrop, Esq., of New Haven, which will, no doubt, be thought the most valuable appendage to the History of their great ancestor.

The title page, dedication, and preface of the former edition are here added.

A

JOURNAL

OF THE

TRANSACTIONS AND OCCURRENCES IN THE SETTLEMENT OF MASSACHUSETTS AND THE OTHER NEW ENGLAND COLONIES, FROM THE YEAR 1630 TO 1644.

WRITTEN BY

JOHN WINTHROP, ESQ.,

FIRST GOVERNOUR OF MASSACHUSETTS,

AND NOW FIRST PUBLISHED FROM A CORRECT COPY OF THE ORIGINAL MANUSCRIPT.

Utcumque erit, juvabit tamen, rerum gestarum memoriæ, ipsum consuluisse. — TIT. LIV. PREF.

HARTFORD:
PRINTED BY ELISHA BABCOCK.
MDCC XC.

TO

THE POSTERITY

OF

JOHN WINTHROP, ESQ.,

THE FOUNDER OF THE MASSACHUSETTS COLONY,

AND, FOR MANY YEARS,

THE FATHER AND THE GOVERNOUR OF THAT INFANT SETTLEMENT,

The Following Journal,

WRITTEN BY THEIR ILLUSTRIOUS ANCESTOR,

IS RESPECTFULLY INSCRIBED

BY THEIR MOST OBEDIENT,

HUMBLE SERVANT,

THE EDITOR.

HARTFORD, *July*, 1790.

THE EDITOR'S PREFACE.

THE following Journal was written by John Winthrop, Esq., first governour of Massachusetts. This distinguished gentleman was born at Groton in Suffolk, June 12, 1587. His grandfather was an eminent lawyer, in the reign of Henry VIII. and attached to the reformation. His father was of the same profession; and the governour himself was bred a lawyer, in which character he was eminent both for integrity and abilities. Indeed, he must have had the fairest reputation; for he was appointed a justice of peace at eighteen years of age.

When the design of settling a colony in New England was undertaken, Mr. Winthrop was chosen, with general consent, to conduct the enterprise. His estate, amounting to the value of six or seven hundred pounds sterling a year, he converted into money, and embarked for America, in the forty-third year of his age. He arrived at Salem, with the Massachusetts charter, June 12, 1630. He was many years governour of that infant colony, and conducted himself with such address and unshaken rectitude, as to render his character universally respectable among his cotemporaries, and his memory dear to posterity. He died March 26, 1649.

Mr. Winthrop kept a Journal of every important occurrence, from his first embarking for America, in 1630, to the year 1644. This manuscript, as appears by some passages, was originally designed for publication; and it was formerly consulted by the first compilers of New England history, particularly by Hubbard, Mather, and Prince. But it continued, unpublished and uncopied, in possession of the elder branch of the family, till the late revolution, when Gov. Trumbull of Connecticut procured it, and, with the assistance of his secretary, copied a considerable part of it. Soon after the governour's death, a gentleman, who has a taste for examining curious original papers, which respect his own country, came, by accident, to a knowledge of this manuscript; and, with consent of the governour's heirs, contracted for a copy, merely for his own improvement and amusement. On reading the work, he found it to contain many curious and interesting facts, relating to the settlement of Massachusetts and the other New England colonies, and highly descriptive of the character and views of the first inhabitants. This suggested to him the design of publishing the Journal *complete;* as any abridgment of it would tend to weaken its historical evidence, and put [it] in the power of captious critics to impeach its authenticity. By consent of the descendants of Governour Winthrop, proposals were issued for publishing a small number of copies; and the design is at length accomplished.

The copy here presented to the public was made by John Porter, Esq., the secretary of the late Gov. Trumbull, whose declaration respecting its accuracy, is here annexed. It is an extract from his letter to the editor: —

LEBANON, *January 1st*, 1788.

DEAR SIR,

Agreeable to your request, I send you a copy of Gov. Winthrop's History. The transcribing has required more labor than I at first expected. I carefully examined the original, and, on comparing, found many errors in the first copy; which upon further experience in reading the original, I have been able to correct; as also to fill up many blanks. This has caused me much study, and retarded the completion of the business for some time. You will observe some blanks in the present copy — some of them are so in the original; but, excepting the blanks, I believe this may be depended on as a genuine copy.

I am, dear Sir,
with sentiments of esteem,
your obedient humble servant,
JOHN PORTER.

The original is in the hand-writing common to that age, and is not read without difficulty. The first copy was made during Gov. Trumbull's life, and part of it by the governour himself. The last copy, here given to the world, was taken from the first, and, throughout the whole, compared with the original.[1] The blanks are few, and, as the reader will observe, of no considerable consequence.

Many parts of the work are not interesting to modern readers; but even these are necessary to give future historians an accurate account

---

[1] Caution is due to the reader, lest by misunderstanding this language, the proper merit of Mr. Secretary Porter be transferred to the Editor, who assured me, that he never read the original. The celebrated philologist, *who in his English Dictionary triumphed over the difficulties* of derivation in our etymology from Danish, Russian, Irish, Welsh, German, high or low, Sanscrit, Persian, or Chaldee fountains, might, after exhausting his patience, have reputably shrunk from encounter with the manuscript of Winthrop.

of the first transactions of the settlers, and furnish posterity with a precise knowledge of the characters and manners of their forefathers.

Important institutions, and the general complexion of national government, often originate in the most trivial circumstances, or the minutest traits of character; and without a detail of the most trifling facts in the early history of New England, it will be impossible to understand the nature of their present religious and political establishments.

But, however unimportant particular passages in the following Journal may appear to the body of readers, the substance of the work is highly valuable; and, it is presumed, the historian, the philosopher, and the divine, will be gratified with a publication, which has long been a desideratum among the literati of the New World.

HARTFORD, *July*, 1790.

[To gratify the last surviving son of Professor John Winthrop, F. R. S. I admitted, in the former impression, this curious note on a separate page.]

"*AT ye Feast of St. Michael, Ano* 1607, *my Sister, ye Lady Mildmay, did give me a Stone Pot, tipped and covered wth a Silver Lydd.*"

THE above memorandum was taken out of my great great grandfather, Mr. Adam Winthrop, his notes, and given me, October 13th, 1707, by my cousin John Winthrop, relating to the Stone Pot, given him by his sister one hundred years ago; which Pot is now in my possession.

ADAM WINTHROP,
the son of Adam — the son of Adam — the son of John, governour of Massachusetts — the son of the abovesaid Adam, to whom the Pot was at first given.

BE it remembered, that the "Stone Pot, *tipped and covered with a Silver Lydd,*" descended to me upon the death of my father in 1779; and that it has, on this 29th day of September, 1807, (being the Feast of St. Michael,) been two hundred years in the family, and is now in my possession.

WILLIAM WINTHROP,
the son of John — the son of Adam — the son of Adam — the son of Adam — the son of John, (governour of Massachusetts,) — the son of Adam, to whom the Pot was at first given.

Readers will observe, that, at the top of the page, stands the name of the governour for the time being; references from the text to the notes are marked by Arabick numerals; words doubtful in the original are printed in Italic, as on page 286; words presumed to be deficient are supplied in brackets, as on page 19; words having a pen drawn through them in the original MSS. are denoted by a star before and after, as on page 232; some important omissions in the Hartford edition are marked by a § before and after, as on page 148; the difference in some particular places, between the correct reading and the erroneous one of the first edition, is marked by giving the true word or words in the text between parallel lines before and after, and the wrong word or words between similar lines in the margin below, as on page 3.

In printing Indian names, the spelling of originals, however various at different times, is observed. Great literal correctness has been aimed at, and in general obtained in printing these volumes. Other errors may, certainly, be detected; but all that have met my eye are noted in the following:—

ERRATA.

Vol. I. page	64, line	6 of note 2, for *Stanbridge*, read Stambridge.
" "	91, "	8 of note, for 1663, read 1643.
" "	141, "	11 of note, for *last note*, read last note but one.
Vol. II. "	241, "	15 of note, for *Marvel*, read Marvell.

THE

HISTORY OF NEW ENGLAND.

ANNO DOMINI, 1630, MARCH 29, MONDAY.

Easter Monday.] RIDING at the Cowes, near the Isle of Wight, in the Arbella,[1] a ship of three hundred and fifty tons,

---

[1] This name has been usually spelt Arabella, and thus Neal, Hutchinson, Trumbull, Dr. Holmes, and Judge Davis, besides Eliot and Allen, in their Biographical Dictionaries, following chiefly Josselyn and Mather, have all written it. Other authorities, of less value, though of earlier date, may have strengthened the mistake. Johnson, who probably was personally acquainted with the fact, in his "Wonder-working Providence," doubles the letter *r;* but the additional syllable gains little support from a book, whose innumerable inaccuracies of every sort can scarcely be accounted for by the circumstance of its author living here while his work was printed at London. The grandson of Sir Ferdinando Gorges, in his "America painted to the Life," gives only a meagre abstract of Johnson, and adds no evidence for the common orthography. The celebrated letter from these adventurers, dated on board *this* ship at Yarmouth, 7 April, published in London, 1630, found in Hubbard, 126–128, and the first article in Hutchinson's Appendix, gives the true name. Hubbard, in his narrative of events during the life of Winthrop, is indeed of very little value, except for the closeness with which he copies the Governor's text. The unfailing accuracy of Prince led him beyond Hubbard to original private manuscripts and the Colony Records, for the exact spelling. I testify that such is the original note of the meeting of the assistants, 23 March, on board *this* ship.

The principal vessels, which brought our fathers hither, are remembered by their descendants with no small degree of affection. The Mayflower had been a name of renown, without forming part of this fleet, because in her came the devoted planters of Plimouth, and she had also brought, in the year preceding this, some of Higginson's companions to Salem. Endicot and the first colonists

whereof Capt. Peter Milborne[1] was master, being manned with fifty-two seamen, and twenty-eight pieces of ordnance, (the wind coming to the N. by W. the evening before,) in the morning there came aboard us Mr. Cradock,[2] the late governour, and the masters of his two ships, Capt. John Lowe, master of the Ambrose, and Mr. Nicholas Hurlston, master of the Jewel, and Mr. Thomas Beecher,[3] master of the Talbot, (which three ships rode

---

of Massachusetts in 1628 demand our gratitude for the Abigail. But the circumstance of changing, "in honour of the Lady" Arbella, wife of Isaac Johnson, Esq., the original name of this *admiral* ship, which was the Eagle, makes us confident in the correctness of this name, while it pleases the imagination that would honor the vessel. In his epistle to the Countess of Lincoln, wife of the brother of this lady, Gov. Dudley uses the same letters with Winthrop, in whose MS. the word is more plainly written than almost any other, and we cannot suppose they could be mistaken in so simple a point about one of their most intimate friends. It was, therefore, only in compliance with popular opinion, that this error found place in the former edition; and we may now hope that, in time to come, the correction will be always regarded.

[1] By the company records it appears, the master owned one eighth of the ship.

[2] Matthew Cradock, it is certain, never came to our country, though he maintained a small plantation for fishing at Mistick, in the present bounds of Malden, opposite to Winthrop's farm at Ten Hills. He was long honoured in our annual registers as first governour of the colony; yet, as he was in fact only the head of a commercial company in England, not ruler of the people, his services are adequately acknowledged without retaining his name in that most respectable list. To him is due the honor of the proposal, 28 July, preceding the date of commencement of this History, for transferring the government from the company in London to the inhabitants here, — a measure, of which the benefit was felt more and more every year till the independence of the United States, with which its connexion is apparent. This fact is by Prince, I. 189, verified from the records of that day. His death I refer to 1644, for in our county registry are found deeds of that year from his agent, and in the next year from the agent of his executors. A descendant, George Cradock, Esq., is mentioned by Douglass and Hutchinson as an inhabitant of Boston.

[3] The same master, in the same ship, had the year before brought to Salem the venerable Higginson, the father and pattern of the New England clergy. His relation of the voyage, printed at London, 1630, is preserved in Hutchinson's "Collection of Papers," and more correctly by Young. Hubbard, 128, makes this name Belcher; but this is perhaps a misprint, for Higginson gives it like Winthrop, except that his first syllable has but one *e*. Thomas Beecher is among the early members of Boston church, being No. 112, and he was a representative from Charlestown in the first year, and often afterwards. He was by

then by us, — the Charles, the Mayflower, the William and Francis, the Hopewell, the Whale, the Success and the Trial being still at Hampton[1] and not ready,) when, upon conference, it was agreed, that (in regard it was uncertain when the rest of the fleet would be ready) these four ships should consort together; the Arbella to be admiral, the Talbot vice-admiral, *3 the Ambrose rear-admiral, and the Jewel a captain; and accordingly articles of consortship were drawn between the said captains and masters; whereupon Mr. Cradock took leave of us, and our captain gave him a farewell with four or five shot.

About ten of the clock we weighed anchor and set sail, with the wind at N., and came to an anchor again over against Yarmouth, and the Talbot weighed likewise, and came and anchored by us. Here we met with a ship of Hampton, called the Plantation, newly come from Virginia. Our captain saluted her, and she us again; and the master, one Mr. [blank] *Graves*,[2] came on board our ship, and stayed with us about two or three hours, and in the meantime his ship came to an anchor by us.

Tuesday, 30.] In the morning, about ten of the clock, the wind being come to the W. with fair weather, we weighed and rode nearer Yarmouth. When we came before the town, the castle put forth a flag; our captain saluted them, and they answered us again. The Talbot, which rode farther off, saluted the castle also.

Here we saw, close by the shore of the Isle of Wight, a Dutch ship of one thousand tons, which, being bound to the East Indies, about two years since, in passing ||through the Needles,|| struck upon a rock, and being forced to run ashore to save her men, could never be weighed since, although she

||thither the rudder||

---

the General Court, in May, 1635, Col. Rec. I. 150, appointed "captain of the fort at Castle Island." Hubbard read our MS. as calling the master of the Jewel, Harlston.

[1] This port is usually called Southampton.

[2] I cannot satisfactorily make out this name from the MS., but am convinced the first edition which gave it, Guerns, was wrong, and note my uncertainty in the text. One Graves was mate of the Talbot, in Higginson's voyage, and was so in the present.

lies a great height above the water, and yet she hath some men aboard her.

Wednesday, 31.] The wind continued W. and S. W. with rain. Our captain and some of our company went to Yarmouth for supply of wood and other provisions; (our captain was still careful to fill our empty casks with water).

Thursday, April 1.] The wind continued very strong at W. and by S. with much rain.

Friday, 2.] We kept a fast aboard our ship and the Talbot. The wind continued still very high at W. and S. and rainy. In the time of our fast, two of our landmen pierced a rundlet of strong water, and stole some of it, for which we laid them in bolts all the night, and the next morning the principal was openly whipped, and both kept with bread and water that day.

Saturday, 3.] The wind continued still at W. and with continual storms and rain.

Sunday, 4.] Fair, clear weather. In the morning the wind W. and by N., but in the afternoon S. S. W. This evening the Tal-
*4 bot weighed and went back to the Cowes, because her an-
chor would not hold here, the tide set with so strong a race.

Monday, 5.] The wind still W. and S. with fair weather. A maid of Sir Richard Saltonstall[1] fell down at the grating by the cook-room, but the carpenter's man, who occasioned her fall unwittingly, caught hold of her with incredible nimbleness, and saved her; otherwise she had fallen into the hold.

Tuesday, 6.] Capt. Burleigh, captain of Yarmouth castle, a grave, comely gentleman, and of great age, came aboard us and stayed breakfast, and, offering us much courtesy, he departed, our captain giving him four shot out of the forecastle for his farewell.[2] He was an old sea captain in Queen Elizabeth's time, and, being taken prisoner at sea, was kept prisoner in Spain three years. Himself and three of his sons were captains in Roe's[3] voyage.

---

[1] A copious collection of biographical memoirs of this gentleman and his descendants, of whom our country has justly been proud, may be seen in 2 Hist. Coll. IV. 154–168.

[2] He had paid kind attention to Higginson the year before.

[3] Sir Thomas Roe was named by the king to be of the council in the second charter of Virginia in May, 1609, and was in the same year sent by

The wind was now come about to N. E. with very fair weather.

In the afternoon Mr. Cradock came aboard us, and told us, that the Talbot, Jewel, and Ambrose were fallen down into Stoke's Bay, intending to take their way by St. Helen's Point, and that they desired we could come back to them. Hereupon we came to council, and wrote unto them to take the first opportunity of the wind to fall down to us, and Mr. Cradock presently went back to them, our captain giving him three shot out of the steerage for a farewell.

Our captain called over our landmen, and tried them at their muskets, and such as were good shot among them were enrolled to serve in the ship, if occasion should be.

The lady Arbella and the gentlewomen, and Mr. Johnson[1] and some others went on shore to refresh themselves.

Prince Henry to explore the coast of Guiana. On the dangerous shores at the mouth of the Oronoco he laboured many months with great diligence, and ascended the Maragnon three hundred miles. After his return in 1611, he became a politician, was a member of parliament, and supported the rights of the people in 1614. After that year he was employed, first at the instance of the East India Company, in several embassies. Of these his own relation, after lying in manuscript more than a century, was given to the press; but, I believe, no account is extant of his voyage to America. He sat with John Selden for the University of Oxford in the Long Parliament, and died during the civil war, having obeyed the call of the king in January, 1644, for assembling at Oxford, while his colleague adhered to the majority of the Commons at Westminster. Such was the separation of true patriots frequently occurring in the contest; and the best men of either side, Hampden and Lord Falkland, were happy in meeting early death. He was one of the forty, incorporated in 1620 as the Plimouth Council, whose names may be seen in Belknap's New Hampshire, I. 12, and Hubbard, 217.

1 Of this gentleman, formerly regarded as the founder of Boston, where it is not probable that he ever passed a single night, an interesting account may be found in Hutchinson, I. 22, to which neither myself nor Snow, the diligent historian of Boston, have been able to make much addition. From the first volume of our Probate Records it may be seen, that he was the most liberal contributor to the company's funds. His early death prevented him from contributing much to the stability of the colony he so assiduously promoted at home, for I find no mention of him in our records, but at the Court 7 September, and again, 18 of same, acting with Winthrop in taking inquisition at Charlestown upon one of their company, who died after short illness. His will, made only three weeks before embarkation with our fathers, obtained by me in

*5 Wednesday,[1] 7.] Fair weather, the wind easterly, in the morning a small gale, but in the afternoon it came about to the south. This afternoon our other consorts came up to us, and about ten or twelve Flemings, and all anchored by us, and the masters of the Jewel and of the Ambrose came aboard us, and our captain and they went on shore.

Towards night there came from the W. a Fleming, a small man-of-war, with a Brazil man which he had taken prize, and came to anchor by us.

Thursday, 8.] About six in the morning (the wind being E. and N. and fair weather) we weighed anchor and set sail, and before ten we gat through the Needles, having so little wind as we had much to do to stem the tide, so as the rest of our fleet (we being nine in all, whereof some were small ships, which were bound for Newfoundland) could not get out all then till the ebb. In the afternoon the wind came S. and W. and we were becalmed, so as being not able to get above three or four leagues from the Needles, our captain tacked about, and putting his fore-sheets aback stays, he stayed for the rest of the fleet, and as they came by us we spake to them, and about eight in the evening we let fall an anchor, intending to stop till the ebb. But before ten at night the wind came about to the N. a good gale; so we put up a light in the poop, and weighed and set sail, and by daylight, Friday 9, we were come to Portland; but the other ships being not able to hold up with us, we were forced to spare our mainsail, and went on with a merry gale. In the ||morning|| we descried from the top eight sail astern of
*6 us, (whom Capt. Lowe told us he had seen at Dunnose in the evening.) We supposing they might be Dunkirkers,[2] our

||night||

---

a certified copy at Doctor's Commons, is printed in 3 Mass. Hist. Coll. VIII. 244.

[1] On this day the admirable letter "to the rest of their brethren in and of the Church of England" was addressed by our adventurous pilgrims from Yarmouth, aboard the Arbella. It is most appropriately given by Hutchinson as the first article in the Appendix to his first volume. Only seven of the signers are named, in the 4to pamphlet, printed for John Bellamie, London, 1630, whence Hubbard, 126, derived it.

[2] Dunkirk was then part of the Spanish Netherlands, and the war between England and Spain lasted till December following.

captain caused the gunroom and gundeck to be cleared; all the hammocks were taken down, our ordnance loaded, and our powder-chests and fireworks made ready, and our landmen quartered among the seamen, and twenty-five of them appointed for muskets, and every man written down for his quarter.

The wind continued N. [blank] with fair weather, and after noon it calmed, and we still saw those eight ships to stand towards us; having more wind than we, they came up apace, so as our captain and the masters of our consorts were more occasioned to think they might be Dunkirkers, (for we were told at Yarmouth, that there were ten sail of them waiting for us;) whereupon we all prepared to fight with them, and took down some cabins which were in the way of our ordnance, and out of every ship were thrown such bed matters as were subject to take fire, and we heaved out our long boats, and put up our waste cloths, and drew forth our men, and armed them with muskets and other weapons, and instruments for fireworks; and for an experiment our captain shot a ball of wild-fire fastened to an arrow out of a cross-bow, which burnt in the water a good time. The lady Arbella and the other women and children were removed into the lower deck, that they might be out of danger. All things being thus fitted, we went to prayer upon the upper deck. It was much to see how cheerful and comfortable all the company appeared; not a woman or child that showed fear, though all did apprehend the danger to have been great, if things had proved as might well be expected, for there had been eight against four, and the least of the enemy's ships were reported to carry thirty brass pieces; but our trust was in the Lord of Hosts; and the courage of our captain, and his care and diligence, did much encourage us. It was now about one of the clock, and the fleet seemed to be within a league of us; therefore our captain, because he would show he was not afraid of them, and that he might see the issue before night should overtake us, tacked about and stood to meet them, and when we came near we perceived them to be our friends, — the Little Neptune, a ship of some twenty pieces of ordnance, and her two consorts, bound for the Straits; a ship of || Flushing, || and a Frenchman, and three other English

|| Hampshire, ||

*7 ships bound for Canada and Newfoundland.[1] So when we drew near, every ship (as they met) saluted each other, and the ||musketeers|| discharged their small shot; and so (God be praised) our fear and danger was turned into mirth and friendly entertainment. Our danger being thus over, we espied two boats on fishing in the channel; so every of our four ships manned out a skiff, and we bought of them great store of excellent fresh fish of divers sorts.

Saturday, 10.] The wind at E. and by N. a handsome gale with fair weather. By seven in the morning we were come over against Plimouth.

About noon the wind slacked, and we were come within sight of the Lizard, and towards night it grew very calm and a great fog, so as our ships made no way.

This afternoon Mr. Hurlston, the master of the Jewel, came aboard our ship, and our captain went in his skiff aboard the Ambrose and the Neptune, of which one Mr. Andrew Cole was master. There he was told, that the bark Warwick was taken by the Dunkirkers, for she came single out of the Downs about fourteen days since, intending to come to us to the Wight, but was never heard of since.[2] She was a pretty ship of about eighty tons and ten pieces of ordnance, and was set out by Sir Ferdinando Gorges,[3] Capt. Mason, and others, §for discovery of the great lake in New England,§ so to have inter-

||Mayflower and ours||

---

[1] Johnson, lib. I. c. 14, makes the number of these suspicious sail only four. But though he was, I presume, a passenger in the fleet with Winthrop, his story was probably committed to paper long after the events. Prince, I. 205–6, got into confusion between Johnson and Hubbard, and followed the carelessness of the latter, 129, who represents these ships as "the rest of the fleet," which, we know from Dudley, did not sail before May.

[2] She was not taken, but had put into Plymouth, whence Ambrose Gibbens, a passenger in her, wrote 8 April to his employers; and she came safely to Gorges's plantation at Piscataqua, as Eyre in his letter next year acknowledges. Belknap, N. H. I. Appendix ii.

[3] Of Gorges and Mason, whose names frequently occur in this History, no more perfect account can be expected, than is furnished by Dr. Belknap in the first volume of his admirable American Biography, though we must regret, that the information about Mason is very slight. The manner in which, in this work, Mason's death is related, sub an. 1636 and 1640, is much to be regretted.

cepted the trade of beaver. The master of her was one Mr. Weatherell, whose father was master of one of the cattle ships, which we left at Hampton.

This day two young men, falling at odds and fighting, contrary to the orders which we had published and set up in the ship, were adjudged to walk upon the deck till night with their hands bound behind them, which accordingly was executed; and another man, for using contemptuous speeches in our presence, was laid in bolts till he submitted himself, and promised open confession of his offence.

I should have noted before, that the day we set sail from the Cowes, my son Henry Winthrop went on shore with one of *8
my servants to fetch an ox and ten wethers, which he had provided for our ship, and there went on shore with him, Mr. Pelham[1] and one of his servants. They sent the cattle aboard, but returned not themselves. About three days after, my servant and a servant of Mr. Pelham's came to us to Yarmouth, and told us they were all coming to us in a boat the day before, but the wind was so strong against them, as they were forced on shore in the night, and the two servants came to Yarmouth by land, and so came on ship-board, but my son and Mr. Pelham (we heard) went back to the Cowes and so to Hampton. We expected them three or four days after, but they came not to us, so we have left them behind, and suppose they will come after in Mr. Goffe's[2] ships. We were very sorry they had put themselves upon such inconvenience, when they were so well accommodated in our ship. This was not noted before, because we expected daily their return; and upon this occasion I must add here one observation, that we have many young gentlemen in our ship, who behave themselves well, and are conformable to all good orders.

---

[1] It may be concluded, from the letter of Herbert Pelham, Esq., to Gov. Winthrop, found in Hutch. Coll. 59, that this gentleman was his brother. The list of persons, desiring to become freemen, in 1630, Prince, II. 4, has the name of Mr. William Pelham.

[2] Thomas Goffe, Esq., a merchant of London, had been an adventurer in the New Plimouth settlement, and was one of our original patentees, but never came to this country. He was in the charter named deputy governour of the company, and was at this time an assistant.

About ten at night it cleared up with a fresh gale at N. and by W., so we stood on our course merrily.

Sunday, 11.] The wind at N. and by W. a very stiff gale. About eight in the morning, being gotten past Scilly, and standing to the W. S. W. we met two small ships, which falling in among us, and the Admiral coming under our lee, we let him pass, but the Jewel and Ambrose, perceiving the other to be a Brazil man, and to take the wind of us, shot at them and made them stop and fall after us, and sent a skiff aboard them to know what they were. Our captain, fearing lest some mistake might arise, and lest they should take them for enemies which were friends, and so, through the unruliness of the mariners some wrong might be done them, caused his skiff to be heaved out, and sent Mr. *Graves*,[1] one of his mates and our
*9 pilot, (a discreet man,) to see how things were, who returned soon after, and brought with him the master of one of the ships and Mr. Lowe and Mr. Hurlston. When they were come aboard us, they agreed to send for the captain, who came and showed his commission from the Prince of Orange. In conclusion he proved to be a Dutchman, and his a man-of-war of Flushing, and the other ship was a prize he had taken laden with sugar and tobacco; so we sent them aboard their ships again, and held on our course. In this time (which hindered us five or six ||leagues||) the Jewel and the Ambrose came foul of each other, so as we much feared the issue, but, through God's mercy, they came well off again, only the Jewel had her foresail torn, and one of her anchors broken. This occasion, and the sickness of our minister and people, put us all out of order this day, so as we could have no sermons.

Monday, 12.] The wind more large to the N. a stiff gale, with fair weather. In the afternoon less wind, and our people began to grow well again. Our children and others, that were sick, and lay groaning in the cabins, we fetched out, and having stretched a rope from the steerage to the mainmast, we made them stand, some of one side and some of the other, and

||days||

---

[1] He was afterwards master of a vessel, perhaps, in several voyages, and, I think, settled in our country; Prince, II. 4, makes him a rear-admiral.

sway it up and down till they were warm, and by this means they soon grew well and merry.

Tuesday, 13.] The night before it was calm, and the next day calm and close weather, so as we made little way, the wind with us being W.

Wednesday, 14.] The wind S. W. rainy weather, in the morning.

About nine in the forenoon the wind came about to N. N. W. a stiff gale; so we tacked about and steered our course W. S. W.

This day the ship heaved and set more than before, yet we had ||but few|| sick, and of these such as came up upon the deck, and stirred themselves, were presently well again; therefore our captain set our children and ||[2]young|| men to some harmless exercises, which the seamen were very active in, and did our people much good, though they would sometimes play the wags with them. Towards night we were forced to take in some sail to stay for the vice-admiral, which was near a league astern of us.

[Large blank.]

Thursday, 15.] The wind still at N. N. W. fair weather, but less wind than the day and night before, so as our ship made but little way.

At noon our captain made observation by the cross-staff,
and found we were in forty-seven degrees thirty-seven min- *10
utes north latitude.

All this forenoon our vice-admiral was much to leeward of us; so after dinner we bare up towards her, and having fetched her up and spoken with her, the wind being come to S. W. we tacked about and steered our course N. N. W. lying as near the wind as we could, and about four of the clock, with a stiff gale, we steered W. and by N. and at night the wind grew very strong, which put us on to the W. amain.

About ten at night the wind grew so high, and rain withal, that we were forced to take in our topsail, and having lowered our mainsail and foresail, the storm was so great as it split our foresail and tore it in pieces, and a knot of the sea washed our

||still some|| ||[2]grown||

tub overboard, wherein our fish was a-watering. The storm still grew, and it was dark with clouds, (though otherwise moonlight,) so as (though it was the Jewel's turn to carry the light this night, yet) lest we should lose or go foul one of another, we hanged out a light upon our mizzen shrouds, and before midnight we lost sight of our vice-admiral.

Our captain, so soon as he had set the watch, at eight in the evening called his men, and told them he feared we should have a storm, and therefore commanded them to be ready upon the deck, if occasion should be; and himself was up and down the decks all times of the night.

Friday, 16.] About four in the morning the wind slacked a little, yet it continued §a great storm§ still, and though in the afternoon it ||blew not|| much wind, yet the sea was so high as it tossed us more than before, and we carried no more but our mainsail, yet our ship steered well with it, which few such ships could have done.

About four in the afternoon, the wind still W. and by S. and rainy, we put on a new foresail and hoisted it up, and stood N. W. All this day our rear-admiral and the Jewel held up with us.

This night was very stormy.

All the time of the storm few of our people were sick, (||[2]except the women,|| who kept under hatches,) and there appeared no fear or dismayedness among them.

[Large blank.]

Saturday, 17.] The wind S. W. very stormy and boisterous. All this time we bore no more sail but our mainsail and foresail, and we steered our course W. and by N.

*11 This day our captain told me, that our landmen were very nasty and slovenly, and that the gundeck, where they lodged, was so beastly and noisome with their victuals and beastliness, as would much endanger the health of the ship. Hereupon, after prayer, we took order, and appointed four men to see to it, and to keep that room clean for three days, and then four others should succeed them, and so forth on.

The wind continued all this day at S. W. a stiff gale. In

||cleared with|| ||[2]though no men||

the afternoon it cleared up, but very hazy. Our captain, about four of the clock, sent one to the top to look for our vice-admiral, but he could not descry him, yet we saw a sail about two leagues to the leeward, which stood toward the N. E.

We were this evening (by our account) about ninety leagues from Scilly, W. and by S. At this place there came a swallow and lighted upon our ship.

Sunday, 18.] About two in the morning the wind N. W.; so we tacked about and steered our course S. W. We had still much wind, and the sea went very high, which tossed our ship continually.

After our evening sermon, about five of the clock, the wind came about to S. E. a good gale, but rainy; so we steered our course W. S. W. and the ship's way was about nine leagues a watch; (a watch is four hours).

This day the captain sent to top again to discover our vice-admiral. We descried from thence to the eastward a sail, but we knew not what she was.

About seven of the clock the Jewel bare up so near as we could speak each to other, and after we bated some sail; so she went ahead of us, and soon after eight put forth her light.

Monday, 19.] In the morning the wind was come about to the N. W. a good gale and fair weather; so we held our course, but the ship made not so good way as when the wind was large.

This day, by observation and account, we found ourselves to be in forty-eight degrees north latitude, and two hundred and twenty leagues W. from the meridian of London.

Here I think good to note, that all this time since we came from the Wight, we had cold weather, so as we could well endure our warmest clothes. I wish, therefore, that all such as shall pass this way in the spring have care to provide warm clothing; for nothing breeds more trouble and danger of sickness, in this season, than cold.

In the afternoon the wind came to S. W. a stiff gale, with rain; so we steered westerly, till night; then the wind came about to N. W. and we tacked again and stood S. W.

Our rear-admiral being to leeward of us, we bare up to *12
him. He told us all their people were in health, but one of
their cows was dead.

Tuesday, 20.] The wind southerly, fair weather, and little wind. In the morning we stood S. and by E., in the afternoon W. and by N.

Wednesday, 21.] Thick, rainy weather; much wind at S. W. Our captain, over night, had invited his consorts to have dined with him this day, but it was such foul weather as they could not come aboard us.

Thursday, 22.] The wind still W. and by S. fair weather; then W. N. W.

This day at noon we found ourselves in forty-seven degrees and forty-eight minutes, and having a stiff gale, we steered S. W. about four leagues a watch, all this day and all the night following.

Friday, 23.] The wind still W. N. W. a small gale, with fair weather. Our captain put forth his ancient in the poop, and heaved out his skiff, and lowered his topsails, to give sign to his consorts that they should come aboard us to dinner, for they were both a good way astern of us, and our vice-admiral was not yet seen of us since the storm, though we sent to the top every day to descry her.

About eleven of the clock, our captain sent his skiff and fetched aboard us the masters of the other two ships, and Mr. Pynchon,[1] and they dined with us in the round-house, for the lady[2] and gentlewomen[3] dined in the great cabin.

---

[1] William Pynchon, Esq., of whom frequent mention is made in this History, was named an assistant in the Massachusetts charter. Dudley relates, that his wife died here before the return of the ship they came in. Many papers in 2 Hist. Coll. VIII. 227 et seq. give honourable proof of his services. He settled first at Roxbury, but in a few years removed to Springfield, of which town he was the founder, and there lived till 1652, when, "having received some ill treatment" from the government, "on account of his religious principles, he, with Capt. Smith, his son-in-law, went to England, and with them went the minister of the town, the Rev. Mr. Moxon, never to return." See Breck's century sermon. I presume Pynchon had written a book above the spirit of that age; for our government, in a curious letter to Sir Henry Vane, who had, in 1652, advised a different course, give no clear idea of its doctrines. See 3 Hist. Coll. I. 35. His son, John, was of the council in 1665, and many of his descendants are in places of public usefulness in Springfield and its neighborhood and at Salem.

[2] The lady was the wife of Johnson.

[3] Mrs. Phillips, the minister's wife, the two daughters of Sir R. Saltonstall,

This day and the night following we had little wind, so *13
as the sea was very smooth, and the ship made little way.

Saturday, 24.] The wind still W. and by N., fair weather and calm all that day and night. Here we made observation again, and found we were in forty-five degrees twenty minutes, north latitude.

Sunday, 25.] The wind northerly, fair weather, but still calm. We stood W. and by S. and saw two ships ahead of us as far as we could descry.

In the afternoon the wind came W. and by S. but calm still. About five of the clock, the rear-admiral and the Jewel had fetched up the two ships, and by their saluting each other we perceived they were friends, (for they were so far to windward of us as we could only see the smoke of their pieces, but could not hear them). About nine of the clock, they both fell back towards us again, and we steered N. N. W. Now the weather begins to be warm.

Monday, 26.] The wind still W. and by S. close weather, and scarce any wind.

The two ships, which we saw yesterday, were bound for Canada. Capt. Kirk[1] was aboard the admiral. They bare up with us, and falling close under our lee, we saluted each other, and conferred together so long till his vice-admiral was becalmed by our sails, and we were foul one of another; but there being little wind and the sea calm, we kept them asunder with oars, etc., till they heaved out their boat, and so towed their ship away.

They told us for certain, that the king of France had set out six of his own ships to recover the fort from them.

---

and, probably, the wives of Coddington, Dudley, Bradstreet, Nowell, and others, are here intended; as the principal people, except Revell and Pynchon, seem to have been in the Arbella, which was chiefly owned by them.

[1] Probably a brother of Sir David Kirk, or Kertk, as Champlain, in his Voyage, and Charlevoix in his Histoire de la Nouvelle France, choose to spell the name. In the table of contents to the former, it is changed to Quer. Sir David, with his two brothers, Thomas and Lewis, had, the preceding year, taken Quebeck, an event then, and long after, thought of so little consequence, as not to be noticed in Hume's History of England. The name of Kirk will recur in the latter part of this History, when he was governour of Newfoundland, of which he had, in a charter of 1628, been one of the grantees.

About one of the clock Capt. Lowe sent his skiff aboard us, (with a friendly token of his love to the governour,) to desire our captain to come aboard his ship, which he did, and there met the masters of the other ships and Capt. Kirk, and before night they all returned to their ships again, Capt. Lowe bestowing some shot upon them for their welcome.

The wind now blew a pretty gale, so as our ship made some way again, though it were out of our right course N. W. by N.

*14 Tuesday, 27.] The wind still westerly, a stiff gale, with close weather. We steered W. N. W. About noon some rain, and all the day very cold. We appointed Tuesdays and Wednesdays to catechize our people, and this day Mr. Phillips[1] began it.

Wednesday, 28.] All the night, and this day till noon, the

---

1 Of the Rev. George Phillips frequent mention will be found in the following pages, and an elaborate eulogy, with very slight biography, may be seen in the Magnalia. He was of Gonville and Caius College, took his degrees in 1613 and 1617, and for the latter was compelled to submit to subscription. His wife died soon after arrival. In Gov. Bradford's Letter Book, the concluding part of which is preserved in 1 Hist. Coll. III. an epistle to him from Samuel Fuller, of 28 June of this year, only a few days after *our* colonists' arrival at Salem, discovers to us, that Phillips was of a straiter sect than most of the companions of Winthrop. "Here is come over," says he, "with these gentlemen, one Mr. Phillips, (a Suffolk man,) who hath told me in private, that if they will have him stand minister, by that calling, which he received from the prelates in England, he will leave them." This was not the spirit of the first settlers of Massachusetts, until they had lived some years in the wilderness; and I imagine Phillips was overcome, by the persuasion of his friends, to postpone the scruple he had communicated to the Plimouth colonist. Hubbard, 186, lets us a little into the cause of the change: "It is said, that Mr. Phillips was at the first more acquainted with the way of church discipline, since owned by Congregational churches; but being then without any to stand by him, (for wo to him that is alone,) he met with much opposition from some of the magistrates, till the time that Mr. Cotton came into the country, who, by his preaching and practice, did by degrees mould all their church administrations into the very same form, which Mr. Phillips laboured to introduce into the churches before." Yet his name is subscribed to the excellent letter, with Winthrop, Dudley, Johnson, Saltonstall, Fiennes, and Coddington, dated on board the Arbella, wishing to be regarded "as those who esteem it our honour to call the church of England, from whence we rise, our dear mother."

A long list of men, distinguishing the name of Phillips in our country by their civil stations and munificent patronage of institutions of learning and benevolence, descends from this first pastor of Watertown.

wind very high at S. W., close weather, and some rain. Between eleven and twelve, in a shower, the wind came W. N. W., so we tacked about and stood S. W.

Thursday, 29.] Much wind all this night at W. and by N. and the sea went very high, so as the ship rolled very much, because we sailed but with one course; therefore, about twelve, our captain arose and caused the foretopsail to be hoisted, and then the ship went more steady. §He caused the quartermaster to look down into the hold to see if the cask lay fast and the.... §[1]

In the morning the wind continued with a stiff gale; rainy and cold all the day.

We had been now three weeks at sea, and were not come above three hundred leagues, being about one third part of our way, viz., about forty-six north latitude, and near the meri- *15
dian of the || Terceras ||.

This night Capt. Kirk carried the light as one of our consorts.

Friday, 30.] The wind at W. N. W., a strong gale all the night and day, with showers now and then.

We made observation, and found we were in forty-four north latitude. At night the wind scanted towards the S. with rain; so we tacked about and stood N. W. and by N.

Saturday, May 1.] All the night much wind at S. S. W. and rain. In the morning the wind still strong, so as we could bear little sail, and so it continued a growing storm all the day, and towards night so much wind as we bore no more sail but so much as should keep the ship stiff. Then it grew a very great tempest § all the night,§ with fierce showers of rain intermixed, and very cold.

Lord's day, 2.] The tempest continued all the day, with the wind W. and by N., and the sea raged and tossed us exceedingly; yet, through God's mercy, we were very comfortable, and few or none sick, but had opportunity to keep the Sabbath, and Mr. Phillips ||[2]preached|| twice that day. The Am-

||T——s.|| ||[2]prayed||

---

[1] This passage, being interlined, was extremely difficult to be made out, and part of it remains illegible, I think, by the aid of any eyes or glasses.

brose and Jewel were separated far from us the first night, but this day we saw them again, but Capt. Kirk's ships we saw not since.

Monday, 3.] In the night the wind abated, and by morning the sea was well assuaged, so as we bare our foresail again, and stood W. S. W.; but all the time of the tempest we could make no way, but were driven to the leeward, and the Ambrose struck all her sails but her mizzen, and lay a hull. She brake her main yard. This day we made observation, and found we were in forty-three and a half north latitude. We set two ||fighters|| in the bolts till night, with their hands bound behind them. A maid-servant in the ship, being stomach-sick, drank so much strong water, that she was senseless, and had near killed herself. We observed it a common fault in our ||[2]young|| people, that they gave themselves to drink hot waters very immoderately.

Tuesday, 4.] Much wind at S. W., close weather. In the morning we tacked about and stood N. W. and about ten in the morning W. N. W., but made little way in regard of the head sea.

Wednesday, 5.] The wind W. and by S. thick, foggy weather, and rainy; so we stood N. W. by W. At night the
*16 Lord remembered us, and enlarged the wind to the N.; so we tacked about and stood our course W. and by S. with a merry gale in all our sails.

Thursday, 6.] The wind at N. a good gale, and fair weather. We made observation and found we were forty-three and a half north latitude; so we stood full west, and ran, in twenty-four hours, about thirty leagues.

||[3]Four|| things I observed here. 1. That the declination of the pole star was much, even to the view, beneath that it is in England. 2. That the new moon, when it first appeared, was much smaller than at any time I had seen it in England. 3. That all the way we came, we saw fowls flying and swimming, when we had no land near by two hundred leagues. 4. That wheresoever the wind blew, we had still cold weather, and the sun did not give so much heat as in England.

Friday, 7.] The wind N. and by E. a small gale, very fair

||sailors|| ||[2]grown|| ||[3]Some||

weather, and towards night a still calm. This day our captain and Mr. Lowe dined aboard the Jewel.

Saturday, 8.] All the night calm. In the morning the wind S. W. a handsome gale; so we tacked and stood N. W. and soon after, the wind growing more large, we stood W. N. W. with a good gale. About four of the clock we saw a whale, who lay just in our ship's way, (the bunch of his back about a yard above water). He would not ||shun us;|| so we passed within a stone's cast of him, as he lay spouting up water.

Lord's day, 9.] The wind still S. W. a good gale, but close weather and some rain; we held on our course W. N. W. About nine it cleared up, and towards night a great fog for an hour or two.

We were now in forty-four and a half north latitude, and a little west of ||[2] Corvos||.

Monday, 10.] The wind S. S. W. a good gale and fair weather; so we stood W. and by N. four or five leagues a watch, all this day. The wind increased, and was a great storm all the night. About midnight our rear-admiral put forth two lights, whereby we knew that some mischance had befallen her. We answered her with two lights again, and bare up to her, so near as we durst, (for the sea went very high, and she lay by the lee) ||[3]and having hailed her, we thought she had sprung aleak; but she had broken some of her shrouds;|| so we went a little ahead of her, and, bringing our
foresail aback stays, we stayed for her, and, about two *17
hours after, she filled her sails, and we stood our course together, but our captain went not to rest till four of the clock, and some others of us slept but little that night.

Tuesday, 11.] The storm continued all this day, till three in the afternoon, and the sea went very high, so as our ship could make no way, being able to bear no more but our mainsail about midmast high. At three there fell a great storm of rain, ||[4]which laid|| the wind, and the wind shifting into the W. we tacked and stood into the head sea, to avoid the rolling of

||swim up|| ||[2]Cowes||

||[3] but she had broken some of her shrouds. Having hailed her, we learnt she had sprung aleak||

||[4] we layed to||

our ship, and by that means we made no way, the sea beating us back as much as the wind put us forward.

We had still cold weather, and our people were so acquainted with ||storms|| as they were not sick, nor troubled, though we were much tossed forty-eight hours together, viz., twenty-four during the storm, and as long the next night and day following, Wednesday, 12, when as we lay as it were a hull, for want of wind, and rolling continually in a high grown sea. This day was close and rainy.

Complaint was made to our captain of some injury that one of the under officers of the ship had done to one of our landmen. He called him and examined the cause, and commanded him to be tied up by the hands, and a weight to be hanged about his neck; but, at the intercession of the governour, (with some difficulty,) he remitted his punishment.

At night the wind blew at S. E. a handsome gale, with rain; so we put forth our sails and stood W. and by S.

Thursday, 13.] Toward morning the wind came to the south-westerly, with close weather and a strong gale, so as before noon we took in our topsails, (the rear-admiral having split her fore-topsail) and we stood west-southerly.

Friday, 14.] The wind W. S. W., thick, foggy weather, and in the afternoon rainy. We stood W. and by S. and after W. and by N. about five leagues a watch. We were in forty-four and a half. The sun set N. W. and by N. one third northerly. And towards night we stood W.

Saturday, 15.] The wind westerly all this day; fair weather. We tacked twice to small purpose.

Lord's day, 16.] As the 15 was.

Monday, 17.] The wind at S. a fine gale and fair weather. We stood W. and by S. We saw a great drift; so we heaved out our skiff, and it proved a fir log, which seemed to have been many years in the water, for it was all overgrown with barnacles and other trash. We sounded here and found no
*18 ground at one hundred fathom and more. We saw two whales. About nine at night the wind grew very strong at S. W. and continued so, with much rain, till one of the clock; then it ceased raining, but the wind came to the W.

||showers||

with more violence. In this storm we were forced to take in all our sails, save our mainsail, and to lower that so much as we could.

Tuesday, 18.] In the morning the wind slacked, but we could stand no nearer our course than N. and we had much wind all this day. In the afternoon we tacked and stood S. by E. Towards night (our rear-admiral being near two leagues to leeward of us) we bare up, and drawing near her, we descried, || some || two leagues more to leeward, two ships, which we conceived were those two of Capt. Kirk's, which parted from us in the storm, May 2. We had still cold weather.

Wednesday, 19.] The wind S. S. W.; close and rainy; little wind. We tacked again and stood W.; but about noon the wind came full W. a very strong gale; so we tacked again and stood N. by E. and at night we took off our main bonnet, and took in all our sails, save our main-course and mizzen. We were now in forty-four degrees twelve minutes north, and by our account in the midway between the false bank and the main bank. All this night a great storm at W. by N.

Thursday, 20.] The storm continued all this day, the wind as it was, and rainy. In the forenoon we carried our fore-course and stood W. S. W., but in the afternoon we took it in, the wind increasing, and the sea grown very high; and lying with the helm a-weather, we made no way but as the ship drove. We had still cold weather.

[1] In the great cabin, at nine at night, etc., and the next day again, etc. The storm continued all this night.

Friday, 21.] The wind still N. W.; little wind, and close weather. We stood S. W. with all our sails, but made little way, and at night it was a still calm.

A servant of one of our company had bargained with a child to sell him a box worth 3*d.* for three biscuits a day all the voyage, and had received about forty, and had sold them and many more to some other servants. We caused his hands to

|| scarce ||

[1] In the margin of the MS. the word "fast" is written by the governour, and a later reader has put in a ☞ pointing at the paragraph. In this bad weather they were, probably, without food.

be tied up to a bar, and hanged a basket with stones about his neck, and so he stood two hours.

Saturday, 22.] The wind S. S. W. much wind and rain.
*19 Our spritsail laid so deep in as it was split in pieces with a head sea at the instant as our captain was going forth of his cabin very early in the morning to give order to take it in. It was a great mercy of God, that it did split, for otherwise it had endangered the breaking of our bowsprit and topmasts at least, and then we had no other way but to have returned for England, except the wind had come east. About ten in the morning, in a very great fret of wind, it chopt suddenly into the W. as it had done divers times before, and so continued with a small gale and [we] stood N. and by W. About four in the afternoon there arose a sudden storm of wind and rain, so violent as we had not a greater. It continued thick and boisterous all the night.

About seven we descried a sail ahead of us, towards the N. and by E. which stood towards us. Our captain, supposing it might be our vice-admiral, hoisted up his mainsail, which before was struck down aboard, and came up to meet her. When we drew near her we put forth our || ancient, ||[1] and she ||[2] luffed || up to get the wind of us; but when she saw she could not, she bare up, and hoisting up her foresail, stood away before the wind; yet we made all the signs we could, that we meant her no harm, but she would not ||[3] trust || us. She was within shot of us, so as we perceived she was a small Frenchman, which we did suppose had been driven off the bank. When she was clear of us, she stood her course again, and we ours.

This day at twelve we made observation, and were about forty-three, but the storm put us far to the N. again. Still cold weather.

Lord's day, 23.] Much wind, still westerly, and very cold weather.

|| ensign || ||[2] tuffled || ||[3] hail ||

[1] Some modern pen had been drawn through this word, that was originally as I have printed it, and the word given in the first edition was substituted. This unimportant alteration is noted, because it affords me an opportunity of assuring the reader that our MS. has not often been so corrupted.

Monday, 24.] The wind N. W. by N. a handsome gale, and close weather and very cold. We stood S. W. About noon we had occasion to lie by the lee to straighten our mizzen shrouds, and the rear-admiral and Jewel, being both to windward of us, bare up and came under our lee, to inquire if anything were amiss with us; so we heard the company was in health in the Jewel, but that two passengers were dead in the Ambrose, and one other § cow §.

Tuesday, 25.] The wind still N. W.; fair weather, but *20
cold. We went on with a handsome gale, and at noon were in forty-three and a half; and the variation of the compass was a point and one-sixth. All this day we stood W. S. W. about five or six leagues a watch, and towards night the wind enlarged, with a cold dash of snowy rain, and then we ran in a smooth sea about eight or nine leagues a watch, and stood due W.

Wednesday, 26.] The wind still N. W. a good gale and fair weather, but very cold still; yet we were about forty-three. At night we sounded, but found no ground.

Thursday, 27.] The wind N. W. a handsome gale; fair weather. About noon it came about to the S. W. and at night rain, with a stiff gale, and it continued to rain very hard till it was near midnight.

This day our skiff went aboard the Jewel for a hogshead of || meal, || which we borrowed, because we could not come by our own, and there came back in the skiff the master of the Jewel and Mr. ||[2] Revell; ||[1] so our captain stayed them dinner, and sent for Capt. Lowe; and about two hours after din-

|| water || ||[2] Nowell ||

[1] I cannot dissemble the pleasure enjoyed by restoring the true name in this place, nor my surprise at finding the marginal substitute in the hand of the scrupulous Prince.

John Revell, Esq., was among those adventurers to New Plimouth, who, in 1626, assigned their interest to the colonists by an indenture, preserved by Bradford in 1 Hist. Coll. III. 47. He had been chosen one of our assistants in October preceding, and was one of those five undertakers to reside here for the management of the joint stock of the company, five others being in England. Yet he returned in the Lyon after a few weeks' visit, before the first meeting of the assistants. He was probably too rich to adventure life and fortune with us.

ner, they went aboard their own ships, our captain giving Mr. ||Revell|| three shot, because he was one of the owners of our ship.

We understood now, that the two which died in the Ambrose were Mr. Cradock's servants, who were sick when they came to sea; and one of them should have been left at Cowes, if any house would have received him.

In the Jewel, also, one of the seamen died — a most profane fellow, and one who was very injurious to the passengers, though much against the will of the master.

At noon we tacked about and stood W. and by N. and so continued most part of that day and night following, and had much rain till midnight.

Friday, 28.] In the morning the wind veered to the W. yet we had a stiff gale, and steered N. W. and by N. It was so great a fog all this day, as we had lost sight of one of our ships,
*21 and saw the other ||[2]sometimes much|| to leeward. We had many ||[3]fierce|| showers of rain throughout this day.

At night the wind cleared up, and we saw both our consorts fair by us; so that wind being very scant, we tacked and stood W. and by S. A child[1] was born in the Jewel about this time.

Saturday, 29.] The wind N. W. a stiff gale, and fair weather, but very cold; in the afternoon full N. and towards night N. and by E.; so we stood W.

Lord's day, 30.] The wind N. by E. a handsome gale, but close, misty weather, and very cold; so our ship made good way in a smooth sea, and our three ships kept close together. By our account we were in the same meridian with Isle Sable, and forty-two and a half.

Monday, 31.] Wind N. W. a small gale, close and cold weather. We sounded, but had no ground. About noon the wind came N. by E. a stiff, constant gale and fair weather, so as our ship's way was seven, eight, and sometimes twelve leagues a watch. This day, about five at night, we expected

||[3]Nowell|| ||[2]some leagues|| ||[3]fine||

---

[1] A note in the margin, "ergo fil. nullius," is an absurd conclusion of a stranger.

the eclipse, but there was not any, the sun being fair and clear from three till it set.

June 1, Tuesday.] The wind N. E. a small gale, with fair, clear weather; in the afternoon full S., and towards night a good gale. We stood W. and by N. A woman in our ship fell in travail, and we sent and had a midwife out of the Jewel. She was so far ahead of us at this time, (though usually we could spare her some sail,) as we shot off a piece and lowered our topsails, and then she brailed her sails and stayed for us.

This evening we saw the new moon more than half an hour after sunset, being much smaller than it is at any time in England.

Wednesday, 2.] The wind S. S. W., a handsome gale; very fair weather, but still cold; in the evening a great fog. We stood W. and by N. and W. N. W.

Our captain, supposing us now to be near the N. coast, and knowing that to the S. there were dangerous shoals, fitted on a new mainsail, that was very strong, and double, and would not adventure with his old sails, as before, when he had sea-room enough.

Thursday, 3.] The wind S. by W. a good steady gale, and we stood W. and by N. The fog continued very thick, and some rain withal. We sounded in the morning, and again *22
at noon, and had no ground. We sounded again about two, afternoon, and had ground about eighty fathom, a fine gray sand; so we presently tacked and stood S. S. E., and shot off a piece of ordnance to give notice to our consorts, whom we saw not since last evening.

The fog continued all this night, and a steady gale at S. W.

Friday, 4.] About four in the morning we tacked again (the wind S. W.) and stood W. N. W. The fog continued all this day, so as we could not see a stone's cast from us; yet the sun shone very bright all the day. We sounded every two hours, but had no ground. At night we tacked again and stood S. § In the great cabin, fast. §[1]

---

[1] Comparing the close of this paragraph, perhaps, with that of the next following, some careless person had substituted *thanksgiving* for *fast*, and then struck out the whole sentence. The first edition was printed in conformity

Saturday, 5.] In the morning the wind came to N. E. a handsome gale, and the fog was dispersed; so we stood before the wind W. and by N., all the afternoon being rainy. At night we sounded, but had no ground. In the great cabin, thanksgiving.

It rained most part of this night, yet our captain kept abroad, and was forced to come in in the night to shift his clothes.

We sounded every half watch, but had no ground.

Lord's day, 6.] The wind N. E. and after N., a good gale, but still foggy at times, and cold. We stood W. N. W., both to make Cape Sable, if we might, and also because of the current, which, near the west shore sets to the S., that we might be the more clear from the southern shoals, viz., of Cape Cod.

About two in the afternoon we sounded and had ground at about eighty fathom, and the mist then breaking up, we saw the shore to the N. about five or six leagues off, and were (as we supposed) to the S. W. of Cape Sable, and in forty-three and a quarter. Towards night it calmed and was foggy again, and the wind came S. and by E. We tacked and stood W. and by N., intending to make land at Aquamenticus, being to the N. of the Isles of Shoals.

Monday, 7.] The wind S. About four in the morning we sounded and had ground at thirty fathom, and was somewhat calm; so we put our ship a-stays, and took, in less than two hours, with a few hooks, sixty-seven codfish, most of them very great fish, some a yard and a half long, and a yard in compass.
*23 This came very seasonably, for our salt fish was now spent, and we were taking care for victuals this day (being a fish day).

After this we filled our sails, and stood W. N. W. with a small gale. *We hoisted out a great boat to keep our sounding the better.* The weather was now very cold. We sounded at eight, and had fifty fathom, and, being calm, we heaved

with this mutilation. As this was the sixty-eighth day passed on board ship, and the wind was adverse, the passengers might well keep a fast; and show their gratitude for the favorable gale the next day by thanksgiving.

out our hooks again, and took twenty-six cods; so we all feasted with fish this day. A woman was delivered of a child in our ship, stillborn. The woman had divers children before, but none lived, and she had some mischance now, which caused her to come near a month before her time, but she did very well. At one of the clock we had a fresh gale at N. W. and very fair weather all that afternoon, and warm, but the wind failed soon.

All the night the wind was W. and by S. a stiff gale, which made us stand to and again, with small advantage.

Tuesday, 8.] The wind still W. and by S., fair weather, but close and cold. We stood N. N. W. with a stiff gale, and, about three in the afternoon, we had sight of land to the N. W. about ten leagues, which we supposed was the Isles of Monhegan, but it proved Mount Mansell.[1] Then we tacked and stood W. S. W. We had now fair sunshine weather, and so pleasant a || sweet air || as did much refresh us, and there came a smell off the shore like the smell of a garden.

There came a wild pigeon into our ship, and another small land bird.

Wednesday, 9.] In the morning the wind easterly, but grew presently calm. Now we had very fair weather, and warm. About noon the wind came to S. W.; so we stood W. N. W. with a handsome gale, and had the main land upon our starboard all that day, about eight or ten leagues off. It is very high land, lying in many hills very unequal. At night we saw many small islands, being low land, between us and the main, about five or six leagues off us; and about three leagues from us, towards the main, a small rock a little above

||scene here||

[1] Now Mount Desert. I presume the name had been given in honor of Sir Robert Mansell, the highest naval officer of England, and one of the patentees in the great patent for New England, usually called the Plimouth charter, of King James, 3 November, 1620, which, in the title page of his History of Connecticut, Trumbull incautiously says, had been "never before published in America," when it may be found in Haz. I. 103 et seq. See North Amer. Review, VIII. 117, where is found an examination of that work, ascribed to a gentleman thoroughly acquainted with the geography and history of this country.

water. At night we sounded and had soft oozy ground at
*24 sixty fathom; so, the wind being now ||scant|| at W. we tacked again and stood S. S. W. We were now in forty-three and a half. This high land, which we saw, we judged to be at the W. cape of the great bay, which goeth towards Port Royal, called Mount Desert, or Mount Mansell, and no island, but part of the main.[1] In the night the wind shifted oft.

Thursday, 10.] In the morning the wind S. and by W. till five. In the morning a thick fog; then it cleared up with fair weather, but somewhat close. After we had run some ten leagues W. and by S. we lost sight of the former land, but made other high land on our starboard, as far off as we could descry,[2] but we lost it again.

The wind continued all this day at S. a stiff, steady gale, yet we bare all our sails, and stood W. S. W. About four in the afternoon we made land on our starboard bow, called the Three Turks' Heads, being a ridge of three hills upon the main, whereof the southmost is the greatest. It lies near Aquamenticus. We descried, also, another hill, more northward, which lies by Cape Porpus. We saw, also, ahead of us, some four leagues from shore, a small rock,[3] not above a flight shot over, which hath a dangerous shoal to the E. and by S. of it, some two leagues in length. We kept our ||2luff|| and weathered it, and left it on our starboard about two miles off. Towards night we might see the trees in all places very plainly, and a small hill to the southward of the Turks' Heads. All the rest of the land to the S. was plain, low land. Here we had a fine fresh smell from shore. Then, lest we should not get clear of the ledge of rocks, which lie under water from within a flight shot of the said rock, (called Boone Isle,) which we had now brought N. E. from us, towards Pascataquac, we tacked and stood S. E. with a stiff gale at S. by W.

Friday, 11.] The wind still S. W., close weather. We stood

||set|| ||2left||

1 But it is an island.

2 This was, undoubtedly, the White Hills, which the sun, at that season of the year, arrays in exquisite brilliance, frequently mistaken for that of clouds, as I have often observed.

3 "Called Boone Isle," is the governour's marginal note.

to and again all this day within sight of Cape Ann. The Isles of Shoals were now within two leagues of us, and we saw a ship[1] lie there at anchor, and five or six shallops under sail up and down.

We took many mackerels, and met a shallop, which stood from Cape Ann towards the Isles of Shoals, which be- *25
longed to some English fishermen.[2]

Saturday, 12.] About four in the morning we were near our port. We shot off two pieces of ordnance, and sent our skiff to Mr. Peirce[3] his ship (which lay in the harbour, and had been there [blank] days before). About an hour after, Mr. Allerton[4] came aboard us in a shallop as he was sailing to Pema-

---

1 Probably the ship was a fishing vessel, bringing no planters. These islands have never been populous. When R. Mather stopped there in 1635, he says, there were two families and about forty persons; so that we may conclude, most of them were transient residents.

2 Here is inserted, on a whole page of the original MS., a chart of the shore of Maine, Isles of Shoals, Boone Isle, Cape Ann, etc., with remarks on the appearance of the various landmarks on the several days, depth of water, bottom, bearings, distances, etc.

3 William Peirce deserves honourable mention among the early navigators between Old England and New. He made many voyages, of which the earliest known by me was in 1623, in the Ann, the sixth vessel, whose arrival in our bay, since the foundation of Plimouth, is mentioned. See Morton and Gov. Bradford in Prince, I. 114, 119, 121, 139. Edward Winslow, afterwards governour of Plimouth, and the celebrated commissioner of Cromwell in Admiral Penn's West India expedition, in that ship then returned with Peirce. He was, in 1629, in the Massachusetts Company's employment, master of the Mayflower, Haz. I. 278, and was now in the service of the Plimouth people, for whom, with Allerton, he had brought in the ship Lyon, this spring, from Bristol, many of their Leyden brethren. Hubbard unvaryingly, except on page 82, gives his name *Peirse*. So the Probate Record spells it, and so by himself, as I have seen, was it written. In another part of this volume his name will recur as the maker of the first American Almanac, viz., for 1639. He was killed at Providence, one of the Bahamas, in 1641, as will be seen in this History.

4 He was one of the principal men in Plimouth colony, of the memorable number of one hundred who came in the first ship, and the first assistant chosen in that government. Dr. Eliot laments, that the later years of Allerton are not illustrated by public services; but, we may presume, they would have been, had he, as our New England Biographer erroneously says, "spent the remainder of his days with the people of Plimouth." Notice of him will be found more than once in later portions of this work; and the reader,

quid. As we stood towards the harbour, we saw another shallop coming to us; so we stood in to meet her, and passed through the narrow strait between Baker's Isle and Little Isle, and came to an anchor a little within the islands.

After Mr. Peirce came aboard us, and returned to fetch Mr.
*26 Endecott,[1] who came to us about two of the clock, and
with him Mr. Skelton[2] and Capt Levett.[3] We that were

---

who would know of him what diligent inquiry could redeem from oblivion, must consult the invaluable edition of Morton's Memorial by Judge Davis, and Bacon's memoir, in 3 Mass. Hist. Coll. VII. 243, with the appendix of that Vol. Hutchinson, whose accuracy of information may generally be relied on, erroneously says, he left this country for England to settle there, but adds, "his male posterity settled in Maryland. If they be extinct, Point Alderton, [in Boston harbour,] which took his name, will probably preserve it many ages." The latest notice of him I have found, is in the second volume of our County Registry of *Deeds*, p. 192, where is recorded a receipt by Isaac Allerton, senior, merchant, of New Haven, 29 November, 1653, for one hogshead and four barrels of mackerel from Evan Thomas, vintner, of Boston, to adventure for half profits. A letter, in my possession, of J. Davenport, 4 August, 1658, mentions *young* Allerton coming from the *Dutch* to New Haven.

[1] This distinguished father of Massachusetts had, near two years before, been sent to found the plantation in the settlement of Salem, the oldest town in the colony. He had a commission, in 1629, from the company to act as governour, which was, of course, superseded by the arrival of Winthrop with the charter. With the history of his adopted country, that of Endecott is interwoven, till the time of his death, 15 March, 1665. He served four years as deputy governour, and sixteen years as governour, being at the head of administration a longer time than any other under the old patent, exceeded under the new charter by Shirley alone, and that only by one year. The farm which he cultivated, remains in possession of an honorable descendant; and one pear tree, planted by the governour on it, is said still to repay his care, bearing fruit in its old age.

[2] Samuel Skelton, pastor of Salem, came the year before in the same fleet with Higginson. The notices of his history are very brief; that of his death will be found in this volume, 2 August, 1634. His wife died 15 March, 1631, as we learn from Dudley, who says, "she was a godly and helpful woman; she lived desired, and died lamented, and well deserves to be honorably remembered."

[3] No satisfactory information has been obtained, by searching every quarter for some account of this gentleman, unless it may be he who died at sea about two years after this date, by which event some indiscreet letters fell into the hands of our adversaries, as will be seen in this work, 22 February, 1633. It might be conjectured, that we should identify him with Christopher Levett, *Esq.*, named in 1623, by the council of New England, under the great charter,

of the assistants, and some other gentlemen, and some of the women, and our captain, returned with them to Nahumkeck, where we supped with a good venison pasty and good beer, and at night we returned to our ship, but some of the women stayed behind.

In the ||mean time most of our|| people went on shore upon the land of Cape Ann, which lay very near us, and gath- *27
ered store of fine strawberries.

An Indian came aboard us and lay there all night.

Lord's day, 13.] In the morning, the sagamore[1] of Agawam and one of his men came aboard our ship and stayed with us all day.

About two in the afternoon we descried the Jewel; so we manned out our skiff and wafted them in, and they went as near the harbour as the tide and wind would suffer.

Monday, 14.] In the morning early we weighed anchor, and the wind being against us, and the channel so narrow as we

||morning the rest of the||

---

with Capt. Francis West and the governour of Plimouth for the time being, assistants to Robert Gorges, who had a commission to be general governour; and he published, at London, 1628, A Voyage into New England, begun in 1623, and ended in 1624, which is reprinted in 3 Mass. Hist. Coll. VIII. 159. But this is improbable; for those constituents were adversaries to our humble colony, and the representative would not have been at Salem on good terms with Endecott and Skelton; and that title seems hardly consistent with our text, being in those times very sparingly given, especially by Morton, the honest annalist of Plimouth, from whom all my information of that gentleman is derived. Nor do I more incline to the notion, that the person mentioned was Thomas Levet, who, with John Wheelwright, Augustine Story, Thomas Wite, and William Wentworth, is said to have purchased of four Indian sagamores, 17 May, 1629, a large tract of land in New Hampshire, by a very formal, though, it will be proved, a spurious deed, preserved in Belknap's New Hampshire, I. Appendix i. In that paper they are indeed called "all of the Massachusetts Bay in New England." The church of Exeter had, in 1639, with Wheelwright, after his banishment from our colony, a member of that name, Haz. I. 463; but I imagine none of Wheelwright's followers had yet come to our country. From a long correspondence, in 1816 and 1817, with which the late Rev. Dr. Bentley of Salem favoured me, I obtained little more than his opinion that Winthrop here intended Lovett, one of Roger Conant's companions, ancestor of a numerous and respectable family in Beverly. But the arguments, though plausible, did not convince.

[1] Hubbard, 130, calls him Masconomo.

could not well turn in, we warped in our ship and came to an anchor in the inward harbour.

In the afternoon we went with most of our company on shore, and our captain gave us five pieces.

[Large blank.]

Thursday, 17.] We went to Mattachusetts,[1] to find out a place for our sitting down. We went up Mistick River about six miles.[2]

We lay at Mr. Maverick's,[3] and returned home on Saturday.

---

1 It would now seem strange to use this expression, 'From Salem we went to Massachusetts;' but the name, though sometimes more comprehensive, generally included only the country lying around the inner bay, usually called Boston harbour, from Nahant to Point Alderton.

2 We must presume the reckoning to be from Conant's, afterwards called Governour's Island, on which now Fort Warren stands, or at least from Maverick's on Noddle's Island, because, being accustomed now to say, Mistick River empties into Charles River, or Boston harbour, at the easterly point of Charlestown, one would consider it little over three miles to the limit of boat navigation. The geography was then unknown or unsettled, and Mistick, at high tide, might as well appear the principal river, as Charles. Dudley speaks of Charlestown as "three leagues up Charles River," but he means undoubtedly to represent its mouth at the outer lighthouse.

3 Maverick was seated on Nottle's or Noddle's Island, and was a gentleman of good estate; but the time of his arrival in our country, I believe, has never been ascertained. As no assessment for the brief campaign against Merry Mount, 1628, is laid on him, perhaps he was not then here; yet I conclude from Johnson's language, lib. I. chap. xvii, he came in that year or the next. At a court 1 April, 1633, the first volume of our Colony Records, p. 96, informs us, "Noddle's Island is granted to Mr. Samuel Maverick, to enjoy to him and his heirs forever, yielding and paying yearly at the general court to the governour for the time being, either a fat wether, a fat hog, or £10 in money, and shall give leave to Boston and Charlestown to fetch wood continually, as their need requires, from the southern part of the said island." Winisemet Ferry, both to Charlestown and Boston, was also granted to him forever. Josselyn, who visited him 10 July, 1638, calls him, p. 12, "the only hospitable man in all the country, giving entertainment to all comers gratis;" but in the chronological observations, p. 252, appended to his Voyages, he is strangely confounded, as the father of Samuel Maverick, Esq., the royal commissioner in 1664, with the Rev. John Maverick, minister of Dorchester. Samuel was not one of our church members, being, says Hutchinson, an Episcopalian. But so were all our fathers. Johnson, in the passage before referred to, designates him as "an enemy to the reformation in hand, being strong for the lordly prelatical power." This circumstance, perhaps, saved him from much trouble in

As we came home,[1] we came by Nataskott, and sent for *28
Capt. Squib ashore — (he had brought the west-country people, viz., Mr. Ludlow,[2] Mr. Rossiter,[3] Mr. Maverick,[4] § etc., to the bay, who were set down at Mattapan,) § — and ended a difference[5] between him and the passengers; whereupon he sent his boat to his ship, (the Mary and John,) and at our

---

the earlier years of his residence; but in the progress of this History he will be seen involved in difficulty with the party of Dr. Child, petitioners for enlargement of privileges. He died 10 March, 1664.

[1] He means to Salem.

[2] The name of Roger Ludlow often occurs in our early history. At the last general court of the company in England, he was chosen an assistant in the room of Samuel Sharp, who had the year before come over to Salem in the same ship with Skelton. He was one of the founders of Dorchester, whence, in about five years, he removed to Windsor, of which he may be called the father. In Connecticut he was deputy governour several times, but he seems to have been unquiet in his domicile, for in 1639 he removed from Windsor and founded Fairfield. In 1654 he removed in disgust to Virginia, where, perhaps, in his advanced years, he became stationary. Eliot has drawn his character with discrimination. From Hubbard, 165, we learn, that he was brother-in-law of Endecott, whom he rivalled in ardour of temperament.

[3] Edward Rossiter, Esq., one of the assistants, Hutchinson informs us, was of a good family in the west of England, whence all the Dorchester people came. He was one of the principal encouragers of the settlement at that place, the first town in the ancient county of Suffolk, unless Quincy or Weymouth may dispute the honour. He died in a few months.

[4] Of the Rev. John Maverick I learn nothing, before his coming to Dorchester, but that he had been a preacher about forty miles from Exeter in Old England; and, after his arrival, so little, except what will be found in our History, during the few years of his life, that it may be unnecessary to prolong this note.

[5] The cause of this difference, probably, is found in the landing of the passengers from the ship, in which they sailed 20 March, and arrived 30 May. Capt. Roger Clap, who was one of the sufferers, informs us in his brief memoirs, "when we came to Nantasket, Capt. Squeb, who was captain of that great ship of four hundred tons, would not bring us into Charles River, as he was bound to do, but put us ashore, and our goods, on Nantasket Point, and left us to shift for ourselves in a forlorn place in this wilderness;" and a little farther on, "Capt. Squeb turned ashore us and our goods, like a merciless man." Trumbull, in a note on Vol. I. p. 8, of his History of Connecticut, several of whose first settlers came in this vessel, says, the master "was afterwards obliged to pay damages for this conduct." He leaves us to conjecture his authority, which was perhaps a contemporaneous manuscript of some gentleman of greater age and distinction than Clap.

*29 ||parting|| gave us five pieces. At our return we found the Ambrose in the harbour at Salem.

Thursday, July 1.] The Mayflower and the Whale arrived safe in Charlton harbour. Their passengers were all in health, but most of their cattle dead, (whereof a mare and horse of mine). Some ||[2]stone|| horses came over in good plight.

Friday, 2.] The Talbot[1] arrived there. She had lost fourteen passengers.

My son, Henry Winthrop,[2] was drowned at Salem.

Saturday, 3.] The Hopewell, and William and Francis arrived.

Monday, 5.] The Trial arrived at Charlton, and the Charles at Salem.

Tuesday, 6.] The Success arrived. She had [blank] goats and lost [blank] of them, and many of her passengers were near starved, etc.

Wednesday, 7.] The Lion went back to Salem.[3]

||firing|| ||[2] few||

---

[1] This ship had parted company with the rest, on 15 April, in a storm.

[2] Delicacy permitted the author to say no more of this son, whose name in the original MS. is denoted only by the initials; but this brief sentence from Hubbard, 131, will be easily indulged: "A sprightly and hopeful young gentleman he was, who, though he escaped the danger of the main sea, yet was unhappily drowned in a small creek, not long after he came ashore, even the very next day, July the 2d, after his landing, to the no small grief of his friends, and the rest of the company." He was baptized 19 January, 1607, o. s. It will be recollected, that he, with Mr. Pelham, had accidentally lost his passage in the ship with his father, to find another in one of those remaining at Southampton. His father's touching notice of his untimely death will be found in the first letter to his wife from America, given in the Appendix A. From the language the conclusion is unavoidable, that the young man had been married before they came from England, leaving his wife with her mother-in-law; and from a previous letter, written 2 March, after taking leave, she was, I presume, in an advanced state of pregnancy. The genealogy of the family mentions, that he married a Fones, his cousin, and left issue a daughter, who was baptized Martha, on Sunday, 9 May, 1630. He was the second son, and of the age of twenty-two years at his death.

[3] Whence she came *back*, is matter of conjecture, for in the text it has not been told, that she left Salem, after being first found by our author in that harbour on his arrival. I am induced to think, from a comparison of Prince, I. 201, 207, 241, contrary to his opinion of her landing Ashley at Penobscot in May, that she had gone there in June from Salem, being in the employment of

Thursday, 8.] We kept a day of thanksgiving in all the plantations.

[Large blank.[1]]

Thursday, August 18.] Capt. Endecott and —— Gib- *30
son[2] were married by the governour and Mr. Wilson.[3]

Saturday, 20.] The French ship called the Gift, came into the harbour at Charlton. She had been twelve weeks at sea, and lost one passenger and twelve goats; she delivered six.

Monday we kept a court.[4]

---

the Plimouth people, probably, and not of ours. After this return our governour made a contract with the master to go to the nearest port in England for provisions.

[1] Another ship, with passengers, came in on 31 July, see Bradford's Letterbook, in 1 Mass. Hist. Coll. III. 76, Fuller's letter of 2 August, 1630, to him. By a letter of 14 August, from the Governour to his son, in the appendix, it appears that the ship was Hewson's. Thomas Hewson, or Huson, a member of the Company in London, like Cradock, its former Governour, maintained a plantation for himself, which was, I think, at Marblehead.

[2] In Prince, I. 178, is preserved a letter from Cradock, in London, to Endecott, of the year before, from which we learn, that Endecott brought a wife from England, of the time of whose death we are ignorant. Morton, the scandalous author of New English Canaan, insinuates, that she perished by the quackery of Fuller of Plimouth. Two seasons of disease had afflicted the colonists at Salem, and the highest seem, equally with the lowest, to have been exposed to its power. By the kindness of the late Rev. William Bentley, the diligent historian of Salem, I learn that the name of this second wife was Elizabeth, and, from our Probate Records, that she survived her husband.

[3] Of the Rev. John Wilson's biography abundant materials are furnished by this History and most other books about our early affairs, and most copiously by Mather, which are happily abbreviated by the amiable Eliot in his New England Dictionary, and Emerson in his History of the First Church. His will is in our Probate Records, VI. p. 1. Having been minister at Sudbury, he was well known to his neighbour, our author, before their undertaking this work of leaving their native country.

[4] Johnson says, this court was holden 23 August, on board the Arbella. As he adds, that Winthrop was then chosen governour, and Dudley, deputy, which I agree with Prince in thinking improbable, since they had before been chosen in England, and our records have no trace of such election, it may also be doubted whether the assistants' meeting was held on shipboard. The record says, the court was at Charlton, and, we may imagine, the "great house" would have been the most convenient place. He is, however, right in his date, and the reader will remark, that, in noting events a few weeks before and after this time, the governour seems to fail of his usual diligence. It may be ac-

*31 Friday, 27.] We, of the congregation, kept a fast, and

---

counted for, either by his grief on account of his son's death, or anxiety from the extraordinary press of business in the circumstances of the new colony. The two preceding dates are erroneous. The 20th of August was Friday, not Saturday. Endecott's marriage, if it were on Thursday, was solemnized on the 19th, or if on the 18th it was Wednesday. The name of the month is indeed inserted, in the MS., not against the line in which the wedding is mentioned, but the next. But the dates before and after convince me, that August, and not July, is the date intended for Endecott's union; and I gather a slight confirmation of my judgment from the fact of his absence from this court. Johnson was, also, at Salem, near his dying wife.

The transactions of this *first* court are sufficiently interesting to excuse the extract from Prince, quoting the Colony Records: "Aug. 23. The first court of assistants held at Charlestown. Present Gov. Winthrop, Deputy Gov. Dudley, Sir Richard Saltonstall, Mr. Ludlow, Rossiter, Nowell, T. Sharp, Pynchon, and Bradstreet; wherein the first thing propounded is, How the ministers shall be maintained, Mr. Wilson and Phillips only proposed; and ordered, that houses be built for them with convenient speed at the public charge. Sir R. Saltonstall undertook to see it done at his plantation for Mr. Phillips; and the governour at the other plantation for Mr. Wilson; Mr. Phillips to have thirty pounds a year, beginning at the first of September next; Mr. Wilson to have twenty pounds a year till his wife come over, beginning at 10 July last; all this at the common charge, those of Mattapan and Salem excepted. Ordered, that Morton of Mount Wollaston, be sent for presently; and that carpenters, joiners, bricklayers, sawyers, and thatchers, take no more than two shillings a day, under pain of ten shillings to giver and taker."

Such was the first formal legislation of Massachusetts. But in March following, artificers were left at liberty to agree for their wages, Prince, II. 23, from Colony Records, though I am sorry to observe, that, two years after, the wisdom of experience was slighted, and the absurd policy of legal rates restored. For many years, this interference with the freedom of contracts was more or less severe, but the very means of enforcing it, probably, conduced to the abolition of the prejudice. It was left to the freemen of the several towns, from time to time, as occasion might require, to agree among themselves about the prices and rates of all workmen's labour and servants' wages; and to exceed those rates was made penal. In the adjustment, great diversity would soon arise in different places, to prevent which, it was provided, that if any town had cause of complaint against the freemen of any other town, for allowing greater wages than themselves, it should be in the power of the county court to adopt uniform regulations. During the war of our revolution, it is within the recollection of many, that, to counteract the inevitable embarrassment arising from the depreciation of the paper currency, arbitrary values were affixed to all commodities by an agreement, which was shown by experiment to be impracticable, after reason had in vain proved it unjust. See President Kirkland's Life of Fisher Ames, p. xi.

chose Mr. Wilson our teacher,[1] and Mr. Nowell[2] an elder,[3] *31

---

[1] Between the offices of teacher and pastor there was, we know, some slight difference in the early times; for, on Cotton's arrival three years after, he was chosen teacher, Wilson having a year before been made pastor. Yet these terms, though at first distinct, soon became convertible, and not much can with certainty be known of the distinction. Eliot says, — Biographical Dictionary, SKELTON, — "Mr. Skelton, being farther advanced in years, was constituted pastor of Salem church, Mr. Higginson, teacher." That author, however, in his Essays on the Ecclesiastical History of Massachusetts, felt the same difficulty as I have; for he says, 1 Hist. Coll. VII. 271, "we, who make no such distinction of offices, think it strange, that there should have been such difference between pastor and teaching elders; for we suppose any man, who can feed the people with knowledge, is qualified for one office equally with another. But it appears from the ecclesiastical history of this country, that A VERY GREAT DISTINCTION was made in the early state of their settlement. They esteemed many to be excellent *teachers*, whom they would not endow with the pastoral care." This seems to me too strongly stated. Cotton was an older and a greater man than Wilson, yet the latter was pastor. Higginson cannot be postponed to Skelton, except for his years; and as he took his degrees at Cambridge, 1609, being then of Jesus College, and 1613, being then of St. John's, while Skelton, who was of Clare Hall, was two years later, he was advanced enough in years to be either pastor or teacher. Maverick, the teacher of Dorchester, was older than Warham. Several instances in other towns of inferiority of the talents, if not character, of the pastor may be found, I think, in our early churches. Still the reason of Dr. Eliot's distinction may be supported by the rule of the clerical constitutions. See Trumbull, I. 282, 283, and the numerous authorities.

[2] Increase Nowell, Esq., had been chosen an assistant in England, and was a person of high consideration in the colony, of which he was long secretary. He died poor, 1 November, 1655. 3 Hist. Coll. I. 47.

[3] This office of *ruling* elder was generally kept up hardly more than fifty years, though in a few churches it continued to the middle of the last century, much reduced, however, in importance, and hardly distinguishable from that of deacon. The title of elders is retained from the beginning as a name for ministers. Prince, I. 92, delineates from high authorities the difference between *teaching* and *ruling* elders, thus: "Pastors, or teaching elders, who have the power both of overseeing, teaching, administering the sacraments, and ruling too, being chiefly to give themselves to studying, teaching, and the spiritual care of the flock, are therefore to be maintained." "Mere ruling elders, who are to help the pastors in overseeing and ruling; that their offices be not temporary, as among the Dutch and French churches, but continual. And being also qualified in some degree to teach, they are to teach only occasionally, through necessity, or in their pastor's absence or illness; but being not to give themselves to study or teaching, they have no need of maintenance. In less than two years, it will be seen in this History, a question arose, whether the

*32 and Mr. Gager and Mr. Aspinwall,[1] deacons. We used imposition of hands, but with this protestation by all, that

offices of magistrate and ruling elder might be filled at the same time by the same person. This may in our days appear quite unimportant, as the elder was not required to give himself to study or teaching, and was allowed no maintenance by the congregation. But in the primitive times it was so important, that our fathers of Boston took the advice of distant churches. Perhaps it was intended, by those who raised the inquiry, only to make Nowell lay down one of his titles. Happily he preferred to retain the station that demanded most service, and continued a magistrate.

The comparative disesteem, into which the office of ruling elder soon fell, was very pathetically lamented by many of the early planters in their later years. In a tract, by Joshua Scottow, 1691, under the whimsical title of "Old Men's Tears for their own Declensions, mixed with Fears of their and Posterities' further falling off from New England's primitive Constitution," this sad presage of portending judgments is thus treated: "It 's not unknown, that some churches, in laying their foundation, did solemnly promise and covenant, before God, and one to another, that they would be furnished with two teaching and two ruling elders; but it 's not attended to. It was not for want of maintenance; no, religion hath brought forth riches, but the daughter hath devoured the mother, as was said and observed of old."

"Where are the ruling elders, who as porters were wont to inspect our sanctuary gates, and to take a turn upon the walls? Is not the remembrance of such an officer almost lost and extinct, though the scripture and the platform of church discipline expressly declare for them, and set out their particular charge and work? It was an affecting question put forth by one of about fifty years old, born in the communion of our churches, concerning ruling elders, what these men were, who were formerly so called; professing, in time of their minority, there were such men to their remembrance, but since had forgotten what they were, and therefore desired resolution."

He proceeds to relate, that it is "questioned by some among us, whether such an officer be jure divino, or any rule for them in God's word, which occasions a reverend elder to take up the argument against such, and bewails the neglect of them in the churches, as a sad omen of their turning popular or prelatical, and if so, then to be regulated either by lord brethren or lord bishops. Is not this a great derogation from Christ's authority to say, that deacons may serve the churches' turn, who may officiate to do these elders' work? Is it not a preference of men's politics before Christ's institutes? Did not the practice of men's prudentials prove the ruin of the churches and rise of Antichrist? That our colleges by God's blessing should afford materials for teaching elders, and that our churches should grow so barren, as not to bring forth, nor educate men qualified for the other, may seem to portend a threatening of Christ's departure from them, as to conjugal communion."

[1] Frequent notice of William Aspinwall will be found in this History. He had come over with his wife, I presume, in the fleet with Winthrop, and cer-

it was only as a sign of election and confirmation, not of *33
any intent that Mr. Wilson should renounce his ||ministry|| he received in England.

||money||

---

tainly was in high esteem with our people until the unhappy controversy about antinomianism, in which, being on the side of the majority of Boston church, he was too important to get off with impunity. With the other disfranchised or discontented members, he removed to Rhode Island, which they purchased 24 March, 1638; and was wise enough, after the heat subsided, to return. He was the first secretary of that colony. His official signature is found afterwards in our records, as notary publick, to protests of bills of exchange. I have seen a very curious tract, entitled, "A brief Description of the Fifth Monarchy, or Kingdom that shortly is to come into the World; the Monarch, Subjects, Officers and Laws thereof, and the surpassing Glory, Amplitude, Unity, and Peace of that Kingdom, etc. And in the Conclusion there is added a Prognostick of the Time, when the Fifth Kingdom shall begin. By William Aspinwall. N. E." Its title-page is garnished with several texts of scripture distorted in the usual style of that day. "London, printed by M. Simmons, and are to be sold by Livewell Chapman at the Crown in Popeshead Alley, 1653." It contains fourteen pages. After showing, "that there is such a thing to be expected in the world as a fifth monarchy," from Daniel's vision, fulfilled in part by the execution of Charles I., he anticipates a farther progress from the destruction of all other kings, though "they have a little prolonging in life granted after the death of Charles Stuart." He comforts himself with the confidence, that "the space will be short; it will be but for a season and time; and then will their lives go for it, as well as Charles; and then, these four monarchies being destroyed, the fifth kingdom or monarchy follows immediately." Proceeding through his inquiries of "the Sovereign, (Jesus Christ,) subjects, officers, and laws of that kingdom," his fanatical vaticination favours us with "some hint of the time when the kingdom shall begin," which he had wit enough to delay so long, that the event might not probably injure the credit of the *living* soothsayer. "Know, therefore, that the uttermost durance of Antichrist's dominion will be in the year 1673, as I have proved from scripture in a brief chronology, ready to be put forth." Cromwell, whose power was just then preparing to be established, knew well the dangerous tendency of such jargon, unless when used by himself; but though he applied the civil arm to many other dreamers of King Jesus, I believe he left the New England seer to the safety of oblivion or contempt. A more useful work, with a well-written preface by him, was two years after printed in London, by the same printer, for the same Chapman, with the ludicrous prænomen, "An abstract of Laws and Government," etc., collected and digested by John Cotton, of Boston, in N. E. in his life time, presented to our General Court, "and now published after his death by William Aspinwall." This evidence of his talents is preserved in 1 Hist. Coll. V. 187. Our Registry of Births mentions, of his children, Edward, born 26 September,

September 20.] Mr. Gager died.[1]

*34 30.] About two in the morning, Mr. Isaac Johnson died; his wife, the lady Arbella, of the house of Lincoln,[2] being dead about one month before. He was a holy man, and wise, and died in sweet peace, leaving some[3] part of his substance to the colony.

The wolves killed six calves at Salem, and they killed one wolf.

1630, died 10 October following; Hannah, born 25 December, 1631; Elizabeth, (his wife's name,) born 30 September, 1633; Samuel, 30 September, 1635; Ethlan, 1 March, 1637; Dorcas, 14 February, 1640. But of him or his family we know nothing after some years. The respectable family bearing this name in our times, of which Thomas, H. C., 1804, Consul of the United States at London, is now the oldest, does not descend from him, but Peter Aspinwall, from Lancashire, I think, in England, whose will is in our Register, lib. VIII. 67.

[1] William Gager, whose election is mentioned in the former paragraph, Gov. Dudley calls "a right godly man, a skilful chyrurgeon." An allowance by the company, from the public treasury, was made him, on account of his office, but this practice did not continue. He was reckoned of the governour's household; and his son John is remembered by our author in his will. See Appendix. This son was, probably, a youth, and went with the governour's son to New London, where, in September, 1659, he complained with others to the commissioners of the United Colonies against some Indian outrage. Haz. II. 412. The name is, perhaps, perpetuated by descendants in Connecticut; at least, in Trumbull, II. 532, a William Gager, of the second church of Lebanon, is among the ministers, 27 May, 1725.

[2] Mather calls it "the best family of any nobleman then in England." Collins's Peerage informs us, that Thomas, third Earl of Lincoln, who was descended of a family that came in with William the Conquerer, had by one wife eight sons and nine daughters. Two sons and four daughters died young. One daughter, Frances, married John, son and heir of Sir Ferdinando Gorges; another, Susan, married John Humfrey; a third is the lady mentioned in the text. Dudley and Bradstreet, two other of our assistants, had lived many years in the family, so that a close relation to New England would be acknowledged by the brother of this lady, Theophilus, the fourth earl, who came to his title on the death of his father, 15 January, 1619. He was a warm patriot on the parliament's side in the civil war, but, after the captivity of the king, being inclined to moderation, was imprisoned and accused of treason by the usurping power of the army, which subverted, under Cromwell's direction, all the principles of the constitution. The earl was in reputation at the restoration, and bore a part in the solemnities of crowning Charles II.; and descendants of his grandfather, Henry Fiennes, the second Earl of Lincoln, I believe, enjoy their hereditary honours with the augmented title of Duke of Newcastle.

[3] Instead of *some*, was first written *a good.*

Thomas Morton[1] adjudged to be imprisoned, till he were sent

[1] Notice of the court, at which this sentence passed, being the second, held 7 September, is omitted by the author. Prince, I. 248, gives, from the Colony Records, the proceedings at full length: "Ordered, that Thomas Morton of Mount Wollaston shall presently be set in the bilbowes, and after sent prisoner to England by the ship called the Gift, now returning thither; that all his goods shall be seized to defray the charge of his transportation, payment of his debts, and to give satisfaction to the Indians for a canoe he took unjustly from them; and that his house be burnt down to the ground in sight of the Indians, for their satisfaction for many wrongs he has done them."

This settlement at Mount Wollaston, called Merry Mount by Morton, had been begun in 1625 by Capt. Wollaston. In the Memorial of Nathaniel Morton, the pious secretary of Plimouth colony, a full history of its sufferings, perhaps an impartial one, may be found. The unhappy subject of this note had some years before been established at Weston's plantation at Wessaguscus. He informs us, in his book, that he arrived in June, 1622, of course, in the Charity. For this publication, called New English Canaan, by Thomas Morton of Clifford's Inn, Gentleman, upon ten Years' Knowledge and Experiment of the Country, printed at Amsterdam by J. F. Stam, 1637, he undoubtedly repented, when again exposed to punishment here in 1644, as will be seen in the history of that time. This work is very rare, only one copy having ever been heard of by me, which was owned by his Excellency John Q. Adams. It is divided into three books; the first treating of the Indians; the second, of the natural history; the last, of the people planted there, their prosperity, what remarkable incidents have happened since, together with the tenets and practice of their church. This part, in thirty-one chapters, is written in an allegorical style, shadowing the principal characters under fictitious names, insomuch that it has to a great degree become hardly intelligible. Endecott suffers his vengeance under the appellation of Littleworth, and Winthrop is aptly called Joshua, and sirnamed Temperwell. Dedicating his work to the lords of the privy council, he says, "it is but a widow's mite, yet all that rapine and wrong hath left me to bring from thence." Laudatory verses are prefixed by Sir Chr. Gardiner and two others, and some of his own poetry is occasionally interspersed. In the 23 chapter of the third book, his own story of his sufferings is told, which we of this age may read without much injury to our forefather's memory: "A court is called of purpose for mine host, he there convented, and must hear his doom, before he go. Nor will they admit him to capitulate, and know wherefore they are so violent to put such things in practice against a man they never saw before. Nor will they allow of it, though he decline their jurisdiction."

"There they all, with one assent, put him to silence, crying out, Hear the governour, Hear the governour, who gave this sentence against mine host at first sight," as above from the Records. He ascribes to the governour a reason, which the character of the age may induce us to believe was really uttered, "because the habitation of the wicked should no more appear in Israel."

He styles himself "of Clifford's Inn, Gent." but his namesake, the Memorialist, from whom all later authors have taken every thing to his discredit, calls him "a pettifogger at Furnival's Inn." No doubt he was a common disturber of the whole country, for the expenses of the expedition against him by Standish, in 1628, were assessed on eight different plantations, in several of which there was little religious sympathy with the worthies of Salem and Plimouth.

Thomas Morton is the first writer, who gave currency to the ludicrous report of a vicarious punishment, for which New England has been jeered in former and later times. But justice to him requires me to add, that he mentions the fact only as a proposal, that was not agreed to, and thus overthrows the *possibility*, which Hubbard, 77, supposes, that justice "might be executed not on him that most deserved, but on him that could be best spared, or who was not like to live long, if he had been let alone." He has, indeed, given the fact (which is put beyond doubt by the contemporary relation of Winslow) that the *guilty* man was hanged. See Purchas's Pilg. lib. X. c. 5, Prince, I. 131, and 1 Hist. Coll. VIII. 266. A judicious note, on p. 333 and 4, of the Chronicles of the Pilgrims contains the sum of the matter; but the author relies too much on the authority of Prince, in support of his mistaken report, that Morton did not come over till March, 1625. Low as is our value of the character of Thomas Morton, yet why should we hesitate to believe his first line of ch. 2 in Book I. or the plainer statement opening ch. I. of the next Book in New English Canaan, "in the Moneth of June, auno salutis 1622, It was my chance to arrive in the parts of New England with thirty servants," etc., etc.? What motive could he have to misdate? Dr. Young will correct this in his next edition of the Chronicles.

Butler's Hudibras has admirably enlarged the ground-work, and decorated the edifice:

Our brethren of New England use
Choice malefactors to excuse,
And hang the guiltless in their stead,
Of whom the churches have less need.

* * * * * * * * *

A precious brother having slain,
In time of peace, an Indian,

* * * * * * * * *

The mighty Tottipotimoy †
Sent to our elders an envoy,
Complaining sorely of the breach
Of league, held forth by brother Patch.

* * * * * * * * *

For which he crav'd the saints to render
Into his hands, or hang the offender.
But they, maturely having weighed,
They had no more but him of the trade,—

† The poet may be excused for misappropriating the name of a sachem in Virginia.

into England, and his house burnt down, for his many injuries offered to the Indians, and other misdemeanours. Capt. *35
Brook, master of the Gift, refused to carry him.[1]

[Large blank.]

Finch, of Watertown, had his wigwam burnt and all his *36
goods.

Billington[2] executed at Plimouth for murdering one.

Mr. Phillips, the minister of Watertown,[3] and others, had their hay[4] burnt.

A man that served them in a double
Capacity, to preach and cobble, —
Resolv'd to spare him; yet to do
The Indian Hogan Mogan too
Impartial justice, in his stead did
Hang an old weaver that was bed-rid.

1 Dudley says, he was sent home in December by the Handmaid.

2 Of John Billington, and the circumstances of this case, it is remarkable, that no mention is made in Morton's New England Memorial, though written "with special reference to the first colony thereof, called Plimouth." Morton, the slanderer, alludes to the murder in a trifling manner. Something may be learned of it from Hubbard, 101, and Prince, II. 2, 3, extracting from Gov. Bradford's Register, a work unhappily lost. Hutchinson has perhaps digested all that can be known, in his Appendix, II. 413, in which he relates, that, on a doubt of their authority to inflict capital punishment, Winthrop's advice was sought and followed.

Billington had come over in the first ship, and was soon distinguished among that sober people; for we find, Prince, I. 103, he was guilty of the *first offence* in the colony, being in March, 1621, "convented before the whole company for his contempt of the captain's lawful command with opprobrious speeches; for which he is adjudged to have his neck and heels tied together." The family were four in number. John, his son, in the summer following, was five days lost in the woods, and preserved by the Indians. His son Francis had in January before discovered the lake, that from him has the name of Billington Sea. Gov. Bradford, writing to Cushman, June, 1625, says of the father, "Billington still rails against you, and threatens to arrest you, I know not wherefore; he is a knave, and so will live and die." 1 Hist. Coll. III. 37. This is much nearer to prophecy than many sayings which have been so regarded.

3 This name is presumed to have been given by Saltonstall; but the reason for his choice must be conjectured. A hamlet, called Waterton, which Sir Richard would often pass near in going to or returning from London, on journeys from his estate in Yorkshire, is in the parish of Luddington, on the Isle of Axholme, on the west side of Trent, not far from its junction with the Humber.

4 Prince, II. 3, who had not then acquired so perfect a knowledge of the au-

The wolves killed some swine at Saugus.

*37 A cow died at Plimouth, and a goat at Boston,[1] with eating Indian corn.

October 23.] Mr. Rossiter,[2] one of the assistants, died.

25.] Mr. Colburn[3] (who was chosen deacon by the congregation a week before) was invested by imposition of hands of the minister and elder.

The governour, upon consideration of the inconveniences which had grown in England by drinking one to another, restrained it at his own table, and wished others to do the like, so as it grew, by little and little, to disuse.[4]

---

thor's chirography, as his late experience furnished, in transcribing this passage, gave *houses*, instead of *hay*.

[1] This is the first notice, in this work, of the name of the town, which had been given by the court of assistants, 7 September preceding, with those of Dorchester and Watertown. We may be confident, therefore, that the settlement had made good progress, though Gorges postpones it to the next spring. Here is proof, that the name of our chief city of New England was given, not, as often is said, after the coming of Cotton, but three years before.

[2] Hutchinson, I. 17, could give little account of this gentleman.

[3] William Colburn was a gentleman of great influence in Boston, and representative of the town in 1635, 6 and 7. The name is spelt with seven or eight variations, and his own signature, in a deed now before me, is Colbron, though the scrivener began, I, William Coleborne. He was long a ruling elder, after ceasing to be deacon, and died 1 August, 1662. His will is in our Probate office, lib. I. 400.

[4] In the MS. volume of this work last found, I discovered a loose paper, containing reasons for a law against this custom, written, probably, by Winthrop, which appears sufficiently interesting, to inquirers into the customs of our fathers, to justify its insertion.

"(1.) Such a law as tends to the suppressing of a vain custom (quatenus it so doth) is a wholesome law. This law doth so, — ergo. The minor is proved thus: 1. Every empty and ineffectual representation of serious things is a way of vanity. But this custom is such: for it is intended to hold forth love and wishes of health, which are serious things, by drinking, which, neither in the nature nor use, it is able to effect; for it is looked at as a mere compliment, and is not taken as an argument of love, which ought to be unfeigned, — ergo. 2. To employ the creature out of its natural use, without warrant of authority, necessity or conveniency, is a way of vanity. But this custom doth so, — ergo.

"(2.) Such a law as frees a man from frequent and needless temptations to dissemble love, etc. (quatenus it so doth) is a wholesome law. But this doth so, — ergo."

On such arguments a law was passed, as may be seen, 10 mo. 1639.

29.] The Handmaid arrived at Plimouth, having been twelve weeks at sea, and spent all her masts, and of twenty-eight cows she lost ten. She had about sixty passengers, who came all well; John Grant, master.

Mr. Goffe wrote to me, that his shipping this year had utterly undone him.

She brought out twenty-eight heifers, but brought but seventeen alive.[1]

November 11.] The master came to Boston with Capt. Standish[2] and two gentlemen passengers, who came to plant here, but having no testimony, we would not receive them. *38

10.] [blank] Firmin, of Watertown, had his wigwam burnt. Divers had their hay-stacks burnt by burning the grass.

27.] Three of the governour's servants were from this day to the 1 of December abroad in his skiff among the islands, in bitter frost and snow, being kept from home by the N. W. wind, and without victuals. At length they gat to Mount Wollaston,[3] and left their boat there, and came home by land. Laus Deo.

December 6.] The governour and most of the assistants, and others, met at Roxbury, and there agreed to build a town fortified upon the neck between that and Boston, and a committee was appointed to consider of all things requisite, etc.

14.] The committee met at Roxbury, and upon further consideration, for reasons, it was concluded, that we could not have a town in the place aforesaid: 1. Because men would be forced to keep two families. 2. There was no running water; and if there were any springs, they would not suffice the town. 3. The most part of the people had built already,

---

[1] This is easily rendered consistent with loss of ten by supposing, that it became necessary to kill one for food, from the unusual length of the passage. I do not think the governour erased this sentence.

[2] Miles Standish is treated by Dr. Belknap, in his American Biography, with such felicity, that it cannot be necessary for me to protract this note any further than to advise the reader, who desires more knowledge of him, to consult Judge Davis's edition of Morton.

[3] For some account of the first settlement in this place, which is the north-eastern promontory of Quincy, formerly of Braintree, see note on page 34.

and would not be able to build again. So we agreed to meet at Watertown that day sen'night, and in the meantime other places should be viewed.

Capt. Neal[1] and three other gentlemen came hither to us.
*39 He came in the bark Warwick, this summer, to Pascataqua, sent as governour there for Sir Ferdinando Gorges and others.

21.] We met again at Watertown, and there, upon view of a place a mile beneath the town, all agreed it a fit place for a ||fortified||[2] town, and we took time to consider further about it.

24.] Till this time there was (for the most part) fair, open weather, with gentle frosts in the night; but this day the wind came N. W., very strong, and some snow withal, but so cold as some had their fingers frozen, and in danger to be lost. Three of the governour's servants, coming in a shallop from

||beautiful||

---

[1] Walter Neal, whose name will occur several times in the early parts of this History, had, in September preceding, as appears from the letter of Thomas Eyre, in Belknap's N. H. I. Appendix ii. promised to discover the lakes, in which the chief purpose of his employers, probably, was to secure a monopoly of the beaver trade. The vessel, as is before mentioned in the text, p. 7, had been fitted out in March, perhaps with Neal on board, to join, as was thought, the fleet, which brought Winthrop and his companions; but from her not joining, they feared she had been captured by the Dunkirkers. As the scheme of the adventurers would require secrecy and despatch, perhaps the report of their intention to join our fleet was only a pretence. She arrived late in May; for the letter of Eyre acknowledges "a good account of your times spent from the first of June." Neal left New England in August, 1633, as appears in this work and articles vi. vii. and viii. of the Appendix above-mentioned; and nothing more is known of him, but the forgery of his name to a deed, as a witness, a little more than a year before the probable date of his first arrival.

[2] Dr. Holmes, in his History of Cambridge, 1 Hist. Coll. VII. 6, and American Annals, I. 262, note 1, was led into error by the former edition of this work. "A fit place for a *beautiful* town" it certainly was; but our fathers, at that time, were chiefly solicitous for the *security* of their dwellings. This note, however, is made, not so much to correct the mistake, as to express my high sense of the value of that writer's labours. His accuracy is wonderfully preserved through two large volumes, surpassing that of all other authors on American history, except Prince, the interruption of whose work is a misfortune that can never wholly be compensated, because we can never retrieve the loss of his materials.

Mistick, were driven by the wind upon Noddle's[1] Island, and forced to stay there all that night, without fire or food; yet, through God's mercy, they came safe to Boston next day, but the fingers of two of them were blistered with cold, and one swooned when he came to the fire.

26.] The rivers were frozen up, and they of Charlton could not come to the sermon at Boston till the afternoon at high water.

Many of our cows and goats were forced to be still || abroad || for want of houses.

28.] Richard Garrett,[2] a shoemaker of Boston, and one of the congregation there, with one of his daughters, a young maid, and four others, went towards Plimouth in a shallop, against the advice of his friends; and about the Gurnett's Nose the wind overblew so much at N. W. as they were *40
forced to come to a ||[2]killock|| at twenty fathom, but their boat drave and shaked out the ||[3]stone, || and they were put to sea, and the boat took in much water, which did freeze so hard as they could not free her; so they gave themselves for lost, and, commending themselves to God, they disposed themselves to die; but one of their company espying land near Cape Cod, they made shift to hoist up part of their sail, and, by God's special providence, were carried through the rocks to the shore, where some gat on land, but some had their legs frozen into the ice, so as they were forced to be cut out. Being come on shore they kindled a fire, but, having no hatchet, they could get little wood, and were forced to lie in the open air all night, being extremely cold. In the morning two of their

||aboard|| ||[2]hillock|| ||[3]stern||

---

[1] Prince, II. 29, giving the names of several admitted, in May following, freemen of the colony, among whom is William Noddle, adds in a note, "Perhaps Noddle's Island might derive its name from him."

[2] The word is printed thus by me, although the governour's MS. rather looks like Garrard, because that was the true name of the sufferer. Prince makes the same correction, taking the story from our author. Hubbard, 138, has it Garn; but the *original* MS. of that author, who borrowed wholly from Winthrop, was, perhaps, more faithful in its representation. In the First Church Records, I find Garrett's name, as a member, No. 55, and he was, undoubtedly, one of the passengers in the fleet of 1630.

company went towards Plimouth, (supposing it had been within seven or eight miles, whereas it was near fifty miles from them). By the way they met with two Indian squaws, who, coming home, told their husbands that they had met two Englishmen. They thinking (as it was) that they had been shipwrecked, made after them, and brought them back to their wigwam, and entertained them kindly; and one of them went with them the next day to Plimouth, and the other went to find out their boat and the rest of their company, which were seven miles off, and having found them, he holp them what he could, and returned to his wigwam, and fetched a hatchet, and built them a wigwam and covered it, and gat them wood (for they were so weak and frozen, as they could not stir;) and Garrett died about two days after his landing; and the ground being so frozen as they could not dig his grave, the Indian hewed a hole about half a yard deep, with his hatchet, and having laid the corpse in it, he laid over it a great heap of wood to keep it from the wolves. By this time the governour of Plimouth had sent three men to them with provisions, who being come, and not able to launch their boat, (which with the strong N. W. wind was driven up to the high water mark,) the Indian returned to Plimouth and fetched three more; but before they came, they had launched their boat, and with a fair southerly wind were gotten to Plimouth, where another of their company died, his flesh being mortified with the frost; and the two who went towards Plimouth died also, one of them being not able to get thither, and the other had his feet so frozen as he died of it after. The girl escaped best, and one Harwood,[1]
*41 a godly man of the congregation of Boston, lay long under the surgeon's hands; and it was above six weeks

[1] Harwood was one of the earliest brethren of the church, being No. 27. From the Colony Records, I. 82, it may be learned, that our court of assistants, 16 August following, ordered, "that the executors of Richard Garrett shall pay unto Henry Harwood the sum of twenty nobles, according to the proportion that the goods of the said Richard Garrett shall amount unto." This looks little like satisfaction of a debt, legally considered, and must, I think, be a provision, out of the estate of the dead, for the danger and suffering, into which the living man had been led by him. As such it may be considered an imitation of oriental jurisprudence.

before they could get the boat from Plimouth; and in their return they were much distressed; yet their boat was very well manned, the want whereof before was the cause of their loss.

January.] A house at Dorchester was burnt down.

February 11.] Mr. Freeman's[1] house at Watertown was burned down, but, being in the daytime, his goods were saved.

5.] The ship Lyon, Mr. William Peirce, master, arrived at Nantasket. She brought Mr. Williams,[2] (a godly ‖ minis-

---

[1] Samuel Freeman, I am told, came from Devonshire, and was one of the chief planters at Watertown. His name is in the list of persons *desiring* to be made freemen, Prince, II. 4; but the record of his admission I find not till seven or eight years after. Tradition in the family informs of his return home. His elder son, Henry, it is said, died in 1672, on the paternal estate, and that branch of the family ceased with his grandchildren. Edmund Freeman, one of the earliest settlers at Sandwich, assistant of Plimouth colony in 1640 and following years, and John Freeman, one of the fathers of Eastham, assistant in that colony in 1660 and following years, are by tradition reported to have been brothers of this Watertown gentleman; but it is not known whether it were a son or grandson Edmund, who in 1646 married Rebecca, daughter of Gov. Prence, who had previously married his widowed mother. Part of the governour's estate at Eastham is still enjoyed by descendants of the Freeman race. This name is extremely common in the county of Barnstable, and has sent out its branches to other parts widely. My friend, the late Rev. Dr. James Freeman, who died 14 November, 1835, a most careful student of our geography, and early history, was great, great, great grandson of the first Samuel. Watertown Records show, "Samuel, the son of Samuel and Apphia Freeman, born 11 (3), 1638."

[2] The biography of Roger Williams deserved more attention than it had thirty years ago received, but would lead me too far from my present undertaking, even were not the attempt to do full justice to his merit above my ability. In our common books he is said to have studied at the University of Oxford, and his life proves he had there learned more than in that day was commonly taught. Had Belknap lived to enlarge the number of volumes of his American Biography, his assiduity and judgment would have raised this pilgrim, whose name for some generations was oppressed with calumny, to a rank inferior, non longo intervallo, only to the two Winthrops, Brewster, Bradford, and Penn. For the effect that bigotry and folly produced in Massachusetts, we refer to Hubbard, 208, who transcribed his facts from Morton, and to Mather, too long the chief authority in our ecclesiastical affairs, though justice was done nearly one hundred and twenty years since by the reverend historian of Rhode Island. From the utter condemnation that most of our theologians of the first and second generation denounced against him, for vindicating the liberty of worshipping God according to the light of conscience, Williams was partially preserved by an incon-

*42 ter, ||[1]) with his wife, Mr. Throgmorton,[2] [blank] Perkins,
||man||

---

sistency, to which he was led in the latter years of his life by aversion to the Quakers; and this temporary change to intolerance gained him the title of "child of light," which the blameless policy and virtue of a long administration in the flourishing plantation of Providence had not deserved. The amiable historian of Salem, and the author of New England Biographical Dictionary, were, in our times, the first to confer due honour on his character. The examination *provoked* by the former does little injury to any but the writer of Remarks in 1 Hist. Coll. VII. introd. Deficiency in all former accounts of this great, *earliest* assertor of religious freedom, has been well supplied by a gentleman, whose elegance and perspicuity of style are fully known. Several quires of original letters of Williams have been seen by me, transcribed by or for the Rev. Mr. Greenwood of this city; and other materials are abundant. He lived to a good old age, and deserves peculiar honour from virtuous politicians for his conduct to the Indians, and from men of science for his researches into their language. In Benedict's General History of the Baptists, I. 473, it is said, that he received a liberal education under the patronage of the great Sir Edward Coke. The authority for this is the records of Williams's own church at Providence. I have examined that volume, and regret to say, that it was compiled within sixty years, probably by Gov. Hopkins. He is there said to have studied the law with the same oracle, but, perhaps, it was rather under his advice. The traditions in this case may be worth more than such traditions usually are. Williams certainly displays a knowledge of general principles of equity and jurisprudence beyond many practitioners of the science in that time, after all allowances for his rigid rejection of many harmless points, which will be disclosed in this History. From a memorandum on the back of a letter of Williams to Mrs. Ann Sadler, about 1652, I ascertain, that the Lord Chief Justice had favored him so far as to procure his admission at a school of high distinction, called Sutton's Hospital, now the Charter House. Mrs. Sadler was daughter of Sir Edward Coke. Letters of Williams and of Mrs. Sadler are in the Library of Trinity College, Cambridge. See Elton's Life of R. W., pp. 96–109.

1 In the original MS. this word has been tampered with, perhaps by some zealot; yet it appears clearly enough to be Winthrop's usual abbreviation for that which is restored in the text, and Prince read it as I do.

2 We may think, he was that George Thockmorton, freeman, 18 May, 1631; yet his baptismal name may be John. John Throgmorton, from a note in Hutchinson, I. 371, it appears, was thought, by the fiery Hugh Peter, worthy of the same persecution that drove Williams to Providence. The original letter is preserved by our Historical Society. From Callender we learn, that he followed his spiritual guide, and by him he is mentioned in a letter of 1638, 3 Hist. Coll. I. 172. The name is perpetuated at Salem, as the Rev. Dr. Bentley informed me, by Throgmorton's Cove.

[blank] ||Ong,||[1] and others, with their wives and children, about twenty passengers, and about two hundred *43
tons of goods. She set sail from Bristol, December 1. She had a very tempestuous passage, yet, through God's mercy, all her people came safe, except Way[2] his son, who fell from the spritsail yard in a tempest, and could not be recovered, though he kept in sight near a quarter of an hour. Her goods also came all in good condition.

8.] The governour went aboard the Lyon, riding by Long Island.

9.] The Lyon came to an anchor before Boston, where she rode very well, notwithstanding the great drift of ice.

10.] The frost brake up; and after that, though we had many ||[2]snows|| and sharp frost, yet they continued not, neither were the waters frozen up as before. It hath been observed, ever since this bay was planted[3] by Englishmen, viz., seven years, that at this day the frost hath broken up every year.

||Augre|| ||[2]storms||

---

[1] This word has perplexed me much. It was certainly given wrong in the former edition, for the first letter is a capital *O*. Presuming that the others were *n*, *y*, *e*, and that the governour wrote the word as frequently pronounced, I once inserted Olney, with much confidence in the substitution, as by Salem church Thomas Olney was excommunicated, Hutchinson, I. 371, for uniting in the errors with Williams. But it is actually written Onge, a name so unusual, that it was not adopted before I found, by Watertown Records, Frances Ong, widow, buried 12 (9), 1638, and in our county Register, 1643, a mortgage to the children of the deceased, and in 1646 a deed from Simon Onge of that town.

Of Perkins, I am less able to speak with certainty, because the name is very common, but conclude he was not the man designed in an order of our assistants, 3 April, 1632, "that no person whatsoever shall shoot at fowl upon Pullen Point or Noddle's Island, but that the said places shall be preserved for John Perkins to take fowl with nets," Mass. Rec. I. 85; for he is the same, whose sentence for drunkenness is given by Hutchinson, I. 385. But the gentleman mentioned in the text, probably, sat down, with Williams and his other fellow passengers, at Salem; to confirm which opinion, the reverend historian of that town assured me, that, from the earliest time, the name of Perkins has been found in possession of estates in that part of Salem since become Topsfield.

[2] Way was of Dorchester, as, I presume, the name again occurring, 26 July next, refers to the same person, who was one of the principal men in that town.

[3] This planting in Boston harbour deserves and will reward inquiry. In the

*44 The poorer sort of people (who lay long in tents, etc.)

---

autumn of 1622 Weymouth, under the aboriginal name of Wessaguscus, Wessaguscusset, Wessagussett, Wichaguscussett, or Wessagusquassett, had been planted by a small colony from England, sent by Thomas Weston; but the settlement was broken up the following year. See Winslow's Relation, 1 Hist. Coll. VIII. 248–271. A company under Capt. Robert Gorges, (son of Sir F.) together with the Rev. William Morell, reoccupied the same spot in a few months after. They, in November, 1623, lost all their goods and provisions at Plimouth by fire, occasioned by the carelessness of the sailors celebrating, I presume, the anniversary of the gunpowder plot with less discretion than loyalty. From this and other misfortunes, the design was next year relinquished. See Bradford, in Prince, I. 141–144. Morell continued above a year in the country, and wrote a poetical, but not very particular account of the land and its productions, reprinted in English and Latin, 1 Hist. Coll. I. 125. Perhaps some stragglers remained on the soil. In 1625 Mount Wollaston was occupied by the captain of that name. This was in Quincy. Here was that disorderly band, among whom Morton, of whom see page 34, exhibited his talent for mischief. This settlement, I believe, was permanent, though the high authority of Gov. Dudley's Narrative, 1 Hist. Coll. VIII. 37, makes it vanish; and, if permanent, must be considered the oldest of Massachusetts colony, unless Weymouth should assert a claim of vitality through its state of suspended animation. Hubbard, 107, informs us, that, the same year, Nantasket was planted by Lyford, Oldham, and Conant, persons discontented with the unseasonable rigour of their brethren of Plimouth. Not long, however, did they remain there; at least Lyford and Conant went to Cape Ann, where some gentlemen of Dorchester, in Old England, attempted to establish a fishing station; but Conant soon removed thence to Salem, where Endecott, in 1628, found him. Hutchinson, I. 15, makes this last removal of Conant to be in the autumn of 1626, and adds, "I find mention made of planters at Winisimet about the same time, who probably removed there from some of the other plantations." From Hubbard, 105, we learn, that David Thomson, a Scotchman, who had been sent over in 1623 by Gorges, Mason, and their associates, and was seated at Piscataqua, "removed down into Massachusetts Bay within a year after." But I doubt, that Hubbard, who is not usually precise, except when he copies, has antedated this emigration of Thomson; for Gov. Bradford, in Prince, I. 161, mentions his abiding at Piscataqua in 1626. The business, however, in which he united, in the summer of that year, with the Plimouth colonists, seems to have been connected with an intention of seeking better quarters, which he found in an island of our harbour that has ever since borne his name. This island, with the neck of land (Squantum) on the neighbouring continent, Hubbard, from the Colony Records, says, "was confirmed to him and his heirs by the court of Massachusetts."

Of the exact time when Maverick first pitched his tent on Noddle's Island, or Thomas Walford at Charlestown, or William Blaxton at Boston, we shall,

were much afflicted with the scurvy, and many died, espe-

---

probably, remain forever uninformed. Walford was found in possession by the Spragues, who went from Salem soon after arriving there in 1629. That Blaxton had occupied our peninsula several years, and with no slight advantage, we may presume from the expenses assessed on the several plantations, from Plimouth northward, for the campaign against Morton at Merry Mount, in 1628; his proportion, though the least, being more than one third of that to be paid by the settlers at Salem, before the coming of Endecott. With him, too, was probably included the Winisimet people, if there were any, and Walford and Maverick, if they had dwellings. The apportionment of the charges, from Bradford, in 1 Hist. Coll. III. 63, is interesting: —

Plimouth	£2.10	Natascot	£1.10
Naumkeak	1.10	Thomson	0.15
Pascataquack	2.10	Blaxton	0.12
Jeffrey and Burslem	2.00	Edward Hilton	1.00
		Total	£12.7

It is not in my power to determine the residence of Jeffery and Burslem, but conjecture would fix it either at Cape Ann, or, more probably, Weymouth, from the latter town a Mr. Bursley being found a deputy so early as 1636.

Blaxton removed a few years after Winthrop's arrival, and seated himself about thirty-five miles to the southward, near the place which the famous Roger Williams soon rendered illustrious by the name of Providence, where a river, which flows into the harbour of that city, still bears the name of this pilgrim. See a memoir in 2 Hist. Coll. X. 170, which gives the time of his death 26 May, 1675, and contains all that the assiduous antiquary of Plimouth could rescue from the shades of forgetfulness. I am able to add only, that by our Colony Records he took the freeman's oath 18 May, 1631, being the first admission, and that in our Town Records it appears he "was married to Sarah Stephenson, widow, 4 July, 1659, by John Endecott, governour. He well improved his new estate, and the apples on his farm were long in high repute. 2 Hist. Coll. IX. 174.

An approximation to the time of Blaxton's coming to Boston is easily obtained. Lechford, who wrote in 1641, thus speaks of him: "One Mr. Blaxton, a minister, went from Boston, having lived there *nine* or *ten* years, because he would not join with the church; he lives near Mr. Williams, but is far from his opinions." Now, to ascertain when he withdrew from this spot first planted by him, is all that remains, and we may find reason, I believe, to reckon it the spring of 1635. That he was unjustly driven away, is an opinion not to be entertained for a moment. As all the right of soil, which the government at home could give, was by the charter given to our governour and company, we shall be convinced of the equity in their treatment, by reading their Records, I. 97. At a court, 1 April, 1633, "It is agreed, that Mr. Wm. Blaxton shall

*45 cially at Boston and Charlestown;[1] but when this ship came and || brought store || of juice of lemons, many recovered speedily. It hath been always observed here, that such as fell into discontent, and lingered after their former conditions in England, fell into the scurvy and died.

18.] Capt. Welden,[2] a hopeful young gentleman, and an experienced soldier, died at Charlestown of a consumption, and was buried at Boston with a military funeral.

Of the old planters, and such as came the year before, there

|| brought us good stores ||

---

have fifty acres of ground set out for him near to his house in Boston to enjoy forever." All this right be sold next year to the other inhabitants, of whom none, now recollected, had so large a portion. See the depositions of Odlin, Walker, Hudson and Letherland about this purchase, 2 Hist. Coll. IV. 202. This evidence, taken after the tyrannical proceedings in chancery in 1683, against our charter, showed that all titles were in danger on our side of the ocean, states the price agreed to be six shillings for every householder in town, still reserving six acres for the grantor. The Town Records of that day, on the second *surviving* page, confirm the evidence; "10 November, 1634, at a general meeting upon public notice, it was agreed that Edmund Quincy, Samuel Wilbore, William Balstone, Edward Hutchinson the elder, and William Cheeseborough the constable, shall make and assess all these rates, viz., a rate for £30 to Mr. Blaxton, a rate for cow's keeping, etc., etc." This sum was, undoubtedly, the consideration for his sale, and, taking from the depositions the proportion for each, would show the number of householders one hundred. I desire the reader to correct an error in Shaw's Description of Boston, 308, where he has *Blackstone*, instead of Balstone, one of a committee in this month to divide the lands among the inhabitants. Blaxton, probably removed the following spring. If so, and he had resided here as long as Lechford, who visited him at his new plantation, reports, he arrived at Boston in 1625 or 1626.

Mr. Felt thinks, he arrived in 1623, with Robert Gorges; and my opinion is that he came not before 1625, and with Capt. Wollaston. Perhaps he abandoned his associates at Braintree, when they received Morton. He was of Emanuel College, Cambridge, where, on taking his degrees of A. B. and A. M., 1617 and 1621, he subscribed the requisite declarations, as I saw the signatures, by his own hand, William Blaxton.

[1] This is the first instance of thus spelling the name.

[2] By Dudley, 1 Hist. Coll. VIII. 45, the loss of this gentleman is lamented in these terms: "Amongst others, who died about this time, was Mr. Robert Welden, who, in the time of his sickness, we had chosen to be captain of one hundred foot, but before he took possession of his place, he died, the *sixteenth* of February, and was buried as a soldier, with three vollies of shot." Our MS. is very plain

were but two, (and those servants,) which had the scurvy in all the country. At Plimouth not any had it, || no not || of those, who came this year, whereof there were above sixty. Whereas, at their first planting ||[2]there,|| near the half of their people died of it. *46

A shallop of Mr. Glover's[1] was cast away upon the rocks about Nahant, but the men were saved.

Of those which went back in the ships this summer, for fear of death or famine, etc., many died by the way and after they were landed, and others fell very sick and low, etc.

The Ambrose, whereof Capt. Lowe was master, being new masted at Charlton, spent all her masts near Newfoundland, and had perished, if Mr. Peirce, in the Lyon, who was her consort, had not towed her home to Bristol. Of the other ships[2] which returned, three, viz., the Charles, the Success, and the Whale, were set upon by Dunkirkers, near Plimouth in England, and after long fight, having lost many men, and being much torn, (especially the Charles,) they gat into Plimouth.

The provision, which came to us this year, came at excessive rates, in regard of the dearness of corn in England, so as every bushel of wheat-meal stood us in fourteen shillings, peas eleven shillings, etc. Tonnage was at £6.11.[3]

||nor out|| ||[2]time||

---

in its date, and the discrepancy may be reconciled by referring it to the funeral honours, though Prince, II. 20, was not of this opinion. No. 91 of the members of Boston church is, "Elizabeth Welden, gone to Watertown," perhaps the widow of the captain.

[1] John Glover was one of the chief men of Dorchester, and many times a deputy in the general court, from which station his services raised him to be an assistant. Johnson, lib. I. chap. xiv. calls him "a man strong for the truth, a plain, sincere, godly man, and of good abilities."

[2] A strange misapprehension by Hubbard, 140, who postpones to the following spring the voyage of these ships returning in the autumn, after bringing to this country the colony, with the relation of which our History begins, arose solely from his failing to observe, that the report of their disasters was brought hither by the Lyon, which, after towing one of them, the Ambrose, home, had left England, 1 December. His mistake would have been impossible, had he, as Prince, II. 19, combined the more perspicuous narrative of Dudley, on this subject, with that of Winthrop.

[3] We find this last sentence in the margin of the original MS. The extrem-

*47 22.] We held a day of thanksgiving for this ship's arrival, by order from the governour and council, directed to all the plantations.

---

ity of want here, before the arrival of the Lyon, may be judged of from the anticipations announced by Winthrop in his letters. See Appendix. Mather says, probably from tradition, that the governour "was distributing the last handful of meal in the barrel unto a poor man distressed by the wolf at the door;" and the language of Capt. Clap, one of the sufferers, Prince II. 10, is much more satisfactory, because less figurative. Having been furnished with an original letter of the venerable John Rogers, of Dedham in Old England, father of *our* Nathaniel, addressed, probably, in November, 1630, to John Winthrop, jun., at Bristol, "or, in his absence, to Mr. Pelham of Buers," on this *foreseen* evil, I think it worth insertion: —

"Good Mr. Winthrop, — I hope you have my letters with certain moneys that I sent to you to intreat you, of all love, to provide some little matter of butter and meal for such as I named, wherein I earnestly entreat your loving faithfulness and care to procure it and direct it to them, to Jeffery Ruggles, late of Sudbury, he is the chief. But this day I have received so lamentable a letter from one John Page, late of Dedham, that hath his wife and two children there, and he certifies me, that unless God stir up some friends to send him some provision, he is like to starve. Now I pity the man much, and have sent you twenty shillings, entreating you, for God's sake, to provide such a barrel of meal as this money will reach unto, and direct it over to John Page with this my letter enclosed. In which I pray God move your heart to be very careful, for it stands upon their lives; and it cuts me to the heart to hear that any of our neighbours should be like to famish. If we could possibly help to prevent it, I should be glad. So, ceasing to trouble you farther, I commend you and the weighty business you are about to the blessing of Almighty God, who speed it happily.

"I sent a letter to your father, which was directed to Mr. Harwood. I beseech you be a help to the safe sending of it.

Your worship's in the Lord,
JOHN ROGERS.

"Good Mr. Pelham, — If, in Mr. Winthrop's absence, this letter should come to your hand, I beseech you, good Sir, that you would be so good as fulfil the contents of it. I shall be much thankful unto you."

Ruggles died before the relief left England, as appears by letter of the Governour in the Appendix.

The Charlestown Records mention, that a fast had been appointed for the next day after this ship's coming, but this happy arrival caused the government to order a thanksgiving.

I have the original bill of Capt. Peirce for the governour's stores, as follows: —

[March 16.] About noon the chimney of Mr. Sharp's[1] *48

Provisions to be made at Bristol for the worshipful John Winthrop, Governour.

	£. s. d.
Wheat meal, 34 hhds. cont'g 8 bushels per hhd. at 8*s.* 6*d.* per bush.	115. 2.0
Peas, 15 hhds. cont'g 7 bushels, at 6*s.* per bushel	32. 2.0
Oatmeal, 4 hhds. cont'g 32 bushels, at 10*s.* per bushel	16. 0.0
Beef and pork, 4 hhds.	24. 0.0
Cheese, 15 cwt. at 30*s.* per cwt. cask and all	22.10.0
Butter, 5 kinderkins, at 38*s.*	9.10.0
Suet, 6 firkins	8. 0.0
Seed barley, 14 bushels	2.16.0
Seed rye, 1 hhd.	1.10.0
Oakum, 1 cwt.	0.12.0
For 20 (unknown) of cask, at 14*s.*	7. 0.0
For haling, craneing, and lightering, at 2*s.* 8*d.*	2.13.4
For one half freight	40. 0.0
	280.11.4
More paid out to the apothecary for provision, for the cask	6. 6.4
Paid out for Samuel Sampson for his passage	3. 0.0
Paid him more for to bring him up to London	1.10.0
Paid more for him for physic and diet at Bristol	2.10.0
Paid for 300 trees	6. 0.0
	299.17.8

1 Thomas Sharp, Esq., was an assistant chosen in England, and probably a passenger in the fleet with Winthrop; for he was present at the first court here, and the last in England on board the Arbella. He is the sixth member of Boston church. We conclude, that he made no preparations for rebuilding his house; for in a fortnight after this disaster he left America, and no account of his return is known. Nor was this the only misfortune that might induce him to go home: the death of his daughter, perhaps, had before fixed his resolution, if she deserved to be valued above, or even equally, with the wives of Johnson, Phillips, Coddington, and Pynchon, as by Dudley, 1 Hist. Coll. VIII. 44: "Upon the third of January died the daughter of Mr. Sharp, a godly virgin, making a comfortable end, after a long sickness. The plantation here received not the like loss of any woman, since we came hither, and therefore she well deserves to be remembered in this place."

Another Sharp, Samuel, perhaps brother of Thomas, had been, in England, chosen an assistant, but was superseded before embarking, because the company then designed to consider themselves a corporation in London. They, however, desired Endecott to regard him as united in the commission with others, for his advisers. He accompanied Skelton in the George Bonadventure, and while on his passage, the deed of the Indian sachems to Wheelwright and others of the

house in Boston took fire,[1] (the splinters being not clayed at the top,) and taking the thatch burnt it down, and the wind being N. W., drove the fire to Mr. Colburn's house, being [blank] rods off, and burnt that down also, yet they saved most of their goods.

23.] Chickatabot[2] came with his sannops and squaws, and presented the governour with a || hogshead || of Indian corn.
*49 After they had all dined, and had each a small cup of sack and beer, and the men tobacco, he sent away all his men and women, (though the governour would have stayed them, in regard of the rain and thunder). Himself and one squaw and one sannop stayed all night, and, being in English clothes, the governour set him at his own table, where he behaved himself as soberly, etc., as an Englishman. The next day after dinner he returned ||[2]home,|| the governour giving him cheese and peas and a mug and some other small things.

|| bushel || ||[2] here ||

---

lower part of New Hampshire, to which his name as a witness is forged, purports to be executed. His friends, I presume, were restrained from choosing him an assistant again by that scruple, of the propriety of uniting in the same person the offices of ruling elder and magistrate, which compelled Nowell to forego the least honourable service. Elder Sharp died in 1658, as the historian of Salem writes, 1 Hist. Coll. VI. 243.

1 Gov. Dudley's account of this fire, 1 Hist. Coll. VIII. 46, seems worth transcribing, with the judicious comment: "The like accident of fire also befel Mr. Sharp and Mr. Colburn, upon the seventeenth of this March; both whose houses (which were as good and as well furnished as the most in the plantation) were in two hours' space burned to the ground, together with much of their household stuff, apparel, and other things; as also some goods of others, who sojourned with them in their houses; God so pleasing to exercise us with corrections of this kind, as he hath done with others. For the prevention whereof in our new town, intended this summer to be builded, we have ordered, that no man there shall build his chimney with *wood*, nor cover his house with thatch, which was readily assented unto; for that divers other houses have been burned since our arrival."

2 This sachem lived near the Neponset River, probably on the eastern side, as there Wood, in his map, 1634, places his wigwam, but his power, no doubt, reached several miles around. Dudley, who calls him Chickatalbot, says, he oppressed Weston's plantation, and intended to destroy it. Notice of his death will be found November, 1633. His son, Josiah, grandson, Jeremy, and great grandson, Charles Josiah, succeeded in the humble sovereignty. See the excellent History of Dorchester, 1 Hist. Coll. IX. 160, 161.

26.] John[1] Sagamore and James his brother, with divers sannops, came to the governour to desire his letter for recovery of twenty beaver skins, which one Watts in England had *forced* him of. The governor entertained them kindly, and gave him his letter with directions to Mr. Downing[2] in England, etc.

The night before, alarm was given in divers of the plantations. It arose through the shooting off some pieces at Watertown, by occasion of a calf, which || Sir Richard Saltonstall || had lost; and the soldiers were sent out with their pieces to ||[2]try || the wilderness from thence till they might find it.

29.] Sir Richard Saltonstall and his two daughters, and one of his younger sons, (his two eldest sons remained still in the country,) came down to Boston, and stayed that night at the governour's, and the next morning, by seven of the clock, accompanied with Mr. Peirce and others in two shallops, they departed to go to the ship riding at Salem. The gov- *50
ernour gave them three ||[3]drakes ||[3] at their setting sail,

||blank|| ||[2]search|| ||[3]ducks||

---

[1] In assigning the residence of these Indians to the neighbourhood of Watertown, or between the Charles and Mistick Rivers, I rely on my slight information of them. A few days before, this Sagamore with one of his subjects had made complaint of the burning of two of their wigwams, of which an account is given by Dudley; but Prince, II. 21, from the Colony Records, enlarges the information by the circumstance, that Sir R. Saltonstall was ordered to make satisfaction, which he did by seven yards of cloth, because the mischief had been occasioned by one of his servants.

[2] Emanuel Downing was of the Inner Temple, and related to Winthrop by marriage of his sister, Lucy. Before coming over, he sent three of his children. In our Church Records, under November, 1633, I find, "Mary Downing, kinswoman to our brother John Winthrop, governour," admitted, No. 182. From several letters brought by her, I am satisfied, she was the daughter of this gentleman. He lived several years, in great esteem, at Salem, which he often represented in the general court, and was father of the celebrated Sir George Downing, ambassador both of Cromwell and Charles II. in Holland, of whom mention will be found in the second volume of this History. Ann, the youngest daughter of Emanuel, was the second wife of the venerable Gov. Bradstreet; but as the first died so late as 16 September, 1672, I presume the second gave no increase to the governour's family. She had been wife of that Capt. Gardner, killed in Philip's war, at the great swamp fight, 19 December, 1675.

[3] To mention, that discharges of artillery are intended by this phrase,

the wind being N. W. a stiff gale and full sea. Mr. Sharp went away at the same time in another shallop.

About ten of the clock, Mr. Coddington[1] and Mr. Wilson, and divers of the congregation, met at the governour's, and there Mr. Wilson, praying and exhorting the congregation to love, etc., commended to them the exercise of prophecy[2] in his absence, and designed those whom he thought most fit for it, viz., the governour, Mr. Dudley,[3] and Mr. Nowell the elder.

---

would be unnecessary, had not the erroneous reading of the former edition permitted a careless reader to suppose, that birds were given for food on the voyage.

[1] William Coddington, whose name is sometimes spelt Cottington, probably from the sound resembling that of Lord Cottington, then of the privy council, was a gentleman of great estate and influence in Boston, where, it is said by Callender, he built the first brick house. He was one of the earliest assistants, treasurer of the colony for some time, and is always mentioned with great esteem by our author, until the unhappy separation caused by the antinomian controversy. His name as a member of our church is not earlier than No. 92, and that of his wife, who died in the first season, is not found. On his return from England, in 1633, he brought another wife, Mary, who is among our church members No. 158. Besides what may be learned of him from these pages, the Biographical Dictionaries of Eliot and Allen, and still more the candid century discourse of the modest historian of Rhode Island, dedicated to his grandson, give ample attestation to the talents and integrity of Coddington, who was the father of that colony, and many years its governour.

[2] After Wilson's departure, only the churches of Salem, Dorchester, and Watertown were supplied with pastors. Since Dorchester had two ministers, Warham and Maverick, it may appear strange, that one of them was not spared for a season to the principal congregation in the colony, including the dwellers at Boston, Charlestown, and Newtown; but perhaps their duties were so diverse, as pastor and teacher, that each was considered as necessary as either. The people of Roxbury had now, indeed, united themselves to Dorchester, as their church records show, Prince, II. 64, yet in November before, we may be sure, from their assessment, Prince, II. 6, they had been part of Wilson's charge. This "exercise of prophecy," or office of preaching, was well entrusted, however, to the three eldest magistrates, though the instructions of Dudley and Nowell were probably rendered less serviceable by their severe tempers than the mild wisdom of Winthrop.

[3] Of Thomas Dudley, little information should be expected in the narrow limits of this note. Something may be learned from Mather, though his habit of intermeddling in politics, 1 Hist. Coll. III. 137, made the governour's family, probably, distrustful of his authority, and therefore the Magnalia contains this curious passage: "I had prepared and intended a more *particular* account of

Then he desired the governour to commend himself and the rest to God by prayer; which being done, they accom- *51

---

this gentleman; but not having any opportunity to commit it unto the *perusal* of any descended from him, (unto whom I am told it will be unacceptable for me to publish anything of this kind, by *them* not perused,) I have laid it aside, and summed all up in this more *general account*."

Being the first deputy governour in the colony, many years governour, and, when he filled neither of these offices, one of the assistants, his history must be embodied in that of his country; and the diligence of Eliot has gleaned almost all that the Records omitted. A hardness in public, and rigidity in private life, are too observable in his character, and even an eagerness for pecuniary gain, which might not have been expected in a soldier and a statesman. Gov. Belcher wrote an epitaph for him:—

Here lies Thomas Dudley, that trusty old stud,
A bargain's a bargain, and must be made good.

Dudley lost, in 1643, the wife he brought over, of whose children are known, Samuel, Ann, Patience, Mercy, and Sarah; but he married again the next year, and the celebrated Gov. Joseph was child of the second wife. Perhaps he had, older or younger than Samuel, Thomas, bred at Emanuel, where he took his degrees 1626 and 1630; but certainly he did not come to our country. Samuel married Mary, daughter of Gov. Winthrop, in 1632, I presume, for she was received of the church, as his wife, in this year, and our Records verify the baptisms of their children, Thomas, 9 March, 1634; John, 28 June, 1635; Samuel, 2 August, 1639. Why these children were baptized here, when the father was not a church member, though the mother was, must be referred to a liberality of practice much controverted in after times, and even to the present day. He was some time at Salisbury, and deputy from that town 1641, settled at Exeter in 1650, where he was a preacher, and is called a person of good capacity and learning. Belknap's New Hampshire, I. 48, in note.

His daughter, Ann, married, at sixteen years of age, to Bradstreet, before our colonists left England, bore him eight children. She is the most distinguished of the early matrons of our land by her literary powers, of which proof is given in a volume of poems, the second edition of which, printed at Boston, 1678, by John Foster, in a very respectable 12mo of 255 pages, is now before me. It does credit to her education, and is a real curiosity, though no reader, free from partiality or friendship, might coincide in the commendation of the funeral elegy by Rev. John Norton:—

Could Maro's muse but hear her lively strain,
He would condemn his works to fire again.
* * * * * * * *
Her breast was a brave palace, a *broad street*,
Where all heroic ample thoughts did meet,
Where nature such a tenement had ta'en,
That other souls, to hers, dwelt in a lane.

panied him to the boat, and so they went over to Charlestown to go by land[1] to the ship. This ship set sail from Salem, *52 April 1, and arrived at London (all safe) April 29.[2]

April.] The beginning of this month we had very much rain and warm weather. It is a general rule, that when the wind blows twelve hours in any part of the east, it brings rain or snow in great abundance.

4.] Wahginnacut, a sagamore upon the River Quonehtacut which lies west of Naragancet, came to the governour at Boston, with John Sagamore, and Jack Straw, (an Indian, who had lived in England and had served Sir Walter *Raleigh*, and was now turned Indian again,) and divers of their sannops, and brought a letter to the governour from Mr. Endecott to this effect: That the said Wahginnacut was very desirous to have some Englishmen to come plant in his country, and offered to find them corn, and give them yearly eighty skins of beaver, and that the country was very fruitful, etc., and wished that there might be two men sent with him to see the country. The governour entertained them at dinner, but would send none with him. He discovered after, that the said sagamore

---

Patience was wife of Major Gen. Denison; Mercy, of Rev. John Woodbridge; and Sarah was the unhappy partner of Major Benjamin Keayne, and more unhappy after his repudiation of her, though a new husband was procured.

The grandson, Thomas, was graduated at Harvard College in 1651, fourteen years before his uncle Joseph, and died in 1655. His will comes but a few pages after that of his grandfather in our first volume of Records. Of so distinguished descendants as the sons of the second governour, Paul, chief justice of the province, and William, speaker of the representatives, it cannot be necessary to speak. Eliot has done better than any one else will ever attempt.

1 That is, to Salem. Dudley's letter went by this ship, in which were embarked Coddington and Wilson, as well as Sharp and Saltonstall with three of his children. The two first returned soon; the others came no more. So many persons of distinction went in this vessel, that the court's order, of 1 March preceding, for the transportation of some unquiet spirits, I imagine, could not be thoroughly executed. Mr. Aleworth, Mr. Weaver, Mr. Plastow, Mr. Shuter, Cobbet, Wormewood, Sir Chr. Gardiner, and Mr. Wright, "or so many of them as the ship can carry," were ordered to be sent to England "as persons unmeet to inhabit here." The knight, who caused so much uneasiness, and Plastow, are afterwards named in the Records as present, though Hutchinson hastily gave Gardiner passage in this ship.

2 This sentence is by the governour given in the margin.

is a very treacherous man, and at war with the Pekoath (a far greater sagamore). His country is ||not above|| five days' journey from us by land.

12.] At a court holden at Boston, (upon information to the governour, that they of Salem had called[1] Mr. Williams to the office of a teacher,) a letter was written from the court to Mr. Endecott to this effect: That whereas Mr. Williams had refused to join with the ||[2]congregation|| at Boston, because they *53
would not make a public declaration of their repentance for having communion with the churches of England, while they ||[3]lived|| there; and, besides, had declared his opinion, that the magistrate might not punish the breach of the Sabbath, nor any other offence, ||[4]as it|| was a breach of the first table;[2] therefore, they marvelled they would choose him without advising with the council; and withal desiring him, that they would forbear to proceed till they had conferred about it.[3]

||at about|| ||[2] churches|| ||[3] tarried|| ||[4] that||

[1] In opposition to this extraordinary interference, as we should now think it, of the civil power in election of a church officer, Bentley informs us, the congregation of Salem received him, on this same day, as teacher. He succeeded Higginson, the time of whose death is mistaken by that author, 1 Hist. Coll. VI. 244. Certainly it was not 15 March, 1630, unless Dudley, 1 Hist. Coll. VIII. 40, Hubbard, 120, and the Memorialist of Plimouth, are in a strange error. Hubbard's precise date, 6 August, is probable, as it differs little, if at all, from Dudley, and is consistent with Morton. See mention of his death in a letter of our author, 9 September, 1630, in Appendix. At what time the violence of opposition, by such as had no real interest in the transaction, caused Williams to separate from his affectionate people, does not clearly appear; but in this History it will appear, that he was driven out of the jurisdiction, and had found refuge at Plimouth, before 25 October, 1632.

[2] All, who are inclined to separate that connection of secular concerns with the duties of religion, to which most governments, in all countries, have been too much disposed, will think this opinion of Roger Williams redounds to his praise. The laws of the first table, or the four commandments of the decalogue first in order, should be rather impressed by early education than by penal enactments of the legislature; and the experience of Rhode Island and other States of our Union is perhaps favorable to the sentiment of this earliest American reformer. By a restoration of the true reading in the text, the sentiment is made more distinct. Too much regulation was the error of our fathers, who were perpetually arguing from analogies in the Levitical institutions, and encumbering themselves with the yoke of Jewish customs.

[3] From the Records of the Colony, I. 71, I introduce another sentence of

13.] Chickatabot came to the governour, and desired to buy some English clothes for himself. The governour told him, that English sagamores did not use to truck; but he called his tailor and gave him order to make him a suit of clothes;
*54 whereupon he gave the governour two large skins of coat beaver, and, after he and his men had dined, they departed, and said he would come again three days after for his suit.

14.] *We began a court of guard upon the neck between Roxbury and Boston, whereupon should be always resident an officer and six men.*

An order was made §last court,§ that no man should discharge a piece after sunset, except by occasion of alarm.

15.] Chickatabot came to the governour again, and he put him into a very good new suit from head to foot, and after he set meat before them; but he would not eat till the governour had given thanks, and after meat he desired him to do the like, and so departed.

---

this court: "Thomas Walford of Charlton is fined £10, and is enjoined, he and his wife, to depart out of the limits of this patent before the 20th day of October next, under pain of confiscation of his goods, for his contempt of authority and confronting officers, etc." This severity must be regretted; for he was the first Englishman at that place, being by the Spragues (who went thither, in 1629, from Endecott's company at Salem) found there a *smith;* but it is not told for whom he was labouring. Prince, I. 175, from the Records of the town. Walford was, however, a valuable man at Piscataqua, being one of two trustees or wardens for the church property. Conf. Hubbard, 220, and 1 Hist. Coll. X. 64. In a record of the court, only a month later than that in the text, I observe, that, being fined £2, "he paid it by killing a wolf." But our rulers distrusted him; for, 3 September, 1633, "it is ordered, that the goods of Thomas Walford shall be sequestered and remain in the hands of *Ancient* Gennison, to satisfy the debts he owes in the bay to several persons." John Walford, probably a son of this person, was by the king named, in 1692, one of the council to Gov. Allen. Belknap's N. H. I. 193. One Jane Walford, perhaps the wife of Thomas, was, in 1656, persecuted by her neighbours as a witch, and, ten or twelve years later, recovered damages against one for calling her by that odious name.

At the same court, in an action of battery by Thomas Dexter against Endecott, a jury was empanneled, and their names are given, whose verdict was £10 damages. For an account of this strange affair, see the very curious letter of the defendant, Hutchinson's Coll. 52, in which the meek ruler of Salem permits himself to say, "If it were lawful to try it at blows, and he a fit man for me to deal with, you should not hear me complain."

21.] The house of John Page[1] of Watertown was burnt by carrying a few coals from one house to another: a coal fell by the way and kindled in the leaves.

One *Mr. Gardiner, (calling himself* Sir Christopher Gardiner,[2] knight of the golden || melice, ||) being accused to have *55
two wives in England, was sent for; but he had intelligence, and escaped, and travelled up and down among the In-

|| blank ||

---

[1] John Page is among the first freemen, admitted at the general court of all the company next month, when the number was 118, not 110, as Johnson, lib. I. c. 17, has it. He fell into another error, in mistaking the *desire* to become freemen, expressed at the court in October preceding, for the *admission*. From Prince, II. 29, who makes only 116 take the oath of freemen, the reason of my differing is, that I count, in the original Record of the Colony, two more names, viz., Robert Coles and Thomas Dexter, which indeed were afterwards erased, but it is evident that they could not have been inserted by the secretary, unless justly entitled to the place. Besides, there is the *old* enumeration of the three columns of names, 44, 40, and 34, to make up my reckoning. We know, that Dexter was disfranchised some years after, and Coles probably was.

Of Page, I know only what is given in the fine letter of Rogers on p. 47; that he was of Dedham in Old England, and had, on coming over, a wife and two children; and, from the Colony Records, that, at the first general court, in October, 1630, held at Boston, he was made constable of Watertown; and, from the Watertown Records of Births, "Daniel, the son of John and Phebe Page, born 10 August, 1634."

[2] I apprehend, that the original cause of dislike to Sir Chr. Gardiner by our colonists, or of his enmity to the company, must be forever left to uncertain conjecture. He arrived, probably, in 1630, but at which plantation, or in what vessel, our early writers leave us uninformed. "Some miscarriages, for which he should have answered," is the doubtful phrase, in which Morton assigns the reason of his flight from Massachusetts; and Hubbard, 149–153, who does some service by correcting the chronology of the Plimouth historian, has enlarged his slender narrative only by an humble sarcasm. The accusation mentioned in the text should have been supported by a warrant from England to arrest the culprit; but as no such legal cause of imprisonment is noted, and he seems to have escaped, on returning to England, any suspicion or even inquiry, we may safely conclude, that Gardiner's disaffection to the worship of our churches first rendered him obnoxious to the charge of popery, for which the evidence afterwards appeared sufficient. The letter of Winthrop to Bradford, 5 May, the day after the prisoner's arrival, preserved in Prince, II. 27, was composed in a temper, the mildness of which scarcely comports with the writer's belief of the misconduct imputed to the knight by the later historian. See two letters, written from Bristol, 1632, to London, by Thomas Wiggin, in which Gardiner's

dians about a ||month;|| but, by means of the governour of Plimouth, he was taken §by the Indians§ about Namasket,[1] and brought to Plimouth, and from thence he was brought, by Capt. Underhill[2] and his Lieut. Dudley,[3] May 4, to Boston.

16.] There was an alarm given to all our towns in the night, by occasion of a piece which was shot off, (but where could not be known,) and the Indians having sent us word the day before, that the Mohawks were coming down against them and us.

17.[4]] A general court at Boston. The former governour was chosen again, and all the freemen of the commons were

||week||

---

case is treated of, after his arrival in England. They are printed in 3 Mass. Hist. Coll. VIII. 320 et seq.

Dudley, in his letter to the Countess of Lincoln, informs her, that "G. arrived here a month before us;" and so we may infer, that he had come in Pierce's ship, the Lion, with fellow passengers of a soberer life. About the two wives, he was quite free in relation, as also, how G. avoided the arrest by the messengers sent to his house, "which was seven miles from" Boston, probably on the south side of Neponset. D. mentions the arrest of a young woman, who had accompanied G. from England, not being either of the wives. Having extorted confession from this paramour, they sent her for examination, to London, in the same ship with Saltonstall, Coddington, and Wilson.

[1] This name belonged to part of the tract, now included in Middleborough; but the lines of Indian geography were probably not very precise, or are forgotten.

[2] Of John Underhill, his errors, fanaticism, and hypocrisy, sufficient notice will be found in subsequent pages, and in most of the early histories of our country; but all, I think, derived from this work. He was early a member of our Boston church, being No. 57, and one of the first deputies in the general court. After removal from Massachusetts to Piscataqua, where he staid not long, he was living in good repute at New Haven colony, as is proved by his election as a representative from Stamford in 1643, Trumbull, I. 124, and by Gov. Welles's letter, eleven years later, in Hutchinson's Coll. 253. In 1655 he dwelt on Long Island, as appears in Haz. I. 341.

[3] This is thought to be that son of Gov. Dudley, who married Winthrop's daughter, mentioned in note on page 51. He died, probably, at Exeter, in 1683. New Hamp. Hist. Coll. II. 238. Mather does not rank him with the ministers.

[4] Prince, II. 28, remarks the error of this date. The court was held on 18th, being the day prescribed by the charter.

sworn to this government. At noon, Cheeseborough's[1] house was burnt down, all the people being present.

27.] There came from Virginia into Salem a pinnace *56
of eighteen tons, laden with corn and tobacco. She was bound to the north, and put in there by foul weather. She sold her corn at ten shillings the bushel.

June 14.] At a court, John Sagamore and Chickatabot being told at last court of some injuries that their men did to our cattle, and giving consent to make satisfaction, etc., now one of their men was complained of for shooting a pig, etc., for which Chickatabot was ordered to pay a small skin of beaver, which he presently paid.

At this court one Philip Ratcliff,[2] a servant of Mr. Cradock,

---

[1] William Cheeseborough, or Chesbrough, was one of the earliest members of Boston church, and in 1634 chosen constable of the town. He moved soon after to Mount Wollaston, where he lived several years, and had a considerable estate. His character is known, by being one of the two appointed for Boston, to unite with committees from other towns in advising the governour and council about raising a public stock, as hereafter mentioned in this History, May, 1632. That measure, as Prince supposed, was, undoubtedly, the natural introduction of a house of representatives. In October, 1640, he was deputy for Braintree, and the same person, whom Trumbull, I. 234, makes first planter of Stonington, coming thither from Rehoboth in 1649. He had some trouble in Connecticut about title to his lands, but soon prevailed; and among the principal people, enumerated soon after by the same author, are William, Elisha, and Samuel Cheeseborough, the two latter being his sons. I find, however, William witness to a deed of land in or near Rehoboth, so late as 1658; yet the distance in those days was thought so little of, that we may suppose he was on a short visit to old neighbours. Descendants are found in Connecticut.

[2] A foreign hand has inserted in the text the Christian name of the culprit; but as it is true, we should not complain of the interpolation. In our Colonial Records, vol. I. 86, is found the sentence, as in the governour's text, with an addition of some importance, — a fine of £40. The offence is there stated, with a little more precision, "for uttering malicious and scandalous speeches against the government, and *the church of Salem*, etc., as appeareth by a particular thereof proved upon oath." No trace of this evidence is known, and the etc. must go unexplained, though the proof would be quite curious, if we may trust the brother libeller, Morton, who represents Ratcliff, by the name of "Mr. Innocence Faircloth, by Mr. Mathias Charterparty sent over," as an injured man, whose chief offence was, asking payment of his debts in his sickness. The New English Canaan aggravates the cruelty of the judgment by the additional circumstances of boring and slitting his tongue, branding his face, and whipping in

being convict, ore tenus, of most foul, scandalous invectives against our churches and government, was censured to be whipped, lose his ears, and be banished the plantation, which was presently executed.

25.] There came a shallop from Pascataqua, which brought news of a small English ship come thither with provisions and some Frenchmen to make salt. By this boat, Capt. Neal, gov-
*57 ernour of Pascataqua, sent a packet of letters to the governour, directed to Sir Christopher Gardiner, which, when the governour had opened, he found it came from Sir Ferdinando Gorges, (who claims a great part of the Bay of Massachusetts). In the packet was one letter to Thomas Morton, (sent prisoner before into England upon the lord chief justice's warrant:) by both which letters it appeared, that he had some secret design to recover his pretended right, and that he reposed much trust in Sir Christopher Gardiner.

These letters we opened, because they were directed to one, who was our prisoner, and had declared himself an ill willer to our government.[1]

27.] There came to the governour Capt. *Southcot*[2] of Dor-

---

every plantation; but the adversary felt a momentary emotion of candor, when he wrote, that Sir Chr. Gardiner's interference with Gov. Winthrop prevented the execution of part of it.

Still I am compelled to regret the cruelty of the punishment, and am not surprised at the dissatisfaction it produced in England. A letter in my possession to J. Winthrop, jun., from his relative, Edward Howes, London, 3 April, 1632, says, "I have heard divers complaints against the severity of your government, especially Mr. Endecott's, and that he shall be sent for over, about cutting off the lunatic man's ears, and other grievances."

1 The task of justifying this breach of confidence, in opening the letters of Gorges, forwarded by his agent, might, to many politicians, appear easy; but I shall merely remark, that a little dislike of the proceeding is by the governour indicated, by giving this paragraph only in the margin, and, probably, at a later date. Perhaps, as in the case of Ratcliff, some other of the council is chargeable with the influence that moved the court.

2 Southcot was one of the principal planters of Dorchester, 1 Hist. Coll. IX. 150; but this is all the information obtained of him, except, from Capt. Clap, we may infer, what is not probable, that the "worthy gentleman, Mr. William Southcot, about three miles from the city of Exeter," with whom he first went to live, is the same person. Prince, II. 32, from the Colony Records, shows, that, at a court, 26 July following, "Captain Southcot hath liberty to go for

chester, and brought letters out of the White Angel, (which was lately arrived at Sauco). She brought [blank] cows, goats, and hogs, and many provisions, for the bay and for Plimouth. Mr. Allerton returned in this ship, and by him we heard, that the Friendship, which put out from Barnstable [blank] weeks before the Angel, was forced home again by extremity of foul weather, and so had given over her voyage. This ship, the Angel, set sail from [blank].

July 4.] The governor built a bark at Mistick,[1] which was launched this day, and called the Blessing of the Bay.

6.] A small ship of sixty tons arrived at Natascott, *58
Mr. Graves master. She brought ten passengers from London. They came with a patent to Sagadahock, but, not liking the place, they came hither. Their ship drew ten feet, and went up to Watertown, but she ran on ground twice by the way. These were the company called the Husbandmen, and their ship called the Plough. Most of them proved familists and vanished away.[2]

13.] Canonicus' son, the great sachem of Naraganset, came to the governour's house with John Sagamore. After they had

---

England, promising to return with all convenient speed." Thomas Southcot was one of the original patentees of Massachusetts, came in company with Winthrop, had leave to go home in the fleet, under condition; but he probably came not back.

[1] I imagine this was the author's residence, during the summer, for the first two or three years, and that Boston then became his constant home; though, from the disagreement between him and Dudley, related hereafter under date of August, 1632, it seems, that he was prevented from sitting down at Newtown only by the affection borne by the people of Boston towards him. The court of assistants, 6 September, 1631, as by the Records, I. 82, is shown, "granted to Mr. Governour six hundred acres of land, to be set forth by metes and bounds, near his house at Mistick, to enjoy to him and his heirs forever." He called this farm Ten Hills, — a name it has retained ever since. It is in the town of Charlestown, nearly opposite the entrance of Malden River into the Mistick, where they form a broad bay.

[2] This last sentence was, as might be supposed by the reader, and as the original proves, added after the lapse of some time. Gentlemen, who remained in England, I suppose, had fitted out the expedition; for, it appears by the Colony Records, I. 89, that, 5 June, 1632, the court "ordered, that the goods of the company of Husbandmen shall be inventoried by the beadle, and preserved here for the use and benefit of the said company."

dined, he gave the governour a skin, and the governour requited him with a fair pewter pot, which he took very thankfully, and stayed all night.

14.] The ship called the Friendship, of Barnstable, arrived at Boston, after she had been at sea eleven weeks, and beaten back again by foul weather. She set sail from Barnstable again about the midst of May. She landed here eight heifers, and one calf, and five sheep.

21.] The governour, and deputy, and Mr. Nowell, the elder of the congregation at Boston, went to Watertown to confer with Mr. Phillips, the pastor, and Mr. Brown,[1] the elder of the congregation there, about an opinion,[2] which they had pub-
*59 lished, that the churches of Rome were true churches. The matter was debated before many of both congregations, and, by the approbation of all the assembly, except three, was concluded an error.

22.] The White Angel came into the bay. She landed here twenty-one heifers.

26.] A small bark of Salem, of about twelve tons, coming towards the bay, John Elston[3] and two of Mr. Cradock's fish-

---

[1] Richard Brown is among those, who first applied for admission as freemen, and, by an order, 5 November, 1633, in Colony Records, I. 105, I find, is "allowed by the court to keep a ferry over Charles River against his house, and is to have two pence for every single person he so transports, and one penny a piece, if there be two or more." He seems to have been a person of consequence, and was the representative of Watertown in the first, second, fourth, ninth, and many following courts of deputies. But no information of him, more than our author's, is obtained, except in Hubbard, 187, who, after saying "he was discharged from his office," which certainly was a good thing, though meant as no honour, because it permitted him to come into civil service, adds, "He was a man of good understanding, and well versed in the discipline of the separation, having been a ruler in one of their churches in London, where he was known to be very violent and passionate in his proceedings." Still he commends him for "his faithfulness and care of Dr. Ames and Mr. Robert Parker, safely conveying them (being himself one that kept a wherry) aboard their vessel at Gravesend, when they were pursued by some that would willingly have shortened their journey."

[2] Of this opinion, more will be found in future pages. To rigid Puritans it seemed, no doubt, very strange; for only the high church party entertained it; and all the unintelligible wonders of the Apocalypse were usually employed to prove the bishop of Rome to be Antichrist.

[3] Of this man I know nothing. Prince reckons him one of Cradock's servants.

ermen being in her, and two tons of stone,[1] and three ‖hogsheads‖ of train oil, was overset in a gust, and, being buoyed up by the oil, she floated up and down ‖[2]forty-eight hours, and the three men sitting upon her, till Henry Way his‖ boat, coming by, espied them and saved them.

29.] The Friendship set sail for the Christopher Islands, and ran on ground behind ‖[3]Conant's‖[2] Island.

30.] The White Angel fell down for Plimouth, but, the wind not serving, she came to an anchor by Long Island, and ran on ground a week after, near Gurnett's Nose.

Mr. Ludlow, in digging the foundation of his house at Dorchester, found two pieces of French money: one was coined in 1596. They were in several places, and above a foot within the firm ground.[3]

August 8.] The Tarentines, to the number of one hundred, came in three canoes, and in the night assaulted the wigwam of the sagamore of Agawam, by Merimack, and slew seven men, and wounded John Sagamore, and James, and some others, (whereof some died after,) and rifled a wigwam *60

‖barrels‖ ‖[2]till then, when a‖ ‖[3]C——‖

---

[1] I am satisfied that Prince, II. 32, is mistaken in reading this word *stores.*

[2] The island has been called Governour's Island, probably, ever since it was, by the court, in April following, demised to Gov. Winthrop; but the rent reserved, being part of the produce, was several times varied. The property remained in the family of the father of Massachusetts, until, within a few years, it has been obtained by the national government for the purpose of fortification.

[3] Perhaps no reader will expect, that the occasion of these coins being lodged here should be satisfactorily ascertained; yet I may be pardoned for offering a conjecture, that they came from a French ship, wrecked at Cape Cod about fourteen years before, whose crew were soon murdered by the savages, except three or four, that were "kept and sent from one sachem to another to make sport with them." Two were redeemed by Dormer, about three years after their calamity, and one died among the Indians, having lived with them long enough to give them some instruction. See Morton's Memorial, sub an. 1620; and Prince, I. 45, relying for his narrative on Bradford and Purchase.

Hubbard, 134, plants some scattering inhabitants, a few years before, at Dorchester; but I know not any proof of such settlement, except these pieces of money. As he, again, p. 186, positively asserts it, we may consider it probable.

where Mr. Cradock's men kept to catch sturgeon, took away their nets and biscuit, etc.[1]

[Large blank.]

19.] The Plough returned to Charlestown, after she had been on her way to the Christopher Islands about three weeks, and was so broke she could not return home.

31.] The governour's bark, called the Blessing of the Bay, being of thirty tons, went to sea.

September 6.] The White Angel set sail from Marble Harbour.

About this time last year the company here set forth a pinnace to the parts about Cape Cod, to trade for corn, and it brought here above eighty bushels. This year again the Salem pinnace, being bound thither for corn, was, by contrary winds, put into Plimouth, where the governour, etc., fell out §with them,§ not only forbidding them to trade, but also telling them they would oppose them by force, even to the spending of their lives, etc.; whereupon they returned, and acquainting the governour of Massachusetts with it, he wrote to the governour of Plimouth this letter, here inserted, with their answer, which came about a month after.[2]

---

[1] Hubbard, 145, says, that the Agawam sachem "was the less pitied of the English," because they heard that he "had treacherously killed some of those Tarratine families." The invaders were from the east. Johnson, lib. I. chap. xxv., in his usual prolix manner, mentions the alarm among the English from this expedition, and the precautions of our fathers; but it is not a very probable story, or at least is much ornamented.

The number of canoes, thirty, in the former edition, appeared to me too large for the forces; and as the Arabic numeral in Winthrop's writing is commonly followed by a :, which easily deceives a common reader, and he had first written *two fishing shallops*, I have determined to reject the cypher, and adhere to my resolution, though both Hubbard, 145, and Prince II. 32, read our MS. 30. On a later page, October 2, 1633, our author observes, that the Indians of Long Island have canoes "so great as one will carry *eighty* men." Had the fierce natives of the eastern shore so small craft for their expedition as to want thirty to carry one hundred?

[2] Since the days of the first generation of the statesmen of the two colonies, it may be presumed, these documents have never been seen; for no other notice of them is known. Perhaps each side desired afterwards to destroy them.

The wolves did much hurt to calves and swine between Charles River and Mistick.[1]

At the last court, a young fellow[2] was whipped for soliciting an Indian squaw to incontinency. Her husband and she *61
complained of the ‖wrong,‖ and were present at the execution, and very well satisfied.

At the same court, one Henry Linne[3] was whipped and banished, for writing letters into England full of slander against our government and orders of our churches.

17.] Mr. Shurd[4] of Pemaquid,[5] sent home James Saga-

‖injury‖

The jealousy of the weaker power seems, in this instance, less reasonable than in some succeeding.

1 This sentence is in the margin.

2 The name of the offender is found in the first volume of our Colony Records, page 82, and, immediately after the sentence, is added by the court, "Upon this occasion it is propounded, whether adultery, either with English or Indian, shall not be punished with death. Referred to the next court to be considered of." At the next court of assistants, held 18 of next month, such an act was adopted, though it could not at first be enforced. It certainly indicates rather the rigorous purity than the wisdom of our early legislators.

3 Lynn, who was of Boston, had been sentenced, in September of the first year, to be whipped. Colony Records, I. 59. Dissatisfaction with this discipline, probably, led to his second offence, which, from the Records, I. 82, consisted only of writing into England "against the government and execution of justice here;" but it may naturally be imagined, that his letters contained some slander of the "orders of our churches," though not included in the judgment against him. His banishment was certainly remitted, though the Records do not mention it; for, in November, 1632, the court fined him "ten shillings, for absenting himself from training." Four years later I find, in our town proceedings, an order about the ranging of his fence.

4 Abraham Shurd, or Shurt, or Short, lived many years at the eastward; for Thomas Gorges, in a letter to Winthrop, Hutchinson's Coll. 114, 28 June, 1643, says, that he had information of the governour's writing to him by that person. From this fact, with the mention of him by our author in June and July, 1644, it is rendered certain, that he was a man of some consideration. In 1662, I have found his testimony, that he was agent of Aldworth and Elbridge at their establishment. He was, therefore, one of those who, under the grant of Sir F. Gorges, Haz. I. 315, had, for three years preceding, lived at this plantation, which was prosperous. Randolph, in his letter to Povey, Hutchinson's Coll. 563, represents one of the name, in June, 1688, as town clerk of Pemaquid, who perhaps was a son of the earliest settler.

5 The president (Sir F. Gorges) and council of New England, in a grant,

more's wife, who had been taken away at the surprise at Agawam, and writ that the Indians demanded [blank] fathom of wampampeague and [blank] skins for her ||ransom.||

27.] At a court, one Josias Plaistowe and two of his servants were censured for stealing corn from Chickatabot and his men, (who were present,) the master to restore two fold, and to be degraded from the title of a gentleman, and fined five pounds, and his men to be whipped.[1]

[Blank.]

*62 October 4.] The Blessing went on a voyage to the eastward.

11.] The governour, being at his farm house at Mistick, walked out after supper, and took a piece in his hand, supposing he might see a wolf, (for they came daily about the house, and killed swine and calves, etc.;) and, being about half a mile off, it grew suddenly dark, so as, in coming home, he mistook his path, and went till he came to a little house of Sagamore John, which stood empty. There he stayed, and having a piece of match in his pocket, (for he always carried about him match and a compass, and in ||[2]summer time snake-weed,||) he made a good fire ||[3]near|| the house, and lay down upon some old mats, which he found there, and so spent the night, sometimes walking by the fire, sometimes singing psalms, and sometimes getting wood, but could not sleep. It was (through God's mercy) a ||[4]warm|| night; but a little before day it began to rain, and, having no cloak, he made shift by a long pole to climb up into the house. In the morning, there came thither

||remission|| ||[2]the former there spake need|| ||[3]and warmed|| ||[4]weary||

---

29 February, 1631, to Aldworth and Elbridge, Haz. I. 315, recite, that their people or servants had occupied the mouth of the river three years or more.

1 Copying exactly the sentence of the court, appears to me the best explanation of this passage: "It is ordered, that Josias Plastowe shall (for stealing four baskets of corn from the Indians) return them eight baskets again, be fined £5, and hereafter to be called by the name of Josias, and not Mr. as formerly he used to be; and that William Buckland and Thomas Andrew shall be whipped for being accessary to the same offence." We must conclude, therefore, that our fathers thought the whipping of the servants a lighter punishment than the degradation of the master.

an Indian squaw, but perceiving her before she had opened the door, he barred her out; yet she stayed there a great while essaying to get in, and at last she went away, and he returned safe home, his servants having been much perplexed for him, and having walked about, and shot off pieces, and hallooed in the night, but he heard them not.

22.] The governour received a letter from Capt. Wiggin[1] of Pascataquack, informing him of a murder committed the third of this month at Richman's Isle, by an Indian sagamore, called Squidrayset, and his company, upon one Walter Bagnall, called Great Watt, and one John P——, who kept with him. They, having killed them, burnt the house over *63
them, and carried away their guns and what else they liked. He persuaded the governour to send twenty men presently to take revenge; but the governour, advising with some of the council, thought best to sit still awhile, partly because he heard that Capt. Neal, etc., were gone after them, and partly because of the season, (it being then frost and snow,) and want of ||boats|| fit for that expedition. This Bagnall was sometimes servant to one in the bay, and these three years had dwelt alone in the said isle, and had gotten about £400 ||[2]most in goods.|| He was a wicked fellow, and had much wronged the Indians.

25.] The governour, with Capt. Underhill and others of the officers, went on foot to Sagus, and next day to Salem, where they were bountifully entertained by Capt. Endecott, etc., and, the 28th, they returned to Boston by the ||[3]ford|| at Sagus River, and so over at Mistick.

A plentiful crop.

30.] The governour, having erected a building of stone at

||boots|| ||[2]interest in government|| ||[3]fort||

---

[1] Thomas Wiggin was agent, or governour, of the upper plantation, as Neal was of the lower. He was a worthy man, without doubt; for the Puritan peers, Say and Brooke, employed him as their representative, and he gave evidence in favor of our people against Gorges and Mason. In 1650, after the union of New Hampshire with our colony, he became one of the assistants, Hutch. I. 150, and, two years later, was among the commissioners to receive the submission of the inhabitants of Maine. Probably descendants perpetuate his name.

Mistick, there came so violent a storm of rain, for twenty-four hours, from the N. E. and S. E. as (it being not finished, and laid with clay for want of lime) two sides of it were washed down to the ground; and much harm was done to other houses by that storm.

§ Mr. Pynchon's boat, coming from Sagadahock, was cast away at Cape Ann, but the men and chief goods saved, and the boat recovered.§ [1]

November 2.] The ship Lyon, William Peirce master, arrived at Natascot. There came in her the governour's wife,[2]
*64 § his eldest son, and his wife, § [3] and others of his children, and Mr. Eliot,[4] a minister, and other families, being in all

---

1 Our author wrote this sentence in the margin; but Prince understood it, very justly, to refer to the same storm, in which the governour's new building had received such injury.

2 In the latter part of this History, 1647, notice of this lady's death will be found. She was the governour's third wife, and the mother of all his children named in this work, except John, Henry, Mary, and Forth. In an Almanac of 1617, belonging to Adam Winthrop, Esq., father of the governour, against 17th September, is this note: "My son rid first to Maplested." At 12 January, he remarks, "This day J. W., the elder, is twenty-nine years old;" at 12 February, "This day J. W., the younger, is eleven years old; at 10 August, "This day I, A. W., am sixty-nine years old." He used the same little book for a register next year; for, in another part, I find it written, "that on Friday the 24th of April, 1618, my son's third wife came first to Groton. She was married to him the 29th day of the same month at Great Maplested, anno 1618." Her baptismal name was Margaret, and her admission at our church was, probably, on the first Sunday after arrival, her number being 111, next to John Eliot.

3 Her name was Martha, admitted of our church, No. 130, her husband being 121. She was daughter of Thomas Fones, an apothecary of London, married after Gov. Winthrop came over, bore no children, and died early at Agawam, before it obtained the name of Ipswich. In one of the letters in Appendix the governour mentions his *sister* Painter, and I have a letter of Mr. Painter to John Winthrop the younger, before leaving England, on this voyage with his mother, in which the writer speaks of his *sister*, whom his correspondent was to accompany, and of his *daughter* Winthrop. It is printed in 3 Mass. Hist. Coll. IX. 231. I presume Painter had married the widow of Fones.

4 This was the celebrated apostle of the Massachusetts Indians, whose fame has been too widely diffused in Europe and America to need any addition from the humble pen of the editor. He joined Boston church, No. 110, and our pages will show how soon he was removed to higher usefulness. Just praise is

about sixty persons, who all arrived in good health, having been ten weeks at sea, and lost none of their company but two children, whereof one was the governour's daughter Ann, about one year and a half old,[1] who died about a week after they came to sea.

3.] The wind being contrary, the ship stayed at Long Island, but the governour's son[2] came on shore, and that night

---

given him in 1 Hist. Coll. VIII. 5, by his amiable namesake of the last generation. He was of Jesus College, Cambridge, where he took his degree of B. A., 1622.

1 From the age of the daughter, thus mentioned, we conclude, that her father had never seen her. She was baptized 20 April, 1630. The situation of his wife in the spring of the preceding year, (see Appendix,) was the reason, probably, why she did not accompany him. As if a fatality attended the name, this was his third child called Ann.

2 This distinguished gentleman, the governour, for many years, of Connecticut, whose name will frequently recur in our History, was the heir of all his father's talents, prudence, and virtues, with a superior share of human learning. His birth was on 12 February, 1605–6, his father having married, 16 April preceding, being then only seventeen years and three months old, Mary, daughter of John Forth, Esq., of Great Stanbridge, Essex. By that wife, as we learn from a letter to the eldest son, published by Mather, II. 32, which I consider the most valuable part of the Magnalia, our author had three sons and three daughters. The sons were John, Henry, and Forth. Of the daughters, Mary alone lived; the others, called Ann, died in a few days. All the children of that union, except the subject of this note, he says, were deceased before the date of that letter, 1643.

Belknap has honoured the son in his American Biography, though we regret much the brevity of the memoir. He probably relied too far upon Mather, as we are sure he did in the life of the father. Mather, speaking of John, jun., with his customary carelessness, says, he was "not above twenty-three years of age" when chosen assistant, in 1632. Two sons, Fitz-John, born 14 March, 1638, and Wait-Still, born 27 February, 1641–2, and five daughters, survived him, and are remembered in his will in the Registry of Suffolk, lib. VI. fol. 156. He died in Boston, 5 April, 1676. He was a member of Boston church, and his wife, Martha, soon after coming. She was sister of Elizabeth, who married the governour's second son, Henry; and they were daughters of Ann, the governour's sister. Of course each married her first cousin. Martha died in a few years, and the family memoirs say, was buried at Ipswich. All his children were born of the second wife, Elizabeth, the eldest, of the same name with her mother, baptized July, 1636. Who was the second wife, has been much disputed. In a letter of Roger Williams, 12 July, 1654, soon after returning from England, to John Winthrop of Connecticut, he says, "I had no

*65 the governour went to the ship, and lay aboard all night;

---

letters for you, but yours were all well. I was at the lodgings of Major Winthrop and Mr. Peters, but I missed them. Your brother flourisheth in good esteem, and is eminent for maintaining the freedom of the conscience, as to matters of belief, religion, and worship. Your father Peters preacheth the same doctrine, though not so zealously as some years since; yet cries out against New English rigidities and persecutions, their civil injuries and wrongs to himself, and their unchristian dealing with him in excommunicating his distracted wife. All this he told me in his lodgings at Whitehall, those lodgings which I was told were Canterbury's; but he himself told me that the library, wherein we were together, was Canterbury's, and given him by the parliament. His wife lives from him, not wholly, but much distracted. He tells me, he had but two hundred a year, and he allowed her four score per annum of it. Surely, Sir, the most holy Lord is most wise in all the trials he exerciseth his people with. He told me, that his affliction from his wife stirred him up to action abroad, and when success tempted him to pride, the bitterness in his bosom comforts was a cooler and a bridle to him." In letters in the Appendix, from our historian to his son, he speaks of *my brother* Peter, and *my sister* Peter; but this might only refer to Christian fellowship. But another letter of Williams to Winthrop of Connecticut, 6 February, 1659–60, giving premature rumour of Peter's death, seemed to settle the matter: " Sir, you were not long since the son of two noble fathers, Mr. John Winthrop and Mr. H. Peters. It is said, they are both extinguished. Surely, I did ever, from my soul, honour and love them, even when their judgments led them to afflict me."

However fair might be the inference, often drawn, that Winthrop had married a daughter of Peters, it is clearly wrong. The " only child " to whom " A dying father's last legacy " was addressed by Hugh Peters, was Elizabeth, to whose mother he was not married until some years after Winthrop's second marriage. By his former wife Peters had not, therefore, any child living in 1660. The Winthrop traditional genealogy makes the second wife of John, first Governour of the United Colony of Connecticut, Elizabeth, baptized 27 November, 1614, daughter of Col. Edward Reed of Essex. Her he brought from England in 1635, and she was mother of all his children. Elizabeth, the daughter of Hugh Peters, was born at Salem, 1640.

Peters was only six years older than John Winthrop, jun., and could not, by his first wife, have had any child above twelve years old, when Winthrop married his second.

Fitz-John, who was a captain in Col. Read's regiment at the restoration, in 1660, continued to reside in Connecticut, of which he was governour, by ten annual elections, from 1698 to his death, 27 November, 1707. Thus father, son, and grandson died in the highest office, to which the affections of the people could exalt them. He was twice married, had an only child, Mary, who became wife of Col. John Livingston. Wait-Still, after living in Connecticut during the life of his father, with whom he was colleague commissioner of the United

and the next morning, the wind coming fair, she came to an anchor before Boston.

Colonies, in 1675, removed to Boston during the usurpation of the charter rights by Andros, to whom he and his brother, the governour, were made counsellors. Hutchinson, I. 317. In the spirit of that oppressor, we know, he did not sympathize; for, on the breaking out of the Boston revolution, he was made by the patriots commander of the militia. He was named of the council by the new charter of William and Mary; but why Increase Mather permitted his name of baptism, in that instrument, to be curtailed to Wait, I cannot divine, unless he thought the dissyllable, as one word, sounding Puritanick, might be unpleasant to courtly ears. But that middle name was derived from intermarriage of Adam, his great grandfather, with the family of Still, the Puritan Bishop of Bath and Wells; and this gentleman was not designated by a perverse simplicity, which characterized the age. He was afterwards chief justice of the superior court of Massachusetts, and died 7 November, 1717. His wife was Mary, daughter of Hon. William Browne of Salem. The inventory of his estate, that was divided between his son John, of New London, born in Boston, 26 August, 1681, and his daughter, Ann, wife of Thomas Lechmere, surveyor of the customs in Boston, returned January, 1717–18, found in lib. XX. fol. 91, of Suffolk Registry, appraises the property over £3000, of which the Elizabeth Islands and stock thereon made £2000. In the settlement of the estate, a controversy arose, from the decision of which, in Connecticut, for his sister, John appealed to the king in council, and obtained an ultimate decree in his favor, consistent with the laws of England, and overruling those of the colony. See an account in Trumbull's Connecticut, II. 54; but observe a strange mistake of the reverend author, who makes the parties children of the last governour of the family, who was their uncle. He was chosen into the Royal Society, of which his grandfather had been, from its beginning, a valued correspondent, and remained to his death in England. Eliot's Biographical Dictionary contains a valuable extract of the dedication to him of the 40th volume of their Transactions. The family have preserved many communications of Sir Robert Boyle, Sir Kenelm Digby, Oldenburgh, and other distinguished naturalists, to the first governour of Connecticut, and many of the second generation after, to this descendant. I have been favoured with a copy of the recommendation by Sir Hans Sloane and three other members, 10 January, 1733, in favor of the "grandson of the learned John Winthrop, Esq., who was one of the first members of this society, and who, in conjunction with others, did greatly contribute to the obtaining our charter, to whom the Royal Society, in its early days, was not only indebted for various ingenious communications, but their museum still contains many testimonies of his generosity, especially of things relating to the natural history of New England." He is the third of the name in Harvard College Catalogue, 1700, married a daughter of Gov. Joseph Dudley, and died 1 August, 1747. Of seven children, two were sons, John Still, born at New London, 15th January, 1720, and Basil. The latter died a bach-

*66 4.] The governour, his wife and children,[1] went on shore, with Mr. Peirce, in his ship's boat. The ship gave them six or seven pieces. At their landing, the captains, with their companies in arms, entertained them with a guard, and divers vollies of shot, and three drakes; and divers of the as-
*67 sistants and most of the people, of the near plantations, came to welcome them, and brought and sent, for divers days, great store of provisions, as fat hogs, kids, venison, poultry, geese, partridges, etc., so as the like joy and manifestation of love had never been seen in New England. It was a great marvel, that so much people and such store of provisions could be gathered together at so few hours' warning.

11.] We kept a day of thanksgiving at Boston.

17.] The governour[2] of Plimouth came to Boston, and lodged in the ship.

23.] Mr. Peirce went down to his ship, which lay at Nantascot. Divers went home with him into England by Virginia,

---

elor. One daughter married Gov. Wanton of Rhode Island. John Still married, 4 September, 1750, Jane, only daughter of Francis Borland of Boston, by whom he had John, H. C., 1770, Jane, Francis B., Ann, William, Joseph, Mary, Thomas L., and died at New London, 6 June, 1776. Francis B. died at New York, leaving four sons and three daughters. From the second of the sons, Francis B., I have derived most of the original papers, that illustrate the private affairs of the family. Ann married the late David Sears, Esq., of Boston; William was of New York; Joseph of Charleston, S. C.; and Thomas L., H. C., 1780, a distinguished gentleman of Boston, who died 22 February, 1841. By a second wife, daughter of William Sheriff, a British officer, John Still had six children, of whom three survived in 1825, viz., Benjamin, of New York, married a daughter of Peter Stuyvesant, Esq., descendant of his ancestor's great antagonist; Robert, an admiral in the British navy; Elizabeth Sebor of Middletown, Conn.

[1] Besides Henry, one son, probably Stephen, came with his father. The other children, to come with John, jun., could only have been Mary, Forth, Adam, Deane, Samuel, and Ann; but Forth had died in England some few months before their embarkation, and I doubt not, that the letter of Ursula Sherman, in the Appendix, relates to him. The loss of Ann on the voyage has just been told in the text. Deane was left to pursue his education until 1635, when he came in the Abigail with his brother, John, who had gone home the preceding year.

[2] William Bradford, whose character is sufficiently illustrated in Belknap's American Biography.

as Sir Richard Saltonstall his eldest son[1] and others; and they were six weeks in going to Virginia.

The congregation at Watertown (whereof Mr. George Phillips was pastor) had chosen one Richard Brown for their elder, before named, who, persisting in his opinion of the truth of the Romish church, and maintaining other errors withal, and being a man of a very violent spirit, the court wrote a letter to the congregation, directed to the pastor and brethren, to advise them to take into consideration, whether Mr. Brown were fit to be continued their elder or not; to which, after some weeks, they returned answer to this effect: That if we would take the pains to prove such things as were objected against him, they would ||endeavour|| to redress them.

December 8.] The said congregation being much divided about their elder, both parties repaired to the governour for assistance, etc.; whereupon he went to Watertown, with the deputy governour and Mr. Nowell, and the congregation being assembled, the governour told them, that being come to settle peace, etc., they might proceed in three distinct respects: 1. As the magistrates, (their assistance being desired). 2. As members of a neighbouring congregation. 3. Upon the answer which we received of our letter, which did no way satisfy us. But the pastor, Mr. Phillips, desired us to sit with them as members of a neighbouring congregation only, whereto the governour, etc., consented.

Then the one side, which had first complained, were ||[2]moved to open|| their grievances; which they did to this effect: That they could not communicate with their elder, being guilty of errors, both in judgment and conversation. After much debate of these things, at length they were reconciled, and agreed *68
to seek God in a day of humiliation, and so to have a solemn ||[3]uniting;|| each party promising to reform what hath been amiss, etc.; and the pastor gave thanks to God, and the assembly brake up.[2]

||undertake|| ||[2]noticed to exhibit|| ||[3]writing||

[1] He came back, with a wife, in the Susan and Ellen, 1635.

[2] The subject of this controversy is thus introduced by the ecclesiastical historian of Massachusetts in 1 Hist. Coll. IX. 21: "Very particular mention is

January 27.] The governour, and some company with him, went up by Charles River about eight miles above Watertown, and named the first brook, on the north side of the river, (being a fair stream, and coming from a pond a mile from the river,) Beaver Brook, because the beavers had shorn down divers great trees there, and made divers dams across the brook. Thence they went to a great rock, upon which stood a high stone, cleft in sunder, that four men might go through, which they called Adam's Chair, because the youngest of their company was Adam[1] Winthrop. Thence they came to another brook, greater than the former, which they called Masters' Brook, because the eldest of their company was one John Masters.[2]

---

made of an elder in the church at Watertown, much to his honour in an age of bigotry, though censured by worthy men, who were influenced by the spirit of the age."

1 He was the second son of the governour's third wife, and now nearly twelve years of age, admitted to the freemen's oath 2 June, 1641. In the Suffolk Registry of Deeds, I. 25, is found an indenture, by which John Winthrop, Margaret his wife, and Adam their son, grant the island, called the Governour's Island, to Henry Dunster, president of Harvard College, and Capt. George Cooke, to the use of said Adam and Elizabeth Glover, and the heirs of their two bodies, remainder to the said Adam and his heirs, reserving to the governour and his wife one third of the apples, pears, grapes, and plums yearly growing. This was made on consideration of a marriage contracted and intended between the said Adam and Elizabeth, and bears date 1 February, 1641–2. He died 24 August, 1652, and the inventory of his estate, taken 4 September, is entered in our Probate Records, II. 64. His son, of the same name, is the first of the family in the catalogue of Harvard College, 1668, was named of the council in the charter of William and Mary, and died August, 1700: and the grandson, of the same name, son of Adam, second in H. C., 1694, was of the council, and died 2 October, 1743. Administration of his estate is in our Probate Records, XXXVI. 221. His son, Adam, the fourth, born 12 Aug., 1706, H. C., 1724, married Mary, daughter of Hugh Hall, Esq., of Boston, was clerk of our judicial courts, died 12 December, 1744. His will is in our Probate Records, XXXVII. 194. John, brother of the last Adam, H. C., 1732, was a member of the Royal Society, and distinguished as a professor at the University. The Dictionaries of Eliot and Allen duly honor him. The professor had four sons at the University; John, 1765, lived in Boston, a merchant; Adam, 1767, was master of a vessel in Gov. Hancock's employment, and in the Downs was knocked overboard and lost; James, 1769, a man of much curious erudition; William, 1770, the last survivor, died 1825. Of these, John alone was married, and had issue, John, H. C., 1796, and Adam, H. C., 1800.

2 Masters was at this time, I presume, an inhabitant of Watertown, though

Thence they came to another high pointed rock, having a *69
fair ascent on the west side, which they called Mount Feake, from one Robert Feake,[1] who had married the governour's daughter-in-law.[2] On the west side of Mount Feake, they went up a very high rock, from whence they might see all over || Neipnett, || and a very high hill due west, about forty miles off, and to the N. W. the high hills by Merrimack, above sixty miles off.[3]

February 7.] The governour, Mr. Nowell, Mr. Eliot, and others, went over Mistick River at Medford, and going N. and by E. among the rocks about two or three miles, they came to a very great pond, having in the midst an island of about one acre, and very thick with trees of pine and ||[2]beech; || and the pond had divers small rocks, standing up here and there in it, which they therefore called Spot Pond.[4] They went all about

|| Whipcutt || ||[2]birch ||

---

the preceding year he lived, perhaps, at Newtown, where he made a dock, paid for by contribution of the whole colony. See Prince, II. 30, 31, 60, and Dr. Holmes's History of Cambridge, in 1 Hist. Coll. VII. 8, 10. Cambridge Records say, he died 21 December, 1639, and his wife five days after. His will, dated 19 December, 1639, is one of the earliest in our Probate Registry, being, vol. I. 11.

[1] At a court, 4 September following, he was "chosen into the place of lieutenant to Capt. Patrick," and he represented Watertown in the first, second, third, fifth, sixth, seventh, and eighth courts of deputies; but my information of him reaches little farther than that, he united with Patrick, 1640, in the purchase of Greenwich, Conn., Trumbull, I. 116; but he continued at Watertown, and died there in 1663, having several years been insane. The same gentleman is meant, where Hazard, II. 214, has erroneously given *Fenner*, as I know from the original act of the commissioners, preserved in the archives of the Massachusetts Historical Society. In Frothingham's valuable History of Charlestown, p. 66, his name is printed Heake, as a witness to grant from Indian Sachems. This arose from mistake of the double *f*, the initial letter. In a very accurate description of Waltham, in 2 Hist. Coll. III. 261, the scene of this early survey, we are informed, that the name of the mountain is perpetuated.

[2] She was widow of his son Henry.

[3] The very high hill is Wachusett, the only elevation in Massachusetts, that justly asserts the name of mountain, east of Connecticut river, though several heights claim it. The Merrimack hills are, I think, the spurs of Monadnock, usually called the Peterborough Mountains.

[4] Succeeding generations have reverenced the first nomination.

it upon the ice. From thence (towards the N. W. about half a mile,) they came to the top of a very high rock, beneath which, (towards the N.) lies a goodly plain, part open land, and part woody, from whence there is a fair prospect, but it being then close and rainy, they could see but a small distance. This place they called Cheese Rock, because, when they went
*70 to eat somewhat, they had only cheese, (the governour's man forgetting, for haste, to put up some bread).

14.] The governour and some other company went to view the country as far as Neponsett, and returned that night.

[Large blank.]

17.] The governour and assistants called before them, at Boston, divers of Watertown; the pastor and elder by letter, and the others by warrant. The occasion was, for that a warrant being sent to Watertown for levying of £8, part of a rate of £60, ordered for the fortifying of the new town, the pastor and elder, etc., assembled the people and delivered their opinions, that it was not safe to pay moneys after that sort, for fear of bringing themselves §and posterity§ into bondage. Being come before the governour and council, after much debate, they acknowledged their fault, confessing freely, that they were in an error, and made a retractation and submission under their hands, and were enjoined to read it in the assembly the next Lord's day. The ground of their error was, for that they took this government to be no other but as of a mayor and aldermen, who have not power to make laws or raise taxations without the people; but understanding that this government was rather in the nature of a parliament, and that no assistant could be chosen but by the freemen, who had power likewise to remove the assistants and put in others, and therefore at every general court (which was to be held once every year) they had free liberty to consider and propound anything concerning the same, and to declare their grievances, without being subject to question, or, etc., they were fully satisfied; and so their submission was accepted, and their offence pardoned.[1]

---

[1] In the objection of these gentlemen of Watertown, there was much force, for no power was by the charter granted to the governour and assistants to raise money by levy, assessment or taxation. Indeed, the same may be said of the

March 5.] The first court after winter. It was ordered, *71

right of making general orders or laws; for the directors of the company, or court of assistants, could only be executive. The company, or great body of the corporation, however, submitted at first to the mild and equal temporary usurpation of the officers, chosen by themselves, which was also justified by indisputable necessity. So simply patriarchal was the government, and so indifferent was the majority of the settlers to retain their full charter rights, that, at the first *general court, or meeting of the whole company*, held at Boston, 19 October after their arrival, "for the establishing of the government, it was propounded, if it were not the best course, that the freemen should have the power of choosing assistants, when there are to be chosen, and the assistants, from amongst themselves, to choose a governour and deputy governour, who, with the assistants, should have the power of making laws and choosing officers to execute the same. This was fully assented unto by the general vote of the people and erection of hands." Col. Rec. I. 62. Such an extraordinary surrender of power proves, that no jealousy was excited by the former assumption, by the governour and assistants, of the legislative, in addition to the executive and judicial functions, with which the charter seems to invest them. From the circumstance of omission of any mention, by our author, of that general court, we may conclude, that the grant was not viewed as very important. The crudity of their political system is farther evidenced by the neglecting to notice in the Records the choice of assistants the next year after such enlargement of their authority, especially if we remember, that, besides the governour and deputy, only five of the council remained, though the charter required eighteen. The manner of the early elections also, which was by proposing the former tenant of office for the new year, and calling for a show of hands, rendered the continuance of the assistants almost certain. But though the secretary has left no trace of the exercise of their rights, at the general meeting of May, 1631, in the choice of assistants, the people appear to have made inquiry on the subject, since it is recorded, I. 72, after notice of the election of governour and deputy, as follows: "For explanation of an order made the last general court, holden the 19th October last, it was ordered now, with full consent of all the *commons* then present, that, once in every year, at least, a general court shall be holden, at which court it shall be lawful for the commons to propound any person or persons, whom they shall desire to be chosen assistants, and if it be doubtful, whether it be the greater part of the commons or not, it shall be put to the poll. The like course to be holden, when they, the said commons, shall see cause, for any defect or misbehaviour, to remove any one or more of the assistants."

The cause of uneasiness, the second year, was, we may presume, the small number that constituted the supreme council or parliament. We may be certain, at least, that no inequality in the proportion of burdens sharpened the opposition to the assessment in the text; for of the thirty pounds levied in July preceding, Boston and Watertown had each *five*, and each paid equally in the subsequent rate. It might, by modern conjecture, be supposed, that the Water-that the courts (which before were every three weeks) should now be held the first Tuesday in every month.[1]

Commissioners appointed to set out the bounds of the towns.

14.] The bark Warwick arrived at Natascott, having been at Pascataquack and at Salem to sell corn, which she brought
*72 from Virginia. At her coming into Natascott, with a S. E. wind, she was in great danger, by a sudden gust, to be cast away upon the rocks.

19.] She came to Winysemett.

Mr. Maverick, one of the ministers of Dorchester, in drying a little powder, (which took fire by the heat of the fire pan,) fired a small barrel of two or three pounds, yet did no other harm but singed his clothes. It was in the new meeting-house, which was thatched, and the thatch only blacked a little.

April 3.] At a court at Boston, the deputy, Mr. Dudley, went away before the court was ended, and then the secretary delivered the governour a letter from him, directed to the governour and assistants, wherein he declared a resignation of his deputyship and place of assistant; but it was not allowed.

At this court an act was made expressing the governour's power, etc., and the office of the secretary and treasurer, etc.[2]

---

town people were less satisfied with the object of the present expenditure; but this would be erroneous, for the other plantations would derive as little protection as they from this palisado; yet Dudley and Bradstreet were the only members of the court, by which the rate was levied, who lived at Newtown. To the agitation of this subject, we may refer the origin of that committee of two from each town to advise with the court about raising public moneys, "so as what they should agree upon should bind all," which will be found a few pages onward, under date of May of this year. This led to the representative body, having the full powers of all the freemen, except that of elections.

[1] An order of extraordinary character was passed at this court, "that no planter within the limits of this jurisdiction, returning for England, shall carry either money or beaver with him, without leave from the governour (for the time being) under pain of forfeiting the money or beaver so intended to be transported." No comment can increase our sense of the dangerous power thus given, nor display the folly of such inhibition.

[2] No mention of the resignation of Dudley is found in the Colony Records; and it is remarkable, that equal disregard of these acts about the governour, secretary, and treasurer is evinced, though to us they appear very important. One *curious* occurrence is, however, preserved there: "Thomas Knower was

9.] The bark Warwick, and Mr. Maverick's pinnace, went out towards Virginia.

12.] The governour received letters from Plimouth, signifying, that there had been a broil between their men at Sowamset and the Naraganset Indians, who set upon the English house there to have taken Owsamequin,[1] the sagamore of Packanocott, who was fled thither with all his people for refuge; and that Capt. Standish, being gone thither to relieve the three English, which were in the house, had sent home in all haste for more men and other provisions, upon intelligence that Canonicus, with a great army, was coming against them. Withal they writ to our governour for some powder to be sent with all possible speed, (for it seemed they were unfurnished). Upon this the governour presently despatched away the messenger with so much powder as he could carry, viz., twenty-seven pounds.

16.] The messenger returned, and brought a letter from the governour, signifying, that the Indians were retired from Sowams to fight with the Pequins, which was probable, because John Sagamore and Chickatabott were gone with all their men, §viz., John Sagamore with thirty, and Chickatabott with [blank]§ to Canonicus, who had sent for them.

A wear was erected by Watertown men upon Charles *73
River, three miles above the town, where they took great store of shads.

A Dutch ship brought from Virginia two thousand bushels of corn, which was sold at four shillings sixpence the bushel.

May 1.] The governour and assistants[2] met at Boston to consider of the deputy his deserting his place. The points discussed were two. The 1st, upon what grounds he did it: 2d, whether it were good or void. For the 1st, his main reason was for public peace; because he must needs discharge his conscience in speaking freely; and he saw that bred disturbance, etc. For the 2d, it was maintained by all, that he could not

---

set in the bilbows for threatening the court, that if he should be punished, he would have it tried in England, whether he was lawfully punished or not."

[1] Formerly called Massassoiet, father of the celebrated Philip.

[2] Undoubtedly this was a private meeting, for notice of it is not found in the Records.

leave his place, except by the same power which put him in; yet he would not be put from his contrary opinion, nor would be persuaded to continue till the general court, which was to be the 9th of this month.

Another question fell out with him, about some bargains he had made with some poor men, members of the same congregation, to whom he had sold seven bushels and an half of corn to receive ten for it after harvest, which the governour and some others held to be oppressing usury,[1] and within compass of the statute; but he persisted to maintain it to be lawful, and there arose hot words about it, he telling the governour, that, if he had thought he had sent for him to his house to give him such usage, he would not have come there; and that he never knew any man of understanding of other opinion; and that the governour thought otherwise of it, it was his weakness. The governour took notice of these speeches, and bare them with more patience than he had done, upon a like occasion, at another time. Upon this there arose another question, about his house. The governour having ||formerly|| told him, that he did not well to bestow such cost about wainscotting and adorning his house, in the beginning of a plantation, both in regard of the necessity of public charges, and for example, etc., his answer now was, that it was for the warmth of his house, and the charge was little, being but clapboards nailed to the
*74 wall in the form of wainscot. These and other speeches passed before dinner. After dinner, the governour told ||[2]them,|| that he had heard, that the people intended, at the next general court, to desire, that the assistants might be chosen anew every year, and that the governour might be chosen by the whole court, and not by the assistants only. Upon this, Mr. Ludlow[2] grew into passion, and said, that then we should

||freely|| ||[2]him||

[1] Common sense vindicated her rights long since in Massachusetts, though she has not yet obtained a full triumph in all dealings between man and man. The proviso in our statute against usury, 1783, c. 55, directs, that "nothing in this act shall extend to the letting of cattle, or other usages of the like nature, in practice amongst farmers, etc., *as hath been heretofore accustomed.*"

[2] This name standing here, as in the first edition, though the reader was informed, in its list of errata, *four* in number, at the end, that it should be DUD-

have no government, but there would be an interim, wherein every man might do what he pleased, etc.) This was answered and cleared in the judgment of the rest of the assistants, but he continued stiff in his opinion, and protested he would then return back into England.

Another ||business|| fell out, which was this. Mr. Clark[1] of Watertown had complained to the governour, that Capt. Patrick,[2] being removed out of their town to Newtown, did compel them to watch near Newtown, and desired the governour, that they might have the ordering within their own town. The governour answered him, that the ordering of the watch did properly belong to the constable; but in those towns where the captains dwelt, they had thought fit to leave it to them, and since Capt. Patrick was removed, the constable might take care of it; but advised him withal to acquaint the deputy *75
with it, and at the court it should be ordered. Clark went right home and told the captain, that the governour had ordered, that the constable should set the watch, (which was false;)

||question||

LEY, — I must give a short explanation. Our original MS. is plain enough; the copy, too, prepared for the press by the secretary of Connecticut, written in an uncommonly fair hand, now in the archives of our Historical Society, I testify, follows Winthrop. The former editor, as he himself assured me, never read the original; and we must conjecture, and only conjecture, why he did not follow the copy. Ludlow's name had not, in this conference, been mentioned before, as Dudley's had. By his correction of the text, against the authority of original and copy, the editor must have thought proper to insert Dudley, because he was the *only* person likely to fall into a passion. Had Mr. Webster been conversant with the early history of Connecticut, he would have better judged the character of Ludlow.

1 John Clark, the constable, was appointed by the court early in this year.

2 He came in the fleet, it is probable, with the governour, as a military leader and instructer; for, at the court of assistants, 28 September, 1630, we find, Prince, II. 1, that fifty pounds were assessed on the plantations for him and Underhill. I suppose their pay was raised, as the colony became more able to bear the expense. At a court, 4 March, 1633, thirty pounds were levied, as their half year's compensation. Col. Rec. I. 96. Patrick was admitted a freeman in May, 1631; but for any farther information of him, except about his removing to Connecticut, it is in my power to do no more than refer to the second volume of this History, in which his death is commemorated, near the close of 1643.

but the captain answered somewhat rashly, and like a soldier, which being certified to the governour by three witnesses, he sent a warrant to the constable to this effect, that whereas some difficulty was fallen out, etc., about the watch, etc., he should, according to his office, see due watch should be kept till the court had taken order in it. This much displeased the captain, who came to this meeting to have it redressed. The governour told the rest what he had done, and upon what ground; whereupon they refused to do anything in it till the court.

While they were thus sitting together, an Indian brings a letter from Capt. Standish, then at Sowams, to this effect, that the Dutchmen (which lay for trading at Anygansett or Naragansett) had lately informed him, that many Pequins (who were professed enemies to the Anagansetts) had been there divers days, and advised us to be watchful, etc., giving other reasons, etc.

Thus the day was spent and no good done, which was the more uncomfortable to most of them, because they had commended this meeting to God in more earnest manner than ordinary at other meetings.

May 8.][1] A general court at Boston. Whereas it was (at our first coming) agreed, that the freemen should choose the assistants, and they the governour, the whole court agreed now, that the governour and assistants should all be new chosen every year by the general court, (the governour to be always chosen out of the assistants;) and accordingly the old governour, John Winthrop, was chosen; accordingly all the rest as before, and Mr. Humfrey[2] and Mr.

[1] The charter fixed Wednesday the 9th, and Prince thus quotes it from the Colony record.

[2] This distinguished planter deserves greater honor than he has received from the brief note of Hutchinson, which Eliot transcribed, but could not enlarge. Allen has forgotten to name him; but his importance in the colony will be observed from many passages of this History. He had been chosen deputy governour at a general court of our company in England, 20 October, 1629, though our annual registers, that used to record, in their list of gentlemen who had filled that office, the name of Goffe, who never came to our country, omitted that of Humfrey. He was also one of the original patentees of the colony of Connecticut. Haz. I. 318. An adventurous desire of planting new colonies consumed his estate; and all wish to end his life with us must have been de-

Coddington also, because they were daily expected.[1] *76

The deputy governour, Thomas Dudley, Esq., having submitted the validity of his resignation to the vote of the court, it was adjudged a nullity, and he accepted of his place again, and the governour and he being reconciled the day before, all things were carried very lovingly amongst all, etc., and the people carried themselves with much silence and modesty.

John Winthrop, the governour's son, was chosen an assistant.

A proposition was made by the people, that every company of trained men might choose their own captain and officers; but the governour giving them reasons to the contrary, they were satisfied ||without|| it.

Every town chose two men to be at the next court, to advise with the governour and assistants about the raising of a public stock, so as what they should agree upon should bind all, etc.[2]

||with||

---

stroyed by the shocking calamities in his family, of which notice will be found in these pages, under date of November, 1641. If any reader would excuse his natural indignation, felt on perusal of the narrative of Hubbard, 379, when obscurely commenting on these sufferings, which he almost calls a judgment for the offence of leaving our country, he may recollect, that the full relation of Winthrop was then lying before Hubbard, and then study the character of the afflicted father in his letter to our author, 4 September, 1646, in Hutchinson's Coll. 159. No praise of the subject of this note can be equivalent to that epistle.

Humfrey was brother-in-law of Isaac Johnson, having married Susan, sister of the lady Arbella. From his connexion with the Earl of Lincoln, I presume, that he was *not* the person, *honored* by an order of the celebrated "High Court of Justice," 20 January, 1648-9, "that Sir Henry Mildmay be desired to deliver unto John Humphreys, Esq., the sword of state in his custody, which said sword, the said Mr. Humphreys is to bear before the lord president of this court." Perhaps he had no connexion with those proceedings, which, in a few days, terminated in the execution of his sovereign. I have been favored with four letters from him to John Winthrop, the younger, of 18 August and 4 November, 1631, 21 June, and 3 December, 1632; the first directed for him "at the Dolphin, Mr. Humfries' house, in Sandwich," when preparing to come over with his father's wife and his own, the other three to him here at Boston, all written before Humfrey left England. They are full of pious reflections and encouragement to the plantation; but give no assistance to merely historical inquiries.

[1] But Humfrey did not come before 1634, and Coddington not until 1633.

[2] Prince, II. 60, gives, from the Colony Records, the names of the gentlemen that formed this embryo of a parliament: —

This court was begun and ended with speeches for the, etc., as formerly.

*77 The governour, among other things, used this speech to the people, after he had taken his oath: That he had received gratuities from divers towns, which he received with much comfort and content; he had also received many kindnesses from particular persons, which he would not refuse, lest he should be accounted uncourteous, etc.; but he ||professed,|| that he received them with a trembling heart, in regard of God's rule, and the consciousness of his own ||[2]infirmity;|| and therefore desired them, that hereafter they would not take it ill, if he did refuse presents from particular persons, except they were from the assistants, or from some special friends; to which no answer was made; but he was told after, that many good people were much grieved at it, for that he never had any allowance towards the charge of his place.

24.] The fortification upon the Corn Hill at Boston was begun.

25.] Charlestown men came and wrought upon the fortification.

Roxbury the next, and Dorchester the next.

26.] The Whale arrived with Mr. Wilson,[1] Mr. Dummer,[2]

||expressed|| ||[2]inconformity||

---

1. Mr. Oldham and Mr. Masters, for Watertown.
2. Robert Coles and John Johnson, for Roxbury.
3. Mr. William Colbron and William Cheesbrough, for Boston.
4. Richard Wright and ——— ———, for Sagus.
5. Mr. Lockwood and Mr. Spencer, for Newtown.
6. Mr. Gibbons and Mr. Palmer, for Charlestown.
7. Mr. Conant and Peter Palfrey, for Salem.
8. William Felps and John Gallard, for Dorchester.

[1] Wilson brought his wife.

[2] Richard Dummer will be frequently mentioned in this History, and Hutchinson and Eliot have well preserved his reputation. It is less remarkable, that the former fell into an error of three years in the date of this gentleman's arrival, than that the latter copied it, with Winthrop in his possession. The mistake of one letter of the name in the former edition, however, prevented Eliot, perhaps, from obtaining the fact from the text, though it had been correctly given by Prince. In this place, it may be proper to observe another error in

and about thirty passengers, all in health; and of seventy cows lost but two. She came from Hampton, April 8th. Mr. Graves was master.

June 5.] The William and Francis, Mr. Thomas master,
with about sixty passengers, whereof Mr. Welde[1] and old *78
Mr. Batchelor[2] (being aged 71) were, with their families,

---

the New England Biography of Dummer. He was of Roxbury, not Boston, before his settlement at Newbury. In the antinomian controversy, he was of the heterodox, or weaker party, and of course punished for his opinions. With others of the same principles, he purchased Rhode Island; but soon after returned to Massachusetts; and even Johnson praises him. He was grandfather of the celebrated Jeremy Dummer; and of Lieut. Gov. William Dummer, founder of Dummer Academy.

[1] Of Thomas Welde enough, it may seem, to an indifferent reader, will be found in the progress of this History, or in the Dictionaries of Eliot and Allen. But as he figures in one of the most important events of our colonial history, and himself furnished a Narrative of it, I shall not be restrained from honoring him further in these notes, at a more proper place. It may now only be necessary to suggest, connected with Eliot's compliment, that "we may suppose him a very prudent and judicious man," the cautions of the same author, in the history of his celebrated namesake, before referred to. 1 Hist. Coll. VIII. 7 and 8. Welde had suffered in England from the follies of the bishops. See the interesting letters of Henry Jacie, in 3 Hist. Coll. I. 235. There was a brother of the clergyman, Joseph, at Roxbury; and, I believe, of both, certainly of Thomas, descendants are spread in the land.

[2] This unfortunate gentleman, Stephen Batchelor, whose name does not occur in either of the Biographical Dictionaries, will often be noticed in the pages of this work, about the close of 1635, while he remained at Lynn, in November, 1641, when he was pastor at Hampton, and in July, 1644, when he was restrained from the exercise of his office at Exeter. Hubbard, 193, mentions Newbury, as another scene of his disquiet, which might be in the progress from Lynn to Hampton; and in Belknap's New Hampshire, I. 37 and 52, his name is introduced. An unfavorable opinion of Batchelor seems to have prevailed soon after his arrival; for, in our Colony Records, I. 93, I find, he was, at a court, 3 October, 1632, "required to forbear exercising his gifts as a pastor or teacher publicly in our patent, unless it be to those he brought with him, for his contempt of authority, and till some scandals be removed." But, at the court, 4 March following, he was relieved from this inhibition. Johnson, in the wretched verses, with which he usually closes his notice of the distinguished men of the colony, advises him, as if he were alive at the period, when his age of ninety must have disinclined him to regard the precept,

"Teach thyself with others thou hast need;
Thy flowing fame unto low ebb is brought."

and many other honest men; also, the Charles of Barnstable, with near eighty cows and six mares, Mr. Hatherly,[1] the merchant, and about twenty passengers, all safe, and in health. They set sail, viz., the William and Francis from London, March the 9th, and the Charles from || Barnstable, || April 10th, and met near Cape Ann. Mr. Winslow[2] of Plimouth came in the William and Francis.[3]

12.] The James, Mr. Grant master, arrived. Her passage was eight weeks from London. ||[2]She|| brought sixty-one heifers and lost forty, and brought twelve passengers.

*79 13.] A day of thanksgiving in all the plantations, by public authority, for the good success of the king of Sweden, and Protestants in Germany, against the emperour, etc., and for the safe arrival of all the ships, they having not lost one person, nor one sick among them.

§ 14.] The governour was invited to dinner aboard the Whale. The master fetched him in his boat, and gave him three pieces at his going off.§

The French came in a pinnace to Penobscot, and rifled a trucking house belonging to Plimouth, carrying thence three hundred weight of beaver and other goods.[4] *They took also one Dixy Bull and his shallop and goods.*

One Abraham ||[3]Shurd|| of Pemaquid, and one Capt. Wright,[5] and others, coming to Pascataquack, being bound for

||Portsmouth|| ||[2]He|| ||[3]Sheert||

[1] It is not to be expected, that any thing can be added by me to the acquisitions of the antiquary, who duly honors Timothy Hatherly, "the principal founder and father of the town of Scituate," in his History of that place.

[2] To the life of Edward Winslow, governour of Plimouth, a great man in all circumstances, the elaborate work of Dr. Belknap has afforded sufficient care; but whatever, beyond the American Biographer, can be acquired by diligence and adorned by affection, must be read in Judge Davis's edition of Morton's Memorial. A very interesting letter from Winslow, at Barbados, March, 1654–5, on Cromwell's great expedition against the Spanish West Indies, in which he died, is contained in Thurloe's State Papers, published by Birch, III. 250.

[3] Names of several other passengers in this ship, as also of those in the James, are preserved in 4 Mass. Hist. Coll. 92 and 93.

[4] Ample account is given of this hostile, or felonious, transaction, by Gov. Bradford, preserved by Prince, II. 62.

[5] I presume this to be the same person, who was one of two chosen for

this bay in a shallop with £200 worth of commodities, one of the seamen, going to light a pipe of tobacco, set fire on a barrel of powder, which tare the ||boat|| in pieces. That man was never seen: the rest were all saved, but the goods lost.

The man, that was blown away with the powder in the boat at Pascataquack, was after found[1] with his hands and feet torn off. This fellow, being wished by another to forbear to take any tobacco, till they came to the shore, which was hard by, answered, that if the devil should carry him away quick, he would take one pipe. Some in the boat were so drunk and fast asleep, as they did not awake with the noise.

A shallop of one Henry Way of Dorchester, having been missing all the winter, it was found that the men in her, being five, were all killed treacherously by the eastern Indians.

Another shallop of his being sent out to seek out the other, was cast away at Aquamenticus, and two of the men drowned.[2] A fishing shallop at Isle of Shoals was overset. One
Noddle, an honest man of Salem, ||[2]carrying|| wood in a *80
canoe, in the South River, was overturned and drowned.

||bark|| ||[2]running||

Sagus, about a public stock, as mentioned in a note on page 76. Hubbard, 195, makes all the people in the boat belong to Pemaquid; but I give little credit to him, because it is evident, that he took all his information from Winthrop, in this place, and copied him so carelessly as to give the year 1633.

[1] Mather introduced this accident, sixty-five years after, into a sermon, Magn. VI. with a ridiculous addition, of the body being found in *the woods long after*, torn in pieces.

[2] My chief object, in this note, is to observe an error in the History of Dorchester, by the Rev. Dr. T. M. Harris. In 1 Hist. Coll. IX. 152, after inserting the substance of the two preceding sentences, on the authority of Hubbard, 198, then existing only in MS., instead of Winthrop, from whom Hubbard took his story, with a trifling addition, which probably is a mistake, that *Way* with his company perished by the Indians, — these absurd remarks are added, from Hubbard, but ascribed to our author: "Thus ofttimes, he that is greedy of gain troubles his own house; and, instead of acquiring a little pelf of this world, loses his own life in the conclusion; which hath been observed as very remarkable on many, who have followed that course of life." Some gratitude might be due to Hubbard, perhaps, had he enlarged the facts, as well as the words, of the text; but as his work was written nearly fifty years after the occurrence of an event so comparatively unimportant, I am convinced, that he carelessly added the murder of Way, without any information, having intended

July.] At a training at Watertown, a man of John ||Oldham's,||[1] having a musket, which had been long charged with pistol bullets, ||[2]not|| knowing of it, gave fire, and shot three

||Alden's|| ||[2]and||

---

nothing more than to transcribe, as usual with him, the contemporary narrative. From the silence of Winthrop on a particular, which would have been the principal incident of the tragedy, as reported at the time, and from the subsequent expedition of another shallop of *his*, that Way was *not* killed, would be a probable conclusion; but this is rendered certain by the MS. annals of Blake of Dorchester, who, under 1667, mentions his death at the mature age of eighty-four years.

[1] Copious materials for the character of this person are found in Morton's Memorial, 74–82, condensed by Hubbard, 92–94, who suggests to our judgment some reasonable cautions in perusing the Plimouth secretary. The contemporary, Gov. Bradford, in Prince, I. 149, 153, 154, affords also some better information, which proves that Oldham was much disliked. But he was so far restored to the affections of the first colonists, after some years, as to be intrusted with their letters to England, in June, 1628, when Thomas Morton was sent home a prisoner. 1 Hist. Coll. III. 63. Oldham was, probably, very enterprising, and less disposed to overlook this world, in his regard for the next, than most of his early neighbours. His boldness and acquaintance with the natives, and perhaps disaffection to the rigid church discipline of the separatists at Plimouth, rendered him not unacceptable to our planters, though he desired to pursue a course independent of their territorial rights. See, in Hazard, I. 256, and, better, in Young's Chronicles of Mass. 141–171, a most valuable letter from the governour and company to Endecott in 1629. This planter was certainly held in respect in this colony; for he was one of that assembly, mentioned in May preceding, page 76, and was chosen from Watertown, where dwelt many gentlemen, esteemed even by the authority of Plimouth. He had, perhaps, seated himself at Watertown, before the arrival of Winthrop, coming over after the fleet that brought Higginson, Skelton, and Sharp; or he may have come in the great fleet of 1630; but we are confident he was not here in season to witness the Indian deed to Wheelwright. Trumbull, in two places, I. 34 and 72, erroneously called him of Dorchester, one of Warham's congregation. Oldham's favor with the Narragansetts, and murder by some of those of Block Island, which was a principal incitement in Massachusetts to the great Pequot war, will be found hereafter in this History.

In copying the relation of the accident mentioned in the text, Prince assumes the date of it to be Monday, 2 July, because, at a court on the 3d, the first order that passed, was, "that the captain and other officers take a special care to search all pieces brought into the field, for being charged with shot or bullets; and that no person whatever shall, at any time, charge any piece of service with bullets or shot, other than for defence of their houses, or at command from the captain, upon such penalty as the court shall think meet to inflict."

men, two into their bodies, and one into his hands;[1] but *81
it was so far off, as the shot entered the skin and stayed there, and they all recovered.

The congregation at Boston wrote to the elders and brethren of the churches of Plimouth, Salem, etc., for their advice in three questions: 1. Whether one person might be a civil magistrate and a ruling elder at the same time? 2. If not, then ||which|| should be ||[2]laid down?|| 3. Whether there might be divers pastors in the same church? — The 1st was agreed by all negatively; the 2d doubtfully; the 3d doubtful also.

[Large blank.]

The strife in Watertown congregation continued still; but at length they gave the separatists a day to come in, or ||[3]else|| to be proceeded against.

5.] At the day, all came in and submitted, except John Masters, who, though he were advised by divers ministers and others, that he had offended in turning his back upon the sacrament, and departing out of the assembly, etc., because ||[4]they|| had then admitted a member whom he judged unfit, etc.; yet he persisted. So the congregation (being loath to proceed against him) gave him a further day; 8, at which time, he continuing obstinate, they excommunicated him; but, about a fortnight after, he submitted himself, and was received in again.

[Blank.]

At Watertown there was (in the view of divers witnesses) a great combat between a mouse and a snake; and, after a long fight, the mouse prevailed and killed the snake. The ||[5]pastor|| of Boston, Mr. Wilson, a very sincere, holy man, hearing of it, gave this interpretation: That the snake was the devil; the mouse was a poor contemptible people, which God had brought hither, which should overcome Satan here, and dispossess him of his kingdom. Upon the same occasion, he told the governour, that, before he was resolved to come into this country, he dreamed he was here, and that he saw a church arise out of

||what|| ||[2]best done|| ||[3]all|| ||[4]he|| ||[5]minister||

[1] Prince, II. 63, reads this word *head*. It does not look so to me.

the earth, which grew up and became a marvellous goodly church.

*82 After many ||imparlances|| and days of humiliation, by those of Boston and Roxbury, to seek the Lord for Mr. Welde his disposing, and the advice of those of Plimouth being taken, etc., at length he resolved to sit down with them of Roxbury.

[Large blank.]

August 3.] The deputy, Mr. Thomas Dudley, being still discontented with the governour, partly for that the governour had removed the frame of his house, which he had set up at Newtown, and partly for that he took too much authority upon him, (as he conceived,) renewed his complaints to Mr. Wilson and Mr. Welde, who acquainting the governour therewith, a meeting was agreed upon at Charlestown, where were present the governour and deputy, Mr. Nowell, Mr. Wilson, Mr. Welde, Mr. Maverick, and Mr. Warham.[1] The conference being begun with calling upon the Lord, the deputy began, — that howsoever he had some ||[2]particular|| grievances, etc.; yet, seeing he was advised by those present, and divers of the assistants, to be silent in them, he would let them pass, and so come first to complain of the breach of promise, both in the governour and others, in not building at Newtown. The governour answered, that he had performed the words of the promise; for he had a house up, and seven or eight servants abiding in it, by the day appointed: and for the removing of his house, he

||importunings|| ||[2]public||

---

[1] John Warham receives little notice from Eliot and Allen, to which, after consulting their authorities, I presume nothing can be added. Fuller, in his letter to Bradford, June, 1630, 1 Hist. Coll. III. 74, mentions his colloquy on religion with the people of Dorchester, till *he was weary*. "Mr. Warham holds, that the visible church may consist of a mixed people, — godly and openly ungodly; upon which point we had all our conference, to which, I trust, the Lord will give a blessing." This is sufficient, even though not reported, perhaps, with adequate precision, to satisfy us, that this gentleman's opinions were less strict than those of the Plimouth colonists. From Mather's 18th chapter of the 3d book of the Magnalia, devoted to Warham, it would not be easy to learn more of him, than that he preached with notes, went to Windsor, Conn., and was of a melancholy temperament.

alleged, that, seeing that the rest of the assistants went not about to build, and that his neighbours of Boston had been discouraged from removing thither by Mr. Deputy himself, and thereupon had (under all their hands) petitioned him, that (according to the promise he made to them when they first sate down with him at Boston, viz., that he would not remove, except they went with him) he would not leave them; — this was the occasion that he removed his house. Upon these and other speeches to this purpose, the ministers went apart for one hour; then returning, they delivered their opinions, that the governour was in fault for removing of his house so suddenly, without *83 conferring with the deputy and the rest of the assistants; but if the deputy were the occasion of discouraging Boston men from removing, it would excuse the governour a ||tanto,|| but not a ||²toto||. The governour, professing himself willing to submit his own opinion to the judgment of so many wise and godly friends, acknowledged himself faulty.

After dinner, the deputy proceeded in his complaint, yet with this protestation, that what he should charge the governour with, was in love, and out of his care of the public, and that the things which he should produce were but for his own satisfaction, and not by way of accusation. Then demanded he of him the ground and limits of his authority, whether by the patent or otherwise. The governour answered, that he was willing to stand to that which he propounded, and would challenge no greater authority than he might by the patent. The deputy replied, that then he had no more authority than every assistant, (except power to call courts, and ||³precedency,|| for honor and order). The governour answered, he had more; for the patent, making him a governour, gave him whatsoever power belonged to a governour by common law or the statutes, and desired him to show wherein he had exceeded, etc.; and speaking this somewhat apprehensively, the deputy began to be in passion, and told the governour, that if he were so round, he would be round too. The governour bad him be round, if he would. So the deputy rose up in great fury and passion, and the governour grew very hot also, so as they both fell into bitterness; but, by mediation of the mediators, they were

||quanto|| ||²tanto|| ||³proceedings||

soon pacified. Then the deputy proceeded to particulars, as followeth:

1st. By what authority the governour removed the ordnance and erected a fort at Boston. — The governour answered, that the ordnance lying upon the beach in danger of spoiling, and having often complained of it in the court, and nothing done, with the help of divers of the assistants, they were mounted upon their carriages, and removed where they might be of some use: and for the fort, it had been agreed, above a year before, that it should be erected there: and all this was done without any penny charge to the public.

2d. By what authority he lent twenty-eight pounds of powder to those of Plimouth. — Governour answered, it was of his own powder, and upon their urgent distress, their own powder proving naught, when they were to send to the ||rescue|| of their men at Sowamsett.

*84 3d. By what authority he had licensed Edward Johnson[1] to sit down at Merrimack. — Governour answered,

||rest||

---

[1] This person I presume to be the same, of whom mention will recur in our second volume, September, 1643, as one of the leaders of the expedition against Gorton, for which station he seems to be designated by his severe bigotry. He probably came in the fleet with Winthrop, is enumerated with those desiring to be made freemen, 19 October, 1630, and admitted in May following. From the phrase, "at Merrimack," in the text, we must not imagine, that a permanent settlement was made by Johnson; for no such was made for some years, and his residence was Charlestown, probably in the upper part, which became Woburn in 1642. It is strange, that his name is omitted in Eliot's Dictionary, and that Allen has given but seven lines to the enthusiastic historian of "The Wonder-working Providence of Zion's Saviour in New England." This work, published in London, 1654, had become very scarce, and was republished in 2 Hist. Coll. II. III. IV. VII. and VIII., the editor of this History supervising the proof-sheets of that, and faithfully preserving the exact reading of the original, with *most* of its errors, in some instances furnishing a certain or conjectural correction in the margin. Johnson was one year speaker of the house of deputies, as will be seen in another part of this work, and his reputation was maintained by one, at least, of his sons, William, a sturdy supporter of the old charter. Robert, H. C., 1645, is also thought to be one, and to be alluded to by his father, lib. II. c. 19, as acting in the Summer islands. A good account of this pilgrim is furnished by Rev. Mr. Chickering, formerly minister of Woburn, extracted into 2 Hist. Coll. II. 95, — and a letter in the Columbian Centinel, 16

that he had licensed him only to go forth on trading, (as he had done divers others,) as belonging to his place.

4th. By what authority he had given them of Watertown leave to erect a wear upon Charles River, and had disposed of lands to divers, etc. — Governour answered, the people of Watertown, falling very short of corn the last year, for want of fish,[1] did complain, etc., and desired leave to erect a wear; and upon this the governour told them, that he could not give them leave, but they must seek it of the court; but because it would be long before the courts began again, and, if they deferred till then, the season would be lost, he wished them to do it, and there was no doubt but, being for so general a good, the court would allow of it; and, for his part, he would employ all his power in the court, so as he should sink under it, if it were not allowed; and besides, those of Roxbury had erected a wear without any license from the court. And for lands, he had *85
|| disposed of none, || otherwise than the deputy and other of the assistants had done, — he had only given his consent, ||[2]but|| referred them to the court, etc. But the deputy had taken more upon him, in that, without order of court, he had empaled, at Newtown, above one thousand acres, and had assigned lands to some there.

5th. By what authority he had given license to Ratcliff and Grey[2] (being banished men) to stay within our limits. — Gov-

|| not disposed any || ||[2]and||

June, 1819, written by a descendant in the sixth generation, John Farmer, Esq., and, with some improvement, taken into the last volume of his Historical Collections. There are some interesting materials in the work of Johnson, that can be found in no other place; but the style is above or below criticism.

[1] For manure. The husbandry, taught our fathers by the Indians, whose contented indolence permitted them to seek no better compost, with materials for which, especially marine grasses, the shores and woods abounded, lasted, I imagine, not much beyond their exclusive devotion to the cultivation of maize.

[2] Of Ratcliff nothing need be added to the note on page 56. The other culprit was early obnoxious to censure. At the court, 28 September, 1630, he was "enjoined, under the penalty of £10, to attend on the court in person, this day three weeks, to answer divers things objected against him, and to remove himself out of the limits of this patent before the end of March next." Col. Rec. I. 59. His disregard of the latter part of this order was, perhaps,

ernour answered, he did it by that authority, which was granted him in court, viz., that, upon any sentence in criminal causes, the governour might, upon cause, stay the execution till the next court. Now the cause was, that, being in the winter, they must otherwise have perished.

6th. Why the fines were not levied. — Governour answered, it belonged to the secretary and not to him: he never refused to sign any that were brought to him; nay, he had called upon the secretary for it; yet he confessed, that it was his judgment, that it were not fit, in the infancy of a commonwealth, to be too strict in levying fines, though severe in other punishments.

§7th. That when a cause had been voted by the rest of the court, the governour would bring new reasons, and move them to alter the sentence: — which the governour justified, and all approved§.

The deputy having made an end, the governour desired the mediators to consider, whether he had exceeded his authority or not, and how little cause the deputy had to charge him with it; for if he had made some slips, in two or three years' government, he ought rather to have covered them, seeing he could not be charged that he had taken advantage of his authority
*86 to oppress or wrong any man, or to benefit himself; but, for want of a public stock, had disbursed all common charges out of his own estate; whereas the deputy would never lay out one penny, etc.; and, besides, he could shew that under his hand, that would convince him of a greater exceeding his authority, than all that the deputy could charge him with, viz., that whereas Binks and Johnson were bound in open court to appear at next court to account to, etc., he had, out of court,

---

not the only cause of the severity of the sentence in October of the next year, "that Thomas Gray's house at Marble Harbour shall be pulled down, and that no Englishman shall hereafter give house-room to him, or entertain him, under such penalty as the court shall think meet to inflict." The delay in executing this interdict, by the governour, was the honourable occasion of Dudley's accusation of him. But the sentence remained, probably, inoperative; for, so long after as the court, 5 June, 1638, I find the same fellow "censured to be severely whipped, and the former execution of banishment to be inflicted. Col. Rec. I. 225.

discharged them of their appearance. The deputy answered, that the party, to whom they were to account, came to him and confessed that he was satisfied, and that the parties were to go to Virginia; so he thought he might discharge them.

Though the governour might justly have refused to answer these seven articles, wherewith the deputy had charged him, both for that he had no knowledge of them before, (the meeting being only for the deputy his personal grievances,) and also for that the governour was not to give account of his actions to any but to the court; yet, out of his desire of the public peace, and to clear his reputation with those to whom the deputy had accused him, he was willing to give him satisfaction, to the end, that he might free him of such jealousy as he had conceived, that the governour intended to make himself popular, that he might gain absolute power, and bring all the assistants under his subjection; which was very improbable, seeing the governour had propounded in court to have an order established for limiting the governour's authority, and had himself drawn articles for that end, which had been approved and established by the whole court; neither could he justly be charged to have transgressed any of them. So the meeting breaking up, without any other conclusion but the commending the success of it by prayer to the Lord, the governour brought the deputy onward of his way, and every man went to his own home. § See two pages after §.

5.] The sachem, who was joined with Canonicus, the great sachem of Naragansett, called Mecumeh, after Miantonomoh, being at Boston, where [he] had lodged two nights with his squaw, and about twelve sanapps, being present at the sermon, three of his sanapps went, in the meantime, and brake into a neighbour's house, etc. Complaint being made thereof to the governour, after evening exercise, he told the sachem of it, and with some difficulty caused him to make one of his sanapps to beat them, and then sent them out of the town; but brought the sachem and the rest of [the] company to his house, and made much of them, (as he had done before,) which he seemed to be well pleased with; but that evening he departed.

At a court not long before, two of Chickatabott's men *87
were convented and convicted for assaulting some Eng-

lish of Dorchester in their houses, etc. They were put in the bilboes, and Chickatabot required to beat them, which he did.

[Large blank.]

The congregation of Boston and Charlestown began the meeting-house at Boston, for which, and Mr. Wilson's house, they had made a voluntary contribution of about one hundred and twenty pounds.

[Blank.]

14.] Fair weather and small wind, and N. E. at Boston, and, at the same time, such a tempest of wind N. E. a little without the bay, as no boat could bear sail, and one had her mast borne by the board. So again, when there hath [been] a very tempest at N. W. or W. in the bay, there hath been a stark calm one league or two off shore.

This summer was very wet and cold, (except now and then a hot day or two,) which caused great store of musketoes and rattle-snakes. The corn, in the dry, sandy grounds, was much better than other years, but in the ||fatter|| grounds much worse, and in Boston, etc., much shorn down close by the ground with worms.

The windmill was brought down to Boston, because, where it stood near ||[2]Newtown,|| it would not grind but with a westerly wind.

Mr. ||[3]Oldham|| had a small house near the wear at Watertown, made all of clapboards, burnt down by making a fire in it when it had no chimney.

This week they ||[4]had|| in barley and oats, at Sagus, above twenty acres good corn, and ||[5]sown|| with the plough.

Great store of eels and lobsters in the bay. Two or three boys have brought in a bushel of great eels at a time, and sixty great lobsters.

The Braintree[2] company, (which had begun to sit down at

||flatter|| ||[2]Watertown|| ||[3]Pelham|| ||[4]harvested|| ||[5]strove||

---

1 This sentence, in different ink, was probably written some time after the preceding.

2 Deriving their name from a town in Essex, 40 miles from London, where Mr. Hooker was a preacher. It was, like many others, perpetuated, by the affection of the settlers, in Massachusetts; but, on a division of the town, the

Mount Wollaston,) by order of court, removed to Newtown. *88
These were Mr. Hooker's[1] company.

The governour's wife was delivered of a son, who was baptized by the name of William.[2] The governour himself held the child to baptism, as others in the congregation did use. William signifies a common man, etc.

30.] Notice being given of ten sagamores and many Indians assembled at Muddy[3] River, the governour sent Capt. || Underhill, || with twenty musketeers, to discover, etc.; but at Roxbury they heard they were broke up.

September 4.] One Hopkins,[4] of Watertown, was convict for selling a piece and pistol, with powder and shot, to James Sagamore, for which he had sentence to be whipped and branded in the cheek. It was discovered by an Indian, one of James's men, upon promise of concealing him, (for otherwise he was sure to be killed).

[Large blank.]

The ministers afterward, for an end of the difference between

|| C—— ||

---

part, first occupied, nearest the bay, in which Mount Wollaston is included, was called Quincy. See note on page 43.

[1] His company came before their pastor. Of Hooker enough will be found in the Magnalia, in Holmes's History of Cambridge, 1 Hist. Coll. VII. 38, in Trumbull's Connecticut, I. 293, and in the biographical works of Eliot and Allen, to excuse the editor from any farther research. He was bred at Emanuel College, Cambridge, and had his degrees in 1607 and 1611. The high esteem, in which he was held, will often appear in the progress of this work. A line of pious, useful, and honorable descendants have embalmed the memory of their ancestors; and, in a former age, his writings were valued with those of the very first class of New England divines.

[2] Knowing nothing more of this son, I presume he died soon, as our Town Registry does not even enrol his birth. The church record is, "William, son of our brother John Winthrop, governour, baptized 26 of 6, 1632."

[3] This place is now the village of Brookline, the most beautiful in New England; for a very minute account of which, see 2 Hist. Coll. II. 140.

[4] Notice of this misdemeanour, in Colony Records, I. 93, concludes with a suggestion, proving the correct estimate by our ancestors of the dangers of such trade with the Indians, though melancholy experience showed the impracticability of prevention: "Hereupon it was propounded, if this offence should not be punished hereafter by death. Referred to the next court to be determined." Of the offender nothing more is discoverable, than that his given name was Richard.

the governour and deputy, ordered, that the governour should procure them a minister at Newtown, and contribute somewhat towards his maintenance for a time; or, if he could not, by the spring, effect that, then to give the deputy, toward his charges in building there, twenty pounds. The governour accepted this order, and promised to perform it in one of the kinds. But the deputy, having received one part of the order, returned
*89 the same to the governour, with this reason to Mr. Wilson, that he was so well persuaded of the governour's love to him, and did prize it so much, as if ||they|| had given him one hundred pounds instead of twenty pounds, he would not have taken it.

Notwithstanding the heat of contention, which had been between the governour and deputy, yet they ||[2]usually|| met about their affairs, and that without any appearance of any breach or discontent; and ever after kept peace and good correspondency together, in love and friendship.[1]

One Jenkins,[2] late an inhabitant of Dorchester, and now removed to Cape Porpus, went with an Indian up into [the] country with store of goods to truck, and, being asleep in a wigwam ||[3]of|| one of Passaconamy's men, was killed in the night by an Indian, dwelling near the Mohawks' country, who fled away with his goods, but was fetched back by Passaconamy. There was much suspicion, that the Indians had some plot against the English, both for that many Naragansett men, etc., gathered together, who, with those of these parts, pretended to make war upon the Neipnett men, and divers insolent speeches were used by some of them, and they did not frequent our houses as they were wont, and one of their pawawes told us, that there was a conspiracy to cut us off to get our victuals and other substance. Upon this there was a camp pitched at Boston in the night, to exercise the soldiers against

||he|| ||[2]peaceably|| ||[3]with||

---

[1] In a later hand the last clause appears; and it was, perhaps, introduced after the family union between the respective children.

[2] Perhaps the settlement of that portion of the coast of Maine, which is now in the town of Arundel, would not be known to have been made so early, without this sentence of our text. Nothing more of Jenkins is known to me, than here inserted, of the manner of his death.

need might be; and Capt. Underhill (to try how they would behave themselves) caused an alarm to be given upon the quarters, which discovered the weakness of our people, who, like men amazed, knew not how to behave themselves, so as the officers could not draw them into any order. All the rest of the plantations took the alarm and answered it; but it caused much fear and distraction among the common sort, so as some, which knew of it before, yet through fear had forgotten, and believed the Indians had been upon us. We doubled our guards, and kept watch each day and night.

14.] The rumour still increasing, the three next sagamores were sent for, who came presently to the governour.

16, being the Lord's day.] In the evening Mr. Peirce, *90
in the ship Lyon, arrived, and came to an anchor before Boston. He brought one hundred and twenty-three passengers, whereof fifty children, all in health; and ||lost|| not one person by the way, save his carpenter, who fell overboard as he was caulking a port.[1] They had been twelve weeks aboard, and eight weeks from the Land's End. He had five days east wind and thick fog, so as he was forced to come, all that time, by the lead; and the first land he made was Cape Ann.

22.] The Barnstable ship went out at ||[2]Pullen|| Point to Marble Harbour.

27.] A day of thanksgiving at Boston for the good news of the prosperous success of the king of Sweden, etc., and for the safe arrival of the last ship and all the passengers, etc.

October 18.] Capt. Camock,[2] and one Mr. Godfry, a mer-

||left|| ||[2]Helen's||

---

[1] Names of several of these persons, of whom some became the chief men in Connecticut, may be seen in 4 Mass. Hist. Coll. I. 94.

[2] Hubbard, 216, was slightly mistaken in saying, that Cammock came not "to New England till about the year 1633;" and as he, with Henry Josselyn, Belk. N. H. I. 21, was appointed attorney, in a deed of 3 November, 1631, to give possession to Sir F. Gorges and other grantees of the president and council of New England, I conclude, that he had either settled before at Piscataqua, or a little to the eastward, or was at that time projecting the expedition, which he made in the following spring. Sullivan, in his History of Maine, 128, says, that "the council of Plimouth, in the year 1629, granted to Thomas Cammock, five thousand acres in Black Point, now in Scarborough, which are held on the east

*91 chant,[1] came from Pascataquack in Captain Neal his pinnace, and brought sixteen hogsheads of corn to the mill. They went away November [blank].

25.] The governour, with Mr. Wilson, pastor of Boston, and the two captains, etc., went aboard the Lyon, and from

---

side of that town, under the title of that grant, at this day. Cammock was the *nephew* of the Earl of Warwick, and came over in 1663, and died at Scarborough." Perhaps this was designed to show the first voyage, and, if so, the error arose from inadvertently taking the date of John Josselyn's *second* voyage for the first, in 1638, in which this *gentleman*, page 10, informs us, that Cammock, whom he calls "a near kinsman of the earl," was his fellow passenger. But it is plain enough, from the text, that he was here long before. He died, on a voyage to the West Indies, in 1663, and Henry Josselyn married his widow, Margaret.

1 Edward Godfrey was very honorably intrusted by Mason and his joint adventurers, as appears by a letter of 5 December, 1632, preserved in Belknap's N. H., I. Appendix iii. In the charter from Sir F. Gorges, for incorporation of Agamenticus, or Acomenticus, 10 April, 1641, in Haz. I. 472, he is named first of the aldermen. He became governour of the province of Maine before 1651; but was compelled, the following year, to submit, with the other inhabitants of that quarter of the country, to the government of Massachusetts, whose commissioners appointed him, with three others, to hold county courts. Haz. I. 564–577. Yet, in 1658, his hopes of independence seem to have revived; for, in Hutchinson's Coll. 314, we find a petition from York, Kittery, Wells, etc., to his highness, the lord protector, against his design; and from the document next in that collection, a letter from Leverett to the government of Massachusetts, it seems, that Godfrey was the most active or most powerful of the discontented. That petition of the *loyal* inhabitants was a strange libel on their country, representing the parts eastward, which are now found to be much the best, as "uninhabitable, sterile lands, swamps and rocky mountains, as not more than a few shreds are left by the sea shore fit for cohabitation." Any good or evil consequences at that time were prevented by the decease of the great protector. But though the complaints were renewed after the restoration, (see Leverett's letter of 13th September, 1660, in Hutchinson's Coll. 322,) and thus afforded a pretext for the temporary separation directed by the royal commissioners some years after, I know not that any benefit was obtained by Godfrey. He is, perhaps, the gentleman referred to in the Narrative, Hutchinson's Coll. 423, "who refused to submit to the Massachusetts, and suffered great loss by them, showed the commissioners a warrant the Massachusetts made to have him brought to Boston, alive or dead, and now demands justice against them."

The error of Prince, II. 70, who, transcribing this passage from our author, gives *Vesey* instead of Godfrey, must render cautious all decypherers of ancient proper names, in which I have often fallen, for a time, into as great mistakes.

thence Mr. Peirce carried them in his shallop to Wessaguscus. The next morning Mr. Peirce returned to his ship, and the governour and his company went on foot to Plimouth, and came thither within the evening. The governour of Plimouth, Mr. William Bradford, (a very discreet and grave man,) with Mr. Brewster,[1] the elder, and some others, came forth and met them without the town, and conducted them to the governour's house, where they were very kindly entertained, and feasted every day at several houses. On the Lord's day there was a sacrament, which they did partake in; and, in the afternoon, Mr. Roger Williams (according to their custom) propounded a question, to which the pastor, Mr. Smith,[2] spake briefly; then Mr. Williams prophesied; and after the governour of *92
Plimouth spake to the question; after him the elder; then some two or three more of the congregation. Then the elder desired the governour of Massachusetts and Mr. Wilson to speak to it, which they did. When this was ended, the dea-

[1] It would be presumption, without hope, for me to attempt any memoir of Elder William Brewster, after the elaborate account in Belknap's American Biography, II. 252. Yet far higher value belongs to the recent researches of Rev. Joseph Hunter, as exhibited in 4 Mass. Hist. Coll. I. 64-72. Brewster may well be thought the earliest layman of prominent service among the Puritans.

[2] In the governour and company's letter to Endecott, 1629, is contained the earliest notice of the Rev. Ralph Smith, "his difference in judgment in some things from our ministers" being therein referred to as a caution against distraction in the Salem church. Haz. I. 260. His stay at that place, however, was very short; for we learn from Bradford, in Prince, I. 188, that he went to Nantasket, where he was found living "in a poor house, that would not keep him dry," and desired a better residence. Being carried to Plimouth, he became their minister for several years. In Morton, I discern his name only twice, and then with no epithets of reverence or circumstance of importance, except that of making, in 1638, complaint against Gorton; thus being the earliest of the numerous adversaries of the unhappy sectarian. But the History of Plimouth Church, 1 Hist. Coll. IV. 108, written, indeed, so lately as 1760, informs of his resignation of office in 1635, at the request of some of the flock, and partly of his own accord; and therefore I infer, that the controversy with Gorton arose not from his station. In that tract Smith is called "a man of low gifts and parts." How long he continued to reside, where he was so lightly esteemed, is not certainly known; but the latter part of this History, 1645, tells, that the people of Manchester, not then formed into a church body, had employed him to preach to them. Neither Eliot nor Allen have given him a place in their dictionaries. Young, Chron. of Mass. 151.

con, Mr. Fuller,[1] put the congregation in mind of their duty of contribution; whereupon the governour and all the rest went down to the deacon's seat, and put into the box, and then returned.

27.] The wind N. W., Mr. Peirce set sail for Virginia.[2]

31, being Wednesday.] About five in the morning the governour and his company came out of Plimouth; the governour of Plimouth, with the pastor and elder, etc., accompanying them near half a mile out of town in the dark. The Lieut. Holmes,[3] with two others, and the governour's ||mare,||[4] came along with them to the great swamp, about ten miles. When they came to the great river,[5] they were carried over by one Luddam,[6] their guide, (as they had been when they came, the stream being very strong, and up to the crotch;) so the governour called that passage Luddam's Ford. Thence they came to a place called Hue's[7] Cross. The governour, being displeased

||man||

---

1 Samuel Fuller was a gentleman high in esteem at Plimouth. He had been chosen to his office in Holland, with Gov. Carver, whom he accompanied in the first ship. He is duly honored by Eliot, though his article should have been enlarged, from Morton's Memorial, with the date of his death, 1633. Young, Chron. of the Pilgr. 222.

2 In this voyage he was wrecked, six days after, outside of the capes of Virginia. See a good letter from him to his friends at Plymouth, in Prince's annals, 428 of Hale's Edition. His ship was the Lion.

3 After the notice of Holmes, by Judge Davis, in his edition of the New England Memorial, nothing should be expected here to extend the reader's acquaintance with him.

4 Winthrop had gone to Plimouth, on foot, from Wessaguscus, as his narrative just before showed. His friend, the governour of the elder colony, sent him back with his own horse. I have no doubt of the MS., though the former edition had *man*.

5 Now called North River, — a stream rendered important by the great number of ships built upon its banks. See the copious account of Scituate, 2 Hist. Coll. IV. 227.

6 I have not learned any thing of this man, nor been able even to ascertain precisely where the fording place was.

7 Hue could hardly have been of much consequence in the governour's opinion, and we can scarcely justify his displeasure at the trifle. Anticipation of so great an empire as grew in two hundred years from their planting, could not consist with the fear, that Papists might say their religion was first settled here. By the antiquary of Plimouth we are told of "Hewes' Cross Brook," and that

at the name, in respect that such things might hereafter *93
give the Papists occasion to say, that their religion was first planted in these parts, changed the name, and called it Hue's Folly. So they came, that evening, to Wessaguscus,[1] where they were bountifully entertained, as before, with store of turkeys, geese, ducks, etc., and the next day came safe to Boston.

About this time Mr. Dudley, his house, at || Newtown, || was preserved from burning down, and all his family from being destroyed by gunpowder, by a marvellous deliverance; — the hearth of the hall chimney burning all night upon a principal § beam, § and store of powder being near, and not discovered till they arose in the morning, and then it began to flame out.

Mr. John Eliot, a member of Boston congregation, and one whom the ||[2]congregation|| intended presently to call to the office of teacher, was called to be a teacher to the ||[3]church|| at Roxbury; and though Boston laboured all they could, both with the congregation of Roxbury and with Mr. Eliot himself, alleging their want of him, and the covenant between them, etc., yet he could not be diverted from accepting the call of Roxbury, November 5. So he was dismissed.

|| Watertown || ||[2]company|| ||[3]company||

John Hewes was one of the first settlers of Scituate. 2 Hist. Coll. IV. 303. The act of jurisdiction by Winthrop, in thus changing a name within the limits of another colony, was a slight usurpation.

[1] The settlements of this place are mentioned, in order of time, on page 43. In 1624, "some addition to the few inhabitants of Wessaguscus, from Weymouth in England," is given by Prince, I. 150; but his authority being only manuscript letters, written, perhaps, more than a hundred years later, and probably embodying idle traditions, I am not disposed to give much credit to them, especially as the contemporary, Gov. Bradford, remarks with emphasis, ib. 144, that the *second* plantation came to an end in the spring of that very year. Besides, the exquisite diligence of the Annalist found no opportunity even to name the spot again before the year 1628. p. 176. Then the ill conduct of Morton and his clan rendered necessary the interference of "the chief of the straggling plantations from Piscatoway, Naumkeag, Winisimet, Wesaguscusset, Natasco, and other places." This was the celebrated and efficient expedition of Standish. Prince's authority for this is the same chief of Plimouth, whose information is always most minute and satisfactory. Perhaps, in 1627, some settlers had reoccupied the vacant fields.

About a fortnight before this, those of Charlestown, who had formerly been joined to Boston congregation, now, in regard of the difficulty of passage in the winter, and having opportunity
*94 of a pastor, one Mr. James,[1] who came over at this time, were dismissed from the congregation of Boston.[2]

---

[1] He remained at Charlestown little over three years, as, in the progress of this History, will be seen. Thence he removed to New Haven, where he resided some years, except while engaged on a mission, in 1642 and 3, to Virginia; and Eliot has erroneously related, that at New Haven he finished the remainder of his days. Hubbard, 191, says, James "returned back to England, where he was accepted as a faithful minister of the gospel, and continued in that work till the year 1678, at Needham, in Suffolk, which was about the eighty-sixth year of his age, and may yet be living." I am the more disposed to value highly this original information of Hubbard, as it is of so very rare occurrence. Prince, II. 77, is still more full than the contemporary historian. His son, of the same name, by the accounts of the commissioners of the United Colonies, seems to have been in their employment as a teacher of the Indians on Long Island, until 1665; and he is No. 10 of the second classis of the Magnalia. Mather, with his habitual carelessness, sinks the name of baptism of both. Allen omits the name of Thomas James.

[2] In the books of our divines, the order of time, in which the churches of Massachusetts were gathered, has often been noticed; but it will be found, that they have, in general, deferred too easily to the authority of Johnson's Wonder-working Providence. That writer did not, probably, mean to be precise on this point; or, if he did, is entitled to little regard. Holmes, in his History of Cambridge, 1 Hist. Coll. VII. 15, follows the general current; and, though he made a partial correction, 1 Hist. Coll. X. 314, he only increases the injustice on Johnson's authority. The six churches next after Salem, he assigns to 1631, when *not one* was gathered that year. Half were in 1630, and half in 1632. With reference to Boston, he made amends, indeed, in Annals, I. 267, by suggesting, what nobody can fail to acquiesce in, that our church *may* be considered as translated in its organized state from Charlestown; though his expressions, compared with those of page 262, where he enumerates only six, instead of seven, show his timidity. Still his injustice to Watertown remains unexpiated. The scrupulous attention of this most diligent annalist would have protected him from my humble animadversion, in a particular of so slight importance, did he not receive encouragement from companions of the highest character. Judge Davis, in the beautiful address on the anniversary of the Plimouth forefathers' landing, 22 December, 1813, with which the *first* volume of 2 Hist. Coll. appropriately commences, has, page ix, injuriously postponed Watertown to Roxbury and Lynn. In his note F. a severe observer will, indeed, find reason to presume, that the author's judgment would give Watertown priority over those churches, notwithstanding the rank of Johnson. The body of that note, however, is occupied with disputing the claim of Watertown to stand second

The congregation of Watertown discharged their elder, *95
Richard Brown, of his office, for his unfitness in regard of

---

only to Salem. Eliot, in his invaluable essays on our ecclesiastical history, 1 Hist. Coll. X. 26, obeys, against his own knowledge, the direction of Wonder-working Providence; and Harris's History of Dorchester betrays the right to the *second* honor for that church. The Century Sermon of the late Dr. Kendall, in a note on pages 20, 21, irresistibly draws me to his opinion, by which Watertown is determined to a rank equal with Boston. "July 30, 1630, at Watertown, forty men subscribed a church covenant." Now, there can be no evidence, that any others, but Salem and Dorchester, *preceded;* though the right of Wilson's (Boston) church to date from the *same* day is established by Judge Davis's argument from the contemporaneous narrative of Bradford, in Prince, I. 243. We cannot doubt the precedence of Dorchester, and its claim to be reckoned in June, 1630, because, when the first court of assistants, 23 August, provided "how the ministers shall be maintained," and made a common charge on the colony for Wilson's (Boston) and Phillip's (Watertown) salaries, Mattapan and Salem were *excepted.* This, from the Records of Massachusetts, Prince, I. 247, must satisfy every one, that the former was considered in a church state no less than the latter. Our Dorchester settlers had an embodied church, we know, when they left home in March, and undoubtedly had regular ordinances with their two ministers after arrival in Massachusetts, in June. Prince, I. 200. Whether Roxbury, or Lynn, which come in the third year, have records to show which may certainly claim priority, is unknown, probably, to themselves. Books cannot assist us in determining. See Prince, II. 64, 68, and Johnson, lib. I. c. 21, 22.

A strange obliquity of judgment has applied the facts in our text to sustain the precedency of Charlestown to Boston church. The pastor and the flock, rather than the place of their assembly, ought surely to entitle any society of worshippers to be thought the same, and not another. Even if exclusive regard be paid to place, the church of Charlestown loses more than it can gain; for, in September, 1630, the greater part of the congregation lived on this side of the river; and in that month, for the last time, the court of assistants met at Charlestown. *There* the body of the church remained, therefore, less than three months. The worship, afterwards, was always *here;* yet, for twenty-five months more, there was but one church of worshippers from both sides. The History always calls this congregation, — a word, which, unless plainly used as a distinction from those in more intimate brotherhood, must always be understood by the reader as signers of the church covenant, — the congregation of Boston. The dismission of Mr. James, and the thirty-two other brethren, little more than one fourth of the whole, is from Boston to Charlestown. We have every light on this subject, that Prince enjoyed, and are fully justified in forming a different conclusion from his, if his, which is doubtful, be adverse to this now expressed. If reference be made to custom or common law, the identity of a body corporate, like each of our churches, must be shown by its records.

*96 his passion and distemper in speech, having been oft admonished and declared his repentance for it.

21.] The governour received a letter from Capt. Neal, that ||Dixy|| Bull[1] and fifteen more of the English, who kept about the east, were turned pirates, and had taken divers boats, and rifled Pemaquid, etc., — 23. Hereupon the governour called a council, and it was agreed to send his bark with twenty men, to join with those of Pascataquack, for the taking of the said pirates.

22.] A fast was held by the congregation of Boston, and Mr. Wilson (formerly their teacher) was chosen pastor, and [blank] Oliver[2] a ruling elder, and both were ordained by

||D.||

This evidence is, of course, in favor of Boston. In future days, I persuade myself, a contrary opinion will seem as strange, as the assertion in the Historical Sketch of Charlestown, 2 Hist. Coll. II. 164, that Winthrop and his company came in 1629.

To conclude this long note, I solicit indulgence for the following arrangement of the early churches of Massachusetts proper, which to me appears most probable:

I.	Salem, 1629, 6 August.	XVI.	Rowley, 1639, 3 Dec.
II.	Dorchester, 1630, June.	XVII.	Salisbury.
III.	Boston, } 1630, 30 July.	XVIII.	Sudbury, 1640, August.
IV.	Watertown, } 1630, 30 July.	XIX.	Gloucester, 1642.
V.	Roxbury, 1632, July.	XX.	Woburn, 1642, 14 August.
VI.	Lynn, 1632.	XXI.	Hull, 1644, July.
VII.	Charlestown, 1632, 2 Nov.	XXII.	Wenham, 1644, 8 October.
VIII.	Cambridge, 1633, 11 Oct.	XXIII.	Haverhill, } 1645, Oct.
IX.	Ipswich, 1634.	XXIV.	Andover, } 1645, Oct.
X.	Newbury, 1635.	XXV.	Reading, 1645, 5 Nov.
XI.	Weymouth, 1635, July.	XXVI.	Springfield, 1645.
XII.	Hingham, 1635, September.	XXVII.	Manchester.
XIII.	Concord, 1636, 5 July.	XXVIII.	Malden.
XIV.	Dedham, 1638, 8 Nov.	XXIX.	Boston, 2d, 1650, 5 June.
XV.	Quincy, 1639, 17 Sept.		

1 Of this miserable fellow, it cannot be expected, that any memoirs should remain. It seems probable, that the loss of his shallop and goods, *reported*, in June preceding, to be taken by the French, may have led him and his companions to this renunciation of the friendship of the rest of the settlements on the coast. They seem to have committed no outrages. Capt. Clap, in Prince, II. 91, gives the largest account of their operations, and concludes, "Bull got into England; but God destroyed this wretched man."

2 Thomas Oliver, whose name occurs several times in the course of this History, was undoubtedly an estimable and useful man; but little is known of him. He came, in the William and Francis, with his family. Reverence for his eldership, probably, kept him from other services, either offered by his townsmen, or

imposition of hands, first by the teacher, and ||the|| two deacons, (in the name of the congregation,) upon the elder, and then by the elder and the deacons upon the pastor. *97

December 4.] At a meeting of all the assistants, it was agreed, in regard that the extremity of the ||[2]snow|| and frost had hindered the making ready of the bark, and that they had certain intelligence, that those of Pascataquack had sent out two pinnaces and two shallops, above a fortnight before, to defer any further expedition against the pirates till they heard what was done by those; and for that end it was agreed, to send presently a shallop to Pascataquack to learn ||[3]more,|| etc.

5.] Accordingly, the governour despatched away John Gallopp[1] with his shallop. The wind being very great at S. W., he could reach no farther than Cape Ann harbour that

||then|| ||[2]season|| ||[3]news||

---

sought by his own ambition; but he was several years one of the selectmen. He died in the latter part of 1657, I conclude, from finding his will proved, 27 January following, in our Registry, I. 300. She died in 1635. His son, John, H. C., 1645, is honorably mentioned in a later part of this work. His son, Peter, was father of Nathaniel, born 8 March, 1651, of whom the first newspaper printed in North America, the Boston Newsletter, 24 April, 1704, has this notice: "Mr. Nathaniel Oliver, a principal merchant of this place, died April 15, and was decently interred April 18, ætatis 53." The same son, one of the chief founders of Boston Third Church, was also father of the Hon. Daniel Oliver, who died 1732. Of him and the sons, Andrew, lieutenant governour, and Peter, chief justice, distinguished in the political history of the province of Massachusetts Bay, as well as others of the name, full biographies are given by Eliot. They are written with an honorable impartiality, for the want of which, in a son of the chief justice, to whom application was made by a son of the biographer, for leave to copy a small part of his transcript of Hubbard's History, liberal minds will make large estimate of the evils of rancorous remembrance incident to civil conflicts. See 2 Hist. Coll. III. 288. But the denial was of no detriment to any other than the possessor; for every careful student of Hubbard would easily part with half that we have.

[1] Mention is often made of this person, who was a fisherman well acquainted with our harbour, in which an island perpetuates his name. He was admitted of the church 5 January, 1633-4. His will, Prob. Rec. I. 292, made 20 December, 1649, proved 9 February following, signed with a cross, was made, probably, in his last hours. In it he gives forty shillings towards building the new meeting-house, which was that for the Second Church. His son, John, was a captain in the great Narraganset battle, 19 December, 1675, and slain at the head of his company.

night; and the winds blowing northerly, he was kept there so long, that it was January the 2d before he returned.

By letters from Capt. Neal and Mr. Hilton,[1] etc., it was cer-
*98 tified, that they had sent out all the forces they could make
against the pirates, viz., four pinnaces and shallops, and about forty men, who, coming to Pemaquid, were there windbound about three weeks.

It was further advertised, by some who came from Penobscott, that the pirates had lost one of their chief men by a musket shot from Pemaquid; and that there remained but fifteen, whereof four or five were detained against their wills; and that they had been at some English plantations, and taken nothing from them but what they paid for; and that they had given another pinnace in exchange for that of Mr. Maverick, and as much beaver and otter as it was worth more, etc.; and that they had made a law against excessive drinking; and that their order was, at such times as other ships use to have prayer,

---

1 Edward Hilton and his brother William, with a few others, sent by Gorges and Mason, were the first planters of New Hampshire in 1623. See Hubbard, 214. The name of Edward, who was a gentleman of good judgment, is often found in our History; and in 1641, when Massachusetts usurped the jurisdiction of the colony of New Hampshire, he became a magistrate. William had visited New Plimouth, before settling on the Piscataqua, as appears by a letter from him, Haz. I. 120, extracted from "New England's Trials," published, in 1622, by the celebrated John Smith. The note of Hazard, that the vessel, which carried this letter, left New England the beginning of April, 1621, is not given with his usual accuracy. The Mayflower, in which came the first company of one hundred, among whom was not Hilton, was the only vessel, Prince, I. 104, that could leave Plimouth in April, 1621. On recurring to the original authority of Hazard, Purchas's Pilgrims, lib. X. c. 3, page 1840 of vol. IV. compared with Prince, I. 114, I find the Fortune arrived at Plimouth in November, 1621. William Hilton was, therefore, a passenger in her, with the venerable Cushman, and by her, in December of the same year, was his epistle returned. Descendants of one, or both, of these brothers, are found in New Hampshire, of whom one, Winthrop, a distinguished officer in the Indian and French wars, was killed by the savages near his own home, 23 June, 1710. Some genealogical account of the families may be seen in Alden's Collection of Epitaphs, II. 131. One, a grandchild of the above named Winthrop, died in March, 1822, in possession of part of the unalienated estate of two centuries. Gov. Joseph Dudley calls the grandfather his dear *kinsman*, and it is agreeable to find the adoption by this family of a name of baptism from the father of Massachusetts. It is still borne by a gentleman of Newmarket.

they would assemble upon the deck, and one sing a song, or speak a few senseless sentences, etc. They also sent a writing, directed to all the governours, signifying their intent not to do harm to any more of their countrymen, but to go to the southward, and to advise them not to send against them; for they were resolved to ||sink|| themselves rather than be taken: Signed underneath, Fortune le garde, and no ||[2]name|| to it.

January 1.] Mr. Edward Winslow chosen governour of Plimouth, Mr. Bradford having been governour about ten years, and now by importunity gat off.[1]

9.] Mr. Oliver, a right godly man, and elder of the church of Boston, having three or four of his sons, all very young, cutting down wood upon the ||[3]neck,|| one of them, being about fifteen years old, had his brains beaten out with the fall of a tree, which he had felled. The good old father (having the news of it in as fearful a manner as might be, by another boy, his brother) called his wife (being also a very godly woman) and went to prayer, and bare it with much patience and honor.

17.] The governour, having intelligence from the east, that the French had bought the Scottish plantation[2] near Cape Sable, and that the fort and all the ammunition were deliver- *99
ed to them, and that the cardinal, having the managing thereof, had sent some companies already, and preparation was made to send many more the next year, and divers priests and Jesuits among them, — called the assistants to Boston, and the ministers and captains, and some other chief men, to advise what was fit to be done for our safety, in regard the French

||strike|| ||[2]more|| ||[3]rocks||

---

[1] From Prince, II. 75, we learn, that the people of Plimouth this year enacted, "that whoever refuses the office of governour shall pay £20, unless he was chose two years going." A proportional penalty was laid on any refusing to be a counsellor. This severity has become unnecessary for such high offices, though it is found useful to provide similar fines for declining subordinate ones.

[2] We presume this to mean the plantation, for which Sir William Alexander had patents from James I. and Charles I. 10 September, 1621, and 12 July, 1625, soon after ceded to the French. The settlement was at Port Royal.

were like to prove ill neighbours (being Papists;) at which meeting it was agreed, that a plantation and a fort should forthwith be begun at Natascott, partly to be ||some|| block in an enemy's way, (though it could not bar ||2his|| entrance,) and especially to prevent an enemy from taking that passage from us; and also, that the fort begun at Boston should be finished; — also, that a plantation should be begun at Agawam, (being the best place in the land for tillage and cattle,) least an enemy, finding it void, should possess and take it from us. The governour's son (being one of the assistants) was to undertake this, and to take no more out of the bay than twelve men; the rest to be supplied at the coming of the next ships.

A maid servant of Mr. Skelton of Salem, going towards Sagus, was lost seven days, and at length came home to Salem. All that time she was in the woods, having no kind of food, the snow being very deep, and as cold as at any time that winter. She was so frozen into the snow some mornings, as she was one hour before she could get up; yet she soon recovered and did well, through the Lord's wonderful providence.

[Large blank.]

About the beginning of this month of January the pinnaces, which went after the pirates, returned, the cold being so great as they could not pursue them; but, in their return, they hanged up at Richman's Isle an Indian, one Black Will, one of those who had there murdered[1] Walter Bagnall. Three of the pirates' company ran from them and came home.

[Large blank.]

February 21.] The governour and four of the assistants, with three of the ministers, and others, about twenty-six in all, went, in three boats, to view Natascott, the wind W., fair weather; but the wind arose at N. W. so strong, and extreme cold, that they were kept there two nights, being forced to lodge upon the ground, in an open cottage, upon a little old straw,

||stone|| ||2their||

---

[1] That murder was mentioned under date of October, 1631, page 62, a year and a quarter before. The process mentioned in the text is more like revenge than justice. Richman's or Richmond's Isle, is part of Scarborough.

which they pulled from the thatch. Their victuals also *100 grew short, so as they were forced to eat muscles, — yet they were very ||mean,|| — and came all safe home the third day after, through the Lord's special providence. Upon view of the place, it was agreed by all, that to build a fort there would be of too great charge, and of little use; whereupon the planting of that place was deferred.[1]

22, or thereabouts.] The ship William, Mr. Trevore master, arrived at Plimouth with some passengers and goods for the Massachusetts Bay; but she came to set up a fishing at Scituate, and so to go to trade at Hudson's River.

By this ship we had intelligence from our friends in England, that Sir Ferdinando Gorges and Capt. Mason (upon the instigation of Sir Christopher Gardiner, Morton, and Ratcliff) had preferred a petition to the lords of the privy council against us, charging us with many false accusations; but, through the Lord's good providence, and the care of our friends in England, (especially Mr. §Emanuel§ Downing, who had married the governour's sister, and the good testimony given on our behalf by one Capt. Wiggin,[2] who dwelt at Pascataquack, and had been divers times among us,) their malicious practice took not effect. The principal matter they had against us was, the letters of some indiscreet persons among us, who had written against the church government §in England,§ etc., which had been intercepted by occasion of the death of Capt. Levett, who carried them, and died at sea.

26.] Two little girls of the governour's family were sitting under a great heap of logs, plucking of birds, and the wind

||merry||

---

[1] Readers accustomed to receive, with some hesitation, any information from Johnson, will compare the narrative in our text with his, lib. I. c. 28, or as it is reprinted in 2 Hist. Coll. III. 138, 9. A scrutiny of his representation discloses mistakes of the time, making it "the vernal of the year 1634;" of the place, "a small island, about two miles distant from Boston," that is, Castle Island, instead of Nantasket; and of the number, "some eight or ten persons of note." He wrote eighteen years after the event, and shows little precision in any thing but his creed; yet his book is one of the most curious that an inquirer into the manners and institutions of our fathers can peruse.

[2] For some of this testimony, see 3 Mass. Hist. Coll. VIII. 320.

driving the feathers into the house, the governour's wife caused them to remove away. They were no sooner gone, but the whole heap of logs fell down in the place, and had crushed them to death, if the Lord, in his special providence, had not delivered them.

March.] The governour's son, John Winthrop, went, with
*101 twelve[1] ||more,|| to begin a plantation at Agawam, after called Ipswich.

[Large blank.]

One John Edye, a godly man of Watertown congregation, fell distracted, and, getting out one evening, could not be found; but, eight days after, he came again of himself. He had kept his strength and colour, yet had eaten nothing (as must needs be conceived) all that time. He recovered his understanding again in good measure, and lived very orderly, but would, now and then, be a little distempered.[2]

[Blank.]

April 10.] Here arrived Mr. Hodges, one of Mr. Peirce his mates. He came from Virginia in a shallop, and brought news that Mr. Peirce's ship was cast away upon a shoal four miles from Feake[3] Isle, ten leagues to the N. of the mouth of Vir-

||men||

---

1 At the court, 1 April next, it was "ordered, that no person whatsoever shall go to plant or inhabit at Agawam, without leave from the court, except those that are already gone with Mr. John Winthrop, jun." Then follows in the Record, I. 96, the list of the others: "Mr. Clerke, Robert Coles, Thomas Howlett, John Biggs, John Gage, Thomas Hardy, William Perkins, Mr. Thorndike, William Sarjeant," as in Prince, II. 86. Of course, there were three more.

2 The last sentence appears to have been written, as the sense would induce us also to suppose, sometime later than the preceding. A blank had been left for the sufferer's Christian name, which is inserted in a different ink from the rest of the page. From Watertown Records, I find, "Pilgrim, daughter of John and Amie Eddie, born 25 August, 1634; John, son of J. and A. E., born 16 February, 1636–7, died soon; Benjamin, son of J. and A. E., buried 1639; Samuel, son of J. and A. E., born 30 September, 1640." Another daughter is also mentioned of a later date.

3 Probably this name was given as a compliment to the relative of Gov. Winthrop, and may not have been perpetuated. The island is undoubtedly on the ocean side of the eastern shore of Virginia. In the map of Maryland, in Ogilby's History of America, it is called Fetche's Island.

ginia Bay, November 2d, about ||five|| in the morning, the wind S. W., through the negligence of one of his mates, who had the watch, and kept not his lead as he was ||²exhorted||. They had a shallop and their ship's boat aboard. All that went into the shallop came safe on shore, but the ship's boat was sunk by the ship's side, and [blank] men drowned in her, and ten of them were taken up alive into the shallop. There were in the ship twenty-eight seamen and ten passengers. Of these were drowned seven seamen and five passengers, and all the goods were lost, except one hogshead of beaver; and most of the letters were saved, and some other small things, which were driven on shore the next day, when the ship was broken in pieces. They were nine days in much distress, before *102
they found any English. Plimouth men lost four hogsheads, 900[1] pounds of beaver, and 200 otter skins. The governour of Massachusetts lost, in beaver and fish, which he sent to Virginia, etc., near £100. Many others lost ||³beaver,|| and Mr. Humfrey, fish.[2]

[Large blank.]

May.] The William and Jane, Mr. Burdock master, arrived with thirty passengers and ten cows ||⁴or more||. She came in six weeks from London.

[Blank.]

The Mary and Jane arrived, Mr. Rose master. She came from London in seven weeks, and brought one hundred and ninety-six passengers, (only two children died). Mr. Coddington, one of the assistants, and his wife,[3] came in her. In her

||one|| ||²appointed|| ||³skins|| ||⁴one mare||

[1] These figures, taken from the margin, were designed, as I think, to represent the quantity, not the value; the pounds avoirdupois, not, as the former editor had it, pounds sterling. Of this construction I felt confident before knowing the concurrence of Prince, II. 87. He inserts a characteristic letter from Capt. Peirce about the shipwreck.

[2] She was bound to England, after stopping to trade at Virginia, probably to receive tobacco for her fish. The skins from Massachusetts were, of course, destined for London. I have seen several letters from friends in England to John Winthrop, jun., here, acknowledging receipt of epistles sent by this vessel, which, having been drenched in the sea, were hardly legible by his correspondents.

[3] Her name was Mary, and she is the 158th member of Boston church. Cod-

return she was cast away upon Isle Sable, but [blank] men were saved.

By these ships we understood, that Sir Christopher Gardiner, and Thomas Morton, and Philip Ratcliff, (who had been punished here for their misdemeanours,) had petitioned to the king and council against us, (being set on by Sir Ferdinando Gorges and Capt. Mason, who had begun a plantation at Pascataquack, and aimed at the general government of New England for their agent there, Capt. Neal). The petition was of many sheets of paper, and contained many false accusations, (and among some truths misrepeated,) accusing us to intend rebellion, to have cast off our allegiance, and to be wholly separate from the church and laws of England; that our ministers and
*103 people did continually rail against the state, church, and bishops there, etc. Upon which such of our company as were then in England, viz., Sir Richard Saltonstall, Mr. Humfrey, and Mr. Cradock, were called before a committee of the council, to whom they delivered in an answer in writing;[1] upon reading whereof, it pleased the Lord, our gracious God and Protector, so to work with the lords, and after with the king's majesty, when the whole matter was reported to him by Sir Thomas Jermin, one of the council, (but not of the committee, who yet had been present at the three days of hearing, and spake much in the commendation of the governour, both to the lords and after to his majesty,) that he said, he would have them severely punished, who did abuse ||his governour|| and the plantation; that the defendants were dismissed with a favorable order for their encouragement, being assured from some

||this government||

dington had lost the wife he brought in the first expedition, as appears by Dudley's letter, in the great mortality of the seasoning. He went to England early in 1631. Gov. Winthrop, in writing to his son, in a letter of that date, in the Appendix, desires him to favor Coddington's application to his *sister*, whom I presume to be the widow of Henry. But she came over in the latter part of that year, with her mother-in-law, the wife of the governour, and soon married Feake.

[1] A letter from Winthrop to his friend Bradford, giving a relation of this inquiry, and the order of the privy council thereon, preserved in Prince, II.89–91, is worth perusal.

of the council, that his majesty did not intend to impose the ceremonies of the church of England upon us; for that it was considered, that it was the freedom from such things that made people come over to us; and it was credibly informed to the council, that this country would, in time, be very beneficial to England for masts, cordage, etc., if the Sound should be debarred.[1]

We sent forth a pinnace after the pirate Bull, but, after *104
she had been forth two months,[2] she came home, hav-

---

[1] The fears, entertained by our friends in England, while this subject was before the council, will be fully exhibited by extracts from two letters in my possession to J. Winthrop the younger. Edward Howes writes, 18 March, 1632–3, "I am glad, and exceedingly rejoice at your prosperity, and the prosperity of the whole colony, and that it hath pleased God to show his power and mercy upon you all in a wonderful manner, beyond the expectation of the great ones of this land, in delivering you, not from a Spanish powder plot, nor an accounted invincible armada, but from a Spanish-like French infection, which was like to have tainted the halest and best men amongst you, yea all of you, as may appear by the writings and letters written with mine own hand, and sent to your father, my honored friend. Sir, I am the more sensible hereof, in regard I was a daily and hourly auditor and spectator of all the passages, which hath caused me to take it into consideration, that your plantation hath need of some hearty and able friends to back you upon all occasions, which must remain here and have friends at court. I, though not so able as I could wish, (if God saw it good,) yet as hearty as the best, considering Mr. Humfrey's preparation for departure, and my master's desire and resolution to be with you, have betaken myself now, at last, to the study of the laws, and to that purpose have admitted myself as a student of Clifford's Inn. Not that I mean absolutely, or presently, to leave my master, but to enable myself to leave when he is gone, and to retire myself, in the vacation time, to my study, which shall ever tend, to the utmost of my poor ability, to the good and welfare of your plantation and state."

Francis Kirby writes, 26 March, 1633, "Your friends here, who are members of your plantation, have had much to do to answer the unjust complaints made to the king and council of your government there. I understand that you are an assistant, and so have a voice in the weighty affairs of that commonwealth. I know I shall not need to advise you, that the prayers for our king be not neglected in any of your public meetings; and I desire that you differ no more from us in church government, than you shall find that we differ from the prescript rule of God's word, and further I meddle not." Our fathers and all their descendants may be content with so liberal a permission of difference on church government.

[2] Prince, II. 91, gives this word *weeks*. The court, 2 July after, directed the treasurer to pay Lieut. Mason £10 for his services in this expedition; and the

ing not found him. After, we heard he was gone to the French.

A Dutch pink arrived, which had been to the southward a trading.

June 2.] Capt. Stone[1] arrived with a small ship with cows and some salt. The governour of Plimouth sent Capt. Standish to prosecute against him for piracy. The cause ||was, being|| at the Dutch plantation, where a pinnace of Plimouth coming, and Capt. Stone and the Dutch governour having been drinking together, Capt. Stone, upon pretence that those of Plimouth had reproached them of Virginia, from whence he came, seized upon their pinnace, (with the governour's consent,) and offered to carry her away, but the Dutchmen ||[2]rescued|| her; and the next day the governour and Capt. Stone entreated the master of the pinnace (being one of the council of Plimouth) to pass it by, which he promised by a solemn instrument under his hand; yet, upon their earnest prosecution at court, we bound over Capt. Stone (with two sureties) to appear in the admiralty court in England, etc. But, after, those of Plimouth, being persuaded that it would turn to their reproach, and that it could be no piracy, with their consent, we withdrew the recognizance.

15.] Mr. Graves, in the ship Elizabeth[2] Bonadventure, from Yarmouth, arrived with ninety-five passengers, and thirty-four Dutch sheep, and two mares. They came from Yarmouth in six weeks; lost not one person, but above forty sheep.

19.] A day of thanksgiving was kept in all the congrega-
*105 tions, for our delivery from the plots of our enemies, and
for the safe arrival of our friends, etc.

July 2.] At a court it was agreed, that the governour, John Winthrop, should have, towards his charges this year, £150,[3]

||was began|| ||[2]wrested||

---

other charges amounted to £24.7.6, for which see the treasurer's account, in 2 Hist. Coll. VIII. 232, 3.

1 More will be found of this unhappy man in September and January following, and in November, 1634. A very bad report of him, under this latter year, is also given by Morton.

2 Here, at first, a blank had been left for the ship's name, which the governour afterwards inserted.

3 The figures in the MS. are 130, or 150, the 3 being, I think, written upon

and the money, which he had disbursed in public business, as officers' wages, etc., being between two and three hundred pounds, should be forthwith paid.

12.] Mr. Edward Winslow, governour of Plimouth, and Mr. Bradford, came into the bay, and went away the 18th. They came partly to confer about joining in a trade to Connecticut, for beaver and hemp. There was a motion to set up a trading house there, to prevent the Dutch, who were about to build one; but, in regard the place was not fit for plantation, there being three or four thousand warlike Indians, and the river not to be gone into but by small pinnaces, having a bar affording but six feet at high water, and for that no vessels can get in for seven months in the year, partly by reason of the ice, and then the violent stream, etc., we thought not fit to meddle with it.[1]

24.] A ship arrived from Weymouth, with about eighty passengers, and twelve kine, who sate down at Dorchester. They were twelve weeks coming, being forced into the Western Islands by a leak, where they stayed three weeks, and were very courteously used by the Portugals; but the extremity of

---

the 5; but it is observable, that the Colony Record has it only £100. The treasurer's account of all the payments to Winthrop, as referred to in my note above, amounts to £328.10.

[1] Under date of 4 April, 1631, the reader has seen the earliest mention of Connecticut arising in the History of Massachusetts. But, from Bradford's Register, in Prince, II. 94, we may be sure, that Plimouth had entertained views of establishing a plantation there, at an earlier season, and was willing to admit our colonists, her neighbours, to partake the advantage. On the first proposal from the Indian sachem, a sufficient cause for declining to send out a colony, to such a distance, would be found in our weakness; but I am constrained to remark, that the reasons, in the text above assigned, the strength of the current, shoalness of the water, continuance of the ice, and multitude of Indians, look to me more like pretexts, than real motives. Some disingenuousness, I fear, may be imputed to our council, in starting difficulties to deter our brethren of the humble community of Plimouth from extending their limits to so advantageous a situation; for we next season were careful to warn the Dutch against occupation of it, and the following year took possession ourselves. Honest Morton complains, that his people "deserved to have held it, and not by friends to have been thrust out, as, in a sort, they afterwards were;" and his complaint appears very natural, if not unanswerable.

the heat there, and the continual rain brought sickness upon them, so as [blank] died.

*106 Much sickness at Plimouth, and above twenty[1] died of pestilent fevers.

Mr. Graves returned, and carried a freight of fish from hence and Plimouth.

By him the governour and assistants sent an answer to the petition of Sir Christopher Gardiner, and withal a certificate from the old planters[2] concerning the carriage of affairs, etc.

August 6.] Two men servants to one Moodye, of Roxbury, returning in a boat from the windmill, struck upon the oyster bank. They went out to gather oysters, and, not making fast their boat, when the flood came, it floated away, and they were both drowned, although they might have waded out on either side; but it was an evident judgment[3] of God upon them, for they were wicked persons. One of them, a little before, being reproved for his lewdness, and put in mind of hell, answered, that if hell were ten times hotter, he had rather be there than he would serve his master, etc. The occasion was, because he had bound himself for divers years, and saw that, if he had been at liberty, he might have had greater wages, though otherwise his master used him very well.[4]

---

[1] For the number a blank was left, when the line was first written.

[2] Of these *old* planters, we may conjecture the names to be, Blaxton, Jefferies, Maverick, Thomson; and perhaps Bursley, Conant, and Oldham.

[3] Too many instances of more extraordinary providential or fortuitous occurrences, perverted in their interpretation, will be observed in the progress of this History. It was the vice of the age, and indeed of most ages. The great historian of the civil war abounds in such judgments; but on the other side they are still more numerous.

[4] With the incomplete transcript of this paragraph, and in the midst of a sentence, Prince's *third* pamphlet, II. 96, abruptly terminates. To omit here the expression of deepest regret for thus parting with such a companion, would be injurious to his memory. Yet deeper will be the regret of all inquirers after the minute circumstances of New England history, that such a patient and judicious student had not begun his Annals with the discovery by Columbus, rather than the creation of Moses. No other antiquary will ever enjoy advantages equal to his for an exact chronological series of our events; and when great opportunities are afforded, a dozen Hubbards, or a score of Mathers, may rise for one Prince. Civil convulsions, disregard of manuscripts, and the lapse of time, favorable to worms and damp, have each robbed us of many of his

Mr. Graves returned. He carried between five and six thousand weight of beaver, and about thirty passengers. Capt. Walter Neal, of Pascataquack, and some eight of his company, went with him. He had been in the bay above ten days, and came not all that time to see the govournour. Being persua- *107
ded by divers of his friends, his answer was, that he was not well entertained the first time he came hither, and, besides, he had some letters opened in the bay; ||ergo,|| except he were invited, he would not go see him. The 13th[1] day he wrote to the governour, to excuse his not coming to see him, upon the same reasons. The governour returned him answer, that his entertainment was such as time and place could afford, (being at their first coming, before they were housed, etc.) and retorted the discourtesy upon him, in that he would thrust himself, with such a company, (he had five or six gentlemen with him,) upon a stranger's entertainment, at such an unseasonable time, and having no need so to do; and for his letters, he protested his innocency, (as he might well, for the letters were opened before they came into the bay;) and so concluded courteously, yet with plain demonstration of his error. And, indeed, if ||[2]the governour|| should have invited him, standing upon those terms, he had blemished his reputation.

There is mention made before of the answer, which was returned to Sir Christopher Gardiner his accusations, to which the governour and all the assistants subscribed, only the deputy refused. He made three exceptions: 1. For that we termed the bishops reverend bishops; which was only in repeating the ||[3]accuser's words||. 2. For that we professed to believe all the articles of the ||[4]Christian|| faith, according to the scriptures and the common received tenets of the churches

||Government;|| ||[2]he courteously|| ||[3]accusations made|| ||[4]gospel||

---

dearest treasures; but for those which himself made public, all succeeding admirers of the days of old must unite with me in the oblation of highest regard,

"His saltem accumulem donis."

[1] Of the month, not of his visit, I presume to be meant. William Wood, to whom we are obliged for New England's Prospect, printed at London, 1634, went undoubtedly with Graves; for he says, he sailed from Boston, 15th August, 1633.

of England. This he refused, because we differed from them in matter of discipline, and about the meaning of Christ's descension into hell; ||yet|| the faithful in England (whom we account the churches) expound it as we do, and not of a local descent, as some of the bishops do. 3. For that we gave the king the title of sacred majesty, which is the most proper title of princes, *being the Lord's anointed,*[1] and the word a mere civil word, never applied in scripture to any divine thing, but sanctus used always, (Mr. Knox called the ||[2]queen of Scotland|| by the same
*108 title). Yet by no reasons could he be drawn to yield to these things, although they were allowed by divers of the ministers and the chief of Plimouth.

There was great scarcity of corn, by reason of the spoil our hogs had made at harvest, and the great quantity they had ||[3]even|| in the winter, (there being no acorns;) yet people lived well with fish and the fruit of their gardens.[2]

Sept. 4.] The Griffin, a ship of three hundred tons, arrived, (having been eight weeks from the Downs). §This ship was brought in by John Gallop a new[3] way by *Lovell's* Island, at low water, now called Griffin's Gap.§ She brought about

||that|| ||[2]In. of S——|| ||[3]eaten||

---

[1] I am certain, from the difference of the ink, that the pen was drawn through this passage some time after it was written. If it were the governour's pen, his sentiments, but not his principles, were changed in a few years.

[2] At the court, 5 November after, the adoption of two remarkable regulations was caused by this scarcity: 1. "That no man shall give his swine any corn, but such as, being viewed by two or three neighbours, shall be judged unfit for man's meat." 2. "Also, that every plantation shall agree how many swine every person may keep, winter and summer, about the plantation: this order to take place ten days hence."

[3] The *new* way is not so clearly indicated, that I should dare to pilot the reader through it. On first reading this sentence, it seemed as if the passage must be our present ship channel, between Lovell's and George's with Gallop's Islands, and, of course, that Broad Sound was the former common way. But this would be wrong; for the governour has noticed, that, in July, 1643, when La Tour sailed from us with the ships hired here, they went out at Broad Sound, *where no ships of such burden had gone out before, or not more than one.* So I conclude, that our present ship channel is the same that was first used; and that Gallop brought the Griffin in between Lovell's Island and the Great Brewster from the northward. We are confident, that very great changes have occurred in the harbour; and, within the recollection of many, such violences

two hundred passengers, having lost some four, §whereof one was drowned two days before, as he was casting forth a line to take mackerel§. In this ship came Mr. Cotton,[1] Mr. Hooker, and Mr. Stone,[2] ministers, and §Mr. Peirce,§[3]

---

are known, as may justify the conjecture, that the long shoal, to the south-west from the Great Brewster, was solid upland when the bay was first settled.

1 Nothing can be added to the abundant materials offered by this History, and all the contemporary books, which Mather, Hutchinson, Eliot, Allen, and Emerson, have exhausted in their notices of "the great Cotton." The first author derived his name and part of his blood from this spiritual guide of Boston; and the last adorned, in his History of the First Church, all who had preceded himself in ministration at that altar.

2 Samuel Stone was, happily, in favor with the author of the Magnalia; and readers that dread to pursue an inquiry in such a work, will find ample account of him in Trumbull, Eliot's and Allen's Dictionaries, Holmes's History of Cambridge, 1 Hist. Coll. VII.; and in the Plimouth Memorialist, at the date of his death, 1663, an elegy in the worst style of that age. He performed good service with Mason, whom he accompanied as chaplain in the expedition against the Pequots, 1637. See 2 Hist. Coll. VIII. 134. A Body of Divinity, in a catechetical way, by him, in a 4to MS. of 540 pages, is in the library of our Historical Society.

3 He was a gentleman of high repute in Boston, being one of the selectmen with Winthrop and Coddington the next year, and must not be confounded with the mariner, who had the same name of baptism. His freeman's oath, at the general court, 14 May, 1634, was taken at the same time with eighty others, of whom Hooker, Stone, Cotton, Thomas Mayhew, and William Brenton are all, besides Peirce, that have the respectful title, Mr., prefixed to their names. Col. Rec. I. 112. Prince, enumerating the principal members of Boston church, II. 69, has mistaken him for the master of the Lyon, as I infer from finding in their Records but one of the name, and being satisfied, that he could not be honored with such office in the civil line, unless in full communion with the brethren. Yet Prince may be correct; for the admission to our church was several weeks before the dismission of Charlestown people. The name of William Peirce does not appear in the record of Boston first church except as next to those of Rev. Mr. James and his wife, and so the very latest before the formation of Charlestown church. It might therefore be thought, that this fellow passenger with Cotton went to some other church, perhaps that of Cambridge or Watertown. But as it is apparent, that our record, in its few earliest pages, is not original, but copy, I presume the fact of admission of this gentleman was omitted by the scribe supposing the former mention of the other W. P. applied to him. His wife, Bridget, was admitted of our church 2 Feb. 1634, after her husband. A second wife survived him, and had administration of his estate in December, 1669. See Prob. Rec. VII. 2, by which we find his estate much reduced, the inventory amounting only to £85.2, unless another person of the same

*109 Mr. Haynes,[1] (a gentleman of great estate,) Mr. || Hoffe, ||[2] and many other men of good estates. They gat out of England with much difficulty, all places being belaid to have taken Mr. Cotton and Mr. Hooker, who had been long sought for to have been brought into the high commission; but the master being bound to touch at the Wight, the ||[2]pursuivants|| attended there, and, in the mean time, the said ministers were taken in at the Downs. Mr. Hooker and Mr. Stone went presently to Newtown, where they were to be entertained, and Mr. Cotton stayed at Boston. ||[3]On Saturday||[3] evening, the

|| Goffe || ||[2]pursuants|| ||[3]One Sunday||

name, but not the navigator mentioned in a note on page 25, be in that record intended; for administration of the estate of *one* William Peirce was granted, January, 1661, to his wife, Prob. Rec. IV. 66, and the inventory of it is £228.5. Several children survived, of whom the Prob. Rec. VII. 213, affords the names. It is not now easy to refer to each stock the numerous descendants in our country.

[1] There can be no need of saying more of this gentleman than will be found in a few pages of this History, in Trumbull, the Magnalia, and the biographies. He was fortunate in being governour of Massachusetts, and more fortunate in removing after his first year of office, thereby avoiding our bitter contentions, to become father of the new colony of Connecticut.

[2] Drs. Trumbull and Holmes were, by the error of the former edition, led into mistake of this gentleman's name. Atherton Haugh, or Hough, pronounced as the text gives it, was of great influence in Boston, as this work, in its progress, will show. He was early chosen into the council, and afterwards a deputy from Boston in several general courts. I presume he came from Boston in Lincolnshire; for, in 1628, the mayor of that borough was of the same name, probably the same person. His descendants, in male and female lines, if we may judge from the perpetuation of the unusual name of baptism, continued long in Boston and its vicinity; and the derivation through female lines is probably not yet extinct. He died 11 September, 1650.

[3] In any other place, I know not that evidence of a regular religious assembly, on the evening before the first day of the week, can be found. The time was observed as holy in private families for many years; and writings in favor of the custom, nearly a century, are recollected, particularly in 1722, by Stoddard of Northampton, one of the greatest divines of that age in our country. The practice still subsists, with greater or less punctuality, in Connecticut, where, on the evening of Sunday, it is said, many recur to their secular labors; and by the statute of Massachusetts, 1791, c. 58, certain regulations, "respecting the due observation of the Lord's day, shall be construed to extend to the time included between the midnight preceding and the sun setting of the same day."

congregation met in their ordinary exercise, and Mr. Cotton, being desired to speak to the question, (which was of the *110
church,) he showed, out of the Canticles, 6, that some churches were as queens, some as concubines, some as damsels, and some as doves,[1] etc. He was then (with his wife) propounded to be admitted a member. The Lord's day following, he exercised in the afternoon, and being to be admitted, he signified his desire and readiness to make his confession according to order, which he said might be sufficient in declaring his faith about baptism, (which he then desired for his child, born in their passage, and therefore named Seaborn[2]). He gave two reasons why he did not baptize it at sea, (not for want of fresh water, for he held, sea water would have served:) 1, because they had no settled congregation there; 2, because a minister hath no power to give the seals but in his own congregation. He desired his wife might also be admitted a member, and gave a modest testimony of her, but withal requested, that she might not be put to make open confession, etc., which he said was against the apostle's rule, and not fit for women's modesty; but that the elders might examine her in private. So she was asked, if she did consent in the confession of faith

---

[1] Most of the early Protestants and especially the Puritans, paid no less attention to the Song, than to the Wisdom of Solomon; and sometimes, by their extreme fondness for spiritualizing what needs great distortion to make it "profitable for doctrine, for reproof, for correction, for instruction in righteousness," seem to be ignorant of the strong doubts of its canonical authority. Piety is shocked, when prudence is thus slighted.

[2] Of this son, whose name, in the catalogue of Harvard College, is found, Marigena, 1651, a brief note is found in Allen. I am less surprised at the omission of him by Eliot, whose account of the father, is admirable for its propriety, than of his younger brother, John, H. C., 1657, who, after officiating several years as teacher of the Indians, and thirty years as pastor at Plimouth, removed to Charleston, S. C., and there gathered a Congregational church. We cannot here avoid the expression of regret, that, in Ramsay's "History of the Independent or Congregational Church in Charleston," so little is related of him; but the ample account of the Plimouth church, 1 Hist. Coll. IV. 122–128, affords all the information that might be desired. For his acquirements in the language of the aborigines, no man of New England, I presume, except Eliot and Williams, ranks higher. Still, on account of the unhappy cause of his dismission from Plimouth, it was, perhaps, excusable in Eliot's Biographical Dictionary, to avoid notice of the younger John Cotton.

made by her husband, and if she did desire to be admitted, etc.; whereto she answered affirmatively; and so both were admitted, and their child baptized, the father presenting it, (the
*111 child's baptism being, as he did then affirm, in another case, the father's ||incentive|| for the help of his faith, etc).

The said 4th of September, came in also the ship called the Bird, (Mr. Yates master). She brought [blank] passengers, having lost [blank;] and [blank] cows, §having lost [blank;]§ and four mares. She had been twelve weeks at sea, being, at her first coming out, driven northerly to fifty-three.

About ten days before this time, a bark was set forth to Connecticut and those parts, to trade.

John Oldham, and three with him, went over land to Connecticut, to trade. The sachem used them kindly, and gave them some beaver. They ||[2]brought of the hemp, which grows|| there in great abundance, and is much better than the English. He accounted it to be about one hundred and sixty miles.[1] He brought some black lead, whereof the Indians told him there was a whole rock. He lodged at Indian towns all the way.

12.] Capt. John Stone (of whom mention is made before) carried himself very dissolutely in drawing company to drink, etc., and being found upon the bed in the night with one Barcroft's wife, he was brought before the governour, etc., and though it appeared he was in drink, and no act to be proved, yet it was thought fit he should abide his trial, for which ||[3]end|| warrant was sent out to stay his pinnace, which was ready to set sail; whereupon he went to Mr. Ludlow, one of the assistants, and used ||[4]braving|| and threatening speeches against him, for which he raised some company and apprehended him, and brought him to the governour, who put him in irons, and

||instruction|| ||[2]bought of him the hemp that grew|| ||[3]a|| ||[4]——||

1 The former editor, desirous of shortening the road to the capital, put this annotation on the text: "From Boston to Connecticut River, in a direct line, is not more than half that distance." Probably Oldham and his fellow travellers followed winding paths for the convenience of lodging all the way, as in much later times we were compelled to for some part of the route.

kept a guard upon him till the court, (but his irons were taken off the same day). At the court his indictment was framed for adultery, but found *ignoramus* by the great jury; but, for his other misdemeanors, he was fined £100, which yet was not levied of him; and ordered upon pain of death to come here no more, without license of the court; and the woman was bound to her good behaviour.[1]

17.] The governour and council met at Boston, and *112
called the ministers and elders of all the churches, to consider about Mr. Cotton his sitting down. He was desired to divers places, and those who came with him desired he might sit down where they might keep store of cattle; but it was agreed, by full consent, that the fittest place for him was Boston, and in that respect those of Boston might take farms in any part of the bay not belonging to other towns; and that (keeping a || lecture ||) he should have some maintenance out of the treasury. But divers of the council, upon their second thoughts, did after refuse this contribution.[2]

October 2.] The bark Blessing, which was sent to the southward, returned. She had been at an island over against Connecticut, called Long Island, because it is near fifty leagues long, the east part about ten leagues from the main, but the west

|| lecturer ||

---

1 Though the Colony Records, I. 103, in the account of Stone's offence, take not any notice of the supposed adultery, yet the whole severity of the sentence is found there. Hubbard, 156, borrows from them the vituperative language, going, in this instance, beyond our author, whom, almost uniformly, he follows with undeviating prudence. But the judgment mentions assaulting, as part of the misdemeanor, which both the historians overlook.

2 I think the refusal was proper. There was certainly no propriety in making the colony, after Boston was so much increased in wealth and numbers, contribute to the support of her minister, because he was the most able man on this side of the ocean.

The rate of £400, voted at the court, 1 October next, shows the relative importance of the towns. The proportions are, to Boston, Roxbury, Newtown, Watertown, and Charlestown, £48 each; Dorchester, £80; Sagus, £36; Salem, £28; Medford, £12; Wenetsemit and Agawam, £8 each. The aggregate exceeds the amount of the levy by £12; but that does not appear so unexpected as the large tax on Dorchester. Some new comers of large estate had, I imagine, settled in that town.

end not a mile. There they had store of the best wampampeak, both white and blue. The Indians there are a very treacherous people. They have many canoes so great as one will carry eighty men. They were also in the River of Connecticut, which is barred at the entrance, so as they could not find above one fathom of water. They were also at the Dutch plantation upon Hudson's River, (called New Netherlands,) where they were very kindly entertained, and had some beaver and other things, for such commodities as they put off. They showed the governour (called Gwalter Van Twilly)[1] their
*113 commission, which was to signify to them, that the king of England had granted the river and country of Connecticut to his own subjects; and therefore desired them to forbear to build there, etc. The Dutch governour wrote back to our governour, (his letter was very courteous and respectful, as it had been to a very honorable person,) whereby he signified, that the Lords the States had also granted the same parts to the West India Company, and therefore requested that || we || would forbear the same till the matter were decided between the king of England and the said lords.

The said bark did pass and repass over the shoals of Cape Cod, about three or four leagues from Nantucket Isle, where the breaches are very terrible, yet they had three fathom water all over.

[Large blank.]

The company of Plimouth sent a bark to Connecticut, at this time, to erect a trading house there. When they came, they found the Dutch had built there, and did forbid the Plimouth men to proceed; but they set up their house notwithstanding,

||he||

[1] Authentic history preserves little account of the administration of this gentleman. But a work of exquisite humour, in which fiction builds on the ground-work of truth, has fully amplified his renown; and the name of Diedrick Knickerbocker, his panegyrist, will forever remind posterity of "the unutterable ponderings of Walter the doubter." William Smith, History of New York, 4to, London, 1757, dates the arrival of the governour, whom he calls Wouter Van Twiller, in June, 1629. Hubbard, 323, with more than his usual negligence, calls *Kieft* first governour, when he had transcribed, 171, 2, from Winthrop, this and the two following paragraphs, with hardly the change of a letter.

about a mile above the Dutch.[1] This river runs so far northward, that it comes within a day's journey of a part of Merrimack called [blank,] and so runs thence N. W. so near the Great Lake, as [allows] the Indians to pass their canoes into it over land. From this lake, and the hideous swamps about it, come most of the beaver which is traded between Virginia and Canada, which runs forth of this lake; and Patomack River in Virginia comes likewise out of it, or very near, so as from this lake there comes yearly to the Dutch about ten thousand skins, which might easily be diverted by Merrimack, if a course of trade were settled above in that river.[2]

10.] A fast was kept at Boston, and Mr. Leverett,[3] an *114
ancient, sincere professor, of Mr. Cotton's congregation in

---

1 Smith, N. Y. 2, asserts the priority of the Dutch settlement, by erection of a fort in 1623; but there can hardly be a particle of doubt, that an error of ten years must be allowed for, since the negotiations between the Dutch commissioner, De Razier, and the Plimouth colony, in 1627, are so totally silent on the subject of Connecticut, that it is impossible for us to believe they had then formed such an establishment. See 2 Hist. Coll. III. 51–57. See also the Dutch governour, Stuyvesant's, case stated by himself in Haz. II. 262, beginning with an allegation of purchase, by Jacobus Van Corlis, in 1633, and complaining of the expedition of Holmes from Plimouth in October following. See further a full account, by Gov. Bradford, of the origin of the controversy, Hutchinson's Mass. II. 469–71. Trumbull, I. 21, says the Dutch fort was at Hartford; the Plimouth house at Windsor.

2 Here is an ignorance of geography, at which we might be surprised, were not similar instances, in the early times, very common. The Connecticut is, indeed, within a day's journey of the Merrimack; but the passage of Indian canoes into that river, over land, could never have been from the Great Lake. It may have been, with a short portage, from the St. Lawrence. All the beaver trade between Virginia and Canada, by which name is designated the great river of Niagara, Cataraqui, or St. Lawrence, naturally took, through Lake Champlain, the direction of Hudson's River, and was therefore secured to the Dutch. It could not easily have been diverted to the Merrimack or the Potomack.

3 An omission to notice the fact, that this gentleman was father of the celebrated John Leverett, governour of Massachusetts, can only be accounted for by supposing, that Mather, Hutchinson, Holmes, Eliot, and Allen, were all unacquainted with it. Yet our first Church Record mentions it, when announcing the admission of the son, 14 July, 1639. Of Thomas little is mentioned; but we may be sure he came with Cotton, and other gentlemen of Boston in Old England, where he was an alderman; for his entrance to the church was

England, was chosen a ruling elder, and Mr. Firmin,[1] a godly man, an apothecary of Sudbury in England, was chosen deacon, by imposition of hands; and Mr. Cotton was then chosen teacher of the congregation of Boston, and ordained by imposition of the hands §of the presbytery, in this manner: First, he was chosen by all the congregation testifying their consent by erection of hands.§ Then Mr. Wilson, the pastor, demanded of him, if he did ||accept|| of that call. He paused, and then spake to this effect: that howsoever he knew himself unworthy and unsufficient for that place; yet, having observed all the passages of God's providence, (which he ||[2]reckoned|| up in particular) in calling him to it, he could not but ||[3]accept|| it. Then the pastor and the two[2] elders laid their hands upon his head, and the pastor prayed, and then, taking off their hands, laid them on again, and, speaking to him by his name, they did ||[4]thenceforth|| design him to the said office, in the name of the Holy Ghost, and did give him the charge of the congrega-
*115 tion, and did thereby (as by a sign from God) indue him with the gifts fit for his office; and lastly did bless him. Then the neighboring ministers, which were present, did (at the pastor's ||[5]motion||) give him the right hands of fellowship, and the pastor made a stipulation between him and the congregation. When Mr. Cotton accepted of the office, he commended to the congregation such as were to come over, who were of

||except|| ||[2]recorded|| ||[3]except|| ||[4]thereby|| ||[5]notice||

---

in October, 1633, he and his wife, Ann, being Nos. 169 and 170. The date of his death is marked in the church record, 3 April, 1650.

[1] His place was enjoyed but a short time; for, at the town meeting, on 6 October next year, which is the earliest, whose proceedings are preserved in our Town Records, the preceding pages being all lost, Richard Bellingham, Esq., was chosen a selectman, they say, "in the place of Giles Firmin, deceased." He took the freeman's oath 4 March, 1633–4. Eliot has given, with minuteness, the biography of the son, who attended his father across the ocean, and in a few years removed to Ipswich, whence an excellent letter from him to Winthrop, dated 26 December, 1639, is preserved by Hutchinson, Coll. 108; but I must correct his mistake in making the son, instead of the father, deacon of our church. Giles, the younger, married a daughter of the famous Nathaniel Ward, and died in England, 1697, at a great age, having written several devotional pieces, of which some are, as is reported, read in our time.

[2] Oliver and Leverett.

his charge in England, that they might be comfortably provided for.

The same day, Mr. Grant, in the ship James, arrived at Salem, having been but eight weeks between Gravesend and Salem. He brought Capt. Wiggin and about thirty, with one Mr. ‖Leveridge,‖[1] a godly minister, to Pascataquack, (which the Lord Say and the Lord Brook had purchased of the Bristol men,) and about thirty for Virginia, and about twenty for ‖[2]this‖ place, and some sixty cattle. He brought news, that the Richard, a bark of fifty tons, which came forth with the Griffin, being come above three hundred leagues, sprang such a leak, as she was forced to bear up, and ‖[3]was put in at‖ Weymouth.

11.] A fast at Newtown, where Mr. Hooker was chosen pastor, and Mr. Stone teacher, in such a manner as before at Boston.

The wolves continued to do much hurt among our cattle; and this month, by Mr. Grant, there came over four Irish greyhounds, which were sent to the governour by Mr. Downing, his brother-in-law.

[Very large blank.]

November.] A great mortality among the Indians. Chick-

‖L———‖ ‖[2]that‖ ‖[3]put into‖

[1] Brief notice only of this gentleman can be given. William Leveridge joined our church 9 August, 1635, being No. 308. Hubbard, who calls him "an able and worthy minister," says, 221, that, for want of encouragement at Wiggin's plantation of Dover, "he removed more southward, towards Plimouth or Long Island." This want of precision in that historian is especially blamable, as the earlier writer, Johnson, lib. 3. c. 10, had mentioned his residence at Sandwich, and engagement in the pious service of instructing the Indians. At that place notice is taken of him by our author, post, 331, sub an. 1640, as introducing a new practice in celebrating the eucharist. His departure from Sandwich is not related by Judge Davis in his edition of Morton's Memorial, 217; but Hazard, II. 372, 384, informs of his employment, by the commissioners of the United Colonies, as a missionary, in 1657. Seventeen years later, in a letter from Col. Matthias Nicolls of New York to Gov. Winthrop of Connecticut, I find him named thus: "I have given conveyance to your enclosed to Mr. Leveredge, which your honor saith related to some medicinal matter, but have received no return; probably he will find out some other way to give answer to it." He was then, I presume, stationed at Newtown, L. I., with which the best mode of conveyance, from Hartford, was through New York.

*116 atabot, the sagamore of Naponsett, died, and many of his people. The disease was the small pox. Some of them were cured by such means as they had from us; many of their children escaped, and were kept by the English.

Capt. Wiggin of Pascataquack wrote to the governour, that one of his people had stabbed another, and desired he might be tried in the bay, if the party ||died||. The governour answered, that if Pascataquack lay within their limits, (as it was supposed,) they would try him.

A small ship of about sixty tons was built at Medford, and called the Rebecca.

This year a watermill was built at Roxbury, by Mr. Dummer.[1]

The scarcity of workmen had caused them to raise their wages to an excessive rate, so as a carpenter would have three shillings the day, a laborer two shillings and sixpence, etc.; and accordingly those who had commodities to sell advanced their prices sometime double to that they cost in England, so as it grew to a general complaint, which the court, taking knowledge of, as also of some further evils, which were springing out of the excessive rates of wages, they made an order, that carpenters, ||[2]masons,|| etc., should take but two shillings the day, and laborers but eighteen pence, and that no commodity should be sold at above four pence in the shilling more than it cost for ready money in England; oil, wine, etc., and cheese, in regard of the hazard of bringing, etc., [excepted]. The evils which were springing, etc., were: 1. Many spent much time idly, etc., because they could get as much in four days as would keep them a week. 2. They spent much in tobacco and strong waters, etc., which was a great waste to the commonwealth, which, by reason of so many ||[3]foreign|| commodities expended, could not have subsisted to this time, but that it was supplied by the cattle and corn, which were sold to new comers at very dear rates, viz., corn at six shillings the bushel, a cow at £20,—yea, some at £24, some £26,—a

||desired|| ||[2]masters|| ||[3]scarce||

[1] Earlier in the year, the first watermill in the colony had been erected in Dorchester, by Stoughton. See 1 Hist. Coll. IX. 164.

mare at £35, an ewe goat at 3 or £4; and yet many cattle were every year brought out of England, and some from Virginia. Soon after order was taken for prices of commodities, viz., not to exceed the rate of four pence in the shilling above the price in England, except cheese and liquors, etc.

The ministers in the bay and Sagus did meet, once a fortnight, at one of their houses by ||course,|| where some *117
question of moment was debated. Mr. Skelton, the pastor of Salem, and Mr. Williams, who was removed from Plimouth thither, (but not in any office, though he exercised by way of prophecy,) took some exception against it, as fearing it might grow in time to a presbytery or superintendency, to the prejudice of the churches' liberties. But this fear was without cause; for they were all clear in that point, that no church or person can have power over another church; neither did they in their meetings exercise any such jurisdiction, etc.[1]

[Large blank.]

News of the taking of Machias[2] by the French. Mr. Allerton of Plimouth, and some others, had set up a trading wigwam there, and ||[2]left|| in it five men and store of commodities. La Tour,[3] governour of the French in those parts, making claim to the place, came to displant them, and, finding resistance, killed two of the men, and carried away the other three, and the goods.

[Large blank.]

Some differences fell out still, now and then, between the

||commission|| ||[2]lost||

---

[1] By Emerson, in History of the First Church, this is considered as the origin of the Boston Association of Congregational Ministers. He censures the strange bitterness of Hubbard, 189, 190, on this subject.

[2] Permanent establishment of settlers at that port was delayed one hundred and thirty years. See 1 Hist. Coll. III. 144. Of this hostile act, see Vol. II. 125–7.

[3] Of this governour of Nova Scotia, to whom a grant of the country had been made by Sir William Alexander, 30 April, 1630, as extracted from the Suffolk Registry of Deeds, III. 265, by Hazard, I. 307, and confirmed by Cromwell, 9 August, 1656, as in Hazard, I. 616, such perpetual mention will occur in the progress of this History, that it may be necessary to protract this note no farther than by reference, for what is not to be found in our author, to Hutchinson, I. 127–135.

governour and the deputy, which yet were soon healed. It had been ordered in court, that all hands should help to the finishing of the fort at Boston, and all the towns in the bay had gone once over, and most the second time; but those of Newtown being warned, the deputy would not suffer them to come, neither did acquaint the governour with the cause, which was, for that Salem and Sagus had not brought in money for their parts. The governour, hearing of it, wrote friendly to him, showing him that the intent of the court was, that the work should be done by those in the bay, and that, after, the others should pay a proportionable sum for the house, etc., which must be done by money; and therefore desired him that he would send in his neighbours. Upon this,
*118 Mr. Haynes and Mr. Hooker came to the governour to treat with him about it, and brought a letter from the deputy full of bitterness and resolution not to send till Salem, etc. The governour told them it should rest till the court, and withal gave the letter to Mr. Hooker with this speech: I am not willing to keep such an occasion of provocation by me. And soon after he wrote to the deputy (who had before desired to buy a fat hog or two of him, being somewhat short of provisions) to desire him to send for one, (which he would have sent him, if he had known when his occasion had been to have made use of it,) and to accept it as a testimony of his good will; and, lest he should make any scruple of it, he made Mr. Haynes and Mr. Hooker (who both sojourned in his house) partakers with him. Upon this the deputy returned this answer: "Your overcoming yourself hath overcome me. Mr. Haynes, Mr. Hooker, and myself, do most kindly accept your good will; but we desire, without offence, to refuse your offer, and that I may only trade with you for two hogs;" and so very lovingly concluded.—The court being two days after, ordered, that Newtown should do their work as others had done, and then Salem, etc., should pay for three days at eighteen pence a man.

11.] The congregation of Boston met to take order for Mr. Cotton's ||passage|| and house, and his and Mr. Wilson's maintenance. Mr. Cotton had disbursed eighty pounds for his ||[2]passage,|| and towards his house, which he would not have

||pursage|| ||[2]pursage||

again; so there was about £60 raised (by voluntary contribution) towards the finishing of his house, and about £100 towards their maintenance. At this meeting there arose some difference between the governour and Mr. Cottington, who charged the governour, that he took away the liberty of the rest, because (at the request of the rest) he had named some men to set out ||men's|| lands, etc., which grew to some heat of words; but the next Lord's day they both acknowledged openly their failing, and declared that they had been reconciled the next day.

[Large blank.]

26.] Mr. Wilson (by leave of the congregation of Boston, whereof he was pastor) went to Agawam to teach the people of that plantation, because they had yet no minister. Whiles he was there, December 4, there fell such a snow (knee deep) as he could not come back for [blank] days, and a boat, which went thither, was frozen up in the river.[1]

||minister's||

---

[1] Nobody can pretend, I believe, that an equal severity of cold has been twice experienced, at so early a season, for the last hundred years. The 4th of December, corresponding to our 14th by correction of the style, very seldom witnesses, on the sea shore, more than three or four inches depth of snow; and that which falls before Christmas does not often lie longer than two days. The frost, in the text, we should now think more remarkable than the snow; and no boat has probably been frozen up in Ipswich harbour, by the middle of December, within the recollection of any inhabitant. There is distinct reference to a degree of frost, in the year before this, that "hindered the making ready" of the expedition against Bull, the pirate, which, in the present age, would be extraordinary. In 1631 nothing is said of the approach of winter, nor any mention of the weather until 27 January. But the first autumn our author passed here was quite favorable; for he remarks that, till the 24 December, or our 3 January, was, "for the most part, fair, open weather;" yet such severity of "bitter frost and snow," as kept three servants in his boat, without victuals, from 27 November to 1 December, (that is, by our reckoning, from 7 to 11 December,) among the islands of Boston harbour, and finally compelled them to run ashore in Braintree Bay, (see page 38,) would surprise us. Cold came on earlier, it will be observed, in the year after this, in the text; and the man frozen in the snow, in November, on Plumb Island, would, in our days, be unable to find credit for his tale. November, 1635, affords strong proof of severe cold in Connecticut and Plimouth. Even Mr. Webster should have been struck with the circumstance of the freezing of the Connecticut so early as the 15 of that

*119 December 5.] John Sagamore died of the small pox, and almost all his people; (above thirty buried by Mr. Maverick of Winesemett in one day). The towns in the bay took away many of the children; but most of them died soon after.

James Sagamore of Sagus died also, and most of his folks.

---

month, O. S., however he might disregard the deep snow of the following December. Of the winter of 1636 nothing is observed, and perhaps Winthrop forgot the temperature of the sky in the unnatural heat of the controversy about grace. The rigid season of the next year, we shall see, continued one hundred and thirty-nine days.

The opinion is general, but not universal, that our climate is less rigorous than it was known to be soon after the discovery of the country; and we find certainly the mildness of autumn is usually prolonged to the winter solstice. But those who are slow to believe the improvement of temperature in our sky, overpowered by the testimony that establishes the fact of retardation in the advance of winter, discern some compensation, as they imagine, in the later approach of spring. I am confident, however, that the complaint of backwardness in that season, though rendered common by the tenderness of valetudinarians, and the impatience of husbandmen, is generally unjust. If the instances of that duration of cold, in the winter of 1641–2, when the ice was strong enough to bear many passengers together, from Pullen Point to Boston in a straight line, on the day corresponding to our 27 February, continuing even to 3 March, and that great snow of 1644–5, which blocked up the roads three weeks in March, and prevented the court from meeting in Boston, remaining on the ground to 9 of April, N. S., be undervalued in the estimate, as uncommon cases, from which conclusions may not safely be deduced, — it may be answered, that modern wonders in the atmosphere are not greater, and that the experience of Winthrop being short, no greater portion of time than his should now be assumed for a parallel. In the autumn of 1645 the cold came earlier than had ever been known, so that the genial season of that year was shortened at the beginning and end. The aggregate, or mean, of observations for many years, as given, nearly one hundred and seventy years ago, by Hubbard, 20, is here transcribed, in order that every reader may, every season, do something, by observation of the phænomena, in aid of the solution of so interesting a question: "The frost here *useth* to visit the inhabitants so early in the winter, and *ordinarily* tarries so long before it takes its leave in the spring, that the difficulty of subsistence is much increased thereby; for it *commonly* begins to take possession of the earth about the middle of November, (25, N. S.) forbidding the husbandman to meddle therewith any more, till the middle or end of March (25 March, — 9 April, N. S.) not being willing, till that time, to resign up its possession or the hold it hath taken for near two feet below the surface of the earth."

On this subject, which has of late received much elucidation, an Essay by an

John Sagamore desired to be brought among the English, (so he ||was;||) and promised (if he recovered) to live with *120
the English and serve their God. He left one son, which he disposed to Mr. Wilson, the pastor of Boston, to be brought up by him. He gave to the governour a good quantity of wampompeague, and to divers others of the English he gave gifts, and took order for the payment of his own debts and his men's. He died in a persuasion that he should go to the Englishmen's God. Divers of them, in their sickness, confessed that the Englishmen's God was a good God; and that, if they recovered, they would serve him.

It wrought much with them, that when their own people forsook them, yet the English came daily and ministered to them; and yet few, *only two families,* took any ||2infection|| by it. Among others, Mr. Maverick of Winesemett is worthy of *a perpetual*[1] remembrance. Himself, his wife, and servants, went daily to them, ministered to their necessities, and buried their dead, and took home many of their children. So did other of the neighbours.

This infectious disease spread to Pascataquack, where all the Indians (except one or two) died.

One Cowper of Pascataquack, going to an island, upon the Lord's day, to fetch some sack to be drank at the great house, he and a boy, coming back in a canoe, (being both drunk,) *121
were driven to sea and never heard of after.

At the same plantation, a company having made a fire at a

||agreed|| ||2instructions||

---

anonymous author, published at Philadelphia, 1809, will reward attentive perusal. A review of it, by the editor of this work, was printed in the Monthly Anthology, IX. 25. Some years before, a very elaborate, but skeptical dissertation had been offered to the Connecticut Academy of Arts and Sciences, by Noah Webster, Esq., for which, and other ingenious labors, the literary public is more indebted to him than even for the first edition of this History. A learned and judicious examination of that tract, usually ascribed to Professor Farrar of Cambridge, may be seen in the General Repository, IV. 313.

[1] That Maverick was not in full communion with our churches, was not, we may hope, the cause of striking a pen through this honorable epithet. No man seems better entitled by his deeds to the character of a Christian. The MS. appears to testify that the mutilation was not Winthrop's.

tree, one of them said, Here this tree will fall, §and here will I lie; § and accordingly it fell upon him and killed him.

It pleased the Lord to give special testimony of his presence in the church of Boston, after Mr. Cotton was called to office there. More were converted and added to that church, than to all the other churches in the bay,[1] (or rather the lake, for so it were more ‖properly‖ termed,[2] the bay being that part of sea without between the two capes, Cape Cod and Cape Ann). Divers profane and notorious evil persons came and confessed their sins, and were comfortably received into the bosom of the church. Yea, the Lord gave witness to the exercise of prophecy, so as thereby some were converted, and others much edified. Also, the Lord pleased greatly to bless the practice of discipline, wherein he gave the pastor, Mr. Wilson, a singular gift,[3] to the great benefit of the church.

After much deliberation and serious advice, the Lord directed the teacher, Mr. Cotton, to make it clear by the scripture, that the minister's maintenance, as well as all other charges of the church, should be defrayed out of a ‖[2]stock,‖ or treasury, which was to be raised out of the weekly contribution; which accordingly was agreed upon.[4]

‖principally‖ ‖[2]chest‖

---

1 Hubbard, 190, who, with sufficient accuracy, quotes his master, from whom a large part of his History is transcribed, enlarges the expression to "all the rest of the churches in the country." The reputation of Cotton needs no such exaggeration. From his arrival to this time, that is, three months, I was led by curiosity to ascertain from the Records the precise number intended by the text, and found thirty-seven added to the members of the church. The "profane and notorious evil persons" cannot be distinguished in the list; but perhaps, in several, the old disease broke out again. Temporal inducements operated too strongly to swell the company of communicants.

2 The governour first wrote, "so it shall be termed henceforth;" but the name could not be made popular in his day, and has never been thought of since. Yet the situation resembles much those arms of the sea, called lochs by the Scots, loughs by the Irish, and lagoons by the Spaniards.

3 Elder Leverett, as well as Wilson, is, by Hubbard, 190, blessed with this *singular gift* in "the practice of discipline." It certainly belonged to his office.

4 Cotton's arguments are lost, we may presume, for the custom of raising these charges of the church, which was made so clear from the scripture, is totally changed. Our fathers looked too much to a special divine appointment

27.] The governour and assistants met at Boston, and took into consideration a treatise, which Mr. Williams (then of Salem) had sent to them, and which he had formerly written to the governour and council of Plimouth, wherein, among other things, he disputes their right to the lands they possessed here, and concluded that, claiming by the king's grant, they could have no title, nor otherwise, except they compounded with the natives. For this, taking advice with some of the most judicious ministers, (who much condemned Mr. Williams's error and presumption,) they gave order, that he should be convented at the next court, to be censured, etc. There were three passages chiefly whereat they were much offended: 1, for that he chargeth King James to have told a solemn public lie, because in his patent he blessed God that he was the first Christian prince that had discovered this land: 2, for that he chargeth him and others with blasphemy for calling Europe Christendom, or the || Christian || world: 3, for that he did personally apply to our present king, Charles, these three places in the Revelations, viz., [blank.][1] *122

Mr. Endecott being absent, the governour wrote to him to let him know what was done, and withal added divers arguments to confute the said errors, wishing him to deal with Mr. Williams to retract the same, etc. Whereto he returned a very modest and discreet answer. Mr. Williams also wrote to the governour, and also to him and the rest of the council, very submissively, professing his intent to have been only to have written for the private satisfaction of the ||[2]governour|| etc., of

||church|| ||[2]gentlemen||

---

in their management of secular concerns, often forgetting that reason was no less the gift of God, than the ritual of Moses, and that a different state existed in the church, from that which the apostles were compelled, by circumstances, not led by inspiration, to adopt.

[1] Perhaps the same expressions, by another, would have given less offence. From Williams they were not at first received in the mildest, or even the most natural sense; though further reflection satisfied the magistrates, that his were not dangerous. The passages from the Apocalypse were probably not *applied* to the honor of the king; and I regret, therefore, that Winthrop did not preserve them. No complaint of such indiscretion would have been expressed ten years later, when the mother country far outran the colony in these perversions of scripture.

Plimouth, without any purpose to have stirred any further in it, if the governour ||here|| had not required a copy of him; withal offering his book, or any part of it, to be burnt.

At the next court he appeared ||[2]*penitently*||, and gave satisfaction of his intention and ||[3]loyalty||. So it was left, and nothing done in it.

January 21.] News came from Plimouth, that Capt. Stone, who this last summer went out of the bay or lake, and so to
*123 Aquamenticus, where he took in Capt. Norton, putting in at the mouth of Connecticut, in his way to Virginia, where the Pequins inhabit, was there cut off by them, with all his company, being eight.[1] The manner was thus: *Three of his men, being gone ashore to kill fowl, were cut off. Then the sachem, with some of his men, came aboard, and staid with Capt. Stone in his cabin, till Capt. Stone (being alone with him) fell on sleep. Then he knocked him on the head, and all the rest of the English being in the cook's room, the Indians took such pieces as they found there ready charged, and bent them at the English; whereupon one took a piece, and by accident gave fire to the powder, which blew up the deck; but most of the Indians, perceiving what they went about, shifted overboard, and after they returned, and killed such as remained, and burned the pinnace. We agreed to write to the governour of Virginia, (because Stone was one of that colony,) to move him to revenge it, and upon his answer to take further counsel.*[2]

20.] Hall and the two others, who went to Connecticut November 3, came now home, having lost themselves and endured much misery. They ||[4]informed|| us, that the small pox was gone as far as any Indian plantation was known to the

||there|| ||[2]privately|| ||[3]gilt|| ||[4]assured||

---

[1] It was first written *ten or twelve.*

[2] A pen has been drawn diagonally across this narrative in the MS.; and in the margin this direction is given, "See after, November 6, 1634." But it is evident, that this is not superseded by that relation, in fulness of detail at least. Whether the first story were designed to be stigmatized as less credible than the other, when neither could come from the innocent, is left to the judgment of the reader. Both are worth preserving.

west, and much people dead of it, by reason whereof they could have no trade.

At Naragansett, by the Indians' report, there died seven hundred; but, beyond Pascataquack, none to the eastward.

24.] The governour and council met again at Boston, to consider of Mr. Williams's letter, etc., when, with the advice of Mr. Cotton and Mr. Wilson, and weighing his letter, and further considering of the aforesaid offensive passages in his book, (which, being written in very obscure and implicative phrases, might well admit of doubtful interpretation,) they found the matters not to be so evil as at first they seemed. Whereupon they agreed, that, upon his retractation, etc., or taking an oath of allegiance to the king, etc., it should be passed over.

[Very large blank.]

An Englishman of Sacoe, travelling into the country *124
to trade, was killed by the Indians.

[Very large blank.]

30.] John Seales, who ran from his master to the Indians, came ||home|| again. He was at a place twelve miles off, where were seven Indians, whereof four died of the pox while he was there.

[Large blank.]

February 1.] Mr. Cradock's house at Marblehead was burnt down about midnight before, there being then in it Mr. Allerton, and many fishermen, whom he employed that season, who all were preserved by a special providence of God, with most of his goods therein, by a tailor, who sate up that night at work in the house, and, hearing a noise, looked out and saw the house on fire above the oven in the thatch.

This winter was very mild, little wind, and most S. and S. W. but ||2oft|| snows, and great. One snow, the 15th of this month, was near two feet deep all over.

[Large blank.]

Such of the Indians' children as were left were taken by the English, most whereof did die of the pox soon after, three only remaining, whereof one, which the governour kept, was

||here|| ||2after||

called Know-God, (the Indians' usual answer being, when they were put in mind of God, Me no know God).

[Large blank.]

22.] The grampus[1] came up towards Charlestown ||against|| the tide of ebb.

[Large blank.]

This season Mr. Allerton fished with eight boats at Marble Harbour.

[Large blank.]

By this time seventeen fishing ships were come to Richman's Isle and the Isles of Shoals.

March 4.] By order of court a mercate was erected at Boston, to be kept upon Thursday, the fifth day of the week, being the lecture day. Samuel Cole[2] set up the first house for
*125 common entertainment, and John Cogan,[3] merchant, the first shop.

Upon offer of some new comers to give liberally towards the building of a galley for defence of the bay, and upon consultation with divers experienced seamen and others, it was thought fitter for our condition to build a vessel forty feet in length, and twenty-one in breadth, to be ||2minion|| proof, and the upper deck musket proof, to have one sail, and to carry whole culverin and other small pieces, eight in all. This was found to be so chargeable, and so long time ere it could be finished, that it was given over.

||by|| ||2cannon||

---

1 Here some may imagine, as the former editor certainly did, that the name of a ship is intended; but to me it seems evident, that the author designed only to remark the early arrival of that species of fish in our shoal waters.

2 From his being so early a member of the church, No. 42, and his wife, Ann, who died no long time after arrival, standing next, I conclude they came over with Winthrop. His will, dated 21 December, 1666, was proved in the following February.

3 This gentleman, who died in 1658, spelt his name with a double *g*. He left a good estate, of which five hundred acres in Woburn is valued in the inventory at ten pounds. From the Boston Records it appears, he was married, for the second time, as his former wife, Ann, is named in the Church Record of July, 1634, to Mrs. Martha Winthrop, undoubtedly the widow of the author of this History, on 10 March, 1651, by Gov. John Endecott.

At this court all swamps, above one hundred acres, were made common, etc. Also Robert Cole, having been oft punished for drunkenness, was now ordered to wear a red D about his neck for a year.

[Blank.]

7.] At the lecture at Boston a question was propounded about veils. Mr. Cotton concluded, that where (by the custom of the place) they were not a sign of ||the women's subjection,|| they were not commanded by the apostle. Mr. Endecott opposed, and did maintain it by the general arguments brought by the apostle.[1] After some debate, the governour, perceiving it to grow to some earnestness, interposed, and so it brake off.

[Large blank.]

Among other testimonies of the Lord's gracious presence with his own ordinances, there was a youth of fourteen years of age (being the son of one of the magistrates) so wrought upon by the ministry of the word, as, for divers months, he was held under such affliction of mind, as he could not be brought to apprehend any comfort in God, being much humbled and broken for his sins, (though he had been a dutiful child, and not given up to the lusts of youth,) and especially for his blasphemous and wicked thoughts, whereby Satan buffeted him, so as he went mourning and languishing daily; yet, at- *126
tending to the means, and not giving over prayer, and seeking counsel, etc., he came at length to be freed from his temptations, and to find comfort in God's promises, and so, being received into the congregation, upon good proof of his understanding in the things of God, he went on cheerfully in a Christian course, falling daily to labor, as a servant, and as a younger brother of his did, who was no whit short of him in the knowledge of God's will, though his youth kept him from dar-

||a woman's sobriety||

[1] In this opinion Endecott had been instructed by Williams, whose scruple on this subject is ridiculed by Hubbard, 204, 5. That historian makes Cotton preach a sermon at Salem one Sunday morning, which so enlightened the women, that "they appeared in the afternoon without their veils."

ing to offer himself to the congregation.[1]—Upon this occasion

---

[1] Conjecture would confidently apply this anecdote to the writer's own family; for such minute relation could only be expected from a party. The "younger brother" was, no doubt, Deane, born March, 1622–3. Stephen, the governour's son, chiefly alluded to in the text, was, on 16 of this month, received as a member of the church. By his wife, Judith, he had, as I learn from Boston Records, two children, Stephen, born 7 November, 1644, and John, 24 May, 1646. They, probably, both died young. He went to England, as will be seen in the sequel of this History, either in the latter part of 1645, or in 1646, whence he did not return, I believe, but for a short period. I find a power of attorney from him to his brother John, 20 July, 1653, and a deed of 28 February, 1654–5, both executed here. He had before been a deputy, and was exposed in England to suit, because he had been *recorder* of a court, which gave an unsatisfactory judgment in the case of Alderman Berkley. In England he got forward in military and political life. He commanded a regiment, was a member of parliament in Oliver's time, for Scotland, as by letter of George Monk, 30 August, 1656, in Thurloe's State Papers, V. 366, appears; and, being a gentleman of sobriety, was much trusted by the protector. Roger Williams, in a letter to Gov. John of Connecticut, 21 February, 1655–6, gives him the news from England, "Your brother succeeds Major General Harrison." This was the exquisite enthusiast, who troubled Cromwell so much with his anticipation of a kingdom of the saints, as to require his imprisonment. He died early; for in our Registry of Deeds is one of 20 May, 1659, to John Leverett, from Judith in England, therein styled "relict of Stephen Winthrop."

I had supposed, when I wrote the note for his brother John, that the royal gratitude had been expressed to Stephen for assisting the preparation for the great change of 1660, knowing his influence so short a time before the restoration, and therefore postponed to this place the introduction of the following curiosity:—

Letter of King Charles II. to . . . .

BRUSSELLES, 6 *or* 8 *April*, 1660.

I HAVE so good information of the many good offices you have done for me, that I cannot doubt but you will continue the same affection, till you have perfected the work you have begun, which, you may be most assured, will be accompanied with such an acknowledgment from me, that all the world shall take notice of the sense I have of your kindness, and how great an instrument you have been in promoting the happiness of your country. I have no more to ask of you, but to proceed in the same way and method your own understanding suggests to you, and that you will believe I will always be

Your affectionate friend,

CHARLES R.

The foregoing is folded in the common style of letters, but not superscribed,

*127 it is not impertinent (though no credit nor regard be to be had of dreams in these days) to report a dream, which the father of these children had at the same time, viz., that, coming into his chamber, he found his wife (she was a very gracious woman) in bed, and three or four of their children lying by her, with most sweet and smiling countenances, with crowns upon their heads, and *blue ribbons about their leaves.* When he awaked, he told his wife his dream, and made this interpretation of it, that God would take of her children to make them fellow heirs with Christ in his kingdom.

[Large blank.]

Satan bestirred himself to hinder the progress of the gospel, as, among other practices, appeared by this:[1] He stirred up a spirit of jealousy between Mr. James, the pastor of Charlton, and many of his people, so as Mr. Nowell, and some others, who had been dismissed from Boston, began to question their fact of breaking from Boston, and it grew to such a principle of conscience among them, as the advice of the other ministers was taken in it, who, after two meetings, could not agree about their continuance or return.

[Large blank.]

---

though it bears the royal signet on its wax. It has been since labelled, "Regis Angliæ Epistola," and in another place, by a different hand, "King Charles II. Letter to Gov. Winthrop." This letter, which is wholly in the king's handwriting, has been preserved in the Winthrop family; but, the envelope being lost, it cannot be *known* to whom the honor was addressed. I once presumed it was to John, the governour of Connecticut. But he had not been absent from New England. The royal autograph may have been given to him by a friend; for that his majesty addressed it to him, is beyond any appearance of probability. It is much regretted by me, that Bancroft too easily followed my presumption. Monk, afterwards rewarded as Duke of Albemarle, would, probably, have the best claim to the epistle; yet in England there were many others, at that day, justly entitled to similar testimonials.

[1] It is to be regretted, that any jealousy arose in the infant church of Charlestown; yet if Nowell and others doubted the propriety of their separation from the brethren of Boston, we may ascribe their dissatisfaction to finding their pastor to be a man of less useful talents or amiable temper than had been expected. Few in the present age would attribute such a misfortune to the agency of Satan, who has been, says Jortin, "charged with many things, which perhaps he never did." But in our indictments for capital offences, we retained, until very recently, the absurd allegation, "being moved and seduced by the instigation of the devil."

One Mr. Morris,[1] ensign to Capt. Underhill, taking some distaste in his office, requested the magistrates, that he might
*128 be discharged of it, and so was, whereby he gave offence to the congregation of Boston, so as, being questioned and convinced of sin in forsaking his calling, he did acknowledge his fault, and, at the request of the people, was by the magistrates chosen lieutenant to the same company, for he was a very stout man and an experienced soldier.

April 1.] Order was taken for ministering an oath to all house keepers and sojourners, being twenty years of age and not freemen, and for making a survey of the houses and lands of all freemen.

Notice being sent out ||of|| the general court to be held the 14th day of the third month, called May, the freemen deputed two of each town to meet and consider of such matters as they were to take order in at the same general court; who, having met, desired a sight of the patent, and, conceiving thereby that all their laws should be made at the general court, repaired to the governour to advise with him about it, and about the abrogating of some orders formerly made, as for killing of swine

||to||

---

[1] Richard Morris was a person of some consequence in the colony, and probably accompanied Winthrop in the fleet; for he and his wife early became members of the Boston church, being Nos. 64 and 5. He was in the military service, when a body of men, or at least of officers, was kept in pay, in 1632 and 3, as appears from the original account of William Pynchon, the treasurer, and became a deputy in the general court of March, 1635–6, I presume from Roxbury. Being unhappily of that party in religion, which favored Wheelwright and his sister, Mrs. Hutchinson, he signed the petition in favor of the preacher, about which great controversy arose a few years after; and the legislature, 20 November, 1637, had ordered him, with the other dangerous schismaticks, to be disarmed, as in the history of that time will appear. On 6 September of next year, Col. Rec., I. 227, informs us, "Lieut. Morris had leave to depart, (having offended in subscribing the petition or remonstrance,) being advised to forbear meddling with our people in the matters of opinion, least they be farther dealt with; and was advised not to sit down within our limits, and was wished to warn the rest not to sit down within our limits." From this banishment, so gently expressed, for signing a memorial to the court eighteen months before, I know not that he returned. His retreat was Exeter, where, with many of his persecuted brethren, he formed the association, 4 October, 1639, which is preserved in Hazard, I. 463.

in corn, etc. He told them, that, when the patent was granted, the number of freemen was supposed to be (as in like corporations) so few, as they might well join in making laws; but now they were grown to so great a body, as it was not possible for them to make or execute laws, but they must choose others for that purpose: and that howsoever it would be necessary hereafter to have a select company to intend that work, yet for the present they were not furnished with a sufficient number of men qualified for such a business, neither could the commonwealth bear the loss of time of so many as must intend it. Yet this they might do at present, viz., they might, at the general court, make an order, that, once in the year, a certain number should be appointed (upon summons from the governour)
to revise all laws, etc., and to reform what they found 129
amiss therein; but not to make any new laws, but prefer their grievances to the court of assistants; and that no assessment should be laid upon the country without the consent of such a committee, nor any lands disposed of.[1]

---

[1] No country on earth can afford the perfect history of any event more interesting to its own inhabitants than that which is here related. Winthrop seems to have spoken like an absolute sovereign, designing to grant a favor to his subjects, by admitting them to a representation at court. Such was the origin of most of the assemblies, in other nations, of delegates of the people, by whom some influence of the majority is imparted to the government. The enlargement of this kind of civil liberty to that perfect measure, enjoyed in Great Britain and our country, may be traced, with tolerable distinctness, for about five hundred years; but its commencement is very dimly discerned through the mists of antiquity. A long controversy on the origin of parliaments is indeed now at an end; but it terminated with a general acquiescence in that opinion, which assigned their beginning to nearly the same motives as our general courts of deputies.

A natural inquiry arises, what induced this concert among the several towns to send deputies, or why the NOTICE mentioned in the text was given? Since nothing can be found in the Records, previous to this meeting of the deputies, the answer must be left to conjecture; and perhaps no conjecture can be more satisfactory, than that the assistants were become weary of the exercise of all the powers of government, and desired others to participate in the responsibility. For this, however cautious the language of our author, it appears to me very evidently designed. The very humble powers, he proposed that the representative should receive from his constituent, it is hardly necessary to add, were immediately transcended; and the assembly, as it ought, was ever after-

*130 3.] The governour went on foot to Agawam, and because the people there wanted a minister, spent the Sab-

---

wards by itself thought competent to the enaction of any regulation for the public welfare.

It seems proper to transcribe here the earliest mention in our Colony Records, I. 115, of any representation, other than that to raise a public stock, of which ample notice is heretofore taken, in pages 70, 76: "It was further ordered, that it shall be lawful for the freemen of every plantation to choose two or three of each town, before every general court, to confer of and prepare such public business as by them shall be thought fit to consider of at the next general court; and that such persons as shall be hereafter so deputed by the freemen of [the] several plantations, to deal in their behalf in the public affairs of the commonwealth, shall have the full power and voice of all the said freemen derived to them for the making and establishing of laws, granting of lands, etc., and to deal in all other affairs of the commonwealth, wherein the freemen have to do, the matter of election of magistrates and other officers only excepted, wherein every freeman is to give his own voice." This is one of the first acts of the representatives.

The proceedings of this *first* general court of delegates, 14 May, 1634, begin on the preceding page, in the margin of which are the names of twenty-four persons, who were, I have no doubt, deputies from only eight towns, being not *two*, as the text has it, but three for each town. As the occasion is so interesting, it may be agreeable to the reader to have here inserted the names of the FIRST representatives of Massachusetts, in the same order as in the Record: "MR. GOODWIN, MR. SPENCER, MR. TALCOTT; MR. FEAKES, MR. BROWN, MR. OLDHAM; MR. BEECHER, MR. PALMER, ROBERT MOULTON; MR. COXEALL, EDMOND QUINSEY, CAPT. JOHN UNDERHILL; JOHN JOHNSON, WILLIAM HEATH, MR. ALCOCK; MR. ISRAEL STOUGHTON, WILLIAM FELPES, GEORGE HULL; CAPT. TURNER, MR. WILLIS, MR. EDWARD TOMLINS; MR. HOLGRAVE, MR. CONANT, FRANCIS WESTON." The first three were of Newtown; the others of Watertown, Charlestown, Boston, Roxbury, Dorchester, Sagus, and Salem, in equal numbers, according to this order. But, in this assignment of the individuals to the several towns, I have followed my own judgment; in making up which, the most patient inquiry was rewarded, for all but two or three, with perfect certainty. No specification of the places, from which the deputies came, is inserted, for many years, in the margin of the volume, wherein their names are contained.

Having taken a copy of the names of members in the first *twenty-two* courts, I may add, that the places in the lists are filled without regard to rank of the person, or age of the town. Hingham stands at the top as often as Salem; and those of the same town are not always written next to each other, though so much regularity is commonly found. Perhaps they were often entered by the secretary, as they came in to take their seats. At the courts in May, September, and November, 1637, all the Boston members are named last. This, I pre-

bath with them, and exercised by way of prophecy, and returned home the 10th.

20.] John Coggeshall,[1] gentleman, being dismissed from the church of Roxbury to Boston, though he were well known and approved of the church, yet was not received but by confession of his faith, etc. *131

[Very large blank.]

May 3.] News came of the death of Hockin and the Plimouth man at Kenebeck, (and of the arrival of the ship at Pemaquid, which brought thirty passengers for this place).

The occasion of the death of those men at Kenebeck was

---

sume, was a punishment of their heresy, and regret, that it was not the only punishment.

The ninth town, that sent deputies, was Ipswich, on 4 March next; and the right was extended to Weymouth at the court, 2 September following. Hingham members appear 25 May, 1636. In September after one from Newbury is found among the representatives; and in April following Concord has a place.

[1] This gentleman was of high consideration, represented Boston in the first, second, third, sixth, seventh, eighth, and ninth courts, in the Records of which his name is sometimes written by the secretary, as it was probably pronounced, Coxeall. He was elected for the twelfth, but, with Aspinwall, as we find, Col. Rec. I. 202, "affirming that Mr. Wheelwright is innocent, and that he was persecuted for the truth, was in like sort dismissed from being a member of the court, and order was given for two new deputies to be chosen by the town of Boston." Perhaps the ceremony, mentioned in the text, would have been dispensed with for himself; but his wife and a maid servant, Ann Shelley, were received, at the same time, from the neighboring church, as I learn from the Records of our own. In general, communicants from other churches were received, in early times, with the same liberality as now prevails. At the same court from which he was expelled, 2 November, 1637, "being convented for disturbing the public peace," he "was disfranchised, and enjoined not to speak any thing to disturb the public peace, upon pain of banishment." He was exiled in March following, and retired with his blameless associates to Rhode Island, which they had just before purchased from the natives. In that peaceable settlement he became an assistant, and, in 1647, presided over the colony with a spirit of heterodox charity. See Callender, 30, 42. His son I presume to be the clerk of the general assembly of that colony in 1676. 2 Hist. Coll. VII. 112. Descendants in a right line remain to this day. In 1817 one was a representative in Massachusetts from Somerset, bordering on the state of Rhode Island; and, from some neighboring ports, several masters of ships of this name have of late years been noticed.

this: The Plimouth men had a grant, from the grand patentees of New England, of Kenebeck, with liberty of sole trade, etc. The said Hockin came in a pinnace, belonging to the Lord Say and Lord Brook at Pascataquack, to trade at Kenebeck. Two of the magistrates ||of|| Plimouth, being there, forbad him; yet he went up the river; and, because he would not come down again, they sent three men in a canoe to cut his cables. Having cut one, Hockin presented a piece, and sware he would kill him that went to cut the other. They ||[2]bad|| him do if he durst, and went on to cut it. Thereupon he killed one of them, and instantly one in the Plimouth pinnace (which rode by them, and wherein five or six men stood with their pieces ready charged) shot and killed Hockin.

15.] At the general court at Boston, upon the complaint of a kinsman of the said Hockin, John Alden,[1] one of the said magistrates of Plimouth, who was present when Hockin was slain, being then at Boston, was called and bound with sureties not to depart out of our jurisdiction without leave ||[3]had;|| and withal we wrote to Plimouth to certify them what we had done, and to know whether they would do justice in the cause, (as belonging to their jurisdiction,) and to have a speedy answer, etc. This we did, that notice might be taken, that we did disavow the said action, which was much condemned of all men, and which was feared would give occasion to the king to send a general governour over; and besides had brought us all and the gospel under a common reproach of cutting one another's throats for beaver.[2]

[Blank.]

||at|| ||[2]told|| ||[3]etc.||

---

[1] While the Memorial of Plimouth Colony survives, the name of Alden, a brief account of whom is found in Eliot and Allen, cannot be forgotten. Many of his descendants are in honorable place in various parts of the United States, of whom one was an indefatible antiquary, the president of a college at Meadville in Pennsylvania, to whose Collection of Epitaphs many acknowledgments are due. The ancestor and his genealogical series, down to the present age, are found in Vol. III. 264–274.

[2] Bradford's relation is a little more full; and, as he was a patentee, the reader will find, with pleasure, that his pen was guided by truth, as well as interest. See Appendix to Hutchinson, II. 474–5.. A little farther onward in this History, more will be found on the same subject.

By this time the fort at Boston was in defence, and divers pieces of ordnance mounted in it. *132

[Large blank.]

Those of Newtown complained of straitness for want of land, especially meadow, and desired leave of the ||court|| to look out either for enlargement or removal, which was granted; whereupon they sent men to see Agawam and Merimack, and gave out they would remove, etc.

[Large blank.]

14.] At the general court, Mr. Cotton preached, and delivered this doctrine, that a magistrate ought not to be turned into the condition of a private man without just cause, and to be publicly convict, no more than the magistrates may not turn a private man out of his freehold, etc., without like public trial, etc. This falling in question in the court, and the opinion of the rest of the ministers being asked, it was referred to further consideration.[1]

The court chose a new governour,[2] viz., Thomas Dudley, Esq., the former deputy; and Mr. Ludlow was chosen deputy; and John Haines, Esq., an assistant, and all the rest of the assistants chosen again.

At this court it was ordered, that four general courts should ke kept every year, and that the whole body of the freemen should be present only at the court of election of magistrates, etc., and that, at the other three, every town should send their deputies, who should assist in making laws, disposing lands, etc.[3] Many good orders were made this court. It held three

||council||

[1] Expediency should have kept Cotton silent; for the people are more likely to become jealous, when such a principle is preached, than when it is put in practice. The reverend teacher took his freeman's oath at this court, and had not sufficient experience in the affairs of the country to authorize so strong an expression of his opinion, unless he believed himself directed from on high. Any of his friends could have led him to doubt the suggestion, however, had he pretended such; but he was delivering a sincere opinion of his own forming.

[2] *Chosen by papers*, is written in the margin of our MS.

[3] *Mr. Cottington chosen treasurer*, is in the margin.

days, and all things were carried very peaceably, notwithstanding that some of the assistants were questioned by the freemen for some errors in their government, and some fines imposed, but remitted again before the court brake up. The court was kept in the meeting-house at Boston, *and the new governour and the assistants *were together entertained* at the house of the old governour, as before.*

*133 The week the court was, there came in six ships, with store of passengers and cattle.

[Large blank.]

Mr. Parker,[1] a minister, and a company with him, being about one hundred, went to sit down at Agawam, and divers others of the new comers.

[Very large blank.]

One [blank,] a godly minister, upon conscience of his oath and care of the commonwealth, discovered to the magistrates some seditious speeches of his own son, delivered in private to himself; but the court thought not fit to call the party in question then, being loath to have the father come in as a public accuser of his own son, but rather desired to find other matter, or other witness against him.

24.] Mr. Fleming, master of a ship of Barnstable, went hence to the eastward to cut masts there, and so to return to England. There returned with him Ensign Motham and another.

[Large blank.]

---

[1] Of Thomas Parker, a learned theologian, pupil of the great Archbishop Usher, having passed a short time at Magdalen College, Oxford, notice will often arise in the progress of this work. He finished his preparation for the pulpit at Leyden, and had a school at Newbury in Berkshire, where also he preached; was a bachelor, but stood in place of a father to many divines of the succeeding generation. One who desires to know more of him, may consult Hubbard, 193, the Magnalia, Eliot, Allen, 1 Hist. Coll. VI. 273, and IX. 48, and Brooks's Lives of the Puritans. An error may be corrected in a note to *James* Parker's letter, in Hutch. Coll. 155, where it is supposed, "*he* was *afterwards* one of the ministers of Newbury," which was the place of usefulness assigned to our Thomas. James had preached at Portsmouth *before* going to Barbados. 1 Hist. Coll. X. 39. Rev. James Noyes and his brother Nicholas, came with Parker. They were his cousins.

These ships, by reason of their short passage, had store of provisions left, which they put off at easy rates, viz. biscuit at 20*s.* the hundred; beef at £6 the hogshead, etc.

[Blank.]

Newtown men, being straitened for ground, sent some to Merimack to find a fit place to transplant themselves.

[Blank.]

June 1.] The Thunder, which went to Bermuda the 17th October, now returned, bringing corn and goats from Virginia, (for the weavils had taken the corn at Bermuda before they came there). Ensign Jenyson[1] went in her for pilot, and related, at his return, that there was a very great change in Bermuda since he dwelt there, divers lewd persons || being || become good Christians. They have three ministers, (one a Scotchman,) who ||[2]take|| great pains among them, and had lately (by *134
prayer and fasting) dispossessed one possessed ||[3]with|| a devil. They obtained his recovery while the congregation were assembled.[2]

He brought news, also, of a great ship arrived in Patomack

||having|| ||[3]took|| ||[3]of||

---

[1] William Jennison was of Watertown, from which he was a deputy in the second and many subsequent courts, with higher titles than in the text, as lieutenant and captain.

[2] If this be the story of the traveller, not the belief of the author, giving it civilly, without throwing any shadow on it, we should rejoice at the completeness of the narrative, rather than exhibit regret for its credulity. The miracle wrought by the prayer and fasting of three ministers at Bermuda, has never, to my knowledge, been brought up against Protestantism, though it may be rejected with as much contempt as the numerous ones produced, at a later day, by the Jansenists in France. It has been remarked by a disbeliever, that, while the church of Rome asserts, from its foundation to our times, the regular succession of miraculous gifts of all kinds, the reformed are contented with exorcisms. What kind of *possession* this was, thus exorcised at Bermuda, we know not, unless we infer, from the mode of cure, that the operators attempted a recovery of that species (epilepsy) related by Matthew, xvii. 21, and Mark, ix. 29. Better signs, or better proof, are wanted in such cases, if, for our reception, a modern instance of hearing prayer in heaven is offered; though the weak and the cunning, the deluded or the deluders, have, in all ages, abounded in such impositions. The credibility of the evangelists is supported by the very means, which, to a careless observer, might seem to detract from it; and the truth is more resplendent, when the counterfeit is detected.

River in Virginia, with a governour and colony sent by the Lord Bartimore,[1] who was expected there shortly himself, and that they resisted those of Virginia, who came to trade in that river.

It appeared after, that the king had written to Sir John Harvy,[2] ||knight,|| governour of Virginia, to give all assistance to that new plantation, which was called Maryland by the queen of England; and those who came over were, many of them, Papists, and did set up mass openly.

July.] The Hercules of Dover returned by St. George's to cut masts to carry to England.

The last month arrived here fourteen great ships,[3] and one at Salem.

Mr. Humfrey and the lady Susan, his wife, one of the Earl of Lincoln's sisters, arrived here. He brought more ordnance,
*135 muskets, and powder, bought for the public by moneys given to that end; for godly people in England began now to apprehend a special hand of God in raising this plantation, and their hearts were generally stirred to come ||[2]over||. Among others, we received letters from a godly preacher, Mr. Levinston, a Scotchman in the north of Ireland, whereby he signified, that there were many good Christians in those parts resolved to come hither, if they might receive satisfaction concerning some questions and propositions which they sent over. Likewise, Mr. Humfrey brought certain propositions[4] from some

||king's|| ||[2]to us||

---

[1] Cecil, son of George, Lord Baltimore, against whom nothing can be learned from history but the father's conscientious conversion, and the heir's adherence, to the Romish religion. For their just deserts, which the liberal inhabitants of Maryland will never forget, the reader is referred to Belknap's American Biography, II. 363–380. Candor must be extended to some passages of this History, in which the spirit of the age will appear more prominently than justice.

[2] This gentleman, who had been named by King James, in his last year, of the council for the immediate government of Virginia, Haz. I. 189, was, by Charles, appointed governour, 26 March, 1627. Ib. 234. A new commission for the same place was given him nine years after. Ib. 400.

[3] One of these was the Planter. The bill of lading for the government stores, put on board by Humfrey, who was, probably, a passenger, was dated 7 April. See the account of Treasurer Pynchon, in 2 Mass. Hist. Coll. VIII. 228.

[4] For these propositions of certain peers, and others of the English nobility,

persons of great quality and estate, (and of special note for piety,) whereby they discovered their intentions to join with us, if they might receive satisfaction therein. It appeared further, by many private letters, that the departure of so many of the best, both ministers and Christians, had bred sad thoughts in those behind of the Lord's intentions in this work, and an apprehension of some evil days to come upon England. || Then || it began now to be apprehended by the archbishops, and others of the council, as a matter of state, so as they sent out warrant to stay the ships, and to call in our patent; but, upon petition of the shipmasters, (||[2]attending|| how beneficial this plantation was to England) in regard of the Newfoundland fishing, which they took in their way homeward, the ships were at that time released. But Mr. Cradock (who had been governour in England before the government was sent over) had strict charge to deliver in the patent; whereupon he wrote to us to send it home. Upon receipt of his letter, the governour and council consulted about it, and resolved to answer Mr. Cradock's letter, but not to return any answer or excuse to the council at that time.

[Very large blank.]

§ For the success of the passengers and cattle in the ships: § Divers of the ships lost many cattle; but the two which came from Ipswich,[1] of more than one hundred and twenty, lost but seven. None of the ships lost any passengers, but the Eliza-

||yea|| ||[2]alloging §

with the answers, drawn with great *discretion*, returned two years after, the curious are indebted to Hutchinson's Mass. I. Appendix, 490–5. Following them is a letter of Cotton, to enforce our answers, addressed to the Puritan Lord Say. He says, "Democracy I do not conceive that ever God did ordain as a fit government, either for church or commonwealth. If the people be governours, who shall be governed? As for monarchy, and aristocracy, they are both of them clearly approved, and directed in scripture, yet so as referreth the sovereignty to himself, and setteth up theocracy in both, as the best form of government in the commonwealth, as well as in the church."

[1] The Elizabeth, William Andrews master, and the Francis, of which John Cutting was master, were the Ipswich ships. Names of 102, and 84 passengers, respectively, are printed in 3 Mass. Hist. Coll. X. 140–145. Probably several of the others were not known to the officers of government, or they would have been forbidden.

*136 beth Dorcas,[1] which, having a long passage, and being hurt upon a rock at Scilly, and very ill victualled, she lost sixty passengers at sea, and divers came sick on shore, who all recovered, (through the mercy of God,) except

[Large blank.]

Mr. Humfrey brought sixteen heifers given by a private friend, viz. Mr. Richard Andrews,[2] to the plantation, viz. to every of the ministers one, and the rest to the poor, and one half of the increase of the ministers' to be reserved for other ministers. Mr. Wilson, so soon as he had his, gave it to Mr. Cotton. By Mr. Humfrey's means much money was procured, and divers promised yearly pensions.

[Large blank.]

Six of Newtown went in the Blessing, (being bound to the Dutch plantation,) to discover Connecticut River, intending to remove their town thither.

9.] Mr. Bradford and Mr. Winslow, two of the magistrates of Plimouth, with Mr. Smith, their pastor, came to Boston by water, to confer with some of our magistrates and ministers about their case of Kenebeck. There met hereabout Mr. Winthrop, Mr. Cotton, and Mr. Wilson, and after they had sought the Lord, they fell first upon some passages which they had taken some offence at, but those were soon cleared. Then for the matter itself, it fell into these two points: 1, whether their right of trade there were such, as they might lawfully hinder others from coming there; 2, admitting that, whether in point of conscience, they might so far stand upon their right as to take away or hazard any man's life in defence of it.

For the first, their right appeared to be good; for that, besides the king's grant, they had taken up that place as vacuum domicilium, and so had continued, without interruption or claim of any of the natives, for divers years; and also had, by their charge and providence, drawn down thither the greatest part of

[1] In this ship came Henry Sewall, father of the first Chief Justice, of the name of Samuel.

[2] Of the liberality of this distinguished friend of Massachusetts and Plimouth colonies, further notice will occur in our progress. He was an alderman of the city; and Thomas, probably his brother, became mayor of London.

the trade, by carrying wampampeage thither, which none of the English had known the use of before. For the second, they ||alleged,|| that their servant did kill Hockin to save other of their men, whom he was ready to have shot. Yet they acknowledged, that they did hold themselves under guilt of the breach of the sixth commandment, in that they did hazard ||[2]man's life|| for such a cause, and did not rather wait to preserve their right by other means, which they rather acknowl- *137
edged, because they wished it were not done; and hereafter they would be careful to prevent the like.

The governour and Mr. Winthrop wrote their letters into England to mediate their peace, and sent them by Mr. ||[3]Winslow||.

Sir Ferdinando Gorges and Capt. Mason sent [blank] to Pascataquack and Aquamenticus, with two sawmills, to be erected, in each place one.[1]

[Blank.]

Mr. Cradock wrote to the governour and assistants, and sent a copy of the council's order,[2] whereby we were required to send over our patent. Upon long consultation whether we should return answer or not, we agreed, and returned answer to Mr. Cradock, excusing that it could not be done but by a general court, which was to be holden in September next.

[Blank.]

Mr. Winthrop, the late governour, received a letter from the Earl of Warwick, wherein he congratulated the prosperity of our plantation, and encouraged our proceedings, and offered his help to further us in it.

29.] The governour and council, and divers of the ministers, and others, met at Castle Island, and there agreed upon erecting two platforms and one small fortification to secure ||[4]them both,||[3] and, for the present furtherance of it, they agreed to

||allowed|| ||[2]men's lives|| ||[3]Wilson|| ||[4]the city||

---

[1] Belknap's New Hampshire, Appendix VIII. contains a letter of Mason about these mills, to erect which he sent people with Josselyn, brother of John, the voyager.

[2] A copy of this order is in Hazard, I. 341, taken from Hubbard, 153.

[3] By the error of the first edition, Dr. Holmes was led to remark, in the

lay out £5 a man till a ||rate|| might be made at the next general court. The deputy, Roger Ludlow, was chosen overseer of this work.

August 2.] Mr. Samuel Skelton, pastor of Salem, died.

4.] At the court, the new town at Agawam was named Ipswich, in acknowledgment of the great honor and kindness done to our people which took shipping there, etc.; and a day of thanksgiving appointed, a fortnight after, for the ||[2]prosperous arrival of the others,|| etc.

A letter[1] §was delivered§ to Mr. Winthrop by Mr. Jeffe-
*138 ry,[2] an old planter, written to him from Morton, wherein he related, how he had obtained his long suit, and that a commission was granted for a general governour to be sent over, with many railing speeches and threats against this plantation, and Mr. Winthrop in particular. Mr. Winthrop acquainted the governour and council with it, and some of the ministers.

[Blank.]

This summer was hotter than many before.

[Blank.]

||rule|| ||[2]particular revival of the times||

---

first edition of his Annals, I. 278, that the "metropolis has never *yet* been incorporated with that name."

[1] Never were feelings of triumph more openly, and, as the event showed, incautiously displayed, than in this epistle, for which the author smarted ten years after, as in the History of that time, in our second volume, will be seen. The original deformity is there exhibited. Hubbard, 428, copied it, and most subsequent writers imagined, that to his page, not Winthrop's, were they indebted for the curiosity.

[2] William Jeffery, or Jeffries, was a person of some distinction, settled in our colony before the arrival of the first company of Endecott, sent by the patentees in 1628. His admission as a freeman is noticed among the earliest who were received. Col. Rec. I. 73. I can assign his residence, only by guess, to Weymouth. See note 2, on page 43. He was named, with Blaxton, by Sir Ferdinando Gorges's son, in his abortive grant to Oldham, attorney to give possession of Massachusetts. Conf. Haz. I. 259 and 268. Such a letter Morton could not have sent, without supposing his correspondent would agree with him in dislike of the men, on whom he lavished so bold abuse; and it may almost seem treachery in the receiver to give it up. Perhaps Jeffery was afraid of discovery, or else the Merry Mount rioter was deceived in judging one his friend, who had six years before joined the formidable alliance for his overthrow.

12.] About midnight, one Craford, (who came this summer,) with his brother and servant, having put much goods in a small boat in Charles River, over against Richard Brown his house, overset the boat with the weight of some hogsheads, (as was supposed,) so as they were all three drowned; yet one of them could swim well, and though the neighbors came running forth, instantly, upon their cry, yet none could be saved.

[Large blank.]

Our neighbors of Plimouth and we had oft trade with the Dutch at Hudson's River, called §by them§ New Netherlands. We had from them about forty sheep, and beaver, and brass pieces, and sugar, etc., for sack, strong waters, linen cloth, and other commodities. They have a great trade of beaver, — about nine or ten thousand skins in a year. Our neighbors of Plimouth had great trade also this year at Kenebeck, so as Mr. Winslow carried with him into England, this year, about twenty hogsheads of beaver, the greatest part whereof was traded for wampampeage.

One pleasant passage happened, which was acted by the Indians. Mr. Winslow, coming in his bark from Connecticut to
Narigansett, — and he left her there, — and intending to *139
return by land, he went to Osamekin the sagamore, his old ally, who offered to conduct him home to Plimouth. But, before they took their journey, Osamekin sent one of his men to Plimouth to tell them that Mr. Winslow was dead; and directed him to show how and where he was killed. Whereupon there was much fear and sorrow at Plimouth. The next day, when Osamekin brought him home, they asked him why he sent such word, etc. He answered, that it was their manner to do so, that they might be more welcome when they came home.

[Blank.]

19.] Mr. Bradford and Mr. Collier[1] of Plimouth came to

---

[1] Honorable mention must ever be made of William Collier, Esq., who came over to Plimouth only the year before that of the text. He was chosen an assistant in 1634, and thenceforward until 1666, every year, except 1638, 52 and 53, when he was probably absent, and was one of the two first delegates to the congress of the United Colonies, in 1643.

Boston, having appointed a meeting here the week before, but by reason of foul weather were driven back. They had written to Capt. Wiggin of Pascataquack about the meeting for hearing the cause of Hockin's death.

[Large blank.]

Corn was this year at four shillings the bushel, and some at three shillings, and some cheaper.

[Large blank.]

29.] The ||Dove,|| a pinnace of about fifty tons, came from Maryland upon Patomack River, with corn, to exchange for fish and other commodities. The governour, Leonard Calvert,[1] and two of the commissioners, wrote to the governour here, to make offer of trade of corn, etc., and the governour of Virginia wrote also on their behalf, and one Capt. Young wrote to make offer to deliver cattle here. Near all their company came sick hither, and the merchant died within one week after.

[Blank.]

*140 September 4.] The general court began[2] at Newtown, and continued a week, and then was adjourned ||[2]fourteen|| days. Many things were there agitated and concluded, as fortifying in Castle Island, Dorchester, and Charlestown; also against tobacco, and costly apparel, and immodest fashions; and

||D——|| ||[2]eleven||

---

[1] This gentleman was the brother of Cecil, Lord Baltimore, mentioned in the note on page 134, sent by the patentee as his governour. His name will recur in the progress of this History; but I regret that any information of the events of his administration is confined to its policy, applauded by Belknap, and the minute, but imperfect narrative in Bozman's History of Maryland. The Hon. Charles Calvert, governour of Maryland, a descendant, died 2 February, 1732. A tomb, erected at Annapolis, bore inscriptions in honor of himself and wife, which may be seen in the American Magazine, printed at Boston, 1743, page 74. I believe reputable descendants of this family perpetuate its fame in Maryland.

[2] By the Col. Records, I. 126, the day of assembling is the 3d, not 4th, of September. But it is more important to observe, that no names of deputies appear; so that I regard it only as a second session of the court, adjourned in May, and therefore give the distinction of *second* court to that in March following. Many new members appeared then, and so we find the fact in every succeeding meeting for many years. Perhaps one or more new delegates appeared at this court from some town not represented at the May session.

committees appointed for setting out the bounds of towns; with divers other matters, which do appear upon record. But the main business, which spent the most time, and caused the adjourning of the court, was about the removal of Newtown. They had leave, the last general court, to look out some place for enlargement or removal, with promise of having it confirmed to them, if it were not prejudicial to any other plantation; and now they moved, that they might have leave to remove to Connecticut. This matter was debated divers days, and many reasons alleged pro and con. The principal reasons for their removal were, 1. Their want of accommodation for their cattle, so as they were not able to maintain their ministers, nor could receive any more of their friends to help them; and here it was alleged by Mr. Hooker, as a fundamental error, that towns were set so near each to other.[1]

2. The fruitfulness and commodiousness of Connecticut, and the danger of having it possessed by others, Dutch or English.

3. The strong bent of their spirits to remove thither.

[Large blank.]

Against these it was said, 1. That, in point of conscience, they ought not to depart from us, being knit to us in one body, and bound by oath to seek the welfare of this commonwealth.

2. That, in point of state and civil policy, we ought not to give them leave to depart. 1. Being || we || were now weak and in danger to be assailed. 2. The departure of Mr. Hooker would not only draw many from us, but also divert other friends that would come to us. 3. We should expose them to evident peril, both from the Dutch (who made claim to the same river, and had already built a fort there) and from the Indians, and also from our own state at home, who would not endure they should sit down without a patent in any place which *141
our king lays claim unto.

3. They might be accommodated at home by some enlargement which other towns offered.

|| new ||

[1] In this fifth year of the Colony history, so sadly crowded were the settlers at Newtown, that Watertown was not a mile and a half distant, nor Charlestown more than two miles.

4. They might remove to Merimack, or any other place within our patent.

5. The removing of a candlestick is a great judgment, which is to be avoided.

Upon these and other arguments the court being divided, it was put to vote; and, of the deputies, fifteen were for their departure, and ten against it.[1] The governour and two assistants were for it, and the deputy and all the rest of the assistants were against it, (except the secretary, who gave no vote;) whereupon no record was entered, because there were not six assistants in the vote, as the patent requires. Upon this grew a great difference between the governour and assistants, and the deputies. They would not yield the assistants a negative voice, and the others (considering how dangerous it might be to the commonwealth, if they should not keep that strength to balance the greater number of the deputies) thought it safe to stand upon it. So, when they could proceed no farther, the whole court agreed to keep a day of humiliation to seek the Lord, which accordingly was done, in all the congregations, the 18th day of this month; and the 24th the court met again. Before they began, Mr. Cotton preached, (being desired by all the court, upon Mr. Hooker's instant excuse of his unfitness for that occasion). He took his text out of Hag. ii. 4, etc., out of which he laid down the nature or strength (as he termed it) of the magistracy, ministry, and people, viz., — the strength of the magistracy to be their authority; of the people, their liberty;

---

[1] The error of Hutchinson, in reporting this division of the deputies, and his mistake of the name of the deputy governour, he owed to Hubbard, 173, 4, who copied our author with carelessness surprising even in him. He almost literally transcribed from our text the very form of the argument and partition of the subject; and the numerals are here as plain as in any part of the original MS. On so important a question, we might, a priori, conclude, that every one of the deputies was present; and since their number, at the *first* general court when representatives appeared, was twenty-four, and so small a body never appears again, we may confidently presume, there were now twenty-five, though the enumeration of the body cannot be given precisely, because the Records, in this solitary instance, omit their names. See the last note. Ludlow was the deputy governour; and it seems not very strange, that he opposed the removal, while he was in this office, but adopted that course, after failing to be rechosen next year.

and of the ministry, their purity; and showed how all of these had a negative voice, etc., and that yet the ultimate resolution, etc., ought to be in the whole body of the people, etc., with answer to all objections, and a declaration of the people's duty and right to maintain their true liberties against any un- *142
just violence, etc., which gave great satisfaction to the company. And it pleased the Lord so to assist him, and to bless his own ordinance, that the affairs of the court went on cheerfully; and although all were not satisfied about the negative voice to be left to the magistrates, yet no man moved aught about it, and the congregation of Newtown came and accepted of such enlargement as had formerly[1] been offered them by Boston and Watertown; and so the fear of their removal to Connecticut was removed.

At this court Mr. Goodwin,[2] a very reverend and godly man,

---

[1] Hubbard, 175, read this word *freely*.

[2] William Goodwin is known to us, for many years, only by this notice of his language, as a deputy in the court. The occasion of his disrespect to the assistant, no doubt, arose from the projected migration of his townsmen. He did not represent Newtown in any following legislature, and removed, probably, the next year but one, with a large portion of his constituents, to Connecticut. Nothing more is heard of him until 1654, when a controversy sprang up in the church of Hartford, where Goodwin was ruling elder, between him and Stone, the teacher, which lasted several years, baffling the attempts of the legislature to calm it, and drawing New Haven and Massachusetts into the idle examination. The humble importance of such mighty agitation occupies many pages in Trumbull, I. 311 and following; but Mather, book III. says, the origin of it "has been rendered almost as obscure as the rise of Connecticut River." That author, in his usual diffuse manner, follows up his illustration with allusions to the force of the stream, and the width of its overflow; yet he has omitted the important parallel, of enriching the soil by its inundation. Goodwin was honored by Gov. Hopkins, in being made a trustee in his will. He died at Farmington, 1673, leaving only daughter, from whom the distinguished family of Wadsworth is derived.

I have seen, among the Hutchinson Papers, in the archives of our Historical Society, a tract, of eight and a half folio pages, entitled "The Sentence of the Council held at Boston, September 26, 1659, concerning the long, sad, and afflicting Controversy between the rev. teacher, Mr. Samuel Stone, the honored and dearly beloved brethren of the church of Hartford, on the one part, and the honored and dearly beloved brethren, the withdrawers from the said church, on the other part, since the relapse after the pacification, May 3, 1657." It bears date 7 October, and is signed by Wilson, Chauncey, R. Mather, Allen,

being the elder of the congregation of Newtown, having, in heat of argument, used some unreverend speech to one of the assistants, and being reproved for the same in the open court, did gravely and humbly acknowledge his fault, etc.

*143 18.] At this court were many laws made against tobacco, and immodest fashions, and costly apparel, etc., as appears by the Records; and £600[1] raised towards fortifications and other charges, which were the more hastened, because the Griffin and another ship now arriving with about two hundred passengers and one hundred cattle, (Mr. Lothrop[2] and Mr. Simmes,[3] two godly ministers, coming in the same ship,) there

---

Symmes, Norton, Eliot, Edm. Browne, Cobbet, Sherman, Hubbard, Danforth, Mitchell, and Shepard, among the divines; and R. Russell, Edw. Tyng, and Isaac Heath, of the laity. It appears to be the handwriting of *matchless* Mitchell; but though it refers to "the great labor of the reverend council held at Hartford in '56; the poor service of the church messengers from hence in '57; the several occasional letters from the elders of these parts before and since; and, lastly, the travels of this present assembly," with earnest entreaty for healing the scandalous divisions, — I hope it may not be imputed to any disesteem of the council or the subject, that my curiosity was not sufficiently strong to encounter the labor of perusal of so venerable a manuscript.

1 The apportionment is worth transcribing from the Records, I. 128, as, we may be confident, it represents the relative wealth of the settlements: "Boston, Dorchester, and Newtown, each, £80; Roxbury, £70; Watertown, £60; Sagus and Ipswich, each, £50; Salem and Charlestown, each, £45; Meadford, £26; Wessaguscus, £10; Barecove, £4."

2 With the excellence of the Rev. John Lathrop, we could form little acquaintance in a place, to which every reader would most naturally resort, the Description of Barnstable, in 1 Hist. Coll. III. But the extraordinary errors of that tract, pages 15, 16, or any other writer's deficiency, are all forgotten on perusal of the memoir of him and his posterity, by a descendant, found in 2 Hist. Coll. I. 163. Eliot has afforded two pages to him, and his name is excluded from Allen only by some less desirable matter. A great, great grandson, one of the most sincere and benevolent men of his time, who died since furnishing that narrative of his ancestor, after a long life of devotion to his duties will long be remembered as pastor of the Second Church of Boston. The patriarchal divine at West Springfield, whose sermons have justly been more in repute than those of equal volume by any other American, who deceased since my work on these pages began, deduced his origin from this first clergyman of Scituate. A very numerous line of descendants is found in our country.

3 Zechariah Symmes, the worthy teacher of the church at Charlestown, is

came over a copy of the commission[1] granted to the two archbishops and ten others of the council, to regulate all plantations, and power given them, or any five of them, to call in all patents, to make laws, to raise tythes and portions for ministers, to remove and punish governours, and to hear and determine all causes, and inflict all punishments, even death itself, etc. This being advised from our friends to be intended specially for us, and that there were ships and soldiers provided, given out as for the carrying the new governour, Capt. Woodhouse, to Virginia, but suspected to be against us, to compel us, by force, to receive a new governour, and the discipline of the church *144
of England, and the laws of the commissioners, — occasioned the magistrates and deputies to hasten our fortifications, and to discover our minds each to other; which grew to this conclusion,[2] viz.

[Large blank.]

At this court, as before, the assistants had their ||diet|| at the governour's at Newtown, and the first day all the deputies. He had £100 allowed him for his charges, and £500 more was raised towards fortifications, etc.

30.] About this time one Alderman, of Bear Cove, being about fifty years old, lost his way between Dorchester and Wessaguscus, and wandered in the woods and swamps three days and two nights, without taking any food, and, being near

||dues||

---

sufficiently commemorated in Eliot's Dictionary, where the time of his death is erroneously given 1676, for February 4, 1670–1. Johnson has honored him, and especially his wife, above most of the ministers in the land, lib. I. c. 32. In this History his service to the community is often mentioned; and at the last election of Winthrop, as governour, narrated in this work, he preached the sermon. His descendants, at different times, have been honored in church and state.

The famous Mrs. Ann Hutchinson came over in the same ship with Symmes, as was given in evidence on her trial. See Hutchinson's Mass. II. Appendix.

1 See the commission in Hubbard, 264.

2 What the conclusion was, we may easily judge from the opinion of the ministers, obtained at a meeting 19 January following, as, a few pages onward will appear.

spent, God brought him to Scituate; but he had torn his legs much, etc. Other harm he had none.

October 5.] It being found, that the four lectures did spend too much time, and proved ||over|| burdensome to the ministers and people, the ministers, with the advice of the magistrates, and with consent of their congregations, did agree to reduce them to two days, viz., Mr. Cotton at Boston one Thursday, or the 5th day of the week, and Mr. Hooker at Newtown the next 5th day, and Mr. Warham at Dorchester one 4th day of the week, and Mr. Welde at Roxbury the next 4th day.

Mr. Lathrop, who had been pastor of a private congregation in London, and for the same kept long time in prison, (upon refusal of the oath ex-officio,) being at Boston upon a sacrament day, after the sermon, etc., desired leave of the congregation to be present at the administration, etc., but said that he durst not desire to partake in it, because he was not then in order, (being dismissed from his former congregation,) and he thought it not fit to be suddenly admitted into any other, for example sake, and because of the deceitfulness of man's heart. He went to Scituate, being desired to be their pastor.

14.] It was informed the governour, that some of our people, being aboard the bark of Maryland, the sailors did revile them, calling them holy brethren, the members, etc., and withal did curse and swear most horribly, and use threatening speeches against us. The governour wrote to some of the assistants about it, and, upon advice with the ministers, it was agreed to
*145 call them in question; and to this end (because we knew not how to get them out of their bark) we apprehended the merchant of the ship, being ||[2]on shore,|| and committed him to the marshal, till Mr. Maverick came and undertook that the offenders should be forthcoming.[1] The next day (the governour not being well) we examined the witnesses, and found them fall short of the matter of threatening, and not to agree about the reviling speeches, and, beside, not able to design certainly the men that had so offended. Whereupon (the bark

||very|| ||[2]one Store||

[1] The process was more effectual than regular.

staying only || upon || this) the bail was discharged, and a letter written to the master, that, in regard such disorders were committed aboard his ship, it was his duty to inquire out the offenders and punish them; and withal to desire him to bring no more such disordered persons among us.

Mr. Wilson's hay, being stacked up not well dried, fell on fire, to his great prejudice at this season; fired by his own servants, etc., as they intended to prevent firing.

The weather was very fine and hot, without rain, near six weeks.

The Lords Say and Brook wrote to the governour and Mr. Bellingham,[1] that howsoever they might have sent a man of

|| for ||

[1] Gov. Richard Bellingham's worth is exhibited in the annals of his country, of which he was the last surviving patentee named in the charter, "having spun," says Hubbard, 610, "a long thread of above eighty years." His talents were adapted less for eloquence than advice, as the same writer expresses it, "like a vessel whose vent holdeth no good proportion with its capacity." Hubbard, after observing that his qualifications, as a governour, were rather lessened by his melancholy humour, continues: "He had been bred a lawyer, yet turned strangely, although upon very pious considerations, as some have judged, out of the ordinary road thereof, in the making of his last will and testament, which defect, if there were any, was abundantly supplied by the power of the general court, so as that no prejudice did arise to his successors about his estate." A fact inconsistent with the correctness of the closing suggestion, is, by the recent editor, in the note to Amer. Ed. Hutch. I. 247, asserted. Bellingham and his wife, Elizabeth, who died in a few years, were received into Boston church, 3 August of this year, so that a wrong date of his arrival is given by Eliot; but more observation is deserved by a casual sentence about this gentleman from the same author. He calls him "a very learned man, compared with his contemporaries in New England." This is uttered without the caution that usually distinguishes our New England biographer. Several of the laity were equals, in my opinion, of Bellingham; and,—without naming some of the worthies of Plimouth, Rhode Island, Connecticut, or New Haven,—both the Winthrops, Bradstreet, and Saltonstall his superiors. I speak confidently, but advisedly, that, if we include the clergy, who surely had as good a share of letters as their brethren educated at the same universities of Oxford and Cambridge, there were in New England, at any time between 1630 and 1690, as many sons of those two famous nurseries of learning as would be found in a proportionate number of their fellow subjects in the mother country. Besides which our own college, for four fifths of the time, sent out streams, many of which flowed to make glad the land of their fathers.

In the eulogium of this worthy, by Hubbard, "a notable hater of bribes"

*146 war to beat down the house at Kenebeck, for the death of Hockin, etc., || yet || they thought better to take another course; and therefore desired that some of ours might be joined with Capt. Wiggin, their agent at Pascataquack, to see justice done, etc.

20.] Six men of Salem, going on fowling in a canoe, were overset near Kettle Island, and five of them drowned.

November 5.] At the court of assistants complaint was made by some of the country, (viz., Richard Brown of Water-

|| that ||

---

is part; and in the Granary burial ground, in this city, over his tomb, which now belongs to the family of the late Gov. Sullivan, that honor is repeated: —

> "Virtue's fast friend within this tomb doth lie,
> A foe to bribes, but rich in charity."

Surely the character of the age forbids us to consider these clean hands as *distinguishing* him from other magistrates.

He was of a good family in England, and was recorder of Boston in 1625. In our Registry of Deeds, lib. VIII. 297, is evidence of a gift from the governour to Angola, a negro, of a piece of land on the highway leading to Roxbury, fifty feet square, to him and his children forever, with the language of the donor: "He was the only instrument that, under God, saved my life, coming to me with his boat, when I was sunk in the river between Boston and Winisimet, several years since, and laid hold of me and got me into the boat he came in, and saved my life; which kindness of him I remember."

Something from the will, 28 November, 1672, in Prob. Rec. VII. 271, is worth copying: "Among many other undeserved favors of God towards me, this is none of the least, that, for so long a time, I have lived under the special government of Christ in his church, not without some soul satisfaction through the gracious presence of Christ, who hath walked in the midst of these churches, which I judge have been constituted according to his mind. That I may testify the engagement of my heart to the Lord, being now of perfect memory and understanding, I do dispose," etc. After various devises, he says, "I do freely and willingly dispose and give (after mine and my wife's decease) the farms she hath during her life, and (after the decease of my son and his daughter) my whole estate in Winnisimet, to be an annual encouragement to some godly ministers and preachers, and such as may be such, who shall be by my trustees judged faithful to those principles in church discipline, which are owned and practised in the First Church of Christ in Boston, of which I am a member; a main one whereof is, that all ecclesiastical jurisdiction is committed by Christ to each particular organical church, from which there is no appeal, visible saintship being the matter, and express covenanting the form, of the church." Bellingham was warm in his opposition to the Third, now Old South, Church.

town, in the name of the rest,) that the ensign at Salem was defaced, viz. one part of the red cross taken out. Upon this, an attachment was awarded against Richard Davenport,[1] ensign-bearer, to appear at the next court to answer. Much matter was made of this, as fearing it would be taken as an act of rebellion, or of like high nature, in defacing the king's colors; though the truth were, it was done upon this opinion, that the red cross was given to the king of England by the pope, as an ensign of victory, and so a superstitious thing, and a relique of antichrist. What proceeding was hereupon, will appear after, at next court, in the first month; (for, by reason of the great snows and frosts, we used not to keep courts in the three winter months).

The Rebecka came from Narigansett with five hundred bushels of corn given to Mr. John Oldham. The Indians had promised him ||one thousand|| bushels, but their store fell out less than they expected. They gave him also an island in the Narigansett Bay, called Chippacursett, containing about *one thousand acres,* six miles long, and two miles broad. This is a very fair bay, being above twelve leagues square, with divers great islands in it, a deep channel close to the shore, being rocky. Mr. Peirce took the height there, and found it forty-one degrees, forty-one minutes, being not above half a degree to the southward of us. In his voyage to and fro, he went over the shoals, having, most part, five or six fathom, within half a mile and less of the shore from the north part of Cape Cod to Natuckett Island, which is about twenty leagues — and, in the shallowest place, two and an half fathom. The country on the west of the Bay of Naragansett is all champaign for many miles, but very stony, and full of Indians. He saw there above one thousand men, women, and children, yet the men were

||100||

---

1 This person rose to higher rank, and was several years commander at Castle Island in Boston harbor, where, Hubbard, 642, informs us, he was killed by lightning in July, 1665, to which Hutchinson, I. 253, adds some particulars. Capt. Roger Clap, the next month, was appointed successor. From his Memoirs something may be learned of the spirit and manners of the early settlers, if not of their deeds. Davenport named a daughter, born, soon after, Truecross.

many abroad on hunting. Natuckett is an island full of Indians, about ten leagues in length east and west.

6.] There came to the deputy governour, about fourteen days since, a messenger from the Pekod sachem, to desire our friendship. He brought two bundles of sticks, whereby he signified how many beaver and ||otter|| skins he would give us for that end, and great store of wampompeage, (about two bushels, by his description). He brought a small present with him, which the deputy received, and returned a moose coat of as good value, and withal told him, that he must send persons of greater quality, and then our governour would treat with them.
*148 And now there came two men, who brought another present of wampompeage. The deputy brought them to Boston, where most of the assistants were assembled, by occasion of the lecture, who, calling to them some of the ministers, grew to this treaty with them: That we were willing to have friendship etc.; but because they had killed some Englishmen, viz. Capt. Stone, etc., they must first deliver up ||[2]those who|| were guilty of his death, etc. They answered, that the sachem, who then lived, was slain by the Dutch, and all the men, who were guilty, etc., were dead of the pox, except two, and that if they were worthy of death, they would move their sachem to have them delivered, (for they had no commission to do it;) but they excused the fact, saying that Capt. Stone, coming into their river, took two of their men and bound them, and made them show him the way up the river, which when they had done, he with two others and the two Indians, (their hands still bound,) went on shore, and nine of their men watched them, and when they were on ||[3]sleep|| in the night, they killed them; then going towards the pinnace to have taken that, it suddenly blew up into the air. This was related with such confidence and gravity, as, having no means to contradict it, we inclined to believe it. But, the governour not being present, we concluded nothing; but some of us went with them the next day to the governour.

The reason why they desired so much our friendship was, because they were now in war with the Naragansetts, whom, till this year, they had kept under, and likewise with the Dutch, who had killed their old sachem and some other of their men,

||other|| ||[2]such as|| ||[3]shore||

for that the Pekods had killed some Indians, who came to trade with the Dutch at Connecticut; and, by these occasions, they could not trade safely any where. Therefore they desired us to send a pinnace with cloth, and we should have all their trade.

They offered us also all their right at Connecticut, and to further us what they could, if we would settle a plantation there.

When they came to the governour, they agreed, according to the former treaty, viz. to deliver us the two men, who were guilty of Capt. Stone's death, when we would send for them; to yield up Connecticut; to give us four hundred fathom of wampompeage, and forty beaver, and thirty otter skins; and that we should presently send a pinnace with cloth to trade with them, §and so should be at peace with them, and as friends to trade with them,[1]§ but not to defend them, etc.

The next morning news came, that two or three hundred *149
of the Naragansetts were come to Cohann, viz. Neponsett, to kill the Pekod ambassadors, etc. Presently we ||met at|| Roxbury, and raised some few men in arms, and sent to the Naragansett men to come to us. When they came there were no more but two of their sachems, and about twenty ||[2]more,|| who had been on hunting thereabouts, and came to lodge with the Indians at Cohann, as their manner is. So we treated with them about the Pekods, and, at our request, they promised they should go and come to and from us in peace, and they were also content to enter further treaty of peace with them; and in all things showed themselves very ready to gratify us. So the

||sent out to|| ||[2]men||

---

[1] A cause of the omission, in the first edition, of this member of the sentence is very easily found. The eye of the transcriber, turning from his copy to the original MS., caught, in the latter branch, the words, "trade with them," which close each part, and he supposed it was what he had already transferred to his sheet. Several errors of that edition, as will appear in the progress of our labor, were occasioned in this way. Collations of ancient MSS. afford critics frequent opportunity of detecting such faults, arising from the ὁμοιοτέλευτον, which forms a class of cases excepted from the general rule, that the shorter reading should be preferred. By such a cause the loss of the famous spurious text, 1 John, v. 7, from all the MSS. was formerly, in vain, attempted to be explained.

Pekods returned home, and the Naragansetts departed well satisfied; only they were told in private, that if they did make peace with the Pekods, we would give them part of that wampompeage, which they should give us; (for the Pekods held it dishonorable to offer them any thing as of themselves, yet were willing we should give it them, and indeed did offer us so much for that end[1]).

The agreement they made with us was put in writing, and the two ambassadors set to their marks — one a bow with an arrow in it, and the other a hand.

13.] The Regard, a ship of Barnstable, of about two hundred tons, arrived with twenty passengers and about fifty cattle.

One thing I think fit to observe, as a witness of God's providence for this plantation. There came in this ship one Mans-
*150 field, a poor godly man of Exeter, being very desirous to come to us, but not able to transport his family. There was in the city a rich merchant, one Marshall, who being troubled in his dreams about the said poor man, could not be quiet till he had sent for him, and given him £50, and lent him £100, willing him withal, that, if he wanted, he should send to him for more. This Mansfield grew suddenly rich, and then lost his godliness, and his wealth soon after.[2]

18.] About this time an open pinnace of one Mr. Sewall[3] of

---

1 If any doubt has ever been entertained, in Europe or America, of the equitable and pacific principles of the founders of New England, in their relations with the Indians, the secret history, in the foregoing paragraph, of this negotiation, should dissipate it. By the unholy maxims of vulgar policy, the discord of these unfriendly nations would have been encouraged, and our European fathers should have employed the passions of the aborigines for their mutual destruction. On the contrary, an honest artifice was resorted to for their reconciliation, and the tribute received by us from one offending party was, by a Christian deception, divided with their enemies to procure mutual peace. Such mediation is more useful than victory, and more honorable than conquest.

2 The last sentence is an addition, by the author, at a later time. Perhaps that providence, which sent us a man, who soon lost his character and his property, had better been reverenced in silence.

3 This ancestor of one of the most venerated families, which has given three of its members to preside in the highest court of civil and criminal jurisdiction in Massachusetts, was one of the first settlers at Newbury. The biographies of

Ipswich, going deep laden from Boston, was cast away upon the rocks at the head of Cape Ann, in a N. E. storm; but all the men were saved.

21.] One Willys,[1] a godly man, and member of Boston church, and one Dorety, an honest man, and two boys, going over to Noddle's Island to fetch wood, in a small boat, and none of them having any skill or experience, were cast away in a N. E. tempest, as they came home in the night laden, being then ebbing water. We sent two boats on the Lord's day, (so soon as they were missing, being the 23d,) but they could not find men, or boat, or wood, in any ||part|| of the bay. Three days after, the boat was found at Muddy River, overturned.

27.] The assistants met at the governour's, to advise about the defacing of the cross in the ensign at Salem, where (taking advice with some of the ministers) we agreed to write to Mr. Downing in England, of the truth of the matter, under all our hands, that, if occasion were, he might show it in our excuse; for therein we expressed our dislike of the thing, and our purpose to punish the offenders, yet with as much wariness as we might, being doubtful of the lawful use of the cross in an ensign, though we were clear that fact, as concerning the matter, was very unlawful.

It was then informed us, how Mr. Eliot, the teacher of *151
the church of Roxbury, had taken occasion, in a sermon, to speak of the peace made with the Pekods, and to lay some blame upon ||the ministry|| for proceeding therein, without consent of the people, and for other failings, (as he conceived). We took order, that he should be dealt with by Mr. Cotton, Mr. Hooker, and Mr. Welde, to be brought to see his errour, and to heal it by some public explanation of his meaning; for the people began to take occasion to murmur against us for it.

||place|| ||2 our measures||

Eliot and Allen, and especially the copious Collection of American Epitaphs, by Alden, II. 115, have well perpetuated the memory of his descendants. Henry died at Rowley, 1654; and in Hutchinson, I. Appendix xii. is a letter from Richard Cromwell, during his short enjoyment of the poor title of Lord Protector, to our governour and magistrates, in favor of the son, who was a minister in Hampshire, and came over about his father's estate.

[3] John and Jane Willis are, in the Records of Boston Church, numbered 135, 6; and against their names is written, *dead since*.

It was likewise informed, that Mr. Williams of Salem had broken his promise to us, in teaching publickly against the king's patent, and our great sin in claiming right thereby to this country, etc. and for usual terming the churches of England antichristian. We granted summons to him for his appearance at the next court.

The aforesaid three ministers, upon conference with the said Mr. Eliot, brought him to acknowlege his errour in that he had mistaken the ground of his doctrine, and that he did acknowledge, that, for a peace only, (whereby the people were not to be engaged in a war,) the magistrates might conclude, plebe inconsulto, and so promised to express himself in public next Lord's day.[1]

24.] One Scott and Eliot of Ipswich were lost in their way homewards, and wandered up and down six days, and eat nothing. At length they were found by an Indian, being almost senseless for want of rest, etc.

About the same time one [blank] was twenty-one days upon Plumb Island, and found by chance frozen in the snow, yet alive, and did well. He had been missing twenty days, and himself said he had no food all that time.[2]

December 4.] Was an extraordinary tempest of wind and snow, at N. N. E. which continued twenty-four hours, and after that such frost as, within two days, the whole bay was frozen over, but free again before night.

11.] The lectures at Boston and Newtown returned again to their former course, because the weather was many times so tedious as people could not travel, etc.

This day, after the lecture, the inhabitants of Boston met to choose seven men who should divide the town lands among them.[3] They chose by papers, and in their choice left out

---

[1] In less than twenty years, Eliot had fallen into a worse indiscretion by writing his "Christian Commonwealth," for which, at a later day, he was called by our General Court, to make submission. See 3 Mass. Hist. Coll. IX. 130.

[2] Perhaps he had lost his memory, and reckoned time by his suffering, and not by the almanac.

[3] In his index, the former editor seems to have considered this paragraph as affording an account of the "origin of selectmen in Boston;" and the same

Mr. *Winthrop,* Coddington, and other of the chief men; *152
only they chose one of the elders and a deacon, and the rest of the inferior sort, *and Mr. Winthrop had the greater number before one of them by a voice or two.*[1] This they did, as fearing that the richer men would give the poorer sort no great proportions of land, but would rather leave a great part at liberty for new comers and for common, which Mr. Winthrop had oft persuaded them unto, as best for the town, etc. Mr. Cotton and divers others were offended at this choice, because they declined the magistrates; and Mr. Winthrop refused to be one upon such an election as was carried by a voice or two, telling them, that though, for his part, he did not apprehend any personal injury, nor did doubt of their good ||affection|| towards him, yet he was much grieved that Boston should be the first who should shake off their magistrates, especially Mr. Coddington, who had been always so forward for their enlargement; adding further reason ||²of|| declining this choice, to blot out so bad a precedent. Whereupon, at the motion of Mr. Cotton, who showed them, that it was the Lord's order among the Israelites to have all such businesses committed to the elders, and that it had been ||³nearer|| the rule to have chosen some of each sort, etc., they all agreed to go to a new election, which was referred to the next lecture day.[2]

The reason why some were not willing that the people should

||offering|| ||²for|| ||³never||

---

error was followed even by so careful a writer as Holmes, Annals, I. 279, of the first ed. This, and most other of the towns, had before been governed by such officers, though the title was different. See note 2 on p. 114. That which continued to our times is first used in Boston Records in 1645. See Shaw's Description of Boston, 147.

[1] The author's modesty erased the conclusion of the sentence, and his own name, in the former part.

[2] Our Town Records omit notice of the first election of these seven; but, on the 18th, Winthrop, Coddington, Bellingham, Cotton, Oliver, Colburn, and Baulstone, were chosen, "to divide and dispose of all such lands, belonging to the town, as are not yet in the lawful possession of any particular person, to the inhabitants of the town, according to the order of the court, leaving such portions in common, for the use of new comers, and the further benefit of the town, as in their best discretion they shall think fit. The islands hired by the town to be also included in this order."

have more land in the bay than they might be likely to use in some reasonable time, was partly to prevent the neglect of trades, and other more necessary employments, and partly that there might be place to receive such as should come after; seeing it would be very prejudicial to the commonwealth, if men should be forced to go far off for land, while others had much, and could make no use of it, more than to please their eye with it.

*153 One Abigail Gifford, widow, being kept at the charge of the parish of Wilsden in Middlesex, near London, was sent by Mr. Ball's ship into this country, and being found to be sometimes distracted, and a very burdensome woman, the governour and assistants returned her back by warrant, 18, to the same parish, in the ship Rebecca.

22.] A fast was kept by the church of Charlton, and Mr. Symmes chosen their teacher.

By a letter from Plimouth it was certified, that the Dutch of Hudson's River had been at Connecticut, and came in warlike manner to put the Plimouth men out of their house there; but when they stood upon their defence, they departed, without offering any violence.[1]

11 mo. 13.[2]] The church of Boston kept a day of humilia-

---

[1] In Haz. II. 262, the invaluable proceedings of the commissioners of the United Colonies preserve the Dutch relation of this affair. We must regret to find in Trumbull, I. 36, too much of the feeling of a partisan on this subject. A very judicious explanation of the controversy may be seen in the North American Review, VIII. 85.

[2] Here is discovered the first instance of changing the name of the month, which arose from a weak scruple, as if there were something heathenish in following the Roman nomenclature. Our fathers departed gradually from the church of England, and perhaps their tendency to separation increased faster in the wilderness than it would have done at home. It will be observed, that this work begins on Easter Monday, and, in his margin, that great festival of the church is duly honored by our historian. A slight error, as to the commencement of this change, is found in Hutchinson, I. 428, who seems to attribute it to the Puritanical severity of Vane; but, before his coming, the settlers were well cured of their fondness for the forms, in which they had been educated. From this place, our original MS. usually employs this new enumeration of the great divisions of time, though we may occasionally observe a backsliding to the errors of the author's earlier years. The fantastical custom was maintained for nearly two generations in New England; and the gradual abrogation of it was, no doubt, regarded by the elder planters as a modern defec-

tion for the absence of their pastor and other brethren, gone to England, and like to be troubled and detained there, and for that the Lord had made a breach upon them by those four which were drowned, as is before set down; at which fast Mr. Cotton preached out of Numbers xxxv. 13, and one of the members taught out of that in ||Lamentations||[1] iii. 39: Wherefore doth a living man complain?

19.] All the ministers, except Mr. Ward[2] of Ipswich, *154
met at Boston, being requested by the governour and assistants, to consider of these two cases: 1. What ||[2]we ought to do,|| if a general governour should be sent out of England? 2. Whether it be lawful for us to carry the cross in our banners? — In the first case, they all agreed, that, if a general governour were sent, we ought not to accept him, but defend our lawful possessions, (if we were able;) otherwise to avoid or protract. For the matter of the cross, they were divided, and so deferred it to another meeting.

||Samuel|| ||[2]ought to be done||

---

tion; for, in Johnson's Wonder-working Providence, lib. I. c. 27, we are informed, that the practice was designed "of purpose to prevent the heathenish and popish observation of days, months, and years, that they may be forgotten among the people of the Lord."

[1] The strange error of the first edition, in giving here a wrong book in the Bible, is easily accounted for in note 1 on page 74. The editor was almost as well acquainted with scripture texts as Winthrop, who, we may be sure, is referred to by the passage above.

[2] Of Nathaniel Ward, the author of the celebrated "Simple Cobler of Agawam," almost enough will be found in the course of this History, in the biographies of Eliot and Allen, and in the books cited by the latter, to excuse me from saying more. He was in the church of Standon Massey, near Chipping Ongar, in Essex, about eighteen miles from London, and favored the cause of New England some years before coming over. See a letter from him to Cotton, of December, 1631, given in Hutchinson, I. 120. He was soon after deprived for his non-conformity, and a new rector was inducted 8 August, 1633. Before obtaining that benefice, he had been a curate at St. James, Duke's Place, London, as both places may be found in Newcourt's Repertorium, I. 917 and II. 545. Brook, in his lives of the Puritans, seems ignorant of the title of the book, which has contributed, by its anonymous authorship, to spread most widely his name. Yet he quotes from a writer the strange news, that he "discovered great loyalty to the king, and much solicitude for his majesty's welfare." That work is very attractive for its humor, and curious for its execrable spirit.

About the middle of this month, Mr. Allerton's pinnace came from the French about Port Royal. They went to fetch the two men, which had been carried by the French from Machias, and to demand the goods taken, etc. But Mr. La Tour made them answer, that he took them as lawful prize, and that he had authority from the king of France, who challenged all from Cape Sable to Cape Cod, wishing them to take notice, and to certify the rest of the English, that, if they traded to the east of Pemaquid, he would make prize of them. Being desired to show his commission, he answered, that his sword was commission sufficient, where he had strength to overcome; where that wanted, he would show his commission.

In the end of this month, three men had their boat frozen up at Bird[1] Island, as they were coming from Deer Island, so as they were compelled to lodge there all night; and in the morning they came over the ice to Noddle's Isle, and thence to Molten's Point in Charlestown, and thence over the ice, by Mr. Hoffe's, to Boston. At the same time six others were kept a week at the Governour's Garden; and in the end
*155 gate with their boat to Mattapan Point; for, near all that time, there was no open place between the Garden and Boston, neither was there any passing at Charlestown for two or three days, the wind about the N. W. three weeks, with much snow and extreme frost.

[Very large blank.]

Mo. 12.] About the middle of this month, a ||proper|| young

||promp||

---

[1] This island is not remembered by any person now alive, I believe, as a spot on which men might lodge, although some soil, covered at high tide, permitted a coarse vegetation of grass within sixty years. That soil is now so washed away, that the rocks, on which it rested, are not visible till near low water. So early as 1650, permission to mow the marsh there was granted to Thomas Munt; and the town gave, eight years after, a lease of it for sixty years at an annual rent of twelve pence in silver, or a bushel of salt. Better evidence of the devastation of the ocean, if better were wanted, will be found in a comparison of the modern state of Nix's Mate, so called, on which is barely room for a sea mark, with what it must have been in September, 1636, when the general court granted "twelve acres of land to John Gallop, upon Nixe's Island, to enjoy to him and his heirs forever, *if the island be so much.*"

man, servant to Mr. Bellingham, passing over the ice to Winnesemett, fell in, and was drowned. Divers others fell in, in that and other places, but, by God's providence, were saved.

14.] Capt. Wiggin, governour at Pascataquack, under the Lords Say and Brook, wrote to ||our|| governour, desiring to have two men tried here, who had committed sodomy with each other, and that on the Lord's day, in time of public exercise. The governour and divers of the assistants met and conferred about it, but did not think fit to try them here.[1]

[Large blank.]

Mo. 1. 4.] A general court at Newtown. Mr. Hooker preached, and showed the three great evils.[2]

[Very large blank.]

At this court, one[3] of the deputies was questioned for deny-

||the||

---

1 It is apparent, from inspection of the MS., that the last sentence of this paragraph was written at a later time than the preceding. The desire of Wiggin seems to imply a defect of criminal jurisdiction; but the refusal, on our part, to accept it, was a very prudent measure.

2 Perhaps these evils were evanescent, though it may be otherwise; but posterity, I believe, is deprived of the light shown to our fathers.

3 The name was partly written in the author's MS. but erased. It appears, however, a few pages onward. An explanation worth transcribing is found in Col. Rec. I. 137: "Whereas Mr. Israel Stoughton hath written a certain book, which hath occasioned much trouble and offence to the court; the said Mr. Stoughton did desire of the court, that the said book might forthwith be burnt, as being weak and offensive." Such almost unexampled modesty, in an author, did not, however, propitiate the severe justice of the assembly; for on the same page appears an order, "that Mr. Israel Stoughton shall be disabled for bearing any public office in the commonwealth, within this jurisdiction, for the space of three years, for affirming the assistants were not magistrates." But his disability was removed or overlooked before the expiration of the sentence; for, in December of the year 1636, he was again a deputy, and being orthodox on the subject of the antinomian controversy, was chosen an assistant the following spring. He commanded the forces in the Pequod expedition in the same year. The General Index to 1 Hist. Coll. X. 295, must be wrong in ascribing to *Thomas* Stoughton the erection of the mill at Neponsit; for our Col. Rec. I. 111, mentions, that *Israel* had liberty granted "to build a mill, a wear, and bridge over Neponsit River, and is to sell the alewives he takes there at five shillings the thousand."

Thomas, who went to Windsor, was, I presume, brother of Israel, and, proba-

*156 ing the magistracy among us, affirming that the power of the governour was but ministerial, etc. || He || had also much opposed the magistrates, and ||[2]slighted|| them, and used many weak arguments against the negative voice, as himself acknowledged upon record. He was adjudged by all the court to be disabled for three years from bearing any public office.

One[1] of the assistants was called to the lower end of the table to answer for refusing to pay towards a rate made by the court, and was fined £5, which was after released.

Mr. Endecott was called to answer for defacing the cross in the ensign; but, because the court could not agree about the thing, whether the ensigns should be laid by, in regard that many refused to follow them, the whole cause was deferred till the next general court; and the commissioners for military affairs gave order, in the mean time, that all the ensigns should be laid aside, etc.

At this court brass farthings were forbidden, and musket bullets made to pass for farthings.

A ||[3]commission|| for military affairs was established, ||[4]which|| had power of life and limb, etc.[2]

[Very large blank.]

||and|| ||[2]stigmatized|| ||[3]commissioner|| ||[4]who||

---

bly, came first to New England; for he was admitted freeman in May, 1631, while the same Records show that Israel took the oath 5 November, 1633.

In the latter part of this History it will be found, that Stoughton went to England, and became a lieutenant colonel in the parliament's service, and died during the civil war. He was father of the celebrated William Stoughton, first lieutenant governour named by the crown under the charter of William and Mary, and chief justice in the trial of the witches. In that lamentable delusion his agency may almost be forgiven, by future generations, for his munificence to Harvard College, in which one of the halls perpetuates his memory. Quincy's History of the University well delineates his character. His epitaph, closely imitated from that of Pascal, is in 1 Hist. Coll. II. 10. A bachelor seldom attained such honors in the infancy of our country; but he had preached.

[1] Pynchon was the offender. For the same cause fines were imposed, at the same time, on the towns of Sagus and Salem, and all were released together.

[2] From the greatness of the powers granted to this body, a fuller account than Winthrop has given may reasonably be extracted from Col. Rec. I. 139; "It is ordered, that the present governour, deputy governour, John Winthrop, John Humfrey, John Haynes, John Endecott, William Coddington, William

15.] Two of the elders of every church met at Sagus, *157
and spent there three days. The occasion was, that divers of the brethren of that church, not liking the proceedings of the pastor, and withal making question, whether they were a church or not, did separate from church communion. The pastor and other brethren desired the advice and help of the rest of the churches, who, not thinking fit to judge of the cause, without hearing the other side, offered to meet at Sagus about it. Upon this the pastor, etc., required the separate members to deliver their grievances in writing, which they refusing to do, the pastor, etc., wrote to all the churches, that, for this cause, they were purposed to proceed against them as persons excommunicated; and therefore desired them to stay their journey, etc. This letter being read at a lecture at Boston, (where some of the elders of every church were present,) they all agreed (with consent of their churches) to go presently to Sagus, to stay this hasty proceeding, etc. Accordingly, being met, and both parties (after much debate) being heard, it was agreed, that they were a true church, though not constituted, at first, in due order, yet after consent and practice of a church estate had supplied that defect; and so all were reconciled.

[Large blank.]

Mo. 2.] Some of our people went to Cape Cod, and made

Pynchon, Increase Nowell, Richard Bellingham, Esquires, and Simon Bradstreet, or the major part of them, who are deputed by this court to dispose of all military affairs whatsoever, shall have full power and authority to see all former laws concerning all military men and munition executed; and also shall have full power to ordain or remove all military officers, and to make and tender to them an oath suitable to their places; to dispose of all companies, to make orders for them, and to make and tender to them a suitable oath, and to see that strict discipline and trainings be observed, and to command them forth upon any occasion they think meet; to make either offensive or defensive war; as also to do whatsoever may be farther behoofeful for the good of this plantation, in case of any war that may befal us; and, also, that the aforesaid commissioners, or the major part of them, shall have power to imprison or confine any that they shall judge to be enemies to the commonwealth; and such as will not come under command or restraint, as they shall be required, it shall be lawful for the said commissioners to put such persons to death. This order to continue to the end of the next general court." It was prolonged from court to court, several times, and some new members were occasionally added.

some oil of a whale, which was cast on shore. There were three or four cast up, as it seems there is almost every year.

26.] An alarm was raised in all our towns, and the governour and assistants met at Boston, and sent forth a shallop to Cape Ann, to discover what ships were there. For the fishermen had brought in word to Marblehead, that two ships had been ||hovering|| upon the coast all the day; one of about four hundred tons, and the other three hundred and fifty, and were gone in to Cape Ann. But it proved to be only one ship of eighty tons, bound for Richman's Isle, and the other a small pinnace of ten tons.

30.] The governour and assistants sent for Mr. Williams.
*158 The occasion was, for that he had taught publicly, that a magistrate ought not to tender an oath to an unregenerate man, for that we thereby have communion with a wicked man in the worship of God, and cause him to take the name of God in vain. He was heard before all the ministers, and very clearly ||[2]confuted||. Mr. Endecott was at first of the same opinion, but he gave place to the ||[3]truth||.

Mo. 3. 6.] A general court was held at Newtown, where John Haynes, Esq., was chosen governour, Richard Bellingham, Esq., deputy governour, and Mr. Hough and Mr. Dummer chosen assistants[1] to the former; and Mr. Ludlow, the late deputy, left out of the magistracy. The reason was, partly, because the people would exercise their absolute power, etc., and partly upon some speeches of the deputy, who protested against the election of the governour as void, for that the deputies of the several towns had agreed upon the election before they came, etc. But this was generally ||[4]discussed,|| and the election adjudged good.

Mr. Endecott was also left out, and called into question about the defacing the cross in the ensign; and a committee was chosen, viz., every town chose one, (which yet were voted by all the people,) and the magistrates chose four, who, taking the charge to consider of the offence, and the censure due to it,

||heaving|| ||[2]confessed|| ||[3]teacher|| ||[4]distrusted||

[1] The other assistants were Winthrop, Dudley, Humfrey, Coddington, Pynchon, Nowell, Bradstreet, and Winthrop, jun.

and to certify the court, after one or two hours ||time,|| made report to the court, that they found his offence to be great, viz., rash and without discretion, taking upon him more authority than he had, and not seeking advice of the court, etc.; ||[2]uncharitable,|| in that he, judging the cross, etc., to be a sin, did content himself to have reformed it at Salem, not taking care that others might be brought out of it also; laying a blemish also upon the rest of the magistrates, as if they would suffer idolatry, etc., and giving occasion to the state of England to think ill of us; — for which they adjudged him worthy admonition, and to be disabled for one year from bearing any public office; declining any heavier sentence, because they were persuaded he did it out of tenderness of conscience, and not of any evil intent.[1]

Some petitions of grievances were tendered to the court in the beginning of it, but the court refused to hear any, or to

||they|| ||[2]unwarrantable||

---

[1] Had his conscience been as enlightened as it was tender, he would have conformed to the harmless custom; but, next year, men of soberer judgment were found ready to refuse compliance with bearing the standard of their country, and almost willing to imitate the outrage of Endecott. A tract of nearly thirteen pages, in defence of the cross, by the celebrated Hooker, is among the MSS. of our Historical Society; but I have neither courage nor curiosity enough to study it. We may not imagine, that our ancestors had carefully scrutinized the ecclesiastical fable of the holy sign in Constantine's vision, or were sufficiently instructed to repudiate the consecrated Labarum of the first Christian emperour; and perhaps an Englishman of our times may presume, that there was as much policy, as abhorrence of idolatry, in their dread of the banner of St. George. Yet this presumption would be unfounded. Though there appears, in September preceding, something like prepared opposition to expected tyranny, I do not discover, in these weak scruples about the ensign, any affectation of independence, to which, a few years later, their circumstances offered very powerful inducements.

In the flag of the United States are exhibited white stars in a blue field; but the most punctilious imitator of the severe simplicity of the fathers of New England has never compared our service under it to the heathenish abomination of worshipping the host of heaven. An anecdote of a politic use of these emblems by Barlow, when negotiating at Algiers, proves that a diseased conscience might entertain this scruple, because the imagination can thus apply the object. He said to the Minister of the Dey, There ought to be friendship between our countries, since you worship the moon, and we the stars.

meddle in any ‖courses‖ but making freemen, until the elections were passed.[1] The governour and deputy were elected by papers, wherein their names were written; but the assistants were chosen by papers, without names, viz. the governour propounded one to the people; then they all went out, and came in at one door, and every man delivered a paper into a hat. Such as gave their vote for the party named, gave in a paper with some figures or scroll in it; others gave in a blank.

The new governour, in his speech to the people, declared his purpose to spare their charge towards his allowance this year, partly in respect of their love showed towards him, and partly for that he observed how much the people had been pressed lately with public charges, which the poorer sort did much groan under.[2]

A petition was preferred by many of Dorchester, etc., for
*160 releasing the sentence against Mr. Stoughton the last
general court; but it was rejected, and the sentence affirmed by the country to be just.

Divers jealousies, that had been between the magistrates and deputies, were now cleared, with full satisfaction to all parties.

The matter of altering the cross in the ensign was referred to the next meeting, (the court being adjourned for three weeks,) it being propounded to turn it to the red and white rose, etc., and every man was to deal with his neighbors, to still their minds, who stood so stiff for the cross, until we should fully agree about it, which was expected, because the ministers had

‖causes‖

---

[1] One of these petitions was on the matter of Endecott's censure. The wisdom of this resolution of the court, in which was now assembled all the people entitled to vote for governour and assistants, except those in towns which sent proxies, was strongly exhibited two years later, when, in the contest for the election between Vane and Winthrop, the precedent was followed. A full examination of that subject, with others, may be found in four tracts preserved in Hutch. Coll. 63–101.

[2] The assessment at this court was £200, only one-third of the amount in the autumn before, and it was apportioned thus: — To Dorchester, Boston, and Newtown, £27. 6. 8, each; Roxbury and Watertown, £20, each; Charlestown, Salem, and Sagus, £16, each; Medford, £10; Ipswich and Newbury, £8, each; Wessaguscus, £4. Col. Rec. I. 152.

promised to take ||pains|| about it, and to write into England, to have the judgments of the most wise and godly there.[1]

The deputies having conceived great danger to our state, in regard that our magistrates, for want of positive laws, in many cases, might proceed according to their discretions, it was agreed that some men should be appointed to frame a body of grounds of laws, in resemblance to a Magna Charta, which, being allowed by some of the ministers, and the general court, should be received for fundamental laws.

At this general court, some of the chief of Ipswich desired leave to remove to Quascacunquen, to begin a town there, which was granted them, and it was named Newberry.

Also, Watertown and Roxbury had leave to remove whither they pleased, so as they continued under this government. The occasion of their desire to remove was, for that all towns in the bay began to be much straitened by their own nearness to one another, and their cattle being so much increased.

21.] A Dutch ship of one hundred and sixty tons arrived at Marblehead. Capt. Hurlston came merchant. She came from Christopher Island. She brought one hundred and forty tons of salt, and ten thousand weight of tobacco.

[Blank.]

This island lies in eighteen degrees, and is about thirty miles in compass, inhabited by two colonies, one English and another French. There is in it about four thousand persons. They have three English churches, but the people are very wicked, as the merchant (who dwelt there five years) complained. The salt is made with the sun in a ||²natural|| pan, half a mile from the sea. Their rain begins in September, and continues till February.

Mo. 4. 3.] Here arrived two Dutch ships, who brought *161
twenty-seven Flanders mares, at £34 a mare, and three horses; sixty-three heifers, at £12 the beast; and eighty-eight sheep, at 50*s.* the sheep. They came from the Tessell in five

||prayers|| ||²watering||

[1] Answers of these "most wise and godly" in England have not fallen in my way. The tract of Hooker, before mentioned, in note on page 158, from very slight examination, appears to contain a temperate censure of Endecott.

weeks three days, and lost not one beast or sheep. Here arrived also, the same day, the James, a ship of three hundred tons, with cattle and passengers, which came all safe from Southampton within the same time. Mr. Graves was master, who had come every year for these seven years.[1] 7. The Lord's day there came in seven other ships,[2] and one to Salem, and four more to the mouth of the bay, with store of passengers and cattle. They came all within six weeks.

For preventing the loss of time, and drunkenness, which sometimes happened, by people's running to the ships, and the excessive prices of commodities, it was ordered, that one in each town should buy for all, etc., and should ‖retain‖ the same within twenty days at five per hundred, if any came to buy in that time. But this took no good effect; for most of the people would not buy, except they might buy for themselves; and the merchants appointed could not disburse so much money, etc.; and the seamen were much discontented, yet some of them brought their goods on shore and sold them there.

16.] A bark of forty tons arrived, set forth with twenty servants, by Sir Richard Saltonstall, to go plant at Connecticut.

By a letter from the Lord Say, and report of divers passengers, it was certified to us, that Capt. Mason and others, the adversaries of this colony, had built a great ship to send over the general governour, etc., which, being launched, fell in sunder in the midst.

It appeared likewise, by a copy of a petition sent over to us, that they had divided all this country of New England, viz. between St. Croix in the east, and that of Lord Bartimore, called Maryland, into twelve provinces, disposed to twelve in England, who should send each ten men to attend the general governour coming over; but ‖[2]the project [took] not effect.‖ The Lord frustrated their design.[3]

‖return‖ ‖[2]this proved not effectual‖

---

[1] In the custom-house return of names of passengers by this ship, preserved at the State Paper Office in Westminster, the name of the master for this voyage is written, Cooper. Possibly, Graves was the owner.

[2] Rev. Peter Hobart, wife, and four children, were in one of these.

[3] This idle division of American provinces may be seen in Hubbard, 228.

Two carpenters, going to wash themselves in the river between Mount Woollaston and Wessaguscus, were carried away with the tide, and drowned.

[Large blank.]

24.] Mr. Graves, in the James, and Mr. Hodges, in the *162
Rebecka, set sail for the Isle of Sable for sea-horse (which are there in great number) and wild cows. Mr. John Rose, being cast ashore there in the [Mary and Jane] two years since, and making a small pinnace of the wreck of his ship, sailed thence to the French upon the main, being thirty leagues off, by whom he was detained prisoner, and forced to pilot them to the island, where they had great store of sea-horse ||teeth,|| and cattle, and ||[2]store|| [of] black foxes; and they left seventeen men upon the island to inhabit it. The island is thirty miles long, two miles broad in most places, a mere sand, yet full of fresh water in ponds, etc. He saw about eight hundred cattle, small and great, all red, and the largest he ever saw, and many foxes, whereof some perfect black. There is no wood upon it, but store of wild peas and flags by the ponds, and grass. In the middle of it is a pond of salt water, ten miles long, full of plaice, ||[3]soles,|| etc. The company, which went now, carried twelve landmen, two mastiffs, a ||[4]house,|| and a shallop.

August 26.] They returned from their voyage. They found there upon the island sixteen Frenchmen, who had wintered there, and built a little fort, and had killed some black foxes. They had killed also many of the cattle, so as they found not above one hundred and forty, and but two or three calves. They could kill but ||[5]few|| sea-horse, by reason they were forced to travel so far in the sand as they were too weak to stick them, and they came away at such time as they used to go up ||[6]highest|| to eat green peas. The winter there is very cold, and the snow above knee deep.

Mo. 5. 8.] At the general court, Mr. Williams of Salem was summoned, and did appear. It was laid to his charge, that, being under question before the magistracy and churches for divers dangerous opinions, viz. 1, that the magistrate ought not to punish the breach of the first table, otherwise than in such

||blank|| ||[2]some|| ||[3]blank|| ||[4]horse|| ||[5]five|| ||[6]heights||

cases as did disturb the civil peace; 2, that he ought not to tender an oath to an unregenerate man; 3, that a man ought not to pray with such, though wife, child, etc.; 4, that a man ought not to give thanks after the sacrament nor after meat, etc.; and that the other churches were about to write to the church of Salem to admonish him of these errors; notwithstanding the church had since called him to [the] office of a teacher. Much debate was about these things. The said opinions were adjudged by all, magistrates and ministers, (who were desired
*163 to be present,) to be erroneous, and very dangerous, and the calling of him to office, at that time, was judged a great contempt of authority. So, in fine, ||time|| was given to him and the church of Salem to consider of these things till the next general court, and then either to give satisfaction to the court, or else to expect the sentence; it being professedly declared by the ministers, (at the request of the court to give their advice,) that he who should obstinately maintain such opinions, (whereby a church might run into heresy, apostacy, or tyranny, and yet the civil magistrate could not intermeddle,) were to be removed, and that the other churches ought to request the magistrates so to do.[1]

At this court Wessaguscus was made a plantation, and Mr. Hull,[2] a minister §in England,§ and twenty-one families with him, allowed to sit down there — after called Weymouth.

||there||

---

[1] We ought not to censure more the declaration of the clergy, than the policy of the court in asking their advice. Church and state were too often playing into each other's hands — if so irreverent a phrase may be allowed — and thus sanctifying principles and conduct, which either would not have, singly, ventured to adopt or enforce.

[2] Of reverend Benjamin Hull further account can hardly be obtained, except that, in the MS. journal of Hobart, first minister of Hingham, on 5 May, 1639, I find "Mr. Hull gave his farewell sermon." Mather, in Magnalia, mentions him as minister at the Isles of Shoals. Conf. Magn. book III. with 1 Hist. Coll. VII. 254. Probably the same person, in this history, 3 month, 1643, is called "an excommunicated person, and very contentious;" yet, in the Magnalia, book VII. 65, Mather, describing the perils of Mrs. Heard, at the famous assault by the Indians on Cocheco, in 1689, makes her "daughter of Mr. Hull, a reverend minister, formerly living at Piscataqua." In our second volume, some failure, in propriety, it will be seen, is attributed to his son.

A careful history of Weymouth is much wanted.

A plantation was likewise erected at Bear's Cove, after called || Hingham.||[1]

12.] Mr. Luxon[2] arrived here in a small pinnace. He fished at the Isle of Shoals, as he had done many years, and, returning to sell his fish at market, was taken in foggy *164
weather, and carried into the bay of Port Royal, and there wrecked upon a small island about [blank] leagues from the main. So he built a pinnace, and came hither in her.

[Blank.]

Salem men had preferred a petition, at the last general court, for some land in Marblehead Neck, which they did challenge as belonging to their town; but, because they had chosen Mr. Williams their teacher, while he stood under question of authority, and so offered contempt to the magistrates, etc., their petition was refused till, etc. Upon this the church of Salem write to other churches, to admonish the magistrates of this as a heinous sin, and likewise the deputies; for which, at the next general court, their deputies were not received until they should give satisfaction about the letter.[3]

Mo. 6. Aug. 16.] The wind having blown hard at S. and S. W. a week before, about midnight it came up at N. E. and

|| Kingham ||

---

[1] By this establishment, or erection, of a plantation, we must not understand, that settlements were then first made at the spot, but that a municipal government was permitted there, or that the place was allowed to have deputies in the general court. Wessaguscus had, at the last general court, been assessed; and, at the same time, Joseph Andrews was "sworn constable of Barecove." Many of the inhabitants were made freemen of the colony in the preceding year. The spelling of the name varies between the Colony Records and this History, and each, in different places, has different orthography. Perhaps it sometimes was thought a natural resort of bears; perhaps sometimes the appearance of the cove, at low water, regulated the letters used to express the same sound. The new name was given by the general court, 2 September, 1635, because the pastor and most of his flock came from Hingham, in Norfolk, England.

[2] Josselyn sailed 15 Oct. 1639, from Boston, in the Fellowship, of 170 tons, Luxon master, and arrived at Biddeford in Devon, 24 Nov., as he tells us.

[3] This denial, or perversion of justice, by postponement of a hearing, on a question of temporal right, for some spiritual deficiency in the church or pastor, will not permit us to think, that the judges of Williams were free from all blame in producing his schism.

blew with such violence, with abundance of rain, that it blew down many hundreds of trees, §near the towns,§ overthrew some houses, [and] drave the ships from their anchors. The Great Hope, of Ipswich, being about four hundred tons, was driven on ground at Mr. Hoffe's Point, and brought back again presently by a N. W. wind, and ||ran|| on shore at Charlestown. About eight of the clock the wind came about to N. W. very strong, and, it being then about high water, by nine the tide was fallen about three feet. Then it began to flow again about one hour, and rose about two or three feet, which was conceived to be, that the sea was grown so high §abroad§ with the N. E. wind, that, meeting with the ebb, it forced it back again.

§This tempest was not so far as Cape Sable, but to the south more violent, and made a double tide all that coast§.

In this tempest, the James of Bristol, having one hundred passengers,[1] honest people of Yorkshire, being put into the Isle of Shoals, lost there three anchors; and, setting sail, no can-
*165 vas nor ropes would hold, but she was driven within a cable's length of the rocks ||[2]at|| Pascataquack, when suddenly the wind, coming to N. W., put them back to the Isle of Shoals, and, being there ready to strike upon the rocks, they ||[3]let|| out a piece of their mainsail, and weathered the rocks. In the same tempest a bark of Mr. Allerton's was cast away upon Cape Ann, and twenty-one persons drowned; among the rest one Mr. ||[4]Avery,||[2] a minister in Wiltshire, a

||came|| ||[2]of|| ||[3]cut|| ||[4]Anvey||

---

[1] Among the number were Richard Mather, with his wife and children, and Jonathan Mitchell, the latter quite a youth, both famous names with the early divines of Massachusetts. Mather, and some of the other passengers, were from Lancashire. His original journal of the voyage, a very interesting document, was first published in Young's Chron. of Mass.

[2] This gentleman, whose fate was designed by his companion in adversity to be forever remembered in the name given to the outer rock, Avery's Fall, was cousin of Anthony Thacher, of whom slight notice is taken in the next note. They came to Boston in the James from Southampton, arriving in June before. From a folio page, in double column, of the Magnalia, book III. p. 77, we learn no more of the life of Avery than his latest hours. His baptismal name was John.

godly man, with his wife and six small children, were drowned. None were saved but one Mr. Thacher[1] and his wife, who were cast on shore, and preserved by a powder horn and a bag with a flint, and a goat and a cheese, cast on shore after them, and a truss of bedding, and some other necessaries: and the third day after a shallop came thither to look for another shallop, which was missing in the storm, and so they were preserved. So as there did appear a miraculous providence in their preservation. The general court gave Mr. Thacher £26.13.4, towards his losses, and divers good people gave him besides. The man was cast on shore, when he had been (as he ||thought||) a quarter of an hour beaten up and down by the waves, not being able to swim one stroke; and his wife sitting in the scuttle of the bark, the deck was broke off, and brought on shore, as she stuck in it. One of the children was then cast dead on shore, and the rest never found.

§Gabriel lost at Pemaquid;[2] and Mr. Witheridge and the

||supposed||

---

[1] An admirable letter from this sufferer to his brother Peter, a clergyman of the city of Salisbury, relates all the particulars of this shipwreck, one of the most disastrous that ever afflicted the iron-bound coast of New England. It is the first article in Increase Mather's Remarkable Providences, and gives to that work its chief value. It is given by Young in the Chron. of Mass. The vessel was returning from Ipswich to Marblehead. Anthony's nephew, Thomas, first pastor of the *Third* Church in Boston, who avoided the peril of his uncle by coming round on land, was progenitor of most, I think, who have rendered this name, in church and state, illustrious in Massachusetts. Of the late deceased pastor of the New South Church in this city, Samuel C. Thacher, the companion and friend of my studies from childhood, no language is too powerful to express my admiration. Animæ dimidium meæ. A memoir of his father, the Rev. Dr. Peter Thacher, late of Brattle Street Church, drawn by one who knew well his duty and his undertaking, contains very minute genealogical details. See 1 Hist. Coll. VIII. 277.

Anthony settled at Cape Cod, and from him descended the late George Thacher, one of the Justices of our S. J. C.

[2] This ship, we know, sailed from Bristol, but last from Milford Haven, 22 June preceding, in company with the James, as Mather, who calls her the Angel Gabriel, tells in his journal. He says, she was of 240 tons, with 14 guns; and mentions her loss with "most of the cattle, and other goods, with one seaman; and 3 or 4 passengers did also perish therein, besides two of the passengers that died by the way."

Dartmouth ships cut all their masts at St. George. The tide
*166 rose at Naragansett fourteen feet higher than ordinary,
and drowned eight Indians flying from their wigwams.§[1]

At this time a French ship came with commission from the king of France, (as they pretended,) and took Penobscott, a Plimouth trading house, and sent away the men which were in it, but kept their goods and gave them bills for them, and bad them tell all the plantations, as far as forty degrees, that they would come with eight ships, next year, and displant them all. But, by a letter which the captain wrote to the governour of Plimouth, it appeared they had commission from Mons. Roselly, commander at the fort near Cape Breton, called La Havre, to displant the English as far as Pemaquid, and by it they professed all courtesy to us here.

Mr. Williams, pastor of Salem, being sick and not able to speak, wrote to his church a protestation, that he could not communicate with the churches in the bay; neither would he communicate with them, except they would refuse ||communion|| with the rest; but the whole church was grieved herewith.

[Large blank.]

The Dorchester men being set down at Connecticut, near the Plimouth trading house, the governour, Mr. Bradford, wrote to them, complaining of it as an injury, in regard of their possession and purchase of the Indians, whose right it was, and the Dutch sent home into Holland for commission to deal with our people at Connecticut.

September 1.] At this general court was the first grand jury, who presented above one hundred offences, and, among others, some of the magistrates.[2]

||communication||

---

[1] Hubbard has expanded this account of the tempest, 199–201. Morton's Memorial informs us, that the marks were visible many years; but his "many hundred thousands of trees" are by Hubbard reduced to "*some thousands*." Though the more moderate number be generally preferable, we need not fear, in this instance, to follow the original historian rather than the copyer. Such extent of devastation in the forest has been equalled within our memories, especially from the gale at the autumnal equinox of 1815.

[2] At this court the rate assessed is found in our Colony Records, I. 161, as

At this court Mr. Endecott made a protestation in justification of the letter formerly sent from Salem to the other churches, against the magistrates and deputies, for which he was committed; but, the same day, he came and acknowledged his fault, and was discharged.[1]

Divers lewd servants (viz., six) ran away, and stole a *167
skiff and other things. A commission was granted, at the general court, to Capt. Trask[2] to fetch them and other such from the eastward. He pursued them to the Isle of Shoals, and so to Pascataquack, where, in the night, he surprised them in a house, and brought them to Boston. At next court they were severely whipped, and ordered to pay all charges, etc.

At this court there was granted to Mr. Buckly[3] and [blank]

---

follows: — Newtown and Dorchester, £26.5, each; Boston, £25.10; Watertown, £19.10; Roxbury, £19.5; Salem, £16; Charlestown, £15; Ipswich, £14; Sagus, £11; Medford, £9.15; Newbury, £7.10; Hingham, £6; Weymouth, £4; in all, £200.

1 Mention is made of the letter on a former page. To show the degree of moderation, with which our civil rulers treated ecclesiastical subjects, I give an extract from Col. Rec. I. 163: "Whereas Mr. Roger Williams, one of the elders of the church of Salem, hath broached and divulged divers new and dangerous opinions, against the authority of magistrates; as also writ letters of defamation, both of the magistrates and churches here, and that before any conviction, and yet maintaineth the same without any retraction; it is therefore ordered, that the said Mr. Williams shall depart out of this jurisdiction within six weeks now next ensuing; which, if he neglect to perform, it shall be lawful for the governour and two of the magistrates to send him to some place out of this jurisdiction, not to return any more without license from the court."

"Mr. Samuel Sharp is enjoined to appear at the next particular court, to answer for the letter that came from the church of Salem, as also *to bring the names of those that will justify the same*, or else to acknowledge his offence, under his own hand, for his own particular."

2 He was of Salem, in the History of which town, 1 Hist. Coll. VI. 253, it is related, that he was out in the Pequod war, by which we must, I suppose, understand not Stoughton's, but Endecott's, expedition. His baptismal name was William, as the Colony Records give it among the deputies at all the general courts, from the fourth to the tenth inclusive.

3 Such is the orthography of the original MS. though the head of this family always spelt the name Bulkeley. The character of Rev. Peter Bulkley is so well known by the reader of our early books, and the labors of Eliot and Allen have so successfully transferred to their pages the truth, which a succession of reverend descendants had preserved, that it were supererogation for me to en-

merchant, and about twelve more families, to begin a town at Musketaquid, for which they were allowed six miles upon the river, and to be free from public charges three years; and it was named Concord. A town was also begun above the falls of Charles River.[1]

[Large blank.]

At the Dutch plantation, this summer, a ship's long boat was overset with a gust, and five men in her, who gat upon || her || keel, and were driven to sea four days, in which time three of them dropt off and were drowned; and the fifth day the fourth, being sore beaten, and ||[2]pained || with hunger and thirst, wil-
*168 fully fell off and was drowned. Soon after the wind came up at S. E. and carried the boat, with the fifth man, to the Long Island, and, being only able to creep on shore, he was found by the Indians, and preserved. He was grown very poor, and almost senseless, with hunger and watching, and would say, that he saw such and such come to give him meat, etc.[2]

The Plimouth men had hired the Great Hope, to go to displant the French, and regain their possession at Penobscott. The master, Mr. ||[3]Girling, || was to have for it £200. They sent ||[4]their bark || with him and about twenty men; but when they came, they found the French had notice, and had so strongly intrenched themselves, (being eighteen,) as, having spent near all their powder and shot, the bark left the ship there, and came here to advise with us what further to do; for they had lately lost another bark laden with corn, and could not spare this to send back again. The general court, being assembled, agreed to aid them with men and munition, and therefore wrote to them to send one with commission to treat with us about it, resolving to drive them out, whatsoever it should cost, (yet first

|| the || ||[2]parched || ||[3]Grig || ||[4]her back ||

---

large this note. See President Stiles's opinion, in 2 Hist. Coll. II. 260. There is a good letter of Bulkley in 3 Hist. Coll. I. 47. He came this season in the Susan and Ellen.

[1] It was afterwards named Dedham, and a very valuable history may he read in three Centennial discourses of Rev. Alvan Lamson.

[2] Mather, in book VI. of the Magnalia, appropriately called by him Thaumaturgus, has a little decorated this narrative of mental alienation.

to put them to bear the charge, if it might be;) for we saw that their neighborhood would be very dangerous to us.[1]

The next week they sent Mr. ||Prence||[2] and Capt. ||2 Standish|| to us, with commission to treat. Four of the commissioners gave them a meeting, which grew to this issue,— *169 that they refused to deal further in it, otherwise than as a common cause of the whole country, and so to contribute their part. We refused to deal in it, otherwise than as in their aid, and so at their charge; for indeed we had then no money in the treasury, neither could we get provision of victuals, on the sudden, for one hundred men, which were to be employed. So we deferred all to further counsel.

Mo. 8. 6.] Two shallops, going, laden with goods, to Connecticut, were taken in the night with an easterly storm, and cast away upon Brown's Island, near the Gurnett's Nose, and the men all drowned.[3]

Here arrived two great ships, the Defence and the Abigail,

||Pierce|| ||2 S———||

---

1 Good union followed from the common danger of the two colonies, whose preceding transactions evidently exhibit a mutual jealousy. I subjoin, from Colony Records, 162, September court, all that is there found of this important essay towards an alliance: "Agreed, that Plimouth shall be aided with men and munition to supplant the French at Penobscot. And it was ordered, that Capt. *Sellanova* shall be sent for, to confer with about this business, and recompensed out of the treasury for his pains, if he be not employed." The hard name of the engineer is quite strange to all our antiquaries of this age. It is manifestly a foreign one, probably of some Dutchman, who had seen service at home, and was now thought a fit antagonist for the enemies of the common religion. In a letter of Gov. Winthrop to his son, John, June, 1636, in our Appendix, the same person is mentioned as being arrived in the West Indies. I know not whether he was employed. The expulsion of the French was reserved for the vigorous administration of Cromwell, in 1654, when Sedgwick and Leverett succeeded with little difficulty.

2 This distinguished gentleman, whose name, though commonly in books spelt Prince, is always, as Judge Davis informed me, by himself written as Winthrop has given it, was long governour of Plimouth colony. He will be forever remembered in the pages of the new edition of Morton's Memorial. Every author, who treats of New England, is full of his praise, and my humble efforts are not needed to extend it.

3 A note in 1 Hist. Coll. VIII. 220, by the most accurate geographer of New England, remarks, that this island is become a shoal.

with Mr. Wilson, pastor of Boston, Mr. Shepard,[1] Mr. Jones,[2] and other[3] ministers; amongst others, Mr. Peter,[4] pastor of the English church in Rotterdam, who, being persecuted by the English ambassador, — who would have brought his and other churches to the English discipline, — and not having had his health these many years, intended to advise with the ministers here about his removal.

The special ||goodness|| of the Lord appeared in this, that the passengers came safe and hale in all [the] ships, though some of them long passages, — the Abigail ten weeks from
*170 Plimouth, with two hundred and twenty persons, and
many cattle, infected also with the small pox; yet, etc.[5]

There came also John Winthrop, the younger, with commis-

||providence||

---

[1] It would probably be a needless task, for me to add any thing about Shepard to what is already known in Eliot and Allen, and the authors referred to by the latter. With him, Shepard says, Wilson and Jones were in the Defence, which was very rotten, unfit for such a voyage. His autobiography is now accessible to all, in Young's Chron. of Mass.

[2] Little could be expected from my diligent inquiries, respecting this person, by one that finds nothing but his name known to Mather, who inserts it in his first classis of ministers, or Trumbull, I. 494. Both seem to be ignorant of any thing but what they learn from Winthrop. Before removing to Fairfield, Conn. he was the pastor of Concord. See, in this History, 5 of 5 month, 1636, and 6 of 2 month, 1637.

[3] Probably Flint, Carter, and Walton, mentioned by Johnson, lib. I. c. 31, as coming over this year, are here intended. Perhaps, in his work, the name of Walton is a misprint for *Waltham*, as thus Mather calls a minister, who came from England, with the prænomen William, settled at Marblehead. Flint was admitted of Boston Church 15 November, this year, a fortnight after Vane. John Winthrop, the son of our author, and the son of Sir Henry Vane, came in the Abigail, publicly.

[4] The unhappy celebrity of Hugh Peters, or Peter, as he wrote it himself, will excuse me from giving more than a reference to some of the innumerable books which furnish evidence of his labors, his errors, and his sufferings. He was executed 16 October, 1660. I suppose he got on board the Abigail, privately, in the Downs, coming from Holland.

[5] But of these 220, the names of only 180 are preserved in the custom-house list at London; and of the passengers by the Defence, only 89. No doubt, excellent reason existed for the deficiency. No minister could embark but by evasion. Flint, who came with Bulkley, was, no doubt, a subsidy man, and therefore forbidden.

sion[1] from the Lord Say, Lord Brook, and divers other great persons in England, to begin a plantation at Connecticut, and to be governour there. They sent also men and ammunition, and £2000 in money, to begin a fortification at the mouth of the river.[2]

Here came also one Mr. Henry Vane,[3] son and heir to Sir Henry Vane, comptroller of the king's house, who, being a young gentleman of excellent parts, and had been employed by his father (when he was ambassador) in foreign affairs; yet, being called to the obedience of the gospel, forsook the honors and preferments of the court, to enjoy the ordinances of Christ in their purity here. His father, being very averse to this way, (as no way savoring the power of religion,) would hardly have consented to his coming hither, but that, acquainting the king with his son's disposition and desire, he commanded him to send him hither, and gave him license for three years' stay here.

This noble gentleman, having order from the said lords and others, treated with the magistrates here, and those who were to go to Connecticut,[4] about the said design of the lords, to this issue, — that either the three towns gone thither should give place, upon full satisfaction, or else sufficient room must be found there for the lords and their companions, etc., or else they would divert their thoughts and preparations some other ways.

[Large blank.]

November 1.] Mr. Vane was admitted a member of the church of Boston.

---

1 See the commission in Trumbull, I. 497.

2 He brought his new wife, and his brother Deane, whose name is derived from Sir John Deane, brother of his mother.

3 Few men have done less good with greater reputation than this statesman, whose fame rings in history too loudly to require my aid in its diffusion. The brief, but busy exercise of his faculties here, is exhibited with sufficient minuteness by our author, in whose page is found no deficiency of respect towards the fanatic, who was too much honored, in his early years, when exalted as the rival of the father of Massachusetts.

4 In the Appendix may be seen the propositions, of which the original draft was preserved in the Historical Society's Library, Trumbull Papers, vol. XIX. page 213, until the Court Street fire of 1825.

October.] At this general court, Mr. Williams, the teacher at Salem, was again convented, and all the ministers in the bay being desired to be present, he was charged with the said two letters,—that to the churches, complaining of the magis-
*171 trates for injustice, extreme oppression, etc., and the other to his own church, to persuade them to renounce communion with all the churches in the bay, as full of antichristian pollution, etc. He justified both these letters, and maintained all his opinions; and, being offered further conference or disputation, and a month's respite, he chose to dispute presently. So Mr. Hooker was appointed to dispute with him, but could not reduce him from any of his errors. So, the next morning, the court sentenced him to depart out of our jurisdiction within six weeks, all the ministers, save one, approving the sentence; and his own church had him under question also for the same cause; and he, at his return home, refused communion with his own church, who openly disclaimed his errors, and wrote an humble submission to the magistrates, acknowledging their fault in joining with Mr. Williams in that letter to the churches against them, etc.

[Large blank.]

15.] About sixty men, women, and little children, went by land toward Connecticut with their cows, || horses, || and swine, and, after a tedious and difficult journey, arrived safe there.

[Very large blank.]

The pinnace, which Sir Richard Saltonstall sent to take possession of a great quantity of land at Connecticut, was, in her return into England, cast away upon the Isle Sable.[1] The men were kindly entertained by the French there, and had passage to Le Havre, some twenty leagues east of Cape Sable, where Monsieur commander of Roselle was governour, who entertained them very courteously, and furnished them with a shallop to return to us, and gave four of their company passage into France, but made them pay dear for their shallop; and in their return,

|| heifers ||

[1] Saltonstall attributes the loss to her detention, both at Boston and at Connecticut River. He thought he had a just claim for satisfaction. See his interesting letter, copied for 2 Hist. Coll. VIII. 42, 3.

they put into Penobscot, at such time as Girling's ship lay there; so that they were kept prisoners there till the ship was gone, and then sent to us with a courteous letter to our governour. A little before, our governour had written to him, (viz. Mons. D'Aulnay,[1]) to send them home to us; but they were come before.

It is useful to observe, as we go along, such especial *172
providences of God as were manifested for the good of these plantations.

Mr. Winslow, the late governour of Plimouth, being this year in England, petitioned the council there for a commission to withstand the intrusions of the French and Dutch, which was likely to take effect, (though undertaken by ill advice, for such precedents might endanger our liberty, that we should do nothing hereafter but by commission out of England;) but the archbishops, being incensed against him, as against all these plantations, informed the rest, that he was a separatist, etc., and that he did marry, etc., and thereupon gate him committed; but, after some few months, he petitioned the board, and was discharged.

[Very large blank.]

Another providence was in the voyage of Mr. Winthrop, the younger, and Mr. Wilson into England, who, returning in the winter time, in a small and weak ship, bound for Barnstaple, were driven by foul weather upon the coast of Ireland, not known by any in the ship, and were brought, through many desperate dangers, into Galloway, where they parted, Mr. Winthrop taking his journey over land to Dublin, and Mr. Wilson by sea, and being come within sight of Lundy, in the mouth of Severn, they were forced back by tempest to Kinsale, where some ships perished in their view. Mr. Wilson, being in Ireland, gave much satisfaction to the Christians there about New England.

---

1 Enough, the reader will probably imagine, about the French governour of that part of Acadia west of the St. Croix, or the eastern half of the present State of Maine, will be found in this History, both of his disappointments and ultimate success. A brief sketch of the whole subject of controversy between him and La Tour, in which many of our people were unhappily involved, may be seen in Hutchinson, I. 127–133. See also note 3 on page 117.

Mr. Winthrop went to Dublin, and from thence to Antrim in the north, and came to the house of one Sir John Clotworthy,[1] the evening before the day when divers godly persons were appointed to meet at his house, to confer about their voyage to New England, by whom they were thoroughly informed of all things, and received great encouragement to proceed on in their intended course. From thence he passed over into Scotland,
*173 and so through the north of England; and all the way he met with persons of quality, whose thoughts were towards New England, who observed his coming among them as a special providence of God.

November 3.] At the court of assistants, John Pratt[2] of Newtown was questioned about the letter he wrote into England, wherein he affirmed divers things, which were untrue and of ill report, for the state of the country, as that here was nothing but rocks, and sands, and salt marshes, etc. He desired respite for his answer to the next morning; then he gave it in writing, in which, by making his own interpretation of some

---

[1] This gentleman became a strenuous asserter of liberty in the long parliament, and, being too easily satisfied with deliverance from tyranny, to coincide with the designs of Cromwell, was, by that hypocrite, with many other early associates, committed to prison. From the text we may not conclude positively, that Clotworthy was one of those who thought of coming to our country; though many, of equal or higher rank and fortune, had such designs, in which most of them were prevented by the government, that had good reason afterwards, says Hume, to repent of such exercise of authority.

Of Hume's wise remark, however, the foundation is not solid, chiefly resting on so poor authority as the Magnalia, I. c. 5, 7. Hutchinson, also, mistook the weight of the document, to which he refers in Vol. I. 42. Too often he yields to Mather, his relative, more than is right. In her Court of Charles I., Lucy Aikin has settled the correct view. See her Vol. I. 472.

[2] Notice of his death will occur in our second volume, sub an. 1645. The answer, in the text alluded to, was so equivocal, that, in an epistle preserved in Hutch. Coll. 106, Sir William Martin says to Winthrop, 29 March, 1636, owning receipt of a copy from Mr. Downing, "In the main I find little difference therein from his letter." This curious apology was transcribed by me from the Colony Records, and printed in 2 Hist. Coll. VII. 126. Pratt had made a contract, in 1629, with our company in London, to come out as a surgeon for the plantation, on a salary. He removed, with most other Newtown people, to Connecticut, in company with Gov. Haynes, as I presume, from finding the same name at their first assembly of deputies in 1639. See Trumbull, I. 103. His death, by shipwreck, will be seen in a later year.

passages, and acknowledging his error in others, he gave satisfaction. This was delivered in under his own hand, and the hands of Mr. Hooker and some of the ministers, and satisfaction acknowledged under the hands of the magistrates.

Mr. Winthrop, jun., the governour appointed by the lords for Connecticut, sent a bark of thirty tons, and about twenty men, with all needful provisions, to take possession of the mouth of Connecticut, and to begin some building.

9.] About this time an open pinnace, returning from Connecticut, was cast away in Manemett Bay; but all the men (being six) were saved, and came to Plimouth, after they had wandered ten days in extreme cold and deep snow, not meeting with any Indian or other person.

26.] There came twelve men from Connecticut. They had been ten days upon their journey, and had lost one of their company, drowned in the ice by the way; and had been all starved, but that, by God's providence, they lighted upon an Indian wigwam. Connecticut River was frozen up the 15th of this month.

Mr. Hugh Peter, preaching at Boston and Salem, moved the country to raise a stock for fishing, as the only probable means to || free || us from that oppression, which the seamen and others held us under.

28.] Here arrived a small § Norsey[1] § bark, of twenty-five tons, sent by the Lords Say, etc., with one Gardiner,[2] an *174
expert engineer or work base,[3] and provisions of all sorts,

|| save ||

---

[1] I never saw this word before; but cannot doubt that it is the same gentilitial as Norwegian, or, of the North Country. *Norse* is common with the poets and others.

[2] From this person, whose name of baptism was Lyon, Gardner's Island and Bay receive their names. Trumbull, I. 61, refers to manuscripts of his, and they certainly might have assisted him with some important illustrations of the origin of the war with the Pequods, during which he commanded the fort at Saybrook. He is also spoken of with respect by Saltonstall, in the letter mentioned in our note on page 171, and by Mason in his History of that war. Gardiner's own History of the same is worth looking into. He was equally brave and intelligent.

[3] The phrase is merely a synonym.

to begin a fort at the mouth of Connecticut. She came through many great tempests; yet, through the Lord's great providence, her passengers, §twelve men, two women§[1] and goods, all safe. Mr. Winthrop had sent, four days before, a bark, with carpenters and other workmen, to take possession of the place, (for the Dutch intended to take it,) and to raise some buildings.

A great shallop, coming from Pascataquack in a N. E. wind with snow, lost her way, and was forced into Anasquam; and going out with a N. W. wind, through the unskilfulness of the men, was cast upon the rocks, and lost £100 worth of goods.

A shallop of William Lovell,[2] laden with goods to Salem, worth £100, was, by foul weather, put into Plimouth, and, coming out, the men went aboard a small bark by the way, and their shallop brake loose and was lost, and, about two months after, was found about Nawset,[3] not much hurt, and the goods were, most of them, saved by some Plimouth men, who had notice of it by the Indians.[4]

[Large blank.]

*175 10ber, 10.] The ship Rebecka, about sixty tons, came from Connecticut, and brought in her about seventy men and women, which came down to the river's mouth to meet the barks which should have brought their provisions; but, not meeting them, they went aboard the Rebecka, which, two days

---

1 This addition to the text of the first edition is from Winthrop's margin.

2 He was, probably, of Dorchester, and from him Lovell's Island, in our harbor, I presume, receives its name.

3 Plimouth people settled there about nine years after, and it has been since called Eastham. See 1 Hist. Coll. VIII. 163.

4 Of the kindness and justice, with which the colonists of Plimouth and Massachusetts had universally treated their uncivilized neighbors, this proof of the honest and friendly conduct of the aborigines towards them is the stronger, because indirect evidence. We ought not to forget, that the native inhabitants of this very spot had indulged a peculiar hatred against the English name, on account of the perfidious conduct, twenty years before, of Hunt, in kidnapping twenty of their tribe, whom he transported for sale in Spain. See the narrative in most of the books on the earlier affairs of America, from Purchas to Holmes. The invaluable work of the latter annalist quotes I. Mather, sub an. 1675, to prove that Christian blood had not been shed in hostility, before that time, in Massachusetts.

before, was frozen twenty miles up the river, but a small rain falling set her free; but coming out, she ran on ground at the mouth of the river, and was forced to unlade. They came to Massachusetts in five days, which was a great mercy of God, for otherwise they had all perished with famine, as some did.

While the Rebecka lay there, the Dutch sent a ‖sloop‖ to take possession of the mouth of the river; but our men gate two pieces on shore, and would not suffer them to land.

The 2d and 3d of this month fell a snow about knee deep, with much wind from the N. and N. E.[1]

Mr. Norton,[2] a godly man, and a preacher in England, coming with his family to the Massachusetts, the ship, wherein he was, was by contrary winds put into Plimouth, where he continued preaching to them all the winter; and although Mr. Smith, their pastor, gave over his place, that he might have it, and the church used him with all respect, and large offers, etc., yet he left them and came to Massachusetts, alleging that his spirit could not close with them, etc.

[Large blank.]

11 mo. January.] The governour and assistants met at Boston to consider about Mr. Williams, for that they were credibly informed, that, notwithstanding the injunction laid upon him (upon the liberty granted him to stay till the spring) not to go about to draw others to his opinions, he did use to entertain company in his house, and to preach to them, even of such points as he had been censured for; and it was agreed to send him into England by a ship then ready to depart. The reason was, because he had drawn above twenty persons to his opinion, and they were intended to erect a plantation about the Naragansett Bay, from whence the infection would easily spread into these churches, (the people being, many of them,

‖ship‖

1 Such depth of snow, at so early a season, though common enough in the interiour, among the hills, has not been known on the seacoast for many years.

2 The history of church and state affords abundant materials for a biography of John Norton, one of the most learned divines that came early to our country, and it has been compiled by Dr. Eliot with more than usual felicity. Mather and Emerson are more copious.

much taken with the apprehension of his godliness). Whereupon a warrant was sent to him to come presently to Boston, to be shipped, etc. He returned answer, (and divers of Salem came with it,) that he could not come without hazard of his life, etc. Whereupon a pinnace was sent with commission to Capt. Underhill, etc., to apprehend him, and carry him aboard the ship, (which then rode at Natascutt;) but, when they came at his house, they found he had been gone three days before; but whither they could not learn.[1]

*176

He had so far prevailed at Salem, as many there (especially of devout women) did embrace his opinions, and separated from the churches, for this cause, that some of their members, going into England, did hear the ministers there, and when they came home the churches here held communion with them.

This month one went by land to Connecticut, and returned safe.[2]

Mr. Hugh Peter went from place to place laboring, both publicly and privately, to raise up men to a public frame of spirit, and so prevailed, as he procured a good sum of money to be raised to set on foot the fishing business, to the value of [blank,] and wrote into England to raise as much more. The intent was to set up a magazine of all provisions and other necessaries for fishing, that men might have things at hand, and for reasonable prices; whereas now the merchants and seamen took advantage to sell at most excessive rates, (in many things two for one, etc.)

Mr. Batchellor of Sagus was convented before the magistrates. The cause was, for that, coming out of England with a small body of six or seven persons, and having since received in many more at Sagus, and contention growing between him and the greatest part of his church, (who had, with the rest, received him for their pastor,) he desired dismission for himself

---

[1] Abundant cause for rejoicing at the failure of this tyrannical order, by which the services of Williams would have been transferred to England, is found in the progress of the life of the founder of Providence.

[2] If it be intended by the author to mention this as matter of felicitation, it probably was because the journey was performed alone.

and his first members, which being granted, upon supposition that he would leave the town, (as he had given out,) he with the said six or seven persons presently ||renewed|| their old ||[2]covenant,|| intending to raise another church in Sagus; whereat the ||[3]most|| and chief of the town being offended, for that it would cross their intentions of calling Mr. Peter or some other minister, they complained to the magistrates, who, foreseeing the distraction which was like to come by this course, had *177
forbidden him to proceed in any such church way, until the cause were considered by the other ministers, etc. But he refused to desist. Whereupon they sent for him, and upon his delay, day after day, the marshal was sent to fetch him. Upon his appearance and submission, and promise to remove out of the town within three months, he was discharged.

18.] Mr. Vane and Mr. Peter, finding some distraction in the commonwealth, arising from some difference in judgment, and withal some alienation of affection among the magistrates and some other persons of quality, and that hereby factions began to grow among the people, some adhering more to the old governour, Mr. Winthrop, and others to the late governour, Mr. Dudley, — the former carrying matters with more lenity, and the latter with more severity, — they procured a meeting, at Boston, of the governour, deputy, Mr. Cotton, Mr. Hooker, Mr. Wilson, and there was present Mr. Winthrop, Mr. Dudley, and themselves; where, after the Lord had been sought, Mr. Vane declared the occasion of this meeting, (as is before noted,) and the fruit aimed at, viz. a more firm and friendly uniting of minds, etc., especially of the said Mr. Dudley and Mr. Winthrop, as those upon whom the weight of the affairs did lie, etc., and therefore desired all present to take up a resolution to deal freely and openly with the parties, and they each with other, that nothing might be left in their breasts, which might break out to any jar or difference hereafter, (which they promised to do). Then Mr. Winthrop spake to this effect: that when it pleased Mr. Vane to acquaint him with what he had observed, of the dispositions of men's minds inclining to the said faction, etc., it was very strange to him, professing solemnly that he knew not of any breach between his brother Dudley and himself,

||removed|| ||[2]covert|| ||[3]rest||

since they were reconciled long since, neither did he suspect any alienation of affection in him or others from himself, save that, of late, he had observed, that some new comers had estranged themselves from him, since they went to dwell at Newtown; and so desired all the company, that, if they had seen any thing amiss in his government or otherwise, they would deal freely and faithfully with him, and for his part he promised to take it in good part, and would endeavor, by God's grace, to amend it. Then Mr. Dudley spake to this effect: that for his part he came thither a mere patient, not with any intent to charge his brother Winthrop with any thing; for though there had been formerly some differences and breaches between them, yet they had been healed, and, for his part, he was not willing to renew them
*178 again; and so left it to others to utter their own complaints. Whereupon the governour, Mr. Haynes, spake to this effect: that Mr. Winthrop and himself had been always in good terms, etc.; therefore he was loath to give any offence to him, and he hoped that, considering what the end of this meeting was, he would take it in good part, if he did deal openly and freely, as his manner ever was. Then he spake of one or two passages, wherein he conceived, that [he] dealt too remissly in point of justice; to which Mr. Winthrop answered, that his speeches and carriage had been in part mistaken; but withal professed, that it was his judgment, that in the infancy of plantation, justice should be administered with more lenity than in a settled state, because people were then more apt to transgress, partly of ignorance of new laws and orders, partly through oppression of business and other straits; but, if it might be made clear to him, that it was an error, he would be ready to take up a stricter course. Then the ministers were desired to consider of the question by the next morning, and to set down a rule in the case. The next morning, they delivered their several reasons, which all || sorted || to this conclusion, that strict discipline, both in criminal offences and in martial affairs, was more needful in plantations than in a settled state, as tending to the honor and safety of the gospel. Whereupon Mr. Winthrop acknowledged that he was convinced, that he had failed in over much lenity and remissness, and would endeavor (by

|| served ||

God's assistance) to take a more strict course hereafter. Whereupon there was a renewal of love amongst them, and articles drawn to this effect: —

1. That there should be more strictness used in civil government and military discipline.

2. That the magistrates should (as far as might be) ripen their consultations beforehand, that their vote in public might bear (as the voice of God).

3. That, in meetings out of court, the magistrates should not discuss the business of parties in their presence, nor deliver their opinions, etc.

4. That trivial things, etc., should be || ended || in towns, etc.

5. If differences fall out among them in public meetings, they shall observe these rules: —

1. Not to touch any person differing, but speak to the cause.

2. To express their difference in all modesty and due respect to the court and such as differ, etc.

3. Or to propound their difference by way of question. *179

4. Or to desire a deferring of the cause to further time.

5. After sentence, (if all have agreed,) none shall intimate his dislike privately; or, if one dissent, he shall sit down, without showing any further distaste, publicly or privately.

6. The magistrates shall be more familiar and open each to other, and more frequent in visitations, and shall, in tenderness and love, admonish one another, (without reserving any secret grudge,) and shall avoid all jealousies and suspicions, each seeking the honor of another, and all, of the court, not opening the nakedness of one another to private persons; in all things seeking the safety and credit of the gospel.

7. To honor the governour in submitting to him the main direction and ordering the business of the court.

8. One assistant shall not seem to gratify any man in undoing or crossing another's proceedings, without due advice with him.

9. They shall grace and strengthen their under officers in their places, etc.

10. All contempts against the court, or any of the magistrates,

|| ordered ||

shall be specially noted and punished; and the magistrates shall appear more solemnly in public, with attendance, apparel, and open notice of their entrance into the court.[1]

[Very large blank.]

Mo. 12. 1.] Mr. Shepherd, a godly minister, come lately out of England, and divers other good Christians, intending to raise a church[2] body, came and acquainted the magistrates therewith, who gave their approbation. They also sent to all the neigh-
*180 boring churches for their elders to give their assistance, at a certain day, at Newtown, when they should constitute their body. Accordingly, at this day, there met a great assembly, where the proceeding was as followeth:

Mr. Shepherd and two others (who were after to be chosen to office) sate together in the elder's seat. Then the elder of them began with prayer. After this, Mr. Shepherd prayed with deep confession of sin, etc., and exercised out of Eph. v. — that he might make it to himself a holy, etc.; and also opened the cause of their meeting, etc. Then the elder desired to know of the churches assembled, what number were needful to make a church, and how they ought to proceed in this action. Whereupon some of the ancient ministers, conferring shortly together, gave answer: That the scripture did not set down any certain rule for the number. Three (they thought) were too few, be-

---

1 Though several principles of sound policy were established, the general result of this conference must, I think, be regretted. When the administration of Winthrop was impeached by Gov. Haynes for too great lenity, it seems natural that such severe tempers as Dudley, and Vane, and Peter, should unite in the attack; and as the rest of the clergy probably agreed with their ardent brother Peter, the maxims of the first governour of the colony would be overruled; but when their united influence was strong enough to compel him to acknowledge his remissness in discipline, we are bound, as in our early history we often are, to lament the undue dictation of the church. It should be remembered, that Haynes and Hooker were, at this very time, preparing to establish themselves as the Moses and Aaron of a new plantation; and they might *decently* have left Massachusetts to be governed by rules, which, though not always observed, had been found beneficial by the earlier inhabitants.

2 As the former church preferred to remove to Connecticut in its corporate state, a new church was gathered, of necessity, in their place, at Newtown. The same formality, it will be seen, was followed at Dorchester. Yet I cannot doubt, that several old members of both remained.

cause by Matt. xviii. an appeal was allowed from three; but that seven might be a fit number. And, for their proceeding, they advised, that such as were to join should make confession of their faith, and declare what work of grace the Lord had wrought in them; which accordingly they did, Mr. Shepherd first, then four others, then the elder, and one who was to be deacon, (who had also prayed,) and another member. Then the covenant was read, and they all gave a solemn assent to it. Then the elder desired of the churches, that, if they did approve them to be a church, they would give them the right hand of fellowship. Whereupon Mr. Cotton, (upon short speech with some others near him,) in the name of their churches, gave his hand to the elder, with a short speech of their assent, and desired the peace of the || Lord Jesus || to be with them. Then Mr. Shepherd made an exhortation to the rest of his body, about the nature of their covenant, and to stand firm to it, and commended them to the Lord in a most heavenly prayer. Then the elder told the assembly, that they were intended to choose Mr. Shepherd for their pastor, (by the name of the brother who had exercised,) and desired the churches, that, if they had any thing to except against him, they would impart it to them before the day of ordination. Then he gave the churches thanks for their assistance, and so left them to the Lord.[1]

At the last general court, it was referred to the military commissioners to appoint colors for ||[2]every|| company; who did accordingly, and left out the cross in all of them,[2] appointing the king's arms to be put into that of Castle Island, and *181
Boston to be the first company.

[Large blank.]

|| Lord's presence || ||[2] each ||

---

[1] Commemoration of this gathering of the present first church of Cambridge, by Rev. William Newell, its pastor, after two hundred years, is duly furnished in an admirable discourse, enriched with an appendix, containing the invaluable Register of the members, by *matchless* Jonathan Mitchell, the successor of Shepherd.

[2] When the parliament, in arms against the king, continued the use of this idolatrous emblem, by order of our court, in a few years, the red cross was restored, "till the state of England shall alter the same, which we much desire." Hazard, I. 554. I suppose the desire abated as the royal cause was depressed; for the banner was the same of the godly and the malignants.

3.] Mr. John Maverick, teacher of the church of Dorchester, died, being near sixty years of age. He was a [blank] man of a very humble spirit, and faithful in furthering the work of the Lord here, both in the churches and civil state.

24.] Mr. Winslow of Plimouth came to treat with those of Dorchester about their land at Connecticut, which they had taken from them. It being doubtful whether that place ‖were‖ within our patent or not, the Plimouth men, about three years since, had treaty with us about joining in erecting a plantation and trade there. We thought not fit to do any thing then, but gave them leave to go on. Whereupon they bought a portion of land of the Indians, and built a house there, and the Dorchester men (without their leave) were now setting down their town in the same place; but, after, they desired to agree with them; for which end Mr. ‖[2]Winslow‖ came to treat with them, and demanded one sixteenth part of their lands, and £100, which those of Dorchester not consenting unto, they brake off, those of Plimouth expecting to have due recompense after, by course of justice, if they went on. But divers resolved to quit the place, if they could not agree with those of Plimouth.[1]

[Large blank.]

25.] The distractions about the churches of Salem and Sagus, and the removal of other churches, and the great scarcity of corn, etc., occasioned a general fast to [be] proclaimed, which, because the court was not at hand, was moved by the elders of the churches, and assented unto by the ministers. The church of Boston renewed their covenant this day, and made a large explanation of that which they had first entered into, and acknowledged such failings as had fallen out, etc.

Mo. 1. 8.] A man's servant in Boston, having stolen from his master, and being threatened to be brought before the magistrates, went and hanged himself. Herein three things ‖[3]were‖ observable: 1. That he was a very profane fellow, given to cursing, etc., and did use to [go] out of the assembly,

‖was‖ ‖[2]Wilson‖ ‖[3]are‖

[1] Some reasonable satisfaction to the Plimouth people, as we learn from Trumbull, I. 66, flowed from this high sense of equity.

upon the Lord's day, to rob his master. 2. The manner *182
of his death, being with a small codline, and his knees touching the floor of the chamber, and one coming in when he was scarce dead, (who was a maid, and while she went to call out, etc., he was past recovery). 3. His discontent, arising from the long time he was to serve his master, (though he were well used). The same day came a letter from his father, out of the Bermuda, with money to buy out his time, etc.

The Rebecka came from Bermuda with thirty thousand weight of potatoes, and store of oranges and ||limes,|| which were a great relief to our people; but their corn was sold to the West Indies three months before. Potatoes were bought there for two shillings and eight pence §the bushel,§ and sold here for two pence the pound.[1]

11.] Some occasions of difference had fallen out between the church of Charlton and Mr. James, their pastor. The teacher, Mr. Simmes, and the most of the brethren, had taken offence at divers speeches of his, (he being a very melancholick man, and full of causeless jealousies, etc.,) for which they had dealt with him, both privately and publicly; but, receiving no satisfaction, they wrote to all the neighboring churches for their advice and help in the case, who, sending chosen men, (most elders,) they met there this day, and finding the pastor very faulty, yet because they had not proceeded with him in a due order, — for of the two witnesses produced, one was the accuser, — they advised, that, if they could not comfortably close, himself and such as stood on his part, (if they would,) should desire dismission, which should be granted them, for avoiding extremities; but if he persisted, etc., the church should cast him out.

30.] Mr. Allerton returned in his pinnace from the French at Penobscott. His bark was cast upon an island, and beat out her keel, and so lay ten days; yet he gate help from Pemaquid, and mended her, and brought her home.

Mr. Wither, in a vessel of fifty tons, going to Virginia, was cast away upon Long Island with a W. N. W. wind. The

||lemons||

[1] For so small a vessel, this was a very good adventure.

company (being about thirty) were, most of them, very profane persons, and in their voyage did much reproach our colony, vowing they would hang, drown, or, etc., before they would come hither again. Seven were drowned in landing; some gate in a small boat to the Dutch plantation; two were killed by the Indians, who took all such goods as they left on shore.
*183 Those who escaped, went towards Virginia in a Dutch bark, and were never heard of after; but were thought to be wrecked, by some Dutch pails, etc., which were found by the Indians thereabout.

Mo. 2. 1.] Mr. Mather[1] and others, of Dorchester, intending

---

[1] This was the father of Increase Mather, president of Harvard College, who was father of the more celebrated Cotton Mather, a name that will forever be perpetuated, while the strange contents of the Magnalia, in which are equally striking his voracious appetite and ill digestion of learning, excite the curiosity of antiquaries. Of all three sufficient accounts will be found in the Biographical Dictionary of Allen, and better still in that of Eliot. Three other sons of Richard, the gentleman named in our text, were clergymen, and are mentioned in these works, as is also a great grandson, who was a minister in Boston; but on them Allen is more minute than Eliot. Richard and his wife, Katharine, were received into Boston church 25 October preceding. He married, in his old age, the widow of the *great* Cotton, and his son, Increase, married a daughter, whence the author of the Magnalia obtained his name of baptism. From the Records of Dorchester First Church I extract this notice: —

"*Richard Mather. Anagram, A third Charmer.*

Third in New England's Dorchester
Was this ordained minister;
Second to none for fruitfulness,
Ability and usefulness.
Divine his charms, years seven times seven,
Wise to win souls from earth to heaven.
Prophet's rewards he gains above,
But great 's our loss by his remove.

Epitaph.

Sacred to God, his servant Richard Mather;
Sons like him, good and great, did call him father.
Hard to discern a difference in degree
'Twixt his bright learning and high piety.
Short time his sleeping dust lies covered down;
So can't his soul, or his deserved renown.
From's birth six lustre's and a jubilee
To his repose; but labored hard in thee,

to begin a new church there, (a great part of the old one being gone to Connecticut,) desired the approbation of the other churches and of the magistrates; and, accordingly, they assembled this day, and, after some of them had given proof of their gifts, they made confession of their faith, which was approved of; but proceeding to manifest the work of God's grace in themselves, the churches, by their elders, and the *184
magistrates, etc., thought them not meet, at present, to be the foundation of a church; and thereupon they were content to forbear to join till further consideration. The reason was, for that most of them (Mr. Mather and one more excepted) had ||builded|| their comfort of salvation upon unsound grounds, viz., some upon dreams and ravishes of spirit by fits; others upon the reformation of their lives; others upon duties and performances, etc.; wherein they discovered three special errors: 1. That they had not come to hate sin, because it was filthy, but only left it, because it was hurtful. 2. That, by reason of this, they had never truly closed with Christ, (or rather Christ with them,) but had made use of him only to help the imperfection of their sanctification and duties, and not made him their sanctification, wisdom, etc. 3. They expected to believe by some power of their own, and not only and wholly from Christ.

Those of Dorchester, who had removed their cattle to Connecticut before winter, lost the greatest part of them this winter; yet some, which came late, and could not be put over the river, lived very well all the winter without any hay. The people also were put to great straits for want of provisions. They eat acorns, and malt, and grains. They lost near £2000 worth of cattle.

7.] At a general court it was ordered, that a certain number of the magistrates should be chosen for life;[1] (the reason

||burdened||

O Dorchester, four more than thirty years.
His sacred dust with thee thine honor rears.

Obiit April 22, 1669."

Other lines, of equal value, may be seen in Johnson, lib. I. c. 32.

[1] Only three years did this council for life subsist. The occasion of the estab-

was, for that it was showed from the word of God, etc., that the principal magistrates ought to be for life). Accordingly, the 25th of the 3d mo. John Winthrop and Thomas Dudley were chosen to this place, and Henry Vane, by his place of governour, was president of this council for his year.[1] It was likewise ordered, that quarter courts should be kept in several places for ease of the people, and, in regard of the || scarcity ||
*185 of victuals, the remote towns should send their votes by proxy[2] to the court of elections; and that no church, etc., should be allowed, etc., that was gathered without consent of the churches and the magistrates.

Mr. Benjamin's[3] house burnt, and £100 in goods lost.

|| streights ||

---

lishment failed with the increase of the troubles in England; and though *the word of God* showed its propriety, jealousy was caused against the body of the magistrates, who easily avoided the unpopularity. See Hubbard, 244, who, however, copied but partially the account furnished by our author of the proceedings of the court in May, 1639. The object of this change in the constitution, I discover, not in the holy scriptures, but in Cotton's epistle to Lord Say. It was, to tempt over here some of the peers, and other leading men, who might expect at home, in due season, to be raised to the upper house, by assuring them of an equal tenure of power on this side of the ocean.

1 This sentence is in Winthrop's margin.

2 It should be remembered, that the general court, for choice of governour and assistants, had formerly consisted of the whole body of the freemen of the jurisdiction assembled at one place, but that proxies were directed at the court in March preceding to be now received, as the Records show: "It is ordered, that the general court to be holden in May next, for election of magistrates, etc. shall be holden at Boston, and that the towns of Ipswich, Newbury, Salem, Sagus, Weymouth, and Hingham, shall have liberty to stay so many of their freemen at home, for the safety of their towns, as they judge needful; and that the said freemen, that are appointed by the town to stay at home, shall have liberty, for this court, to send their voices by proxy."

Another order, immediately following, is worth transcription: "Also it is agreed, that all other towns that are nearer shall send ten of their members out of each town to the said court, completely armed with muskets, swords, shots, etc."

3 Of this person, who, from the title given him by Winthrop, and the amount of his loss by the casualty, was, we may be certain, of some consideration in the colony, I have no other information, but that he was admitted free of the company, 6 November, 1632, lived at Watertown, and died in June, 1645. His will, made in that month, and proved in the next, is in our first volume of

12.] The Charity, of Dartmouth, of one hundred and twenty tons, arrived here, laden with provisions. She came in with a strong N. W. wind, and was in great danger to have been lost between Allerton Point and Natascott; but the Lord, in mercy to his people, delivered her, after she had struck twice, and upon the ||ebb.|| Mr. Peter bought all the provisions at fifty in the hundred,[1] (which saved the country £200,) and distributed them to all the towns, as each town needed.

The church of Salem was still infected with Mr. Williams his opinions, so as most of them held it unlawful to hear in the ordinary assemblies in England, because their foundation was antichristian, and we should, by hearing, hold communion with them; and some went so far as they were ready to separate from the church upon it. Whereupon the church sent two brethren, and a letter, to the elders of the other churches, for their advice in three points: 1. Whether (for satisfying the weak) they might promise not to hear in England any false church. This was not thought safe, because then they *186
would draw them to the like towards the other churches here, who were all of opinion, that it was lawful, and that hearing was not ||[2]church|| communion. 2. If they were not better, to grant them dismission to be a church by themselves. This was also opposed, for that it was not a remedy of God's ordering; neither would the magistrates allow them to be a church, being but three men and eight women; and besides, it were dangerous to raise churches on such grounds. 3. Whether they ought then to excommunicate them, if they did withdraw, etc. This was granted, yet, withal, that if they did not withdraw or run into contempt, they ought, in these matters of difference of opinion in things not fundamental nor scandalous, etc., to bear each with other.

[Very large blank.]

||cliff|| ||[2]holding||

Probate Records, and the inventory in the second. The eldest son is named John, after his father. I presume the second or third generation removed to Norwich, Connecticut, or its neighborhood, and perhaps the alderman of that name, in this city, some years ago, was a descendant.

[1] I suppose fifty per cent. advance is meant. A letter, in the Appendix to this volume, from our author to his son, John, of 26 of this month, takes notice of this purchase, and the amoumt of provisions.

Mo. 3. 15.] Mr. Peter, preaching at Boston, made an earnest request to the church for [blank] things: 1. That they would spare their teacher, Mr. Cotton, for a time, that he might go through the Bible, and raise marginal notes upon all the knotty places of the scriptures. 2. That a new book of ||martyrs|| might be made, to begin where the other had left. 3. That a form of church government might be drawn according to the scriptures. 4. That they would take order for employment of people, (especially women and children, in the winter time;) for he feared that idleness would be the ||[2]ruin|| both of church and commonwealth.

Here arrived a ship, called the St. Patrick, belonging to Sir Thomas Wentworth,[1] deputy of Ireland, one Palmer master. When she came near Castle Island, the lieutenant of the fort went aboard her, and made her strike her flag, which the master took as a great injury, and complained of it to the magistrates, who, calling the lieutenant before them, heard the cause, and declared to the master that he had no commission so to do. And because he had made them strike to the fort, (which had then no colors ||[3]abroad||,) they tendered the master such satisfaction as he desired, which was only this, that the lieutenant, aboard their ship, should acknowledge his error, that so all the ship's company might receive satisfaction, lest the lord deputy should have been informed, that we had offered that discourtesy to his ship, which we had never offered to any before.

*187 25.] Henry Vane, Esq., before mentioned, was chosen governour; and, because he was son and heir to a privy counsellor in England, the ships congratulated his election with a volley of great shot. The next week he invited all the masters (there were then fifteen great ships, etc.,) to dinner. After they had dined, he propounded three things to them: 1. That all ships, which should come after this year, should come to an

||blank|| ||[2]vice|| ||[3]aboard||

---

[1] This friend of New England was afterwards the great Earl of Strafford, with whose labors the king was better pleased than the commons. He expiated his unpopularity on the scaffold; and the success of the unconstitutional means employed for his destruction, gave encouragement to the illegal proceedings against his master.

anchor before they came at the fort, except they did send their boat before, and did satisfy the commander that they were friends. 2. That, before they offered any goods to sale, they would deliver an invoice, etc., and give the governour, etc., twenty-four hours' liberty to refuse, etc. 3. That their men might not stay on shore (except upon necessary business) after sunset. These things they all willingly condescended unto.

31.] Mr. Hooker, pastor of the church of Newtown, and the ||most|| of his congregation, went to Connecticut. His wife was carried in a horse litter; and they drove one hundred and sixty cattle, and fed of their milk by the way.

The last winter Capt. Mason died. He was the chief mover in all the attempts against us, and was to have sent the general governour, and for this end was providing shipping; but the Lord, in mercy, taking him away, all the business fell on sleep, so as ships came and brought what and whom they would, without any question or control.[1]

Divers of the ships this spring, both out of the Downs and from Holland, came in five weeks; and Mr. Ball his ship went from hence to England the 16th of January, and saw land there in eighteen days.

One Miller, master's mate in the Hector, spake to some of our people aboard his ship, that, because we had not the king's colors at our fort, we were all traitors and ||²rebels,|| etc. The governour sent for the master, Mr. Ferne, and acquainted him with it, who promised to deliver him to us. Whereupon we sent the marshal and four sergeants to the ship for him, *188
but the master not being aboard, they would not deliver

||rest|| ||²robbers||

[1] We must always be careful to distinguish between the opinions and the principles of our fathers. The spirit of the age, in which religious controversy had borne or was bearing all its evil fruits, was not a spirit of charity; and the judgment of heaven was, by each party, perpetually invoked against the other. In the wilderness the error increased, but it increased faster at home; and much as we regret the fanaticism of the two first ages of New England, the examples of its baleful influence are more numerous and more shocking, though for a shorter season, in the native land of our ancestors. The disaster of Mason will be mentioned hereafter in more detail. Perhaps his dying declaration, of good will to our country, prevented a heavier condemnation at the tribunal of our author, as it has and will do in the judgment of later times.

him; whereupon the master went himself and brought him to the court, and the words being proved against him by two witnesses, he was committed. The next day the master, to pacify his men, who were in a great tumult, requested he might be delivered to him, and did undertake to bring him before us again the day after, which was granted him, and he brought him to us at the time appointed. Then, in the presence of all the rest of the masters, he acknowledged his offence, and set his hand to a submission,[1] and was discharged. Then the governour desired the masters, that they would deal freely, and tell us, if they did take any offence, and what they required of us. They answered, that, in regard they should be examined upon their return, what colors they saw here, they did desire that the king's colors might be ‖spread‖ at our fort. It was answered, that we had not the king's colors. Thereupon two of them did offer them freely to us. We replied, that for our part we were fully persuaded, that the cross in the ensign was idolatrous, and therefore might not set it in our ensign; but, because the fort was the king's, and maintained in his name, we thought that his own colors might be ‖[2]spread‖ there. So the governour accepted the colors of Capt. Palmer, and prom-

‖suspended‖ ‖[2]suspended‖

[1] If we should infer, from the language of this submission, that it was prepared by some *friendly* hand, we may still derive, from the incident, strong illustration of the regular discipline or severe police maintained by our fathers over the most refractory persons. I find it in Col. Rec. I. 179: "Whereas I, Thomas Millerd, have given out most false and reproachful speeches against his majesty's loyal and faithful subjects, dwelling in the Massachusetts Bay in America, saying that they were all traitors and rebels, and that I would affirm so much before the governour himself, which expressions I do confess (and so desire may be conceived) did proceed from the rashness and distemper of my own brain, without any just ground or cause so to think or speak, for which my unworthy and sinful carriage being called in question, I do justly stand committed, — my humble request therefore is, that, upon this my full and ingenuous recantation of this my gross failing, it would please the governour and the rest of the assistants, to accept of this my humble submission, to pass by my fault, and to dismiss me from further trouble; and this my free and voluntary confession I subscribe with my hand this 9th June, 1636. Thomas Millerd." A new scribe appears in the Records for one or two pages preceding this, and the change of the culprit's name might be charged to him as fairly as to our author. But in another page he has given it like Winthrop.

ised they should be set up at Castle Island. We had conferred over night with Mr. Cotton, etc., about the point. The governour, and Mr. Dudley, and Mr. Cotton, were of opinion, that they might be set up at the fort upon this distinction, *189
that it was maintained in the king's name. Others,[1] not being so persuaded, answered, that the governour and Mr. Dudley, being two of the council, and being persuaded of the lawfulness, etc., might use their power to set them up. Some others, being not so persuaded, could not join in the act, yet would not oppose, as being doubtful, etc.

Mo. 5. 9.] The governour, etc., went to Salem.

Many ships lying ready at Natascott to set sail, Mr. Peter went down and preached aboard the Hector, and the ships going forth met with an east wind, which put them in again; whereupon he stayed and kept the sabbath with them.

5.] Mr. Buckly and Mr. Jones, two English ministers, appointed this day to gather a church at Newtown, to settle at Concord. They sent word, three days before, to the governour and deputy, to desire their presence; but they took it in ill part, and thought not fit to go, because they had not come to them before, § (as they ought to have done, and as others had done before,) § to acquaint them with their purpose.

[Very large blank.]

§ Mr. Winthrop, jun., gave £5 towards the building of the meeting-house at Charlton. I sent it by James Brown.§

20.] John Gallop, with one man more, and two little boys, coming from Connecticut in a bark of twenty tons, intending to put in at Long Island to trade, and being || at || the mouth of the harbor, || [2]were || forced, by a sudden change of the wind, to bear up for Block Island or Fisher's Island, lying before Naragansett, where they espied a small pinnace, which, drawing near unto, they found to be Mr. Oldham's (an old planter, and a member of Watertown congregation, who had been long out a trading, having with him only two English boys,

|| near || || [2] was ||

---

[1] Among these others, I am sorry to observe, was Winthrop himself. See Addenda.

and two Indians of Naragansett). So they hailed || him, || but had no answer; and the deck was full of Indians, (fourteen in all,) and a canoe was gone from her full of Indians and goods. Whereupon they suspected they had killed John Oldham, and the rather, because the Indians let slip and set up sail, being two miles from shore, and the wind and tide being off the shore of the island, whereby they drove towards the main at Naragansett. Whereupon they went ahead of them, and having but two pieces and two pistols, and nothing but duck shot, they bear up near the Indians, (who stood ready armed with guns, pikes, and swords,) and let fly among them, and so
*190 galled them || [2]as || they all gate under hatches. Then they stood off again, and returning with a good gale, they stemmed her upon the quarter and almost overset her, which so frightened the Indians, as six of them leaped overboard and were drowned. Yet they durst not board her, but stood off again, and fitted their anchor, so as, stemming her the second time, they bored her || [3]bow || through with their anchor, and so sticking fast to her, they made divers shot through her, (being but inch board,) and so raked her fore and aft, as they must needs kill or hurt some of the Indians; but, seeing none of them come forth, they gate loose from her and stood off again. Then four or five more of the Indians leaped into the sea, and were likewise drowned. So there being now but four left in her, they boarded her; whereupon one Indian came up and yielded; him they bound and put into hold. Then another yielded, whom they bound. But John Gallop, being well acquainted with their skill to untie themselves, if two of them || [4]be || together, and having no place to keep them asunder, he threw him bound into [the] sea; and, looking about, they found John Oldham under an old seine, § stark naked, § his head cleft to the brains, and his hand and legs cut as if they had been cutting them off, and yet warm. So they put him into the sea; but could not get to the other two Indians, who were in a little room underneath, with their swords. So they took the goods which were left, and the sails, etc., and towed the boat away; but night coming on, and the wind rising, they were forced

|| them || || [2]that || || [3]boom || || [4]were ||

to turn her off, and the wind carried her to the Naragansett shore.[1]

26.] The two Indians, which were with Mr. Oldham, and one other, came from Canonicus, the chief sachem of Naragansett, with a letter from Mr. Williams to the governour, to certify him what had befallen Mr. Oldham, and how grievously they were afflicted, and that Miantunnomoh was gone, with seventeen canoes and || two hundred ||[2] men, to take revenge, etc. But, upon examination of the Indian who was brought prisoner[3] to us, we found that all the sachems of the Nara- *191
gansett, except Canonicus and Miantunnomoh, were the contrivers of Mr. Oldham's death; and the occasion was, because he went to make peace, and trade with the Pekods last year, as is before related. The prisoner said also, that Mr. Oldham's two Indians were acquainted with it; but, because they were sent as messengers from Canonicus, we would not imprison them. But the governour wrote back to Mr. Williams to let the Naragansetts know, that we expected they should send us the two boys, and take revenge upon the islanders; and withal gave Mr. Williams a caution to look to himself, if we should have occasion to make war upon the Naragansetts, for Block Island was under them. And the next day, 27, he wrote to Canonicus by one of those two Indians, and that he had suspicion of him, etc., yet he had sent him back, because he was a messenger, but did expect that, if he should send for the said two Indians, he should send them to us to clear themselves.

30.] Mr. Oldham's two boys were sent home by one of Miantunnomoh his men, with a letter from Mr. Williams, signifying that Miantunnomoh had caused the sachem of Niantick

|| twenty ||

[1] Prince, though usually accurate in chronology to a proverb, in his introduction to Mason's History of the Pequot war, printed at Boston, 1736, republished in our 2 Hist. Coll. VIII. has, page 123, made the murder of Oldham a year earlier.

[2] It would have been no bold exertion of conjectural criticism, to change the reading of the former edition in this place, since a fleet of seventeen sail, even of canoes, would, by *twenty* persons, be weakly manned for warlike revenge; but I assure the reader the MS. was plain.

[3] He is, I presume, the one whom Gallop brought, the *first* taken, the next being thrown overboard.

to send to Block Island for them; and that he had near one hundred fathom of wampom and other goods of Mr. Oldham's, which should be reserved for us; and that three of the seven, which were drowned, were sachems; and one of the two, which were hired by the sachem of Niantick, was dead also. So we wrote back to have the rest of those, which were accessory, to be sent to us, and the rest of the goods, and that he should tell Canonicus and Miantunnomoh, that we held them innocent; but that six other under-sachems were guilty, etc.

Mo. 6. 3.] Samuel Maverick, who had been in Virginia near twelve months, now returned with two pinnaces, and brought some fourteen heifers, and about eighty goats, (having lost ||above|| twenty goats by the way). .One of his pinnaces was about forty tons, of cedar, built at ||[2]Barbathes,|| and brought to Virginia by Capt. Powell, who there dying, she was sold for a small matter. There died in Virginia, (by his relation,) this last year, above eighteen hundred, and corn was there at twenty shillings the bushel, the most of the people having lived a great time of nothing but purslain, etc. It is very strange, what was related by him and many others, that, above sixty miles up James River, they dig nowhere but they find the ground full of oyster shells, and fishes' bones, etc.; ||[3]yea,|| he affirmed that he saw the bone of a whale taken out of the earth (where they digged for a well) eighteen feet deep.

*192 8.] Lieutenant Edward Gibbons,[1] and John Higgin-

||about|| ||[2]blank|| ||[3]yet||

---

[1] Edward Gibbons is named with honor in Eliot's, but not in Allen's Dictionary. He was early admitted into the Boston church, being No. 113, and his piety was probably more approved, because he had belonged to the irregular adventurers of Mount Wollaston. His name very frequently occurs in this History. He was deputy, several years, for Boston, made major general of all our forces, 1649, and in 1650,—not 1644, as Eliot has it,—attained to the high rank of being an assistant. Death closed his services 9 December, 1654. In our Probate Records, II. 147, the inventory of his estate shows a considerable fortune for those times,—£535.6.7; yet the next information is of a special commission, resembling much those of our days, on account of its insolvency. Correction of error in amount of this inventory is offered in Ed. 2 of the Hist. of the Art. Co., p. 60, as if it should be £294.19.6, and the date of return is made 15 of December, 1654. But the editor of that work should have seen on

son,[1] with Cutshamekin, the sagamore of Massachusetts, were sent to Canonicus to treat with him about the murder of John Oldham. 13. They returned, being very well accepted, and good success in their business. They observed in the sachem much state, great command over his men, and marvellous wisdom in his answers and the carriage of the whole treaty, clearing himself and his neighbors of the murder, and offering assistance for revenge of it, yet upon very safe and wary conditions.[2]

25.] The governour and council, having lately assembled the rest of the magistrates and ministers, to advise with them about doing justice upon the Indians for the death of Mr. Oldham, and all agreeing that it should be attempted with expedition, did this day send forth ninety men, distributed to four commanders, — Capt. John Underhill, Capt. Nathaniel Turner,[3] Ensign Jenyson, and Ensign Davenport; and over them all, as general, John Endecott, Esq., one of the assistants, was sent. They were embarked in three pinnaces, and carried two shallops and two Indians with them. They had commission to put to death the men of Block Island,[4] but to spare the women and

---

the page beyond that at which he stopped that the return was on 30 December, and my amount in the former edition was right within a half penny, of which I confess the omission. Gibbons had been too adventurous in the great undertakings of La Tour, and was, beside, unfortunate in trade. An idle tale of his being found in a great ship, 17 July, 1640, in the arctic ocean, near Behring's Straits, when he was five days before in Boston, acting as a selectman, was used by an able writer in the N. A. Rev. for Jan., 1839, p. 131, and explained in the No. for April following, p. 559.

[1] Of this gentleman, who became afterwards a minister of high respectability in his father's place at Salem, and survived all of his generation in the pulpit, good accounts are furnished by Eliot and Allen.

[2] From the minuteness of his description of the Indian court, I think Johnson must have accompanied these ambassadors. See book II. c. 6, of the Wonder-working Providence.

[3] He was representative, in the six first general courts, from Sagus or Lynn; but we have not, except his disaster by fire, mentioned by our author under date of January, 1636–7, any further account of him, than the present service with Endecott.

[4] No degree of veneration for our fathers can lead to hesitation in coinciding with a remark I find in a copy of the first part of this History, formerly owned by Dr. Belknap, that these were "sanguinary orders." The numbers of the island must have been so small, that it was not matter of necessity; and per-

*193 children, and to bring them away, and to take possession of the island; and from thence to go to the Pequods to demand the murderers of Capt. Stone and other English, and one thousand fathom of wampom for damages, etc., and some of their children ||as|| hostages, which if they should refuse, they were to obtain it by force. No man was impressed for this service, but all went voluntaries.

26.] Miantunnomoh, sachem of Naragansett, sent a messenger to us, with a letter from Mr. Williams, to signify to us, that they had taken one of the Indians, who had broken prison and was escaped away, and had him safe for us, when we would send for him, (we had before sent to him ||[2]to|| that end;) and the other (being also of Block Island) he had sent away, (not knowing, as it seemed, that he had been our prisoner,) according to their promise, that they would not entertain any of that island, which should come to them. But we conceived it was rather in love to him; for he had been his servant formerly.

We sent for the two Indians. One was sent us; the other was dead before the messengers came.

A ship of one hundred and twenty tons was built at Marblehead, and called the Desire.[1]

||for|| ||[2]for||

---

haps we may attribute the cruel direction chiefly to the limited knowledge of the new governour.

[1] Being furnished with the original bill of particulars for part of the outfits of this ship, signed William *Peirse*, I transcribe it: "The ship Desire, or the owners thereof, are debited to account of the bark Warwick, or her owners, for these particulars following, taken by order of the Gov. Winthrop:—

1636.	Three falcons and one falconet, cwt. 38.3.0, with the old carriages, at 10*s*.6, per cwt.	£21.5.10
	An old poop lanthorn, 5*s*. and a small crow of iron, 2*s*.6.	7. 6
	Two spindles for vanes, 18*d*. a pump bolt and a wooden brake, all	2. 2
	A small anchor stock, 4*s*. a pistol barrel, 6*d*. and three small tackle hooks, 12*d*. all is	5. 6
	A copper funnel, 6*s*., 2 sponge staves, a rammer and a ladle, all	11. 0
	Eleven falcon shot, 4*s*. a small bell, 3*s*.	7. 0
	A small anchor, esteemed at	2.0. 0
		£24.19. 0

7ber, 8.] At a general court, a levy was made of £1200 to pay the country's debts.[1]

The trade of beaver and wampom was to be farmed, and all others restrained from trading.

23.] A new church was gathered at Dorchester, with approbation of the magistrates and elders, etc.[2] *194

August 24.] John Endecott, Esq., and four captains under him, with twenty men a-piece, set sail. They arrived at Block Island the last of the same. The wind blowing hard at N. E. there went so great a surf, as they had much to do to land; and about forty Indians were ready upon the shore to entertain them with their arrows, which they shot ||oft|| at our men; but, being armed with ||[2]corslets,|| they had no hurt, only one was lightly hurt upon his neck, and another near his foot. So soon as ||[3]one man|| leaped on shore, they all fled. The island is about ten miles long, and four broad, full of small hills, and all overgrown with brush-wood of oak, — no good timber ||[4]in|| it, — so as they could not march but in one file and in the narrow paths.[3] There were two plantations, three miles in sunder, and about sixty wigwams, — some very large and fair, — and ||[5]above|| two hundred acres of corn, some gath-

||off|| ||[2]croslets|| ||[3]our men were|| ||[4]on|| ||[5]about||

---

[1] The apportionment upon the several towns does not appear, it being left to the discretion of a committee. So heavy a contribution could not be made at once, and the order of court was, "one half at three months, and the other at a time to be appointed at the next session."

[2] Being written in the margin, with the day, but not the month, given, this sentence left an uncertainty, from inspection, whether August, to which the subsequent paragraph refers, or September, which had accidentally obtained precedence, were the true date. But the Dorchester Records prove it to be the earlier month. The author wished to bring into one view the whole story of Endecott's expedition, and therefore, after the report of proceedings at September court, inserted the story of the campaign with the marginal date of the day when the fleet departed. Hubbard, 274, copying it, made a careless transcript of the day of the court in the above recital, and neglected, as he usually did, to seek collateral information.

[3] Dr. Stiles, president of Yale College, one of the most diligent antiquaries our country has furnished, made a hasty collation of some parts of the former edition with the original MS. and in this place read *passes*. I am convinced of the correctness of the text.

ered and laid on heaps, and the rest standing. When they had spent two days in searching the island, and could not find the Indians, they burnt their wigwams, and all their matts, and some corn, and staved seven canoes, and departed. They could not tell what men they killed, but some were wounded and carried away by their fellows.

Thence they went to the mouth of the Connecticut, where they lay wind-bound four days, and taking thence twenty men and two shallops, they sailed to the Pequot harbor, where an Indian came to them in a canoe, and demanded what they were, and what they would have. The general told him, he came from the governour of Massachusetts to speak with their sachems. He told him, Sassacus was gone to Long Island. Then he bade him go tell the other sachem, etc. So he departed; and in the mean time our men landed, but with much danger, if the Indians had made use of their advantage,
*195 for all the shore was high, rugged rocks, etc. Then the messenger returned, and the Indians began to gather about our men till there were about three hundred of them; and some four hours past while the messenger went to and fro, bringing still excuses for the sachem's not coming. At ||last|| the general told the messenger, and the rest of the Indians near, the particulars of his commission, and sent him to tell the sachem, that if he would not come to him, nor yield to those demands, he would fight with them. The messenger told him, that the sachem would meet him, if our men would lay down their arms, as his men should do their bows, etc. When the general saw they did but dally, to gain time, he bad them be gone, and shift for themselves; for they had dared the English to come fight with them, and now they were come for that purpose. Thereupon they all withdrew. Some of our men would have made a shot at them, but the general would not suffer them; but when they were gone out of musket shot, he marched after them, supposing they would have stood to it awhile, as they did to the Dutch. But they all fled, and shot at our men from the thickets and rocks, but did us no harm. Two of them our men killed, and hurt others. So they marched up to their town, and burnt all their wigwams and matts, but their corn being

||length||

standing, they could not spoil it. At night they returned to their vessels, and the next day they went ashore on the west side of the river, and burnt all their wigwams, and spoiled their canoes; and so set sail, and came to the Naragansett, where they landed their men, and, the 14th of 7ber, they came all safe to Boston, which was a marvellous providence of God, that not a hair fell from the head of any of them, nor any sick or feeble person among them.[1] As they came by Naragansett, Cutshamakin, an Indian, who went with them for an interpreter, who, being armed with a ||corslet|| and a piece, had crept into a swamp and killed a Pequot, and having flayed off the skin of his head, he sent it to Canonicus, who presently sent it to all the sachems about him, and returned many thanks to the English, and sent four fathom of wampom to Cutshamakin.

The soldiers who went were all voluntaries, and had only their victuals provided, but demanded no pay. The whole charge of the voyage came to about £200. The seamen had all wages.

The Naragansett men told us after, that thirteen of the *196
Pequods were killed, and forty wounded; and but one of Block Island killed.[2]

At the last general court, order was taken to restrain the trade with the Indians, and the governour and council appointed to let it to farm, for a rent to be paid to the treasury.

The inhabitants of Boston, who had taken their farms and lots at Mount Woollaston, finding it very burdensome to have their business, etc. so far off, desired to gather a church there. Many meetings were about it. The great let was, in regard it was given to Boston for upholding the town and church there, which end would be frustrate by the removal of so many chief

||croslet||

[1] Yet I find, at the general court in October, a grant of £5 to "George Munnings, in regard of the loss of his eye in the voyage to Block Island;" and an addition to that grant was made, on the same day, of the fines imposed upon members in that session of four days, for absence at the hour of meeting in the morning, amounting to £3 more.

[2] One prisoner was, by order of court, made a slave for life. If a man, he was preserved contrary to the instructions of the troops, and perhaps against his own desire.

men as would go thither. For helping of this, it was propounded, that such as dwelt there should pay six-pence the acre, yearly, for such lands as lay within a mile of the water, and three-pence for that which lay further off.

[Very large blank.]

A ship of Barnstaple arrived here with eighty heifers.

Another from Bristol arrived, a fortnight after, with some cattle and passengers; §but she had delivered most of her cattle and passengers§ at Pascataquack for Sir Ferdinando Gorge[1] his plantation at Aquamenticus.

Canonicus sent word of some English, whom the Pequods had killed at Saybrook; and Mr. Williams wrote, that the Pequods and Naragansetts were at ||truce,|| and that Miantunnomoh told him, that the Pequods had labored to persuade them, that the English were minded to destroy all Indians. Whereupon we sent for Miantunnomoh to come to us.

[Very large blank.]

Another windmill was erected at Boston, and one at Charlestown; and a watermill at Salem, and another at Ipswich, and another at Newbury.[2]

[Very large blank.]

||war||

---

[1] I take this opportunity of printing the name as Winthrop wrote it, though usually spelt as two syllables. Probably the family had, in early times, as the old books, and Collins's Peerage, give it occasionally, used the writing of Gorge; and the old grammar, for the possessive case, employing the pronominal *his*, led them and all others to dignify it by the final *s*.

[2] With this paragraph closes the regular sequence of narrative in the first volume of MS. For the many happy hours and days spent upon it, no slight share of veneration is by me felt and acknowledged.

§ A CONTINUATION[1] *197

OF THE

HISTORY OF NEW ENGLAND. §

1636.

8ber.] After Mr. Endecott and our men were departed from the Pequod, the twenty men of Saybrook lay wind-bound there, and went to fetch some of the Indians' corn; and having fetched every man one sackful to their boat, they returned for more, and having loaded themselves, the Indians set upon them. So they laid down their corn and gave fire upon them, and the Indians shot arrows at them. The place was open for the distance of musket shot, and the Indians kept the covert, save when they || came || forth, about ten at a time, and discharged their arrows. The English put themselves into a single file, and some ten only (who had pieces ||[2]which || could reach them) shot; the others stood ready to keep them from breaking in upon our men. So they continued the most part of the afternoon. Our men killed some of them, as they supposed, and hurt others; and they shot only one of ours, and he was armed,[2]

|| ran || ||[2] that ||

---

[1] Deeply is the loss of the author's *second* volume of his MS. History regretted by me. On the thirteenth page of my next volume closes the perfect verification of the author's text by collation, though the notes for the lost part of it were saved, when the text was destroyed by fire. Any inquisitive reader can verify only that part of this work which is contained in the first and third volumes of the original MS. of Winthrop, preserved in the Library of the Mass. Historical Society.

[2] The meaning is, with defensive armor. Back and breast pieces of iron were then commonly worn. Those *without* arms had muskets.

all the rest being without arms. He was shot through the leg. Their arrows were all shot compass, so as our men, standing single, could easily see and avoid them; and one was employed to gather up their arrows. At last they emptied their sacks, and retired safe to their boat.

About two days after, five men of Saybrook went up the river about four miles, to fetch hay in a meadow on Pequot
*198 side. The grass was so high as some Pequots, being hid in it, set upon our men, and one, that had hay on his back, they took; the others fled to their boat, one of them having five arrows in him, (but yet recovered). He who was taken was a godly young man, called [blank] Butterfield; (whereupon the meadow was named Butterfield Meadow).[1] About fourteen days after, six of Saybrook, being sent to keep the house in their corn-field, about two miles from the fort, three of them went forth on fowling, (which the lieutenant had *strictly* forbidden them). Two had pieces, and the third only a sword. Suddenly about one hundred Indians ||came|| out of the covert, and ||[2]set|| upon them. ||[3]He|| who had the sword brake through them, (and received only two shot, not dangerous,) and escaped to the house, which was not a bow-shot off, and persuaded the other two to follow him; but they stood still till the Indians came and took them, and carried them away with their pieces. Soon after they burnt down the said house, and some outhouses and haystacks within a bow-shot of the fort, and killed a cow, and shot divers others; but they all came home with the arrows in them.[2]

21.] Miantunnomoh, the sachem of Naragansett, (being sent for by the governour,) came to Boston with two of Canonicus's sons, and another sachem, and near twenty sanaps. Cutshamakin gave us notice the day before. The governour sent

||rose|| ||[2]shot|| ||[3]the man||

---

[1] Hubbard, 252, after faithful transcription of this narrative, of the fate of Butterfield, has added from Ovid, Icarus Icariis nomina *dedit* aquis. We should be well pleased, did other parts of his volume show equal attention to the reader's gratification.

[2] Lyon Gardiner's narrative is very animated; and his objection to the policy of the war at *that* time, and animadversion on Endecott's conduct of it, show much sound judgment. See 3 Mass. Hist. Coll. III. 136, and X. 173.

twenty musketeers to meet him at Roxbury. He came to Boston about noon. The governour had called together most of the magistrates and ministers, to give countenance to our proceedings, and to advise with them about the terms of peace. It was dinner time, and the sachems and their council dined by themselves in the same room where the governour dined, and their sanaps were sent to the inn. After dinner, Miantunnomoh declared what he had to say to us in [blank] propositions, which were to this effect: — That they had always loved the English, and desired firm peace with us: That they would continue in war with the Pequods and their confederates, till they were subdued; and desired we should so do: They would deliver our enemies to us, or kill them: That if any of theirs should kill our cattle, that we would not kill them, but cause them to make satisfaction: That they would now make a firm peace, and two months hence they would send us a present.

The governour told them, they should have answer the *199
next morning.

In the morning we met again, and concluded the peace upon the articles underwritten, which the governour subscribed, and they also subscribed with their marks, and Cutshamakin also. But because we could not well make them understand the articles perfectly, we agreed to send a copy of them to Mr. Williams, who could best interpret them to them. So, after dinner, they took leave, and were conveyed out of town by some musketeers, and dismissed with a volley of shot.

THE ARTICLES.

1. A firm peace between us and our friends of other plantations, (if they consent,) and their confederates, (if they will observe the articles, etc.,) and our posterities.

2. Neither party to make peace with the Pequods without the other's consent.

3. Not to harbor, etc., the Pequods, etc.

4. To put to death or deliver over murderers, etc.

5. To return our fugitive servants, etc.

6. We to give them notice when we go against the Pequods, and they to send us some guides.

7. Free trade between us.

8. None of them to come near our plantations during the wars with the Pequods, without some Englishman or known Indian.

9. To continue to the posterity of both parties.

The governour of Plimouth wrote to the deputy,[1] that we had occasioned a war, etc., by provoking the Pequods, and no more, and about the peace with the Naragansetts, etc. The deputy took it ill, (as there was reason,) and returned answer accordingly, and made it appear, 1. That there was as much done as could be expected, considering they fled from us, and we could not follow them in our armour, neither had any to guide us in their country. 2. We went not to make war upon them, but to do justice, etc., and having killed thirteen of them for four or five, which they had murdered of || ours, || and destroyed sixty wigwams, etc., we were not much behind with them. 3. They had no cause to glory over us, when they saw that they could not save § themselves nor § their houses and corn from so few of ours. 4. If we had left but one hun-
*200 dred of them living, those might have done us as much hurt as they have or are likely to do. 5. It was very likely they would have taken notice of our advantage against them, and would have sitten still, or have sought peace, if God had not deprived them of common reason.

About the middle of this month, John Tilley, master of a bark, coming down Connecticut River, went on shore in a canoe, three miles above the fort, to kill fowl; and having shot off his piece, many Indians arose out of the covert and took him, and killed one other, who was in the canoe. This Tilley was a very stout man, and of great understanding.[2] They cut off his hands, and sent them before, and after cut off his feet. He lived three days after his hands were cut off; and themselves confessed, that he was a stout man, because he cried not in his torture.

About this time two houses were burnt, and all the goods in

|| us ||

---

1 Winthrop had not mentioned his own election to the second place.

2 Lyon Gardiner does not afford us much support of this character of Tilley.

them, to a great value; one was one Shaw at Watertown, and the other one Jackson of Salem, both professors, and Shaw the day before admitted of the former church. This was very observable in Shaw,[1] that he concealed his estate, and made show as if he had been poor, and ‖was‖ not clear of some unrighteous passages.

One Mrs. Hutchinson,[2] a member of the church of Boston, a woman of a ready wit and bold spirit, brought over with her two dangerous errors: 1. That the person of the Holy Ghost dwells in a justified person. 2. That no sanctification can help to evidence to us our justification. — From these two grew many branches; as, 1, Our union with the Holy Ghost, so as a Christian remains dead to every spiritual action, and hath no gifts nor graces, other than such as are in hypocrites, nor any other sanctification but the Holy Ghost himself.

[Large blank.]

There joined with her in these opinions a brother of *201
hers, one Mr. Wheelwright,[3] a silenced minister sometimes in England.

[Large blank.]

‖went‖

---

[1] In the original first stood *both*, instead of *Shaw; they*, instead of *he; their*, instead of *his; they*, instead of *he;* and *were*, instead of *was*, in the progress of the sentence. The alteration was made by Winthrop. We may therefore conclude, that the report against Jackson's character was unfounded, and that he did not *deserve* to have his house and goods burnt by accident.

[2] Being descended from this lady, the editor feels not at liberty to indulge his pen in a memoir, of which all benefit is indeed anticipated by the more honorable labors of a nearer relative, the late Gov. Hutchinson. Time has abated all the venom of the accusations against her, and the futility of most of them will forever forbid the inquiry of reason. Mather, in the middle age, and Eliot, of the present, 1 Hist. Coll. IX. 28–30, give her great credit, as in our text, for powers of mind; and all are strengthened by the orthodox contemporary, Johnson, lib. I. c. 42, who calls her "the masterpiece of women's wit."

[3] A just estimate of this distinguished gentleman may readily be formed from the pages of this History and the volumes of Hutchinson and Eliot. His long life afforded him a triumph over the injustice of intolerance, which attempted hardly any other cure for his errors than banishment. Hubbard marks his death about 1681. Some pleasure may be derived from a jeu de môt of Johnson, to whom we are usually obliged to refer for less valuable qualities. In his verses to the honor of Wilson, alluding to the opposition he encountered

25.] The other ministers in the bay, hearing of these things, came to Boston at the time of ||a|| general court, and entered conference in private with them, to the end they might know the certainty of these things; that if need were, they might write to the church of Boston about them, to prevent (if it were possible) the dangers, which seemed hereby to hang over that and the rest of the churches. At this conference, Mr. Cotton was present, and gave satisfaction to them, so as he agreed with them all in the point of sanctification, and so did Mr. Wheelwright; so as they all did hold, that sanctification did help to evidence justification. The same he had ||[2]delivered|| plainly in public, divers times; but, for the indwelling of the person of the Holy Ghost, he held that still, *as some others of the ministers did,* but not ||[3]union|| with the person of the Holy Ghost, *(as Mrs. Hutchinson and others did,)* so as to amount to a personal union.

[Blank.]

*202 Mr. Cotton, being requested by the general court, with some other ministers, to assist some of the magistrates in compiling a body of fundametal laws, did this court, present a model of Moses his judicials, compiled in an exact

||the|| ||[2]declared|| ||[3]very man||

---

from the supporters of Mrs. Hutchinson, the author of Wonder-working Providence of Zion's Saviour says,

"They thee deprave, thy ministry despise;
By thy thick utterance seek to call men back
From hearing thee: but Christ for thee did rise,
And turned the *wheel-right* over them to crack."

From our Town Records I find, that a daughter of Wheelwright was, in December, 1660, married to Samuel Maverick, soon after one of the royal commissioners to New England. Cotton Mather says, Belknap's New Hampshire, III. Appendix 1., that a daughter of this pilgrim informed him, that her father came in the same ship with Whiting of Lynn; and if this were his first appearance in our country, the authenticity of the famous Indian deed to him, for which, in the same letter, the credulous author of the Magnalia argues, must be rejected. That letter is well worth reading, as an admirable specimen of feeble argument; but the other evidence in the cause is irresistible; and it is not necessary to found an opinion on the incompetency of the advocate. Wheelwright and his wife, Mary, were admitted of Boston church 12 June, 1636, which was soon after arrival.

method, which were taken into further consideration till the next general court.

30.] Some of the church of Boston, being of the opinion of Mrs. Hutchinson, had labored to have Mr. Wheelwright to be called to be a teacher there. It was propounded the last Lord's day, and was moved again this day for resolution. One[1] of the church stood up and said, he could not consent, etc. His reason was, because the church being well furnished already with able ministers, whose spirits they knew, and whose labors God || had || blessed in much love and sweet peace, he thought it not fit (no necessity urging) to put the welfare of the church to the least hazard, as he feared they should do, by calling in one, whose spirit they knew not, and one who seemed to dissent in judgment, and instanced in two points, which he delivered in a late exercise there; 1. That a believer was more than a creature. 2. That the person of the Holy Ghost and a believer were united. Hereupon the governour spake, that he marvelled at this, seeing Mr. Cotton had lately approved his doctrine. To this Mr. Cotton answered, that he did not remember the first, and desired Mr. Wheelwright to explain his meaning. He denied not the points, but showed upon what occasion he delivered them. Whereupon, there being an ||[2]endeavor|| to make a reconciliation, the first replied, that, although Mr. Wheelwright and himself might likely agree about the point, and though he thought reverendly of his godliness and abilities, so as he could be content to live under such a ministry; yet, seeing he was apt to raise doubtful disputations, he could not consent to choose him to that place. Whereupon the church gave way, that he might be called to a new church, to be gathered at Mount Woollaston, ||[3]now|| Braintree.[2]

Divers of the brethren took offence at the said speech against Mr. Wheelwright; whereupon the same brother spake in the congregation the next day to this effect: That, hearing that some of the brethren were offended at his former speech,

|| hath || ||[2]indication|| ||[3]near||

[1] This, we cannot doubt, was Winthrop himself.

[2] A later hand, I suspect Mather's, wrote the two last words.

and for that offences were dangerous, he was desirous to give satisfaction. The offence, he said, was in three things: 1. For
*203 that he had charged the brother in public, and for a thing so long since delivered, and had not first dealt with him privately. For this he acknowledged it was a failing; but the occasion was, that, when he heard the points delivered, he took them in a good sense, as spoken figuratively, seeing the whole scope of his doctrine was sound, and savouring of the spirit of God; but hearing, very lately, that he was suspected to hold such opinions, it caused him to think, he spake as he meant. The 2d cause of offence was, that in his speech appeared some bitterness. For that he answered, that they well knew his manner of speech ||was|| always earnest in things, which he conceived to be serious; and professed, that he did love that brother's person, and did ||[2]honor|| the gifts and graces of God in him. The 3d was, that he had charged him to have held things which he did not. For this he answered, that he had spoken since with the said brother; and for the two points, — that ||[3]a|| believer should be more than a creature, and that there should be a personal union between the Holy Ghost and a believer, — he had denied to hold either of them; but by necessary consequence, he doth hold them both; for he holds, (said he,) that there is a real union with the person of the Holy Ghost, and then of necessity it must be personal, and so a believer must be more than a creature, viz., God-man, even Christ Jesus. For though, in a true union, the two terms may still remain the same, etc., as between husband and wife, he is a man still, and she a woman, (for the union is only in sympathy and relation,) yet in a real or personal union it is not. Now, whether this were agreeable to the doctrine of the church or not, he left to the church to judge; hoping that the Lord would direct our teacher to clear these points fully, as he had well done, in good measure, already. Withal he made this request to the ||[4]brother,|| (which he said he did seriously and affectionately,) that, seeing these ||[5]variances|| grew (and some estrangement withal) from some words and phrases, which were of ||[6]human invention,|| and tended to doubtful disputation, rather than to edification, and had no footing in

||as|| ||[2]know|| ||[3]the|| ||[4]teacher ||[5]uneasinesses|| ||[6]known intention||

scripture, nor had been in use in the purest churches for three hundred years after Christ, — that, for the peace of the church, etc., they might be forborn; (he meant, person of the Holy Ghost, and real union;) and concluded, that he did not intend to dispute the matter, (as not having place or calling thereunto then;) yet, if any brother desired to see what light he walked by, he would be ready to impart it to him. How this was taken by the congregation, did not appear, for no man *204
spake to it.[1]

A day or two after, the same brother wrote his mind fully, with such scriptures and arguments as came to hand, and sent it to Mr. Cotton.

(9.) 8.] A new church was gathered at Sagus, now Lynn. The governour and deputy were not there, being letted by the coming in of a ship, and other occasions. It held the company two days, Mr. Whiting,[2] who was to be the pastor, being very

---

[1] On this subject the prudent advice of our author has, in general, prevailed in New England; and the personality of the Holy Spirit, with other metaphysical or barbarous terminology "of human invention," has seldom, before the last age, entered into the controversial labors of our divines, for whom the language of the scriptures, in their original tongues, appeared sufficient. But Winthrop was less judicious in his conduct than in advice; for, having obtained from Wheelwright a denial of his holding the two dangerous points, that a believer was more than a creature, and that there was a personal union between the Holy Spirit and a believer, he should have been contented. Unhappily he proceeded to prove, that, by *necessary consequence*, both opinions were maintained by the heresiarch of Braintree. We shall never have peace in the church, if muddy-headed religionists are to be made answerable for inferences, which themselves do not deduce from their dogmas. "*Calvinism run to seed*" became, in the view of many Christians, a convenient periphrase for antinomianism; and the creed of the predestinarian, to which one or more of the articles of the Church of England makes near, and the catechism of the Westminster Assembly a nearer approach, is often charged with all the dangerous absurdities of the heathen notions of fate.

[2] We may be very confident, that this notion of our author, of the *unskilfulness* in church matters of the Rev. Samuel Whiting, is an error. He had been in the country but a few months, and Winthrop probably contracted a prejudice against him from his going so soon to join the company of poor Bachellor, which had been subjected to animadversion for its irregularities. It is strange, that Eliot omitted him in his Dictionary; but his memory is duly honoured by Hubbard, 194, Johnson, lib. I. c. 38, and, above all, Mather, III. 156. In the great controversy about the Third, or Old South Church, in Boston, he and his

unskilful in church matters, and those who were to be members not fit for such a work. At last six were accepted, with Mr. Whiting, but with much ado.

12.] A commission was sent out of the chancery in England to some private men here, to examine witnesses in a cause depending || there; || but nothing was done in it, nor any return made.[1]

[Large blank.]

*205 17.] Two ships arrived here from London, and one a week before. They were full of passengers, — men, women, and children. One of them had been from London twenty-six weeks, and between land and land ||[2]eighteen|| weeks; (the other two something less time;) their beer all spent and leaked out a month before their arrival, so as they were forced to stinking water (and that very little) mixed with sack or vinegar, and their other provisions very short and bad. Yet, through the great providence of the Lord, they came all safe on shore, and most of them sound and well liking. They had continual tempests, and when they were near the shore, (being brought two or three days with a ||[3]strong|| east wind,) the weather was so thick all that time ||[4]as|| they could not make land, and the seamen were in great perplexity, when on ||[5]the|| sudden the fog cleared, so as they saw Cape Ann fair on their starboard bow, and presently grew thick again; yet by their compass they made their harbor. There were aboard that ship two godly ministers, Mr. Nathaniel Rogers,[2] and Mr.

||here|| ||[2]sixteen|| ||[3]stronger|| ||[4]that|| ||[5]a||

---

son, Samuel, the minister of Billerica, were much engaged. See Hutch. I. 270–274. He is miscalled Lambert by Neal, History of Puritans, II. 304. It was from regard to Whiting, perhaps, that the town received its name of Lynn, as he had been a preacher in the borough of Lynn Regis in Norfolk.

[1] An unreasonable, though natural jealousy, may be imagined as the ground of this neglect. It might have come to private men from any court of a foreign nation.

[2] Hubbard, 554, thinks "it might be honor enough to say, that he was the son of Mr. John Rogers, the famous preacher of Dedham." His descent from one of the most celebrated of that "noble army of martyrs" seems only a modern tradition, not heard of by either Mather or Hubbard, the latter of whom was likely to know of such a claim, for he married the only daughter of Rogers.

Partridge,[1] and many good people in that and the other *206
ships; and we had prayed earnestly for them; (for a small pinnace of thirty tons, which came out with them, and was come in three weeks before, brought us news of their coming). In one of the other ships, the passengers had but half a pint of drink for a day, fourteen days together; yet, through the Lord's mercy, did all well. One of the ships was overset in the night by a sudden gust, and lay so half an hour, yet righted of herself.

Cattle were grown to high rates; — a good cow, £25 or £30;

Yet high veneration we must bestow on the amiable progenitor of a numerous list of men, who, in several generations, are esteemed among the worthies of New England. His son, John, was president of Harvard College; and a grandson and great grandson were ministers of the same church in Ipswich, which was thus, by four degrees, supplied for over one hundred and twenty years. Other descendants have been distinguished for useful services. Eliot, who is very copious on this family of learned men, quoting the Magnalia, refers to a particular publication of the first Nathaniel; but the highest subject of praise in it is omitted. The tract is in the abundant collection at the Boston Athenæum. It is a letter written from this country to a member of parliament, 17 December, 1643; and though, of course, it favored the cause of liberty and reformation, yet it contains a few lines of merited censure against the dishonorable aspersions on the king by Mercurius Britannicus. In that inflammatory gazette, — a perfect copy of which, containing 130 numbers, from 29 August, 1643, to 18 May, 1646, perhaps a unique in America, and certainly very rare in England, was in my possession at the day of the great fire in Court Street, 1825, — the number 46, 5 August, 1644, bestows some vulgar abuse on the moderation of our peacemaker. Though Rogers's letter was printed under the authority of parliament, being licensed by Calamy, one of the great Westminster divines, the newspaper affects to consider it as part of an Oxford or royal plot, and insinuates, that the king had agents in New England. Such is the reception of truth and decency in a civil war. Mather's name is written in the first page of this curious belligerent volume; but perhaps the author of the Magnalia, in his Life of Rogers, thought it unworthy of the amiable pilgrim, to record with honor the gentle remonstrance in favor of his sovereign.

[2] This gentleman is honored in the Magnalia, Morton's Memorial, and Eliot's and Allen's Dictionaries. He was the first minister of Duxbury, and needs only the mention, which Judge Davis has given him. He left no son. Margaret, wife of John Marshall, and Elizabeth, wife of Rev. Thomas Thacher, were his daughters. Johnson bestows on him and Rogers verses of less value for their beauty than justice. An honorable descendant of George, who came the same year with Rev. Ralph, and perhaps may be thought his brother, was well known for his services in our revolutionary war.

a pair of bulls or oxen, £40. Corn was ||now|| at 5*s.* the bushel, and much rye was sown with the plough this year, for about thirty ploughs were at work. ||[2]Bread||[1] was at 9 and 10*s.* the C.; carpenters at 3*s.* the day, and other ||[3]workmen|| accordingly.

Things went not well at Connecticut. Their cattle did, many of them, cast their young, as they had done the year before.

[Large blank.]

Mons. D'Aulney, captain of Penobscott or Pentagonett, returned answer to the governour's letter, wherein he professed, that they claimed no further than to Pemaquid, nor would unless he had further order; and that he supposed, that the cause why he had no order, etc., was, that the English ambassador had dealt effectually with the cardinal of France for settling the limits for our peace, etc.

The governour, Mr. Vane, a wise and godly gentleman, held, with Mr. Cotton and many others, the indwelling of the person of the Holy Ghost in a believer, and went so far beyond the rest, as to maintain a personal union with the Holy Ghost; but the deputy, with the pastor and divers others, denied both; and the question proceeded so far by disputation, (in writing, for the peace sake of the church, which all were tender of,) as at length they could not find the person of the Holy Ghost in scripture, nor in the primitive churches three hundred years after Christ. So that, all agreeing in the chief matter of substance, viz. that the Holy Ghost is God, and that he doth dwell
*207 in the believers, (as the Father and Son both are said also to do,) but whether by his gifts and power only, or by any other manner of presence, seeing the scripture doth not declare it,—it was earnestly desired, that the word person might be forborn, being a term of human invention, and tending to doubtful disputation in this case.[2]

[Large blank.]

||near|| ||[2]Board|| ||[3]work||

---

[1] I made this alteration by conjecture; for the MS. looks very much like the reading of the former edition, which Dr. Allen, in his Biographical Dictionary, offers reason for preferring.

[2] So much evil has not been caused in New England, as in most other Pro-

10ber.] The governour, receiving letters from his friends in England, which necessarily required his presence there, imparted the same to the council[1] and some others; and, being thereupon resolved of his return into England, called a court of deputies, to the end he might have free leave of the country, etc. They, being assembled in court, and himself declaring the necessity of his departure, and those of the council affirming the reasons to be very urgent, though not fit to be imparted to the whole court, they desired respite to consider thereof till the morning; when one of the assistants using some pathetical passages of the loss of such a governour in a time of such danger as did hang over us, from the Indians and French, the governour brake forth into tears, and professed, that howsoever the causes propounded for his departure were such as did concern the utter ruin of his outward estate, yet he would rather have hazarded all, than have gone from them at this time, if something else had not pressed him more, viz. the inevitable danger he saw of God's judgments to come upon us for these differences and dissensions, which he saw amongst us, and the scandalous imputations brought upon himself, as if he should be the cause of all; and therefore he thought it best for him to give place for a time, etc. Upon this the court concluded that it would not be fit to give way to his departure upon these grounds. Whereupon he recalled himself, and professed, *208
that the reasons concerning his own estate were sufficient to his own satisfaction for his departure, and therefore desired

---

testant countries, by the "*terms of human invention*," not found in the scriptures, nor in the three earliest centuries of the Christian church. Our exemption is chiefly owing to the separation of church and state, which gradually proceeded after the second generation. The early *forbearing* of the personality of the Holy Ghost in their technical theology, after examination of the ante-Nicene fathers, is not more a proof of the learning than of the moderation of the clerical leaders of Massachusetts.

[1] Hubbard, 256, adds, "which at that time consisted but of two, besides himself." In this I doubt the historian of Ipswich is mistaken, and that Vane consulted with the body of assistants, not merely the standing council for life, who were part of the council of assistants. When the house of deputies assembled, as in the next sentence is told, "*those of the council*" must mean the men to whom the governour *imparted* his letters; and no suggestion can be perceived, that it was two, instead of ten or more, who had thus been honored.

the court he might have leave to go; as for the other passage, it slipped him out of his passion, and not out of judgment. Upon this the court consented, silently, to his departure. Then the question was about supply of his place. Some were of opinion, that it should be executed by the deputy; but this scruple being cast in, that if the deputy should die, then the government would be vacant, and none have power to call any court, or to preside therein, etc., it was agreed to call a court of elections, for a new governour and deputy, in case the present deputy should be chose governour; and an order was made, (in regard of the season,) that such as would might send their votes by proxy, in papers sealed up and delivered to the deputies. And so this court was adjourned four days, and two days after the court of elections was to assemble. These things thus passed, divers of the congregation of Boston met together, and agreed that they did not apprehend the necessity of the governour's departure upon the reasons alleged, and sent some of them to declare the same to the court; whereupon the governour expressed himself to be an obedient child to the church, and therefore, notwithstanding the license of the court, yet, without the leave of the church, he durst not go away.[1]

Whereupon a great part of the court and country, who understood hereof, declared their purpose to continue him still in his place, and therefore, so soon as the day of election came, and the country were assembled, it was thought the best way for avoiding trouble, etc., not to proceed to election, but to adjourn the court to the great general court in May. And so the court of deputies, etc., continued still, (for the other court was not called).

At this court the elders of the churches were called, to advise with them about ||discovering|| and pacifying the differences among the churches in point of opinion.[2] The governour

||discontinuing||

---

[1] Hutchinson, I. 55, judiciously regards the conduct of Vane as dissimulation; and though he followed the narrative as authority of Hubbard, not of Winthrop, perhaps few admirers of the ardent republican, who opposed the tyranny of Cromwell, can fail to unite in the opinion.

[2] Notice of this consultation is not contained in the public records, and the

having declared the occasion to them, Mr. Dudley desired, that men would be free and open, etc. Another of the magistrates spake, that it would much further the end they came for, if men would freely declare what they held different from others, as himself would freely do, in what point soever he should be opposed. The governour said, that he would *209
be content to do the like, but that he understood the ministers were about it in a church way, etc., which he spake upon this occasion: the ministers had met, a little before, and had drawn into heads all the points, wherein they suspected Mr. Cotton did differ from them, and had propounded them to him, and pressed him to a direct answer, affirmative or negative, to every one; which he had promised, and taken time for. This meeting being spoke of in the court the day before, the governour took great offence at it, as being without his privity, etc., which this day Mr. Peter told him as ||plainly|| of, (with all due reverence,) and how it had sadded the ministers' spirits, that he should be jealous of their meetings, or seem to restrain their liberty, etc. The governour excused his speech, as sudden and upon a mistake. Mr. Peter told him also, that *before he came,* within less than two years since, the churches were in peace, etc. The governour answered, that the ||[2]light|| of the gospel brings a sword, and the children of the bondwoman would persecute those of the freewoman. Mr. Peter also besought him humbly to consider his ||[3]youth,|| and short experience in the things of God, and to beware of peremptory conclusions, which he perceived him to be very apt unto. He declared further, that he had observed, both in the Low Countries and here, three principal causes of new opinions and divisions thereupon: 1. Pride, new notions lift up the mind, etc. 2. Idleness. 3. [blank.]

Mr. Wilson made a very sad speech[1] of the condition of our churches, and the ||[4]inevitable|| danger of separation, if these

||protimely|| ||[2]liberty|| ||[3]hasty|| ||[4]invoidable||

---

community would, probably, have been more quiet, had the court done no more than their secretary has preserved.

[1] His speech was approved by the court, as from the record, (which luckily consists of only two lines, about the whole controversy,) at the next session, appears.

differences and alienations among brethren were not speedily remedied; and laid the blame upon these new opinions risen up amongst us, which all the magistrates, except the governour and two others, did confirm, and all the ministers but two.

In this discourse ‖one question‖ arose about sanctification. Mr. Cotton, in his sermon that day, had laid down this ground, that evident sanctification was an evidence of justification, and thereupon had taught, that in cases of ‖[2]spiritual‖ desertion, true desires of sanctification was found to be sanctification; and further, if a man were laid so flat upon the ground, as he could see no desires, etc., but only, as a bruised reed, did wait at the feet of Christ, yet here was matter of comfort for this, as found to be true.

*210 The question here grew, whether any of these, or evident sanctification, could be evidence to a man without a concurrent sight of his justification. The governour and Mr. Cotton denied it.

The speech of Mr. Wilson was taken very ill by Mr. Cotton and others of the same church, so as he and divers of them went to admonish him. But Mr. Wilson and some others could see no breach of rule, seeing he was called by the court about the same matter with the rest of the elders, and ‖[3]exhorted‖ to deliver their minds freely and faithfully, both for discovering the danger, and the means to help; and the things he spake of were only in general, and such as were under a common ‖[4]fame.‖ And being questioned about his intent, he professed he did not mean Boston church, nor the members thereof, more than others. But this would not satisfy, but they called him to answer publicly, 31; and there the governour pressed it violently against him, and all the congregation, except the deputy and one or two more, and many of them with much bitterness and reproaches; but he answered them all with words of truth and soberness, and with marvellous wisdom. It was strange to see, how the common people were led, by example, to condemn him in that, which (it was very probable) divers of them did not understand,[1] nor the rule which

‖two questions‖ ‖[2]special‖ ‖[3]expected‖ ‖[4]form‖

[1] That the subject was not well understood, may be, in our days, thought the

he was supposed to have broken; and that such as had known him so long, and what good he had done for that church, should fall upon him with such bitterness for justifying himself in a good cause; for he was a very holy, upright man, and *211
for faith and love inferior to none in the country, and most dear to all men. The teacher joined with the church in their judgment of him, (not without some appearance of prejudice,) yet with much wisdom and moderation. They were eager to proceed to present censure, but the teacher staid them from that, telling them he might not do it, because some opposed it, but gave him a grave exhortation. The next day Mr. Wilson preached, notwithstanding, and the Lord so assisted him, as gave great satisfaction, and the governour himself gave public witness to him.

One of the brethren[1] wrote to Mr. Cotton about it, and laid before him divers failings, (as he supposed,) and some reasons to justify Mr. Wilson, and dealt very plainly with him. Mr. Cotton made a very ||loving|| and gentle answer, clearing his intentions, and persisting in his judgment of Mr. Wilson's of-

||long||

---

very occasion of the bitterness, as in theological controversies is often experienced. Charity should be expected rather from those, who well comprehend any matter of doubt in the faith of the church; for only they know the reasons for both sides, and the difficulty of forming a judgment. Winthrop and Cotton, on opposite sides, were moderate. Wilson's exculpation of himself, in the text, that he did not mean the members of his own church, more than others, appears something like equivocation; for that church was the only one in the colony, wherein any considerable part of the worshippers held these deadly, unintelligible opinions. Some palliation for his timidity is easily found in the unhappy circumstance of all but two or three of the congregation being vexed at his speech, and ready to proceed hastily to censure him for it. The difference, it will be seen, in several passages of this History, was very slight between the orthodox and heretical doctrine, even when men's wits were sharpened to discover that difference; and the indistinct shadows of meaning have, in our time, almost wholly vanished. Perhaps the language of neither would now be employed in definition of the nature or extent of divine influences on the human soul. By then imputing to Cotton what he did not teach, — though his gifted hearers, Vane and Mrs. Hutchinson, might so understand him, — opportunity was afforded, however, for a synod, to perform the important service of settling, as they supposed, the faith of future generations.

[1] Winthrop, by this periphrase, no doubt, means himself.

fence, laying down divers arguments for it. The said brother replied to him in like loving manner, and desired leave to show his letter to Mr. Wilson, which he readily assented unto. But for answer to his arguments, he forbore to reply to Mr. Cotton, (because he was overburdened with business,) but wrote to the two ruling elders,[1] (whom the matter most concerned,) and, by way of defence of Mr. Wilson, answered all Mr. Cotton's arguments.

Upon these public occasions, other opinions brake out publicly in the church of Boston, — as that the Holy Ghost dwelt in a believer as he is in heaven; that a man is justified before he believes; and that faith is no cause of justification. And others spread more secretly, — as that the letter of the scripture holds forth nothing but a covenant of works; and that the covenant of grace was the spirit of the scripture, which was known only to believers; and that this covenant of works was given by Moses in the ‖ten commandments;‖ that there was a seed (viz., Abraham's carnal seed) went along in this, and there was a spirit and life in it, by virtue whereof a man might attain to any sanctification in gifts and graces, and might have ‖[2]spiritual‖ and ‖[3]*continual*‖ communion with Jesus Christ, and yet be damned. After, it was granted, that faith was before justification, but it was only passive, an empty vessel, etc.; but in conclusion, the ground of all was found to be assurance by immediate revelation.

*212 All the congregation of Boston, except four or five, closed with these opinions, or the most of them; but one of the brethren wrote against them, and bore witness to the truth; together with the pastor, and very few others joined with them.

About this time the rest of the ministers, taking offence at some doctrines delivered by Mr. Cotton, and especially at some opinions, which some of his church did broach, and for he seemed to have too good an opinion of, and too much fa-

‖tenth commandment‖ ‖[2]special‖ ‖[3]blank‖

[1] Unfortunately these elders, Oliver and Leverett, were infected with the same hankering after what was called antinomianism, as the great majority of their brethren.

miliarity with those persons, drew out sixteen points, and gave them to him, entreating him to deliver his judgment directly in them, which accordingly he did, and many copies thereof were dispersed about. Some doubts he well cleared, but in some things he gave not satisfaction. The rest of the ministers replied to these answers, and at large showed their dissent, and the grounds thereof; and, at the next general court, held 9th of the 1st, they all assembled at Boston, and agreed to put off all lectures for three weeks, that they might bring things to || some || issue.[1]

One Mr. Glover of Dorchester, having laid sixty pounds of gunpowder in bags to dry in the end of his chimney, it took fire, and some went up the chimney; other of it filled the room and passed out at a door into another room, and blew up a gable end. A maid, which was in the room, having her arms and neck naked, was scorched, and died soon after. A little child, in the arms of another, was scorched upon the face, but not killed. Two men were scorched, but not much. Divers pieces, which lay charged in several places, took fire and went off, but did no harm. The room was so dark with smoke, as those in the house could neither find door nor window, and when neighbors came in, none could see each other a good time for smoke. The house was thatched, yet took not fire; yet when the smoke was gone, many things were found burnt. Another great providence was, that three little children, being at the fire a little before, they went out to play, (though it were a very cold day,) and so were preserved.

12 mo. 22.] The lieutenant ||[2]of|| Saybrook, at the mouth of Connecticut, going out with nine men, armed with swords and pieces, they started three Indians, whom they pursued till they were brought into an ambush of fifty, who came upon them, and slew four of their men, and had they not drawn their

||an|| ||[2]at||

[1] How injurious to the cause of the christian church, this disagreement between the able teacher and the meek pastor was, is evident by observing that no admission of any member is given from 9 January, 1636–7, when No. 372 came in, before 30 December, 1638, near two years. But soon after Cotton came, 37 had joined in three months.

swords and retired, they had been all slain. The Indians were so hardy, as they came close up to them, notwithstanding their pieces.[1]

*213 (11.) 10.] Capt. Turner's house in Sagus took fire by an oven about midnight, and was burnt down, with all that was in it, save the persons. About fourteen days since, a ship called the George of Bristol, laden with cattle and passengers, (having been some time at the Western Islands,) and having spent her mainmast about Cape Cod, and after come near Brewster's Islands, was, by N. W. winds, forced to put into Plimouth.

20.] A general fast was kept in all the churches. The occasion was, the miserable estate of the churches in Germany; the calamities upon our native country, the bishops making havock in the churches, putting down the faithful ministers, and advancing popish ceremonies and doctrines, the plague raging exceedingly, and famine and sword threatening them; the dangers of those at Connecticut, and of ourselves also, by the Indians; and the dissensions in our churches.

The differences in the said points of religion increased more and more, and the ministers of both sides (there being only Mr. Cotton of one party) did publicly declare their judgments in some of them, so as all men's mouths were full of them. And there being, 12 mo. 3, a ship ready to go for England, and many passengers in it, Mr. Cotton took occasion to speak to them about the differences, etc., and willed them to tell our countrymen, that all the strife amongst us was about magnifying the grace of God; one party seeking to advance the grace of God within us, and the other to advance the grace of God towards us, (meaning by the one justification, and by the other sanctification;) and so bade them tell them, that, if there were any among them that would strive for grace, they should come hither; and so declared some particulars. Mr. Wilson spake after him, and declared, that he knew none of the elders or

[1] Trumbull, I. 76, says it was in March, but he is wrong. We have the report of Gardiner, the lieutenant, in 3 Mass. Hist. Coll. III. 143, giving the same date as above. Only two of his men were killed. His narrative is very amusing as well as exact.

brethren of the churches, but did labor to advance the free grace of God in justification, so far as the word of God required; and spake also about the doctrine of sanctification, and the use and necessity, etc., of it; by occasion whereof no man could tell (except some few, who knew the bottom of the matter) where any difference was: which speech, though it offended those of Mr. Cotton's party, yet it was very seasonable to clear the rest, who otherwise should have been reputed to have opposed free grace. Thus every occasion increased the contention, and caused great alienation of minds; and the members of Boston (frequenting the lectures of other ministers) did make much disturbance by public questions, and objections to their doctrines, which did any way disagree from their opinions; and it began to be as common here to distinguish between men, by being under a covenant of grace or a covenant of works, as in other countries between Protestants *214 and Papists.

February 6.] A man of Weymouth (but not of the church) fell into some trouble of mind, and in the night cried out, "Art thou come, Lord Jesus?" and with that leaped out of his bed in his shirt, and, breaking from his wife, leaped out at a high window into the snow, and ran about seven miles off, and being traced in the snow, was found dead next morning. They might perceive, that he had kneeled down to prayer in divers places.

(1.) 9.] The general court began. When any matter about these new opinions was mentioned, the court was divided; yet the greater number far were sound. They questioned the proceeding against Mr. Wilson, for his speech in the last court, but could not fasten upon such as had prejudiced him, etc.; but, by the vote of the greater party, his speech was approved, and declared to have been a seasonable advice, and no charge or accusation.

The ministers, being called to give advice about the authority of the court in things concerning the churches, etc., did all agree of these two things: 1. That no member of the court ought to be publicly questioned by a church for any speech in the court, without the license of the court. The reason was, because the court may have sufficient reason that may excuse the sin, which yet may not be fit to acquaint the church with, being a secret of state. The second thing was, that, in all such heresies or errors of any church members as are manifest and dangerous to the state, the court may proceed without tarrying for the church; but if the opinions be doubtful, etc., they are first to refer them to the church, etc.

At this court, when Mr. Wheelwright was to be questioned for a sermon, which seemed to tend to sedition, etc., near all the church of Boston presented a petition to the court for two things: 1. That as freemen they might be present in cases of judicature. 2. That the court would declare, if they might deal in cases of conscience before the church, etc. This was taken as a groundless and presumptuous act, especially at this season, and was rejected with this answer: That the court had never used to proceed §judicially§ but it was openly; but for matter of consultation and preparation in causes, they might and would be private.

One Stephen ‖Greensmith,‖[1] for saying that all the minis-
*215 ters, except A. B. C.,[2] did teach a covenant of works, was censured to acknowledge his fault in every church, and fined £40.

Mr. Wheelwright, one of the members of Boston, preaching at the last fast, inveighed against all that walked in a covenant of works, as he described it *to be,* viz., such as maintain sanctification as an evidence of justification, etc.[3] and called them antichrists, and stirred up the people against them with much bitterness and vehemency. For this he was called ‖[2]into‖ the court, and his sermon being produced, he justified it, and confessed he did mean all that walk in such a way. Whereupon the elders of the rest of the churches were called, and asked whether they, in their ministry, did walk in

‖Green‖ ‖[2]before‖

---

[1] Greensmith was a person of some consequence, as we should infer from the names of his sureties, which may be seen in Addenda.

[2] From the Records of the general court, I find the names to be, Cotton, Wheelwright, "and, as he thought, Mr. Hooker." His sentence required also sureties in £100. Of the payment of the fine notice will appear in Addenda.

[3] This explanation was in the margin.

such a way. They all acknowledged they did. So, after much debate, the court adjudged him guilty of sedition, and also of contempt, for that the court had appointed the fast as a means of reconciliation of the differences, etc., and he purposely set himself to kindle and increase them.[1] The governour and some few more (who dissented) tendered a pro- *216
testation, which, because it wholly justified Mr. ||Wheel-

||Wilson||

[1] In the archives of the Historical Society, I discovered, many years since, the larger part, being the last thirty-three pages, of this inflammatory discourse, which has never been printed, and probably not read more than once or twice for two hundred years. Having no acquaintance with the handwriting of Wheelwright, though it is an ancient MS., I am not able to ascertain, whether it be copy or original; yet it is probably original, for some comparatively modern preserver has written on a blank leaf, that it "was left in the hands of Mr. John Coggeshall, who was a deacon of the church in Boston." The character of the sermon is, however, of more importance; and I unhesitatingly say, that it was not such as can justify the court in their sentence for *sedition* and *contempt*, nor prevent the present age from regarding that proceeding as an example and a warning of the usual tyranny of ecclesiastical factions. The author's conduct is by himself judged with sufficient severity in two letters, which will appear in this History sub an. 1644. Similar, and often much heavier artillery of reproach, is too often employed in that fortress, within which the brave defenders fear no answer of an adversary's fire.

The followers of Cotton, supporters of Wheelwright, and admirers of Mrs. Hutchinson, have been usually stigmatized as antinomians; and I am well satisfied, that the tendency of their doctrines was, by unscriptural representations of grace, to disparage the value of good works. But by many the same opinion is entertained of the tendency in teaching of the great body of their antagonists. We should never impute conclusions from the premises of one party, drawn by the adversary. With all his ardour against the errors of that time, Winthrop, who well understood them, has not used this term of reproach, though Welde and other inquisitors have trusted much to the influence of an odious name. It is the most common artifice of the "exquisite rancour of theological hatred." Though we may presume it was given, the deluded did not adopt the denomination. I shall not be blamed for an extract from this sermon, which Hutchinson, I. 57, I fear, without having read it, characterizes as "carrying antinomianism to the height." It contains this exhortation: "Thirdly, let us have a care, that we do show ourselves holy in all manner of good conversation, both in private and public; and, in all our carriages and conversations, let us have a care to endeavor to be holy as the Lord is; let us not give occasion to those that are coming on, or manifestly opposite to the ways of grace, to suspect the way of grace; let us carry ourselves, that they may be ashamed to

wright,||[1] and condemned the proceedings of the court, was rejected. The church of Boston also tendered a petition in his behalf, justifying Mr. Wheelwright's sermon. The court deferred sentence till the next court, and advised with the ministers, etc., whether they might enjoin his ||silence,|| etc. They answered, that they were not clear in that point, but desired rather, that he might be commended to the church of Boston to take care of him, etc., which accordingly was done, and he enjoined to appear at the next court. Much heat of contention was this court between the opposite parties; so as it was moved, that the next court might be kept at Newtown. The
*217 governour refused to put it to the vote; the deputy was loath to do it, except the court would require him, be-

||sentence||

---

blame us; let us deal uprightly with those with whom we have occasion to deal, and have a care to guide our families and to perform duties that belong to us; and let us have a care that we give not occasion to others to say, we are libertines or antinomians."

A perfect copy of this sermon, from the state house, with a great body of other old papers, supposed formerly to have belonged to Gov. Hutchinson, was presented to the Historical Society; and from this I find no reason to alter the foregoing opinion. The text was, for the views of his party, admirably chosen from Matt. ix. 15.

Mather, book VII. chap. iii. sect. 3, says, of Wheelwright, "he published a vindication of himself against the wrongs, that by Mr. Welde and by Mr. Rutherford had been done unto him." The scarcity of this tract induces me to enlarge my quotation from the Magnalia: "In this vindication, he not only produces a speech of Mr. Cotton, *I do conceive and profess, that our brother Wheelwright's doctrine is according to God in the points controverted;* but also a declaration from the whole general court of the colony, signed by the secretary, August 24, 1654, upon the petition of Mr. Wheelwright's church at Hampton, in which declaration they profess, that, hearing that Mr. Wheelwright is, by Mr. Rutherford and Mr. Welde, rendered, in some books printed by them, as heretical and criminous, they now signify, that Mr. Wheelwright hath, for these many years, approved himself a sound, orthodox, and profitable minister of the gospel, among these churches of Christ." Wheelwright's first tract is in the British Museum, in answer to Welde.

[1] By following the absurd reading of the first edition, substituting the chief of one party for the head of the other, Emerson, History of First Church, 38, puzzled his readers in a maze, from which they may now easily be extricated.

cause he dwelt in Boston, etc. So the court put it to Mr. Endecott.[1]

21.] Miantunnomoh, etc., sent twenty-six, with forty fathom of wampom and a Pequod's hand. We gave four of the chief ||each|| a coat of ||[2]fourteen|| shillings price, and deferred to return our present till after, according to their manner.

Mo. 2. 1.] Those of Connecticut returned answer to our public letters, wherein they showed themselves unsatisfied about our former expedition against the Pequods, and their expectations of a further prosecution of the war, to which they offer to send men, and signify their unpreparedness to declare themselves in the matter of government, in regard of their engagement to attend the answer of the gentlemen of Saybrook about the same matter.

10.] Capt. Underhill was sent to Saybrook, with twenty men, to keep the fort, both in respect of the Indians, and especially of the Dutch, who, by their speeches and supplies out of Holland, gave ||[3]cause|| of suspicion that they had some design upon it. The men were sent at the charge of the gentlemen of Saybrook, and lent by order of the council here, for fear any advantage should be taken by the adverse party, through the weakness of the place.

6.] The church of Concord kept a day of humiliation at Newtown, for ordination of their elders, and they chose Mr. Buckly teacher, and Mr. Jones pastor. Upon a question moved by one sent from the church of Salem, it was resolved by the ministers there present, that such as had been ministers in England were lawful ministers by the call of the people there, notwithstanding their acceptance of the call of the bishops, etc., (for which they humbled themselves, acknowledging it their sin,[2] etc.,) but being come hither, they accounted themselves no

||sachems|| ||[2]nineteen|| ||[3]occasion||

[1] Boston was punished for its political contumacy, one hundred and thirty years later, by a royal governour in the same manner.

[2] Ordination by a bishop in England must have been thought valid, for by that rite it was, that all the other ministers asserted their claims to office, as we may see at the election, in August, 1630, of Wilson to the first church of Boston. The people also equally respected it. But how it should be a sin, yet a valid entrance or admission to the Christian ministry, can be explained only by such

ministers, until they were called ||to|| another church, and that, upon election, they were ministers before they were solemnly ordained.

The governour, and Mr. Cotton, and Mr. Wheelwright, and the two ruling elders of Boston, and the rest of that church,
*218 which were of any note, did none of them come to this meeting. The reason was conceived to be, because they accounted these as legal preachers, and therefore would not give approbation to their ordination.

3. 2.] Mr. Haynes, one of our magistrates, removed with his family to Connecticut.

12.] We received a letter from him and others, being then at Saybrook, that the Pekods had been up the river at Weathersfield, and had killed six men, being at their work, and twenty cows and a mare, and had killed three women, and carried away two maids.

Mr. Winslow was sent from the governour and council of Plimouth to treat with us about joining against the Pequods. He declared first their willingness to aid us; but that they could not do any thing till their general court, which was not till the first Tuesday in the 4th month. Then he made some objections: as, 1. Our refusal to aid them against the French. 2. Our people's trading at Kenebeck. 3. The injury offered them at Connecticut by those of Windsor, in taking away their land there. 4. Their own poverty, and our ability, which needed not any help from them.

To this answer was made by our governour and deputy: that, 1. We did not desire them to afford aid unto us, but to join against the common enemy, who, if he were not subdued, would prove as dangerous to them as to us, and, he prevailing, would cause all the Indians in the country to join to root out all the English. 2. For our refusal to aid them against the French, the case was not alike, for it was their private quarrel, and they were supposed to have commission from the king of

||by||

---

timid casuists as humbled themselves for their act in submitting to it. Dr. Bacon, in his delightful Historical Discourses, has, in some good degree, explained the matter.

France, and we thought it no wisdom for us to engage ourselves in a war with the king of France; § yet we acknowledged some failing in it. §[1] For our people's trading at Kenebeck, we answered, that we gave no allowance to it, nor had we heard of more than a boat or two that had been there. For the injury done them at Connecticut, we had dealt with them to give satisfaction, but it was not in our power to do them justice in it. || He || alleged also, that this war did not concern them, seeing the Pequods had not killed any of theirs. We answered, that Capt. Stone, etc., for whom this war was begun, were none of ours neither. ||[2] He || alleged further, that, in our first undertaking, they were not acquainted with it till two or three days before our forces were to go forth. We answered, we *219
intended at the first to send only to Block Island, and for that we thought it not needful to trouble them, and our sending them thence to the Pequods was with hope to draw them to parley, and so to some quiet end. We concluded to write further to them from our next court. And whereas they propounded to have us promise to aid them in all their occasions, etc., we answered, that, seeing, when we now treated with them about joining with us, they were at liberty and might withhold, except they saw reason to move them; so we desired to be left free, that we might judge of the reason of any such occasion as might fall out. According hereunto we writ to them the 20th of the 3d month, and gave them some considerations, why they should join with us: as, 1. because, if we should be overcome, it would cost them more to help us, and be less acceptable; 2. if we should prevail without them, it would occasion ill thoughts in our people towards theirs, etc. So we left it to them.

17.] Our court of elections was at Newtown. So soon as the court was set, being about one of the clock, a petition was preferred by those of Boston. The governour would have read it, but the deputy said it was out of order; it was a court ||[3] for || elections, and those must first be despatched, and then their petitions should be heard. Divers others also opposed that course, as an ill precedent, etc.; and the petition, being about

|| They || ||[2] They || ||[3] of ||

[1] This clause was brought from the margin.

pretence of liberty, etc., (though intended chiefly for revoking the sentence given against Mr. Wheelwright,) would have spent all the day in debate, etc.; but yet the governour and those of that party would not proceed to election, except the petition was read. Much time was already spent about this debate, and the people crying out for election, it was moved by the deputy, that the people should divide themselves, and the greater number must carry it. And so it was done, and the greater number by ||many|| were for election. But the governour and that side kept their place still, and would not proceed. Whereupon the deputy told him, that, if he would not go to election, he and the rest of that side would proceed. Upon that, he came from his company, and they went to election;[1] and Mr. Winthrop was chosen governour, Mr. Dudley deputy, and Mr.
*220 Endecott of the standing council;[2] and Mr. Israel Stoughton and Mr. Richard Saltonstall were called in to be assistants; and Mr. Vane, Mr. Coddington, and Mr. Dummer, (being all of ||[2]that|| faction,) were left quite out.

There was great danger of a tumult that day; for those of that side grew into fierce speeches, and some laid hands on others; but seeing themselves too weak, they grew quiet. They expected a great advantage that day, because the remote towns were allowed to come in by proxy;[3] but it fell out, that

||much|| ||[2]the||

[1] A pleasant story of the exertion of Wilson to secure this election is told by Hutchinson, I. 62.

[2] He held this place, without re-election, till the change of the constitution in 1639.

[3] The admission of proxies was justified by experience at the election of the former year, and at the general court in December preceding this course was adopted, as by the record appears: "This court, taking into serious consideration the great danger and damage that may accrue to the state by all the freemen's leaving their plantations to come to the place of elections, have therefore ordered it, that it shall be free and lawful for all freemen to send their votes for elections by proxy, the next general court in May, and so for hereafter, which shall be done in this manner: The deputies, which shall be chosen, shall cause the freemen of their towns to be assembled, and then to take such freemen's votes as please to send by proxy for every magistrate, and seal them up severally, subscribing the magistrate's name on the back side, and so to bring them to the court sealed, with an open roll of the names of the freemen that so send by proxy."

there were enough beside. But if it had been otherwise, they must have put in their deputies, as other towns had done, for all matters beside elections. Boston, having deferred to choose deputies till the election was passed, went home that night, and the next morning they sent Mr. Vane, the late governour, and Mr. Coddington, and Mr. Hoffe, for their deputies; but the court, being grieved at it, found a means to send them home again, for that two of the freemen of Boston had not notice of the election. So they went all home, and the next morning they returned the same gentlemen again upon a new choice; and the court not finding how they might reject them, they were admitted.

Upon the election of the new governour, the serjeants, who had attended the old governour to the court, (being all Boston men, where the new governour also dwelt,) laid down their halberds and went home; and whereas they had been wont to attend the former governour to and from the meetings on the Lord's days, they gave over now, so as the new governour was fain to use his own servants to carry two halberds before him; whereas the former governour had never less than four.[1]

Divers writings were now published about these differ- *221
ences. Among the rest, the magistrates ||set|| forth an

||sent||

[1] Many writers, looking only to the tone of this paragraph in our author, have considered that the officers showed a special discourtesy to him. A strict examination of the complaint, perhaps, may show that it was not very well founded, and certainly exempt these sergeants from the obloquy. The Colony Records, I. 145, instruct us, that, at the general court in March, 1635, it was ordered, "that at every general court there shall be six men appointed by the governour for the time being, out of the town where he lives, to attend with halberds and swords upon the person of the governour, and the rest of the members of the court, during the space of the first day of every general court; and that there shall be two men appointed by the governour, to attend in like manner at every particular court at the public charges." When Haynes was afterwards chosen, the officers for this service, appointed by him, of course belonged to Newtown; when Vane succeeded, he was required to appoint men of Boston; and at this election, after Winthrop was sworn in, he might have appointed the same or others of the same town. But those, whose office ceased with the authority of Vane, are not, it seems to me, to be blamed for declining, without commission anew, to wait on his successor.

apology[1] to justify the sentence of the court against Mr. Wheelwright, which the adverse party had much opposed and spoken evil of, and did also set forth a remonstrance to that end, in which they did not deal fairly; for, in abbreviating Mr. Wheelwright his sermon, they clear altered both the words and meaning of such passages in it, whereat the offence was taken, and which were the ground of the court's sentence.

Mr. Wheelwright also himself set forth a small ||tractate|| about the principal doctrine of his sermon, viz., about the covenant of grace, which was also differing from his sermon.

The other ministers also set out an answer to his sermon, confuting the same by many strong arguments.

Mr. Cotton also replied to their answer very largely, and stated the differences in a very narrow scantling; and Mr. Shepherd, preaching at the day of election, brought them yet nearer, so as, except men of good understanding, and such as knew the bottom of the tenents of those of the other party, few could see where the difference was; and indeed it seemed so small, as (if men's affections had not been formerly alienated, when the differences were formerly stated as fundamental) they might easily have come to reconciliation. For in these particulars they agreed: 1. That justification and sanctification were both together in time; 2. That a man must know himself to be justified, before he can know himself to be sanctified; 3. That the spirit never witnesseth justification without a ||[2]word|| and a work.

The difference was, whether the first assurance be by an absolute promise always, and not by a conditional also, and whether a man could have any true assurance, without sight
*222 of some such work in his soul as no hypocrite could
attain unto.[2]

||treatise|| ||[2]wonder||

[1] It is printed in Welde's Rise, Reign, and Ruin.

[2] Upon such a harmony of the creeds, without want of reverence for the wisdom and sincerity of our ancestors, we may well refer to the language of Solomon, Prov. i. 6, — "the words of the wise and their dark sayings." The simplicity of the gospel seems utterly obscured by this controversy about the priority of sanctification or justification, which may be thought profound, or only absurd, according to the reader's education and ability to "darken counsel by words without knowledge."

At the court Mr. Wheelwright, according as he was enjoined, did appear; but, because a general day of humiliation was appointed, and it was agreed, that all the churches should choose certain men to meet and confer about the differences, the court gave him respite to the next session, (which was appointed the first Tuesday in August,) to bethink himself, that, retracting and reforming his error, etc., the court might show him favor, which otherwise he must not expect. His answer was, that if he had committed sedition, then he ought to be put to death; and if we did mean to proceed against him, he meant to appeal to the king's court; for he could retract nothing. The court told him, that they were clear in the justice of their proceeding, and should judge of his offence as they had done, if it were to do again; but if, upon the conference among the churches, the Lord should discover any further light to them than as yet they had seen, they should gladly embrace it.

The intent of the court in deferring the sentence was, that, being thus provoked by their tumultuous course, and divers insolent speeches, which some of that party had uttered in the court, and having now power enough to have crushed them, their moderation and desire of reconciliation might appear to all.

Having received intelligence from Miantunnomoh, that the Pequods had sent their women and children to an island for their safety, we presently sent away forty men by land to the Narigansetts, and there to take in Miantunnomoh, (and he offered to send sixteen men with || ours, ||) and so, in the night, to set upon them.

We also provided to send one hundred and sixty[1] more

|| us ||

[1] Of this number, the proportion to be raised by the several towns was as follows: Boston, 26; Salem, 18; Ipswich, 17; Sagus, 16; Watertown, 14; Dorchester, 13; Charlestown, 12; Roxbury, 10; Newtown, 9; Newbury, 8; Hingham, 6; Weymouth, 5; Medford, 3; Marblehead, 3. The note in Hutchinson, on I. 76, is wrong, by one figure, in the apportionment of Newtown, many of whose chief men had then lately removed to Connecticut. It will be seen, in a comparison of the several notes on this subject, that the relative population and wealth of our settlements frequently changed. At the general court, in August following, a rate of £400 was thus assessed: Boston, £59.4; Salem,

*223 after them to prosecute the war; and Mr. Stoughton, one of the magistrates, was sent with them, and Mr. Wilson, the pastor of Boston. These two were chosen thus in the open court: Three magistrates were set apart, and one was designed by a lot; also the elders set apart two; and a lot was cast between them in a solemn public invocation of the name of God.

22.] Miantunnomoh sent us word, that Capt. Mason, with a company of the English upon the river, had surprised and slain eight Pequods, and taken seven squaws, and with some of them had redeemed the two English maids.

24.] By letters from Mr. Williams we were certified, (which the next day was confirmed by some who came from Saybrook,) that Capt. Mason[1] was come to Saybrook with eighty English and one hundred Indians; and that the Indians had gone out there, and met with seven Pequods; five they killed; one they took alive, whom the English put to torture; and set all their heads upon the fort. The reason was, because they had tortured such of our men as they took alive.[2]

£45.12; Dorchester, £42.6; Charlestown, £42.6; Ipswich, £34.12; Watertown, £30.8; Roxbury, £30.8; Newtown, £29.12; Sagus, £28.16; Medford, £24.12; Newbury, £16.18; Hingham, £8.10; Weymouth, £6.16. Property and numbers, in a very short period, appear to have been quite unequally distributed between Medford and Marblehead, the latter place having no assessment laid upon it, unless probably as a precinct of Salem, yet was before called on for as many soldiers as the other.

[1] An ample account of Mason is given by Allen, and it seems strange, that Eliot omitted so distinguished a name. That he arrived in 1630, with the first settlers of Dorchester, as Allen asserts, from Trumbull, I. 322, may be an error, as his name is not found before December, 1632, when he went in the expedition after the pirate Bull, of which notice in this volume, 96, 97, may be compared with 2 Hist. Coll. VIII. 232. I *presume* he came in that year, and *know*, that he was admitted a freeman 4 March, 1634–5. Prefixed to his own History of the Pequot War, in which he deserves the principal honor, reprinted 2 Hist. Coll. VIII. 120–153, is a life by the diligent hand of Prince, who would not assign an earlier arrival. His son, John, a captain, was wounded, 19 December, 1675, in the great battle with the Narragansetts, and died in September following. Descendants of this energetic warrior are found in New England, of whom one was the great lawyer, Jeremiah Mason. Abundant correspondence of his with J. Winthrop of Connecticut is preserved.

[2] It was, probably, a mistaken policy, however justifiable the practice of retal-

The Dutch governour sent a sloop to Pequod to redeem the two English maids by what means soever, though it were with breach of their peace with the Pequods.[1] The sloop offered largely for their ransom; but nothing would be accepted. *224
So the Dutch, having many Pequods aboard, stayed six of them, (the rest leaped overboard,) and with them redeemed the two maids, who had been well used by the Pequods, and no violence offered them.[2]

The former governour and Mr. Coddington, being discontented that the people had left them out of all public service, gave further proof of it in the congregation; for they refused to sit in the magistrate's seat, (where Mr. Vane had always sitten from his first arrival,) and went and sate with the deacons, although the governour sent to desire them to come in to him.[3] And upon the day of the general fast, they went from Boston to keep the day at the Mount with Mr. Wheelwright.

Another occasion of their discontent, and of the rest of that party, was an order, which the court had made, to keep out all such persons as might be dangerous to the commonwealth, by imposing a penalty upon all such as should retain any, etc., above three weeks, which should not be allowed by some of the magistrates; for it was very probable, that they expected many of their opinion to come out of England from Mr. || Brierly || his church, etc.[4]

|| B. ||

---

iation may be with nations of nearer similarity of manners. Savages are hardly tamed by kindness; never by severity. I lament, that brave men should be commanded to torture a prisoner of war.

1 This kindness of the Dutch I wish had been longer remembered by their neighbors of Connecticut, especially as mutual charges, without proof, of incitement of the barbarians, are so frequently made by all civilised nations. Of the several causes of the war of 1812, an earnest supporter of the declaration, afterwards President of the United States, speaking of the Orders in Council, said, to " keep them out of sight, is like laying your finger over the unit before a series of noughts, and then arithmetically proving, that they are all nothing."

2 No instance of the worst violence to woman has ever been told of our aborigines. Johnson, lib. II. c. 1, who makes them the " seed of the serpent," says the Indians questioned these maids " to know whether they could make gunpowder."

3 As they ceased to be magistrates, by not being rechosen, they had no right in the seats.

4 In Cotton's Way of Congregational Churches Cleared, in answer to Bayley,

This order, and other differences between the new governour and them, was the cause, that, at his return to Boston, none of them met him; and the serjeants, which had constantly attended the former governour to all public meetings with four halberds, did now refuse to do any such office to the new, alleging that they had done it to the former voluntarily, in respect of his person, not his place. To which it was answered, that there was a double error; 1. Because the place drowns the person, be he honorable or base; 2. In that any compliment of honor, being once conferred upon an office, (though voluntarily,) cannot after be taken away without contempt and injury. The country, taking notice of this, offered to send in
*225 some from the neighboring towns to carry the halberds by course; and upon that the town of Boston offered to send some men, but not the serjeants; but the governour chose rather to make use of two of his own servants.[1]

25.] Our English from Connecticut, with their Indians, and many of the Naragansetts, marched in the night to a fort of the Pequods at Mistick, and, besetting the same about break of the day, after two hours' fight they took it, (by firing it,) and slew therein two chief sachems, and one hundred and fifty fighting men, and about one hundred and fifty old men, women, and children, with the loss of two English, *whereof but one was*[2] killed by the enemy. Divers of the Indian friends were hurt by the ||English,||[3] *because they had not some mark to distinguish

||Pequods||

---

one of the assertors of Presbyterian divine right, he says, speaking of this arbitrary order: "I saw by this means we should receive no more members into our church, but such as must profess themselves of a contrary judgment to what I believed to be a truth." He designed to remove out of the jurisdiction with Davenport, but was dissuaded.

Three tracts on this subject, — A Defence, The Answer, and Replication, — are found in Hutchinson's Coll. 67–100.

1 By the extract from the Records, in a former note on this subject, five pages back, it will be seen, that it was no part of the provision, that those who carried the halberds should be of the rank of serjeants.

2 Mason says, two were killed outright; and thus our author corrects his first relation.

3 The governour had erased *English*, and written *Pequods;* but that is

them from the Pequods, as some of them had.* The story is more fully described in the next leaf.[1]

Presently upon this came news from the Naragansett, that all the English, and two hundred of the Indians, were cut off in their retreat, for want of powder and victuals. Three days after, this was confirmed by a post from Plimouth, with such probable circumstances, as it was generally believed. But, three days after, Mr. Williams, having gone to the Naragansetts to discover the truth, found them mourning, as being confident of it; but that night some came from the army, and assured them all was well, and that all the Pequods were fled, and had forsaken their forts. The general defeat of the Pequods at Mistick happened the day after || our || general fast.

Mo. 4. 3.] Two ships arrived here out of England, (Mr. Peirce was one). In them came the copy of a commission, from the commissioners for New England, to divers of the magistrates here, to govern all the people in New England till further order, etc., upon this pretence, that there was no lawful authority in ||[2]force|| here, either mediate or immediate, from his majesty. *226

Upon the news from Mr. Williams, that the Pequods were dispersed, and some come in and submitted to the Naragansetts, (who would not receive them ||[3]before he|| had sent to know our mind,) the governour and council thought it needless to send so many men, and therefore sent out ||[4]warrants|| only for one half of the two hundred; but some of the people liked not of it, and came to the governour to have all sent. He took it ill; and though three of the ministers came with them to debate the matter, he told them, that if any one, ||[5]discerning|| an error in the proceedings of the council, had come, in a private

||the|| ||[2]form|| ||[3]till they|| ||[4]word|| ||[5]discovering||

manifestly an error, if the following clause be part of the report, which was probably false.

[1] It will not be found, though the author intended to furnish an account. This storming of the Indian fort at Mistick, between New London and Norwich, was an affair reflecting much credit on the commander, whose report, in the History of the war, is very full, accurate, and animated; but he makes the loss of the enemy six or seven hundred, "as some of themselves confessed," and "only seven taken captive, and about seven escaped."

manner, to acquaint ||him|| therewith, etc., it had been well done; but to come, so many of them, in a public and popular way, was not well, and would bring authority into contempt. This they took well at his hands, and excused their intentions. So it was thought fit to send about forty men more, which was yielded rather to satisfy the people, than for any need that appeared.

Upon our governour's letter to Plimouth, our friends there agreed to send a pinnace, with forty men, to assist in the war against the Pequods; but they could not be ready to meet us at the first.

15.] There was a day of thanksgiving kept in all the churches for the victory obtained against the Pequods, and for other mercies.

About this time came home a small pinnace of thirty tons, which had been forth eight months, and was given for lost.[1] She went to the Bermuda, but by continual tempests was kept from ||[2]thence,|| and forced to bear up for the West Indies, and, being in great distress, arrived at Hispaniola, and not daring to go into any inhabited place there, but to go ashore in obscure places, and lived of turtles and *hogs*, etc. At last they were forced into a harbor, where lay a French man-of-war with
*227 his prize, and had surely made prize of them also, but that the providence of God so disposed, as the captain, one ||[3]Petfree,|| had lived at Pascataquack, and knew the merchant of our bark, one Mr. Gibbons. Whereupon he used them courteously, and, for such commodities as she carried, ||[4]freighted|| her with tallow, hides, etc., and sent home with her his prize, which he sold for a small price to be paid in New

||them|| ||[2]hence|| ||[3]Peterfore|| ||[4]furnished||

---

[1] The marginal note is, "Capt. Gib. and Mr. Hill at W. Indies." When we recollect how minute Winthrop usually is in his narrative of such disasters, we may judge how the tale of distress gained by frequent telling, till it grew up to "the wonderful story of Major Gibbons" in the Magnalia, lib. VI. chap. i. § 3. It would with difficulty be understood to refer to the same event in our text, were not the sufferer's name, and his relief by a French *pirate*, sufficient marks of identity to turn us from Mather's Thaumaturgus back to the first relation, probably received from the adventurers' mouths.

England. He brought home an aligarto, which he gave the governour.

20.] Three ships arrived here from Ipswich, with three hundred and sixty passengers.[1] The last being loath to come to an anchor at Castle Island, though hailed by the Castle boat, and required, etc., the gunner made a shot, intending to shoot before her for a warning, but the powder in ||the|| touch-hole being wet, and the ship having fresh way with wind and tide, the shot took place in the shrouds and killed a passenger, an honest man. The next day the governour charged an inquest, and sent them aboard with two of the magistrates (one of them being deputed coroner) to take view of the dead body, and who, upon hearing all the evidence, etc., found that he came to his death by the providence of God.

23.] The governour went to Sagus, and so to Salem and to Ipswich, at all which places the men of the towns met him, and guarded him from town to town, (though not desired nor expected by him,) to show their respect to their governour, and also for his safety, in regard it was reported the Pequods were come this way.[2] He returned again the 28th, being forced to travel all the night by reason of the heat, which was so extreme, as divers of those who were new come on shore, died in their travel a few miles.

26.] There arrived two ships from London, the Hector,

||her||

[1] One of the ships was the John and Dorothy, of which William Andrews was master. His son William was master of another, the Rose of Yarmouth. The other was, I suppose, the Mary Ann, William Goose master. Account of 197 of the passengers, who desired to go, of whom one, with wife and six children, was forbidden by the useless tyranny of the Privy Council, may be read in 4 Mass. Hist. Coll. I. 95-101. Michael Metcalf, a dornix weaver, with wife, nine children, and a servant, came in one of the two former ships. He was a freeman of the city of Norwich, and says he had attempted, in the former year, to escape from the thraldom of Bp. Wren.

[2] Fear of the enemy's enterprise may to us seem unreasonable, considering the numerous plantations between Pequot and Salem; but the inhabitants were few, except on the seaboard. Yet we may believe, that their apprehension for his safety operated much less than a desire to show respect to the governour, especially under the circumstances of slight from those less sound in the faith.

*226 and the [blank]. In these came Mr. Davenport[1] and another[2] minister, and Mr. Eaton[3] and Mr. Hop-

---

[1] Of this celebrated divine, who had been a priest in one of the parishes of London, ample memorials are preserved by all the writers on the early affairs of our country. A sermon preached by him in 1629 is found at the Boston Athenæum. His conduct in concealing the regicides, Whalley and Goffe, has ever been eulogized in part of Connecticut, and was admired by many, who dared not imitate it in Massachusetts. He succeeded Wilson in the First Church of Boston, being the fourth minister in that place, all whose names were John. But his coming from New Haven occasioned one of the most disagreeable controversies with which the affairs of the church have ever troubled our country. The officers of the first church seem to have dealt too subtilely in the affair, and near all the great names of the clergy — Higginson, Cobbet, Whiting, Sherman, Mather, Symmes, and others, including Wilson, son of the former pastor, and Seaborn Cotton, son of the great teacher of the same church — took ground in opposition to Gov. Bellingham and the first church, and in favor of the third church, now the Old South, formed by powerful seceders from the first. Hutchinson, 270–275, has well explained the long protracted agony. Descendants of Davenport have often vindicated their claim to the enjoyment of the talents of their progenitor.

[2] We learn from Trumbull, who erroneously marks the arrival in July, instead of June, that this other minister was Samuel, brother of Gov. Eaton. That author might have read in Mather, that Samuel Eaton, after returning home, died, 9 January, 1665, at Denton in Lancashire.

From the undue brevity of this note, in my former edition, the late Professor J. L. Kingsley, of Yale College, was misled in note H of the Appendix to his admirable Historical Discourse, as he wrote me in May, 1848, on receiving very few words of explanation. His death, on 31 August last, left a void deeply regretted by every student of American History and pure letters.

[3] No character in the annals of New England is of purer fame than that of Theophilus Eaton, governour of the colony of New Haven from its settlement to his death, by twenty annual elections. That his talents were adequate to the station, might be confidently concluded from the fact of his prior service, several years, as representative of Charles I. at the court of Denmark; and the long administration of an infant state without a rival, is irrefragable proof of his prudence and virtue. All the original writers of our history are abundant in his praise, and the later and more judicious inquirers are satisfied with their evidence. The error of Trumbull, I. 99–100, and 231, in asserting that Eaton was three years in the East Indies, and sometime deputy governour of the company trading thither, arose probably from the appellation of *East Country*, used by Mather, from the universal custom of England, at that time, for the regions bordering on the Baltic. It had been avoided by Eliot, Holmes, and Allen; but my respect for the venerable historiographer of Connecticut led me unhesitatingly to adopt his authority, till I saw the cause of his mistake in the

kins,[1] two merchants of London, men of fair estate and of great esteem for religion, and wisdom in outward affairs.

Magnalia. On this pilgrim's character and death, Hubbard, 329, 330, is more valuable and minute than about any other. His death was 7 January, 1657–8.

[1] Edward Hopkins was son-in-law of Gov. Eaton, and, alternately with Haynes, for many years governour of the colony of Connecticut, in which station Eliot erroneously asserts he died. He went to England, probably, in 1652, whence he did not return; though, after the decease of Haynes, he was again chosen governour, in 1654. The time of his death was March, 1657, a few months before his friend Eaton. He was then serving in Oliver's parliament, and also as a commissioner of the army and navy. His liberality to New England was abundantly shown in his will, made 7 or 17 March, 1656–7. Extracts will interest the present age: — "For my estate in New England, (the full account of which I left clear in book there, and the care and inspection whereof was committed to my loving friend, Capt. John Cullick,) I do in this manner dispose: Item, I do give and bequeath unto the eldest child of Mrs. Mary Newton, wife to Mr. Roger Newton, [first minister] of Farmington, and daughter of Mr. Thomas Hooker, deceased, the sum of £30; as also the sum of £30 unto the eldest child of Mr. John Cullick by Elizabeth his present wife, [who was daughter of Col. Fenwick]. Item, I do give and bequeath to Mrs. Sarah Wilson, the wife of Mr. John Wilson, preacher of the gospel, and daughter of my dear pastor, Mr. Hooker, my farm at Farmington, with all the houses, outhouses, buildings, lands, etc., belonging thereunto, to the use of her and the heirs of her body forever. I do also give unto Mrs. Susan Hooker, the relict of Mr. Thomas Hooker, all such debts as are due to me from her, upon the account I left in New England. And the residue of my estate there I do hereby give and bequeath to my father, Theophilus Eaton, Esq., Mr. John Davenport, Mr. John Cullick, and Mr. William Goodwin, in full assurance of their trust and faithfulness in disposing of it according to the true intent and purpose of me the said Edward Hopkins, which is, to give some encouragement in those foreign plantations for the breeding up of hopeful youths, both at the grammar school and college, for the public service of the country in future times. For the estate the Lord hath given me in *this* England, I thus dispose, and my wish is, that £150 per annum be yearly paid per my executor to Mr. David Yale, brother to my dear distressed wife, for her comfortable maintenance, and to be disposed of per him for her good, she not being in a condition fit to manage it herself; and I do heartily entreat him to be careful and tender over her; and my will is, that this be paid quarterly by £37.10 each quarter, and to continue to the end of the quarter after the death of my said wife, and that my executor give good security for a punctual performance hereof. My will also is, that the £30 given me per the will and testament of my brother Henry Hopkins, lately deceased, be given to our sister Mrs. Judith [unknown,] during her natural life, and that it be made up £50 per annum during her life. I do give to my sister Mrs. Margaret Thomson the sum of £50, to be paid her within one year

*229 In the Hector came also the Lord Ley, son and heir of the Earl of Marlborough, being about nineteen years of

---

after my decease. I do give unto my nephew Henry Thomson £800, whereof £400 to be paid within sixteen months after my decease, and the other £400 within six months after the decease of my wife. I do likewise give and bequeath to my niece Katherine Thomson, but now Katherine James, (over and above the portion of £500 formerly given her,) £100. I do also give and bequeath unto my nieces Elizabeth and Patience Dalley, unto each of them, £200, provided they attend the direction of their brother or aunts, or such as are capable to give them advice in the dispose of themselves in marriage. I give unto my brother Mr. David Yale £200; to my brother Mr. Thomas Yale £200, and to my sister Mrs. Hannah Eaton £200. [This was that maiden daughter of Gov. Eaton, who went home with her mother, after his death, married, at London, William Jones, and came again to New Haven in 1660.] My farther mind and will is, that, within six months after the decease of my wife, £500 be made over into New England, according to the advice of my loving friends Major Robert Thomson and Mr. Francis Willoughby, and conveyed into the hands of the trustees before-mentioned, in farther prosecution of the aforesaid public ends, which, in the simplicity of my heart, are for the upholding and promoting the kingdom of the Lord Jesus Christ in those parts of the earth. I do farther give unto my beloved wife a bed, with all furniture belonging unto it, for herself to lie on, and another for the servant maid that waits on her, and £20 in plate for her present use, besides one third part of all my household goods. I give unto Mr. John Davenport, Mr. Theophilus Eaton, Mr. Cullick, each of them, £20, to be made over to them into New England where they are; and my will and pleasure is, that £20 be put into a piece of plate, and presented in my name to my honored friend Dr. Wright, to whom I owe more than that, being much engaged, desiring him to accept it only as a testimony of my respects. I do give unto my servant James Porter £10; unto my maid Margaret £5; unto my maid Mary £2. I do give unto my honored and loving friends Major Robert Thomson and Mr. Francis Willoughby £20 a piece, in a piece of plate, as a token of my respects unto them; and I do give unto my servant Thomas Haytor £20. I do give unto my sister Yale, the wife of Mr. David Yale, £20; as also to John Lollor, a youth now with my sister Eve, £20, to farther him out to be an apprentice to some good trade, and £20 more at the time of his coming to his own liberty, to encourage him to set up his trade, if he continue living so long. I do give unto my nephew Henry Dalley, master of arts in Cambridge, my land in the county of Essex; and, for the payment of all debts, dues, and legacies, do give unto him all my personal estate, and, by these presents, renouncing and making void all other wills and testaments, do declare, constitute, and make him my sole executor, and my good friends Major Robert Thomson and Mr. Francis Willoughby overseers, of this my last will and testament. Signed, sealed, declared, and published by the said Edward Hopkins, Esq., at his house at London, on the 17th day of March in the year of our Lord 1657 to be his last will and testament."

age, who came only to see the country. He was of very *230
sober carriage, and showed much wisdom and moderation
in his lowly and familiar carriage, especially in the ship, where he was much disrespected and unworthily used by the master, one Ferne, and some of the passengers; yet he bare it meekly

---

Mention of the distress of his wife, named Ann, daughter of the widow Ann Yale, who had married Gov. Eaton, which was by loss of her reason, will occur in our second volume. She died 17 December, 1698. Trumbull, I. 233, says, Hopkins's estate, "given in New England, was estimated at about £1000 sterling, and was appropriated to the support of the grammar schools in New Haven, Hartford, and Hadley. The money originally belonged to New Haven and Hartford; but as a considerable number of the people of Hartford afterwards removed to Hadley, and were principal settlers of that town, they received their proportion of the donation."

In six months after the wife's decease, which was above forty years later than the testator's, the £500 out of the English property should have been paid. But the executor and residuary devisee being dead, process in chancery was necessary against *his* executor. Under a final decree by Sir Simon Harcourt, lord keeper, Harvard College has enjoyed, jointly with the grammar school in Cambridge, since 1714, a fund, of which Gov. Dudley and other principal persons, civil and ecclesiastical, to the number of twenty-one, were made first trustees. As the direction from the chancery was to invest the same in lands, a purchase was made, under authority of an act of the province, from the Natick Indians, being about thirteen thousand acres, comprising, with an additional grant from the province, the flourishing town of Hopkinton in Middlesex county, — having its name from this liberal benefactor of New England, — and part of the town of Upton in the county of Worcester. The rent charge of these lands, for many years secured by the commonwealth, amounted to $222,22 annually, until March, 1823, and from thence forward, forever, $666,67 annually, being at the rate of one penny sterling per acre for the first ninety-nine years of the leases, and three pence sterling afterwards. Forever lasted but a short time, for the enhanced rents could not be obtained from the tenants; and by composition with the commonwealth, they were acquitted on receipt from the public treasury, after long disputation, for less than half their legal value, by the trustees. Being one of the trustees, the editor knows the faithful and judicious employment of this charity. The fund, which, notwithstanding the evils of paper money, and occasional injurious denial of rent by some of the tenants, has been increased, now exceeds the sum of thirty thousand dollars. See Quincy's Hist. of Har. Coll. I. 205.

Several letters of Gov. Hopkins to J. Winthrop, jun., were preserved, in vol. XIX. of Trumbull MSS. before the Court street fire, and there is one to our author, 21 June, 1648, printed in Hutchinson's Collection, 225, showing a disposition to return to England, controlled by affection towards his adopted country. It is written with more perspicuity than is usually found in papers of that age.

and silently. When he came on shore the governour was from home, and he took up his lodging at the common inn. When the governour returned, he presently came to his house. The governour offered him lodging, etc., but he refused, saying, that he came not to be troublesome to any, and the house where he
*231 was, was so well governed, that he could be as private there as elsewhere.

We had news of a commission granted in England to divers gentlemen here for the governing of New England, etc.; but instead thereof we received a commission from Sir Ferdinando Gorges to govern his province of New Somersetshire, which is from Cape Elizabeth to Sagadahoc, and withal to oversee his servants and private ||affairs;|| which was observed as a matter of no good discretion, but passed in silence. We excused our not intermeddling, etc., because, being directed to six or five of them, and one of their names being mistaken, and another removed to Connecticut, there were but four in the country; as also for that it did not appear to us what authority he had to grant such a commission. As for the commission from the king, we received only a copy of it, but the commission itself staid at the seal for want of paying the fees.[1]

Mo. 5.] The party, who procured the commission, one George ||[2]Cleves,||[2] brought also a protection under the privy signet for searching out the great lake of Iracoyce, and for the

||officers|| ||[2]Chever||

---

[1] At the State Paper Office in London, I saw, eleven years since, a letter of Gorges, in which he said, he was to be made Governour General of the New England Colonies. It bore date, I think, of 1637.

[2] Cleves was a person of some importance, as, in the second volume of this History, will appear. He was agent or governour under Alexander Rigby, a member of parliament; and in Hazard, I. 570, is a letter from Edward Rigby, son of Alexander, to the inhabitants of Laconia, 19 July, 1652, taking notice of Cleves being in England, and expressing a design to send him back. I should consider it as an approbation, though Sullivan, History of Maine, 315, says, Cleves "was an equivocal character, and acted with great duplicity. He obtained a letter of agency from Sir Ferdinando Gorges, acted as deputy governour to both, and sold lands under the title of each, as appears from the registry of deeds, which he executed." On his next page he remarks on Cleves's unfaithfulness to the son, after the death of the father. I know not whether Cleves lived in Maine afterwards.

sole trade of beaver, and the planting of Long Island, by §articles of§ agreement between the Earl of Sterling, Viscount Canada, and him. Thus this and other gentlemen in England get large circuits of lands, etc., in this country, and are very ready to grant them out to such as will become their tenants, and, to encourage them, do procure commissions, protections, etc., which cost them nothing, but will be at no charge in any right way of plantation, which should be by coming themselves, or sending some of their children, etc.; but now, as they adventure little, so they are sure to lose nothing but their vain hope.[1]

Capt. Stoughton and his company, having pursued the Pequots beyond Connecticut, and missing of them, returned *232
to Pequot River, where they were advertised, that one hundred of them were newly come back to a place some twelve miles off. So they marched thither by night, and surprised them all. They put to death twenty-two men, and reserved two sachems, hoping by them to get Sasacus, (which they promised). All the rest were women and children, of whom they gave the Naragansetts thirty, and our Massachusetts Indians three, and the rest they sent hither.

A pinnace, returning, took a canoe with four Indians near Block Island. We sent to Miantunnomoh to know what they were, and after we discharged all save one, who was a Pequod, whom we gave Mr. Cutting to carry into England.

[Large blank.]

The differences grew so much here, as tended fast to a separation; so as Mr. Vane, being, among others, invited by the governour to accompany the Lord Ley at dinner, *not only* refused to come, (alleging by letter that his conscience withheld him,) *but also, at the same hour, he went over to Nottle's Island to dine with Mr. Maverick, and carried the Lord Ley with him.*[2]

---

[1] This opinion of Winthrop has, in all succeeding times, been confirmed, being not more founded on reason, than verified by experience.

[2] I have no doubt, that every reader will be pleased with the preservation of this anecdote, though erased by the governour; for it strengthens his remark very much.

6.] There were sent to Boston forty-eight women and children. There were eighty taken, as before is expressed. These were disposed of to particular persons in the country. Some of them ran away and were brought again by the Indians our neighbors, and those ||we|| branded on the shoulder.

12.] Ayanemo, the sachem of Niantick, came to Boston with seventeen men. He made divers propositions, which we promised to give answer unto the next day; and then, understanding he had received many of the Pequods, submitting to him since the former defeat, we first demanded the delivery of them, which he sticking at, we refused further conference with him; but the next morning, he came and offered what we desired. So the governour referred him to treat with our captains at the Pequod, and wrote instructions to them how to deal with him, and received his present of ten fathom of wampom. He was lovingly dismissed, with some small things given him.

Here came over a brother[1] of Mrs. Hutchinson, and some other of Mr. Wheelwright's friends, whom the governour thought not fit to allow, as others, to sit down among us, with-
*233 out some trial of them. Therefore, to save others from the danger of the law in receiving of them, he allowed them for four months. This was taken very ill by those of the other party, and many hot speeches given forth about it, and about their removal, etc.

13.] Mr. Stoughton, with about eighty of the English, whereof Mr. Ludlow, Capt. Mason, and [blank,] of Connecticut, were part, sailed to the west in pursuit of Sasacus, etc. At Quinepiack, they killed six, and took two. At a head of land a little short they beheaded two sachems; whereupon they called the place Sachem's Head. About this time they had given a Pequod his life to go find out Sasacus. He went, and found him not far off; but Sasacus, suspecting him, intended to kill him, which the fellow perceiving, escaped in the night, and came to the English. Whereupon Sasacus and Mononotto, their two chief sachems, and some twenty more, fled to

||men||

[1] What ship he came in, who he was, or where he lived, are all unknown.

the Mohawks. But eighty of their stoutest men, and two hundred others, women and children, were at a place within twenty or thirty miles of the Dutch, whither our men marched, and, being guided by a Divine Providence, came upon them, where they had twenty wigwams, hard by a most hideous swamp, so thick with bushes and so quagmiry, as men could hardly crowd into it. Into this swamp they were all gotten. Lieut. Davenport and two or three more, that entered the swamp, were dangerously wounded by the Indian arrows, and with much difficulty were fetched out. Then our men surrounded the swamp, being a mile about, and shot at the Indians, and they at them, from three of the clock in the afternoon till they desired parley, and offered to yield, and life was offered to all that had not shed English blood. So they began to come forth, now some and then some, till about two hundred women and children were come out, and amongst them the sachem of that place, and thus they kept us two hours, till night was come on, and then the men told us they would fight it out; and so they did all the night, coming up behind the bushes very near our men, and shot many arrows into their hats, sleeves, and ||stocks,|| yet (which was a very miracle) not one of ours wounded. When it was near morning, it grew very dark, so as such of them as were left crept out at one place and escaped, being (as was judged) not above twenty at most, and those like to be wounded; for in the pursuit they found some of them dead of their wounds.[1] Here our men gat some booty of kettles, trays, wampom, *234
etc., and the women and children were divided, and sent some to Connecticut, and some to the Massachusetts. The sachem of the place, having yielded, had his life, and his wife and children, etc. The women, which were brought home, reported that we had slain in all thirteen sachems, and that there were thirteen more left. We had now slain and taken, in all, about seven hundred. We sent fifteen of the boys and two women to Bermuda, by Mr. Peirce; but he, missing it, carried them to Providence Isle.[2]

||stockings||

---

[1] For a larger account of this swamp fight, see Mason's History.

[2] We cannot fail, I think, to lament this enslaving of the prisoners, by sale in

Mo. 6.] Mr. Stoughton sailed, with some of his company, from Pequod to Block Island. They came thither in the night, yet were discovered, and our men having killed one or two of them, and burnt some of their wigwams, etc., they came to parley, and, submitting themselves to become tributaries in one hundred fathom wampompeague, and to deliver any that should be found to have any hand in Mr. Oldham's death, they were all received, and no more harm done them.

3.] At our general court, one Greensmith, being censured for saying that all the elders, etc., except two, did preach a covenant of works, etc., he did appeal to the king; but the court, notwithstanding, committed him till, etc.

The Lord Ley, being told that one Ewre had spoken treason against the king, sent for the party, one Brooks, and inquiring of him, he told him that Ewre had said, about twelve months before, that, if the king did send any authority hither against our patent, he would be the first should resist him. This coming to the governour's knowledge, he sent for the parties, and bound them over to the general court. When they came there, Brooks brought his wife to witness with him; but her testimony agreed not with his; also three others (whom he had told it unto) reported it otherwise. So at length they all agreed, and set it under their hands, that Ewre said, that, if there came any authority out of England contrary to the patent, he would withstand it. Now, because here was no mention of the king, and because he never informed any of the magistrates of it, and for that it was evident that he bare malice ||to|| the said Ewre, we saw no cause to take any other of the parties informing, (the rather because themselves did urge it, and she *235
refused longer to speak at all, except she might be put to her oath,) nor any offence which deserved punishment, seeing it is lawful to resist any authority, which was to overthrow the lawful authority of the king's ||[2]grant;|| and so the governour

||of|| ||[2]patent||

---

a foreign country, however it might be excused by a pretended necessity. In that day it was probably justified by reference to the practice or institution of the Jews. Yet that cruel people never sent prisoners so far.

did openly declare, in the court, as justifiable by the laws of England.[1]

3.] The Lord Ley and Mr. Vane went from Boston to the ship, riding at Long Island, to go for England. At their departure, those of Mr. Vane's party were gathered together, and did accompany him to the boat, (and many to the ship;) and the men, being in their arms, gave him divers vollies of shot, and five pieces of ordnance, and he had five more at the castle. But the governour was not come from the court, but had left order with the captain for their honorable dismission.

There was an old woman in Ipswich, who came out of England blind and deaf, yet her son could make her understand any thing, and know any man's name, by her sense of feeling. He would write upon her hand some letters of the name, and by other such motions would inform her. This the governour himself had ||trial of|| when he was at Ipswich.

5.] Mr. Hooker and Mr. Stone came, with Mr. Wilson, from Connecticut by Providence; and, the same day, Mr. Ludlow, Mr. Pincheon, and about twelve more, came the ordinary way by land, and brought with them a part of the skin and lock of hair of Sasacus and his brother, and five other Pequod sachems, who, being fled to the Mohawks for shelter, with their wampom, being to the value of ||[2]five hundred pounds,||[2] were by them surprised and slain, with twenty of their best men. Mononottoh was also taken, but escaped wounded. They brought news also of divers other Pequods, which had been slain by other Indians, and their heads brought to the English; so that now there had been slain and taken between eight and nine hundred. Whereupon letters were sent to Mr. Stoughton and the rest, to call them all home.[3]

A woman of Boston congregation, having been in much trouble of mind about her spiritual estate, at length grew *236

||tried often|| ||[2]£500||

[1] Here is perhaps to be understood an indirect censure of Lord Ley for his interference, and a direct maintenance of the freedom of speech on *such* a topick.

[2] Weight, not money, appears to me the meaning.

[3] A despatch, from Stoughton on service, will be found in the Appendix, letter D.

into ||utter|| desperation, and could not endure to hear of any comfort, etc., so as one day she took her little infant and threw it into a well, and then came into the house and said, now she was sure she should be damned, for she had drowned her child; but some, stepping presently forth, saved the child.[1] See more after.

Mr. Hooker and the rest of the elders, meeting divers days, they agreed (with consent of the magistrates) upon a day of humiliation to be kept in all the churches the 24th of this month; the day for the conference to be the 30th day. At their private meetings some reconciliation was made between Mr. Cotton and Mr. Wheelwright and Mr. Wilson, he professing, that, by his speech in the court, he did not intend the doctrine of Mr. Cotton or Mr. Wheelwright delivered in the public congregation, but some opinions, (||[2]naming|| three or four,) which were privately carried in Boston and other parts of the country; and accordingly Mr. Cotton declared so much in the congregation the Lord's day following. And for the rest of his speech, it was agreed by all the elders to be inoffensive, considering his call thereto by the court. This sudden change was much observed by some, who were privy that Mr. Wilson had professed as much before, both privately to the elders, and publicly in the congregation, and that the said opinions had been delivered to the elders of Boston in writing as those which Mr. Wilson intended.

17.] Mr. Davenport preached at Boston (it being the lecture day) out of that in 1 Cor., I exhort you brethren, etc., that there be no division among you, etc.; wherein, as he fully set forth the nature and danger of ||divisions, and the disorders|| which were among us, etc., so he clearly discovered his judgment against the new opinions and bitter practices which were sprung up here.

||bitter|| ||[2]meaning|| ||[3]disorders and the divisions||

[1] In the margin is written, "Hett's wife distracted." A similar instance of her insanity, in attempting to destroy another of her children, is found in this History five years later, in Vol. II. 65. See also II. 129, for result.

[2] Nothing is more refreshing, in the violence of these contests, which grew more violent as the matter of contest was unintelligible to the many, and the

Mr. Cotton, expounding that in 2 Chron. [blank] of *237
the defection of the ten tribes from Rehoboam, and his preparations to recover them by war, and the prophet's prohibition, etc., proved from that in Numbers, 27. 21, that the rulers of the people should consult with the ministers of the churches upon occasion of any war to be undertaken, and any other weighty business, though the case should seem never so clear, as David in the case of Ziglag, and the Israelites in the case of Gibeah. Judges, etc.

26.] The captain and soldiers returned all from Pequod, having lost but one man, and he died of a flux, and another fell sick of an old infirmity, an asthma. The Indians about sent in still many Pequods' heads and hands from Long Island and other places, and [blank] sachems of Long Island came voluntarily, and brought a tribute to us of twenty fathom of wampom, each of them; and Miantunnomoh sent here some Pequod squaws, which had run from us.

31.] The Naragansetts sent us the ||hands|| of three Pequods, — one the chief of those who murdered Capt. Stone.

[Very large blank.]

Twenty men went in a pinnace to kill sea horse at the Isle of Sable, and after six weeks returned home, and could not find the island; but, after another month, viz., about the [blank] of September, they set forth again with more skilful seamen, with intent to stay there all winter.

Mr. Eaton, and some others of Mr. Davenport's company, went to view Quinepiack, with intent to begin a plantation there. They had many offers here and at Plimouth, and they had viewed many places, but none could content.

[Large blank.]

Some of the magistrates and ministers of Connecticut being here, there was a day of meeting appointed to agree upon some articles of confederation, and notice was given to Plim-

||heads||

---

diversity of opinions not very striking to the few, than the same church retaining, for their Christian instructors, the heads of the opposite parties, Cotton and Wilson. The fact proves, stronger than any argument, the prudence of the pastor and the temper of the teacher.

outh, that they might join in it, (but their warning was so short as they could not come). This was concluded after. See (3.) 1643.

[Very large blank.]

30.] The synod, called the assembly, began at Newtown. There were all the teaching elders through the country, and some ||new|| come out of England, not yet called to any place here, as Mr. Davenport, etc.

The assembly began with prayer, made by Mr. Shepherd, the pastor of Newtown. Then the erroneous opinions, which were
*238 spread in the country, were read, (being eighty[1] in all;) next the unwholesome expressions;[2] then the scriptures abused. Then they chose two moderators for the next day, viz., Mr. Buckly and Mr. Hooker, and these were continued in that place all the time of the assembly. There were about eighty opinions, some blasphemous, others erroneous, and all unsafe, condemned by the whole assembly; whereto near all the elders, and others sent by the churches, subscribed their names; but some few liked not subscription, though they consented to the condemning of them.

||were||

---

[1] If any in our times have such insatiable curiosity, as to desire more particular information of the incomprehensible jargon contained in these errors, the exact numeration of which was eighty-two, imputed to the followers of Cotton and supporters of Wheelwright, with the antinomian explanations of Mrs. Hutchinson, that she denied, the whole is written in "A short Story of the Rise, Reign, and Ruin of Antinomians, Familists, and Libertines, that infected the Churches of New England," by Thomas Welde, who was one of the chief inquisitors. The edition, London, 1644, published by the author, is in the Boston Athenæum; a second edition, London, 1692, in Harvard College Library. The work has not, I presume, been often quoted within a century. It was relied upon in the famous "Testimony of the Pastors of the Churches in the Province of Massachusetts Bay at the Annual Convention in Boston, 25 May, 1743," protesting against the spreading of many antinomian and familistical errors, occasioned by the itinerant labors of Whitefield, Tennent, and their disciples, by which, for some years, was produced the greatest religious excitement ever known in New England. It was happy that the government did not employ the same means of conversion as in 1637.

[2] They amounted to nine, in stating which, with their confutation, three pages of Welde's book is occupied.

Some of the church of Boston, and some others, were offended at the producing of so many errors, as if it were a reproach laid upon the country without cause; and called to have the persons named, which held those errors. To which it was answered and affirmed by many, both elders and others, that all those opinions could be proved, by sufficient testimony, to be held by some in the country; but it was not thought fit to name the § parties, because this assembly had not to do with § persons, but doctrines only. Yet this would not satisfy some, but they oft called for witnesses; and, because some of the magistrates declared to them, (when they refused to forbear speech unseasonably, though the moderators desired them,) that, if they would not forbear, it would prove § a civil § disturbance, and then the magistrate must interpose, they objected against this, as if the magistrate had nothing to do in this assembly. So as he was forced to tell one of them, that, if he would not forbear, but make trial of it, he might see it executed. Upon this some of Boston departed from the assem- *239 bly, and came no more.[1]

After the errors condemned, there were five points in question, between Mr. Cotton and Mr. Wheelwright on the one part, and the rest of the elders on the other part, *which were after reduced to three,* and those after put into such expressions as Mr. Cotton and they agreed, but Mr. Wheelwright did not:—

1. The first was about our union with Christ. The question was, whether we were united before we had active faith. The consent was, that there was no marriage union with Christ before actual faith, which is more than habitual.

---

[1] Perhaps it may seem reasonable, to doubt the usefulness of such a declaration of errors, that might not, at least many of them, have entered into the heads of the speculatists, unless they had been thus branded. But, "'tis glorious sport, to see the engineer hoist with his own petard."

In his 'Way of Congregational Churches,' p. 63, Cotton, answering many gross charges of Bailey's Dissuasive, as to his concurrence in Mrs. Hutchinson's errors, says with much force: "Such as endeavored the healing of these distempers did seem to me to be transported with more jealousies, and heats, and paroxysms of spirit than would well stand with brotherly love, or the rule of the gospel." Ten years after the agitations, this was his opinion; and it may safely be taken for the judgment of all succeeding time.

2. The second was, about evidencing justification §by sanctification.§ The consent was, that some saving sanctifications (as faith, etc.) were coexistent, concurrent, and coapparent (or at least might be) with the witness of the Spirit always.

3. That the new creature is not the person of a believer, but a body of saving graces in such a one; and that Christ, as a head, doth enliven or quicken, preserve and act the same, but Christ himself is no part of this new creature.

4. That though, in effectual calling, (in which the answer of the soul is by active faith, wrought at the same instant by the Spirit,) justification and sanctification be all together in them; yet God doth not justify a man, before he be effectually called, and so a believer.

5. That Christ and his benefits may be offered and exhibited to a man under a covenant of works, but not in or by a covenant of works.[1]

In the first handling of these questions, either party delivered their arguments in writing, which were read in the assembly, and, after, the answers to them, which spent much time without any effect; but after they came to open dispute, the questions were soon determined; for so they came to understand each other better.

Mo. 7.] The last day of the assembly other questions were debated and resolved: —

*240 1. That though women might meet (some few together) to pray and ||edify|| one another; yet such a set assembly, (as was then in practice at Boston,) where sixty or more did meet every week, and one woman (in a prophetical way, by resolving questions of doctrine, and expounding scripture) took upon her the whole exercise, was agreed to be disorderly, and without rule.[2]

||advise||

---

[1] We must regret, rather than wonder, that consent in the faith, after a synod on high points of doctrine, not deduced simply, perhaps not deducible, from the scriptures, is generally obtained by expressing the propositions in language, either unintelligible or designedly ambiguous. The peace of the church is restored by darkness.

[2] A *prophetical way* has been often followed, at meetings of women in Boston, and is, I think, in our days, without censure. The conduct of the female

2. Though a private member might ask a question publicly, after sermon, for information; yet this ought to be very wisely and sparingly done, and that with leave of the elders: but questions of ‖reference,‖ (then in use,) whereby the doctrines delivered were reproved, and the elders reproached, and that with bitterness, etc., was utterly condemned.

3. That a person, refusing to come to the assembly, to abide the censure of the church, might be proceeded against, though absent; yet it was held better, that the magistrates' help were called for, to compel him to be present.

4. That a member, differing from the rest of the church in any opinion, which was not fundamental, ought not for that to forsake the ordinances there; and if such did desire dismission to any other church, which was of his opinion, and did it for that end, the church whereof he was ought to deny it for the same end.[1]

22.] The assembly brake up; and it was propounded by the governour, that they would consider, that, seeing the Lord had been so graciously present in this assembly, that matters had been carried on so peaceably, and concluded so comfortably in all love, etc., if it were not fit to have the like meeting once a year, or, at least, the next year, to settle what yet remained to be agreed, or if but to nourish love, etc. This motion was well liked of all, but it was not thought fit to conclude it.[2]

‖blank‖

---

assembly in 1637, however, so much resembles party making, that the resolution of the synod is approved by the editor, though it bears hard on his great, great, great, great grandmother.

[1] Such resolutions as the two last must, by modern Congregationalists, be thought very tyrannical; and any proceedings of churches conformable to them would be utterly disregarded by the aggrieved. The law would now protect one, instead of compelling him, in case of refusal to go to church to hear his own censure.

[2] General experience in Christendom, since the council at Jerusalem in the days of the apostles, has shown, that, instead of tending to "*nourish love*," synods have served only to engender strife and debate, to rend anew the seamless coat of their master, and in his name to utter a new commandment, that men hate one another. If this first synod of New England produced peace, as we cannot but acknowledge it did, it was by the encourage-

*241 There was a motion made also by the governour, that, whereas there was difference among the churches about the maintenance of their ministers, it might be agreed what way was most agreeable to the rule of the gospel; but the elders did not like to deal in that, lest it should be said, that this assembly was gathered for their private advantage.[1]

26.] Mr. Davenport (as he had been before requested by the assembly) preached out of Phil. 3: 16, wherein he laid down the occasions of differences among Christians, etc., and declared the effect and fruit of the assembly, and, with much wisdom and sound argument, persuaded to unity, etc.

The diet of the assembly was provided at the country's charge, as also the fetching and sending back of those which came from Connecticut. It came to, in all, [blank].[2]

[Large blank.]

28.] Two men were hanged at Boston for several murders. The one, John Williams, a ship-carpenter, who, being lately come into the country, and put in prison for theft, brake out of prison with one John Hoddy, ||whom,|| near the great pond, in the way to Ipswich, beyond Salem, he murdered, and took away his clothes and what else he had, and went in them to Ipswich, (where he had been sent to prison,) and was there again apprehended; and though his clothes were all bloody, yet he would confess nothing, till about a week after, that the body of Hoddy was found by the kine, who, smelling the blood, made such a roaring, as the cow-keeper, looking about, found the dead body covered with a heap of stones.

The other, William Schooler, was a vintner in London, and had been a common adulterer, (as himself did confess,) and had wounded a man in a duel, for which he fled into the Low

||when||

---

ment of the magistrate to the evangelical process of banishment, which was soon inflicted by the civil arm, after the ecclesiastical head had failed in its remedies.

[1] This disinterested spirit of the assembly, when invited by the chief civil authority of the colony to consider of their own maintenance, must never be recollected without honor.

[2] From the Colony Records, where we ought to look, I am unable to supply this blank. The synod lasted twenty-four days.

Country, and from thence he fled from his captain and came into this country, leaving his wife (a handsome, neat woman) in England. He lived with another fellow at Merrimack, and there being a poor maid at Newbury, one Mary Sholy, *242
who had desired a guide to go with her to her master, who dwelt at Pascataquack, he inquired her out, and agreed, for fifteen shillings, to conduct her thither. But, two days after, he returned, and, being asked why he returned so soon, he answered, that he had carried her within two or three miles of the place, and then she would go no farther. Being examined for this by the magistrates ||at|| Ipswich, and no proof found against him, he was let go. But, about a year after, being impressed to go against the Pequods, he gave ill speeches, for which the governour sent warrant for him, and being apprehended, (and supposed it had been for the death of the maid, ||[2]some|| spake what they had heard, which might occasion suspicion,) he was again examined, and divers witnesses produced about it. Whereupon he was committed, arraigned, and condemned, by due proceeding. The ||[3]effect|| of the evidence was this: —

1. He had ||[4]lived|| a vicious life, and now lived like an atheist.

2. He had sought out the maid, and undertook to carry her to a place where he had never been.

3. When he crossed Merrimack, he landed in a place three miles from the usual path, from whence it was scarce possible she should get into the path.

4. He said he went by Winicowett house, which he said stood on the contrary side of the way.

5. Being, as he said, within two or three miles of Swamscote, ||[5]where|| he left her, he went not thither to tell them of her, nor staid by her that night, nor, at his return home, did tell any body of her, till he was demanded of her.

6. When he came back, he had above ten shillings in his purse, and yet he said she would give him but seven shillings, and he carried no money with him.

7. At his return, he had some blood upon his hat, and on

||of|| ||[2]soon|| ||[3]estate|| ||[4]led|| ||[5]when||

his skirts before, which he said was with a pigeon, which he killed.

8. He had a scratch on the left side of his nose, and, being asked by a neighbor how it came, he said it was with a bramble, which could not be, it being of the breadth of a small nail; and being asked after by the magistrate, he said it was with his piece, but that could not be on the left side.

9. The body of the maid was found by an Indian, about half a year after, in the midst of thick swamp, ten miles short of the place he said he left her in, and about three miles from the place where he landed by Merrimack, (and it was after seen
*243 by the English,) the flesh being rotted off it, and the clothes laid all on an heap by the body.

10. He said, that soon after he left her, he met with a bear, and he thought that bear might kill her, yet he would not go back to save her.

11. He brake prison, and fled as far as Powder Horn Hill, and there hid himself out of the way, for fear of pursuit, and after, when he arose to go forward, he could not, but (as himself confessed) was forced to return back to prison again.

At his death he confessed he had made many lies to excuse himself, but denied that he had killed or ravished her. He was very loath to die, and had hope he should be reprieved; but the court held him worthy of death, in undertaking the charge of a shiftless maid, and leaving her (when he might have done otherwise) in such a place as he knew she must needs perish, if not preserved by means unknown. Yet there were some ministers and others, who thought the evidence not sufficient to take away his life.[1]

(8.) 7.] The Wren, a small pinnace, coming from Connecticut, was taken in a N. E. storm, and forced to anchor near Conyhassett, where she drave upon the rocks, and was wrecked, but all the men were saved.

12.] A day of thanksgiving kept in all the churches for ||our victories|| against the Pequods, and for the success of the

||a victory||

[1] Doubts might reasonably be entertained; for the first and last circumstances, to say nothing of more than half of the others, are of very uncertain tendency.

assembly; but, by reason of this latter, some of Boston would not be present at the public exercises. The captains and soldiers, who had been in the late service, were feasted, and, after the sermon, the magistrates and elders accompanied them to the door of the house where they dined.

[Large blank.]

(9.) 1.] Miantunnomoh, the Naragansett sachem, came to Boston. The governour, deputy, and treasurer, treated with him, and they parted upon fair terms. He acknowledged that all the Pequod country and Block Island were ours, and promised that he would not meddle with them but by our leave. We gave him leave to right himself for the ‖wrongs‖ which ‖[2]Janemoh and Wequash Cook‖ had done him; and for the wrong they had done us, we would right ourselves in our own time.

A young man, coming alone in a skiff from Newtown, in a N. E. storm of wind and snow, was found dead in his *244 boat, with a half-crown piece in his mouth.

One Jewell, master of a bark, was drowned. The manner was this. He was bound to the Isle of Sable, to relieve our men there. His bark had lain near a week at Natascott, waiting for him, but he staid at Boston drinking, and could not be gotten away. Mo. x. When he went, there was committed to his care a rundlet of strong water, sent to some there, he promising, that upon his life, it should not be touched; but, as he went down in his bark's skiff, he went on shore at the castle, and there drank out about a gallon of it, and at night went away; but, it being very cold and dark, they could not find their bark, and Jewell his hat falling into the water, as they were ‖[3]rowing‖ back to look for it, he fell into the water, near the shore, where it was not six feet deep, and could not be recovered.

There was great hope that the late general assembly would have had some good effect in pacifying the troubles and dissensions about matters of religion; but it fell out otherwise.[1]

‖injuries‖ ‖[2]J. and N. Cook‖ ‖[3]coming‖

[1] By this generation, an erroneous zeal for God in their fathers should be regarded with tenderness. We are not much endangered in this respect by their example; yet it is proper to look at their conduct, for it may be a warning.

For though Mr. Wheelwright and those of his party had been
*245 clearly confuted and confounded in the assembly, yet
they persisted in their opinions, and were as busy in nourishing contentions (the principal of them) as before. Whereupon the general court, being assembled in the 2 of the 9th month, and finding, upon consultation, that two so opposite parties could not || contain || in the same body, without apparent hazard of ruin to the whole, agreed to send away some of the principal; and for this a fair opportunity[1] was offered by the

||continue||

If the state had left this obscure controversy, where it belonged, to the unsound heads but pure hearts of the deluded, it might soon have subsided in silence. Hutchinson, I. 73, thinks posterity might have been ignorant that such a woman as his ancestor ever existed. The proceedings of the first council of Ephesus, A. D. 431, which condemned Nestorius and his harmless errors, may be found in Gibbon's Decline and Fall, chap. XLVII. Metaphysical doctrines then influenced, as they have often since, the concerns of the state, and the rights of citizens were judged by their opinions on religion; while the supreme magistrate, instead of an impartial arbiter, became the furious leader or blind follower of the dominant faction. "Ephesus, the city of the Virgin, was defiled with rage and clamor, with sedition and blood; the rival synods darted anathemas and excommunications from their spiritual engines; and the court of Theodosius was perplexed by the adverse and contradictory narratives of the Syrian and Egyptian factions. During a busy period of three months, the emperor tried every method, except the most effectual means of indifference and contempt, to reconcile this theological quarrel."

The deliberations at Ephesus terminated in the establishment of a dogma about the double nature of the Founder of our religion; but this benefit, for which the unholy assembly has since been venerated under the title of the third œcumenical council, appears rather the result of passion than of argument, and relies more on the fraud of man than the authority of scripture. Similar indecencies may not be found in the ecclesiastical assemblies of New England; but there is some parallelism in the object and the result; and the sarcasms of the adversary are in no small degree justified. For seventeen centuries, the occasions to blaspheme are almost as numerous as the synods.

1 *Pretence* would have been as proper a word as *opportunity*, and a strange pretence it seems. If by the remonstrance an indignity were offered to the March court, by all rules of proceeding, either of reason or practice, the same body, and not another, should have passed its animadversion on the contempt. Yet a new court was chosen in May, and held, as our author shows, a second session in August, without taking any notice of the previous offence. Perhaps it might have been imprudent to punish, before Sir H. Vane and Lord Ley departed; and such a probable inference is fortified by a passage in Welde's pre-

remonstrance or petition, which they preferred to the court the 9th of the 1st month, wherein they affirm Mr. Wheelwright to be innocent, and that the court had condemned the truth of Christ, with divers other scandalous and seditious speeches, (as appears at large in the proceedings[1] of this court, which were faithfully collected and published soon after the court brake up,) subscribed by more than sixty of that faction, whereof one || William || Aspinwall, being one, and he that drew the said petition, being then sent as a deputy for Boston, was for the same dismissed, and after called to the court and disfranchised and banished.[2] John Coggeshall was another deputy, who, though his hand || were || not to the petition, yet, professing *246
himself to approve it, etc., was also dismissed, and after disfranchised. Then the court sent warrant to Boston to send other deputies in their room; but they intended to have sent the same men again; but Mr. Cotton, coming amongst them,

|| Mr. || ||² was ||

---

face. There was still another general court, in September after the dissolution of the synod, and Aspinwall was a member of that court; yet, though it must have been known, that the foul spirit exhibited in the petition was not purged away by the scientific confutation, the sleeping honor of the March legislature remained without vindication.

1 Unless my opinions be as much perverted by prejudice as those of the majority of the court appear to me, this account of the remonstrance is very unjust; but that every reader may form his own judgment of this "seditious libel," as it was called by authority, I have transcribed it from Welde, p. 23–25, and given it a place in the Appendix, E.

2 The petition was suddenly drawn up, as the audience withdrew from the court, after their censure of Wheelwright; and sentence of banishment was passed on Aspinwall, before it was known that he was the penman. Welde, 30, considers it "an overruling hand of God; for, the *next day*, it was discovered, that he was the man that did frame the petition, and drew many to subscribe to it, and some had their names put to it without their knowledge, and in his first draught there were other passages so foul, as he was forced to put them out, and yet many had not subscribed but upon his promise, that it should not be delivered without advice of Mr. Cotton, which was never done." Perhaps the passages erased before presenting were an aggravation of the crime in the opinion of the reverend casuist, whose judgment is so blinded by passion, that he seems an unfortunate advocate, rather than an impartial reporter. Of the misrepresentation about Cotton, and of the forged signatures, no light is obtained from Winthrop or the public records.

dissuaded them with much ado.[1] Then the court sent for Mr. Wheelwright, and, he persisting to justify his sermon, and his whole practice and opinions, and refusing to leave either the place or his public exercisings, he was disfranchised and banished. Upon which he appealed to the king, but neither called witnesses, nor desired any act to be made of it. The court told him, that an appeal did not || lie ; || for by the king's grant we had power to hear and determine without any reservation, etc. So he relinquished his appeal, and the court gave him leave to go to his house, upon his promise, that, if he were not gone out of ||[2]our|| jurisdiction within fourteen days, he would render himself to one of the magistrates.[2]

The court also sent for Mrs. Hutchinson, and charged her with divers matters, as her keeping two public lectures every week in her house, whereto sixty or eighty persons did usually resort, and for reproaching most of the ministers (viz., all except Mr. Cotton) for not preaching a covenant of free grace, and that they had not the seal of the spirit, nor were able ministers of the New Testament; which were clearly proved against her, though she sought to shift it off. And, after many speeches to and fro, at last she was so full as she could not contain, but vented her revelations; amongst which this was

||lay|| ||[2]the||

---

1 Coddington was the other representative of Boston, and probably did not sign the remonstrance; yet he approved it, I suppose, as much as Coggeshall. In place of Aspinwall and Coggeshall, the Town Records inform us, that, 6 November, William Colbron and John Oliver were chosen; but, at the same court, the latter was " dismissed from being a deputy for justifying the seditious libel, called a remonstrance or petition." Col. Rec. I. 203. The town had spirit enough to forbear further exercise of their right for that session; but Oliver, and Hough, who was of the same party, were members of the two following courts. This John Oliver, I presume, was brother of Thomas, the ruling elder.

2 Hubbard, 368, almost confesses, that the government " had overdone in passing the sentence." This treacherous candor, had Wheelwright died thirty years sooner, might not have been observed. At the end of his Mercurius Americanus, London, 1645, in reply to Welde's virulent book of the year before, the sufferer says: " It was marvellous he got thither," that is, to Piscataqua, " at that time, when they expelled him, by reason of the deep snow in which he might have perished."

one, that she had it revealed to her, that she should come into New England, and should here be ||persecuted,|| and that God would ruin us and our posterity, and the whole state, for *247
the same. So the court proceeded and banished her; but, because it was winter, they committed her to a private house,[1] where she was well provided, and her own friends and the elders permitted to go to her, but none else.

The court called also Capt. Underhill, and some five or six more of the principal, whose hands were to the said petition; and because they stood to justify it, they were disfranchised, and such as had public places were put from them.[2]

The court also ordered, that the rest, who had subscribed the petition, (and would not acknowledge their fault, and which near twenty[3] of them did,) and some others, who had been

||presented||

---

[1] It will be seen, a few pages onward, that this house was in Roxbury. The Colony Record of her banishment, I. 203, informs us, that she "was committed to Mr. Joseph Welde," one of the deputies from that town, and brother of the clergyman there, Thomas, the sad historian of the controversy, who had shown himself sufficiently desirous of convincing her of her errors, and was not a little soured by his ill success. To be taken from her husband, children, and friends, and committed to a prison in another town, even at the house of so good a man as Joseph Welde, might not be agreeable process of conversion; but when subjected to the perpetual buzzing of the clerical tormentor, she must have been more than woman, not to prove incorrigible.

[2] Underhill excused himself, like a soldier, but in vain. "He insisted much," says Welde, "upon the liberty which all states do allow to military officers for free speech, etc., and that himself had spoken sometimes as freely to Count Nassau."

[3] Only *ten* names of those, who "acknowledged their sin in subscribing the seditious writing, and desired to have their names crossed out," are found in the Records of that session; and one of *them*, Ralph Mousall, a representative at the court in September, 1638, "for speeches formerly spoken by him in approbation of Mr. Wheelwright, was dismissed from being a member of this court." Rec. I. 227. We are left then to the supposition, that the governour enlarges the number of the converts, or else that, at a future day, when the violence of party was assuaged, reconciliation with the offended majesty of a *different* court was encouraged, without noticing the fact in their proceedings. Yet there is entered, so late as 13 May, 1640, the submission of "Mr. Henry Flint." But the victory over him was well deserving of notice, as he was a distinguished

chief stirrers in these contentions, etc., should be disarmed. This troubled some of them very much, especially because they were to bring them in themselves; but at last, when they saw no remedy, they obeyed.[1]

---

young man, then chosen minister at Braintree, where his settlement, which should have taken place at the same time with Tompson's, 19 November, 1639, was delayed till 17 March after. No doubt this postponement was, to afford him liberal opportunity for this recantation. The commendation of him by Johnson, lib. I. c. 37, and again, lib. II. c. 18, for his industry against the same "sinful opinions" appears, to us who know the whole, rather ludicrous. Mather's biography of Flint, Magnalia, III. c. 19, is remarkable, even in him, for its nothingness.

[1] In no part of the history of any of the United States, perhaps, can a parallel be found for this act, the remarkable circumstances of which justify a long transcript from the Colony records, vol. I. 207–8.

"Whereas the opinions and revelations of Mr. Wheelwright and Mrs. Hutchinson have seduced, and led into dangerous errors, many of the people heare in Newe England, insomuch as there is just cause of suspition, that they, as others in Germany, in former times, may, upon some revelation, make some suddaine irruption upon those that differ from them in judgment: for prevention whereof, it is ordered, that all those, whose names are underwritten, shall, (upon warning given or left at their dwelling houses,) before the 30th day of this month of November, deliver in at Mr. Cane's house at Boston all such guns, pistols, swords, powder, shot, and match, as they shall bee owners of, or have in their custody, upon paine of tenn pound for evry default to bee made thereof; which armes are to bee kept by Mr. Cane till this court shall take further order therein. Also it is ordered, upon like penalty of X £, that no man, who is to render his armes by this order, shall buy or borrow any guns, swords, pistols, powder, shot, or match, untill this court shall take further order therein."

"The names of Boston men to bee disarmed: Capt. John Underhill, Mr. Thomas Oliver, William Hutchinson, William Aspinwall, Samuel Cole, William Dyer, Edward Rainsfoard, John Button, John Sanfoard, Richard Cooke, Richard Fairbanks, Thomas Marshall, Oliver Mellows, Samuel Wilbore, John Oliver, Hugh Gunnison, John Biggs, Richard Gridley, Edward Bates, William Dinely, William Litherland, Mathewe Iyans, Henry Elkins, Zaccheus Bosworth, Robert Rice, William Townsend, Robert Hull, William Pell, Richard Hutchinson, James Johnson, Thomas Savage, John Davy, George Burden, John Odlin, Gamaliel Wayte, Edward Hutchinson, William Wilson, Isaack Grosse, Richard Carder, Robert Hardings, Richard Wayte, John Porter, Jacob Eliot, James Penniman, Thomas Wardell, William Wardell, Thomas Matson, William Baulston, John Compton, Mr. Parker, William Freeborn, Henry Bull, John Walker, William Salter, Edward Bendall, Thomas Wheeler, Mr. Clarke, Mr. John Coggeshall."

All the proceedings of this court against these persons *248
were set down at large, with the reasons and other observations, and were sent into England to be published there, to the

---

"The like order is taken for other towns, changing the names of those who shall deliver their armes, and keepe them.

"The names of Salem men to bee disarmed: Mr. Scrugs, Mr. Alfoot, Mr. Commins, goodman Robert Moulton, goodman King, to deliver their arms to Leift. Damfort.

"The names of Neweberry men to bee disarmed are Mr. Dummer, Mr. Easton, Mr. Spencer, to bee delivered to the cunstable of the towne.

"The names of Roxberry men to bee disarmed are Mr. Edward Denison, Richard Morris, Richard Bulgar, and William Denison, Philip Sherman, to bee delivered to goodman Johnson.

"The names of Ipswich men to bee disarmed are Mr. Foster and Samuel Sherman, which are to deliver their armes to Mr. Bartholomewe.

"The names of Charlestowne men to be disarmed are Mr. George Bunker, and James Browne, who are to deliver their armes to goodman Thomas Line."

"It was ordered, that if any that are to bee disarmed acknowledge their sinn in subscribing the seditious libell, or do not justify it, but acknowledge it evill to two magistrates, they shall bee thereby freed from delivering in their armes according to the former order."

"The towne of Roxberry is required to take order for the safe custody of Mrs. Hutchinson, and if any charge arise, to be defrayed by her husband."

The full and overflowing measure of an honorable and Christian revenge, for this indignity to the lineal ancestor of the editor, was enjoyed by him, little more than thirty-seven years after, when he was commander in chief of all the Massachusetts forces, in the beginning of King Philip's war, and the blood of his sons was shed for his country. He was representative for Boston in 1654, and very often after, as well as for Hingham, and Andover; speaker of the house by five annual elections, and member of the council in 1680, and until his death, 14 February, 1682.

Another of these disarmed gentlemen, Edward Hutchinson, son of the prophetess, and brother-in-law of Savage, representative for Boston, 1658, fell by the mortal wound received in Indian ambuscade near Quaboag, at which town he died, 19 August, 1675, in an honorable rank. His will is in our Probate Records, Vol. VI. 95. His son, the Hon. Elisha Hutchinson, who died 10 December, 1717, aged 77, was father of Hon. Thomas, born 30 January, 1674, who died 3 December, 1739. This last was father of Thomas, born 9 September, 1711, H. C. 1727, the celebrated historian and unhappy governour of Massachusetts, who died 3 June, 1780. Of this latter Eliot gives an account more full and judicious than of any other in his admirable volume.

*249 end that *all* our godly friends might not be discouraged from coming to us, etc.[1]

---

[1] In the margin was written, in a hand I thought to be Cotton Mather's, "This was printed by Mr. Wells about seven years after." The misspelling of the author's name is strange. From diligent examination of Welde's book, I think he must be held answerable for 72 of its 85 pages; and that Gov. Winthrop wrote what is printed from the top of p. 46 to the third line of p. 59. This is entitled, "A Brief Apology in Defence of the General Proceedings of the Court," [probably Winthrop had written, Proceedings of the General Court,] "holden at Boston, the ninth day of the first month, 1636, against Mr. J. Wheelwright, a member there, by occasion of a Sermon," etc. etc. Welde, who went home in 1641, did not until 1644 publish his "Short Story of the Rise, Reign, and Ruin of the Antinomians, etc., that infected the churches of New England; and how they were confuted by the assembly of ministers there; as also of the magistrates' proceedings in Court against them; together with God's strange and remarkable judgments from heaven upon some of the chief fomenters of these Opinions, and the lamentable death of Mrs. Hutchinson; very fit for these times, here being the same Errors amongst us, and acted by the same spirit. Published at the instant request of sundry, *by one that was an eye and ear witness of the carriage of matters there.*" Quotations follow from Ephes. 4 : 14, and 2 Peter, 3 : 17. "London: printed for Ralph Smith, at the sign of the Bible, in Cornhill, near the Royal Exchange, 1644." The book opens with a short address, followed by sixteen very curious pages of preface, and a postscript, to which is signed the name of T. Welde.

The intent of the address to the reader, is to convince him, that T. W. met with the book, "newly come forth of the press," and was earnestly desired "to perfect it by laying down the order and sense of this story, (which in the book is omitted;") and that the names of the parties in our troubles thus being "already in print without any act of his," he thought it "requisite that God's great works should be made known," whereupon he drew up the following preface, "*with some additions to the conclusion of the book.*"

No small reason to presume, that this is altogether a pretence on the part of the virulent pamphleteer, would be drawn from inspection of the copy of the work in the British Museum. It is in the wonderful collection, by Thomason, of the pamphlets published from 1640 to 1660, of near thirty thousand pieces, in almost two thousand volumes, and is found in Vol. 143 of the small quartos, there marked 19 Feb. 1643, as the gatherer was careful, he says, "that the very day is written upon most of them that they came out."

Very trifling importance would attach, however, to the question of Welde's concern in the publication; and we might slightly regard his indication of himself on the title-page, that does not bear his name, as "an eye and ear witness of the carriage of matters," had not the over-cunning writer caused another title-page to be affixed to the *same* work, omitting solely the address and preface. It has every word, and part of a word, and abbreviation of names,

After this, many of the church of Boston, being highly offended with the governour for this proceeding, were earnest with the elders to have him called to account for it; but they were not forward in it, and himself, understanding their intent, thought fit to prevent such a public disorder, and so took occasion to speak to the congregation to this effect: —

1. That if he had been called, etc., he would have desired, first, to have advised with the elders, whether the church had power to call in question the proceedings of the civil court.

2. He would have consulted with the rest of the court,

---

and exactly the same references and figures, on every page, as the former book, from p. 1 to 66, and *Finis* inclusive. Yet, to mystify a heedless observer, it is entitled, "Antinomians and Familists condemned by the Synod of Elders in New England; with the proceedings of the Magistrates against them, and their Apology for the same; together with a memorable example of God's judgments upon some of those persons, etc.;" and most exact copy of the last words and figures of the imprint, "London: published for Ralph Smith at the sign of the Bible, etc., 1644." It seems, as if the types had never been disturbed; and to a skilful eye this test is decisive. My attention to this extraordinary instance of bibliographical disingenuity was drawn in March, 1851, by Dr. Harris, the learned librarian of our University, where it is preserved; but probably it imposed upon nobody until within two or three years. Certainly, in some ancient chirography, of which this substituted title-page is probably the sole possessor, as I presume no other copy can be found in the world, (for Thomason had not heard of it, we may be sure,) it is branded, "By Mr. Wells." What a sneaking device it was, need not be argued. Nor can any one, it seems to me, hesitate to ask the unanswerable question, What did Welde mean by acknowledging in *his* preface "SOME ADDITIONS TO THE CONCLUSION OF THE BOOK," when not a word, or letter, or comma, or figure, is added to the last six pages or any part of what, for a shield of his own cowardice, he wished to have pass as a new edition of a work heretofore issued from the press?

No doubt was ever expressed about the *true* title-page, "A Short Story, etc." by Baylie, in Dissuasive, 1645; by Wheelwright, in Mercurius Americanus, 1645, both at London; or by Cotton, 1648; by our own General Court, 1654, as in note to p. 216, ante; by the author of "A Glass for the People of New England," 1676, as quoted by Hutchinson, I. 72, charging Rev. Samuel Clark of London with "taking the lie out of his brother Welde's Short Story" into his book, "God's judgments against heresy;" or by Mather, or by the London publisher of the *second* edition, 1692; or by the careful antiquary, Prince, in Catal. of N. E. Library; or by Chauncey, or Eliot, or any other of our New England divines; and perhaps the reader may think I have derived too much gratification from disclosing the shameless infirmity or petty malice of the ecclesiastical historian. Let it go for the least skilful of all attempts at deception:

whether he might discover the ||counsels|| of the court to this assembly.

3. Though he knew, that the elders and some others did know, that the church could not inquire into the justice and proceedings of the court, etc.; yet, for the ||[2]satisfaction|| of such as did not, and were willing to be satisfied, he would declare his mind herein.

4. He showed, that, if the church had such power, they must have it from Christ, but Christ had disclaimed it in his practice ||[3]and|| by rule, as Luke [blank,] Matt. [blank;] and the scripture holds not out any rule or example for it; and though Christ's kingly power be in his church, yet that is not that kingly power whereby he is King of kings and Lord of lords, for by that kings reign and princes, etc. It is true, indeed, that magistrates, as they are church members, are accountable to the church for their failings, but that is when they are out of their calling; for we have examples of the highest magistrates in the same kind, as Uzzia, when he would go offer incense in the
*250 temple, the officers of the church called him to account, and withstood him. But when Asa put a prophet in prison, and when Salam put out Abiathar from the priesthood, (the one being a good act and the other ill,) yet the officers of the church did not call either of them to account for it. If a magistrate shall, in a private way, take away a man's goods or his servants, etc., the church may call him to account for it; but if he doth thus in pursuing a course of justice, (though the thing be unjust,) yet he is not accountable, etc.

5. For himself, he did nothing in the cases of the brethren, but by the advice and direction of our teacher and other of the elders. For in the oath, which was administered to him and the rest, etc., there was inserted, by his advice, this clause,—In all causes wherein you are to give your vote, etc., you are to give your vote as in your judgment and conscience you shall see to be most for the public good, etc.; and so for his part he was persuaded, that it would be most for the glory of God, and the public good, to pass sentence as they did.

||concerns|| ||[2]sanctification|| ||[3]as||

---

an anonymous title-page to a pamphlet, of which "additions to the conclusion," probably of seven pages, were before confessed.

6. He would give them one reason, which was || a || ground for his judgment, and that was, for that he saw, that those brethren, etc., were so divided from the rest of the country in their judgment and practice, as it could not stand with the public peace, that they should continue amongst us. So, by the example of Lot in Abraham's family, and after Hagar and Ishmael, he saw they must be sent away.[1]

Mo. 11.] The church at Roxbury dealt with divers of their members, (who had their hands to the petition,) and spent many days in public meetings to have brought them to see their sin in that, as also in the corrupt opinions which they held, but could not prevail with them.[2] So they proceeded to two or three admonitions, and, when all was in ||[2]vain,|| they cast them out of the church. In their dealing with them, they took some of them in plain lies and other foul distempers.

[Blank.]

9.] Divers of the elders went to Weymouth, to reconcile the differences between the people and Mr. Jenner,[3] whom they *251
had called thither with intent to have him their pastor. They had good success of their prayers.

13.] About thirty persons of Boston going out in a fair day to Spectacle Island to cut wood, (the town being in great want

|| the || ||[2] union ||

---

[1] That such examples from the private history of the Jewish patriarchs were alleged as justification of the intolerance of the ruling party, should not lessen our esteem of the general prudence of Winthrop, which, on the main subject of inquiry before the church, is exhibited with great happiness, and must have satisfied, or silenced, all opponents.

[2] Yet the mild and candid Thomas Welde was pastor there.

[3] Thomas Jenner remained not long at Weymouth, though he represented the town in general court, May, 1640; for, in Hutchinson's Coll. 111, is a letter, and a good one, from him, early in 1641, at Saco. He had been made free of the colony 8 December, 1636. Lechford, 45, speaks of him as residing in Maine. Weymouth seems to have been peculiarly unfortunate in its ministers, the first five having all been transplanted. Hull, Jenner, and Lenthall, appear in this History; Newman removed to Rehoboth; and when they were happy with Thacher, in the second generation, he was, in 1669, transferred to Boston. I presume Jenner went home to England; for, in Hazard, II. 78, a letter of Edward Winslow, London, 17 April, 1651, speaks of a purchase of his library for Harvard College, he being poor, and then living in Norfolk.

thereof,[1]) the next night the wind rose so high at N. E. with snow, and after at N. W. for two days, and then it froze so hard, as the bay was all frozen up, || save || a little channel. In this twelve of them gate to the Governour's Garden, and seven more were carried in the ice in a small skiff out at Broad Sound, and kept among Brewster's Rocks, without food or fire, two days, and then the wind forbearing, they gate to Pullin Point, to a little house there of Mr. Aspenwall's. Three of them gate home the next day over the ice, but their hands and feet frozen. Some lost their fingers and toes, and one died. The rest went from Spectacle Island to the main, but two of them fell into the ice, yet recovered again.

In this extremity of weather, a small pinnace was cast away upon Long Island by Natascott, but the men were ||[2]saved,|| and came home upon the ice.

[Large blank.]

16.] The powder and arms of the country, which were kept at Boston, were, by order of the last court, carried to Roxbury and Newtown.[2]

This year a plantation was begun at Tecticutt by a gentlewoman, an ancient maid, one Mrs. Poole.[3] She went late

|| except || ||[2] found ||

---

[1] It may seem strange, that a scarcity of wood should occur so soon after the settlement of the town; but we must remember its narrow dimensions within the peninsula, and presume that none was brought in from the country. By the accident which befel one of elder Oliver's sons cutting wood *on the neck* in January, 1632–3, we see there was then wood enough for the occasions of the people; and the Town Records, for three or four years later, contain frequent regulations of the manner and quantity in which the inhabitants might there be supplied. The forest was *now* probably exhausted; and in a letter, giving an account of the same disaster recorded in the text, the governour says to his son, "we at Boston were almost ready to break up for want of wood." Still there was plenty on the islands in the harbor. The continuance of our city has never been materially endangered since 1637 for want of fuel.

[2] We can assign no other reason for this measure than the religious opinions of the majority of Boston, by which the condition of the other party was rendered unsafe. As their faith was so unsound as to require the government to disarm them, there was little need of powder in the magazine.

[3] She was probably encouraged in her perilous undertaking by the Rev. William Hooke, a gentleman born, as the old phrase was, from Hampshire, who was the spiritual guide of the new settlement until he removed to New Haven.

thither, and endured much hardship, and lost much cattle. *252
Called, after, Taunton.[1]

[Blank.]

This was no long time, yet it is variously given, as are also the circumstances of ordination or installation, by Trumbull, I. 280, 286, 296, 493.

Hooke was *teacher* at New Haven, after the return of Samuel Eaton, but went home in 1656. I presume both of them were overshadowed by the powers of Davenport, the pastor. Yet the talents of Hooke were respectable. A very interesting letter from him to Winthrop of Connecticut, about the private intrigues and difficulties of Cromwell, with whom he was in great favor, is preserved in 3 Hist. Coll. I. 181, from Vol. XIX. of Trumbull MSS. Whalley, the regicide, was, I find from MS., brother of his wife, which circumstance may partly account for the devotion shown to him and Goffe at New Haven. Hooke died, 21 March, 1667, says Trumbull, but Mather, on better authority, makes it 1678.

In the Records of Taunton proprietors, which I have examined, in setting out Mrs. Poole's lot, May, 1639, reference is made to Hooke's lot. She was, I think, accompanied by some relatives; for in the town books is found, "Timothy Poole, the son of Mr. William Poole, died the 15th of December, 1667. He was drowned in a little pond at Nesquabinausit, where it was thought he did swim in after a goose which he had shot." In this most ancient town of Bristol county, the curious traveller may see a fair slab, formerly laid over the grave of this virgin mother of Taunton, now removed to the common burial-ground, having this inscription: —

"Here rest the remains
of Mrs. Elizabeth Pool,
a native of Old England,
of good family, friends, and prospects,
all which she left, in the prime of her life,
to enjoy the religion of her conscience
in this distant wilderness;
a great proprietor of the township
of Taunton,
a chief promoter of its settlement
and its incorporation 1639–40,
about which time she settled near this spot;
and, having employed the opportunity
of her virgin state
in piety, liberality,
and sanctity of manners,
died, May 21st, A. D. 1654, aged 65;
to whose memory
this monument is gratefully erected
by her next of kin,
John Borland, Esquire,
A. D. 1771."

[1] A town so early settled as Taunton should have some history; and as it is

*253 Another plantation was begun (and called Sandwich) about fifteen miles beyond Plimouth, towards Cape Cod, by many families, which removed from Sagus, otherwise Lynn.[1]

[Blank.]

Upon occasion of the censures of the court upon Mrs. Hutchinson and others, divers other foul errors were discovered, which had been secretly carried by way of inquiry, but after were maintained by Mrs. Hutchinson and others; and so many of Boston were tainted with them, as Mr. Cotton, finding how he had been abused, and made (as himself said) their stalking horse, (for they pretended to hold nothing but what Mr. Cotton held, and himself did think the same,) did spend most of his time, both publicly and privately, to discover those errors, and to reduce such as were gone astray. And also the magistrates, calling together such of the elders as were near, did spend two days in consulting with them about the way to help the growing evils.

Some of the secret opinions were these: —

That there is no inherent righteousness in a child of God.

That neither absolute nor conditional ||promises|| belong to a Christian.

That we are not bound to the law, not as a rule, etc.

That the Sabbath is but as other days.

That the soul is mortal, till it be united to Christ, and then it is annihilated, and the body also, and a new given by Christ.

||praises||

---

not included in Prince's list of deficiencies, I presume, that, in the immense collection of that most diligent antiquary, more than a century since, one was contained, but now gone, with his other MS. treasures, to the winds, the worms, or the flames. The first volume of Bristol county's Registry of Deeds contains a more recent confirmation of lands of Titicut, purchased in 1637, by Mrs. Poole, in behalf of the town of Taunton.

[1] If no other lover of the things of old will undertake to set in order the annals of Sandwich, the public may well expect the favor from the historian of Plimouth. The possession of the faculty is evidence of the call to such a work.

Such was my hope, twenty-eight years ago. The beloved annalist of Plimouth died four years after its expression; and we do not know that the work is begun by another.

That there is no resurrection of the body.

[Very large blank.]

Mo. 12.] Divers gentlemen and others, being joined in a military company, desired to be made a corporation, etc. But the council, considering (from the example of the Pretorian band among the Romans, and the Templars in Europe) how dangerous it might be to erect a standing authority of military men, which might easily, in time, overthrow the civil power, thought fit to stop it betimes. Yet they were allowed to be a company, but subordinate to all authority.[1]

About this time the Indians, which were in our fami- *254
lies, were much frightened with Hobbamock (as they call the devil) appearing to them in divers shapes, and persuading them to forsake the English, and not to come at the assemblies, nor to learn to read, etc.

26.] Mr. Peirce, in the Salem ship, the Desire, returned from the West Indies after seven months. He had been at Providence, and brought some cotton, and tobacco, and negroes,[2] etc., §from thence,§ and salt from Tertugos. Dry fish and strong liquors are the only commodities for those parts. He met there two men-of-war, set forth by the lords, etc., of Providence with letters of mart, who had taken divers prizes from the Spaniard, and many negroes.

A reason for this jealousy will appear in the course of a few paragraphs onward; but this company, now known as the Ancient and Honorable Artillery, soon triumphed over such scruples, and has enjoyed, in a remarkable manner, the countenance of the government of colony, province, and commonwealth. The History of this military band was published, in 1820, by Zechariah G. Whitman, Esq. Keayne, its first captain, was orthodox, as we see from the order in a preceding note, page 248, that the arms of the disaffected of Boston should be surrendered at his house. His creed was more correct than his practice, on which a few remarks by the historian, and some exemplification by the editor, will appear.

2 Perhaps the unavoidable conclusion from this passage is, that slaves were brought here for sale. It was an unhappy exchange for the Indians, — fifteen boys and two women, — he had carried out, (see page 234;) though perhaps the blacks were happier than their red brethren. A few years later, we shall see a very honorable testimony of our fathers against the horrible practice of taking the negroes from their native land.

Mo. 1.] While Mrs. Hutchinson continued at Roxbury, divers of the elders and others resorted to her, and finding her to persist in maintaining those gross errors beforementioned, and many others, to the number of thirty or thereabout, some of them wrote to the church at Boston, offering to make proof of the same before the church, etc., 15; whereupon she was called, (the magistrates being desired to give her license to come,) and the lecture was appointed to begin at ten. (The general court being then at Newtown, the governour and the treasurer, being members of Boston, were permitted to come down, but the rest of the court continued at Newtown.) When she appeared, the errors were read to her. The first was, that the souls of men are mortal by generation, but, after, made immortal by Christ's purchase. This she maintained a long time; but at length she was so clearly convinced by reason and scripture, and the whole church agreeing that sufficient had been delivered for her conviction, that she yielded she had been in an error. Then they proceeded to three other errors:
*255 1. That there was no resurrection of these bodies, and that these bodies were not united to Christ, but every person united hath a new body, etc. These were also clearly confuted, but yet she held her ||own;|| so as the church (all but two of her sons) agreed she should be admonished, and because her sons would not agree to it, they were admonished also.[1]

||error||

[1] Bating what is incomprehensible, and may be rejected rather as nonsense than heresy, we should easily imagine, that a construction in the mildest sense would have found little damnable error in these opinions. It was well that the projector of such novelties was not branded as an atheist, or Sadducee, denying the resurrection and future life altogether. Controversialists easily impute to the dogmas of their opponents consequences drawn only by the imputers, and then fasten on the new doctrines the opprobrium of their false inferences.

The doctrine of resurrection of the body, apparently of heathen origin, though incautiously asserted in words by Christians of many communions, I am glad to find so early disputed in Massachusetts. The materialists have indeed the majority on their side from a very early age of our religion, the Author and Finisher of which, in giving instruction to the poor, deemed it unnecessary to explain, what could hardly, in those times, be made intelligible, — the manner of existence in the future state. This part of the creed is not taught in the

Mr. Cotton pronounced the sentence of admonition *256
with great solemnity, and with much zeal and detestation of her errors and pride of spirit. The assembly continued till eight at night, and all did acknowledge the special presence of God's spirit therein; and she was appointed to appear again the next lecture day.

While the general court sate, there came a letter, directed to the court, from John Greene[1] of Providence, who, not long

---

scriptures. But, in his first letter to the church of Corinth, xv. 35–51, the greatest of the apostles has illustrated, as far as the original and *acquired* ignorance of his correspondents could receive the explanation, the subject of a resurrection in a manner perfectly consistent with the refined intellectual philosophy of the spiritualists. Yet he strongly marks the folly of the question, "How are the dead raised, and with what bodies do they come?"

Hutchinson, I. 478, in a note to his chap. 6, which treats of the Indians, quotes Roger Williams as saying, "that when he had discoursed of the creation, of the soul, of the danger of it, and the saving of it, they assented; but when he spake of the resurrection of the body, they cried out, We will never believe this." On that passage Mr. Jefferson, in his margin, had made a remark like this: "This doctrine of the resurrection of the body is, it seems, so absurd as to stagger even the credulity of Indians." Having sent to Washington, for the purpose of verifying this quotation, I find, from my friend's reply, that the words "*had been most carefully scratched out with a penknife.*" To me it seems a proof of more timid than useful friendship.

The future restoration of the *flesh*, as well as the soul, though asserted by speculative expounders of our religion in the second or third age after the apostles, did not become a necessary symbol of faith before the middle of the fourth century. A dignitary of the church of England, higher in learning than station, left, to be published after his death, "An Enquiry when the Resurrection of the Body, or Flesh, was first inserted into the public Creeds," London, 1757. When the reader learns, that A. A. SYKES was the author, he will need no other recommendation of this modest tract.

A profound and original philosopher, to whom revelation owes much for his aid, in "The Light of Nature Pursued," vol. III. 425, offers a striking observation, which shall close this note: "As to the vulgar notion of a resurrection in the same form and substance we carry about at present, the various ways in which it has been expounded, and many difficulties raised upon them all, sufficiently declare it untenable: and the reason ordinarily given, because the body, being partaker in the deed, ought to share in the reward, as well requires a resurrection of the sword a man murders with, or the bank note he gives to charitable uses; for our mind is the sole agent, and our hands are as much instruments as any thing we hold in them."

1 He is, probably, the same gentleman, of whom much will be found in our

before, had been imprisoned and fined, for saying that the magistrates had usurped upon the power of Christ in his church, and had persecuted Mr. Williams and another, whom they had banished for disturbing the peace by divulging their opinions against the authority of the magistrates, etc.; but upon his submission, etc., his fine was remitted; and now, by his letter, he retracted his former submission, and charged the court as he had done before. Now, because the court knew, that divers others of Providence were of the same ill affection to the court, and were probably suspected to be confederate in the same letter, the court ordered, that, if any of that plantation were found within our jurisdiction, he should be brought before one of the magistrates, and if he would not disclaim the charge in the said letter, he should be sent home, and charged to come no more into this jurisdiction, upon pain of imprisonment and further censure.

At this court, divers of our chief military officers, who had declared themselves favorers of the familistical persons and opinions, were sent for, and being told, that the court having
*257 some jealousy of them for the same, and therefore did desire some || good || satisfaction from them, they did ingenuously acknowledge, how they had been deceived and misled by the pretence, which ||[2]was|| held forth, of advancing Christ, and debasing the creature, etc., which since they have found to be otherwise, and that their opinions and practices ||[3]tended|| to dis-

||general|| ||[2]had been|| ||[3]led||

---

second volume, as a chief planter of Warwick, with Gorton and Holden; and from whom the highly respectable family in Rhode Island, of which was the celebrated General Greene, derives its descent. Like most other dwellers in that colony, he was subject to vexation from our government; for, in the Record of proceedings at our court, 1 August, 1637, I observe, "Mr. John Greene of New Providence, having spoken against the magistrates contemptuously, stands bound, in one hundred marks, to appear at the next quarter court to be held the first Tuesday of the 5th month ensuing;" and on 29th of *that* month he was fined £20, and forbid to come into this jurisdiction on pain of fine and imprisonment. His religious opinions seem not to have attracted the wrath of heaven to shorten his days, for he lived long in the land; and his son of the same name was deputy governour of the heterodox colony in 1700. See Callender, 35, 37, 43, 93.

turbance and delusions; and so blessed God, that had so timely discovered their error and danger to them.

At this court, a committee was appointed, of some magistrates, some ministers, and some others, to compile a body of fundamental laws.

Also the elders (who had been requested to deliver their judgments concerning the law of adultery, about which three had been kept long in prison) returned their answer, with the reasons thereof, to this effect: That, if the law had been sufficiently published, they ought to be put to death. Whereupon the court, considering that there had been some ||defect|| in that point, and especially for that it had been oft questioned among the deputies and others, whether that law were of force or not, being made by the court of assistants by allowance of the general court; therefore it was thought safest, that these three persons should be whipped and banished;[1] and the law was confirmed and published.

The Castle Island being found to be very chargeable to maintain the garrison there, and of little use, but only to have some command of ships, which should come hither with passengers, etc., there was a committee appointed to dispose of the ammunition there, etc.[2]

22.] Mrs. Hutchinson appeared again; (she had been licensed by the court, in regard she had given hope of her repentance, to be at Mr. Cotton's house, that both he and Mr. Davenport might have the more opportunity to deal with her;) and the articles being again read to her, and her answer required, she delivered it in writing, wherein she made a retractation of near all, but with such explanations and circumstances as gave no satisfaction to the church; so as she was required to speak further to them. Then she declared, that it was just with God

||dispute||

---

[1] On pain of death for returning, the Colony Record has it.

[2] The rate levied by this court, of £1500, shows a considerable variance from the proportions in August preceding: — Boston, £233.10; Ipswich, £180; Salem, £172.10; Dorchester, £140; Charlestown, £138; Roxbury, £115; Watertown, £110; Newtown, £106; Lynn, £105; Newbury, £75; Medford, £52.10; Hingham, £36; Weymouth, £27; and Mr. Theophilus Eaton, £20.

*258 to leave her to herself, as he had done, for her slighting his ordinances, both magistracy and ministry; and confessed that what she had spoken against the magistrates at the court (by way of revelation) was rash and ungrounded; and desired the church to pray for her. This gave the church good hope of her repentance; but when she was examined about some particulars, as that she had denied inherent righteousness, etc., she affirmed that it was never her judgment; and though it was proved by many testimonies, that she had been of that judgment, and so had persisted, and maintained it by argument against divers, yet she impudently persisted in her affirmation, tó the astonishment of all the assembly. So that, after much time and many arguments had been spent to bring her to see her sin, but all in vain, the church, with one consent, cast her out. Some moved to have her admonished once more; but, it being for manifest evil in matter of conversation, it was agreed otherwise; and for that reason also the sentence was denounced by the pastor, matter of manners belonging properly to his place.

After she was excommunicated, her spirits, which seemed before to be somewhat dejected, revived again, and she gloried in her sufferings, saying, that it was the greatest happiness, next to Christ, that ever befel her.[1] Indeed, it was a happy day to

---

[1] Welde, on his last page, calls her the American Jezabel, and is surprised, in the simplicity of his bigotry, at her hardness of heart in slighting the excommunication, "as she is not affected with any remorse, but glories in it, and fears not the vengeance of God, which she lies under; as if God did work contrary to his own word, and loosed from heaven what his church had bound upon earth." The sober story-teller, who thus "played the God an engine on his foe," closes his book with these appropriate remarks. See my note beginning on page 249. But the blood of this Jezabel — the reader will see the propriety of this hard name, when, in a very few years, she and most of her family were murdered by the Indians near Long Island, as the author of Rise, Reign, and Ruin exultingly relates — the blood of this Jezabel, besides being licked by the dogs, was, in two generations, mixed, by intermarriage, with the more orthodox ἰχωρ of Thomas Welde. His grandson, of the same name, first pastor of the church of Dunstable, gathered 16 December, 1685, took to wife a great granddaughter of this same outcast from heaven and the church of Boston. The sin of the progenitor was, I presume, exhausted by subdivision, or neutralized by admixture; for their son, Habijah S. Welde, was minister of Attleborough. See Alden's Collection of Epitaphs, I. 110, with III. 41.

the churches of Christ here, and to many poor souls, who had been seduced by her, who, by what they heard and saw that day, were (through the grace of God) brought off quite from her errors, and settled again in the truth.

At this time the good providence of God so disposed, divers of the congregation (being the chief men of the party, her husband being one) were gone to Naragansett to seek out a *259
new place for plantation, and taking liking of one in Plimouth patent, they went thither to have it granted them; but the magistrates there, knowing their spirit, gave them a denial, but consented they might buy of the Indians an island in the Naragansett Bay.[1]

After two or three days, the governour sent a warrant to Mrs. Hutchinson to depart this jurisdiction before the last of this month, according to the order of court, and for that end set her at liberty from her former constraint, so as she was not to go forth of her own house till her departure; and upon the 28th she went by water to her farm at the Mount, where she was to take water, with Mr. Wheelwright's wife and family, to go to Pascataquack; but she changed her mind, and went by land to Providence, and so to the island in the Naragansett Bay, which her husband and the rest of that sect had purchased of the Indians, and prepared with all speed to remove unto. For the court had ordered, that, except they were gone with their families by such a time, they should be summoned to the general court, etc.

30.] Mr. Davenport and Mr. Prudden,[2] and a brother of Mr.

---

[1] The *denial* was matter of inference, for the adventurers were resolved to go free of Plimouth as well as Massachusetts; and the *consent* was the advice of equals, not the dictate of superiors. See Callender, 30, who informs us, that these purchasers of Rhode Island formed their civil compact 7 March, and that the cession by the Indian sachems was of the 24th of same month. As twelve of these eighteen associates were members of the church of Boston, the advantage taken of their absence, by "the good providence of God," would be thought, in a day of less ferment, either disadvantageous to a cause, or dishonorable to its supporters.

[2] Peter Prudden, who was first minister of Milford, Conn., was useful in his place, and of high esteem in the colony of New Haven, but nothing more can be learned of him than Dr. Trumbull, I. 294, supplying in part the deficiency of Mather, has told.

Eaton, (being ministers also,) went by water to Quinepiack; and with them many families removed out of this jurisdiction to plant in those parts, being much taken with the opinion of the fruitfulness of that place, and more safety (as they conceived) from danger of a general governour, who was feared to be sent this summer; which, though it were a great weakening to these parts, yet we expected to see a good providence of God in it, (for all possible means had been used to accommodate them here; Charlestown offered them largely, Newbury their whole town, the court any place which was free,) both for possessing those parts which lay open for an enemy, and for strengthening our friends at Connecticut, and for making room
*260 here for many, who were expected out of England this year, and for diverting the thoughts and intentions of such in England as intended evil against us, whose designs might be frustrate by our scatterings so far; and such as were now gone that way were as much in the eye of the state of England as we here.[1]

There came letters from Connecticut to the governour of the Massachusetts, to desire advice from the magistrates and elders here about Sequin and the Indians of the river, who had, underhand, (as was conceived,) procured the Pequods to do that || onslaught || at Weathersfield the last year. The case fell out to be this: Sequin gave the English land there, upon ||[2]contract|| that he might sit down by them, and be protected, etc. When he came to Weathersfield, and had set down his wigwam, they drave him away by force. Whereupon, he not being of strength to repair this injury by open force, he secretly draws in the Pequods. Such of the magistrates and elders as could meet on the sudden returned this answer, viz.: That, if the cause were thus, Sequin might, upon this injury first offered by

||blank|| ||[2] Connecticut||

[1] An excellent letter of Davenport and Gov. Eaton, the fathers of New Haven colony, giving the reasons of their removal, may be seen in the Appendix. It was copied by me from the original, in the hand-writing of the first signer; and is reprinted in 3 Mass. Hist. Coll. III. 165–7, with a very elaborate error of date. See my reference in the preface, and correction of the mistake, eight years before it was committed.

them, right himself either by force or fraud, and that by the law of nations; and though the damage he had done them had been one hundred times more than what he sustained from them, that is not considerable in point of a just war; neither was he bound (upon such an open act of hostility publicly maintained) to seek satisfaction first in a peaceable way; it was enough, that he had complained of it as an injury and breach of covenant. According to this advice, they proceeded and made a new agreement with the Indians of the river.

Another plantation was now in hand at Mattakeese,[1] six miles beyond Sandwich. The undertaker of this was one Mr. Batchellor, late pastor at Sagus, (since called Lynn,) being about seventy-six years of age; yet he walked thither on foot in a very hard season.

He and his company, being all poor men, finding the difficulty, gave it over, and others undertook it.

27.] The Indians of Block Island sent three men with *261
ten fathom of wampom for part of their tribute.

The wife[2] of one William Dyer, a milliner in the New Exchange, a very ||proper|| and fair woman, and both of them notoriously infected with Mrs. Hutchinson's errors, and very censorious and troublesome, (she being of a very proud spirit, and much addicted to revelations,) had been delivered of [a] child some ||[2]few|| months before, §October 17,§ and the child buried, (being stillborn,) and viewed of none but Mrs. Hutchinson and the midwife, one Hawkins's wife, a rank familist

||promp|| ||[2]four||

[1] "Now Yarmouth," is written in the margin. Of that town a collection of Memorabilia is contained in 1 Hist. Coll. V. 54–60. Some correction of a slight error in that tract will be found in a note on Marmaduke Matthews.

[2] Her name was Mary. She had been, with her husband, admitted of Boston church 13 December, 1635. After long enjoying her revelations, in quiet, at Rhode Island, she was unhappily led, about twenty-one years later, again to visit Boston, probably bringing more light, when she was condemned to death as a Quaker. Winthrop, governour of Connecticut, our author's eldest son, inheriting the natural mildness of his father, attempted to save her life; but the bigotry of the age had acquired a severer character, and, for a second return, in June, 1660, she suffered. See Hutchinson, I. 184. Yet her son, at that very time, held an important office in the neighboring colony. The influence of such cruelty could not be favorable.

also; and another woman had a glimpse of it, who, not being able to keep counsel, as the other two did, some rumor began to spread, that the child was a monster. One of the elders, hearing of it, asked Mrs. Hutchinson, when she was ready to depart; whereupon she told him how it was, and said she meant to have it chronicled, but excused her concealing of it till then, (by advice, as she said, of Mr. Cotton,) which coming to the governour's knowledge, he called another of the magistrates and that elder, and sent for the midwife, and examined her about it. At first she confessed only, that the head was defective and misplaced, but being told that Mrs. Hutchinson had ||revealed|| all, and that he intended to have it taken up and viewed, she made this report of it, viz.: It was a woman child, stillborn, about two months before the just time, having life a few hours before; it came hiplings till she turned it; it was of ordinary bigness; it had a face, but no head, and the ears stood upon the shoulders and were like an ape's; it had no forehead, but over the eyes four horns, hard and sharp; two of them were above one inch long, the other two shorter; the eyes standing out, and the mouth also; the nose hooked upward; all over the breast and back full of sharp pricks and scales, like a thornback; the navel and all the belly, with the distinction of the sex, were where the back should be, and the back and hips before, where the belly should have been; be-
*262 hind, between the shoulders, it had two mouths, and in each of them a piece of red flesh sticking out; it had arms and legs as other children; but, instead of toes, it had on each foot three claws, like a young fowl, with sharp talons.[1]

||recalled||

---

[1] From this disgusting story we are authorized by Welde to derive profit, less indeed for doctrine than for reproof. In his preface he favors us with the means of deliverance from the antinomian heresy, — preaching, conferences, the synod, the exertions of the magistrates in disfranchising, fining, or banishing the deluded, and, lastly, the misfortunes of Mrs. Dyer and Mrs. Hutchinson. He thus relates the ultimate cause of success: —

"Then God himself was pleased to step in with his casting voice, and bring in his own vote and suffrage from Heaven, by testifying his displeasure against their opinions and practices, as clearly as if he had pointed with his finger, in causing the two fomenting women, in the time of the height of the opinions, to

The governour speaking with Mr. Cotton about it, he told him the reason why he advised them to conceal it: 1. Because he saw a providence of God in it, that the rest of the women, which were coming and going in the time of her travail, should then be absent. 2. He considered, that, if it had been his own case, he should have desired to have had it concealed. 3. He had known other monstrous births, which had been concealed, and that he thought God might intend only the instruction of the parents, and such other to whom it was || known, || etc. The like apology he made for himself in public, which was well accepted.[1]

(2.)] The governour, with advice of some other of the *263
magistrates and of the elders of Boston, caused the said monster to be taken up, and though it were much corrupted, yet most of those things were to be seen, as the horns and

|| shown ||

---

produce out of their wombs, as before they had out of their brains, such monstrous births, as no chronicle (I think) hardly ever recorded the like." He after asserts, "He that runs may read their sin in these judgments."

This "suffrage from heaven" is introduced in the wrong place, by Welde, unskilfully, as proxy or attorney of the Most High, such is the character he claims; for it appears by the text, that Mrs. Dyer's premature delivery was between the time of the synod and that of the general court, possibly occasioned by the result of the former and the expectation of the latter.

Another New England divine, of purer spirit as of greater name, has left a sermon, to which we may often turn for refreshment, when sickened with these uncharitable denunciations. See Buckminster, last of vol. 1. In the foul records of ecclesiastical history, one is frequently shocked with discoveries of the anger of Providence, asserted with higher presumption and directness than even by the Temanite in his *questions* to his afflicted friend: "Remember, I pray thee, who ever perished, being *innocent?* Or where were the *righteous* cut off?" This detestable spirit belongs not to any particular communion; and that church, which must reproach itself with fewest instances, may still have enough to regret. On occasion of the sudden death of Jovian, Cardinal Baronius, "as being one of the privy council of Heaven, declares, that this emperor was taken out of the world by a divine judgment, because he had made a decent funeral for his predecessor Julian." Jortin's Eccl. Hist.

[1] Apology to Cotton ought to have been made for the inquiry, rather than by him for the concealment, if the suspicion, under which he lay, had been entertained by a people less jealous for the honor of God, and less careful to vindicate it, as they supposed, by ascribing to his displeasure the cross accidents, that befel their opponents.

claws, the scales, etc. When it died in the mother's body, (which was about two hours before the birth,) the bed whereon the mother lay did shake, and withal there was such a noisome savor, as most of the women were taken with §extreme vomiting and purging, so as they were forced to depart; and others of them their children were taken with§ convulsions, (which they never had before nor after,) and so were sent for home, so as by these occasions it came to be concealed.[1]

Another thing observable was, the discovery of it, which was just when Mrs. Hutchinson was cast out of the church. For Mrs. Dyer going forth with her, a stranger asked, what young woman it was. The others answered, it was the woman which had the monster; which gave the first occasion to some that heard it to speak of it. The midwife, presently after this discovery, went out of the jurisdiction; and indeed it was time for her to be gone, for it was known, that she used to give young women oil of mandrakes and other stuff to cause conception; and she grew into great suspicion to be a witch, for it was credibly reported, that, when she gave any medicines, (for she practised physic,) she would ask the ||party,|| if she did believe, she could help her, etc.[2]

||patient||

With good conscience, we may concede, that the Governour acted in this nauseous inquisition; yet if good taste had been allowed to stifle the conscience, we should have thought better of the magistrate.

2 She did not go voluntarily, as by the text we might be led to infer; for our Colony Rec. I. 219, looks very much like banishment: "Jane Hawkins, the wife of Richard Hawkins, had liberty till the beginning of the third month, called May, and the magistrates (if she did not depart before) to dispose of her; and, in the mean time, she is not to meddle in surgery or physic, drink, plaisters, or oils, nor to question matters of religion, except with the elders for satisfaction." I suppose her oil of antinomianism was more dreaded than her oil of mandrakes.

Her "*suspicion to be a witch*," is elegantly expanded, in the Short Story of Welde, to "notorious for familiarity with the devil;" and I am very sorry to remark, that Winthrop himself, at a later period, 1640, gives countenance to the same absurdity. Such intercourse, however, was not made capital for several years, or Welde might then have enjoyed, as *suspicion* of such a crime is hardly less than full proof, the delight imputed to some of his brethren of the clergy, two generations after, in the delusion of 1692.

Another observable passage was, that the father of this monster, coming home at this very time, was, the next Lord's day, § by an unexpected providence, § questioned in the church for divers monstrous errors, as for denying all inherent right- *264
eousness, etc., which he maintained, and was for the same admonished.

12.] A general fast was kept through all the churches, by advice from the court, for seeking the Lord to prevent evil, that we feared to be intended against us from England by a general governour; for the safe arrival of our friends from thence, (very many being expected;) and for establishment of peace and truth amongst us.

21.] Owsamekin, the sachem of Acooerneck, on this side Connecticut, came to the governour and brought a present of eighteen skins of beaver from himself and the sachems of Mohegan beyond Connecticut and Pakontuckett. The occasion was, (as he said,) it was reported, that we were angry with him, and intended to war upon them; so they came to seek peace. The governour received the present, and (having none of the other magistrates at hand to advise with) answered them, that if they had done no wrong to the English, nor aided our enemies, we would be at peace with them; and accordingly signified so much to the magistrates at Connecticut. They took this answer well, and departed with the letter.

23.] This was a very hard winter. The snow lay, from November 4th to March 23d, ||half a|| yard deep about the Massachusetts, and a yard deep beyond Merrimack, and so the more north the deeper, and the spring was very backward. This day it did snow two hours together, (after much rain from N. E.) with flakes as great as shillings. This was in the year 1637.[1]

§24.] The governour and deputy went to Concord to view some land for farms, and, going down the river about four miles, they made choice of a place for one thousand acres for each of them. They offered each other the first choice, but

||one and an half||

---

[1] The writer meant, probably, that the long winter was that of 1637; and the two hours falling of the great flakes of snow occurred on 23 April following.

because the deputy's was first granted, and himself had store of land already, the governour yielded him the choice. So, at the place where the deputy's land was to begin, there were two great stones, which they called the Two Brothers, in remembrance that they were brothers by their children's marriage, and did so brotherly agree, and for that a little creek near those stones was to part their lands. At the court in the 4th month after, two hundred acres were added to the governour's part.§[1]

*265 26.] Mr. Coddington (who had been an assistant from the first coming over of the || government, || being, with his wife, taken with the familistical opinions) removed to Aquiday Island in the Naragansett Bay.

(3.) 2.] At the court of elections, the former governour, John Winthrop, was chosen again. The same day, at night, he was taken with a sharp fever, which brought him near death; but many prayers were put up to the Lord for him, and he was restored again after one month.

This court the name of Newtown was altered, and it was called Cambridge.[2]

The spring was so cold, that men were forced to ||[2]plant|| their corn two or three times, for it rotted in the ground; but, when we feared a great dearth, God sent a warm season, which brought on corn beyond expectation.

(4.) 1.] Between three and four in the afternoon, being clear, warm weather, the wind westerly, there was a great earthquake. It came with a noise like a continued thunder or

||governour|| ||[2]replant||

---

[1] This paragraph is marked by a line down the margin, and "This may be left out" written in the same hand. I prefer to disregard the author's modesty, for the anecdote is interesting, and derives importance from the act of the general court, adopting *the name of the rocks* given by the grantees on their selection of these lands. See Col. Rec. I. 222.

[2] In compliment to the place, where so many of the civil and clerical fathers of New England had received their education, this venerable name (may it ever be preserved!) was undoubtedly bestowed. There were probably, at that time, forty or fifty sons of the University of Cambridge in Old England, — one for every two hundred or two hundred and fifty inhabitants, — dwelling in the few villages of Massachusetts and Connecticut. The sons of Oxford were not few.

the rattling of coaches in London, but was presently gone. It was at Connecticut, at Naragansett, at Pascataquack, and all the parts round about. It shook the ships, which rode in the harbor, and all the islands, etc. The noise and the shakings continued about four minutes. The earth was unquiet twenty days after, by times.[1]

5.] Unkus, alias Okoco, the Monahegan sachem in the twist of Pequod River, came to Boston with thirty-seven men. He came from Connecticut with Mr. Haynes, and tendered the governour a present of twenty fathom of wampom. This was at the court, and it was thought fit by the council to refuse it, till he had given satisfaction about the Pequods he kept, etc. Upon this he was much dejected, and made account we would have killed him; but, two days after, having received good satisfaction of his innocency, etc., and he promising to sub- *266
mit to the order of the English touching the Pequods he had, and the differences between the Naragansetts and him, we accepted his present. And, about half an hour after, he came to the governour, and entertained him with these compliments: This heart (laying his hand upon his breast) is not mine, but yours; I have no men; they are all yours; command me any difficult thing, I will do it; I will not believe any Indians' words against the English; if any man shall kill an Englishman, I will put him to death, were he never so dear to me. So the governour gave him a fair, red coat, and defrayed his and his men's ||diet,|| and gave them corn to relieve them homeward, and a letter of protection to all men, etc., and he departed very joyful.

Many ships arrived this year, with people of good quality and estate, notwithstanding the council's order, that none §such§ should come without the king's license; but God so wrought, that some obtained §license,§ and others came away

||due||

[1] Johnson, lib. II. c. 12, gives very unsatisfactory accounts of this earthquake. He was more engaged in the shaking of the people out of their antinomianism, in which those of his party went, perhaps, as far from propriety as the others from truth. Morton, in his Memorial, is more particular; yet it is evident his pen was not so careful as modern accuracy requires, for he says, "*about* the second of June."

without.[1] The troubles which arose in Scotland about the book of common prayer, and the canons, which the king would have forced upon the Scotch churches, did so take up the king and council, that they had neither heart nor leisure to look after the affairs of New England; yet, upon report of the many thousands, which were preparing to come away, the arch-bishops caused all the ships to be stayed. But, upon the petition of the masters, and suggestion of the great ‖damage‖ it would be to the commonwealth in hindering the Newfound-land trade, which brought in much money, etc., they were presently released. And in this and other passages it plainly appeared, that near all the lords of the council did favor this plantation; and all the officers of the custom house were very ready to further it, for they never made search ‖[2]for‖ any goods, etc., but let men bring what they would, without question or control. For ‖[3]sure the Lord awed their hearts, and‖ they and others (who savoured not religion) were amazed to see men of all conditions, rich and poor, servants and others, offering themselves so readily for New England, when, for furnishing of other plantations, they were forced to send about their stalls, and when they had gotten any, they were forced to keep them as prisoners from running away.

Mo. (6.) 3.] In the night was a very great tempest or hiracano at S. W. which drave a ship on ground at Charlestown, and brake down the windmill there, and did much other harm. It flowed twice in six hours, and about Naragansett it
*267 raised the tide fourteen or fifteen foot above the ordinary spring tides, upright.[2]

Janemoh, the sachem of Niantick, had gone to Long Island

‖danger‖ ‖[2]of‖ ‖[3]since the Lords avowed their party, etc.‖

---

[1] The number of the ships, and of the passengers brought this summer, will be seen two pages onward. Much misapprehension has arisen on this subject. It has been supposed, that the order in Council, for which see Rushworth, under date of 6 April, 1638, or in the abridged ed. vol. II. 496, was executed according to its import, and for that mistake, above is sufficient explanation. Neal, who is too often only the conduit of Mather, in vol. I. 168 of his History of N. E. relies on Magn. for his passengers detained, and enlarges the number I have shown the value of such a tradition in note on p. 172 foregoing.

Our storms in August are often the most violent of any in the year.

and rifled some of those Indians, which were tributaries to us. The sachem complained to our friends of Connecticut, who wrote us about it, and sent Capt. Mason, with seven men, to require satisfaction. The governour of the Massachusetts wrote also to Mr. Williams to treat with Miantunnomoh about satisfaction, or otherwise to bid them look for war.

Upon this Janemoh went to Connecticut, and made his peace, and gave full satisfaction for all injuries.

Two ships, which came over this year much pestered, lost many passengers, and some principal men, and many fell sick after they were landed, and many of them died.[1]

Four servants of Plimouth ran from their masters, and, coming to Providence, they killed an Indian. He escaped, after he was deadly wounded in the belly, and gat to other Indians. So, being discovered, they fled and were taken at the Isle Aquiday. Mr. Williams gave notice to the governour of Massachusetts, and desired advice. He returned answer, that, seeing they were of Plimouth, they should certify Plimouth of them, and, if they would send for them, to deliver them; otherwise, seeing no English had jurisdiction in the place where the murder was committed, neither had they at the Island any || government || established, it would be safest to deliver the principal, who was certainly known to have killed the party, to the Indians his friends, with caution that they should not put

|| governour ||

---

[1] One of the ships so *pestered* was probably the Nicholas, of London, of 300 tons, chartered by Edward Tyng, arriving at Boston 3 July, in which came John Josselyn, gentleman; for five of the passengers died on board. His book is a curiosity, sometimes worth examining, but seldom to be implicitly relied on. Where he speaks, page 20, of Boston as a village of "not above twenty or thirty houses," I suspect the right-hand cipher was lost from his manuscript, or memory; for he printed thirty-six years after. The population certainly required tenfold the number of dwellings reported; and, in this eighth year of the town, the log huts, that he *might* scorn to honor with the name of houses, were very few.

Another of the *pestered* ships probably was the Martin, coming nearly at the same time with the Nicholas. I know, at least, that the nuncupative will of Sylvester Baldwin, one of her passengers, who died on the ocean, was proved 13 July of this year, by Chad Brown, and other fellow-passengers, before Dep. Gov. Dudley. His wife and children are named.

him to torture, and to keep the other three to further consideration.[1]

*268 After this, Plimouth men sent for them, (but one had escaped,) and the governour there wrote to the governour here for advice, especially for that he heard they intended to appeal into England. The governour returned answer of encouragement to proceed notwithstanding, seeing no appeal did lie, for that they could not be tried in England, and that the whole country here were interested in the case, and would expect to || have || justice done. Whereupon they proceeded as appears after.

Many of Boston and others, who were of Mrs. Hutchinson's judgment and party, removed to the Isle of Aquiday; and ||[2]others,|| who were of the rigid separation, and savored anabaptism, removed to Providence, so as those parts began to be well peopled.

[Large blank.]

There came over this summer twenty ships, and at least ||[3]three thousand|| [2] persons, so as they were forced to look out

||see|| ||[2]many|| ||[3]three hundred||

---

[1] A directly opposite course of political motives is assigned by Morton. In the Plimouth secretary's Memorial, our author's advice was not given because the criminals belonged to Plimouth, nor because the English had not jurisdiction where the murder was committed, nor because they of Rhode Island were without any government; but "the Massachusetts refused this trial, as being committed in the jurisdiction of Plimouth, and they of Rhode Island, having apprehended them, delivered them to the aforesaid jurisdiction of Plimouth *on the same grounds.*" Both writers evidently desire to depreciate the new schismatic colony, or colonies, if Providence and Rhode Island be counted two. Winthrop, however, would not deny their independence. In 3 Hist. Coll. I. 171–173, is a very full account, in the original letter of Williams, of all the circumstances of this aggravated and cowardly murder.

[2] Dr. Holmes, Ann. I. 305, of first edition, followed the Webster text without scruple, though his excellent judgment must have observed the probability of error in this number, since the governour immediately adds, all the established plantations would not afford room for so many passengers. In the ship with Josselyn were one hundred and sixty-four; and if the others were as full, the corrected reading of our author, which is plain enough in his MS., is within the limits. In the Diligent of Ipswich, John Martin master, arriving at Boston 10 August, were one hundred and thirty-five, among whom was Rev. Robert Peck, of Old Hingham, as says Daniel Cushing, who, with his father, was of the

new plantations. One was begun at Merrimack, and another four or five miles above Concord, and another at Winicowett.

[Large blank.]

The three prisoners, being brought to Plimouth, and there examined, did all confess the murder, and that they did it to get his wampom, etc.; but all the question was about the death of the Indian, for no man could witness that he saw him dead. But Mr. Williams and Mr. James[1] of Providence made oath, that his wound was mortal, etc. At last two Indians, who, with much difficulty, were procured to come to the trial, (for they still feared that the English were conspired to kill all the Indians,) made oath after this manner, viz.: that if he were *269
not dead of that wound, then they would suffer death. Upon this they three were condemned and executed. Two of them died very penitently, especially Arthur Peach, a young man of good parentage and fair conditioned, and who had done very good service against the Pequods.[2]

The fourth escaped to Pascataquack. The governour sent after him, but those of Pascataquack conveyed him away, and openly withstood his apprehension. It was their usual manner (some of them) to countenance, etc., all such lewd persons as fled from us to them.

(7.) The general court was assembled, in which it was agreed, that, whereas a very strict order was sent from the lords commissioners for plantations for the sending home our patent, upon pretence that judgment had passed against it upon a quo warranto, a letter should be written by the governour, in

---

number. The Bevis of Hampton, of only 150 tons, in which Richard Dummer, this year, brought his family, had sixty-one passengers entered at the Southampton custom-house; and possibly a few others came without license. Hubbard, 242, when transcribing from this part of Winthrop, seems to have been afraid to number either the ships or the passengers. He often avoids the most valuable incidents of his story.

[1] I know nothing more of this gentleman than Williams, in his letter, 3 Hist. Coll. I. 172, mentions of his humane endeavors for the sufferer; and in another letter in MS., early in 1649, he notices his return from England, with a full cargo of goods, which were saved from the wreck of the vessel on Rhode Island.

[2] He came a few years before, from Virginia. One of the men executed was Thomas Jackson; the other, John Barnes.

the name of the court, to excuse our not sending of it; for it was resolved to be best not to send it, because then such of our friends and others in England would conceive it to be surrendered, and that thereupon we should be bound to receive such a governour and such orders as should be sent to us, and many bad minds, yea, and some weak ones, among ourselves, would think it lawful, if not necessary, to accept a general governour. The copy of the letter is reserved, etc., in form of a petition. See the after fol. 74.[1]

At this court a law was made about such as should continue excommunicated six months, and for public thankgiving for the arrival of the ships, and for the coming on of harvest beyond expectation, etc. This law was after repealed.[2]

At this court, also, Capt. Underhill (being about to remove to Mr. Wheelwright) petitioned for three hundred acres of land promised him formerly; by occasion whereof he was questioned about some speeches he had used in the ship lately, in his return out of England, viz., that he should say, that we were zealous here, as the Scribes and Pharisees were, and as Paul was before his conversion, etc., which he denying, they were
*270 proved to his face by a sober, godly woman, whom he had seduced in the ship, and ||drawn|| to his opinions, (but she was after freed again). Among other passages, he told her how he came to his assurance, and that was thus: He had lain under a spirit of bondage and a legal way five years, and could get no assurance, till at length, as he was taking a pipe of tobacco, the Spirit set home an absolute promise of free grace with such assurance and joy, as he never since doubted of his good estate, neither should he, though he should fall into sin. He would not confess nor deny this, but took exceptions at the court for crediting one witness against him, etc., and withal

||drew||

---

1 The reference is to the page of the governour's MS., where, unluckily, the letter could not be found, nor in any other place.

2 A rate of £400 was levied by this court in the following proportions:— Boston, £57.14.9; Ipswich, £46.10; Salem, £44.11.3; Dorchester, £36.16.3; Charlestown, £35.13; Cambridge, £34.17.6; Roxbury and Lynn, each, £31; Watertown, £29.1.3; Newbury, £27.2.6; Hingham, £11.2.10; Weymouth, £7.15; and Medford, £6.15.8.

said, that he was still of the same opinion he had been, etc. Whereupon he was demanded, if he were of the same opinion he had been in about the petition or remonstrance. He answered, yes, and that his retractation was only of the manner, not of the matter. Whereupon his retractation (which he had lately delivered to the governour, to be presented to this court) was read, wherein he professeth how the Lord had brought him to see his sin in condemning the court, and passing the bounds of modesty and submission, which is required in private persons, etc., and in what trouble of spirit he had been for it, etc. Upon this, the court committed him for abusing the court with a show of retractation, and intending no such thing; and the next day he was called again and banished. The Lord's day following, he made a speech in the assembly, showing that, as the Lord was pleased to convert Paul as he was in persecuting, etc., so he might manifest himself to him as he was taking the moderate use of the creature called tobacco. He professed withal, that he knew not wherein he had deserved the sentence of the court, and that he was sure that Christ was his, etc. The elders reproved him for this speech; and Mr. Cotton told him, that he brake a rule in condemning publicly the sentence of the court, before he had privately convinced the magistrates, or some of them; and told him, also, that, although God doth often lay a man under a spirit of bondage, when he is walking in sin, as Paul was, yet he never sends such a spirit of comfort but in an ordinance, as he did to the same Paul by Ananias; and ||ergo|| advised him well to examine the revelation and joy which he had.

The next Lord's day, the same Capt. Underhill, having been privately dealt with upon suspicion of incontinency with a neighbor's wife, and not hearkening to it, was publicly questioned, and put under admonition. The matter was, for that the woman being young, and beautiful, and withal of a jovial spirit and behavior, he did daily frequent her house, and was divers times found there alone with her, the door being *271
locked on the inside. He confessed it was ill, because it had an appearance of evil in it; but his excuse was, that the woman was in great trouble of mind, and sore temptations, and

||so||

that he resorted to her to comfort her; and that when the door was found locked upon them, they were in private prayer together. But this practice was clearly condemned also by the elders, affirming, that it had not been of good report for any of them to have done the like, and that they ought, in such case, to have called in some brother or sister, and not to have locked the door, etc. They also declared, that once he procured them to go visit her, telling them that she was in great trouble of mind; but when they came to her, (taking her, it seems, upon the sudden,) they perceived no such thing. See the issue of this after, (9,) 1638, and (10,) 13, 38.

[Large blank.]

Mrs. Hutchinson, being removed to the Isle of Aquiday, in the Naragansett Bay, after her time was fulfilled, that she expected deliverance of a child, was delivered of a monstrous birth, which, being diversely related in the country, (and, in the open assembly at Boston, upon a lecture day, declared by Mr. Cotton to be twenty-seven || several lumps of man's seed, without any alteration, or mixture of any thing from the woman, || and thereupon gathered, that it might signify her error in denying inherent righteousness, but that all was Christ in us, and nothing of ours in our faith, love, etc.) hereupon the governour wrote to Mr. Clarke,[1] a physician and a preacher to those of the

||singula frusta vel globulos seminis masculini sine ulla mutatione aut mixtura de femina||

[1] John Clarke was one of the most distinguished gentlemen of Rhode Island, of which colony he was long agent in England, during the *reigns* of Oliver, of Richard, and part of that of Charles II. The Baptist church of Newport owns him for its father. He published, in 1652, a book, entitled "Ill News from New England, or a Narrative of New England's persecution, wherein is declared, that, while Old England is becoming New, New England is becoming Old," etc., etc., etc., in which he introduced the substance of a tract, issued the preceding year, called "A Brief Discourse touching New England, and particularly Rhode Island; as also a faithful and true relation of the prosecution of Obadiah Holmes, John Crandall, and John Clarke, merely for conscience towards God, by the principal members of the church or commonwealth of the Massachusetts in New England, which rules over that part of the world." This tract was probably by the same hand.

Some light may be derived by us from a petition of the sufferer, of which the

island, to know the certainty thereof, who returned him *272 this answer: Mrs. Hutchinson, six weeks before her delivery, perceived her body to be greatly distempered, and her spirits failing, and in that regard doubtful of life, she sent to me, etc., and not long after (in ||immoderato fluore uterino||) it was brought to light, and I was called to see it, where I beheld, first unwashed, (and afterwards in warm water,) several lumps, every one of them greatly confused, and if you consider each of them according to the representation of the whole, they were altogether without form; but if they were considered in respect of the parts of each lump of flesh, then there was a rep-

||immoderate fluor and urine||

---

original is preserved, from the colony files, in the Historical Society's library: "To the honored court assembled at Boston. Whereas it pleased this honored court, yesterday, to condemn the faith and order which I hold and practise and, after you had passed your sentence upon me for it, were pleased to express, I could not maintain the same against your ministers, and thereupon publicly proffered me a dispute with them; be pleased by these few lines to understand, I readily accept it, and therefore do desire you would appoint the time when, and the person with whom, in that public place where I was condemned, I might, with freedom, and without molestation of the civil power, dispute that point publicly, where I doubt not but, by the strength of Christ, to make it good out of his last will and testament, unto which nothing is to be added, nor from which nothing is to be diminished. Thus, desiring the Father of lights to shine forth by his power to expel the darkness, I remain your well wisher, John Clarke. From the prison, this 1. 6. 51," i. e. 1 August, 1651.

In 1653 was published "The Civil Magistrate's Power in Matters of Religion modestly debated, etc., etc., etc., with a brief answer to a certain slanderous pamphlet, called Ill News from New England, etc., by Thomas Cobbett of Lynn in N. E." This was written in the violent temper of that day, thought necessary for the orthodox, but now so universally reprobated. Clarke's book is exceedingly rare. A copy was in Prince's New England library, but cannot be found now; nor can I hear of more than one even in Rhode Island. Cobbett's answer, which might certainly be better spared, is preserved, but is very scarce, only a single copy having ever fallen within my reach. Both are in the British Museum; and Col. Aspinwall, our consul, has both. Clarke died, says Benedict, I. 495, in 1676, in the sixty-sixth year of his age, without children. Callender, who is very full in his account of Clarke, 2, 16, 21, 29, 45, 52, 62, 63, 93, marks his death 20 April of that year. From three of his brothers are descended the large family in Rhode Island bearing that name. The article Clarke, John, in Allen's Biographical Dictionary, is the best in that laborious work.

resentation of innumerable distinct bodies in the form of a globe, not much unlike the swims of some fish, so confusedly knit together by so many several strings, (which I conceive were the beginning of veins and nerves,) so that it was impossible either to number the small round pieces in every lump, much less to discern from whence every string did fetch its original, they were so snarled one within another. The small globes I likewise opened, and perceived the matter of them (setting aside the membrane in which ||it was involved,||) to be partly wind and partly water. Of these several lumps there were about twenty-six, according to the relation of those, who more
*273 narrowly searched into the number of them. I took notice of six or seven of some bigness; the rest were small; but all as I have declared, except one or two, which differed much from the rest both in matter and form; and the whole was like the [blank] of the liver, being simular and every where like itself. When I had opened it, the matter seemed to be ||[2]blood|| congealed. The governour, not satisfied with this relation, spake after with the said Mr. Clarke, who thus cleared all the doubts: The lumps were twenty-six or twenty-seven, distinct and not joined together; there came no secundine after them; six of them were as great as his fist, and one as great as two fists; the rest each less than other, and the smallest about the bigness of the top of his thumb. The globes were round things, included in the lumps, about the bigness of a small Indian bean, and like the pearl in a man's eye. The two lumps, which differed from the rest, were like liver or congealed blood, and had no small globes in them, as the rest had. Mr. Cotton, next lecture day, acknowledged his error, etc., and that he had his information by a letter from her husband, etc.[1]

||they were involumed|| ||[2]hard||

---

[1] Having been favored with the original letter of Clarke, I testify that the author's transcription is sufficiently accurate, and nearly literal. It might be unnecessary to add, on this offensive subject, the introduction of which, at a religious lecture, it seems hardly possible to justify, that Clarke says, he was sent to once and again, and that he considered her condition was both doubtful and dangerous, and that he was somewhat unwilling to meddle, at least before her delivery, but only advised to procure some medicines from the bay proper

21.] A ship of Barnstaple arrived with about eighty passengers, near all western people. There came with them a godly minister, one Mr. Matthews.[1]

Here arrived a small Spanish frigate with hides and *274
tallow. She was a prize taken by Capt. Newman, who was set out with letters of mart by the lords, etc., of the Isle of Providence.

This year there came a letter from Mr. Thomas || Mewtis, || clerk of the council in England, directed to Mr. Winthrop, (the present governour,) and therein an order from the lords commissioners for foreign plantations, (being all of the council,) wherein they straightly required the patent to be sent home by the first ship, etc. This letter and order were produced at the

||M ||

---

for the occasion; for "I conceived," he adds, "if it were a child, it was dead, but rather that it was not, but such a thing as afterward it proved." It is strange, that the word, which the governour leaves blank, is, plainly, *lobe* in the original letter. On the margin of the letter, the governour has added what Clarke told him, nearly as given in the text, with this slight variation: "the globes were like pearls, about the bigness of a sloe."

[1] Very diligent inquiry has been followed with some success in tracing the course of this clergyman, of whom most of our early books take very slight notice. He was a Welshman, bred at Oxford, matriculated, in his 18th year, at All Souls Coll. Lechford, 41, mentions him as living in Plimouth patent. He was probably at Yarmouth, where there is a tradition, that he was one of their first ministers. See 1 Hist. Coll. V. 59. The diligent author of that tract is certainly mistaken in supposing, that Miller was the *first*, and Matthews (whose given name was Marmaduke) the *second* minister there. Miller, who was at Yarmouth when Johnson wrote, preached first at Rowley; and we may safely conclude, that he did not go to Yarmouth before Matthews left it. I am quite confident it was not before 1642. Matthews had removed from that place, and spent some time at Hull, about the year 1650, whence, though, as Johnson says, he "lost the approbation of some able, understanding men, among both magistrates and ministers, by weak and unsafe expressions in his teaching," he was, nevertheless, called to the church at Malden. A very humble confession of his darkness, and ignorance, and weak expressions, signed by him, though written by another, of 28 October, 1651, is preserved in the archives of the Historical Society, and, with other papers on the subject, of prior date, is printed in 3 Hist. Coll. I. 29–32. The hints of the author of Wonder-working Providence are more expressive than his verses usually are, lib. III. c. 7. He was one of the magistrates appointed for a scrutiny of the faith and doctrines of Matthews.

general court last past, and there agreed not to send home the patent, but to return answer to the lords by way of humble petition, which was drawn up and sent accordingly. These instruments are all among the governour's papers, and the effect of them would be here inserted.[1]

25.] Being the third day of the week, and two days before the change, the wind having blown at N. E. all the day, and rainy in the night, was a mighty tempest, and withal the highest tide, which had been seen since our coming into this country; but, through the good providence of God, it did little harm. About fourteen days after, the wind having been at N. W. and then calm ||here,|| came in the greatest eastern sea, which had been in our time. Mr. Peirce (who came in a week after) had that time a very great tempest three days at N. E.[2]

A remarkable providence appeared in a case, which was tried at the last court of assistants. Divers neighbors of Lynn, by agreement, kept their cattle by turns. It fell out to the turn of one Gillow to keep them, and, as he was driving them forth, another of these neighbors went along with him, and kept him so earnestly in talk, that his cattle strayed and gate in the corn. Then this other neighbor left him, and would not help him recover his cattle, but went and told another how he had kept Gillow in talk, that he might lose his cattle, etc. The cattle, getting into the Indian corn, eat so much ere they could be gotten out, that two of them fell sick of it, and one of them
*275 died presently; and these two cows were that neighbor's, who had kept Gillow in talk, etc. The man brings his action against Gillow for his cow, (not knowing that he had witness of his speech); but Gillow, producing witness, etc., barred him of his action, and had good costs, etc.

||turn||

---

1 Hubbard, 268–271, has laid us under obligation by preserving both documents.

2 Emanuel Downing, a lawyer from London, with his wife and children, at least those of them, who had not before joined their uncle, Winthrop, came, I suppose, with Peirce, arriving early in October. He and Lucy his wife, the sister of our author, were admitted of Salem church 4 November next. She was born 9 January, 1601.

The court, taking into consideration the great disorder || general || through the country in costliness of apparel, and following new fashions, sent for the elders of the churches, and conferred with them about it, and laid it upon them, as belonging to them, to redress it, by urging it upon the consciences of their people, which they promised to do. But little was done about it; for divers of the elders' wives, etc., were in some measure partners in this general disorder.[1]

[Large blank.]

8ber.] About two years since one Mr. Bernard, a minister at Batcomb in Somersetshire in England, sent over two books in writing, one to the magistrates, and the other to the elders, wherein he laid down arguments against the manner of our gathering our churches, etc., which the elders could not answer till this time, by reason of the many troubles about Mrs. Hutchinson's opinions, etc. Mr. Cotton also answered another book sent over in defence of set form of prayer. This I suppose was Mr. Ball's book.[2]

About this time was very much rain and snow, in six weeks together; scarce two days without rain or snow. This was observed by some as an effect of the earthquake.[3]

(9.) 8.] A church was gathered at Dedham with good approbation; and, 28th, Mr. Peck[4] ordained teacher at Hingham.

|| proceeding ||

---

[1] The wives of clergymen have been, since that day, generally exempt from such charges.

[2] It will not be expected, that an account of Bernard's books should be given here, especially as they were not, I believe, printed, probably, being too good for the character of the age. See Eliot, in 1 Hist. Coll. IX. 16. In his Lives of the Puritans, Brook II. 458, has a good account of Richard Bernard, who died March, 1641. He enumerates his works, among which are not these tracts.

[3] To mark the relation of cause and effect in atmospheric phenomena, is a dangerous exercise of imagination. Example may, however, serve, better than precept, to dissuade from such idle philosophy as that in the text. One of the books, blending practical wisdom with amusement, by which Miss Edgeworth favored the last age, makes a venerable observer of events regard "Tenderden steeple as the cause of Goodwin sands." I think there is evidence, that this anecdote belongs to the famous Sir Thomas More.

[4] Little can be learned of this reverend gentleman, except from old records

*276 By order of the last general court, the governour wrote a letter to Mr. Burdet,[1] Mr. Wiggin, and others of the plantation of Pascataquack, to this effect: That, whereas there had been good correspondency between us formerly, we could not but be sensible of their entertaining and countenancing, etc., some that we had cast out, etc., and that our purpose was to survey our utmost limits, and make use of them. Mr. Burdet returned a scornful answer, and would not give the governour his title, etc. This was very ill taken, for that he was one of our body, and sworn to our government, and a member of the church

---

in Hingham, by which I find, he had been a preacher at Hingham in Norfolk in Old England, whence came almost all of the progenitors of the present inhabitants of that ancient town, preserving the same name in Massachusetts. The teacher was Robert Peck; but the contemporary MS. of Hobart, the pastor, collated by me, informs, that, 27 October, 1641, he sailed for England, and, another ancient writing adds, "with his wife and son Joseph." I presume he found religion so free at home, that he had no inducement to return. He and Joseph Peck, probably a brother, were made freemen here 13 March, 1638–9. Both have the appropriate Mr. prefixed. Joseph was very soon after a representative in the general court. Notice of his removal from the jurisdiction will occur in our second volume.

Hubbard, 279, though literally extracting this paragraph, in his usual manner, has thrown the chronology into strange confusion, making it 1640, by disregard of Winthrop's arrangement of dates. Johnson, lib. II. c. 9, has made the gathering of Dedham church a year too early.

[1] Of the few instances, in which any advantage is derived from Hubbard, our acquaintance with this person is one. He was minister at Dover; and the historian of Ipswich informs us, 221, 353, that Burdet, "upon a pretended quarrel with the bishops and ceremonies of the church of England, had, about the year 1634, left Yarmouth in England," and came "to Salem, where he was received a member of their church, and was employed to preach among them for a year or more, being an able scholar, and of plausible parts and carriage. But finding the discipline of the church as much too strict for his loose conscience as the other was in pretence too large, he left his brethren at Salem, out of love to his friends at Piscataqua, where he continued for some time in good esteem (at least in appearance) with Mr. Wiggans, that had the power of a governour thereabouts, until he declared himself of what sort he was." Our Records show his admission as a freeman 2 September, 1635. The conclusion of his doings in America will appear in this History, 1640. He had been silenced in England; and I marvel at the charge by Winthrop, that he had intelligence with the prelatical party at home. His wife and children were in distress there, according to the county history of Bloomfield.

of Salem; so as the governour was purposed to summon him to appear at our court to answer his contempt; but, advising with the deputy about it, he was dissuaded from it, the rather for that, if he should suffer in this cause, it would ingratiate him more with the archbishops, (with whom he had intelligence, etc.) but his council was rather to undermine him by making him thoroughly known, etc., to his friends in Pascataquack, and to take them from him. Whereupon the governour wrote to Edward Hilton, declaring his ill dealing, (and sent a copy of his letter,) and advising them to take heed how they put themselves ‖into‖ his power, etc., but rather to give us a proof of their respect towards us, etc. — He intimated withal how ill it would relish, if they should advance Capt. Un- *277
derhill, whom we had ‖[2]thrust‖ out for abusing the court with ‖[3]feigning‖ a retractation both of his seditious practice and also of his corrupt opinions, and after denying it again, and for casting reproach upon our churches, etc.; signifying withal, that he was now found to have been an unclean person, (for he was charged by a godly young woman to have solicited her chastity under pretence of Christian love, and to have confessed to her, that he had his will oftentimes of the cooper's wife, and all out of strength of love,) and the church had sent for him, and sent him a license to come and go, under the hands of the governour and deputy; but he refused to come, excusing himself, by letters to the elders, that the license was not sufficient, etc., and, by letters to the governour, that he had no rule to come and answer to any offence, except his banishment were released; but to the matter he was charged with, he gave no answer, but sought an evasion. Pascataquack men had chosen him their governour before the letter came to them.

13.] The governour went by water to Salem, where he was entertained with all the respect that they could show him. The ‖[4]12‖ he returned by land, and they sent six of their chief military officers with carbines to guard him to Boston.[1]

‖under‖ ‖[2]cast‖ ‖[3]framing‖ ‖[4]14th‖

[1] Both dates are plain in the MS., but it is not certain where the correction should be made. The first edition, assuming the former to be correct, and that

17.] Roger Herlakenden,[1] one of our magistrates, about
*278 thirty[2] years of age, second son of [blank][3] Herlakenden of || Earl's Colne || in Essex, Esq., died at Cambridge of the small pox. He was a very godly man, and of good use both in the commonweath and in the church. He was buried with military honor, because he was lieutenant colonel. He left behind a virtuous *gentlewoman* and two daughters. He died in great peace, and left a sweet memorial behind him of his piety and virtue.

§ 10. 2.] Ezekiel Rogers,[4] son of Richard Rogers of Weath-

|| Karlscoke ||

---

the governour returned next day, altered the second date to 14. To me it seems more probable, that the day of return, being in the body of the paragraph, is right. Perhaps he went on the 10th, and spent Sunday with Endecott, returning on Monday, 12th, and writing the notice the next day.

[1] The brother of this gentleman, Richard, is, by Dr. Holmes, from the Cambridge Records, 1 Hist. Coll. VII. 10, mentioned as one of the earliest proprietors. But he never came over. Roger had arrived in 1635, Hubbard, 233, says, in the same ship with Vane. He was admitted freeman 3 March, 1635–6, with Shepherd, Peter, Vane, and other distinguished men, and, on 25 May following, at the general election, chosen one of the assistants, to which place he was re-elected in the two following years. It is proof of the solid judgment of so young a man. In the questions about Mrs. Hutchinson he took a part, as appears in that most curious and minute article of the Appendix to History of Massachusetts, II. 500. Some humble verses in honor of Harlackenden are afforded by Johnson, lib. I. c. 32. His will, in our Probate Records, I. 13, without date, was probably made two years or more before his death, since he makes Gov. Haynes one of his executors with his brother Richard. In it he takes notice of his estate in England, called "Colne Park, or the Little Lodge," and of one daughter only, though provision is made for the probability of another child. He was, I believe, a cousin of Lord Roper, and had probably been brought up under the ministry of Shepherd in his native country. See Neal's Puritans, II. 282, and Shepherd's autobiography. To enjoy the spiritual aid of the same gentleman, he purchased Dudley's estate at Newtown.

[2] He was born 1 October, 1611, and was only 27 years old.

[3] The father, born 22 July, 1568, was named Richard.

[4] No inadequate notices of Ezekiel Rogers may be found in the progress of our History, in Johnson, lib. II. 11, and, above all, in Mather's Magnalia. Eliot and Allen have well abbreviated these authorities; but the former misdates his death. He was a man of very high influence for a portion of his life, and his epitaph on *our* Hooker is thought by Hubbard, 541, worthy of preservation. The tardy justice of our age erected a monument to Rogers in 1805.

ersfield in Essex, a worthy son of so worthy a father, lying at Boston with some who came out of Yorkshire with him, where he had been a painful preacher many years, being desirous to partake in the Lord's supper with the church of Boston, did first impart his desire to the elders, and having given them satisfaction, they acquainted the church with it, and before the sacrament, being called forth by the elders, he spoke to this effect, viz.: that he and his company (viz. divers families, who came over with him this summer) had, of a good time, withdrawn themselves from the church communion of England, and that for many corruptions which were among them. But, first, he desired, that he might not be mistaken, as if he did condemn all there; for he did acknowledge a special presence of God there in three things: 1, in the soundness of doctrine in all fundamental truths; 2, in the excellency of ministerial gifts; 3, in the blessing upon the same, for the work of conversion and for the power of religion, in all which there appeared more, etc., in England than in all the known world besides. Yet there are such corruptions, as, since God let them see some light therein, they could not, with safe conscience, join any longer with them. The first is, their national church; second, their hierarchy, wholly antichristian; third, their dead service; fourth, their receiving (nay, compelling) all to partake of the seals; fifth, their abuse of excommunications, wherein they enwrap many a godly minister, by causing him to pronounce their sentence, etc., they not knowing that the *fear* of the excommunication lies in that. Hereupon they bewailed before the Lord their sinful partaking so long in those corruptions, and entered a covenant *279
together, to walk together in all the ordinances, etc.

1639. 10. 3.] Being settled at Rowley,[1] they renewed their church covenant, and their call [blank] of Mr. Rogers to the office of pastor, according to the course of other churches, etc.§

(10.) 6.] Dorothy Talbye was hanged at Boston for murder-

---

[1] No doubt this name was adopted from the place in Yorkshire in Old England, where their pastor had labored, and most of themselves had enjoyed his services. He had there long been well esteemed by Toby Matthews, the Archbishop of York.

ing her own daughter, a child of three years old.[1] She had been a member of the church of Salem, and of good esteem for godliness, etc.; but, falling at difference with her husband, through melancholy or spiritual delusions, she sometimes attempted to kill him, and her children, and herself, by refusing ‖ meat,‖ saying it was so revealed to her, etc. After much patience, and divers admonitions not prevailing, the church cast her out. Whereupon she grew worse; so as the magistrate caused her to be whipped. Whereupon she was reformed for a time, and carried herself more dutifully to her husband,[2] etc.; but soon after she was so possessed with Satan, that he persuaded her (by his delusions, which she listened to as revelations from God) to break the neck of her own child, that she might free it from future misery. This she confessed upon her apprehension; yet, at her arraignment, she stood mute a good space, till the governour told her she should be pressed to death, and then she confessed the indictment. When she was to receive judgment, she would not uncover her face, nor stand up, but as she was forced, nor give any testimony of her repentance, either then or at her execution. The cloth, which should have covered her face, she plucked off and put between the rope and her neck. She desired to have been beheaded, giving this reason, that it was less painful and less shameful. After a swing or two, she catched at the ladder. Mr. Peter, her late pastor, and Mr. Wilson, went with her to the place of execution, but could do no good with her. Mr. Peter gave an exhortation to the people to take heed of revelations, etc., and of despising the ordinance of excommunication as she had done; for when it was to have been denounced against her, she turned her back, and would have gone forth, if she had not been stayed by force.

‖ water ‖

[1] This child was baptized at Salem, 25 December, 1635, by the strange name of Difficulty.

[2] The unfortunate husband, whose life had been attempted by her, was, after her execution, excommunicated "for much pride and unnaturalness to his wife." See the letter of Hugh Peter in Hutchinson, I. 420. The original has been seen by me. Perhaps Peter regretted his treatment of Talby, after his own wife was distracted.

One Capt. Newman, being set forth with commission *280 from the Earl of Holland, governour of the Westminster company, and the Earl of Warwick, and others of the same company, to spoil the Spaniard within the limits of their grant in the West Indies, after he had taken many of their small vessels, etc., returned home by the Massachusetts in a small pinnace, with which he had taken all || his || prizes, (for his great ship was of no use for that purpose). He brought many hides and much tallow. The hides he sold here for £17.10 the ||[2] score ; ||[1] the tallow at 29*s.* the hundred ; and set sail for England (10,) 1. He was after cast away at ||[3] Christopher's || with a very rich prize, in the great hyrracano, 1642.

13.] A general fast was kept upon the motion of the elders to the governour and council. The chief occasion was, the much sickness of pox and fevers spread through the country, (yet it was to the east and south also,) the apparent decay of power of religion, and the general declining of professors to the world, etc. Mr. Cotton, in his exercise that day at Boston, did confess and bewail, as the churches', so his own security, sloth, and credulity, whereupon so many and dangerous errors had gotten up and spread in the church ; and went over all the particulars, and showed how he came to be deceived ; the errors being framed (in words) so ||[4] near || the truths which he had preached, and the falsehood of the maintainers of them, who usually would deny to him what they had delivered to others, etc. He acknowledged, that such as had been seducers of others (instancing in some of those of the Island, though he named them not) had been justly banished. Yet he said, that such as had been only misled, and others, who had done any thing out of a misguided conscience, (not being ||[5] grossly || evil,) should be borne withal, and first referred to the church, and if that could not heal them, they should rather be imprisoned, fined, or, etc., than banished, ||[6] *qua* || it was likely no other church would receive them.

|| the || ||[2] stone || ||[3] blank || ||[4] were || ||[5] greatly || ||[6] tho' ||

1 Having the printed copy before me, as I collated the MS., the error of the former edition, it must be confessed, escaped me at two readings ; but happening to reflect on the extreme disproportion of price and value, a closer inspection of

Those who were gone with Mrs. Hutchinson to Aquiday fell into new errors daily. One Nicholas Easton,[1] a tanner, taught,
*281 that gifts and graces were that antichrist mentioned Thess., and that which withheld, etc., was the preaching of the law; and that every of the elect had the Holy Ghost and also the devil indwelling. Another, one Herne, taught, that women had no souls, and that Adam was not created in true holiness, etc., for then he could not have lost it.

Those who went to the falls ||at|| Pascataquack, gathered a church, and wrote to our church to desire us to dismiss Mr. Wheelwright to them for an officer; but, because he desired it not himself, the elders did not propound it. Soon after came his own letter, with theirs, for his dismission, which thereupon was granted. Others likewise (upon their request) were also dismissed thither.

The governour's letter to Mr. Hilton, about Mr. Burdet and Capt. Underhill, was by them intercepted and opened; and thereupon they wrote presently into England against us, §discovering what they knew of our combination to resist any authority, that should come out of England against us, etc.;§ for they were extremely moved ||[2]at|| the governour's letter, but could take no advantage by it, for he made account, when he wrote it, that Mr. Hilton would show it them. And, upon this, Capt. Underhill wrote a letter to Mr. Cotton, full of high and threatening words against us; but he wrote another, at the same time, to the governour in very fair terms, entreating an obliterating of all that was past, and a bearing with human infirmities, etc., disavowing all purpose of revenge, etc. See after, (1,) 1639.

The devil would never cease to disturb our peace, and to raise up ||[3]instruments|| one after another. Amongst the rest, there was a woman in Salem, one Oliver his wife, who had suffered somewhat in England for refusing to bow at the name of Jesus, though otherwise she was conformable to all their

||of|| ||[2]by|| ||[3]insurgents||

---

the original easily undeceived me, and led to the restoration of the true text, though vexed with a bad chirography.

[1] " One Milton, a blind man," derogates nothing from the author of Paradise

orders. She was (for ability of speech, and appearance of zeal and devotion) far before Mrs. Hutchinson, and so the fitter instrument to have done hurt, but that she was poor and *282
had little acquaintance. She took offence at this, that she might not be admitted to the Lord's supper without giving public satisfaction to the church of her faith, etc., and covenanting or professing to walk with them according to the rule of the gospel; so as, upon the sacrament day, she openly called for it, and stood to plead her right, though she were denied; and would not forbear, before the magistrate, Mr. Endecott, did threaten to send the constable to put her forth. This woman was brought to the court for disturbing the peace in the church, etc., and there she gave such peremptory answers, as she was committed till she should find sureties for her good behavior. After she had been in prison three or four days, she made || means || to the governour, and submitted herself, and acknowledged her fault in disturbing the church; whereupon he took her husband's bond for her good behavior, and discharged her out of prison. But he found, after, that she still held her former opinions, which were very dangerous, as, 1. That the church is the heads of the people, both magistrates and ministers, met together, and that these have power to ordain ministers, etc. 2. That all that dwell in the same town, and will profess their faith in Christ Jesus, ought to be received to the sacraments there; and that she was per-

|| blank ||

Lost. Nicholas Easton is distinguished, with only four others, out of a list of fifty-four freemen admitted at a general court, 3 September, 1634, by the title of respect. It may be seen, Colony Rec. I. 113, that the Rev. Messieurs Parker and Noyes were admitted at the same time, and I conclude, that he accompanied them. In March after, Easton was deputy from Ipswich, and he probably followed his spiritual guide to Newbury. From his occupation, mentioned in the text, no conclusion to his discredit can be drawn; for that employment, in a new country, is found the most useful and profitable for men of good education and estate. Large capital is often invested in that business, and we need not suppose it was mere handicraft. He was governour at Rhode Island four years, and the station was five years filled by one, whom I presume to be his son, John Easton. See 1 Hist. Coll. VI. 144, 145, and Callender, 42, 93.

suaded, that, if Paul were at Salem, he would call all the inhabitants there saints. 3. That excommunication is no other but when Christians withdraw private communion from one that hath offended.[1]

About five years after, this woman was adjudged to be whipped for reproaching the magistrates. She stood without tying, and bare her punishment with a masculine spirit, glorying in her suffering. But after (when she came to consider the reproach, which would stick by her, etc.) she was much dejected about it. She had a cleft stick put on her tongue half an hour, for reproaching the elders, (6,) 1646.[2]

At Providence, also, the devil was not idle. For whereas, at
*283 their first coming thither, Mr. Williams and the rest did make an order, that no man should be molested for his conscience, now men's wives, and children, and servants, claimed liberty hereby to go to all religious meetings, though never so often, or though private, upon the week days; and because one ||Verin||[3] refused to let his wife go to Mr. Williams so oft as she was called for, they required to have him censured. But there stood up one Arnold,[4] a witty man of their own company,

||Udrin||

[1] A favorable construction would surely find no deadly errors in these opinions; and certainly imprisonment appears not very appropriate means for conviction. I doubt that the apostle pointed at much more blameable notions, and even practices, in the church of Corinth, than he would have found at Salem, though he bestows the epithet *saints* on the members of the former. Mrs. Oliver thought, probably, there was too much power assumed by the elders.

[2] This paragraph comes in where the author had long left a blank. I fear more reproach attached to the elders, with all who pitied the sufferer, than if her tongue had been left loose.

[3] Of this unusual name I have met with no recurrence, except in Hutchinson, I. 203, where he informs us of the trial and imprisonment of Philip Verin, as a Quaker.

[4] Benedict Arnold was governour of Rhode Island thirteen years. 1 Hist. Coll. VI. 144, 145. In 1657, with Gov. Coddington, he purchased Cononicut Island. 1 Hist. Coll. V. 217. He will often be mentioned in this History as a great friend of Massachusetts, especially in negotiation with the Indians, whose language was better known to him and his son, of the same name, than most other of our people. I do not ascertain whether the anecdote in the text belongs to him or William Arnold. See Callender, 35, 43, 80, 93.

and withstood it, telling them that, when he consented to that order, he never intended it should extend to the breach of any ordinance of God, such as the ||subjection|| of wives to their husbands, etc., and gave divers solid reasons against it. Then one Greene (who hath married the wife of one Beggerly,[1] whose husband is living, and no divorce, etc., but only it was said, that he had lived in adultery, and had confessed it) he replied, that, if they should restrain their wives, etc., all the women in the country would cry out of them, etc. Arnold answered him thus: Did you pretend to leave the Massachusetts, because you would not offend God to please men, and would you now break an ordinance and commandment §of God§ to please women? Some were of opinion, that if ||[2]Verin|| would not suffer his wife to have her liberty, the church should dispose her to some other man, who would use her better. Arnold told them, that it was not the woman's desire to go so oft from home, but only Mr. Williams's and others. In ||[3]conclusion,|| when they would have censured ||[4]Verin,|| Arnold told them, that it was against their own order, for ||[5]Verin|| did ||[6]that he did|| out of conscience; and their order was, that no man should be censured for his conscience.

Another plot the old serpent had against us, by sowing jealousies and differences between us and our friends at Connecticut, and also Plimouth. This latter was about our *284
bounds. They had planted Scituate, and had given out all the lands to Conyhassett. We desired only so much of the marshes there, as might accommodate Hingham, which being denied, we caused Charles River to be surveyed, and found it come so far southward as would fetch in Scituate and ||[7]more;|| but this was referred to a meeting between us.[2]

||submission|| ||[2]Udrin|| ||[3]court after|| ||[4]Udrin|| ||[5]Udrin|| ||[6]that, and did it|| ||[7]Concord||

[1] The circumstances of the separation, which may be seen in Addenda, sub an. 1636, will excuse our belief, that the charge against Greene is altogether invidious.

[2] Relative to this survey of Charles River, and the line between Plimouth and Massachusetts colonies, which frequently was matter of controversy, the

The differences between us and those of Connecticut were divers; but the ground of all was their ||shyness|| of coming under our government, which, though we never intended to make them subordinate to us, yet they were very jealous, and therefore, in the articles of confederation, which we propounded to them, and whereby order was taken, that all differences, which might fall out, should be ended by a way of peace, and never to come to a necessity or danger of force, — they did so alter the chief article, as all would have come to nothing. For whereas the article was, That, upon any matter of difference, two, three, or more commissioners of every of the confederate colonies should assemble, and have absolute power (the greater number of them) to determine the matter, — they would have them only to meet, and if they could agree, so; if not, then to report to their several colonies, and to return with their advice, and so to go on till the matter might be agreed; which, beside that it would have been infinitely tedious and extreme chargeable, it would never have attained the end; for it was very unlikely, that all the churches in all the plantations would ever have accorded upon the same propositions.[1]

*285 These articles, with their alterations, they sent to our general court at Newtown, the [blank] of the 5th, by Mr.

||sickness||

---

earliest notice in our Colony Records, I. 228, is 6 September, 1638: "The town of Dedham is desired to spare two that are most fit to go with goodman Woodward and goodman Johnson, (if he can spare time,) or another to be got in his room, to lay out the most southermost part of Charles River, and to have five shillings a day a piece." Woodward was often employed in such business, and, at the same court, was ordered to survey the line north of Merrimack. He was admitted of Boston church 8 December, 1633, being No. 194.

[1] If the liability to disagreement in the consultations of the churches had been regarded as an objection against submitting to them other matters of state, we might not so frequently have to lament the proceedings of our fathers. Whenever any course, that might proceed to a result of extreme injustice, cruelty, or tyranny, was contemplated by the civil rulers, the sanction of the churches or of the elders was usually solicited, and too often obtained. Such is the consequence of uniting the wisdom of magistrates and ecclesiastics in concerns belonging exclusively to either. See the matter well stated by our author in the last article of Addenda, next volume.

Haynes, Mr. Pincheon, and John Steele.[1] The court, finding their alteration, and the inconveniences thereof, would take the like liberty to add and alter; (for the articles were drawn only by some of the council, and never allowed by the court). This they excepted against, and would have restrained us of that liberty, which they took themselves; and one of their three commissioners, falling in debate with some of our deputies, said, that they would not meddle with any thing that was within our limits; which being reported to the court, they thought it seasonable we should stand upon our right, so as, though we were formerly willing that Agawam (now Springfield) should have fallen into their government, yet, seeing they would not be beholden to us for any thing, we intended to keep it; and accordingly we put it in as an article, that the line between us should be, one way, the Pequod River, (viz. south and north,) and the other way, (viz. east and west,) the limits of our own grant. And this article we added: That we, etc., should have liberty to pass to and fro upon Connecticut, and they likewise. To these articles all their commissioners offered to consent, but it was thought by our court, (because of the new articles,) that they should first acquaint their own court with it. And so their commissioners departed.

After this, we understood that they went on to exercise their authority at Agawam. Whereupon the governour wrote to ||them|| to desire them to forbear until the line was laid out,

||him||

---

[1] Steele was one of the first settlers of Hartford, called Newtown, because most of the early inhabitants went from that town with Hooker and Haynes; but the Connecticut village changed its name very soon, probably before that in our neighborhood. Windsor was first called Dorchester, and Weathersfield Watertown, after the chief fountains of their blood in Massachusetts. This gentleman was a deputy in our general court 4 March, 1634–5, and again in September following; and was also one of those appointed by the authority of Massachusetts to administer justice among the people of the new colony until they formed a government for themselves. See Hutchinson, I. 99, from the Colony Records. He was *now* one of the magistrates or assistants of Connecticut, and, when their first court of deputies assembled, in 1639, was one of that body. Trumbull, I. 79, 103. The time of his death is unknown to me. I suppose descendants are numerous.

with advice about some other things, as by the copy of the letter appears. After a long time, Mr. Ludlow (in the name of their court) returned answer, which was very harsh; and in fine declared, that they thought it not fit to treat any further before they had advice from the gentlemen of Saybrook, etc. The governour acquainted the council and magistrates with this
*286 letter; and, because they had tied our hands (in a manner) from replying, he wrote a private letter to Mr. Haynes, wherein he lays open their mistakes (as he called them) and the apparent causes of offence, which they had given us; as by || disclaiming || to their Naragansetts to be bound by our former agreement with them, (which they would never make till the wars were ended,) by making a treaty of agreement with the Naragansetts and Monhigans, without joining us, or mentioning us to that end, (though we had by letter given them liberty to take us in,) and by binding all the Indians (who had received any Pequods) to pay tribute for them all to them || at || Connecticut, etc. (All these things are clearly to be seen in the letters.) *These and the like miscarriages in point of correspondency were conceived to arise from these two errors in their government: 1. They chose divers *scores* men, who had no learning nor judgment, which might fit them for those affairs, though otherwise men holy and religious. 2. By occasion hereof, the main burden for managing of state business fell upon some one or other of their ministers, (as the phrase and style of these letters will clearly discover,) who, though they were men of singular wisdom and godliness, yet, stepping out of their course, their actions wanted that blessing, which otherwise might have been expected.*[1]

15.] The wind at N. E., there was so great a tempest of wind and snow all the night and the next day, as had not been since our time. Five men and youths perished between Matta-

|| disinclining || ||[2] of ||

[1] These lines were so effectually erased, that, for some years, my desire of decyphering them was baffled; but, after twice abandoning the task, I gradually obtained, with the aid of a gentleman much skilled in reading difficult MS., a sufficient confidence in all but one word.

pan and Dorchester,[1] and a man and a woman[2] between Boston and Roxbury. || Anthony || Dick,[3] in a bark of thirty *287
tons, cast away upon the head of Cape Cod. Three were starved to death with the cold; the other two got some fire and so lived there, by such food as they saved, seven weeks, till an Indian found them, etc. Two vessels bound for Quinipiack were cast away at Aquiday, but the people saved. Much other harm was done in staving of boats, etc., and by the great tides,

|| Arthur ||

---

[1] Our information cannot denote the line between the English and the Indian places, the names of which are commonly applied indiscriminately. The historian of Dorchester leaves me to conjecture; and my supposition is, that the neck, of old called Dorchester Neck, now annexed to the metropolis by the designation of South Boston, was Mattapan. The early settlement of the English was made near the present *first* church, and between that and South Boston the face of the country was bad enough for one to be lost in without an extreme tempest of snow. It is to be understood from the text, that the disaster occurred by land, not water.

[2] A very full relation of these persons perishing with cold on Boston Neck is given by Johnson, with characteristic deficiency of precision as to date, against which all readers should perpetually guard, lib. II. c. 15. "To end this year, 1639, the Lord was pleased to send a very sharp winter, and more especially in strong storms of weekly snows, with very bitter blasts. And here the reader may take notice of the sad hand of the Lord against two persons, who were taken in a storm of snow, as they were passing from Boston to Roxbury, it being much about a mile distant, and a very plain way. One of Roxbury sending to Boston his servant maid for a barber-chirurgeon to draw his tooth, they lost their way in their passage between, and were not found till many days after, and then the maid was found in one place, and the man in another, both of them frozen to death; in which sad accident this was taken into consideration by divers people, that this barber was more than ordinary laborious to draw men to those sinful errors, that were formerly so frequent, and now newly overthrown, — by the blessing of the Lord upon the endeavor of his faithful servants with the word of truth, — he having a fit opportunity, by reason of his trade, so soon as any were set down in his chair, he would commonly be cutting of their hair and the truth together; notwithstanding some report better of the man, the example is for the living; the dead is judged of the Lord alone." The barber-surgeon was William Dinely, whose name is on p. 248, with others of those disarmed for heresy. His son, born ten days after his father perished, was baptized 6 January following, by the name, Fathergone.

[3] I know nothing more of this man than that he had come to Plimouth in 1623, that Capt. Clap, in his Memoirs, mentions his having been taken by the pirate Bull, and that he received his information from Dick's own mouth.

which exceeded all before. This happened the day after a general fast, which occasioned some of our ministers to stir us up to seek the Lord better, because he seemed to discountenance the means of reconciliation. Whereupon the next general court, by advice of the elders, agreed to keep another day, and to seek further into the causes of such displeasure, etc.; which accordingly was performed.

(11.) 14.] The earthquake, which had continued at times since the 1st of the 4th, was more generally felt, and the same noise heard in many places.

30.] A church was gathered at Weymouth with approbation of the magistrates and elders. It is observable, this church, having been gathered before, and so that of Lynn, could not hold together, nor could have any elders join or hold with them. The reason appeared to be, because they did not begin according to the rule of the gospel, which when Lynn had found and humbled themselves for it, and began again upon a new foundation, they went on with a blessing.

The people of this town of Weymouth had invited one Mr. || Lenthall ||[1] to come to them, with intention to call him to be
*288 their minister. This man, though of good report in England, coming hither, was found to have drank in some of Mrs. Hutchinson's opinions, as of justification before faith, etc.,

|| Leathall ||

---

[1] Hubbard, 275, carefully copies his master, but neglects to enlarge our knowledge of this clergyman. I learn from Lechford, that he, soon after, found him at Newport, "out of office and employment, and lives very poorly." From the proceedings in our Colony Records, I. 241, we find his name of baptism was Robert. Callender, 62, gives all the further information that can be obtained, and confirms my conjecture that he returned home: "They procured [for a religious teacher] Mr. Lenthal of Weymouth, who was admitted a freeman here August 6, 1640. And, August 20, Mr. Lenthal was by vote called to keep a public school for the learning of youth, and for his encouragement there was granted to him and his heirs one hundred acres of land, and four more for an house lot. It was also voted, that one hundred acres should be laid forth, and appropriated for a school, for encouragement of the poorer sort to train up their youth in learning; and Mr. Robert Lenthal, while he continues to teach school, is to have the benefit thereof. But this gentleman did not tarry here very long. I find him gone to England the next year but one." It seems, the New Lights of Rhode Island were willing to have advantage of the old light.

and opposed the gathering of our churches in such a way of mutual stipulation as was practised among us. From the former he was soon taken off upon conference with Mr. Cotton; but he stuck close to the other, that only baptism was the door of entrance into the church, etc., so as the common sort of people did eagerly embrace his opinions, and some labored to get such a church on foot as all baptized ones might communicate in without any further trial of them, etc. For this end they procured many hands in Weymouth to a blank, intending to have Mr. || Lenthall's || advice to the frame of their call; and he likewise was very forward to become a minister to them in such a way, and did openly maintain the cause. But the magistrates, hearing of this disturbance and combination, thought it needful to stop it betimes, and ||[2]ergo|| they called Mr. ||[3]Lenthall,|| and some of the chief of the faction, to the next general court in the 1 month, where Mr. ||[4]Lenthall,|| having before conferred with some of the magistrates and of the elders, and being convinced both of his error in judgment, and of his sin in practice to the disturbance of our peace, etc., did openly and freely retract, with expression of much grief of heart for his offence, and did deliver his retractation in writing, under his hand, in the open court; whereupon he was enjoined to appear at the next court, and in the mean time to make and deliver the like recantation in some public assembly at Weymouth. So the court stopped for any further censure by fine, or, etc., though it was much urged by some.

At the same court one Smith was convicted and fined £20 for being a chief stirrer in the business; and one Silvester *289
was disfranchised; and one Britton, who had spoken reproachfully of the answer, which was sent to Mr. Barnard his book against our church covenant, and of some of our elders, and had sided with Mr. || Lenthall, || etc., was openly whipped, because he had no estate to answer, etc.

||Leathall's|| ||[2]so|| ||[3]Leathall|| ||[4]Leathall|| ||[5]Leathall||

---

[1] Of this extraordinary tyranny (I can appropriate no milder word) all that our court has left on record is here extracted from vol. I. 240:

"13 of 1, 1638–9, John Smyth, for disturbing the public peace by combining with others to hinder the orderly gathering of a church at Weymouth, and to

Mo. 1.] A printing house was begun at Cambridge by one Daye, at the charge of Mr. Glover, who died on sea hitherward. The first thing which was printed was the freemen's oath; *the next was an almanac made for New England by Mr. William Peirce, mariner;* the next was the Psalms newly turned into metre.[1]

§ A plantation was begun by Sandwich, and was called Yarmouth, in Plimouth jurisdiction.§

Another plantation was begun upon the north side of Merrimack, called Sarisbury, §now Colchester;§ another at Win-

---

set up another there, contrary to the orders here established, and the constant practice of all our churches, and for undue procuring the hands of many to a blank for that purpose, is fined £20, and committed during the pleasure of court or the council.

"Richard Silvester, for going with Smyth to get hands to a blank, was disfranchised, and fined £2.

"Mr. Ambrose Marten, for calling the church covenant a stinking carrion, and a human invention, and saying he wondered at God's patience, feared it would end in the sharp, and said the ministers did dethrone Christ and set up themselves; he was fined £10, and counselled to go to Mr. Mather, to be instructed by him.

"Mr. Thomas Makepeace, because of his novel disposition, was informed, we were weary of him, unless he reform."

These two latter offenders are supposed by me to be among the conspirators for a free church, because their offences and sentences are related next after the former, and Mather was the minister nearest to Weymouth. It is observable, that nothing is said of Britton's crime or punishment. It was, probably, thought unnecessary to burden the record with such a case, though we should, in modern times, think very differently. Lechford says, "he was whipped eleven stripes," and his guilt is by that author represented as "saying that some of the ministers in the bay were Brownists."

Yet a very humane and judicious critic, in 3 Mass. Hist. Col. III. 403, the late admirable James Bowdoin, doubted the soundness of this charge of "extraordinary tyranny."

[1] The history of printing, at least in America, has been illustrated with exemplary diligence, in two amusing volumes, by Isaiah Thomas, who treats of his own profession with equal skill and affection. The place, where it was first practised in these English colonies, has been ever since devoted to the cause of letters, by the establishment of a College, having the widest fame of any on this side of the Atlantic, though long intervals have elapsed without the exercise of the press.

icowett, called Hampton, which gave occasion of ‖some‖ difference between us and some of Pascataquack, which *290 grew thus: Mr. Wheelwright, being banished from us, gathered a company and sat down by the falls of Pascataquack, and called their town Exeter; and for their enlargement they dealt with an Indian there, and bought of him Winicowett, etc., and then wrote to us what they had done, and that they intended to lot out all these lands in farms, except we could show a better title. They wrote also to those whom we had sent to plant Winicowett to have them desist, etc. These letters coming to the general court, they returned answer, that they looked at this their dealing as against good neighborhood, religion, and common honesty; that, knowing we claimed Winicowett as within our patent, or as vacuum domicilium, and had taken possession thereof by building an house there above two years since, they should now go and purchase an unknown title, and then come to ‖²inquire‖ of our right. It was in the same letter also manifestly proved, that the Indians having only a natural right to so much land as they had or could improve, so as the rest of the country lay open to any that could and would improve it, as by the said letter more at large doth appear.[1]

In this year one James ‖³Everell,‖[2] a sober, discreet man, and two others, saw a great light in the night at Muddy River. When it stood still, it flamed up, and was about three yards square; when it ran, it was contracted into the figure of a swine: it ran as swift as an arrow towards Charlton, and so up and down about two or three hours. They were come down

‖sore‖ ‖²deny‖ ‖³Everett‖

---

[1] From this paragraph my suspicion was first excited of the authenticity of the Indian deed to Wheelwright, the first article in Appendix to Belknap's New Hamp. I. The scrutiny has convinced me, that it is a forgery; but the length of the inquiry renders it expedient to postpone it to the Appendix H.

[2] He was a man of reputation, activity, and good estate in Boston many years afterwards. With his wife, Elizabeth, he had been received into Boston church 20 of July, 1634, being Nos. 239, 240. His will, made 11 December, 1682, proved 2 February following, is found in our Probate Registry, vol. VI. 400.

in their lighter about a mile, and, when it was over, they found themselves carried quite back against the tide to the place they came from. Divers other credible persons saw the same light, after, about the same place.[1]

*291 The general court, in the 7th mo. last, gave order to the governour to write to them of Pascataquack, to signify to them, that we looked at it as an unneighborly part, that they should encourage and advance such as we had cast out from us for their offences, before they had inquired of us the cause, etc. (The occasion of this letter was, that they had aided Mr. Wheelwright to begin a plantation there, and intended to make Capt. Underhill their governour in the room of Mr. Burdett, who had thrust out Capt. Wiggin, set in there by the lords, etc.) Upon this, Capt. Underhill (being chosen governour there) wrote a letter to a young gentleman, (who sojourned in the house of our governour,) wherein he reviles ||the|| governour with reproachful terms and imprecations of vengeance upon us all. This letter being showed to the governour and council, the governour, by advice, wrote the letter to Edward Hilton as is before mentioned, page [blank,] mo. 10, 13. The captain was so nettled with this letter, and especially because his adulterous life with the cooper's wife at Boston was now discovered, and the church had called him to come and make answer to it; but he made many excuses, as want of liberty, being a banished man, (yet the governour and council had sent him a safe conduct,) and upon his pretence of the insufficiency of that, the general court sent him another for three months. But, instead of coming, he procured a new church at Pascataquack of some few loose men (who had chosen one Mr.

||our||

[1] This account of an ignis fatuus may easily be believed on testimony less respectable than that which was adduced. Some operation of the devil, or other power beyond the customary agents of nature, was probably imagined by the relaters and hearers of that age, and the wonder of being carried a mile against the tide became important corroboration of such a fancy. Perhaps they were wafted, during the two or three hours' astonishment, for so moderate a distance, by the wind; but, if this suggestion be rejected, we might suppose, that the eddy, flowing always, in our rivers, contrary to the tide in the channel, rather than the meteor, carried their lighter back.

Knolles,[1] a weak minister, lately come out of England, and rejected by us for holding some of Mrs. Hutchinson's opinions) to write to our church at Boston in his commendation, wherein they style him the right worshipful, their honored governour; all which notwithstanding, the church of Boston proceeded with him; and, in the mean time, the general court wrote to all the chief inhabitants of Pascataquack, and sent them a copy of his letters, (wherein he professeth himself to be an instrument ordained of God for our ruin,) to know, whether it were with their privity and consent, that he sent us such a defiance, etc., and whether they would maintain him in such practices against us, etc. *292

Those of Pascataquack returned answer to us by two several letters. Those of the plantation disclaimed to have any hand in his miscarriages, etc., and offered to call him to account, etc., whensoever we would send any to inform against him. The others at the river's mouth disclaimed likewise, and showed their indignation against him for his insolences, and their readiness to join in any fair course for our satisfaction; only they desired us to have some compassion of him, and not to send any forces against him.

After this, Capt. Underhill's courage was abated, for the chiefest in the river fell from him, and the rest little regarded him, so as he wrote letters of retractation to divers; and, to

---

1 Hanserd Knollys is a name of considerable repute among the early Baptists in England, where, like the other divines of our first settlers, he had been episcopally ordained. After a residence of a few years in our country, the account of which, little creditable to his morals, will appear in other parts of this History, he returned home. Something of his sufferings, for the new doctrines, at the hands of the persecuting parliament and Independents, during the great age of anarchy, will be found in Toulmin's edition of Neal's Puritans, III. 551, 2, 3. He was persecuted by the other side, in the following age of prelatical domination, and his sufferings were probably of use to him. Hubbard, 356, has preserved the famous Bastwick's play upon his name, — Absurdo Knowless. His reputation was so much improved in his latter days, that Mather, III. calls him *godly*, and assures us he died "a good man in a good old age." Belknap, N. H. I. 45, with precision, notices his years and death, "Sept. 19, 1691, Ætat. ninety-three." Eliot includes him, but Allen does not.

In his notice of Knollys, who left an autobiography, Brook had large materials, and seems to have well used them. Lives of the Puritans, III. 491.

show his wisdom, he wrote a letter to the deputy and the court, (not mentioning the governour,) wherein he sent the copies of some of the governour's letters to Pascataquack, supposing that something would appear in them either to extenuate his fault, or to lay blame upon the governour; but he failed in both, for the governour was able to make good what he had written.

[Large blank.]

16.] There was so violent a wind at S. S. E. and S. as the like was not since we came into this land. It began in the evening, and increased till midnight. It overturned some new, strong houses; but the Lord miraculously preserved old, weak cottages.[1] It tare down fences, — people ||ran|| out of their houses in the night, etc. There came such a rain withal, as raised the waters at Connecticut twenty feet above their meadows, etc.

*293 The Indians near Aquiday being pawwawing in this tempest, the devil came and fetched away five of them. Quere.[2]

At Providence things grew still worse; for a sister of Mrs. Hutchinson, the wife of one Scott,[3] being infected with Anabaptistry, and going last year to live at Providence, Mr. Williams was taken (or rather emboldened) by her to make open profession thereof, and accordingly was rebaptized by one

||came||

---

[1] If the new houses were higher, we may reasonably doubt the *miracle*. The oak breaks and the willow bends, according to the laws of nature, not by their suspension.

[2] The last word seems to be of a later date. *Perhaps* the story staggered the credulity of Mather. But if the author meant only, that a violent flood, raised by the prince of the power of the air, carried off these natives and drowned them, we may regret the consequence, at least as much as we deride the manner of expression. A greater loss from such cause is related in this volume, 166, August, 1635.

[3] Richard Scott, shoemaker, had been admitted of Boston church 28 August, 1634, being No. 265, and is, I presume, the same person, who, with Greene, Holliman, the two Arnolds, and others, derived title in the lands of Providence under Williams. Callender, 43.

Holyman,[1] a poor man[2] late of Salem. Then Mr. Williams rebaptized him and some ten more. They also denied the bap tizing of infants, and would have no magistrates.[3]

At Aquiday, also, Mrs. Hutchinson exercised publicly, and she and her party (some[4] three or four families) would have no magistracy. She sent also an admonition to the church of Boston; but the elders would not read it publicly, because she was excommunicated. By these examples we may see how dangerous it is to slight the censures of the church; for it was apparent, that God had given them up to || strange || delu- *294
sions. Those of Aquiday also had entertained two men, whom the church of Roxbury had excommunicated, and one of them did exercise publicly there. For this the church of Boston called in question such of them as were yet their members; and Mr. Coddington, being present, not freely acknowledging his sin, (though he confessed himself in some fault,) was solemnly admonished.

This is further to be observed in the delusions which this people were taken with: Mrs. Hutchinson and some of her

|| strong ||

---

[1] Ezekiel Holliman, founder, with eleven others, of the first Baptist church in America, is well spoken of, as a man of gifts and piety, by those who knew him best. See Benedict. At our general court, March, 1637–8, being summoned, "because he did not frequent the public assemblies, and for seducing many, he was referred by the court to the ministers for conviction." Of the execution of such a sentence, to the uttermost, we should in vain look for a record, and perhaps it may be thought a reward rather than a punishment. They who are found guilty of entertaining other notions than the court are seldom in a good temper for conviction after judgment. The dissenter thanked his judges, I suppose, for the opportunity of a conference.

[2] Hubbard, 338, in transcribing this passage, candidly changes "poor man" into "mean fellow." The ministers failed, probably, to enlighten his conscience.

[3] If the like assertion of rejecting magistracy, which, in the text immediately after, is made about Rhode Island, be untrue, as will be clearly proved, we may doubt this alleged insanity of the people at Williams's plantation. When shall we have a true history of Rhode Island, with the temper of Callender and the opportunities of Hutchinson?

[4] *Save* is given by Hubbard instead of "some;" but although the MS. has not become more legible in the intervening hundred and forty years, I prefer my eyesight to his, as may our readers the sense of the passage.

adherents happened to be at prayer when the earthquake was at Aquiday, etc., and the house being shaken thereby, they were persuaded, (and boasted of it,) that the Holy Ghost did shake it in coming down upon them, as he did upon the apostles.

[Blank.]

(2.)] A plantation was begun between Ipswich and Newbury. The occasion was this: Mr. Eaton and Mr. Davenport having determined to sit down at Quinipiack, there came over one Mr. Ezekiel Rogers, second son of that truly faithful servant of God, Mr. Richard Rogers of Weathersfield in England, and with him some twenty families, godly men, and most of them of good estate. This Mr. Rogers, being a man of special note in England for his zeal, piety, and other parts,[1] they labored by all means to draw || with them || to Quinipiack, and had so far prevailed with him, being newly come, and unacquainted with the state of the country, as they had engaged him; yet, being a very wise man, and considering that many of quality[2] in England did depend upon his choice of a fit place for them, he agreed upon such ||[2]propositions || and cautions, as, though they promised to fulfil them all, (whereupon he sent divers of his people thither before winter,) yet, when it came to, they were not able to make good what they had promised. Whereupon he consulted with the elders of the bay, and, by their advice, etc., holding his former engagement released, he and his people took that place by Ipswich; and because some farms had been granted by Ipswich and Newbury, which would be prejudicial to their plantation, they bought out the owners, disbursing

|| him || ||[2]proposals ||

---

1 In Oliver's History of Beverley in Yorkshire appears sufficient evidence of the esteem in which Rogers was held. Complaint being made in Chancery of gross misapplication of funds, by Queen Elizabeth bestowed on the church of St. Mary in that borough, a commission was issued to inquire by a jury or otherwise. It was directed to the Archbishop of York, the Earl of Cumberland, three baronets, six knights, eight esquires, and seven clergymen, of whom the first named was our Richard Rogers.

2 Mather mentions two names of persons, Sir William Constable and Sir Matthew Boynton, who designed to accompany him.

therein about £800; and he sent a pinnace to Quinipiack to fetch back the rest of his people; but Mr. Eaton and Mr. Davenport, and others of Connecticut, (being impatient of the loss of him and his people,) staid the pinnace, and sent a messenger with letters of purpose to recover him again. This *295
made him to desire the elders to assemble again, and he showed them the letters they sent, (which wanted no arguments, though some truth;[1]) but he made the case so clear, by letters which had passed between them, etc., as they held him still free from all engagement; and so he returned answer to them, and went on with his plantation.

[Large blank.]

The Indians of Block Island sent, for their tribute this year, ten fathom of wampompeak.

One Mr. Howe,[2] of Lynn, a godly man, and a deputy of the last general court, after the court was ended, and he had dined, being in health as he used to be, went to pass over to Charlestown, and, being alone, he was presently after found dead upon the strand, being there (as it seemed) waiting for the boat, which came soon after.

(3.) 2.] Mr. Cotton, preaching out of the 8 of Kings, 8, taught, that when magistrates are forced to provide for the maintenance of ministers, etc., then the churches are in a declining condition. There he showed, that the ministers' maintenance should be by voluntary contribution, not by lands, or revenues, or tithes, etc.; for these ||have|| always been accompanied with pride, contention, and sloth, etc.[3]

||things had||

---

[1] The exertions of the New Haven gentlemen, to acquire so important a confederate as Rogers, might lead to a little exaggeration; but the insinuation of falsehood against such characters, as Eaton and Davenport, needs not to be repelled. As they harmonized in symbols of doctrine and church forms with our colonists, so rude a charge upon them is more extraordinary than many suggestions we find against the lovers of episcopacy or the latitudinarians of Rhode Island.

[2] Edward Howe had been representative in all the courts the year preceding. There was, in Lynn, another Howe, perhaps brother of Edward, named Daniel, of whom, in the progress of this History, something will be told.

[3] Cotton did not often preach more sound doctrine, though I am not satis-

11.] The two chief sachems of Naragansett sent the governour a present of thirty fathom of wampom, and Sequin, the sachem of Connecticut, sent ten fathom.

At Aquiday the people grew very tumultuous, and put out Mr. Coddington and the other three magistrates, and chose Mr. William Hutchinson only, a man of a very mild temper and weak parts, and wholly guided by his wife, who had been the
*296 beginner of all the former troubles in the country, and still continued to breed disturbance.[1]

---

fied with the pertinency of the text, which was, undoubtedly, in the second book.

[1] Here I may redeem the pledge, given in note 3, on page 293, of showing this relation erroneous. The Hon. Samuel Eddy, many years secretary of the state of Rhode Island, and a consistent asserter of the doctrine of religious liberty, for which his fellow-citizens may feel as great obligation, as I do for his antiquarian diligence in furnishing the State Papers, 2 Hist. Coll. VII. 75–113, besides other valuable information, has supplied the evidence. In a letter of 18 January, 1817, now before me, after quoting from Hubbard, 338, 9, what that historian had copied from our text, he adds: "Now this, not to notice the contradiction, is altogether without foundation, and contrary to the whole tenor of the records, which admit of no such construction. On the first settlement of the island, they chose Coddington (7th 1st month, 1638, the day of their incorporation) their judge. He remained sole judge until the 2d of the 11th month, 1638, when they chose three elders to his assistance, viz. Nicholas Easton, John Coggeshall, and William Brenton. These all continued in office until the 12th of the 1st month, 1640, when they ordered their chief magistrate to be called governour, the next, deputy governour, and Easton, Coggeshall, *William Hutchinson*, and John Porter assistants, for one year. This was the only time that William Hutchinson was chosen to office. The four following years, Coddington and Brenton were re-elected. 1641, Coggeshall, Robert Harding, William Balston, and John Porter, were chosen assistants. The three following years, they were all re-elected. In 1642, according to Hutchinson, (Vol. I. p. 72,) William Hutchinson died on Rhode Island. The same year, according to Hubbard, Mrs. Hutchinson and family 'removed to some place under the Dutch,' and were destroyed by the Indians."

"The fact, in itself, is, to be sure, of not much importance; though it removes from Mrs. Hutchinson a part of the evidence of her being a meddling and troublesome woman. But, so far as it shows the materials from which the historian composed his narrative, it is of considerable importance. Vague reports ought never to be adopted in opposition to records. Neither ought they to be adopted at all, but *as such;* and not then, until the proper sources of information have been examined. I am apprehensive, that much of what has been said, and continues to be said, of the first settlers of this state, is founded

They also gathered a church in a very disordered way; *297
for they took some excommunicated persons, and others

---

on the same kind of authority. I purpose hereafter to show something of this in the case of Gorton, who appears to have been the common butt of all the early, and some late writers, than whom, I am persuaded, no one of the first settlers of this country has received more unmerited reproach, nor any one suffered so much injustice. His opinions on religious subjects were, probably, somewhat singular, though certainly not more so than those of many at this day. But that was *his* business; his opinions were his own, and he had a *right* to them."

My correspondent died before fulfilment of his promise about Gorton. But he was told, that Hubbard is *innocently* chargeable with following materials from which he did not so much *compose*, as compile, or rather copy, his work. To prevent all succeeding writers from looking into the historian of Ipswich, as an *original* authority, for any fact which Winthrop had related, I subjoin to this protracted note two considerations, from which the just value of his book may be ascertained.

1. Hutchinson, the most diligent and exact of all writers of colonial history, since Winthrop, whose work he could not see, at the opening of his labors, mentions his apparatus: "among the rest a manuscript history of Mr. WILLIAM HUBBARD, which is carried down to the year 1680, but, *after* 1650, contains *but few facts*." Now, our author's work brings the series of events to 1649, when he died. Yet, though Hubbard was in the prime of life for the thirty years following, he seems to have slighted most of the occurrences, in which he should have felt the deepest interest, if he had not also felt his incapacity to appear the relater of them. A small part of his volume was, certainly, compiled from several scarce tracts relative to the discovery of our coast and the early voyages to it; and, for any thing of date preceding 1630, his information is sometimes authentic, and often curious. A collation with Morton's Memorial will, however, prove the facility with which Hubbard transcribed whole pages in succession, even from a printed book. But from the time when Winthrop came to his aid, he generously relies on him, and deems the labor of copying sufficient. So that more than seven eighths of his volume, between 1630 and 1650, is borrowed, usually by specific extracts, occasionally with unimportant changes, from the text of the Father of Massachusetts. It must be acknowledged, however, that, sometimes, he wisely abbreviates; though much more frequently he slides over circumstances, as dates or numbers, in which the chirography of the MS. would have given him too much trouble to be accurate. I would recommend to any studious lover of our early history to go through from pages 128 to 536 of Hubbard, and in his margin to note the corresponding passages from this History.

2. Dr. Holmes, in his invaluable Annals, a work which almost compensates for our loss of the accuracy of Prince, referred, between pages 255 and 347 of Vol. I. in his first edition, narrating events within the limits of time, for which Winthrop could and did afford assistance, not less than one hundred and seven times to the MS. of Hubbard. Now fifty-six of these citations are of passages

who were members of the church of Boston and not dismissed.[1]

*298 6.] The two regiments in the bay were mustered at Boston, to the number of one thousand soldiers, able men, and well armed and exercised. They were ||led,|| the one by the governour, who was general of all, and the other by the deputy, who was colonel, etc. The captains, etc., showed themselves very skilful and ready in divers sorts of skirmishes and other military actions, wherein they spent the whole day.[2]

One of Pascataquack, having opportunity to go into Mr. Burdet his study, and finding there the copy of his letter to the archbishops, sent it to the governour, which was to this effect:

||headed||

---

taken literally by Hubbard from our History, and three fourths of the remaining fifty-one are such as the Ipswich historian adopted, with alterations utterly trivial, from the same authority. Printing, therefore, lamentably reduced the value of that MS., as all antiquaries, it may be presumed, would acknowledge higher veneration for written than printed evidence. Yet the scrupulous annalist may easily be absolved from censure; for, when his volumes were put forth, it had never been considered, whence Hubbard derived his treasures. Those which could not be found in the first edition of Winthrop, must have been sought in Hubbard; and of the fourteen last citations by Dr. Holmes, within the space above-mentioned, eleven will be seen, from the part of the History now published, to be literal extracts. All this process of verification, the work of a few hours, if not too easily credited by my readers, will afford, to any who attempt it, sufficient amusement, and at the same time furnish infallible means of ascertaining the relative value of the testimony furnished by each of the witnesses, Hubbard and Winthrop.

1 Those members of Boston church who had been driven by intolerance to the new region, if they gathered a church at all, must do it in a disordered way; for they might well apprehend, that an application for dismission would be rejected, and perhaps punished by excommunication. The anathema against the outcasts, I suppose, belongs also to all who receive them. In 2 Hist. Coll. X. 184, is a long letter of Cotton, in the name of the church of Boston, to Francis Hutchinson, at Aquettinck, or Rhode Island, refusing dismission, though it appears to have been solicited on two grounds, of his remote situation rendering it impossible for him to perform the duties of his covenant at Boston, and also of his natural obligation to attend upon his parents.

2 Wonder-working Providence is chiefly valued for its account of the military array of the people in their several settlements, lib. II. c. 26, the author having been better acquainted with the use of the sword than the Bible, though so frequently ambitious of exhibiting his dexterity in handling the word.

That he did delay to go into England, because he would fully inform himself of the state of the people here in regard of allegiance; and that it was not discipline that was now so much aimed at, as sovereignty; and that it was accounted ||perjury|| and treason in our general courts to speak of appeals to the king.

The first ships, which came this year, brought him letters from the archbishops and the lords commissioners for plantations, wherein they gave him thanks for his care of his majesty's service, etc., and that they would take a time to redress such disorders as he had informed them of, etc., but, by reason of the much business now lay upon them, they could not, at present, accomplish his desire. These letters lay above fourteen days in the bay, and some moved the governour to open them; but himself and others of the council thought it not safe to meddle with them, nor would take any notice of them; and it fell out well, by God's good providence; for the letters, (by some means) were opened, (yet without any of their privity or consent,) and Mr. Burdet threatened to complain of it to the lords; and afterwards we had knowledge of the contents of them by some of his own friends.

The governour received letters from Mr. Cradock, and in them another order from the lords commissioners, to this effect: That, whereas they had received our petition upon their former order,[1] etc., by which they perceived, that we were taken with some jealousies and fears of their intentions, etc., they did accept of our answer, and did now declare their intentions to be only to regulate all plantations to be sub- *299
ordinate to the said commission; and that they meant to continue our liberties, etc., and therefore did now again peremptorily require the governour to send them our patent by the first ship; and that, in the mean time, they did give us, by that order, full power to go on in the government of the people until we had a new patent sent us; and, withal, they added threats of further course to be taken with us, if we failed.

This order being imparted to the next general court, some

||piracy||

[1] See page 269.

advised to return answer to it. Others thought fitter to make no answer at all, because, being sent in a private letter, and not delivered by a certain messenger, as the former order was, they could not proceed upon it, because they could not have any proof that it was delivered to the governour; §and order was taken, that Mr. Cradock's agent, who delivered the letter to the governour, etc., should, in his letters to his master, make no mention of the letters he delivered to the governour,§ seeing his master had not laid any charge upon him to that end.

Mr. Haynes, the governour of Connecticut, and Mr. Hooker, etc., came into the bay, and staid near a month. It appeared by them, that they were desirous to renew the treaty of confederation with us, and though themselves would not move it, yet, by their means, it was moved ||to|| our general court, and accepted; for they were in some doubt of the Dutch, who had lately received a new governour,[1] a more discreet and sober man than the former, and one who did complain much of the injury done to them at Connecticut, and was very forward to hold correspondency with us, and very inquisitive how things stood between us and them of Connecticut, which occasioned us the more readily to renew the former treaty, that the Dutch might not take notice of any breach or alienation between us.

22.] The court of elections was; at which time there was a small eclipse of the sun. Mr. Winthrop was chosen governour again, though some laboring had been, by some of the elders §and others§ to have changed, not out of any dislike of him, (for they all loved and esteemed him,) but out of their fear lest it might make way for having a governour for life, which some had propounded as most agreeable to God's institution and the practice of all well ordered states. But neither the governour

||by||

[1] His name was William Kieft; and of him frequent notice will occur in the interminable negotiations between the Dutch and our New England colonies. It is hardly necessary to refer the reader, for amusement at his expense, to Knickerbocker's New York.

nor any other attempted the thing; though some jealousies *300
arose which were increased by two occasions. The first was, there being want of assistants, the governour and other magistrates thought fit (in the warrant for the court) to propound three, amongst which Mr. Downing, the governour's brother-in-law, was one, which they conceived to be done to strengthen his party, and therefore, though he were known to be a very able man, etc., and one who had done many good offices for the country for these ten years, yet the people would not choose him.[1] Another occasion of their jealousy was, the court, finding the number of deputies to be much increased by the addition of new plantations, thought fit, for the ease both of the country and the court, to reduce all towns to two deputies.[2] This occasioned some to fear, that the magistrates intended to make themselves stronger, and the deputies weaker, and so, in time, to bring all power into the hands of the magistrates; so as the people in some towns were much displeased with their deputies for yielding to such an order. Whereupon, at the next session, it was propounded to have the number of deputies restored; and allegations were made, that it was an infringement of their liberty; so as, after much debate, and such reasons given for diminishing the number of deputies, and clearly proved that their liberty consisted not in the number, but in the thing, divers of the deputies, who came with intent to reverse the last order, were, by force of reason, brought to uphold it; so that, when it was put to the vote, the last order

---

[1] It is by no means remarkable, that this measure caused some jealousy. For the exact phraseology employed, on this occasion, by the assistants, see Addenda. Yet I find this memorandum on the last page of our first volume of Colony Records, in 1641: "Mr. Flint, Mr. Symonds, Mr. Dummer, Mr. Tyng, Mr. Downing, and Mr. Pyncheon, are to be propounded to the towns for new magistrates."

[2] Foresight, rather than experience, must have led to the adoption of this remedy; for the number of deputies, at the court in March preceding, amounted only to thirty-three, and had never been greater. But, in fact, the smaller towns had not exercised their full right, and the change was probably made, because two might represent either of the other towns as well as three. Perhaps it was thought, that not more than two fit men could be found in some towns.

for two deputies only was confirmed. Yet, the next day, a petition was brought to the court from the freemen of Roxbury, to have the ‖third deputy‖ restored. Whereupon the reasons of the court's proceedings were set down in writing, and all objections answered, and sent to such towns as were unsatisfied with this advice, that, if any could take away those reasons, or
*301 bring us better for what they did desire, we should be ready, at the next court, to repeal the said order.[1]

The hands of some of the elders (learned and godly men) were to this petition, though suddenly drawn in, and without due consideration, for the lawfulness of it may well be questioned: for when the people have chosen men to be their rulers, and to make their laws, and bound themselves by oath to submit thereto, now to combine together (a lesser part of them) in a public petition to have any order repealed, which is not repugnant to the law of God, savors of resisting an ordinance of God; for the people, having deputed others, have no power

‖three deputies‖

---

[1] Early practice and law seem to have established the equality of representation from towns; though it was, after a few years, restricted in some degree. Towns having less than twenty freemen were allowed but one deputy, and those less than ten, none, though the freemen of such towns were permitted to unite in election with the next towns. A "liberty of sending or not sending deputies" was very early exercised by the towns, and allowed by the house. It has constantly been enjoyed since, subject, however, to a discretion of the body in imposing fines for neglect; and, though a little more restricted under the provincial than the colony government, is perfectly well settled under our present constitution as an independent state. From the date in the text, Boston, like most of the other towns, sent only two members. In 1680 the number was increased again to three, and, after the first session under the charter of William and Mary, was raised to four. This was our complement, nearly ninety years, till the commencement of our national independence. By the charter of William and Mary, every town was authorized in the first house to have two representatives; but that first general court was by the charter empowered to declare and fix the apportionment to each town. In the exercise of this authority, leave was granted to towns of thirty freeholders to have one member; towns of one hundred and twenty freeholders, two members; and Boston, alone, four. A complete list of representatives from Boston to the commencement of the revolution in 1775 is given in 2 Hist. Coll. X. 23–29. Probably one or two additions for vacancies might, however, be made to it, had I leisure to spend as many hours as the formation of it cost.

to make or alter laws, but are to be subject; and if any such order seem unlawful or inconvenient, they ||were|| better prefer some reasons, etc., to the court, with manifestation of their desire to move them to a review, than peremptorily to petition to have it repealed, which amounts to a plain reproof of those whom God hath set over them, and putting dishonor upon them, against the tenor of the fifth commandment.

There fell out at this court another occasion of increasing the people's jealousy of their magistrates, viz.: One of the elders, being present with those of his church, when they were to prepare their votes for the election, declared his judgment, that a governour ought to be for his life, alleging for his authority the practice of all the best commonwealths in Europe, and especially that of Israel by God's own ordinance.[1] But *302
this was opposed by some other of the elders with much zeal, and so notice was taken of it by the people, not as a matter of dispute, but as if there had been some plot to put it in practice, which did occasion the deputies, at the next session of this court, to deliver in an order drawn to this effect: That, whereas our sovereign lord, King Charles, etc., had, by his patent, established a governour, deputy and assistants, that therefore no person, chosen a counsellor *for life,* should have any authority as a magistrate, except he were chosen in the annual elections to one of the said places of magistracy established by the patent. This being thus bluntly tendered, (no mention being made thereof before,) the governour took time to consider of it, before he would put it to vote. So, when the court was risen, the magistrates advised of it, and drew up another order to this effect: That whereas, at the court in [blank,] it was ordered, that a certain number of magistrates should be chosen to be a standing council for life, etc., whereupon some had gathered that we had erected a new or-

||had||

[1] Who gave such impolitic counsel, supported by the preposterous analogies, is unknown to me. The ministers were perpetually meddling with the regimen of the commonwealth; and we have frequent occasion to regret, that their references to the theocracy of Israel were received as authority, rather than illustration.

der of magistrates not warranted by our patent, this court doth therefore declare, that the intent of the order was, that the standing council should always be chosen out of the magistrates, etc.; and therefore it is now ordered, that no such counsellor shall have any power as a magistrate, nor shall do any act as a magistrate, etc., except he be annually chosen, etc., according to the patent; and this order was after passed by vote. That which led those of the council to yield to this desire of the deputies was, because it concerned themselves, and they did more study to remove these jealousies out of the people's heads, than to preserve any power or dignity to themselves above others; for till this court those of the council, viz., Mr. Endecott, had stood and executed as a magistrate, without any annual election, and so they had been ||reputed|| by the elders and all the people till this present. But the order was drawn up in this form, that it might be of less observation and freer from any note of injury to make this alteration rather by way of explanation of the fundamental order, than without any cause shown to repeal that which had been established by serious advice of the elders, and had been in practice two or
*303 three years without any inconvenience.[1] And here may be observed, how strictly the people would seem to stick to their patent, where they think it makes for their advantage, but are content to decline it, where it will not warrant such liberties as they have taken up without warrant from thence, as appears in their strife for three deputies, etc., when as the patent allows them none at all, but only by inference, etc., voting by proxies, etc.

The governour acquainted the general court, that, in these two last years of his government, he had received from the Indians, in presents, to the value of about £40, and that he had

||reported||

[1] This appears a very idle scruple of the assistants. Since they consented to give up the substance, it was unwise to permit any jealousy about the form. Election for life has, in no other instance, I believe, obtained for any legislative or executive office in our country. Annual choice gives admirable opportunity for our people to show their stability; and a gentleman is much longer in office usually in the New England states than in those where the people vote only at periods of two or three years.

spent about £20 in entertainments of them and in presents to their sachems, etc. The court declared, that the presents were the governour's due, but the tribute was to be paid to the treasurer.[1]

[Blank.]

15.] Mr. Endecott and Mr. Stoughton, commissioners for us, and Mr. Bradford and Mr. Winslow for Plimouth, met at Hingham about deciding the difference between us concerning our bounds. Our commissioners had full power to determine, etc.; but theirs had not, although they had notice of it long before, and themselves had appointed the day. Whereupon the court ordered, that those of Hingham should make use of all the land near Conyhassett to the ||creek|| next Scituate, till the court should take further order; and a letter was directed to the governour ||[2]of|| Plimouth to the same effect, with declaration of the reasons of our proceeding, and readiness to give them a further meeting. The charges of their commissioners' diet ||[3]was|| defrayed by us, because they met us within our own jurisdiction.

Those of Exeter replied to our answer, standing still to maintain the Indians' right, and their interest thereby. But, in the mean time, we had sent men to discover Merrimack, and found some part of it about Penkook to lie more northerly than *304
forty-three and a half. § So § we returned answer to them, that, though we would not relinquish our interest by priority of possession for any right they could have from the Indians, yet, seeing they had professed not to claim any thing which should fall within our patent, we would look no further than that in respect of their claim.

One Mr. Ryall,[2] having gotten a patent at Sagadahoc out of

||crook|| ||[2]at|| ||[3]were||

[1] A rate of £1000, levied by this court, Rec. I. 250, was thus assessed:— Boston, £144.10.1; Ipswich, £111.18.11; Salem, £111.13.11; Dorchester, £93.7.9; Cambridge, £91.19.9; Charlestown, £85.15.10; Watertown, £81.17.1; Lynn, £79.19.6; Roxbury, £74.12.6; Newbury, £67.8.3; Hingham, £33.14.5; Weymouth, £23.2.

[2] In a diligent search amidst all accessible stores of information, very little knowledge on the subject of this gentleman's grant has been acquired, and, of this little, not a word from Gorges, under whom the title was derived. Very

the grand patent,[1] wrote to our governour and tendered it to our government, so as we would send people to possess it. The governour acquainted the general court with it, but nothing was done about it, for we were not ready for such a business, having enough || to do || at home.

[Large blank.]

26.] Mr. Hooker being to preach at Cambridge, the governour and many others went to hear him, (though the governour did very seldom go from his own congregation upon the Lord's day).[2] He preached in the afternoon, and having gone on, with much strength of voice and intention of spirit, about a quarter of an hour, he was at a stand, and told the people, that God had deprived him both of his strength and matter, etc., and so went forth, and about half an hour after returned again, and went on to very good purpose about two hours.

There was at this time a very great ||[2]drouth || all over the country, both east and west, there being little or no rain from the 26th of the 2d month to the 10th of the 4th; so as the corn generally began to wither, and great fear there was it would all
*305 be lost. Whereupon the general court conferred with the elders, and agreed upon a day of humiliation about a week after. The very day after the fast was appointed there fell a good shower, and, within one week after the day of hu-

|| besides || ||[2] dearth ||

short and unsatisfactory reference is made to it in some proceedings under the authority of President Danforth, acting by power from Massachusetts, above forty years after, which may be seen in Sullivan's History of the District of Maine, 182–4. The name of Royal's River in North Yarmouth is, probably, deduced from this person, whose descendants, of the male line, pronouncing the name as it is spelt in the text, I am informed, are still remaining in the neighborhood of their early domain.

[1] By this *grand patent* is not intended, I presume, the original patent of 18 Jac. I., 3 November, usually called the Plimouth Charter, but one of much narrower limits, 15 Car. I., 3 April, which may be found in Haz. I. 442–455. Royal's letter must have been written immediately after the king's grant, in anticipation of which he, probably, had made his arrangements with Gorges.

[2] Gov. Winthrop's travelling on Sunday, for such a purpose, must not, I suppose, be considered unnecessary. His example would justify the many others. Such instances are now almost unknown.

miliation was past, we had such store of rain, and so seasonably, as the corn revived and gave hope of a very plentiful harvest. When the court and the elders were met about it, they ||considered|| of such things as were amiss, which might provoke God against us, and agreed to acquaint their churches therewith, that they might be stirred up to bewail and reform them.

(4.)] We were much afraid this year of a ||[2]stop|| in England, by reason of the complaints which had been sent against us, and the great displeasure which the archbishops and others, the commissioners for plantations, had conceived and uttered against us, both for those complaints, and also for our not sending home our patent. But the Lord wrought for us beyond all expectation; for the petition, which we returned in answer of the order sent for our patent, was read before the lords and well accepted, as is before expressed; and ships came to us from England and divers other parts with great store of people and provisions of all sorts.

About this time our people came from Isle Sable. A bark went for them, on the 2 of the 1 month, but by foul weather she was wrecked there, and of her ruins they made a small one, wherein they returned. It was found to be a great error to send thither before the middle of the 2 month. They had gotten store of seal oil and skins, and some horse teeth and black fox skins; but the loss of the vessel, etc., overthrew the hope of the design.

The island is very healthful and temperate. We lost not one man in two years, nor any sick, etc.

(5.)] The rent at Connecticut grew greater, notwithstanding the great pains ||[3]which|| had been ||[4]taken|| for healing it; so as the church of Weathersfield itself was not only divided from the rest of the town, etc., but, of those seven which were the church, four fell off; so as it was conceived, that thereby the church was dissolved, which occasioned the church of Watertown here (which had divers of ||[5]their|| members there, not yet dismissed) to send two of their church to look after their members, and to take order with them. But the contention and alienation of minds was such, as they could not bring them to

||conferred|| ||[2]step|| ||[3]we|| ||[4]taking|| ||[5]her||

any other accord than this, that the one party must remove to some other place, which they both consented to, but still the difficulty remained; for those three, who pretended themselves
*306 to be the church, pleaded that privilege for their stay, and the others alleged their multitude, etc., so as neither would give place, whereby it seemed, that either they minded not the example of Abraham's offer to Lot, or else they wanted Abraham's spirit of peace and love.

This controversy having called in Mr. Davenport and others of Quilipiack, for mediation, and they not according with those of Connecticut about the case, gave advantage to Satan to ||sow|| some seeds of contention between those plantations also; but, being godly and wise men on both parts, things were easily reconciled.[1]

In this month there arrived two ships ||[2]at|| Quilipiack. One was of three hundred and fifty tons, wherein came Mr. Fenwick[2] and his lady and family to make a plantation at Saybrook upon the mouth of Connecticut. Two other plantations were begun beyond Quilipiack, and every plantation intended a peculiar government.

There were also divers new plantations begun this summer here and at Plimouth, as Colchester[3] upon Merrimack, Sudbury

||straw|| ||[2]of||

---

1 From Trumbull, I. 120, 1, it appears, the reconciliation was not very easy, and was at last effected by the separation of the dissonant parts. Stamford was settled in consequence.

2 George Fenwick, Esq., would surely deserve more consideration than he has received from the writers about our country, neither Eliot nor Allen having thought his name required insertion in their volumes, and even Trumbull being apparently negligent of one of the principal fathers of Connecticut. This probably resulted from his return to England, and there ending his days in high office, of which some influence will appear in our second volume. Hutchinson, I. 100, 1, gives the fullest account of him and his friendly regards to our country. He had come to Boston in May, 1636, but went home, probably, the same year, after ascertaining the capacity and value of his colony at the mouth of Connecticut. The two ships were the first, and, I suppose, the last, that ever came from London to New Haven. His wife died at Saybrook, where her monument is still extant. She was daughter, I believe, of Sir Arthur Haslerig. He died early in 1657.

3 At the court of October, 1640, this place was ordered to be called Salisbury. This seems, from page 289, to have been its first name.

by Concord, (Winicowett was named Hampton,) Yarmouth and Barnstaple by Cape Cod.

[Large blank.]

Capt. Underhill, having been dealt with and convinced of his great sin against God and the churches and state here, etc., returned to a better mind, and wrote divers letters to the governour and deputy, etc., bewailing his offences, and craving pardon. See after, (1,) 5, 39, and (7,) 3, 40.

There was sent to the governour ||the|| copy of a letter written into England by Mr. Hansard Knolles of Pascataquack, wherein he had most falsely slandered this government, as that it was worse than the high commission, etc., and that here was nothing but oppression, etc., and not so much as a face *307
of religion. The governour acquainted one of Pascataquack, Mr. Knolles his special friend, with it. Whereupon Mr. Knolles became very much perplexed, and wrote to the governour, acknowledging the wrong he had done us, and desired that his retractation might be published. The governour sent his letter into England, and kept a copy of it. See more of this after, (12,) 20, 1639.

At Providence matters went after the old manner. Mr. Williams and many of his company, a ||[2]few|| months since, were in all haste rebaptized, and denied communion with all others, and now he was come to question his second baptism, not being able to derive the authority of it from the apostles, otherwise than by the ministers of England, (whom he judged to be ill authority,) so as he conceived God would raise up some apostolic power. Therefore he bent himself that way, expecting (as was supposed) to become an apostle; and having, ||[3]a little|| before, refused communion with all, save his own wife, now he would preach to and pray with all comers. Whereupon some of his followers left him and returned back from whence they went.

(6.) 27.] Here came a small bark from the West Indies, one Capt. ||[4]*Jackson*|| in her, with commission from the Westminster company to take prize, etc., from the Spaniard. He brought much wealth in money, plate, indico, and sugar. He

||a|| ||[2]some|| ||[3]no title|| ||[4]Sackett||

sold his indico and sugar here for £1400, wherewith he furnished himself with commodities, and departed again for the West Indies.[1]

A fishing trade was begun at Cape Ann by one Mr. || Maurice || Tomson,[2] a merchant of London; and an order was made, that all stocks employed in fishing should be free from public charge for seven years. This was not done to encourage foreigners to set up fishing among us, (for all the gains would be returned to the place where they dwelt,) but to encourage our own people to set upon it, and in expectation that Mr. Tomson, etc., would, ere long, come settle with us.

*308 (7.)] Here was such store of exceeding large and fat mackerel upon our coast this season, as was a great benefit to all our plantations. Some one boat with three men would take, in a week, ten ||[2]hogsheads,|| which was sold at Connecticut for £3.12 the ||[3]hogshead.||

There were such swarms of small flies, like moths, came from the southward, that they covered the sea, and came flying like drifts of snow; but none of them were seen upon the land.[3]

(7.) 17.] A church was gathered at the Mount.

4.] At the general court at Boston, one Mr. Nathaniel

||Maverick|| ||[2]hundreds|| ||[3]hundred||

---

1 Josselyn, in his Voyages, p. 26, mentions his finding at Boston, on arrival, 27 September of this year, captain Jackson in the Queen of Bohemia, a privateer.

2 Of this gentleman I know very little. Francis Kirby, in a letter to John Winthrop, jun., 26 December, 1631, says: "Capt. B. who was employed by my cousin, Maurice Thomson and company, for the trade of beaver in the River of Canada, is now arrived here. . . . . He hath brought in here about three thousand pounds weight of beaver, and they are now hastening to set forth a small ship only for that river, hoping to be there before Capt. Kirk, who (I hear) is to fetch his men from Quebec, and yield up the castle again to the French this next summer." Probably Thomson was not tempted to come to New England, except for temporary purpose about this fishing establishment.

3 In 2 Hist. Coll. IV. 230, a large account of the mackerel fishery on the south shore of Massachusetts Bay informs us, that the appearance of such insects is "a welcome herald to the fisherman." That memoir is worth consulting by all the curious.

Eaton,[1] brother to the ||merchant|| at Quilipiack, was convented and censured. The occasion was this: He was a schoolmaster, and had many scholars, the sons of gentlemen and others of best note in the country, and had entertained one Nathaniel Briscoe,[2] a gentleman born, to be his usher, and to do some other things for him, which might not be unfit for a scholar. He had not been with him above three days but he fell out with him for a very small occasion, and, with reproachful terms, discharged him, and turned him out of his doors; but, it being then about eight of the clock after the Sabbath, he told him he should stay till next morning, and, some words growing between them, he struck him and pulled him into his house. Briscoe defended himself, and closed with him, and, being parted, he came in and went up to his chamber to lodge there. Mr. Eaton sent for the constable, who advised him first to *309
admonish him, etc., and if he could not, by the power of
a master, reform him, then he should complain to the magistrate. But he caused his man to fetch him a cudgel, which was a walnut tree plant, big enough to have killed a horse, and a yard in length, and, taking his two men with him, he went

||magistrate||

[1] Slight mention of this unhappy man will be found in Addenda. He had been admitted a freeman of our colony 9 June of the preceding year. What became of him, after 1646, is known only from Mather, who says, he went from Virginia to England, there lived privately until the restoration, then conformed to the ceremonies of the church by law established, was settled at Biddeford, persecuted the dissenters, from whom he had *apostatized*, and died in prison for debt. He undoubtedly had very high encouragement to continue at the head of the newly established college; for, in the Court Records, I. 252, of May preceding the date in the text, I find a grant "to Mr. Nathaniel Eaton five hundred acres, if he continue his employment for his life, to be to him and his heirs." Further evidence of the resolution of the government in supporting that institution, is found, at the same court, in two orders: 1. "That a letter should be sent to Mr. Humfrey to send in the £100, which is in his hand, to further the college." 2. "Mr. Endecott, Mr. Downing, and Mr. Hawthorne are to dispose of the house, which Mr. Peters bought, as they can, and return the money for the college."

[2] Of him I know nothing, unless he be the author of a very curious letter from England, 7 Sept. 1652, on which proceedings more curious were had here by our government. See 3 Hist. Coll. I. 32–35.

up to Briscoe, and caused his men to hold him till he had given him two hundred stripes about the head and shoulders, etc., and so kept him under blows (with some two or three short intermissions) about the space of two hours, about which time Mr. Shepherd and some others of the town came in at the outcry, and so he gave over. In this distress Briscoe gate ‖out‖ his knife, and struck at the man that held him, but hurt him not. He also fell to prayer, (supposing he should have been murdered,) and then Mr. Eaton beat him for taking the name of God in vain. After this Mr. Eaton and Mr. Shepherd (who knew not then of these passages) came to the governour and some other of the magistrates, complaining of Briscoe for his insolent speeches, and for crying out murder and drawing his knife, and desired that he might be enjoined to a public acknowledgment, etc., The magistrates answered, that they must first hear him speak, and then they would do as they should see cause. Mr. Eaton was displeased at this, and went away discontented, etc., and, being after called into the court to make answer to the information, which had been given by some who knew the truth of the case, and also to answer for his neglect and cruelty, and other ill usage towards his scholars, one of the elders (not suspecting such miscarriages by him) came to the governour, and showed himself much grieved, that he should be publicly produced, alleging, that it would derogate from his authority and reverence among his scholars, etc. But the cause went on notwithstanding, and he was called, and these things laid to his charge in the open court. His answers were full of pride and disdain, telling the magistrates, that they should not need to do any thing herein, for he was intended to leave his employment. And being asked, why he used such cruelty to Briscoe his usher, and to other his scholars, (for it was testified by another of his ushers and divers of his scholars, that he would give them between twenty and thirty stripes at a time, and would not leave till they had confessed what he required,) his answer was, that he had this rule, that he would not give over correcting till he had subdued the party to his will. Being also questioned about the ill and scant diet of his boarders, (for, though their friends gave large allowance, yet their diet was ordinarily nothing but

‖at‖

porridge and pudding, and that very homely,) he put it off *310
to his wife.[1] So the court dismissed him at present,

[1] An examination of the lady followed, I presume, for the former secretary of the commonwealth furnished me a paper, which can hardly refer to any other transaction than this. Some overseer of the college, probably, either magistrate or clergyman, wrote it from the confession or dictation of the accused party: "For their breakfast, that it was not so well ordered, the flower not so fine as it might, nor so well boiled or stirred, at all times that it was so, it was my sin of neglect, and want of that care that ought to have been in one that the Lord had intrusted with such a work. Concerning their beef, that was allowed them, as they affirm, which, I confess, had been my duty to have seen they should have had it, and continued to have had it, because it was my husband's command; but truly I must confess, to my shame, I cannot remember that ever they had it, nor that ever it was taken from them. And that they had not so good or so much provision in my husband's absence as presence, I conceive it was, because he would call sometimes for butter or cheese, when I conceived there was no need of it; yet, forasmuch as the scholars did otherways apprehend, I desire to see the evil that was in the carriage of that as well as in the other, and to take shame to myself for it. And that they sent down for more, when they had not enough, and the maid should answer, if they had not, they should not, I must confess, that I have denied them cheese, when they have sent for it, and it have been in the house; for which I shall humbly beg pardon of them, and own the shame, and confess my sin. And for such provoking words, which my servants have given, I cannot own them, but am sorry any such should be given in my house. And for bad fish, that they had it brought to table, I am sorry there was that cause of offence given them. I acknowledge my sin in it. And for their mackerel, brought to them with their guts in them, and goat's dung in their hasty pudding, it's utterly unknown to me; but I am much ashamed it should be in the family, and not prevented by myself or servants, and I humbly acknowledge my negligence in it. And that they made their beds at any time, were my straits never so great, I am sorry they were ever put to it. For the Moor his lying in Sam. Hough's sheet and pillow-bier, it hath a truth in it: he did so one time, and it gave Sam. Hough just cause of offence; and that it was not prevented by my care and watchfulness, I desire [to] take the shame and the sorrow for it. And that they eat the Moor's crusts, and the swine and they had share and share alike, and the Moor to have beer, and they denied it, and if they had not enough, for my maid to answer, they should not, I am an utter stranger to these things, and know not the least footsteps for them so to charge me; and if my servants were guilty of such miscarriages, had the boarders complained of it unto myself, I should have thought it my sin, if I had not sharply reproved my servants, and endeavored reform. And for bread made of heated, sour meal, although I know of but once that it was so, since I kept house, yet John Wilson affirms it was twice; and I am truly sorry, that any of it was spent amongst them. For beer and bread, that

*311 and commanded him to attend again the next day, when, being called, he was commanded to the lower end of the table, (where all offenders do usually stand,) and, being openly convict of all the former offences, by the oaths of four or five witnesses, he yet continued to justify himself; so, it being near night, he was committed to the marshall till the next day. When the court was set in the morning, many of the elders

---

it was denied them by me betwixt meals, truly I do not remember, that ever I did deny it unto them; and John Wilson will affirm, that, generally, the bread and beer was free for the boarders to go unto. And that money was demanded of them for washing the linen, it's true it was propounded to them, but never imposed upon them. And for their pudding being given the last day of the week without butter or suet, and that I said, it was miln of Manchester in Old England, it's true that I did say so, and am sorry, they had any cause of offence given them by having it so. And for their wanting beer, betwixt brewings, a week or half a week together, I am sorry that it was so at any time, and should tremble to have it so, were it in my hands to do again."

The above is an exact copy of all that is written by that hand; but on the next page is found, in a more difficult, but uncommonly beautiful chirography, "and whereas they say, that sometimes they have sent down for more meat, and it hath been denied, when it have been in the house, I must confess, to my shame, that I have denied them oft, when they have sent for it, and it have been in the house."

In the archives of the State House it is not probable that any document more minute or entertaining can be preserved; nor would this seem of importance and gravity appropriate to this work, were it not connected with the history of the college, and highly illustrative of our author's text. That no complaints against Mrs. Eaton had been brought down from antiquity, when her husband suffered perpetual malediction, is perhaps owing to the gallantry of our fathers. Her accomplishments as a housewife appear equal to the gentleness of the head of the college. Her adherence to the religion in which she was educated, might have been as frail as his, had she not been lost on a voyage with her children to Virginia the next year. The commons of the students have often been matter of complaint, but, I believe, have never since occupied the attention of the government of the state.

Of the two men referred to by Mrs. Eaton, Wilson was son of the pastor of Boston, graduated in the first class, 1642, and, Mather says, "continued, unto old age, a faithful, painful, useful minister of the gospel" in Medfield. Hough was son of Atherton, the assistant, and was the second minister of Reading. Why he received not the usual degree is unknown. See Johnson, lib. II. c. 25. In our Town Records I find, "Mr. Samuel Haugh, pastor of the church at Reading, deceased at Mr. Hezekiah Usher's house in Boston, 30 March, 1662." The Moor was probably a slave.

came into the court, (it being then private for matter of consultation,) and declared how, the evening before, they had taken pains with him, to convince him of his faults; yet, for divers hours, he had still stood to his justification; but, in the end, he was convinced, and had freely and fully acknowledged his sin, and that with tears; so as they did hope he had truly repented, and therefore desired of the court that he might be pardoned, and continued in his employment, alleging such further reasons as they thought fit. After the elders were departed, the court consulted about it, and sent for him, and there, in the open court, before a great assembly, he made a very solid, wise, eloquent, and serious (seeming) confession, condemning himself in all the particulars, etc. Whereupon, being put aside, the court consulted privately about his sentence, and, though many were taken with his confession, and none but had a charitable opinion of it; yet, because of the scandal of *312
religion, and offence which would be given to such as might intend to send their children hither, they all agreed to censure him, and put him from that employment. So, being called in, the governour, after a short preface, etc., declared the sentence of the court to this effect, viz.: that he should give Briscoe £30, fined 100 ||marks,|| and debarred teaching of children within our jurisdiction. A pause being made, and expectation that (according to his former confession) he would have given glory to God, and acknowledged the justice and clemency of the court, the governour giving him occasion, by asking him if he had ought to say, he turned away with a discontented look, saying, "If sentence be passed, then it is to no end to speak." Yet the court remitted his fine to £20, and willed Briscoe to take but £20.

The church at Cambridge, taking notice of these proceedings, intended to deal with him. The pastor moved the governour, if they might, without offence to the court, examine other witnesses. His answer was, that the court would leave them to their own liberty; but he saw not to what end they should do it, seeing there had been five already upon oath, and those whom they should examine should speak without oath, and it was an ordinance of God, that by the mouths of two or three

||blank||

witnesses every matter should be established. But he soon discovered himself; for, ere the church could come to deal with him, he fled to Pascataquack, and, being pursued and apprehended by the governour there, he again acknowledged his great sin in flying, etc., and promised (as he was a Christian man) he would return with the messengers. But, because his things he carried with him were aboard a bark there, bound to Virginia, he desired leave to go fetch them, which they assented unto, and went with him (three of them) aboard with him. So he took his truss and came away with them in the boat; but, being come to the shore, and two of them going out of the boat, he caused the boatsmen to put off the boat, and because the third man would not go out, he turned him into the water, where he had been drowned, if he had not saved himself by swimming. So he returned to the bark, and presently they set sail and went out of the harbor. Being thus gone, his creditors began to complain; and thereupon it was found, that he was run in debt about £1000, and had taken up most of this money upon bills he had charged into England upon his brother's agents, and others whom he had no such relation to. So his estate was seized, and put into commissioners' hands, to be divided among his creditors, allowing somewhat for the
*313 present maintenance of his wife and children. And, being thus gone, the church proceeded and cast him out. He had been sometimes initiated among the Jesuits,[1] and, coming into England, his friends drew him from them, but, it was very probable, he now intended to return to them again, being at this time about thirty years of age, and upwards. See after.

7. 17.] Mount Woollaston had been formerly laid to Boston; but many poor men having lots assigned them there, and not able to use those lands and dwell still in Boston, they petitioned the town first to have a minister there, and after to have leave to gather a church there, which the town at length (upon some small composition) gave way unto. So, this day, they gathered a church after the usual manner, and chose one Mr. Tomson,[2]

---

[1] His cruelty and injustice might have been as great, if the Jesuits had had no share in his education; though, I fear, the author intended to refer the fruits to the soil, rather than the tree.

[2] Satisfactory accounts of William Tompson may be seen in Eliot's and Allen's

a very gracious, sincere man, and Mr. Flint, a godly man also, their ministers.[1]

Mo. 9.] At a general court holden at Boston, great complaint was made of the oppression used in the country in sale of foreign commodities; and Mr. Robert Keaine,[2] who kept a shop in *314
Boston, was notoriously above others observed and com-

Dictionaries, in the Magnalia, III., Johnson, lib. II. c. 7, 10 and 18, and lib. III. c. 1 and 11, larger in Morton, sub. an. 1666, the year of his death, and, best of all, in the century sermon of Hancock, his successor in the church of Braintree, now of Quincy. In our day, a later successor, Rev. W. P. Lunt, D. D., in two very happy discourses on the second centenary, has supplied all that diligence and affection could furnish. He had been some years in the country, perhaps; for the Records of Dorchester, which I have inspected, according to the views of the historian of that town, 1 Hist. Coll. IX. 191, reckon him among their members in 1636. But I suspect that was two years before his admission. The scrutinizing author must have concluded, that he was a different person from the future minister of the adjoining town; for he adds, of him "I cannot obtain any information." He was admitted freeman 13 May, 1640. Most of the materials used by later writers were found in our author, the most interesting event in his pilgrimage here being the mission to Virginia, of which a full account will be found in the next volume. The first mention of him, after that in the text, will show, that he "had been an instrument of much good at Acomenticus." The Braintree Records mention the birth of his son, Joseph, 1 May, 1640, Benjamin, 14 July, 1642, and death of his wife in January following. Benjamin was graduated at Harvard College in 1662. Him I consider the author of the verses in praise of Whiting, which are, probably, the best in the Magnalia. A tribute in verse, of greater justice than beauty, is entered in the Roxbury Church Records on the lamentable death of Tompson's wife, while he was absent on the service of his master. It was supposed by John Farmer, the assiduous genealogist, that the celebrated Benjamin Thomson, Count Rumford, descended from this first pastor of Braintree; but he afterwards favored me with evidence of a different derivation.

[1] Our MS. had first "*their pastor*," after "Tomson," and "*teacher*," to end the sentence; and, as the alteration was made by the governour, I infer that the distinction was disregarded at the election.

[2] This gentleman is, probably, the same with one whose name is the last signed to a letter of encouragement of the plantation at Plimouth, 7 April, 1624, preserved by Gov. Bradford in 1 Hist. Coll. III. 28, and who united with others, in all forty-two, in a loan of £1800 sterling, by which its life was preserved. Ib. 48. Being received into Boston church 20 March, 1635-6, we may conclude, he had come over in the preceding autumn, probably with Wilson in October. At the general election, in May following, he was admitted to the freeman's oath, at the same time with Samuel Appleton, Henry Flint, and

plained of; and, being convented, he was charged with many par-
*315 ticulars; in some, for taking above six-pence in the shilling
profit; in some above eight-pence; and, in some §small§

Daniel Maude, who alone, out of sixty-two that day sworn, have the prefix of respect.

Of the curious subject, introduced to our notice by the text, inquiry had, at the former session of the same court, in September, been instituted; and, from the language of the Record, I. 269, "Capt. Keayne was willed to return Sarah King her necessary clothes again," we may presume, the case was a flagrant one. It is evident, however, that much more tenderness was shown towards him than delinquents usually received; for we find, at the assistants' quarter court, four pages later, in the same volume, this note: "There is £10 delivered the governour by one that had failed by taking too great prices for his commodities. He hath satisfied the parties, whom he sold the commodities unto." At the general court in May after the date in the text, I find, Col. Rec. I. 276, "Mr. Robert Keayne had £120 of his fine remitted him; so that there remains only £80 to be paid by him." He was not the only person of eminence liable to this animadversion, though the proceedings against him went further than in any other case within my knowledge. Indeed, the attempt to prevent demand of high price for any commodity, however willing the purchaser may be to give it, is preposterous and destructive to all commerce between man and man. Sedgwick was admonished for a like frailty, in asking the money's worth for his goods. Before this scandal, Keayne had been four times chosen from Boston to the general court; and, after the evil report had passed over, was several times elected, and became speaker in October, 1646, but only for one day. Unhappily, he fell under obloquy again: a less probable, though more injurious accusation was preferred, of which a very particular relation is, in subsequent pages, given by our author. He certainly stood high in the estimation of the government; for, in May, 1639, a grant of four hundred acres had been made to him, when others of no larger quantity were made to several gentlemen of the first rank in the colony. He was brother-in-law of Wilson.

Keayne died 23 March, 1655–6. His will, proved 2 May after, written with his own hand — for no other hand could have been so patient — at different times, beginning 1 August, 1653, is a most extraordinary instrument, commencing on page 116 of our first volume of Records in Probate office, and filling one hundred and fifty-eight folio pages. It would be an idle affectation to say, that it has been all studied by me, though most parts were cursorily examined; for no reader of this work would exact of its editor such an unprofitable labor. An abridgment of several pages could easily be afforded here, for it was made; but when thirty pages of the will are occupied about the animadversion of the court on his extortion, as explained in our text, with inculpation of his prosecutor for cruel and unfounded allegations in that and another affair, and thirty pages more given to explanation of his accounts in many different books, with the order and reasons, plentiful enough, of dividing his estate, — the most things, above two for one; and being hereof convict, (as appears by the records,) he was fined £200, which came thus to pass: The deputies considered, apart, of his fine, and set it at £200; the magistrates agreed but to £100. So, the court being divided, at length it was agreed, that his fine should be £200, but he should pay but £100, and the other should be respited to the further consideration of the next general court. By this means the magistrates and deputies were brought to an accord, which otherwise had not been likely, and so much trouble might have grown, and the offender escaped censure. For the cry of the country was so great against oppression, and some of the elders and magistrates had declared such detestation of the corrupt practice of this man (which was the more observable, because he was wealthy and sold dearer than most other tradesmen, and for that he was of ill report for the like covetous practice

---

minute antiquary becomes weary with the trifles. Yet there are several curious parts. The ample declaration of his correct faith, that fills two of the early pages, hardly compensates, however, for the anxiously refined, but equivocal, morality, by which, towards the end, he excuses himself. Between his only child, Benjamin, and a daughter of Gov. Dudley, "an unhappy and uncomfortable match" is spoken of in this will; and that union, perhaps, with other disagreeable circumstances, compelled the son to return to the land of his fathers, where he died, I presume, in 1668. In August of that year, administration of the estate was granted, which he reckoned at £4000. The male line ended with Benjamin, whose only child, Ann, married Edward Lane, a merchant from London, who died here; and she next married Nicholas Paige, to whom, in 1683, with his wife, was granted admin. de bonis non of Robert's estate. His widow married Samuel Cole. Much amusement, and some knowledge, may be gained from the abstract of his will in Genealog. Reg. VI. 89 and 152.

The chief claims of Robert to be remembered, must arise from his activity in founding the Artillery Company, of which he was captain, and which is fondly remembered in the endless testament. See the History of that institution for other particulars. A large 4to MS. of his is preserved in the archives of the Historical Society, chiefly composed of the sermons or expositions of Cotton, as taken, probably in church, by the owner. It contains, besides, two very curious cases of ecclesiastical discipline, in which all the church members deliver their opinions on the matters,—one against Mrs. Hibbins, the other against Serjeant Richard Wait. The lady was cast out; the serjeant continued in the affection of the body. The report of brethren sent to Rhode Island, to warn the dwellers there of contumacy, is also given; and a few other trifles. He left, among other liberal bequests, a large one to Harvard College, still preserved in their exhibit.

in England, that incensed the deputies very much against him). And ||sure|| the course was very evil, especial circumstances considered: 1. He being an ancient professor of the gospel: 2. A man of eminent parts: 3. Wealthy, and having but one child: 4. Having come over for conscience' sake, and for the advancement of the gospel here: 5. Having been formerly dealt with and admonished, both by private friends and also by some of the magistrates and elders, and having promised reformation; being a member of a church and commonwealth now in their infancy, and under the curious observation of all churches and civil states in the world. These added much aggravation to his sin in the judgment of all men of understanding. Yet most of the magistrates (though they discerned of
*316 the offence clothed with all these circumstances) would have been more moderate in their censure: 1. Because there was no law in force to limit or direct men in point of profit in their trade. 2. Because it is the common practice, in all countries, for men to make use of advantages for raising the prices of their commodities. 3. Because (though he were chiefly aimed at, yet) he was not alone in this fault. 4. §Because all men through the country, in sale of cattle, corn, labor, etc., were guilty of the like excess in prices. 5.§ Because a certain rule could not be found out for an equal rate between buyer and seller, though much labor had been bestowed in it, and divers laws had been made, which, upon experience, were repealed, as being neither safe nor equal. Lastly, and especially, because the law of God appoints no other punishment but ||[2]double|| restitution; and, in some cases, as where the offender freely confesseth, and brings his offering, only half added to the principal. After the court had censured him, the church of Boston called him also in question, where (as before he had done in the court) he did, with tears, acknowledge and bewail his covetous and corrupt heart, yet making some excuse for many of the particulars, which were charged upon him, as ||[3]partly|| by pretence of ignorance of the true price of some wares, and chiefly by being misled by some false principles, as 1. That, if a man lost in one commodity, he might help himself in the price of another. 2. That if, through

||since|| ||[2]two|| ||[3]particularly||

want of skill or || other occasion, || his commodity cost him more than the price of the market in England, he might then sell it for more than the price of the market in New England, etc. These things gave occasion to Mr. Cotton, in his public exercise the next lecture day, to lay open the error of such false principles, and to give some rules of direction in the case.

Some false principles were these: —

1. That a man ||[2]might|| sell as dear as he can, and buy as cheap as he can.

2. If a man lose by casualty ||[3]of|| sea, etc., in some of his commodities, he may raise the price of the rest.

3. That he may sell as he bought, though he paid too dear, etc., and though the commodity be fallen, etc.

4. That, as a man may take the advantage of his own skill or ability, so he may of another's ignorance or necessity.

5. Where one gives time for payment, he is to take like recompense of one as of another.

The rules for trading were these: —

1. A man may not sell above the current price, i. e., such a price as is usual in the time and place, and as another *317
(who knows the worth of the commodity) would give for it, if he had occasion to use it; as that is called current money, which every man will take, etc.

2. When a man loseth in his commodity for want of skill, etc., he must look at it as his own fault or cross, and therefore must not lay it upon another.

3. Where a man loseth by casualty of sea, or, etc., it is a loss cast upon himself by providence, and he may not ease himself of it by casting it upon another; for so a man should seem to provide against all providences, etc., that he should never lose; but where there is a scarcity of the commodity, there men may raise their price; for now it is a hand of God upon the commodity, and not the person.[1]

4. A man may not ask any more for his commodity than his

||otherwise|| ||[2]may|| ||[3]at||

[1] Perhaps this excuse would usually be offered.

selling price, as Ephron to Abraham, the land is worth thus much.

[Large blank.]

The cause being debated by the church, some were earnest to have him excommunicated; but the most thought an admonition would be sufficient. Mr. Cotton opened the causes, which required excommunication, out of that in 1 Cor. 5. 11. The point now in question was, whether these actions did declare him to be such a covetous person, etc. Upon which he showed, that it is neither the habit of covetousness, (which is in every man in some degree,) nor simply the act, that declares a man to be such, but when it appears, that a man sins against his conscience, or the very light of nature, and when it appears in a man's whole conversation. But Mr. Keaine did not appear to be such, but rather upon an error in his judgment, being led by false principles; and, beside, he is otherwise liberal, as in his hospitality, and in church communion, etc. So, in the end, the church consented to an admonition.[1]

Upon this occasion a question grew, whether an admonition did bar a man from the sacrament, etc. Of this more shall be spoken hereafter.

*318 Being now about church matters, I will here insert another passage in the same church, which fell out about the same time. Their old meeting-house, being decayed and too small, they sold it away, and agreed to build another, which workmen undertook to set up for £600. Three hundred they had for the old,[2] and the rest was to be gathered by voluntary

---

[1] For this unusual instance of moderation in the church, whose corrective hand, in such an offence, had been more appropriately exercised than that of the magistrate, we may find two reasons: 1, that Keayne's principal accuser belonged to the country; the sympathies of Boston people, of whom many, being traders, must have felt the futility of several of the allegations against their craft, were therefore less strongly excited; 2. Wilson, the pastor of the church, was his brother-in-law. Keayne, in his will, says, Winthrop was prejudiced against him, but changed his opinion on the matter shortly before his death, and designed to have moved the court for restitution of the fine.

[2] In our Registry of Deeds are found, Vol. III. 386, the depositions in perpetuam rei memoriam, taken July, 1660, before Endicott, Gov., and Bellingham, Deputy Governour, of William Colbron, aged 67, heretofore deacon, now

contributions, as other charges were. But there grew a great difference among the brethren, where this new one should stand. Some were for the green, (which was the governour's first lot, and he had yielded it to the church, etc.;) others, viz., the tradesmen, especially, who dwelt about the market place, desired it might stand still ‖near‖ the market, lest in time it should divert the chief trade from thence. The church referred it to the judgment and determination of five[1] of the brethren, who agreed, that the fittest place (all things considered) would be near the market; but, understanding that many of the brethren were unsatisfied, and desired rather it might be put to a lot, they declared only their opinions in writing, and respited the full determination to another general meeting, thinking it very unsafe to proceed with the discontent of any considerable part of the church. When the church met, the matter was debated to and fro, and grew at length to some earnestness, etc.; but, after Mr. Cotton had cleared it up to them, that the removing it to the green[2] would be a damage to such as dwelt by the market, who had there purchased and built at great charge, but it would be no damage to the ‖[2]rest‖ to have it by the § market, because it would be no less, but rather more convenient for them, than where the former stood, they all yielded to have it set by the § market place; and, though some remained still in their opinion, that the green were the fitter place, yet, for peace sake, they yielded to the rest by keeping silence while it passed. This good providence and overruling hand of God caused much admiration and acknowledgment of special mercy

‖nearer‖ ‖[2]most‖

---

ruling elder, James Penn, then one of the members, now a ruling elder, and James Johnson, then one of the members, now one of the deacons, relative to this sale to Robert Thompson, of London, merchant, now resident in Boston. The price for the old meeting-house, and the land, with *exact* dimensions, was, they say, £160.

[1] Instead of "five of the brethren," was originally written "*the governour and four others.*" We easily understand the cause of the change.

[2] The green, the governour's first lot, was the corner of the street, part of which was afterwards taken for the Third, or Old South Church. Prince, who was minister of that church above a hundred years after, — Advertisement to Annals, II. — says, Winthrop "deceased in the very house I dwell in."

to the church, especially considering how long the like contention had held in some other churches, and ||with what|| difficulty they had been accorded.[1]

(7.) At the court of assistants, one Marmaduke Percy, of
*319 Salem, was arraigned for the death of one [blank,] his apprentice. The great inquest found the bill for murder; the jury of life and death could not agree; so they were adjourned to the next court, and Percy was let to bail by the governour and some other of the magistrates, after the court. At the court in 10ber, the prisoner appeared, and the jury being called, had further evidence given them, which tended to the clearing of Percy; yet two of the jury dissented from the rest, who were all agreed to acquit him. In the end it had this issue, that these two were silent, and so the verdict was received. The cause was this: The boy was ill disposed, and his master gave him unreasonable correction, and used him ill in his diet. After, the boy gate a bruise on his head, so as there appeared a fracture in his skull, being dissected after his death. Now, two things were in the evidence, which made the case doubtful; one, the boy his charging his master, before his death, to have given him that wound with his meatyard and with a broomstaff (for he spake of both at several times;) the other was, that he had told another, that his hurt came with the fall of a bough from a tree; and other evidence there was none.

4.] At the general court, etc., the inhabitants of the upper part of Pascataquack, viz. Dover, etc., had written to the governour to offer themselves to come under our government. Answer was returned them, that, if they sent two or three of their company, with full commission, under all their hands, to conclude, etc., it was like the court would agree to their propositions. And now, at this court, came three with commission to agree upon certain articles annexed to their commission, which being read, the court appointed three to treat with them; but, their articles being not reasonable, they stood not upon them, but confessed that they had absolute commission to con-

||which without||

[1] The spot on which the new edifice was erected, is now covered by Joy's buildings.

clude by their discretion. Whereupon the treaty was brought to a conclusion to this effect: That they should ||be|| as Ipswich and Salem, and have courts there, etc., as by the copy of the agreement remaining with the recorder doth appear. This was ratified under ||[2]our|| public seal, and so delivered to them; only they desired a promise from the court, that, if the people did not assent to it, (which yet they had no fear of,) they might be at liberty, which was granted them.[1]

Those of Exeter sent the like propositions to the court; but not liking (it seems) the agreement, which those of Dover had made, they repented themselves, and wrote to the court, *320
that they intended not to proceed.

[Large blank.]

At this court there fell out some contestation between the governour and the treasurer.[2] Nicholas Trerice[3] being defendant in a cause, wherein Mr. Hibbins,[4] brother-in-law to the treasurer, was plaintiff, for £500, which the searchers took from him in the ship, whereof Trerice was master, and the defendant having answered upon oath to certain interrogatories ministered unto him, (and which were read to him before he took his oath,) and the treasurer pressing him again with the same interrogatory, the governour said, he had answered the same directly before. The treasurer thereupon said, (angerly,) Sir, I speak not to you. The governour replied, that time was very precious, and, seeing the thing was already answered, it was fit to proceed. Thereupon the treasurer stood up, and said, if he might not have liberty to speak, he would no longer

||fare|| ||[2]a||

[1] Much more of the terms, on which these settlements were taken under our jurisdiction, will appear two or three years later.

[2] The marginal note is, "Difference between the governour and Mr. Bellingham."

[3] He was of Charlestown.

[4] Of the services of William Hibbins much will appear in the progress of this work. He was a deputy from Boston in the autumn of the following year, though admitted only in May a freeman, and again in 1641 and 1643. In this latter he was chosen an assistant. Hutchinson, I. 173, gives as much of his character as can well be ascertained beyond the means furnished by Winthrop He died 23 July, 1654.

sit there. The governour replied, that it was his place to manage the proceedings of the court, etc. The treasurer then said, You have no more to do in managing the business here than I. At which the governour took offence, as at an injury done to his place, and appealed to the court to declare, whether he might not enjoin any of the magistrates silence, if he saw cause. The deputy governour, at first apprehension, gainsaid it; but, presently, both himself and the rest of the magistrates (for the deputies were without, staying till this cause should be ended) did agree, that he might so do for a particular time; and if the party, so enjoined silence, were unsatisfied, he might appeal to the whole court, who might give him liberty to speak, though the governour had restrained him. So the governour pressed it no further, yet expected that the court would not have suffered such a public affront to the governour to have passed without due reproof, etc. But nothing was done, save only the secretary and some one other spake somewhat of their
*321 dislike of it; neither did it occasion any falling out between the governour and treasurer, for the governour held himself sufficiently discharged, after he had referred it to the consideration of the court, so as, if they did not look at it as a public injury, he was willing to account of it accordingly.[1]

---

[1] A strange and lamentable consequence of this controversy, in which Hibbins was cast, may be seen in Hubbard, 574. Some have said, he remarks, that the loss "so discomposed his wife's spirit, that she scarce ever was well settled in her mind afterward, but grew very turbulent in her passion, and discontented, on which occasions she was cast out of the church, and then charged to be a witch, giving too much occasion, by her strange carriage, to common people so to judge." The unhappy woman might, perhaps, have been early cured by a ducking stool. A long controversy, in 1640, before the church, about some scolding, which terminated in a public admonition and subsequent excommunication, is recorded in Keayne's MS. before mentioned; but to me it is not, and to others would not probably appear, a very attractive subject. Hutchinson, I. 173, informs us, that, though the magistrates refused to accept the verdict, yet it was the general court that condemned her for witchcraft; and the common people afterwards, with their accustomed manner, implied the judgments of God in the disasters of those who had given way, so unjustly, to the opinions of the same people. For the facts in support of his remark, he is indebted to Hubbard, ut supra. She suffered the punishment of death for the ridiculous crime, the year after her husband's decease; her brother, Bellingham, not exerting,

There happened a memorable thing at Plimouth about this time. One Keysar, of Lynn, being at Plimouth in his boat, and one Dickerson with him, a professor, but a notorious thief, was coming out of the harbor with the ebb, and the wind southerly, a fresh gale; yet, with all their skill and labor, they could not, in three hours, get the boat above one league, so as they were forced to come to an anchor, and, at the flood, to go back to the town; and, as soon as they were come in, the said Dickerson was arrested upon suspicion of a gold ring and some other pieces of gold, which, upon search, were found about him, and he was there whipped for it.[1]

The like happened at Boston about two years before. Schooler, who was executed for murder, as before is mentioned, had broke prison and was escaped beyond Winisemett, but there he was taken with such an astonishment, etc., as he could go no further, but was forced to return to Boston. These and many other examples of discovering hypocrites and *322
other lewd persons, and bringing them under their deserved punishments, do (among other things) show the presence and power of God in his ordinances, and his blessing upon his people, while they endeavor to walk before him with uprightness.

At Kennebeck, the Indians wanting food, and there being store in the Plimouth trading house, they conspired to kill the English there for their provisions; and some Indians coming

---

perhaps, his highest influence for her preservation. Her will, made in prison, immediately follows, in the Records, that of Keayne, who could not have been pleased with her. She had three sons by a former husband. Of her will, in which she desired decent burial, near her late husband, abstract is given in Genealog. Reg. VI. 287, 8. Six or seven of the most respectable gentlemen of Boston were named by her overseers of it. Rev. John Norton said, she was hanged for having more wit than her neighbors.

[1] It is in vain to regret, that such paragraphs are preserved in this History. The spirit of the age had prepared the people for such false impressions, and, in the perpetual glooms of the wilderness, their imagination gradually stole away the supremacy from judgment. The subsequent paragraph, remarking the *likeness* of the event there related, which is natural enough, would induce us to refer the astonishment, by which the escape of the criminal was prevented, to the *boat*, rather than the offender.

into the house, Mr. Willet,[1] the master of the house, being reading in the Bible, his countenance was more solemn than at other times, so as he did not look cheerfully upon them, as he was wont to do; whereupon they went out and told their fellows, that their purpose was discovered. They asked them, how it could be. The others told them, that they knew it by Mr. Willet's countenance, and that he had discovered it by a book that he was reading. Whereupon they gave over their design.

The people had long desired a body of laws, and thought their condition very unsafe, while so much power rested in the discretion of magistrates. Divers attempts had been made at former courts, and the matter referred to some of the magistrates and some of the elders; but still it came to no effect; for, being committed to the care of many, whatsoever was done by some, was still disliked or neglected by others. At last it was referred to Mr. Cotton and Mr. Nathaniel Warde,[2] etc., and each of them framed a model, which were presented to this general court, and by them committed to the governour and deputy and some others to consider of, and so prepare it for the court in the 3d month next. Two great reasons there were,

---

[1] From New England's Memorial we learn, that Capt. Thomas Willet was highly esteemed in Plimouth colony, being, in 1651, elected an assistant; and, by the choice for thirteen successive years to the same office, in that most strictly republican jurisdiction, we may be confident of his well deserving the affections of the people. It is unnecessary for me to add more than a reference to Judge Davis's edition of that work, in which his services with the Dutch, and settlement afterwards at New York, are particularly related. Descendants are, I believe, known in honorable stations.

[2] In December, 1641, the labors of these legislators were perfected, as this History will show. The result was printed in London immediately after. An Abstract may be found by the curious in 1 Hist. Coll. V. 171–192, with an account of a second edition by Aspinwall. We may be sure, that Winthrop could not be mistaken in ascribing to Ward the principal honor of the work, though Cotton has often enjoyed it. Perhaps any one of twenty, in the civil or clerical line, had contributed as much as Cotton, though his name would carry the greatest weight.

From a thorough examination of the whole subject, by Hon. F. C. Gray, introductory to a reprint of the code, in 3 Hist. Coll. VIII. 191, it appears, that the abstract was Cotton's; but the Laws and Liberties, a far more important work, was prepared by Ward.

which caused most of the magistrates and some of the elders not to be very forward in this matter. One was, want of sufficient experience of the nature and disposition of the people, considered with the condition of the country and other circumstances, which made them conceive, that such laws would be fittest for us, which should arise pro ||re nata|| upon occasions, etc., and so the laws of England and other states grew, and therefore the fundamental laws of England are called ||[2]customs, consuetudines.|| 2. For that it would professedly transgress the limits of our charter, which provide, we shall made no laws repugnant to the laws of England, and that we were assured we must do. But to raise up laws by practice and custom had been no transgression; as in our church discipline, and in matters of marriage, to make a law, that marriages should not be solemnized by ministers, is repugnant to the laws of England; but to bring it to a custom by practice for the magistrates to perform it, is no law made repugnant, etc. At length (to satisfy the people) it proceeded, and the two models were digested with divers alterations and additions, and abbreviated and sent to every town, (12,) to be considered of first by the magistrates and elders, and then to be published by the constables to all the people, that if any man should think fit, that any thing therein ought to be altered, he might acquaint some of the deputies therewith against the next court. *323

[Large blank.]

By this time there appeared a great change in the church of Boston; for whereas, the year before, they were all (save five or six) so affected to Mr. Wheelwright and Mrs. Hutchinson, and those new opinions, as they ||[3]slighted|| the present governour and the pastor, looking at them as men under a covenant of works, and as their greatest enemies; but they bearing all patiently, and not withdrawing themselves, (as they were strongly solicited to have done,) but carrying themselves lovingly and helpfully upon all occasions, the Lord brought about the hearts of all the people to love and esteem them more than ever before, and all ||[4]breaches|| were made up, and the church was saved from ruin beyond all expectation; which could

||rei natura|| ||[2]custos consuetusdinis|| ||[3]perceived|| ||[4]breeches||

hardly have been, (in human reason,) if those two had not been guided by the Lord to that moderation, etc. And the church (to manifest their hearty affection to the governour, upon occasion of some strait he was brought into through his bailiff's unfaithfulness) sent him £200.

There was now a church gathered at the Mount, and Mr.
*324 Tomson (a very holy man, who had been an instrument of much good at Acomenticus) was ordained the pastor the 19th of the 9th month.

(10.)] At the general court, an order was made to abolish that vain custom of drinking one to another, and that upon these and other grounds:

1. It was a thing of no good use.

2. It was an inducement to drunkenness, and occasion of quarrelling and bloodshed.

3. It occasioned much waste of wine and beer.

4. It was very troublesome to many, especially the masters and mistresses of the feast, who were forced thereby to drink more oft than they would, etc. Yet divers (even godly persons) were very loath to part with this idle ceremony, though (when disputation was tendered) they had no ||list,|| nor, indeed, could find any arguments, to maintain it. Such power hath custom, etc.

Mr. Ezekiel Rogers, of whose gathering of a church in England mention was made before, being now settled with his company at ||[2] Rowley,|| was there ordained pastor, etc.

3.] There were so many lectures now in the country, and many poor persons would usually resort to two or three in the week, to the great neglect of their affairs, and the damage of the public. The assemblies also were (in divers churches) held till night, and sometimes within the night, so as such as dwelt far off could not get home in due season, and many weak bodies could not endure so long, in the extremity of the heat or cold, without great trouble, and hazard of their health. Whereupon the general court ordered, that the elders should be desired to give a meeting to the magistrates and deputies, to consider about the length and frequency of church assemblies, and to make return to the court of their determinations, etc. This was

||life|| ||[2] Roxbury||

taken in ill part by most of the elders and other of the churches, so as that those who should have met at Salem, did not meet, and those in the bay, when they met with the magistrates, etc., at Boston, expressed much dislike of such a course, alleging their tenderness of the church's liberties, (as if such a precedent might enthrall them to the civil power, and as if it would cast a blemish upon the elders, which would remain to posterity, that they should need to be regulated by the civil magistrate, and also raise an ill savour of the people's coldness, that would complain of much preaching, etc., — when as liberty for the ordinances was the main end (||professed||) of our coming hither). To which it was answered, 1. That the order *325
was framed with as much tenderness and respect as might be in general words, without mentioning sermons or lectures, so as it might as well be taken for meetings upon other occasions of the churches, which were known to be very frequent. 2. It carried no command, but only an expression of a desire. 3. ||[2]It|| concluded nothing, but only to confer and consider. 4. The record of such an order will be rather an argument of the zeal and forwardness of the elders and churches, as it was of the Israelites', when they offered so liberally to the service of the tabernacle, as Moses was forced to restrain them.[1] Upon this interpretation of the court's intent, the elders were reasonably satisfied, and the magistrates finding how hardly such propositions would be digested, and that, if matters should be further pushed, it might make some breach, or disturbance at least, (for the elders had great power in the people's hearts, which was needful to be upheld, lest the people should break their bonds through abuse of liberty, which divers, having ||[3]surfeited

||proposed|| ||[2]I|| ||[3]forfeited||

---

[1] "Much more than enough for the service of the work which the Lord commanded," Exodus xxxvi. 5, was the occasion of the order by Moses to restrain the free offerings. Yet it seems, from the history, they were brought only in the *morning*. In the ten preceding chapters, the contribution exacted, under that remarkable economy of the house of Israel, appears sufficiently burdensome. Pious services were, however, by our ancestors, given, in many instances, with greater liberality than by the chosen people; but the reference to their theocracy, in the text, will be thought, I presume, the most valuable and ingenious of all those that occur in our early history.

of,|| were very forward to incite others to raise mutinies and foment dangerous and groundless jealousies of the magistrates, etc., which the wisdom and care of the elders did still prevail against; and indeed the people themselves, generally, through the churches, were of that understanding and moderation, as they would easily be guided in their way by any rule from scripture or sound reason:) in this consideration, the magistrates and deputies, which were then met, thought it not fit to enter any dispute or conference with the elders about the number of lectures, or for appointing any certain time for the continuance of the assemblies, but rested satisfied with their affirmative answer to these two propositions: 1. That their church assemblies might ordinarily break up in such season, as people that dwell a mile or two off might get home by daylight. 2. That, if they were not satisfied in the declaration of our intentions in this order of court, that nothing was attempted herein against the church's liberties, etc., they would truly acquaint us with the reasons of their unsatisfiedness; or, if we heard not
*326 from them before the next court, we should take it for granted, that they were fully satisfied. They desired, that the order might be taken off the record; but for that it was answered, that it might not be done without consent of the general court; only it was agreed unto, that the secretary might defer to enter it in the book till the mind of the court might be known.

(12.) 20.] One Mr. Hanserd Knolles, a minister in England, who came over the last summer in the company of our familistical opinionists, and so being suspected and examined, and found inclining that way, was denied residence in the Massachusetts; whereupon he went to Pascataquack, where he began to preach; but Mr. Burdett, being then their governour and preacher, inhibited him. But, he being after removed to Acomenticus, the people called Mr. Knolles, and in short time he gathered some of the best minded into a church body, and became their pastor, and Capt. Underhill being their governour, they called ||their|| town Dover. But this Mr. Knolles, at his first coming thither, wrote a letter to his friends in London, wherein he bitterly inveighed against us, both against our

||this||

magistrates and churches, and against all the people in general, (as by the copy of his letter sent over to our governour may appear). The governour gave him notice thereof, and, being brought to a better judgment by further consideration and more experience, he saw the wrong he had done us, and was deeply humbled for it, and wrote to the governour to that effect, and desired a safe conduct, that he might come into the bay to give satisfaction, etc., for he could have no rest in his spirit until, etc.; which being sent him under the governour his hand, (with consent of the council,) §he came,§ and, upon a lecture day at Boston, (most of the magistrates and elders in the bay being there assembled,) he made a very free and full confession of his offence, with much aggravation against himself, so as the assembly were well satisfied. He wrote also a letter to the same effect to his said friends in England, which he left with the governour to be sent to them.

Capt. Underhill, also, being struck with horror and remorse for his offences, both against the church and civil state, could have no rest till he had obtained a safe conduct to come and give satisfaction; and accordingly, (1,) 5, at a lecture at Boston, (it being then the court time,) he made a public confession both of his living in adultery with Faber's wife, (upon suspicion whereof the church had before admonished him,) and attempting the like with another woman,[1] and also the injury he had done to our state, etc., and acknowledged the justice of the court in their proceeding against him, etc. Yet all his *327
confessions were mixed with such excuses and extenuations, as did not give satisfaction of the truth of his repentance, so as it seemed to be done rather out of policy, and to pacify the sting of his conscience, than in sincerity. But, however, his offences being so foul and scandalous, the church presently cast him out; which censure he seemed to submit unto, and, for the time he staid in Boston, (being four or five days) he was very much dejected, etc.; but, being gone back, he soon recovered his spirits again, or, at least, gave not that proof of a broken heart, as he gave hope of at Boston. For (to ingratiate himself with the state of England, and with some gentlemen

---

[1] Jane, wife of Robert Holmes, of Cambridge, says our church record.

at the river's mouth, who were very zealous that way, and had lately set up common prayer, etc.) he sent thirteen men armed to Exeter to fetch one Gabriel Fish, who was detained in the officer's hands for speaking against the king, the magistrates of Exeter being then in the bay to take advice what to do with him; and besides, when the church and people of Dover desired him to forbear to come to the next court, till they had considered of his case, and he had promised so to do, yet, hearing that they were consulting to remove him from his government, he could not refrain, but came and took his place in the court; and though he had offered to lay down his place, yet, when he saw they went about it, he grew passionate, and expostulated with them, and would not stay to receive his dismission, nor would be seen to accept it, when it was sent after him. Yet they proceeded, and chose one Roberts[1] to be president of the court, and, soon after, they returned back Fish to Exeter, which was considerately done §of them,§ for it had been a dangerous precedent against them, being a weak plantation, if the commissioners from the lords of the council, who were daily expected, should have taken occasion to have done the like by them, though they held themselves to be out of that province, which was granted to Sir Ferdinando Gorges. Besides this, in the open court he committed one of his fellow magistrates for rising up and saying he would not sit with an adulterer, etc. But the chief matter, ||which they produced|| against him, was, that, whereas he himself was the mover of them to break off their agreement with us, he had written to
*328 our governour, and laid it upon the people, especially upon some among them; and for this they produced against him a letter from our governour, written to one of their commissioners in answer to a letter of his, wherein he had discovered the captain's proceeding in that matter. Soon after this the captain came by water into the bay to tender (as he said) satis-

||for which they proceeded||

---

[1] Of this gentleman nothing is known to me, unless he be the John Roberts appointed marshal, in 1680, under the new administration by royal commission in that year, Belknap's N. H. Farmer's Ed., 91, and who next year resigned, or Thomas Roberts, one of the principal landholders of Dover. Ib. 122.

faction to the church. This was taken by some of the magistrates as a very presumptuous act, and they would have had him imprisoned, supposing that his safe conduct would not bear him out, having been once here and returned back again; but that ||counsel|| was not approved, because the time of his safe conduct was not expired, and it was thought very dangerous to our reputation to give the least occasion of reproach in this kind, seeing it might be objected against us to our great prejudice, ||[2]where|| we should not have opportunity to clear our innocency. But the church, not being satisfied of his repentance, would not admit him to public speech. So, after one week, he returned home.

In this winter, in a close, calm day, there fell divers flakes of snow of this form *, very thin, and as exactly pointed as art could have cut them in paper, or, etc.

(1.) 24.] The church of Boston sent three brethren, viz., Capt. Edward Gibbons, Mr. Hibbins, and Mr. Oliver[1] the

||council|| ||[2]when||

---

[1] John, son of the ruling elder, is, probably, the gentleman intended. Notice of his death will appear in our second volume, sub an. 1646. In Keayne's MS. it appears, that, in our church, early in 1640, "a motion was made by such as have farms at Rumney Marsh, that our brother Oliver may be sent to instruct their servants, and to be a help to them, because they cannot many times come hither, nor sometimes to Lynn, and sometimes nowhere at all." On this much debate followed. His father spoke first: "I desire what calling my son hath to such a work, or by what rule of God's word may the church send out any ot her members to such as are not of the church." Cotton answered, at some length. Two of the lay brethren proposed objections, to which Wilson briefly replied, and the subject was postponed. On 23 March, Wilson made a full statement of the general consent of the church, and the candidate closed thus: "Serjeant Oliver. I desire to speak a word or two to the business of Rumney Marsh. I am apt to be discouraged in any good work, and I am glad, that there is a universal consent in the hearts of the church; for if there should have been variety in their thoughts, or compulsion of their minds, it would have been a great discouragement. But, seeing a call of God, I hope I shall employ my weak talent to God's service; and, considering my own youth and feebleness to so great a work, I shall desire my loving brethren to look at me as their brother, to send me out with their constant prayers." From his will, I find, he married a daughter of John Newgate, and left three children, two sons, and a daughter, who afterwards married a gentleman of the name of Wiswell. Rumney Marsh is now Chelsea. It is a little strange, that a people settled on a spot so difficult

*329 younger, with letters to Mr. Coddington and the rest of our members at Aquiday, to understand their judgments in divers points of religion, formerly maintained by all, or divers of them, and to require them to give account to the church of their unwarrantable practice ||in|| communicating with excommunicated persons, etc. When they came, they found that those of them, who dwell at Newport, had joined themselves to a church there newly constituted, and thereupon they refused to hear them as messengers of our church, or to receive the church's letters.[1] Whereupon, at their return, the elders and most of the church would have cast them out, as refusing to hear the church; but, all being not agreed, it was deferred.

||of||

---

to have religious instruction at the neighboring parishes, should have continued so long a time out of church state. The first sentence of the Records of the Chelsea parish is, October 19, 1715, "This day the church was gathered at Rumney Marsh, and Mr. Thomas Cheever was ordained their pastor." For this information I was indebted to the kindness of the late pastor, Dr. Joseph Tuckerman. Undoubtedly the population was small, as it continued until the last twenty years.

[1] By Keayne's MS. it appears, the place was called Portsmouth, a name since appropriated to another town, of much less magnitude, on the island. Coggeshall, for the refractory brethren, it seems, inquired of these spiritual commissioners, "what power one church hath over another church?" Oliver relates, that "they denied our commission, and refused to let our letter be received; and they conceive, one church hath not power over the members of another church, and do not think they are tied to us by our covenant. So we were fain to take all their answers by going to their several houses. Mr. Hutchinson told us, he was more nearly tied to his wife than to the church: he thought her to be a dear saint and servant of God. We came then to Mrs. Hutchinson, and told her, that we had a message to do to her from the Lord and from our church. She answered, There are lords many, and gods many; but I acknowledge but one Lord. Which lord do you mean? We answered, we came in the name but of one Lord, and that is God. Then, saith she, so far we agree; and where we do agree, let it be set down. Then we told her, we had a message to her from the church of Christ in Boston. She replied, she knew no church but one. We told her, in scripture the Holy Ghost calls them churches. She said, Christ had but one spouse. We told her, he had in some sort as many spouses as saints. But for our church, she would not acknowledge it any church of Christ." The report of this unprofitable mission was made 16 March.

18.] Mr. Norris[1] was ordained teacher of the church of Salem, there being present near all the elders of the other *330
churches, and much people besides.

21.] The White Angel, a small ship of Bristol, went from hence, and arrived there in twenty-four days; and, the same year, the Desire, a ship built at Marblehead, of one hundred tons, went from hence in the summer, and arrived at Gravesend, in the Thames, in twenty-three days.

Our neighbors of Plimouth had procured from hence, this year, one Mr. Chancey,[2] a great scholar, and a godly man,

---

[1] Edward Norris is commemorated with due honors in Eliot's Biographical Dictionary. Our regret, that so important a name eluded the search of Allen, though a descendant of our age is well remembered for his pious liberality, will not be vain, if the second edition of that gentleman's volume, which has been long preparing, supply the deficiency, and go beyond his predecessor. Norris arrived in our country, probably, the year before his ordination, which was the period that the church had to form their estimate of his merit. He was not admitted a freeman till May, 1640. He had been a minister in England, yet Johnson has not named him. Much influence in the state was exerted by him, of which evidence will appear in this History; and, four years after Winthrop's death, in the famous schism of the commissioners of the four United Colonies, he took side against the principles of the Massachusetts court, who resisted the war with the Dutch. War had been raging two years between the respective mother countries; yet our people were wise enough to keep at peace on this side of the Atlantic. Those who hoped to gain by a war were very eager for its declaration, and charged the pacific temper of Massachusetts to any thing but its true cause. Norris was, happily, unsuccessful, though he quoted the curse against Meroz, which religious or political enthusiasm has commonly found effectual. See his letter of 3 May, 1653, in Hazard, II. 256. The president of the council, the amiable Bradstreet, was averse to war; but Norris's parishioner, Hawthorne, the other commissioner of Massachusetts, was urgent for it. Before the gradual influence of the false reports from New Haven and Connecticut had overcome the disinclination of Massachusetts to the unjust war, news was received that in the third year hostilities were closed in Europe.

[2] An excuse for neglecting great labor of inquiry about this celebrated scholar, who, after the honor conferred on him of two professorships by his alma mater, the University of Cambridge in England, became head of our own College, is afforded by the elaborate biography, written by a descendant of great name, preserved in 1 Hist. Coll. X. 171. Perhaps, however, the ancestor's doctrines are a little softened in that tract. He was of Trinity College. Mather mentions his verses on the death of Queen Ann, 1619. I have seen, in the Boston Athenæum, the Cantabrigiensium Dolor et Solamen, on the death of

intending to call him to the office of a teacher; but, before the fit time came, he discovered his judgment about baptism, that the children ought to be dipped and not sprinkled; and, he being an active man, and very vehement, there arose much trouble about it. The magistrates and the other elders there, and the most of the people, withstood the receiving of that practice, not for itself so much, as for fear of worse consequences, as the annihilating our baptism, etc. Whereupon the church there wrote to all the other churches, both here and at Connecticut, etc., for advice, and sent Mr. Chancey's arguments. The churches took them into consideration, and ||returned|| their several answers, wherein they showed their dissent from him, and clearly confuted all his arguments, discovering withal some great mistakes of his about the judgment
*331 and practice of antiquity.[1] Yet he would not give over his opinion; and the church of Plimouth, (though they could not agree to call him to office, yet,) being much taken with his able parts, they were very loath to part with him. He

||wrote||

James and accession of Charles, 1625, containing his Greek and Latin verses, signed Car. Chauncy, Coll. Trin. Bac. Theol. His two unimportant opinions, relative to the time of celebrating the eucharist, and the mode of baptism, were no obstacles to his advancement, even in that age of narrow and scrupulous formality. It is a little remarkable, that the two first presidents of Harvard College adopted opinions on the form of baptism adverse to that of all the other divines and laicks of the colony.

[1] If nothing of greater value, than these answers of the churches, were lost by us, we should less regret the extent of our ignorance of the thoughts and actions of our fathers. From Keayne's MS. it appears, that answer by Boston church was made, 21 June, to a question and desire from the church of Plimouth, "whether it be lawful to use sprinkling in baptism, or rather dipping; Mr. Chauncy being of the mind, that it is a violation of an ordinance to use sprinkling instead of dipping." In the illustrious descendant's Life of his ancestor, there may be some mistake on this point. Yet an equal error is, perhaps, discernible in the text, as to the confutation, and finding mistakes about "the judgment and practice of antiquity." Fortunately, it is a matter, on which little depends; and the churches here would do wisely to allow, as a large part of the antipædobaptists in England are liberal enough to do, that the substance of Christianity is of infinitely higher importance than this form of expressing our devotion to it, and that a controversy, which cannot be settled, had better be dropped.

did maintain, also, that the Lord's supper ought to be administered in the evening, and every Lord's day; and the church at Sandwich (where one Mr. Leveridge was minister) fell into the practice of it; but that being a matter of no great ill consequence, save some outward inconvenience, there was little stir about it. This Mr. Chancey was after called to office in the church of Scituate.

One Palmer,[1] of Hingham, and two others, (being ancient and skilful seamen,) being in a shallop of ‖ten‖ tons, in an easterly wind, by Peddock's Island, were overset; yet one of them had the sheet in his hand, and let fly; but it was too late, having but little ballast in her; yet it pleased God, there came by, soon after, a pinnace, which espied them sitting upon her ‖[2]side,‖ yet deep in the water, and took them up, but the shallop was not heard of after.

Many men began to inquire after the southern parts; and the great advantages supposed to be had in Virginia and the West Indies, etc., made this country to be disesteemed of many; and yet those countries (for all their great wealth) have sent hither, both this year and formerly, for supply of clothes and other necessaries; and some families have forsaken both Providence and other the Caribbee Islands and Virginia to come live here. And though our people saw what meagre, unhealthful countenances they brought hither, and how fat and well liking they became soon, yet they were so taken with the ease *332 and plenty of those countries, as many of them sold their estates here to transport themselves to Providence; among whom the chief was John Humfrey, Esq., a gentleman of special parts of learning and activity, and a godly man, who had been one of the first beginners in the promoting of this plantation, and had labored very much therein. He, being brought low in his estate, and having many children, and being well known to the lords of Providence, and offering himself to their service, was accepted to be the next governour. Whereupon he

‖100‖ ‖[2]shrouds‖

[1] Hingham Records show, that John Palmer came over in September, 1635, and those of the colony, that he was made free 13 March, 1638-9. Nothing more of him is known by me.

labored much to draw men to join with him. This was looked ‖at, both‖ by the general court, and also by the elders, as an unwarrantable course; for though it was thought very needful to further plantation of churches in the West Indies, and all were willing to endeavor the same; yet to do it with disparagement of this country, (for they gave out that they could not subsist here,) caused us to fear, that the Lord was not with them in this way. And, withal, some considerations were propounded to them by the court, which diverted some of them, and made others to pause, upon three points especially: 1. How dangerous it was to bring up an ill report upon this good land, which God had found out and given to his people, and so to discourage the hearts of their brethren, etc. 2. To leave a place of rest and safety, to expose themselves, their wives and children, to the danger of a potent enemy, the Spaniard. 3. Their subjection to such governours as those in England shall set over them, etc. Notwithstanding these considerations, divers of them persisted in their resolutions, and went about to get some ship or bark to transport them; but they were still crossed by the hand of God.[1]

Mo. 3. 17.] Joseph Grafton[2] set sail from Salem, the 2d day in the morning, in a ‖[2]ketch‖ of about forty tons, (three men and a boy in her,) and arrived at Pemaquid (the wind easterly) upon the third day in the morning, and there took in some

‖upon‖ ‖[2] Cavye‖

[1] "That the Lord was not with them," in their design to draw off people from Massachusetts to the West Indies for a permanent plantation, we may as confidently believe, as did Winthrop and the majority who remained; yet it is desirable to disavow the notion, that their difficulties in the attempt prove, that they "were still crossed by his hand."

[2] He had been made free at the general election in May, 1637. The relation in the text proves the prosperity of the plantation at Pemaquid, no less than the activity of Grafton. In the next volume it will be seen, that his vessel, carrying provisions to La Tour, was taken by D'Aulney, and the crew were very ill treated. His son, Joseph, died at Barbados, February, 1671, leaving two children, of whom his father was made guardian, in Sept. following, until "they come to age to choose a guardian to themselves." Descendants are known, among whom is one of the same name in this city.

twenty cows, oxen, etc., with hay and water for them, and *333
came to an anchor in the bay the 6th[1] day, about three after noon.

It came over by divers letters and reports, that the Lord Say did labor, by disparaging this country, to divert men from coming to us, and so to draw them to the West Indies; and, finding that godly men were unwilling to come under other governours than such as they should make choice of themselves, etc., they condescended to articles somewhat suitable to our form of government, although they had formerly declared themselves much against it, and for a ||meer aristocratie,|| and an hereditary magistracy to be settled upon some great persons, etc.

The governour also wrote to the Lord Say about the report aforesaid, and therein showed his lordship, how evident it was, that God had chosen this country to plant his people in, and therefore how displeasing it would be to the Lord, and dangerous to himself, to hinder this work, or to discourage men from supplying us, by abasing the goodness of the country, which he never saw, and persuading men, that here was no possibility of subsistence; whereas there was a sure ground for his children's faith, that, being sent hither by him, either he saw that the land was a good land, and sufficient to maintain them, or else he intended to make it such, etc. To this letter his lordship returned answer, (not denying that which was reported of him, nor the evidence of the Lord's owning the work, but) alleging, that this was a place appointed only for a present refuge, etc., and that, a better place being now found out, we were all called to remove thither.

[Very large blank.]

||more aristocratic||

---

[1] Days of the week are meant, the sixth being Saturday, and his voyage began on Monday. The same scruple, which led to change of the months, caused the names of the days to be offensive, and induced the fathers to reckon the less, as well as greater divisions of time, by numerals. Adherence to this custom still distinguishes the Quakers. Still Winthrop felt no scruple about making this entry, on Sunday, of the quick despatch, of the vessel from Salem to Pemaquid, and return with cargo, within the secular days.

APPENDIX.

A 1.

Dear Son,

Though I have received no letters yet from you, I cannot pass by any opportunity, without some testimony of my fatherly affection, and care of your welfare, for which respect I am content to have you absent from me in so far a distance; for I know, that, in respect of yourself, patria ubicunque bene, and in respect of the Almighty, his power and providence is alike in all places; and for mine own comfort, it shall be in your prosperity and well-doing wheresoever.

Because I cannot so oft put you in mind of those things, which concern your good, as if you were nearer to me, it must be your care the better to observe and ruminate those instructions, which I give you, and the better to apply the other good means, which you have. Especially labor, by all means, to imprint in your heart the fear of God, and let not the fearful profaneness and contempt of ungodly men diminish the reverent and awful regard of his Great Majesty in your heart. But remember still, that the time is at hand, when they shall call the [mountains to] hide them from the face of Him, whom now they slight and neglect, etc.

I have written to you more largely by one Mr. Southwell, and now am at little leisure. When you write back, let me know the state of your college, etc., and how you like, etc., and remember my love to your reverend tutor. Your grandfather, grandmother, and mother, salute and bless you. Your brothers and sister are in health, (I praise God). The Lord, in mercy, season your heart with his grace, and keep you from the lusts of youth and the evil of the times. So I rest

Your loving father,

JOHN WINTHROP

Groton, August 6, 1622.

To my beloved Son, John Winthrop, *at the College in Dublin, d'd.*

A 2.

My beloved Son,

I beseech the Lord to bless thee with grace and peace. I give him thanks for thy welfare, and hope, through his mercy, that this infirmity, which is now upon thee, shall turn to thy health. I received two letters from thee, written (I perceive) in haste; but they were welcome to me and the rest, to your grandmother, mother, etc., who all rejoice in your good liking. I sent you two letters, a good while since, which I hope will not miscarry, though they be long in going. The further you are from me, the more careful I am of your welfare, both in body and soul; the chief means whereof lyeth in your own endeavor. Your friends may pray for you and counsel you, but your own diligence and watchfulness must be added to make you blessed. God hath provided you a liberal portion of outward good things. You must labor to use them soberly, and to consider, that your happiness lyeth not in meat, drink, and bodily refreshings, but in the favor of God for your part in a better life. I purposed to send you, by this bearer, such books as you writ for; only Aristotle I cannot, because your uncle Fones is not at London to buy it; and I know not whether you would have Latin or Greek. I purpose also to send you some cloth for a gown and suit; but for a study gown, you were best buy some coarse Irish cloth. I shall (if God will) write to you again by Mr. Olmsted. For the carriage of such things as I send you by John Hutton, you must remember to pay him, because I cannot tell here what they will come to. I have written to your uncle to send over my gelding. If you see that he forget it, you may put him in mind. Your grandfather and grandmother will write to you. Your mother salutes you with her blessings. We are all in health, (I praise God). Remember my love to your good tutor. The Lord in mercy bless and keep you, and direct and prosper your study. Amen. So I rest

Your loving father,

JOHN WINTHROP.

Groton, August 31, 1622.

To my beloved Son, John Winthrop, *at the College near Dublin.*

A 3.

My dearly beloved Son,

I do usually begin and end my letters with that, which I would have the A and Ω of all thy thoughts and endeavors, viz., the blessing of the Almighty to be upon thee, not after the common valuation of God's blessings, like the warming of the sun to a hale, stirring body; but that blessing, which faith finds in the sweet promises of God and his free favor, whereby the soul hath a place of joy and refuge in all storms of adversity. I beseech the Lord to open thine eyes, that thou mayest see the riches of this grace, which will abate the account of all earthly vanities: and if it please him to give thee once a taste of the sweetness of the true wisdom, which is from above, it will season thy studies, and give a new temper to thy soul. Remember, therefore, what the wisest saith, The fear of the Lord is the beginning of wisdom. Lay this foundation, and thou shalt be wise indeed.

I am very glad to hear, that you like so well in Ireland. If your profiting in learning may be answerable, it will much increase my comfort. I was not greatly troubled to hear that your body did break out, but rather occasioned to bless God, that sent you so good a means of future health. I must needs acknowledge the great care and kindness of your uncle and aunt towards you. It may be much to your good, if you be careful to make right use of it, as I hope you do; for I hear you love your study well. You must have special care, that you be not ensnared with the lusts of youth, which are commonly covered under the name of recreations, etc. I remember the counsel of a wise man, Quidquid ad voluptatis seminarium pullulat, venenum puta. Think of it, (dear son,) and especially that of Paul to Timothy, Exhort young men that they be sober minded.

I sent you some books by J. Hutton. I could not then buy the rest, nor such cloth, etc., which I would have sent you, because your uncle Fones was not then in London; and I have no friend else, that I can make bold with. I have now a piece of cloth to make your doublet and hose, if I can send it by Mr. Olmested; if not, then desire your uncle to fit you there; it is only some little more in the price; and I have found, that, except one send by some friend, the carriage and custom (besides the hazard) costs so much, as there will be little saved. You may line your gown with some warm baize, and wear it out, for else you will soon outgrow it; and if you be not already in a frieze jerkin, I wish you to get one speedily; and howsoever you clothe yourself when you stir, yet be sure to keep warm when you study or sleep. I send you no money, because you may have of your uncle what you need. I hope you will be honestly frugal, and have respect to my great charge and small means, which I shall willingly extend to the utmost to do you good. Your grandfather, grandmother, and mother salute and bless you. We all, with your brothers and sister, are in health, (I praise God). Forth is at Bury; but he fell so between two forms, as he had like, between both, to have fallen back to Boxford.

Your uncle Gostlin[1] and aunt are in health, and he means to write to you. Your good host and hostess at Bury inquire much of you, and desire always to be remembered to you; so did your master there, when I last saw him.

I purpose to write two or three lines to your good tutor, in token of my thankful acceptance of his loving pains with you.

We are daily in expectation of Mr. Olmested's coming by us, who appointed to have set forth on his journey above a fortnight since; otherwise I had adventured some letters by London before this, though we received none from you since John Hutton came to us. I hear not yet of my gelding. It will be fit, that, at the quarter's end, (if your uncle forget it,) you ask him money for your tutor. The Lord bless you ever. So I rest

Your loving father,
JOHN WINTHROP.

October 16, 1622.

Commend me to Mr. Downes the stationer.

To my beloved Son, JOHN WINTHROP, *at Trinity College in Dublin, Ireland, d'd.*

A 4.

MY SWEET WIFE,

Blessed be God, by whose providence and protection I am come safe to London. Here I find them all in health, and a great deal of kind welcome; only thy company is wanting, which they much desire.

I doubt my brother's coming to Ipswich will be deferred till the spring; for Mr. Hore (who should hire his house) and he are broken off. Thus man purposeth, but God disposeth. O, that we could learn, at length, to trust his wisdom, love, power, etc., and cast our care upon him, and leave our own carnal wisdom, fear, confidence, etc. Then should it go well with us assuredly; then should we have our rest in that true peace, which passeth understanding. But it is our wretched infidelity that keeps good things from us. Let us, therefore, pray earnestly, and labor for this precious faith; it will recompense all our cost.

For such news as is here, this bearer can sufficiently inform you, and so may spare my labor; and, besides, I am hasted into the city about my business. When I shall return, I cannot yet tell, but thy love will

---

[1] Thomas Gostlin married 5 January, 1612, Jane, sister of the author, who was baptized at Groton, 17 June, 1592.

make me lose no time. Therefore, for the present, with my brother's and sister's kind salutations to thee and to my parents, to whom I commend my love and duty, I heartily commend thee and our little ones, and all our family, to the gracious protection and blessing of the Lord. So I rest

Thy faithful, loving husband,
JOHN WINTHROP.

London, October 19, 1622.

A 5.

MY DEAR SON,

I received your letters, with the bill of charges inclosed, etc. I bless God for the continuance of your health, but especially for the good seed of his true fear, which I trust is planted, and grows daily in you. I perceive you lose not your time, nor neglect your study, which, as it will be abundantly fruitful to my comfort, so much more to your own future and eternal happiness, and especially to the glory of him, who hath created you to this purpose. I pray continually, that God will please to establish your heart, and bless these good beginnings. For the money, which you have spent, I will pay it, and what else your uncle shall appoint me, so soon as I receive my rents. And for your expenses, seeing I perceive you are considerate of my estate, I will have as great regard of yours; and so long as your mind is limited to a sober course, I will not limit your allowance less than to the uttermost of mine own estate. So as, if £20 be too little, (as I always accounted it,) you shall have £30; and when that shall not suffice, you shall have more. Only hold a sober and frugal course, (yet without baseness,) and I will shorten myself to enlarge you. For your apparel, desire your uncle to furnish you for this present; and, if I can find out a means to send you things against winter at a more easy rate, I will provide for you, as I would have done before this, but that I thought (the charges of sending and hazard considered) you were as good provide them there. Your mother is lately delivered of another son,[1] (his name is Deane,) and is reasonable well, (I praise God,) with your grandmother, brothers, sister, uncle and aunt Gostlin, etc.; but your grandfather is very weak, and (we fear) in his last sickness.[2] They all salute you, and rejoice in your welfare. Goodman Hawes was here, and salutes

---

[1] Baptized two days before the date of this letter.

[2] He was buried three days after.

you also. Remember my love to your tutor, etc. The Lord bless you always. Amen.

Your loving father,
J. WINTHROP.

I wrote to you lately, and to your uncle and aunt; and, since, I wrote another letter to your aunt.

March 25, 1623.

To my beloved Son, JOHN WINTHROP, *at Trinity College, in Dublin, d'd, Ireland.* . . .Rec'd April 26.

A 6.

SON JOHN,

The blessing of the Lord be upon thee, and upon thy studies unto a most happy success. I received divers letters from thee since Christtide, and I have written three. I hope thou hast received them before this. I bless God, and am heartily refreshed to hear of thy health and good liking; especially to see those seeds of the fear of God, which (I hope and daily pray) will arise to timely fruit. He who hath begun that good in you, will perfect it unto the day of the Lord Jesus; only you must be constant and fervent in the use of the means, and yet trust only to God's blessing.

I was purposed to defer writing to you till your uncle Gostlin should have come; but his journey being put off on the sudden, I am enforced to borrow of the night to write these few lines unto thee. Concerning thy charges, I have written my mind in a former letter; but, lest that hath miscarried, know that my good persuasion of thy tender regard of my estate, and confidence of a sober course, shall make me to extend myself to the farthest of my ability for thy good, be it £30 per annum, or more, if occasion be. And though I have sent over no money all this time, it was not through my neglect of thee, but upon that assurance, which I had of thy uncle and aunt their care of thee, he himself willing me to send no money till he sent for it; and now, since Mr. Good is dead, I know not to whom to pay it. But make you no question, for (God willing) I will discharge every groat. And for your apparel and books, I find it so difficult and troublesome, etc., to send things over, as I would wish you to provide there for the present.

I have written to your uncle of the change, that it hath pleased the Lord to make in our family.[1] The Lord give us and you to make a

[1] This refers, probably, to the death of Gov. Winthrop's father.

right use of it. Time will not permit me to write more. Your grandmother and mother salute and bless you. Remember me very kindly to your good tutor and Mr. Downes, etc.

Your loving father,

J. WINTHROP.

April 20, 1623.

Send me word, in your next, how Mr. Olmsted and that plantation prospers. I wish oft God would open a way to settle me in Ireland, if it might be for his glory there.

Commend me to my little cousins, and to my god-daughter, Susannah Mitton, to Richard, and the rest of the family.

To my loving Son, JOHN WINTHROP, *at the College in Dublin, Ireland.*

A. 7.

MY WELL BELOVED SON,

I received thy letters of the 26 of May this 26 of June; and, the messenger being presently to return, I cannot satisfy myself in writing to thee as I desire. Let it suffice for the present, that I humbly praise our heavenly Father for his great mercy towards thee, in all respects; especially for the hope, which I conceive, that he hath pleased to make thee a vessel of glory for thy salvation in Christ Jesus. And I heartily rejoice, that he hath withdrawn thy mind from the love of those worldly vanities, wherewith the most part of youth are poisoned, and hath given thee to discern of, and exercise thyself in, things that are of true worth. I see by your epistle, that you have not spent this year past in idleness, but have profited even beyond my expectations. The Lord grant that thy soul may still prosper in the knowledge of Jesus Christ, and in the strength of the Spirit, as thy mind is strengthened in wisdom and learning; for this gives the true lustre and beauty to all gifts, both of nature and industry, and is as wisdom with an inheritance. I am sure, before this, you have knowledge of that, which, at the time when you wrote, you were ignorant of, viz. the departure of your grandfather;[1] (for I wrote over twice since). He hath finished his course, and is gathered to his people in peace, as the ripe corn into the barn. He thought long for the day of his dissolution, and welcomed it most gladly. Thus is he

---

[1] Adam, born 10 August, 1548.

gone before, and we must go after in our time. This advantage he hath of us, he shall not see the evil, which we may meet with ere we go hence. Happy those, who stand in good terms with God and their own conscience. They shall not fear evil tidings; and in all changes they shall be the same.

The rest of us (I praise God) are in health. Your grandmother and mother salute and bless you in the Lord. We all think long to see you; and, it is like, myself shall (if it please God) go over to you, before I shall be willing you should take so great a journey, and be so long withdrawn from your happy studies to come to us. It satisfieth me, that I know you are well, and can want nothing, and that (I believe) God blesses you. I shall continue to pray for you, and will not be wanting, to my power, to further your good in every thing; and know this, that no distance of place, or length of absence, can abate the affection of a loving father towards a dutiful, well-deserving child. And in that I have not sent you money all this time, it is upon that assurance, which I have of your uncle's and aunt's care of you, and his free offer to forbear me till he should send. But I have written to him to receive £30, or £40, of some of Dublin, who have occasion to use money in London, and they shall not fail to receive it again at my brother Fones his [house,] upon the first demand. For Cooper's Dictionary,[1] I will send it you as soon as I can; but it is so difficult and hazardable, (especially now, since Mr. Good died,) as I cannot tell how to convey that, or any thing else to thee. Remember my kind love to your good tutor. And so, in haste, I end; and, beseeching daily the Lord Jesus Christ to be with thee and bless thee, I rest

Your loving father,

JO. WINTHROP.

GROTON, *June* 26, 1623.

To my [torn off] JOHN WINTHROP, *at Trinity College, in Dublin, Ireland.* Rec'd Aug. the 1st.

A. 8.

MY DEAR SON,

The Lord bless thee, and multiply his graces in thee, to the building up of that good work, which (I well hope) is truly begun in thee, and wherein I rejoice daily, and bless God, who hath pleased to call thee

---

[1] This volume is now in the library of the Historical Society.

and keep thee in that good course, which yields hope to all the friends of thy future happiness. Be watchful, good son, and remember, that, though it be true, in some cases, that principium est dimidium totius, yet, in divinity, he who hath attained beyond the middest, must still think himself to have but new begun; for, through the continual instigation of Satan, and our own proneness to evil, we are always in danger of being turned out of our course; but God will preserve us to the end, if we trust in him, and be guided by his will.

I received no letters from you since that in Latin, wherein you wrote for Cooper's Dictionary, which I sent you since by London; and I have wrote twice since. I purpose to send by this bearer, Samuel Gostlin, a piece of Turkey grogram, about ten yards, to make you a suit; and I shall have a piece of good cloth against winter, to make you a gown; all my care is how to get it well conveyed. I would have sent you some other things, with some remembrancers to your aunt and cousins, but that the occasion of sending this messenger was so sudden as I could not provide them. If your uncle come over to Chester, you may come with him, and there I hope to see you. Be directed by him and your tutor; for, though I much desire to see you, yet I had rather hear of your welfare than hazard it. And if your uncle mean to come further than Chester, I would wish you not to come over now, for I am not willing you should come to Groton this year, except your uncle shall much desire your company. Remember my kind love to your good tutor, and to Mr. Downes, and excuse me to your aunt, that I write not to her, for I have not leisure; and, if occasion be, impart my joy in her safe deliverance, which we long much to hear of. What remains, this bearer can inform you of all our affairs. Put him in mind (as from me) to be sober, and beware of company. Your grandmother and mother salute and bless you; your uncle Gostlin and aunt salute you; your master at Bury,[1] (to whom I wish you to write at leisure,) your good host and hostess, salute you also. — Vale.

JOHN WINTHROP.

Groton, *August* 12, 1623.

You shall receive by Samuel a twenty-two shilling piece, if he have not occasion to spend it by the way.

[The superscription of this letter is wanting.]

---

[1] The grammar school at Bury St. Edmunds, where Forth was occupying the room of John, has preserved, I believe, a good reputation to our day.

A. 9.

MY WELL BELOVED SON,

I beseech our God and heavenly Father, through Christ, to bless thee; and I humbly praise his holy name for his great mercy towards thee hitherto, which is a great occasion of my rejoicing. For there is nothing in this world, that can be like cause of private comfort to me as to see the welfare of my children; especially when I may have hope, that they belong to Christ, and increase his kingdom, and that I shall meet them in glory, to enjoy them in life eternal, when this shade of life shall be vanished. Labor (my dear son) to have in highest esteem the favor of this God, whose blessing is better than life, and reacheth to eternity. Make him thy joy, by trusting in him with all thy heart; and nourish the peace of a pure conscience in an undefiled body. I am glad also to hear, that thou declinest the evil company and manners of the place thou livest in, and followest thy study with good fruit. Go on, and God will still prosper thee. To fall back will be far worse than never to have begun; but I hope better of thee. Your grandmother, mother, brothers, and sister are in health, (I praise God). How we do all here at London, this bearer can tell you. Your uncle (Fones) wishes well to you. I would have you write him a Latin epistle at your leisure. You must be careful to visit your aunt, and help her to be cheerful in this time of your uncle's absence. Commend me heartily to your reverend tutor; and think not of seeing England till you may bring a hood at your back.

It shall satisfy me, in the mean time, to hear of your welfare, which I daily pray for. And so I commend thee to the Lord, and rest

Your loving father,

JOHN WINTHROP.

LONDON, *October 3d*, 1623.

I send two books by Richard. One of them is for your aunt; the other for yourself. Read it over and again, and God give a blessing with it.

To my beloved Son, JOHN WINTHROP, *at Trinity College, in Dublin, Ireland, d'd.* . . . Rec'd Nov. 14, 1623.

A. 10.

[A fragment of a letter.]

I SENT you in January last the books, which you wrote for. Imagines Deorum is very dear and hard to get. I could not find a second in London. It is a book that may be of some use, for the praise and antiquity of the monuments, abused by the superstition of succeeding times; but you must read it with a sober mind and sanctified heart. Your grandmother and mother are in health, (I bless God,) and do salute and bless you. Your brothers and sister, and the rest of your friends, are likewise in health; only Adam hath a sore ague. Let me hear, by your next, how your aunt bears this long absence of your uncle, and how things agree in Ireland, at Mont Wealy, and elsewhere; and what success hath been of the proclamation. Our parliament here is begun with exceeding much comfort and hope. The treaty about the Spanish match is now concluded, by king, prince, and parliament, to be at an end; and, it is very like, we shall not hold long with Spain. The Duke of Richmond and Lenox died suddenly that morning the parliament should have begun. The Duke of Buckingham hath quit himself worthily, and given great satisfaction to the parliament. God send a good end to these happy beginnings. This bearer comes suddenly upon me, and is but a stranger. Therefore I end; and, with loving salutations to your reverend tutor, and your kind friend, his substitute, with Mr. Downes, your little cousins, Richard, etc., I rest

Your loving father,

JOHN WINTHROP.

GROTON, *March* 7, 1623.

To my loving Son, JOHN WINTHROP, *at Trinity College, in Dublin, Ireland, d'd.* . . . Rec'd March 29, 1624.

A. 11.

MY GOOD SON,

I received your letter, and do bless God for the continuance of your health, and of all our good friends at London; but I had no letters from any of them. For the matter which you write of, I can give you no advice; for I must deal plainly and faithfully with all men, and especially with my inward friends. So it is, that I have had lately some speech with my cousin Waldegrave, about matching you with his younger daughter, which I have referred to your own liking; but yet I cannot in honesty enter treaty for another till he hath some determinate answer. It is a religious and a worshipful family; but how the woman will like you, I know not, for she is somewhat crooked. I will neither persuade you to that, nor dissuade you from this or any other, which you shall desire, that may be fitting for my estate, and hopeful of comfort to you, which is not to be judged of only by wealth and person, but by meet parts and godly education. I trust you will mind well that saying, Deliberandum est diu, quod statuendum est semel.

I praise God, we continue all in health, as you left us, and, when you are weary of London, will be glad to see you and your sister at home; but take your own time before the holidays. Your grandmother and mother salute and bless you and your sister. Your mother thanks you for the things which you sent her. Remember us very kindly to your uncles and aunts, and to all our cousins and good friends. The good Lord guide, protect, and bless you in all your ways.

Your loving father,

JOHN WINTHROP.

November 21, 1626.

I pray buy me a pair of stirrup stocks, the warmest you can get; and when you go near the bridge, on Fish Street Hill dwells one, that sells lines and packthread, — buy some lines to raise up the long net, and some packthread to do it. A hair line were best for the leads.

To my loving Son, JOHN WINTHROP, *d'd.*

A. 12.

MY GOOD SON,

I wrote the last week so far as my paper would reach. I hope you received my letters, which I desire to understand from you, for Jarvice his man had them. I bless God for your health and welfare; but we now think long to have you at home, for your brother[1] is to return to Cambridge, and then we shall be alone; but if there be any good occasion to stay you still, I will not urge your hasty return. Touching the

---

[1] Forth, who had, in April before, been admitted of Emanuel, and matriculated 4 July, in the rank of pensioner. He was buried at Groton, 23 November, 1630, having been betrothed to Ursula Sherman.

matter of Mr. Pettuall, (though I can give no direct answer where nothing is propounded, yet) thus much in general, where I may have more money, I can depart with the more land. I pray God give you wisdom and grace to discern of meet gifts and disposition, that may promise hope of a comfortable life in the fear of God; otherwise (if you can so content your own mind) you were best live as you are. But I commit this, and all other our affairs, to the only wise providence of our heavenly Father.

We have had much ado for a minister, since Mr. Simonds refused it. Groton church did not afford such variety of gifts in divers years before. We have many suitors, that would take it at a mean rate; but for such as are worthy, all the difficulty is to get maintenance enough. We are now (by God's providence) like to fasten upon a godly man, one Mr. Lea,[1] a curate at Denston in Suffolk, a man of very good parts, but of a melancholic constitution, yet as sociable and full of good discourse as I have known. All the parish are very earnest with me to take him; but I have taken a little respite, because he is but a stranger to me, but well known to divers in the town.[2] He was Mr. Simond's pupil. I purpose to send up £10 for my A. B. if I can hear of any fit party; if not, you should receive some money of your uncle Downing for Mr. John Brande. Lay out £10 of that, and I will restore it, for I have the money by me. Be not known to any body of any money you receive for Mr. Brande; but fail not to write me word this week of the receipt of it. You may speak to your uncle about it, lest he should forget it. Mr. Rogers hath set forth a little book of faith. Buy it. I want a pair of plain, ordinary knives, and some leaf tobacco and pipes. You may buy these things at your leisure; as likewise some packthread and lines, hemp ones, if you will. Your grandmother

---

1 He was afterwards settled there. The name was William Leigh. I have had a letter of 13 May, 1628, from him at Groton "to the worshipful, his most loving patron, John Winthrop, Esq., at London," announcing the birth of a son, and his baptism, by the name of John, on Sunday preceding, at which Mrs. Winthrop, our governour's wife, stood godmother. He was son of Ralph, and married Eliz. Newton, daughter of a fellow of St. Johns, Cambridge, and a preacher at Bury St. Edmunds. Of another William Leigh, fellow of Christ's College, Cambridge, Calamy says, he was "a serious, single-hearted man, of good abilities, very laborious in the work of the ministry; one of the classis of Manchester. He was grievously afflicted with the stone, which at last cut him off in 1664, about fifty years of age. He wrote an English elegy on the death of Dr. Samuel Bolton, and one in Latin on the death of Mr. Bright of Emanuel."

2 The writer was patron of the living, which was in the diocese of Norwich, of which Harsnet was Bishop.

and mother salute and bless you. The good Lord bless you ever. Farewell.

Your loving father,

JOHN WINTHROP.

January 9, 1626.

I should have sent up some fowls this week, if they had been fat.

To my loving Son, JOHN WINTHROP, *at the House of Mr. Downing, at the Sign of the Bishop, over against the Conduit, in Fleet street, London, d'd.*

A. 13.

MY GOOD SON,

I received your letter from Gravesend, and do bless God for your safe arrival there; but I heard not from you since, which I impute to the sudden departure of your captain out of the Downs upon the duke's coming thither. But I hope to hear from you soon, for I long to understand how you fare, and what entertainment you find with your captain, that accordingly I may be stirred up to prayer for you, and to bless God for his mercies towards you. I know not what further advice to give you, than you have already received, and your own observation, upon occasion, shall direct you. Only be careful to seek the Lord in the first place, and with all earnestness, as he who is only able to keep you in all perils, and to give you favor in the sight of those, who may be instruments of your welfare; and account it a great point of wisdom, to keep diligent watch over yourself, that you may neither be infected by the evil conversation of any, that you may be forced to converse with, neither that your own speech or behavior be any just occasion to hurt or ensnare you. Be not rash, upon ostentation of valor, to adventure yourself to unnecessary dangers; but, if you be lawfully called, let it appear, that you hold your life for him, who gave it you, and will preserve it unto the farthest period of his own holy decree. For you may be resolved, that, while you keep in your way, all the cannons or enemies in the world shall not be able to shorten your days one minute. For my part, as a father, who desires your welfare as mine own, I cease not daily to commend you to God, beseeching him to preserve, prosper, and bless you, that I may receive you again in peace, and have assurance of enjoying you in a better life, when your course here shall be finished. Your friends here (I praise God) are all in health, and are daily mindful of you. Let me hear from you so soon and oft as you may conveniently. Remember my love and service to your good captain. The Lord bless you ever. So I rest

Your loving father,
JO. WINTHROP.

LONDON, *June* 6, 1627.

To my loving Son, JOHN WINTHROP, *attending upon Capt. Best, in his Majesty's Ship the Due Repulse, at Portsmouth, d'd.*

[The Duke of Buckingham sailed from Portsmouth 27 June.]

A. 14.

MINE OWN DEAR HEART,

I praise God, we are all in health at Chelmsford this morning. My son F. came to us last night about ten of the clock. Our two boys are lusty travellers, and God's providence hath fitted them with so good means for their carriage, as we could not desire better. I thank thee for thy kind tokens. I have nothing to return thee but love and prayers for thee and thine. The blessing of the Lord be upon thee and them. My son Hen. must go by Maplested.[1] Pray him to call to my brother Tindale[2] for £100, and bring it with him. It is in gold. Send John Hardinge when thou wilt. Commend us to all our friends, broth. G. and sister, Mr. Leigh, goodwife Cole, all at Castleins, and all that love us. We all here salute you all. You must divide it at leisure, with my love and blessing to all our children and the rest in our family. Farewell, my sweet wife, and be of good comfort. The Lord is with us. He hath sent his servants to bless us, and we shall be blessed. Kiss me, my sweet wife. Farewell.

Thy faithful husband,
JO. WINTHROP.

This Saturday morning.

Nov. 1627. *To* Mrs. MARG. WINTHROP, *at Groton, with haste.*

---

[1] Soon after this letter Henry went to Virginia.

[2] Sir John Tindal, a master in chancery, was, probably, the father of this gentleman and of Gov. Winthrop's third wife. He was assassinated 12 November, 1616, for making a report against a suitor, in a cause of comparatively trifling amount. The murderer was examined 16 November, and the next day hanged himself in prison. See the Works of Bacon, Lord Chancellor, V. 452–455, and VI. 133.

A. 15.

Most dear and loving Husband,

I cannot express my love to you, as I desire, in these poor, lifeless lines; but I do heartily wish you did see my heart, how true and faithful it is to you, and how much I do desire to be always with you, to enjoy the sweet comfort of your presence, and those helps from you in spiritual and temporal duties, which I am so unfit to perform without you. It makes me to see the want of you, and wish myself with you. But I desire we may be guided by God in all our ways, who is able to direct us for the best; and so I will wait upon him with patience, who is all-sufficient for me. I shall not need to write much to you at this time. My brother Gostling can tell you any thing by word of mouth. I praise God, we are all here in health, as you left us, and are glad to hear the same of you and all the rest of our friends at London. My mother and myself remember our best love to you, and all the rest. Our children remember their duty to you. And thus, desiring to be remembered in your prayers, I bid my good husband good night. Little Samuel thinks it is time for me to go to bed; and so I beseech the Lord to keep you in safety, and us all here. Farewell, my sweet husband.

Your obedient wife,

MARGARET WINTHROP.

[Probably late in 1627, because "*Little Samuel*" was born in August of that year.]

A. 16.

Loving Son,

I received your letter, and I bless God for your welfare, begging of him daily, that your soul may prosper as your body doth; and if this care be in your heart, (as I hope it is,) you shall do well, for this rule God hath set us to walk by,—first to seek the kingdom of heaven, then will he see to us for other things. So as I dare avouch it for infallible truth, that he who doth otherwise takes a preposterous course to happiness, and shall not prosper. Should not a man trust his Maker, and rest upon the counsel of his Father, before all other things? Should not the promise of the holy Lord, the God of truth, be believed above all carnal, false fears and shallow ways of human wisdom? It is just with God to harden men's hearts in their distrust of his faithfulness, because they dare not rely upon him. But such as will roll their ways upon the Lord, do find him always as good as his word. I bless his name, we all continue in health, and this day I expect your brother from Cambridge. I wish you could meet with some safe means to send to your brother Henry. I have found two sturdy youths, that would go to him. If Capt. Powell return not soon, I shall fear he hath miscarried, and then shall we see God's providence, that your brother returned not with him.

I cannot come up till the week after Easter; but you may know Mr. Featherstone's resolution in the mean time. I pray, inquire how things go in the parliament, and write to me of them; but things which are doubtful, let pass. If the commission for the navy be dissolved, what employment hath your captain then? for it seems he was lately put into it. When you see him or her, commend me kindly to them.

We want a little tobacco. I had very good, for seven shillings a pound, at a grocer's, by Holburn Bridge. There be two shops together. It was at that which is farthest from the bridge, towards the Conduit. If you tell him, it is for him that bought half a pound of Verina and a pound of Virginia of him last term, he will use you well. Send me half a pound of Virginia. I would gladly hear of a chamber in the Temple, or in some other convenient place; for that I have is much too dear.

I have many letters to write: therefore I end; and, with my love and blessing to you, I commend you to the protection and good government of the Lord, and rest

Your loving father,

JO. WINTHROP.

March 18, 1627.

I think to send my brother Downing a greyhound.

To my loving Son, JOHN WINTHROP, *at the House of Mr. Downing, near the Conduit, in Fleet Street, London, d'd.*

A. 17.

SON JOHN,

I received your letter and the books you sent, for which I do thank you. I bless God for the continuance of your health and welfare, which, through his mercy, we all here also enjoy; only myself have a sore hand, which makes me that I cannot write. For the note, which you mentioned in your letter, I received it not. I desire to hear from you concerning Mr. Featherstone's resolution, and whether you have inquired out a chamber for me, or else to take order, that I may have that I had before. I pray send me down six of Mr. Egerton's cattle. For the stuff for the gowns, you may buy it of some olive color, or such like. Either let there be several colors, or else the velvet for the capes of several colors. Remember us all to your uncles and aunts and the rest of our friends. Pray your uncle Downing to send me an answer of my last week's letter, and thank your aunt Downing for her kind love and prayers, and excuse my not writing to them all, for my hand is so as I am not able. Your grandmother and mother salute and bless you. So, with my love and blessing to you, I commend you to the protection, direction, and good providence of our heavenly Father, and rest

Your loving father,

JOHN WINTHROP.

March 31, 1628.

To my very loving Son, JOHN WINTHROP, *d'd, London.*

A. 18.

SON JOHN,

I received your letter, with the things you sent. I do praise God for the continuance of your health and welfare. For myself, my hand is so ill as I know not when I shall be able to travel. It hath pleased God to make it a sharp affliction to me. I hope he will dispose it for my good, and, in his due time, send me deliverance. For your journey intended, seeing you have a resolution to go to sea, I know not where you should go with such religious company, and under such hope of blessing; only I am loath you should think of settling there, as yet, but to be going and coming are best, and afterward to do as God shall offer occasion. You may adventure somewhat in the plantation at the present, and hereafter more, as God shall give enlargement. If Mr. Featherstone will not deal, I will look no further; but your uncle Fones shall have it, and the odd £50 may be for your occasions. Commend me heartily to all your uncles and aunts. Desire them to be mindful of me in their prayers. Thank your aunt Downing for her kind letter. Tell her I see she now means to work upon the advantage in setting me upon the score for letters when I want my hand to free myself. Put your uncle Downing in mind again of my chamber, and tell him, that this day my brother Gostling and another shall go about the business he did write of. Tell him also, that Peter Alston is dead. Commend me to Edward, and desire him to get me out a privy seal against John Carver, Clarcke and Eliza his wife, at the suit of Mr. Attorney, on the behalf of Thomas Foule. In the business concerning your voyage,[1] I pray be advised by your uncle and other your worthy friends, who are experienced in these affairs; but, above all, seek direction and blessing from God. And so, being forced to use another's pen, so as I am not at that freedom to write as I would, I end; and, with your grandmother's and mother's salutation and blessing unto you, I commend you to the gracious providence, direction, and rich blessing of the Almighty. Farewell.

Your loving father,

JOHN WINTHROP.

April 7, 1628.

As soon as I am able to stir about the house, I will look out those geometrical instruments and books, and send them unto you, and any thing else that you will write for.

To his loving Son, Mr. John Winthrop, *at Mr. Fones's House in the Old Bailey, London, d'd.*

A. 19.

My most sweet Husband,

How dearly welcome thy kind letter was to me, I am not able to express. The sweetness of it did much refresh me. What can be more pleasing to a wife, than to hear of the welfare of her best beloved, and how he is pleased with her poor endeavors! I blush to hear myself commended, knowing my own wants. But it is your love that conceives the best, and makes all things seem better than they are. I wish that I may be always pleasing to thee, and that those comforts we have in each other may be daily increased, as far as they be pleasing to God. I will use that speech to thee, that Abigail did to David, I will be a servant to wash the feet of my lord. I will do any service wherein I may please my good husband. I confess I cannot do enough for thee; but thou art pleased to accept the will for the deed, and rest contented.

I have many reasons to make me love thee, whereof I will name two: First, because thou lovest God; and, secondly, because that thou lovest me. If these two were wanting, all the rest would be eclipsed. But I

---

[1] To Turkey.

must leave this discourse, and go about my household affairs. I am a bad housewife to be so long from them; but I must needs borrow a little time to talk with thee, my sweet heart. The term is more than half done. I hope thy business draws to an end. It will be but two or three weeks before I see thee, though they be long ones. God will bring us together in his good time; for which time I shall pray. I thank the Lord, we are all in health. We are very glad to hear so good news of our son Henry. The Lord make us thankful for all his mercies to us and ours. And thus, with my mother's and my own best love to yourself and all the rest, I shall leave scribbling. The weather being cold, makes me make haste. Farewell, my good husband; the Lord keep thee.

Your obedient wife,

MARGARET WINTHROP.

GROTON, *November* 22.[1]

I have not yet received the box; but I will send for it. I send up a turkey and some cheese. I pray send my son Forth such a knife as mine is. Mrs. Hugen would pray you to buy a cake for the boys.

I did dine at Groton Hall yesterday; they are in health, and remember their love. We did wish you there, but that would not bring you, and I could not be merry without thee. Mr. Lee and his wife were there; they remember their love. Our neighbor Cole and goodman Newton have been sick, but somewhat amended again. I fear thy cheese will not prove so good as thou didst expect. I have sent it all, for we could not cut it.

A. 20.

RIGHT HONORABLE,

After the exhibition of my service to your lordship and my lady, I crave pardon, if these rude lines presume to kiss your honor's hands. My duty and respect to your honor urgeth me to give some testimony thereof; and your noble favors have obliged me to present this as a small earnest of my thankfulness, and the service which I owe, and desire to perform, whensoever your lordship shall please to command.

---

[1] It might seem as early as 1621 or 2, before the death of Adam, lord of the manor of Groton; but the mention of Lee, or Leigh, would certainly make it as late as 1627, and the news from Henry must make it 1628.

Here is no news worth your honor's intelligence. We are this day setting sail from the Castles. So, wishing your honor a happy beginning, and prosperous continuance of this new year, and many more to succeed, I humbly take my leave, resting, etc.

CASTLES OF HELLESPONT, *December* 26, 1628.

[The above is a rough draught of a letter "To Sir Peter Wich, Lord Ambassador at Constantinople," found among papers of John Winthrop, jun. The same paper contains, in cypher, probably the same words. It is mentioned, that he was sailing "for Venice," which words are erased, that fact being known to his correspondent. The writer had, no doubt, accompanied this very celebrated minister, either as secretary of legation, or private secretary; most likely the latter. He was now on his return to England.

A. 21.

SON HENRY,

It is my daily care to commend you to the Lord, that he would please to put his true fear into your heart, and the faith of the Lord Jesus Christ, that you may be saved, and that your ways may be pleasing in his sight. I wish also your outward prosperity, so far as may be for your good. I have been sick, these seven or eight weeks, near unto death; but the Lord hath had mercy on me to restore me; yet I am not able to go abroad.

I sent you by Capt. Powell a letter, and in it a note of such things as I likewise sent you by him, in a chest with two locks, whereof the keys were delivered to his brother, who went master of the ship. The things cost me about £35; but, as yet, I have received nothing towards it. I sent divers times to Capt. Powell about your tobacco, but my man could never see it, but had answer, I should have it, or money for it. But there was ten pounds of it, by your appointment, to be delivered to one and the worth of four paid to another, which made me that I knew not what course to take; besides, I found, by the rolls you sent to me and to your uncles, that it was very ill-conditioned, foul, and full of stalks, and evil colored; and your uncle Fones, taking the judgment of divers grocers, none of them would give five shillings a pounds for it. I desired Capt. Powell, (coming one day to see me,) that he would help me with money for it, which he promised to do; but, as yet, I hear not from him. I would have sent you some other things by Mr. Randall; but, in truth, I have no money, and I am so far in debt already, to both your uncles, as I am ashamed to borrow any more. I have disbursed a great deal of money for you, more than my estate will bear. I paid for your debts since you went, above £30, besides £4.10*s.* to Annett and Dixon, and now £35. Except you send commodity to raise money, I can supply you no further. I have many other children that are unprovided for, and I see my life is uncertain. I marvel at your great undertakings, having no means, and knowing how much I am in debt already. Solomon saith, He who hasteth to be rich, shall surely come to poverty. It had been more wisdom and better becoming your youth, to have contained yourself in a moderate course, for your three years; and by that time, by your own gettings and my help, you might have been able to have done somewhat. But this hath been always the fruit of your vain, overreaching mind, which will be your overthrow, if you attain not more discretion and moderation with your years. I do wonder upon what ground you should be led into so gross an error as to think, that I could provide ten such men as you write for, and disburse a matter of £200, (when I owe more already than I am able to pay, without sale of my land,) and to do this at some two or three months' warning. Well, I will write no more of these things. I pray God, make you more wise and sober, and bring you home in peace in his due time. If I receive money for your tobacco before Mr. Randall go, I will send you something else; otherwise you must be content to stay till I can. Your brother (as I wrote to you) hath been in the Levant above this half year, and I look not for him before a year more. Your friends here are all in health. Your uncles and aunts commend them to you; but they will take none of your tobacco; only your uncle Tindale and aunt (whom you write your kinswoman upon the outside of your tobacco) thank you for theirs. I sent you, also, two boys, (for men I could get none,) such as Capt. Powell carried over; but I knew not what to do for their binding, being not able then either to walk or write, and they being but youths. For news, here is little but what, I suppose, this bearer can tell you. We shall have peace with France. The Dutch have taken from the Spaniard, in the West Indies, a very great prize of silver, gold, etc., and have brought it safe home. The king of Bohemia, and his oldest son, going aboard to see it, in their return were cast away. The king was saved, but the prince and many others were lost.

Sir Nathaniel Barnardiston,[1] and Sir William Springe, are knights of the parliament for Suffolk. All the gentlemen have been long since set

---

[1] He was returned again, on the popular side, with Sir Philip Parker, in the great reformation parliament of 1640.

at liberty. Sir Francis Barrington is at rest in the Lord. Sir Henry Mildmay, of Graces, is sheriff of Essex, and Mr. Gurdon for Suffolk.

I have staid sending my letter above a week since I wrote it, expecting some money from Capt. Powell, according to his promise, that I might have sent you some other things; but I hear of none. Therefore I will end, and defer till some other occasion. So, again, I commend you to the blessing, protection, and direction of the Lord, and rest

Your loving father,

JO. WINTHROP.

LONDON, *this* 30 *of January*, 1628.[1]

A. 22.

MY GOOD SISTER,

I have been too long silent to you, considering mine own consciousness of that great debt, which I owe you for your love and much kindness to me and mine. But, I assure you, it is not through want of good will to you; but having many letters to write weekly, I take my ease, to include you in my brother's.

I partake with you in that affliction,[2] which it pleaseth the Lord still to exercise you and my good brother in. I know God hath so fitted and disposed your mind to bear troubles, as your friends may take the less care for you in them. He shews you more love, in enabling you to bear them comfortably, than you could apprehend in the freedom from them. Go on cheerfully, (my good sister,) let experience add more confidence still to your patience. Peace shall come. There will be a bed to rest in, large and easy enough for you both. It is preparing in the lodging appointed for you in your Father's house. He that vouchsafeth to wipe the sweat from his disciples' feet, will not disdain to wipe the tears from those tender, affectionate eyes. Because you have been one of his mourners in the house of tribulation, you shall drink of the cup of joy, and be clothed with the garment of gladness, in the kingdom of

---

[1] This letter was addressed to Virginia, whither the young adventurer had gone fourteen months before, and whence he was then on his voyage home.

[2] Referring, no doubt, to the last sickness of her husband. Fones made his will 14 April, 1629, and died next day. It was proved at Doctors' Commons on 29. His wife Priscilla and John Winthrop were named Excors. His son, Samuel, and daughters Eliz. and Martha were to be, by directions therein, brought up by John Winthrop, and —— White, Esq., of the Temple; and daughter Mary by her mother Priscilla. All the children were minors.

his glory. The former things, and evil, will soon be passed; but the good to come shall neither end nor change. Never man saw heaven, but would have passed through hell to come at it. Let this suffice as a test of my true love to you, and of the account I make of the happiness of your condition. I commend you to his good grace, who is all-sufficient; and so, with my mother's, my wife's, and mine own salutation to yourself, and my good brother, and all my cousins, I rest

Your loving brother,

JO. WINTHROP.

March 25, 1628.[1]

I pray remember my love to your brother, Mr. Burgesse.

I pray tell my brother, that his tenant Gage desires him to forbear him £10 till Whitsuntide.

To my very loving Sister, Mrs. Fones, *at her House in the Old Bailey, London, d'd.*

A. 23.

[The date of this letter is, by probable conjecture, as late as 1629.]

My good Wife,

I wrote to thee this week by Roger Mather, but shall expect no other letter from thee, because of thy journey to Maplested, from whence I hope thou art safely returned. Blessed be the Lord, our good God, who watcheth over us in all our ways to do us good, and to comfort us with his manifold blessings, not taking occasion by our sins to punish us as we deserve. Through his mercy it is, that I continue in health, and that, to my great joy, I hear well of thee and our family. The Lord teach us the right use of all his blessings, and so temper our affections towards the good things of this life, as our greatest joy may be, that our names are in the book of life, that we have the good will of our heavenly Father, that Christ Jesus is ours, and that by him we have right to all things. Then, come what will, we may have joy and confidence.

My sweet wife,—I am sorry that I cannot now appoint the time, that I hope to return, which cannot be the next week; though, it is like, my

---

[1] This was, certainly, the old year, but written by mistake. No doubt it was the first day of 1629, by the lawful mode of reckoning.

sister Fones,[1] or some of her company, will come down then; but you shall hear more the beginning of next week.

Mr. Fowle.

For news I have but one to write of, but that will be more welcome to thee than a great deal of other. My office is gone, and my chamber, and I shall be a saver in them both. So, as I hope, we shall now enjoy each other again, as we desire. The Lord teach us to improve our time and society to more use for our mutual comfort, and the good of our family, etc., than before. It is now bed time; but I must lie alone; therefore I make less haste. Yet I must kiss my sweet wife; and so, with my blessing to our children, and salutation to all our friends, I commend thee to the grace and blessing of the Lord, and rest

Thy faithful husband,

JO. WINTHROP.

My brother D. and sister, and sister F. commend them to thee.

To his very loving wife, Mr. WINTHROP,
at her House in Groton.

A. 24.

MY GOOD WIFE,

Although I wrote to thee last week by the carrier of Hadleigh, yet, having so fit opportunity, I must needs write to thee again; for I do esteem one little, sweet, short letter of thine (such as the last was) to be well worthy two or three from me. How it is with us, these bearers can inform thee, so as I may write the less. They were married on Saturday last, and intend to stay with thee till towards the end of the term; for it will be yet six weeks before they can take their voyage.[2] Labor to keep my son at home as much as thou canst, especially from Hadleigh.[3] I began this letter to thee yesterday at two of the clock,

---

[1] Thomas Fones, Apothecary at the Three Fawns, Old Bailey, married 20 Feb. 1604, Anna, sister of the author. She died 16 May, 1619, and he took another wife, 28 August, 1621, and died 15 April, 1629.

[2] From this it is evident, that Henry, who had married his cousin, Eliz. Fones, on 25 April, 1629, designed to return to Virginia, with his new wife. His views, probably, were changed by want of funds, and before the year ended, he undertook with his father the New England scheme of colonization.

[3] The nearest market town on the east, as Sudbury was on the west. Each five or six miles from Groton.

thinking to have been large, but was so taken up by company and business, as I could get but hither by this morning. It grieves me that I have not liberty to make better expression of my love to thee, who art more dear to me than all earthly things; but I will endeavor that my prayers may supply the defect of my pen, which will be of best use to us both, inasmuch as the favor and blessing of our God is better than all things besides. My trust is in his mercy, that, upon the faith of his gracious promise, and the experience of his fatherly goodness, he will be our God to the end, to carry us along through this course of our pilgrimage, in the peace of a good conscience, and that, in the end of our race, we shall safely arrive at the haven of eternal happiness. We see how frail and vain all earthly good things are.[1] There is no means to avoid the loss of them in death, nor the bitterness which accompanyeth them in the cares and troubles of this life. Only the fruition of Jesus Christ and the hope of heaven can give us true comfort and rest. The Lord teach us wisdom to prepare for our change, and to lay up our treasure there, where our abiding must be forever. I know thou lookest for troubles here, and, when one affliction is over, to meet with another; but remember what our Saviour tells us: BE OF GOOD COMFORT, I HAVE OVERCOME THE WORLD. See his goodness; He hath conquered our enemies beforehand, and, by faith in him, we shall assuredly prevail over them all. Therefore, (my sweet wife,) raise up thy heart, and be not dismayed at the crosses thou meetest with in family affairs or otherwise; but still fly to him, who will take up thy burden for thee. Go thou on cheerfully, in obedience to his holy will, in the course he hath set thee. Peace shall come. Thou shalt rest as in thy bed; and, in the mean time, he will not fail nor forsake thee. But my time is past; I must leave thee. So I commend thee and all thine to the gracious protection and blessing of the Lord. All our friends here salute thee; salute thou ours from me. Farewell, my good wife. I kiss and love thee with the kindest affection, and rest

Thy faithful husband,

JO. WINTHROP.

April 28, 1629.

Let John Bluet[2] be satisfied for his horse.

---

1 His wife had, no doubt, written to him of the death of his mother a few days before.

2 He was, two years before, steward of the manor of Groton, of which Winthrop was lord, after his father's death.

A. 25.

The largeness and truth of my love to thee makes me always mindful of thy welfare, and set me on work to begin to write before I hear from thee. The very thought of thee affords me many a kind refreshing: What will then the enjoying of thy sweet society, which I prize above all worldly comforts?

Yet, such is the folly and misery of man, as he is easily brought to contemn the true good he enjoys, and to neglect the best things, which he holds only in hope, and both upon an ungrounded desire of some seeming good, which he promiseth to himself. And if it be thus with us, that are Christians, who have a sure word to direct us, and the holy faith to live by, what is the madness and bondage of those, who are out of Christ? Oh! the riches of Christ! Oh! the sweetness of the word of grace! It ravisheth my soul in the thought hereof, so as, when I apprehend but a glimpse of the dignity and felicity of a Christian, I can hardly persuade my heart to hope for so great happiness. Let men talk what they will of riches, honors, pleasures, etc.; let us have Christ crucified, and let them take all besides. For, indeed, he who hath Christ, hath all things with him; for he enjoyeth an all-sufficiency, which makes him abundantly rich in poverty, honorable in the lowest abasements, full of joy and consolation in the sharpest afflictions, living in death, and possessing eternity in this vale of misery. Therefore bless we God for his free and infinite mercy, in bestowing Christ upon us. Let us entertain and love him with our whole hearts; let us trust in him, and cleave to him with denial of ourselves, and all things besides, and account our portion the best in the world; that so, being strengthened and comforted in his love, we may put forth ourselves to improve our life and means to do him service. There are very few hours left of this day of our labor: then comes the night, when we shall take our rest. In the morning we shall awake unto glory and immortality, when we shall have no more work to do; no more pain or grief to endure; no more care, fear, want, reproach, or infirmity; no more sin, corruption, or temptation.

I am forced to patch up my letters, here a piece and there another. I have now received thine, the kindly fruits of thy most sweet affections. Blessed be the Lord for the welfare of thyself and all our family.

I received letters from my two sons with thee. Remember my love and blessing to them, and to my daughter Winthrop, for whose safety I give the Lord thanks. I have so many letters to write, as I cannot write to them now. Our friends here are in reasonable health, and desire to be kindly remembered to you all. Commend me to all my good friends, my loving neighbors, goodman Cole, and his wife, to whom we are always much beholden. I will remember M——— her gown and petticoat, and the children's girdles. So, with my most affectionate desires of thy welfare, and my blessing to all our children, I kiss my sweet wife, and commend thee and all ours to the gracious protection of our heavenly Father, and rest

Thy faithful husband,
still present with thee in his most unkind absence,
JO. WINTHROP.

May 8, 1629.

I am sorry for my neighbor Bluet's horse; but he shall lose nothing by him. Tell my son Henry I will pay the money he writes of.

A. 26.

MOST LOVING AND GOOD HUSBAND,

I have received your letters. The true tokens of your love and care of my good, now in your absence, as well as when you are present, make me think that saying false, Out of sight out of mind. I am sure my heart and thoughts are always near you, to do you good and not evil all the days of my life.

I hope, through God's blessing, your pains will not be altogether lost, which you bestow upon me in writing. Those serious thoughts of your own, which you sent me, did make a very good supply instead of a sermon. I shall often read them, and desire to be of God's family, to whom so many blessings belong, and pray that I may not be one separated from God, whose conscience is always accusing them. I shall not need to write to you of any thing this week. My son and brother Gostling can tell you how we are. And I shall think long for your coming home. And thus, with my best love to you, I beseech the Lord to send us a comfortable meeting in his good time. I commit you to the Lord.

Your loving and obedient wife,
MARGARET WINTHROP.

For my very loving Husband, JOHN WINTHROP, Esq., *these deliver.*

[Probably in May, 1629.]

A. 27.

MY SWEET HUSBAND,

I rejoice in the expectation of our happy meeting; for thy absence hath been very long in my conceit, and thy presence much desired. Thy welcome is always ready; make haste to entertain it.

I was yesterday at a meeting at goodman Cole's, upon the going of the young folk to Dedham, where many thanks were given to God for the reformation of the young man, and amendment of his life. We had also a part in their prayers. My dear husband, I will now leave writing to thee, hoping to see thee shortly. The good Lord send us a comfortable meeting. And thus, with my due respect to thyself, brother and sister D., sister Fanny,[1] son John, and the rest. My daughter remembers her duty to you all; thinks long for her husband. I received the things you sent, and thank you heartily for them. I will take order with my man to buy some trimming for my gown. And so I bid my good husband farewell, and commit him to the Lord.

Your loving and obedient wife,

MARGARET WINTHROP.

I pray buy a Psalter for Deane.[2] I can get none here.

To my very loving Husband these deliver.

[Probably, 1629.]

A. 28.

SIR,

My humble duty remembered to you and my mother, may you please to understand, that I received your letters, that by William Ridley on Wednesday, and your other yesterday, rejoicing much to hear of your welfare, with the rest of our good friends, which I desire much with my own eyes to behold. Therefore I purpose, God willing, to make all haste down the next week, hoping to accept of Mr. Gurdon's kind offer, if I can. For the business of New England, I can say no other thing, but that I believe confidently, that the whole disposition thereof is of the Lord, who disposeth all alterations, by his blessed will, to his own

---

[1] Perhaps I mistook this name for Fones.

[2] He was baptized 23 March, 1622-3.

glory and the good of his; and, therefore, do assure myself, that all things shall work together for the best therein. And for myself, I have seen so much of the vanity of the world, that I esteem no more of the diversities of countries, than as so many inns, whereof the traveller that hath lodged in the best, or in the worst, findeth no difference, when he cometh to his journey's end; and I shall call that my country, where I may most glorify God, and enjoy the presence of my dearest friends. Therefore herein I submit myself to God's will and yours, and, with your leave, do dedicate myself (laying by all desire of other employments whatsoever) to the service of God and the company herein, with the whole endeavors, both of body and mind. The Conclusions, which you sent down, I showed my uncle and aunt, who like them well. I think they are unanswerable; and it cannot but be a prosperous action, which is so well allowed by the judgments of God's prophets, undertaken by so religious and wise worthies of Israel, and intended to God's glory in so special a service. My aunt Goulding remembereth her love to you. She saith, it is not yet discharged, that she knoweth. Here is certain news, that the Dutch have taken Wesel. So, desiring your prayers and blessing, I commend you to the Almighty's protection, and rest

Your obedient son,

JOHN WINTHROP.

London, *August* 21, 1629.

I pray remember my love to my brothers and sisters and all our friends, whom I hope shortly to see.

The father's letters, referred to by the son, are not preserved. From our own Colony Records we know, that, on 28 July preceding, at the meeting, or general court of the company, in London, Gov. Cradock proposed, that, for the advancement of the plantation, the inducing persons of worth and quality to transplant themselves and families thither, and other weighty reasons, to transfer the government to those who shall inhabit there, and not continue the same subordinate to the company here. Prince, I. 189, 190; and see page 2, note 2. At the meeting, Aug. 28, a special committee was raised to debate this subject, pro and con, and, the next day, the resolution was adopted, the benefit of which has been felt every day from that to the present. The Conclusions spoken of by the son were, no doubt, a paper of considerations for the plantation, with an answer to several objections, printed in Hutchinson's Coll. 27–31, probably drawn by our author. I have had in my possession the larger part of the original in the well known hand of the elder Gov. Winthrop. That draft of considerations was published, Mr. Felt says, Ann. I. 69, by Higginson before he embarked; which I regard as extremely improbable, for H. had enough to do between the latter part of March, when he proposed to come over in the employment of the Governour and company, he then living in the centre of England, and 25 April, when with his large family he embarked. Very apparent is the connexion between

A. 29.

My dear Wife,

I praise the Lord that I hear of thy welfare, and of the rest of our family. I thank thee for thy most kind letter, and especially that sweet affection, from whence it flows. I am sorry I cannot come down to thee, as I hoped; but there is no remedy. The Lord so disposeth as I must stay yet (I doubt) a fortnight, but, assure thyself, not one day more than I must needs.

I pray thee have patience. God, in his due time, will bring us together in peace. We are now agreed with the merchants, and stay only to settle our affairs. I have not one quarter of an hour's time to write to thee. Therefore thou must bear with me, and supply all defects of remembrances. The Lord bless thee, my sweet wife, and all ours. Farewell.

Thy faithful husband,

JO. WINTHROP.

Send not up my horses till I send for them.

October.

[Early in the month, and, no doubt, 1629.]

A. 30.

Son,

I received your letter, and do heartily bless the Lord for the continuance of your welfare, beseeching him to sanctify you more and more, for his glory and your own salvation.

For the business you write of concerning your brother, I have conferred with him, and shall be as glad as any of his stay here, if he can take any good order for his estate there. What he will do, I know not yet; but I think he will be with you soon. I would gladly have you

---

this paper and the compact for emigration by a powerful company. Had so valuable a document been published more than four months prior to that meeting, we should have some reference to the fact, at least, if not to the convincing argument of the writer. An agreement to transport themselves and families to New England, was, on the Wednesday after this letter, made at Cambridge, by Sir Richard Saltonstall, Thomas Dudley, William Vassall, Nich. West, Isaac Johnson, John Humfrey, Thomas Sharp, Increase Nowell, John Winthrop, William Pynchon, Kellam Browne, William Colburn, which may be seen in Hutchinson's Coll. 25, or in Young's Chron. of Mass. 281.

here betimes next week; but, being it will be Monday sennight before we shall get forth of town, it will be chargeable to keep all the horses here so long. Therefore, if you can find any company to come up with, you may be here on Tuesday or Wednesday; otherwise, you may stay a day or two the longer, and let John come with you; for I would not have you ride alone. I have sent down all the late news from New England. I would have some of you read it to your mother, and let Forth copy out the observations and all that follows from the ☞, and the letter in the end, and show it Mr. Mott and others, that intend this voyage.[1] Your uncle and aunts are all in health, and salute you and the rest of ours, etc. Commend me to your uncle G. and a. and all the rest of our loving friends, that ask of me. So, with my love and blessing to yourself, your brothers and sister, salutations to our young company, I end, and rest

Your loving father,

JO. WINTHROP.

October 9, 1629.

[*To*] *his loving Son,* JOHN WINTHROP, *at Groton, Suffolk, d'd.*

A. 31.

MY DEAR WIFE,

I must needs write to thee by this bearer, though I can write little, in regard of my much business. I praise God, I came safe hither, where I found all in health, and so (through his mercy) we continue. I have sent down my horses, because I am like to stay somewhat longer than I made account of; but I shall make what haste I can back. Here is much news: Divers great personages questioned and committed; but the cause yet uncertain. St. Christopher's is taken by the Spaniard, and the English there honestly sent home. The same is reported of the Barbethes, but not so certain; but, if it be, the people are all safe. Some would discourage us with this news; but there is no cause, for neither are we in the like danger: and, besides, God is with us, and will surely keep us. I shall take time to write to thee again in the end of the week. So, for this time, with all our hearty salutations to thyself, my good sister Fones, and the rest of our friends,

---

[1] Probably this refers to the letters received a few days before from Higginson. See Young's Chron. of Mass. 235 et seq.

with my love and blessing to all our children, I commend thee to the Lord. So I kiss my sweet wife, and rest

Thy faithful husband,

JO. WINTHROP.

November 11, 1629.

My son remembers his duty to thee and his aunt,[1] and love to all, etc.

To his very loving Wife, Mrs. WINTHROP *the elder, at Groton, Suffolk, d'd.*

A. 32.

MY DEAR WIFE,

I have many things to thank thee for this week, — thy most kind letter, fowls, puddings, etc.; but I must first thank our heavenly Father, that I hear of thy health and the welfare of all our family; for I was in fear, because I left thee not well. But thus is the Lord pleased still to declare his goodness and mercy to his unworthy servants. Oh that we could learn to trust in him, and to love him as we ought!

For my care of thee and thine, I will say nothing. The Lord knows my heart, that it was one great motive to draw me into this course. The Lord prosper me in it, as I desire the prosperity of thee and thine. For this end, I purpose to leave £1500 with thy friends, if I can sell my lands, which I am now about, but, as yet, have done nothing. I purpose (if God will) to be at home the next week. I am forced to keep John here for my business, which now comes so heavy upon me, as I can spare no time for aught else. The Lord in mercy bring us well through all our troubles, as I trust he will. Thou must bear with my brevity. The Lord bless and keep thee, and all our children, and company. So I kiss my sweet wife, and rest

Thy faithful husband,

JO. WINTHROP.

My brother and sister[2] salute you all. Let the cow be killed against I come home; and let my son Henry provide such peas as will porridge well, or else none.[3]

January 15, 1629.

---

[1] Probably Fones, but it may be Gostlin. F. was a widow, but G. had her own family, and was less likely to be on a visit to Groton Hall; as, we know, sister F. was, by subsequent letters of both husband and wife, in January after.

[2] Downing, I doubt not.

[3] In preparation for his projected voyage, with his father, to New England.

A. 33.

My dear Wife,

I praise God, we came safe to London, and continue in health, and found all well here. Thus it pleaseth the Lord to follow us with his blessings, that we might love him again. I find here so much to do, as I doubt I shall not come down these three weeks; but, thou mayest be sure, I will stay no longer than my occasions shall enforce me.

I must now begin to prepare thee for our long parting, which grows very near. I know not how to deal with thee by arguments; for if thou wert as wise and patient as ever woman was, yet it must needs be a great trial to thee, and the greater, because I am so dear to thee. That which I must chiefly look at in thee, for a ground of contentment, is thy godliness. If now the Lord be thy God, thou must show it by trusting in him, and resigning thyself quietly to his good pleasure. If now Christ be thy Husband, thou must show what sure and sweet intercourse is between him and thy soul, when it shall be no hard thing for thee to part with an earthly, mortal, infirm husband for his sake. The enlargement of thy comfort in the communion of the love and sweet familiarity of thy most holy, heavenly, and undefiled Lord and Husband, will abundantly recompense whatsoever want or inconvenience may come by the absence of the other. The best course is to turn all our reasons and discourse into prayers; for he only can help, who is Lord of sea and land, and hath sole power of life and death.

It is now near eleven of the clock, and I shall write again ere long (if God will). The good Lord bless thee and all thy company. My broth. and sister salute you all. Commend my hearty love to my good sister F. and all the rest. Tell her I wrote to Mr. Dummer so soon as I came to town; and, if I can, I will speak with him, before John go down. So I kiss my sweet wife, and rest

Thy frail, yet faithful husband.

JO. WINTHROP.

January 31, 1629.

A. 34.

My most dear Husband,

I should not now omit any opportunity of writing to thee, considering I shall not long have thee to write unto. But, by reason of my unfitness at this time, I must entreat thee to accept of a few lines from me, and not to impute it to any want of love, or neglect of my duty to thee, to whom I owe more than I shall ever be able to express. My request now shall be to the Lord to prosper thee in thy voyage, and enable thee and fit thee for it, and give all graces and gifts for such employments as he shall call thee to. I trust God will once more bring us together before you go, that we may see each other with gladness, and take solemn leave, till we, through the goodness of our God, shall meet in New England, which will be a joyful day to us. I send thee here enclosed letters from Mr. P. My good sister F. remembers her love to you, and, it seemeth, hath written so earnestly to Mr. P. not to come, that he doth forbear to come till he hear more. I think she would have you send him word to come as soon as he can, being desirous to speak with him before you go; but it must not come from herself, for she will write to him to stay still.[1] She saith, that he shall not need to provide any thing but a house, for she will furnish it herself. And thus, with my best wishes to God for thy health and welfare, I take my leave, and rest

Thy faithful, obedient wife,

MARGARET WINTHROP.

January the last.

[The superscription of this letter, written, without doubt, 1629-30, is wanting.]

A. 35.

MY SWEET WIFE,

The opportunity of so fit a messenger, and my deep engagement of affection to thee, makes me write at this time, though I hope to follow soon after. The Lord our God hath oft brought us together with comfort, when we have been long absent; and, if it be good for us, he will do so still. When I was in Ireland, he brought us together again. When I was sick here at London, he restored us together again. How many dangers, near death, hast thou been in thyself! and yet the Lord hath granted me to enjoy thee still. If he did not watch over us, we need

---

[1] This coquetry of Priscilla, the widow of Fones, is agreeable enough. She soon after married this gentleman, the Rev. Henry Painter, of Exeter, who had, I think, been husband of the mother of Ursula Sherman, to whom Forth, the third son of the governour, was betrothed. See 3 Mass. Hist. Coll. IX. 231, for a letter of Painter to Winthrop's eldest son, just before embarking with his mother.

not go over sea to seek death or misery: we should meet it at every step, in every journey. And is not he a God abroad as well as at home? Is not his power and providence the same in New England that it hath Job 5. been in Old England? If our ways please him, he can command deliverance and safety in all places, and can make the stones of the field and the beasts, yea, the raging seas, and our very enemies, to be in league with us. But, if we sin against him, he can raise up evil against us out of our own bowels, houses, estates, etc. My good wife, trust in the Lord, whom thou hast found faithful. He will be better to thee than any husband, and will restore thee thy husband with advantage. But I must end, with all our salutations, with which I have laden this bearer, that he may be the more kindly welcome. So I kiss my sweet wife, and bless thee and all ours, and rest

Thine ever,

JO. WINTHROP.

February 14, 1629.

Thou must be my valentine, for none hath challenged me.

To MARG. WINTHROP, *the elder, at Groton.*

A. 36.

MINE OWN SWEET SELF,

I bless God, our heavenly Father, we are all come safe to Maplested, where we find all in health. I have nothing to write to thee, but an expression of my dearest and most faithful affection to thee, and my dear children and friends with thee. Be comfortable and courageous, my sweet wife. Fear nothing. I am assured the Lord is with us, and will be with thee. Thou shalt find it in the needful time. Cleave to thy faithful Lord and Husband, Christ Jesus, into whose blessed arms I have put thee, to whose care I have and do commend thee and all thine. Once again I kiss and embrace my sweet wife. Farewell; the Lord bless thee and all thy company. Commend me to all, and to all our good friends and neighbors, and remember Monday and Friday between five and six.

Thy faithful husband,

JO. WINTHROP.

My son Henry must come by Maplested to seal a writing, which I left there.

To my very loving Wife, MRS. WINTHROP, *at Groton.*

[Dated, probably, latter part of February, 1629–30.]

A. 37.

LONDON, *March* 2, 1629.

MINE OWN DEAR HEART,

I must confess, thou hast overcome me with thy exceeding great love, and those abundant expressions of it in thy sweet letters, which savour of more than an ordinary spirit of love and piety. Blessed be the Lord our God, that gives strength and comfort to thee to undergo this great trial, which, I must confess, would be too heavy for thee, if the Lord did not put under his hand in so gracious a measure. Let this experience of his faithfulness to thee in this first trial, be a ground to establish thy heart to believe and expect his help in all that may follow. It grieveth me much, that I want time and freedom of mind to discourse with thee (my faithful yokefellow) in those things, which thy sweet letters offer me so plentiful occasion for. I beseech the Lord, I may have liberty to supply it, ere I depart; for I cannot thus leave thee. Our two boys and James Downing, John Samford and Mary M. and most of my servants, are gone this day towards South Hampton. The good Lord be with them and us all. Goodman Hawes was with me, and very kindly offers to bring his wife to Groton about the beginning of April, and so stay till thyself and my daughter[1] be in bed; so as thou shalt not need take care for a midwife. Ah, my most kind and dear wife, how sweet is thy love to me! The Lord bless thee and thine with the blessings from above and from beneath, of the right hand and the left, with plenty of favor and peace here, and eternal glory hereafter. All here are in health, (I praise God,) and salute thee. Remember my love and blessing to our children, and my salutations to all as thou knowest. So I kiss and embrace thee, and rest

Thine ever,

JO. WINTHROP.

A. 38.

MINE ONLY BEST-BELOVED,

I now salute thee from South Hampton, where, by the Lord's mercy, we are all safe; but the winds have been such as our ships are not yet come. We wait upon God, hoping that he will dispose all for the best

---

[1] I suppose this was Henry's wife. Her daughter Martha was baptized, at Groton, 9 May following.

unto us. I supposed I should have found leisure to have written more fully to thee by this bearer; but here I meet with so much company and business, as I am forced to borrow of my sleep for this. I purpose to redeem this loss before I go hence, and to write to divers of my friends. I must entreat thee to supply this defect by remembering me in the kindest manner to them all. And now (my dear wife) what shall I say to thee? I am full of matter and affection toward thee, but want time to express it. I beseech the good Lord to take care of thee and thine; to seal up his loving kindness to thy soul; to fill thee with the sweet comfort of his presence, that may uphold thee in this time of trial; and grant us this mercy, that we may see the faces of each other again in the time expected. So, loving thee truly, and tender of thy welfare, studying to bestow thee safe, where I may have thee again, I leave thee in the arms of the Lord Jesus, our sweet Saviour, and, with many kisses and embracings, I rest

Thine only, and ever thine,

JO. WINTHROP.

SOUTH HAMPTON, *March* 14, 1629.

The good Lord bless our children and all thy company.

Do thou bless these here, and pray pray for us.

Give Mrs. Leigh many thanks for her horse, and remember to requite it.

A. 39.

MY DEAR WIFE,

I wrote to thee, when I went from South Hampton, and now I must salute thee and take leave together from the ship. God be blessed, the wind is come very fair, and we are all in health. Our children[1] remember their duties and desire thy blessing. Commend me to all our good friends, as I wrote in my former letter, and be comfortable, and trust in the Lord, my dear wife, pray, pray. He is our God and Father; we are in covenant with him, and he will not cast us off. So, this once more, I kiss and embrace thee and all my children, etc., etc.

Thy faithful husband,

JO. WINTHROP.

From aboard the Arbella, riding at the COWES, *March* 22, 1629.

---

[1] Henry, and, probably, Stephen.

A. 40.

My good Son,

We are now going to the ship, under the comfort of the Lord's gracious protection and good providence. I pray have care so to walk with God in faith and sincerity, as, by his blessing, we may meet with joy. There is newly come into our company, and sworn an assistant, one Sir Brian Janson of London, a man of good estate, and so affected with our society, as he hath given £50 to our common stock, and £50 to the joint stock. He desires to be acquainted with you.

I pray pay Bulbrooke of Wenham such money as his provisions cost him, about 30 or 40*s.* and receive £12 of goodman Pond for the rest of his son's two cows, (I had £10 before,) and ask him for their passage £10. You shall receive £5 for Edward Palsford, which John S. hath order for. I pray pay Mr. Goffe such money as you shall receive direction for from your uncle Downing.

We are now come safe (I praise God) to the Cowes. The wind is now very fair, (God be praised,) and we are preparing to set sail this night. The Lord in mercy send us a prosperous voyage. Farewell, my dear son. The Lord bless you and all my children and friends. Commend me to them all, as if I named them; for I am in great straits of leisure. So I rest

Your loving father,

JO. WINTHROP.

March 22, 1629.

To my very loving Son, Mr. John Winthrop, *at Groton, Suffolk, d'd.*

A. 41.

My faithful and dear Wife,

It pleaseth God, that thou shouldst once again hear from me before our departure, and I hope this shall come safe to thy hands. I know it will be a great refreshing to thee. And blessed be his mercy, that I can write thee so good news, that we are all in very good health, and, having tried our ship's entertainment now more than a week, we find it agree very well with us. Our boys are well and cheerful, and have no mind of home. They lie both with me, and sleep as soundly in a rug (for we use no sheets here) as ever they did at Groton; and so I do myself, (I praise God). The wind hath been against us this week and more; but this day it is come fair to the north, so as we are preparing (by God's assistance) to set sail in the morning. We have only four ships ready, and some two or three Hollanders go along with us. The rest of our fleet [1] (being seven ships) will not be ready this sennight. We have spent now two Sabbaths on shipboard very comfortably, (God be praised,) and are daily more and more encouraged to look for the Lord's presence to go along with us. Henry Kingsbury hath a child or two in the Talbot sick of the measles, but like to do well. One of my men had them at Hampton, but he was soon well again. We are, in all our eleven ships, about seven hundred persons, passengers, and two hundred and forty cows, and about sixty horses. The ship, which went from Plimouth, carried about one hundred and forty persons, and the ship, which goes from Bristowe, carrieth about eighty persons.[2] And now (my sweet soul) I must once again take my last farewell of thee in Old England. It goeth very near to my heart to leave thee; but I know to whom I have committed thee, even to him who loves thee much better than any husband can, who hath taken account of the hairs of thy head, and puts all thy tears in his bottle, who can, and (if it be for his glory) will bring us together again with peace and comfort. Oh, how it refresheth my heart, to think, that I shall yet again see thy sweet face in the land of the living! — that lovely countenance, that I have so much delighted in, and beheld with so great content! I have hitherto been so taken up with business, as I could seldom look back to my former happiness; but now, when I shall be at some leisure, I shall not avoid the remembrance of thee, nor the grief for thy absence. Thou hast thy share with me, but I hope the course we have agreed upon will be some ease to us both. Mondays and Fridays, at five of the clock at night, we shall meet in spirit till we meet in person. Yet, if all these hopes should fail, blessed be our God, that we are assured we shall meet one day, if not as husband and wife, yet in a better condition. Let that stay and comfort thy heart. Neither can the sea drown thy husband, nor enemies destroy, nor any adversity deprive thee of thy husband or children. Therefore I will only take thee now and my sweet children in mine arms, and kiss and embrace you all, and so leave you with my God. Farewell, farewell. I bless you all in the name of

---

[1] See page 2.

[2] The ship from Plymouth was the Mary and John, which carried Maverick, Warham, and Roger Clap. From Bristol came the Lion, William Pierce master.

FAC SIMILE OF PART OF A LETTER FROM GOV. WINTHROP TO HIS WIFE.— See Vol. I. P. 368.9. Appendix A. 41.

And now (my sweet soule) I must once againe take my last farewell of thee in old England, it goeth verye neere to my heart to leave thee, but I know to whom I have comitted thee, even to him, who loves thee much better than any husband can, who hath taken account of the haires of thy head, & puts all thy teares in his bottle, who can, & (if it be for his glorye) will bringe us togither againe wth peace & comfort. oh how it refresheth my heart, to thinke that I shall yet againe see thy sweet face in the lande of the livinge: that lovely countenance, that I have so much delighted in, & beheld wth so great contente! I have hitherto been so taken up wth businesse, as I could seldome looke backe to my former happinesse, but now when I shall be at some leysure, I shall not avoid the remembrance of thee nor the greife for thy absence: thou hast thy share wth me, but I hope, the course we have agreed upon wilbe some ease to us both, mundayes & frydayes at 5: of the clocke at night, we shall meet in spirit till we meet in person. yet if all these hopes should faile, blessed be or God, that we are assured, we shall meet one day, if not as husband & wife, yet in a better condition, let that staye & comfort thy heart, neither can the sea drowne thy husband, nor enemyes destroye, nor any adversity deprive thee of thy husband or children, therefore I will only take thee now & my sweet children in mine armes, & kisse & embrace you all & so leave you wth my God. farewell farewell. I blesse you all in the name of the Lord Jesus; I salute my daughter Winth: Matt: Nan: & the rest, & all my good neighbors & friends. pray all for us. farewell.

Comend my blessinge to my sonne John, I cannot now write to him, but tell him I have comitted thee & thine to him, labour to drawe him yet nearer to God & he wilbe the surer staffe of comfort to thee. I cannot name the rest of my good frends, but thou canst supplye it. I wrote a weeke since to thee & Mr Leigh & divers others.

Thine wheresoever Jo: Winthrop

from Aboard the Arbella rydinge at the Cowes march 28 1630.

the Lord Jesus. I salute my daughter Winth. Matt.[1] Nan.[2] and the rest, and all my good neighbors and friends. Pray all for us. Farewell. Commend my blessing to my son John. I cannot now write to him; but tell him I have committed thee and thine to him. Labor to draw him yet nearer to God, and he will be the surer staff of comfort to thee. I cannot name the rest of my good friends, but thou canst supply it. I wrote, a week since, to thee and Mr. Leigh, and divers others.

Thine wheresoever,

JO. WINTHROP.

From aboard the Arbella, riding at the COWES, *March* 28, 1630.

I would have written to my brother and sister Gostling, but it is near midnight. Let this excuse; and commend my love to them and all theirs.

To MARG. WINTHROP, *the elder, at Groton.*

A. 42.

MY LOVE, MY JOY, MY FAITHFUL ONE,

I suppose thou didst not expect to have any more letters from me till the return of our ships; but so is the good pleasure of God, that the winds should not serve yet to carry us hence. He will do all things in his own time, and that shall be for the best in the end. We acknowledge it a great mercy to us, that we went not out to sea on Monday, when the wind was fair for one day; for we had been exposed, ever since, to sore tempests and contrary winds. I praise God, we are all in good health, and want nothing. For myself, I was never at more liberty of body and mind these many years. The Lord make me thankful and wise to improve his blessings for the furtherance of his own work. I desire to resign myself wholly to his gracious disposing. Oh that I had an heart so to do, and to trust perfectly in him for his assistance in all our ways. We find him still going along with us. He hath brought in the heart of the master of our ship to afford us all good respect, and to join with us in every good action. Yesterday he caused his seamen to keep a fast with us, wherein the Lord assisted us

[1] I presume this was Martha Fones, niece of the Governour, who married her cousin John.

[2] Possibly, Ann Gostlin, another niece.

and our minister very comfortably; and when five of the clock came, I had respite to remember thee, (it being Friday,) and to parley with thee, and to meet thee in spirit before the Lord. After supper, we discovered some notorious lewd persons of our own company, who, in time of our fast, had committed theft, and done other villanies, for which we have caused them to be severely punished.

I am uncertain whether I shall have opportunity to send these to thee; for, if the wind turn, we shall soon be gone. Therefore I will not write much. I know it will be sufficient for thy present comfort, to hear of our welfare; and this is the third letter I have written to thee, since I came to Hampton, in requital of those two I received from thee, which I do often read with much delight, apprehending so much love and sweet affection in them, as I am never satisfied with reading, nor can read them without tears; but whether they proceed from joy, sorrow, or desire, or from that consent of affection, which I always hold with thee, I cannot conceive. Ah, my dear heart, I ever held thee in high esteem, as thy love and goodness hath well deserved; but (if it be possible) I shall yet prize thy virtue at a greater rate, and long more to enjoy thy sweet society than ever before. I am sure thou art not short of me in this desire. Let us pray hard, and pray in faith, and our God, in his good time, will accomplish our desire. Oh, how loath am I to bid thee farewell! but, since it must be, farewell, my sweet love, farewell. Farewell, my dear children and family. The Lord bless you all, and grant me to see your faces once again. Come, (my dear,) take him and let him rest in thine arms, who will ever remain,

Thy faithful husband,

JO. WINTHROP.

Commend my love to all our friends at Castleins,[1] Mr. Leigh and his wife, my neighbor Cole and his wife, and all the rest of our good friends and neighbors, and our good friends at Maplested, when you see them, and those our worthy and kind friends at Assington,[2] etc. My brother Arthur[3] hath carried himself very soberly since he came

---

1 This was a manor house in Groton, then the seat of the family of Chopton, of which William was head. See Sir John Cullum's History and Antiq. of Hawsted and Hardwick in Co. Suff. The second wife of the Governour, who died 1616, was Thomasine Chopton.

2 Assington was the residence of Brompton Gurdon, Esquire, Sheriff of the county.

3 He was, perhaps, son of Sir John Tindall, father of the writer's wife; but what became of him after this voyage, is not known. Probably he went home. An elder brother was Deane Tindall, Esquire.

self very soberly since he came on shipboard, and so hath Mr. Brand's son,[1] and my cousin Ro. Sampson.[2] I hope their friends shall hear well of them.

From aboard the Arbella, riding before YARMOUTH, *in the* ISLE OF WIGHT, *April* 3, 1630.

To my very loving Wife, Mrs. WINTHROP, *the elder, at Groton, in Suffolk, d'd.*

A. 43.

MY GOOD SON,

I received two letters from you since I came to Hampton, and this is the second I have written back to you. I do much rejoice and bless God for that goodness I find in you towards me and mine. I do pray, and assuredly expect, that the Lord will reward it plentifully in your bosom; for it is his promise to prolong their days, (which includes all outward prosperity,) who give due honor to their parents. Trust him, son, for he is faithful. Labor to grow into nearer communion and acquaintance with him, and you shall find him a good God, and a master worth the serving. Ask of any who have tried him, and they will justify him in his kindness and bounty to his servants. Yet we must not look that he should always give us what we think might be good for us; but wait, and let him take his own way, and the end will satisfy our expectation.

Our ship and the Talbot are now at Yarmouth; but the Jewell and Ambrose are put back unto the Cowes. We have had very tempestuous weather, with the wind at S. W. so as some ships, which went out at the Needles before us, are driven back again; and we intend not to stir till we see the wind settled. I would wish women and children not to go to sea till April, and then to take shipping at London. If we had done so, it had eased us of much trouble and charge. There lie now at Cowes two ships of Holland, bound, one to the Streights, and the other

---

[1] The Brands were of Polstead Hall in Polstead or Edwardston, parishes close to Groton. I think this son applied to be made freeman in Oct. 1630, but he probably went home. At least he never took the oath.

[2] Sampson was an ancient knightly family of Sampson's Hall in Kersey, near Groton. John, the father of "cousin Robert," married Bridget Clopton, sister of the second wife of Winthrop. Most of the information on this page, and two or three more, was given me in 1842 by Richard Almack, Esquire, a careful and liberal antiquary of Long Melford.

to the East Indies, of one hundred tons a piece, which, putting to sea in February, spent their masts, and, with much difficulty, and loss of near one hundred men, are come in hither. There came in lately by us a ship from Virginia, laden with tobacco. The master came aboard us, and told us, that they want corn there. She was fourteen weeks outward, and yet lost but one man. I pray certify me, by the next occasion, what the wine cost for the common use, and if you have laid out any more in that kind, that I may perfect my account.

I pray prepare money so soon as you can, that I may be clear with Mr. Goffe and others, and that my part in the joint stock may be made up.

Sir Nath. Barnardiston desired to put in money into our joint stock. Remember my love and respect to him, and if he will put in £50, take it as part of the £200, which I have put in already, except you have money enough to supply more.

Yesterday we kept a fast aboard our ship and in the Talbot. Mr. Phillips exercised with us the whole day, and gave very good content to all the company, as he doth in all his exercises, so as we have much cause to bless God for him.

In the Talbot a woman was lately delivered of a son, and both like to do well.

For other things, which concern my affairs at home, I refer them to your care and the good providence of the Almighty.

Commend my love to all our good friends, as you have occasion, — to my daughter Winthrop, your sister and cousin, and to Mr. Leigh, Mr. Nutt and that family, and to all at Castleins, and the rest, whom I can't now name; and the Lord bless, direct, and prosper you in all your ways. So farewell, my good son.

Your loving father,

JO. WINTHROP.

From aboard the Arbella, riding before
YARMOUTH, *April* 5, 1630.

Our long stay here hath occasioned the expense of much more money than I expected, so as I am run much in Mr. Goffe's debt. I pray get up some money so soon as you can, and pay him £150, or so much as you can get.

To [*my very loving Son,*] Mr. [JOHN WINTHROP,]
Groton, in Suffolk, d'd.

A. 44.

CHARLETON *in* NEW ENGLAND, *July* 16, 1630.

MY DEAR WIFE,

Blessed be the Lord, our good God and merciful Father, that yet hath preserved me in life and health to salute thee, and to comfort thy long longing heart with the joyful news of my welfare, and the welfare of thy beloved children.

We had a long and troublesome passage, but the Lord made it safe and easy to us; and though we have met with many and great troubles, (as this bearer[1] can certify thee,) yet he hath pleased to uphold us, and to give us hope of a happy issue.

I am so overpressed with business, as I have no time for these or other mine own private occasions. I only write now, that thou mayest know, that yet I live and am mindful of thee in all my affairs. The larger discourse of all things thou shalt receive from my brother Downing, which I must send by some of the last ships. We have met with many sad and discomfortable things, as thou shalt hear after; and the Lord's hand hath been heavy upon myself in some very near to me. My son Henry! my son Henry! ah, poor child! Yet it grieves me much more for my dear daughter. The Lord strengthen and comfort her heart, to bear this cross patiently. I know thou wilt not be wanting to her in this distress. Yet, for all these things, (I praise my God,) I am not discouraged; nor do I see cause to repent or despair of those good days here, which will make amends for all.

I shall expect thee next summer, (if the Lord please,) and by that time I hope to be provided for thy comfortable entertainment. My most sweet wife, be not disheartened; trust in the Lord, and thou shalt see his faithfulness. Commend me heartily to all our kind friends at Castleins, Groton Hall, Mr. Leigh and his wife, my neighbor Cole, and all the rest of my neighbors and their wives, both rich and poor. Remember me to them at Assington Hall, and Codenham Hall,[2] Mr. Brand, Mr. Alston, Mr. Mott, and their wives, goodman Pond, Charles Neale, etc. The good Lord be with thee and bless thee and all our children and servants. Commend my love to them all. I kiss and embrace thee, my dear wife, and all my children, and leave thee in his

---

[1] Some neighbor, or, perhaps, Revell, one of the assistants, who came in the Jewel, and went back in the Lion, the first returning ship from this side.

[2] It was in Boxford, adjoining Groton, the ancient seat of Sir Joseph Brand.

arms, who is able to preserve you all, and to fulfil our joy in our happy meeting in his good time. Amen.

Thy faithful husband,

JO. WINTHROP.

I shall write to my son John by London.

To my very loving Wife, Mrs. WINTHROP, *the elder, at Groton, in Suffolk, near Sudbury. From* NEW ENGLAND.

A 45.

MY GOOD SON,

The blessing of God all-sufficient be upon thee ever. Amen.

It hath pleased the Lord to bring us hither in peace, (blessed be his name). For the course of our voyage, and other occurrents, you shall understand them by a journal, which I send with my letters to your uncle D. We had a comfortable passage, and I found that love and respect from Capt. Milburne our master, as I may not forget. I pray (if he be returned before you come hither) take occasion to see him, and remember my kind salutations to him and his wife.

It is like you shall hear (before this come to you) how the Lord hath disposed of your brother Hen. The Lord teach you and the rest by it to remember your Creator in the days of your youth, and to improve your time in his service, while it lasts.

The unexpected troubles and necessities, which are fallen upon us, will bring a great deal of business and care upon thee; but be not discouraged. It is the Lord, who hath cast it upon thee, and he will uphold and deliver thee.

We are forced to send to Bristowe for supply of provisions, by Mr. Peirce and Mr. Allerton, for which I have given them a bill of exchange. You must needs take order, the money may be provided presently for them, for they can't stay. If all means fail, Mr. Revel hath promised to help me with £100. He hath a bill also for money for provisions, which I took up of him here; so have divers others, which you must take care to see paid.

For the freight for the ships, you shall receive some bills from Sir Richard, Mr. Johnson, and Mr. Dudley; but it is doubtful whether their moneys will be ready. What you can provide of theirs and mine, be sure the Talbot be first discharged, for they will not tarry. There is much likewise to be paid to Mr. Beecher, which may stay awhile. There are other moneys to be paid to Mr. Peirce, which must be provided. If all means fail, you may try Doctor Wright; but I hope you have sold the land, and then that care is at an end. For Mr. Goffe, he hath failed exceedingly in his undertaking, so as he is in debt to many of us, and hath had a great deal more of me than his due. Therefore pay him no more. I will send you the account for him and rest, whom I undertook for.

I shall expect your mother and you and the rest of our company here the next spring, if God will. For directions for your passage, I have written about it to your uncle D. and your mother, and I am tired out with writing and much business. Commend my love and blessing to your brother Forth, and your sister M., my neice, Matt. and the rest of our family, and my kind salutations to all my good friends and neighbors, who inquire of us, and to Mr. Nicolson.

For your sister Winthrop,[1] if she will come over, I will provide for her as mine own; if not, she hath a bond of £400. Yet you know there is not so much due to her; for your brother had much money of me out of the £400 I had of him, besides what he ought to your sister Mary. Yet, if it be to be had, I would pay it her, as it can be raised; but then she must give me a general release.

If money be brought to you or your uncle Downing for goodman Lockwood, let Mr. Peirce be paid his bill of provisions for him, and bring the rest with you.

For Forth's coming over, I leave it to my sister Painter[2] her disposing. If they come, they shall be welcome. These afflictions we have met with need discourage none, for the country is exceeding good, and the climate very like our own; only people must come well provided, and not too many at once. Pease may come, if he will, and such other as you shall think fit, but not many, and let those be good, and but few servants, and those useful ones.

Take order that a copy of my relation, etc., be sent to Sir Nath. Barnardiston, and my excuse of not writing to him and Sir Wm. Springe, with my salutations to them both; and if Sir Nath. hath put in no money, let him forbear still.

You must call to Mr. Andrews in Bowe Lane for £20, which Mr. Pincheon hath appointed for you, and you are to pay it, and £30 more, to Mr. Rich. Andrews, at the Mermaid in Cheapside; but you must first inquire if it were lent to us, as we were promised at Hampton. It may

---

1 Widow of Henry.

2 Widow of Fones, who had married Rev. Mr. P. of Exeter; as to her daughter-in-law, Ursula Sherman, Forth was then betrothed, by my conjecture.

be paid soon after Michaelmas next. There is also £208 to be paid to Mr. Cradock, or Mr. Woodward at his house in St. Bartl. near the Exchange, September 8, for which Mr. Johnson and I stood bound; but, if it be not ready, I think Mr. Cradock will get it continued.

Here is a barrel of neat of Bulbroke's of Wenham. If I did not pay for it, let it be paid.

If you reckon with Mr. Wall, thus it stands: You receive of him by Mr. Chamber (to whom I desire to be kindly remembered)

The passage for himself, his wife, and a servant, comes to	£16.10
For one cow, ...	15.02
For tonnage of his goods, ...	11.00
	42.12

Demand the rest of him, and certify me of it.

Henry Kingsbury hath appointed money to be paid to you by [blank].

John Warren hath appointed money to be paid to you by the bond he left with you. He owes beside £10, beside his present provisions.

Demand of Stone and Bragge of Neyland, £15. You have bond for it.

Mr. Goffe's and my account stands thus:

He received of me in England at several payments . .	£642.00
More of me for my brother Downing	107.02
You have paid him since, by my direction from Hampton	
He is to discount for two mares and a horse, (one Mr. Brand's,) which died by the way	27.00
He is allowed for ninety-six passengers, at £4	384.00
For twenty-four cows, (ten being for my broth. D.) . .	361.00
For thirty-two tons of goods, at £3.	

I must end. The Lord God Almighty bless you, and send you all hither in peace. Farewell, my dear son.

Your loving father,

JO. WINTHROP.

Commend me to old Pond, and tell him both his sons are well, and remember their duty to him. He must needs send his son John some more provisions, for much of that he brought was spoiled by the way. You must demand money of him. His reckoning stands thus:

His passage and goods come to . . . . . , ...	£27.00
One cow	15.00
	42.00

I had of him, £10.04.
Rest due, . . 32.00.

Charlton, *July* 23, 1630.

For the country itself, I can discern little difference between it and our own. We have had only two days, which I observed more hot than in England. Here is as good land as I have seen there, but none so bad as there. Here is sweet air, fair rivers, and plenty of springs, and the water better than in England. Here can be no want of any thing to those, who bring means to raise out of the earth and sea.

To my very loving Son, Mr. John Winthrop,
at Groton, in Suffolk, d'd.

A. 46.

Charleton, *in* New England, *August* 14, 1630.

My good Son,

I received your letters by Mr. Huson's ship, and do much rejoice, and bless the Lord for the good news of all your welfares. For our condition here, and our voyage hither, I wrote to you, about a fortnight since, by Mr. Revel, but more fully in a journal and relation, which I sent to your uncle Downing; yet I could [not] make any perfect relation, for want of time and leisure, and I am still as much straitened as before, so as I must refer you and all my friends to my former report as it is. Withal I sent a card of our voyage at sea, which Capt. Milborne drew for me. I wrote, also, how the Lord's hand had been very heavy upon our people in these parts, and that which I conceived to be the reason why so many fell sick, and so many died, and what course you should take when your mother is to come hither, etc. I can now only write a word or two for direction about our affairs; and so I shall leave my blessing with you.[1] First, for the land, (if it be not already sold,) you must sell it speedily, for much debt will lie upon us. For Mr. Appleton, take no money of him, for he can have no cows: there came not on shore one half of them. I had £15 of Mrs. Sands for a cow for

---

[1] Perhaps this letter went by the Arbella.

her brother Goffe; but he could have none now: ergo, if she will not have him have it at next return, let her have her money again.

Pay Mr. Goffe no more money, but require the remainder; and, if he refuse to pay it, it were well his bond were put in suit. If you have money to spare, send over some more cows and goats, and bring £100 with you, or 2.

The beef we had of Mr. Stretton is as sweet and good as if it were but a month powdered. You shall know of other things by your mother's letters.[1] We have powder and pieces enough, but want flints and bird-shot and store of chalk. But I must end. The Lord bless you, and send you hither in safety. Farewell, my good son.

Your loving father,

JO. WINTHROP.

To my very loving Son, Mr. John Winthrop, *at Groton, Suffolk, d'd.*

A. 47.

My dear Wife,

The blessing of God all-sufficient be upon thee and all my dear ones with thee forever.

I praise the good Lord, though we see much mortality, sickness, and trouble, yet (such is his mercy) myself and children, with most of my family, are yet living, and in health, and enjoy prosperity enough, if the affliction of our brethren did not hold under the comfort of it. The lady Arbella is dead, and good Mr. Higginson, my servant, old Waters of Neyland, and many others. Thus the Lord is pleased still to humble us; yet he mixes so many mercies with his corrections, as we are persuaded he will not cast us off, but, in his due time, will do us good, according to the measure of our afflictions. He stays but till he hath purged our corruptions, and healed the hardness and error of our hearts, and stripped us of our vain confidence in this arm of flesh, that he may have us rely wholly upon himself. The French ship, so long expected, and given for lost, is now come safe to us, about a fortnight since, having been twelve weeks at sea; and yet her passengers (being but few) all safe and well but one, and her goats but six living of eighteen. So as now we are somewhat refreshed with such goods and provisions as she brought, though much thereof hath received damage by wet. I praise God, we have many occasions of comfort here, and do hope, that our

---

[1] We have not these letters.

days of affliction will soon have an end, and that the Lord will do us more good in the end than we could have expected, that will abundantly recompense for all the trouble we have endured. Yet we may not look at great things here. It is enough that we shall have heaven, though we should pass through hell to it. We here enjoy God and Jesus Christ. Is not this enough? What would we have more? I thank God, I like so well to be here, as I do not repent my coming; and if I were to come again, I would not have altered my course, though I had foreseen all these afflictions. I never fared better in my life, never slept better, never had more content of mind, which comes merely of the Lord's good hand; for we have not the like means of these comforts here, which we had in England. But the Lord is all-sufficient, blessed be his holy name. If he please, he can still uphold us in this estate; but, if he shall see good to make us partakers with others in more affliction, his will be done. He is our God, and may dispose of us as he sees good.

I am sorry to part with thee so soon, seeing we meet so seldom, and my much business hath made me too oft forget Mondays and Fridays. I long for the time, when I may see thy sweet face again, and the faces of my dear children. But I must break off, and desire thee to commend me kindly to all my good friends, and excuse my not writing at this time. If God please once to settle me, I shall make amends. I will name now but such as are nearest to thee, my brother and sister Gostlin, Mr. Leigh, etc., Castleins, my neighbor Cole and his good wife, with the rest of my good neighbors, tenants, and servants. The good Lord bless thee and all our children and family. So I kiss my sweet wife and my dear children, and rest

Thy faithful husband,

JO. WINTHROP.

I would have written to Maplested, if I had time. Thou must excuse me, and remember me kindly to them all.

This is the third letter I have written to thee from New England.[1]

September 9, 1630.

---

[1] And much do we regret the absence of the second.

A. 48.

MY GOOD SON,

The good Lord bless you ever.

I have written to your mother and to your uncle Downing at large of all things here, to which I must refer you, in regard of my much business and little leisure here.

I shall expect your mother and you and the rest of my company here next spring, (if God will). I pray take order (if it be possible) to make even reckoning with all before you come over, and get a good ship and forty hogsheads of meal at least, well cleansed from the bran, and laid abroad three or four days before it be packed; peas and oatmeal, well dried, as much as you can; good store of dry, Suffolk cheese, brought loose, or packed in very dry malt; butter and tried suet; sugar and fruit; pepper and ginger; store of coarse rugs, both to use and sell; a hogshead of wine vinegar, and another of verjuice, both in good casks and iron-bound. We have lost much by bad casks. Bestow every thing in even hogsheads, if you can; for it will save much in the charge of freight. Bring some good oil, pitch, and tar, and a good piece of an old cable to make oakum; for that which was sent is much lost. Some more cows would be brought, especially two new milch, which must be well mealed and milked by the way, and some goats, especially sheep, (if they can be had). Bring some store of garlick and onions, and conserve of red roses, alum, and aloes, oiled skins, both calf and sheep, and some worsted ribbing of several sizes. This is the third letter I have written to you from here. Commend me to all our friends. My love and blessing to your brother and sisters, your sister Winthrop and cousin Matt. My love and service to Mr. Gurdon and his wife. Salutations to Mr. Jacy, Mr. Chamber, and the rest of the good ministers, Mr. Nott and Mr. Brand. I laid out £15 to Mr. Goffe for a cow for his son. Commend me to all my good neighbors, Mr. Jarrold, William Pond, and the rest. Those who were to have cows delivered here, and failed, must have their money again, my cousin [blank] of Battlesden, £20. I can think of no other, but Mrs. Sands, £15. Commend me to her; and if you see them at Graces,[1] remember me to them. The Lord bless you. Farewell.

Your loving father,

JO. WINTHROP.

September 9, 1630.

---

[1] Where lived Henry Mildmay, not Sir Henry, the regicide.

A. 49.

My sweet Wife,

The blessing of the Almighty be upon thee and thine forever.

There is a ship arrived at Plimouth, some thirty miles from us, which came from London the 10th of August, and was twelve weeks at sea in such tempests as she spent all her masts; yet, of sixty passengers, she lost but one. All the rest (through the Lord's great mercy) are safe and in health. Edy of Boxted, who came in her, told me, a fortnight since, that he had many letters in the ship for me; but I hear not yet of them, which makes me now (having opportunity to send to Plimouth) to write these few lines to thee, lest the ship should be gone before I have received my letters, and can return answer to them. Thou shalt understand by this, how it is with us since I wrote last, (for this [is] the third or fourth letter I have written to thee since I came hither,) that thou mayest see the goodness of the Lord towards me, that, when so many have died, and many yet languish, myself and my children are yet living and in health. Yet I have lost twelve of my family, viz. Waters and his wife, and two of his children, Mr. Gager and his man Smith of Buxall and his wife and two children, the wife of Taylor of Haverill and their child: my son H. makes the twelve. And, besides many other of less note, as Jeff. Ruggle of Sudbury, and divers others of that town, (about twenty,) the Lord hath stripped us of some principal persons, Mr. Johnson and his lady, Mr. Rossiter, Mrs. Phillips and others unknown to thee. We conceive, that this disease grew from ill diet at sea, and proved infectious. I write not this to discourage thee, but to warn thee and others to provide well for the sea, and, by God's help, the passage will be safe and easy, how long soever. Be careful (I entreat thee) to observe the directions in my former letters; and I trust that that God, who hath so graciously preserved and blessed us hitherto, will bring us to see the faces of each other with abundance of joy. My dear wife, we are here in a paradise. Though we have not beef and mutton etc., yet (God be praised) we want them not; our Indian corn answers for all. Yet here is fowl and fish in great plenty. I will here break off, because I hope to receive letters from thee soon, and to have opportunity of writing more largely. I will say nothing of my love to thee, and of my longing desires towards thee. Thou knowest my heart. Neither can I mention salutations to my good friends, other than in general. In my next, I hope to supply all. Now the Lord, our good God, be with thee and all my children and company with thee. Grace and peace be with

and one of L. Kedby his sons.

you all. So I kiss my sweet wife and all my dear children, and bless you in the Lord. Farewell.

Thy faithful husband,

JO. WINTHROP.

Boston, *in* Mattachusets, *November* 29, 1630.

Thou must excuse my not writing to my son John and other of my friends at this time; for I defer it till I receive my letters.

To Marg. Winthrop, *the elder, at Groton, d'd.*

A. 50.

My dear Wife,

I have small hope, that this should come to thy hands, in regard of the long stay of the ship here, so as thou mayest be well onward of thy way hither before these can come to England.[1] Therefore I write little to thyself and my son, and those whom I expect to see here shortly, if it shall so please the Lord. And blessed be his holy and glorious name, that he hath so far magnified his mercy towards us, that, when so many have been laid in their graves since we parted, yet he hath pleased to preserve us unto this hope of a joyful meeting, that we may see the faces of each other again, the faces of our children and sweet babes. These things I durst scarce think of heretofore; but now I embrace them oft, and delight my heart in them, because I trust, that the Lord, our God, who hath kept me and so many of my company in health and safety among so many dead corpses, through the heat of the summer and the cold of winter, and hath also preserved thee in the peril of childbirth, and upheld thy heart in the midst of so many discouragements, with the life of all thy company, will, of his own goodness and free mercy, preserve us and ours still, that we shall meet in joy and peace, which I daily pray for, and shall expect in the Lord's good time; who still continue his favor and blessing upon thee and our sweet babes and all thy company. For our little daughter, do as thou thinkest best. The Lord direct thee in it. If thou bringest her, she will be more trouble to thee in the ship than all the rest. I know my

---

1 Yet she came, with her family, in the same ship that carried her this advice, the Lion, which got back 2 Nov. See p. 63.

sister will be tender of her, till I may send for her. Bring Amy and Ann Gostlin with thee, if thou canst. If they come not, they will much wrong themselves. They need fear no want here, if they will be guided by God's word; otherwise they can look to prosper nowhere. I praise God, I want nothing but thee and the rest of my family. Commend my love and blessing to them all, and to all my neighbours and friends; but I have desired my brother Gostlin to perform that. Remember to bring juice of lemons to sea with thee, for thee and thy company to eat with your meat as sauce. But of these things, my son hath direction. So again I kiss thee my sweet wife, and commend thee and all ours to the Lord, and rest

Thine,

March 28, 1631. JO. WINTHROP.

A. 51.

My good son,

The blessing of the Almighty be upon thy soul and life forever.

Among many of the sweet mercies of my God towards me in this strange land, where we have met many troubles and adversities, this is not the least, and that which affords much comfort to my heart, that he hath given me a loving and dutiful son. God all-sufficient reward thee abundantly for all thy care and pains in my affairs, and for all that love and duty thou hast showed to thy good mother. I doubt not but thou shalt find it in outward blessings, for thou art under the promise of having thy dysprolona gcd; but I desire especially thou mayest find it in the manifestations of the good will of the Lord towards thee, and in those spiritual blessings, which may fatten thy soul.

This ship staying so long here, I am almost out of hope, that my letters should come to thy hands; for, though I think very long till I see you all here, yet I would rather you stayed, though it were two or three months, to come with Mr. Peirce, partly because of his skill and care of his passengers, and partly that we might be the better provided of housing, &c. to entertain you. For we are much straitened yet that way, and we have had divers houses burnt, and now, within these two days, Mr. Sharp and Mr. Colburne, both of our town, had their houses burnt to the ground, and much goods lost. Thus it pleaseth the Lord still to humble us. I doubt not but he will do us the more good at the last.

I have written to your uncle D. concerning all our business, fearing you should be come away. I have sent the assignment sealed. I left all my bonds and writings in my cupboard at Groton, or else at London.

Bring no provision with you, but meal, and peas, and some oat-meal, and sugar, fruit, figs, and pepper, and good store of saltpetre, and conserve of red roses, and mithridate, good store of pitch, and ordinary suet or tallow. Bring none but wine vinegar, and not much of that, and be sure that the cask be good; store of oiled calves-skins of the largest; and the strongest welt leather shoes and stockings for children; and hats of all sizes. If you could bring two or three hundred sheep-skins and lamb-skins, with the wool on, dyed red, it would be a good commodity here; and the coarsest woollen cloth, (so it be not flocks,) and of sad colours, and some red; millstones, some two foot and some three foot over, with bracings ready cast, and rings, and mill-bills; store of shoemakers' thread and hobnails; chalk and chalk-line; and a pair or two, or more, of large, steel compasses; store of coarse linen; some birdlime.

When you have cleared all things in England, if you have any money left, you may bring some with you, (not above £100,) and the rest leave with your uncle D. or dispose of it as your own occasions may require. Anywise, Matt. must have £400, and there will be much due to your sister Winthrop, which were best to be left in England. But you must advise with your uncle D. about these things; for I am so full of business here, as I can't think of mine own affairs as I should. You must also consider what you would have for yourself, and how you would employ it.

I never had letter yet from your brother F. If he intends to come hither, it were good he sold his land, and paid his sister her £100, which he promised when I put over his land to him.[1] You shall need bring no more cows, for I have enough. The good Lord bless you, and bring you and all my company hither in safety. So I rest

Your loving father,

JO. WINTHROP.

MASSACHUSETTS, *March* 28, 1631.

I hope the Lord hath provided a good husband for your sister

---

[1] Forth died so late in the preceding November, that Peirce, who left Bristol in the Lion on Dec. first, had not brought the sad news to the Governor. He was buried at Groton, 23 Nov. 1630.

Winthrop.[1] Mr. Coddington is well affected to her. If he proceed, I wish you to further it; for he is a godly man, and of good estate.[2]

To my very loving Son, Mr. JOHN WINTHROP, *at London, d'd.*
If he be come away, my brother Downing may open this letter.

A. 52.

MY DEAR SON,

Blessed be our good God, who hath not failed us, but hath given us cause of most unspeakable joy, for the good news, which we have heard out of New England. Mr. Wilson had been with me before thy letters came to my hands, but brought me no letter. He speaks very well of things there, so as my heart and thoughts are there already. I want but means to carry my body after them. I am now fully persuaded, that it is the place wherein God will have us to settle in; and I beseech him to fit us for it, that we may be instruments of his glory there. This news came very seasonable to me, being possessed with much grief for thee, hearing how things went concerning thy wife's jointure. But now I have cast off that, and hope God will turn all to the best. If thou canst but send me over when Mr. Wilson goeth back, I shall be very, very glad of his company.[3] If thy manifold employments will not suffer thee to go with me, I shall be very sorry for it; for I would be glad to carry all my company with me. But I will not say any more of this till I hear from thee, how things may be done. I pray consider of it, and give me the best counsel you can. Mr. Wilson is now in London, and promised me to come and see you. He cannot yet persuade his wife to go, for all he hath taken this pains to come and fetch her. I marvel what mettle she is made of.[4] Sure she will yield at last, or else we shall want him exceedingly in New England. I desire to hear what

---

[1] She came with her sister Martha, who had married 8 Feb. preceding her cousin, John Winthrop, to whom this despatch is addressed; and here she married, very soon after arrival, Robert Feake. See p. 69.

[2] He remained in England, until April, 1633, but got a different wife to bring here in his second visit.

[3] Better than her desire was the action of her son, for he brought her above six months before Wilson came away.

[4] Her admission to Boston church is of 20 March, 1635-6. But she came in 1632 with her husband, and they had Mary, born 12, baptized 15 Sept. 1633, I believe their only child born on our side of the water. She was wife of Rev. Samuel Danforth of Roxbury.

news my brother Downing hath; for my husband writ but little to me, thinking we had been on our voyage. And thus, with my love to thyself, my daughter, and all the rest of my good friends, I desire the Lord to bless and keep you, and rest

Your loving Mother,
MARGARET WINTHROP.

I received the things you sent down by the carrier this week, and thank my daughter for my band. I like it well. I must, of necessity, make me a gown to wear every day, and would have one bought me of some good strong black stuff, and Mr. Smith to make it of the civilest now in use. If my sister Downing would please to give him some directions about it, he would make it the better.

[May or June, 1631.]

A. 53.

My worthy and beloved Brother,

I am told by my mother,—and she showed me a letter, which you have very kindly written to my father,—that you will repay certain money, that was taken up in London, by reason of my troubles occasioned by God's providence in that my so much desired match with your dearest brother, which the Lord otherwise ordered, and brought his estate into your hands. The Lord prosper it unto you and yours. I shall truly pray for you, and desire your prayers may be before the Lord for me, who am left to pass through the miseries of a troublesome pilgrimage. I thank you for the continuance of your love. My father and mother are very kind unto me, and will not be wanting, I know, in their love. But, though the Lord should greatly increase your estate by the loss of my dearest friend, and the lessening of my poor portion, and laying other hindrances upon me, yet shall I never think my love ill settled upon one, that loved me so dearly, though he could leave me nothing but his prayers for me and the interest I have in your love, whose kindness is so clearly manifested, like the kindness of Ruth, to the living and to the dead.[1] The £30 you writ of was taken up of my uncle Talley; besides which, the £10 my father's man brought with him,

---

[1] If our language can exhibit any letter of a female hand, earlier in date than this, and more likely to be read with delight a thousand years after, it is not within my recollection.

and the £5 of Mr. Brinscely, and £8 from my uncle Downing, goeth out of that sum of £50 in his hands, which my father Paynter was willing mother should add to my portion, which was but £250 before, for your brother. And now that is all spent, excepting very little. But in all this I do submit myself patiently to the will of God, and take it as the least part of that great affliction. I do not mention any of this to press you, good brother; neither are you bound, but as the consideration of God's dealing, both with you and your brother and me, shall move you. Your promises were your kindness. I could not deserve them, forlorn and desolate as I was. Yet they were comfortable in that case, and I still thank you, and pray the Lord to reward you.

The mare I confess I should desire to get down, if it might stand with your good liking. I hope to ride to Sutton[1] upon her shortly. Mr. Brinscely knows how to send her down by the carrier. I am ashamed to put all these things in a letter, which your well known love and ready kindness would prevent me in, if I could but see you, nay, hath prevented. My father and mother desire to see you all, if it be possible, though they have little hope, by reason of my father's employments. Pray remember my unfeigned love to my sister your wife, and my sister Elizabeth Winthrop. Pray certify her, that I received her loving letter, and excuse me to her, that I have not now written to her. I should be very thankful, if you would be pleased to let me hear from you, the messenger of your welfare being always welcome, and much rejoicing the heart of me.

Your ever-loving sister,
URSULA SHERMAN.

My mother remembereth her love to yourself and your wife, and thanks you both for your kind tokens you sent her by me. She desires to be excused for not writing you at this time.

From EXETER, *June* 18, 1631.

To my worthy and very loving Brother, Mr. JOHN WINTHROP, *at Groton in Suffolk, d'd.*

This letter comes from a maiden betrothed to Forth,[2] who was left in England, when his father came over; and his first letter to John in England leaves it to his sister Painter's disposing, whether Forth should come or not. Another, of March, 1631, mentions him. He was third child of the Gov. by his first wife, Mary, daughter and heir of John Forth, Esquire of Stondon in Essex; or as given on p. 64, Great Stambridge. The correction is made on authority of Sir Charles Geo. Young, the

[1] Near Plymouth.

[2] A letter from Painter to John Winthrop, Jr., which is quite serviceable in explaining relations, is printed in 3 Mass. Hist. Coll. IX. 231.

present Garter in the Herald's College, furnished to Richard Almack, Esquire, of Melford. I suppose it was the same Stondon Massey, of which Nathaniel Ward was rector, before he came to New England. It belongs to the diocese of Rochester. Forth was entered, in April, 1626, of Emanuel College, Cambridge. Henry Painter, of Exeter, one of the celebrated Assembly of Divines at Westminster, married the mother of the above-mentioned lady.

A. 54.

MY DEAR SON,

I hope the Lord hath carried you safe to England, with our most dear Mr. Warner,[1] and the rest of our good brethren and friends. There is nothing befallen since your departure, but Mr. Peirce came from Naraganset, three days after, with five hundred bushels of corn only. At the court it was informed, that some of Salem had taken out a piece of the cross in their ensign; whereupon we sent forth an attachment to bring in the parties at the next court, where they are like to be punished for their indiscreet zeal, for the people are generally offended with it. Mrs. W.[2] was at first very much affected with her husband's departure, but she is now well pacified. I intend to send this letter by Capt. Underhill, who hath leave to go see his friends in Holland. If he come to you, he can inform you of all things here. As I was writing this, Richard came in and told me, the dogs had killed an old wolf this morning in our neck. She made more resistance than both the former. I have many things to write to you about, for such necessaries as are to be provided and sent over; but this occasion is sudden, and I can't think of them, but shall write more largely by Mr. P. if the Lord will. Yourself know what will be needful, and therefore may consider accordingly. Remember copperas, white and green, and two or three pounds of Paracelsus's plaister, and some East Indian bezoar, store of sail cloth, nails, cordage, pitch, tallow and wick, steel spades and shovels, two hand saws and small axes, the best of all, whatever they cost. Commend us to all our good friends where you be come, Mr. W. and the rest, your uncles, aunts, &c. Advise Mr. W. to keep close by all means, and make haste back. The good Lord bless and prosper you, that we may see your face with joy. Your mother, &c. salute and bless you. Farewell.

November 6, 1634.

To my loving Son, Mr. JOHN WINTHROP, *d'd. at Mr. Downing his Chamber, in the Inner Temple Lane, London.*

---

1 Undoubtedly Wilson is meant.

2 Perhaps this means Wilson's wife.

A. 55.

My good Son,

The Lord bless thee ever.

I wrote to you by Capt. Underhill, who went hence in Mr. Babb's ship; since which time here arrived a ship from Barnstable of two hundred tons, Mr. Packers master. She brought about twenty passengers and forty cattle. She lost but two, and yet was seventeen weeks outward bound, whereof five in Ireland. She now returns empty with Mr. Peirce, by whom I send these.

All things continue as when you left us; only Mrs. Warham is dead, and Mr. Hooker's young son, (who died of the small pox, which are very rife at Newtown,) and two men of our town, Willys and Doretye; and two lads were cast away in a great tempest at N. E. on Friday, November 21, in the night, between Noddle's Island and Boston, in a small boat, which they had overladen with wood. Myself and divers others were in the same tempest, not without some peril, but the Lord preserved us. Mr. Sewall's boat was then in the cove at the head of Cape Ann, and broken to pieces, but the men and goods saved. The pestilent fever hath taken away some at Plimouth; among others, Mr. Prence the governour his wife, and Mr. Allerton's wife.

We met the last week, to consider about the business of the ensign at Salem, and have written a letter to my brother Downing, wherein, under our hands, we signify our dislike of the action, and our purpose to punish the offenders.[1]

I wrote to you in my former letter about divers things, which we should have need of, which I will here insert also, with addition of some others.

The Pekods sent two embassies to us. The first time, they went away without answer. The next time, we agreed a peace with them, (for friendly commerce only,) which was that they desired, having now war with the Dutch and Narigansetts, upon these terms, viz., that they should deliver us those men, who killed Capt. Stone, etc., and surrender up to us their right in Conecticott, which they willingly agreed unto, and offered us a great present of wampompeag, and beavers, and otter, with this expression, that we might, with part thereof, procure their peace with the Narigansetts, (themselves standing upon terms of honor, not to offer any thing of themselves).

---

[1] Six lines are here perfectly erased, possibly at the time of writing, but it may be since.

Winter hath begun early with us. The bay hath been frozen all over, but is now open again; and we had a snow last week of much depth in many places. It came with so violent a storm, as it put by our lecture for that day. I wish that, in your return, you would observe the winds and weather, every day, that we may see how it agrees with our parts.

Mr. Ward continues at your house this winter, and Mr. Clerk (to give him content) in his own. Mr. Cl. finds much fault with your servants John and Sarah, and tells me they will not earn their bread, and that Ned is worth them all.

Spades and shovels.

Felling axes, and other small axes.

Nails of 6, 10 and 20.

Piercer bitts.

Sithes for grass, and two brush sithes.

Copperas, white and green.

Emplastrum Paracelsi, two or three lb.

Emplastrum de mim.

Trading cloth, good store, if money may be had.

Brown thread, and hair buttons, and a hogshead of twine for herring nets.

Shoes, two soaled, strong, and the best Irish stockings and wash leather stockings.

Strong cloth suits, unlinen and linen suits of canvas.

Suet, tallow, and wick.

A carpenter, and a husbandman, and a rope-maker, and a cooper.

Some muskets.

Store of brimstone.

A brake for hemp.

Bring the more of all necessaries, because this is the last we shall have without custom.

If my brother Tindale would let you have £100, you may give him assurance of so much in cattle here, to be presently set out for my wife and her children, with the increase, or for £200, if he will.

Commend us to all our good friends, your aunt Downing, and uncle G. and aunts, those at Maplested, Graces, Assington, Groton, Charter-House, Sir Richard S. and his son, and all the rest, as you have occasion, Mr. Kirby, etc., and Mr. Howes; and make haste back. And if there be any matter of importance, write by the first fishing ships. Direct your letters to Capt. Wiggin, or Mr. Hilton. Your mother and the rest are in health, (I praise God). We all salute you. The good Lord direct, keep and bless you. Farewell, my good son.

December 12, 1634.

To my dear Son, Mr. JOHN WINTHROP, *at the House of Mr. Downing, in Lincoln's Fields, near the Golden Lion Tavern, London, d'd.*

A. 56.

SON,

I went to Ten Hills this morning, with your mother and your wife, to have seen goodman Bushnell; but the Lord had taken him away half an hour before we came there. So I made haste down to send you notice of it; but the ship was under sail before I came, which gives me no time to write further to you, for I must send the boat presently after her. You shall receive of Mr. Hodges the key of one of his chests, where the seeds are; the key of the other can't be found; so you must break it open. There is in one of them a rundlet of *honey*, which she desires may be sent to her against she lie down. She desires you to take an inventory of all he hath there. We are all in health, I praise God for it. Your two men you left sick, your wife and mother, and all of us, salute you and your good company. The Lord bless and prosper you. Farewell, my good son.

This 28 *of the* 1 *mo.* 1636.

To my very loving Son, Mr. WINTHROP, Jun. *Governour of Conecticott, d.*

A. 57.

SON,

Blessed be the Lord, who hath preserved and prospered you hitherto.

I received your letters by the Blessing, which arrived here the 14 of this present, and is to return to you with Mr. Pincheon's goods, so soon as she can be laden. By her I shall (God willing) write to you of other things, which I may now omit. Your wife and all our family (I praise God) are in health. I think you will have no letter from her till the Blessing come. It hath been earnestly pressed to have her go to Virginia for Mr. Maverick and his corn; but I have no heart to it at this season, being so perilous both to the vessel, (for worms,) and especially the persons. I will never have any that belong to me come there, if I can avoid it; but Mr. Mayhew hath taken order the Rebecca shall go, if she can be met with.

The Lord, in much mercy, sent us a ship[1] the 12 of this present with provisions; but she had put in at Pascataqua, and sold much there; for she brought only thirty-nine hogsheads of meal, twenty-five of peas, eight of oatmeal, forty of malt, and some beef, and prunes, and aqua-vitæ, eighteen thousand of [unknown]. My brother Peter bought it all, and divided it among all the

[Here about sixteen lines are gone, the paper being torn.]

Queen of Bohemia her eldest son is in England, and no speech of any stop of shipping hither, nor of the general governour, more than divers years before. This ship came in eight weeks from Dartmouth, and saith, there had not been an easterly wind in England fourteen weeks before.

For home news,—the general court hath ordained a standing council for life, and quarterly courts to be kept at Ipswich, Salem, Newtown, and Boston; and four courts in the year at Boston, for greater causes, and for appeals. Mr. Allerton is returned, but had a very ill voyage. His bark lay ten days upon the rock, and beat out all her keel; and so, the second time, Mr. Mayhew and he could get but little provisions, and at extreme rates, but six hogsheads of bread, and few peas. I can get but one barrel of peas of Mr. Allerton, which I will send you. Some pork they brought, but so lean as I have not seen the like salted. The Indians killed up all their swine, so as Capt. Lovell had none; but you shall have beef instead of it. I have sent to Ipswich for your cattle and your servant; for it will be great loss to keep them there. I will take the others from Mr. Mayhew so soon as grass is up.

[The same deficiency as above-mentioned.]

I sent you two letters lately, one by Mr. Hodges, and the other by Mr. Oldham, wherein I certified you of the death of goodman Bushnell, one whom you will miss above all the rest. I had him down to Boston, to do him what honor I could at his burial. Your carpenter and the other fellow (who, I think, truly fears God) are recovering, and, I hope, shall be able to come to you in the Blessing. I pray send me some saltpetre; for I suppose it was a means, through God's blessing, to save one of their lives, being far spent in a fever.

---

[1] See p. 185 ante.

I purpose to send you some milch goats and swine. The prunes I suppose you may sell such of them as you can't spend. The butt cost £10, and should weigh near one thousand pounds. The aquavitæ was put aboard by my brother Peter's order, without my appointment. It cost £22. What you will not spend of it, you may sell to the Dutch for profit enough.

I sent you two letters by Mr. Tilly. [A line and a half erased.] Your brother Stephen was desirous to come to you. If you have any employment for him, you may keep him; otherwise you may return him back.

This ship is bound for the Isle of Sable. If you will send the Blessing with her, she may be here time enough a month hence. But two things I fear: first, that here will be no men nor provisions to set her forth with: the second, that both of them will not be of sufficient strength against the French; for this ship hath not above fourteen men. Neither would I send any of ours without taking leave of the French.

I think the bark goeth away in the morning. Therefore I here end, with salutations to all our friends with you, Mr. Gardiner and his wife, etc. Your mother saluteth you; your wife writes. The Lord in mercy preserve, guide, prosper and bless you in all your ways. Farewell, my good son.

Mr. Hooker and his company intend to set forth three weeks hence.[1]

This 26 *of the* 2 *mo.* 1636.

This night we hear of a ship arrived at Pemaquid, and of twenty-four ships upon the seas, bound hither.

To my very loving Son, Mr. WINTHROP, Jun. *Governor of the new Plantation upon Connecticut, d'd.*

A. 58.

QUENETICUT, *May* 16, 1636.

SIR,

John Wood being returned without any corn, I shall now desire, that I may be supplied, by the first shipping that arrive with any store of provisions, with ten or twelve hogsheads of meal, five or six hogsheads

[1] But he did not for a fortnight later.

of peas, two or three barrels of oatmeal, two hogsheads of beef; for, if we should want, I see no means to be supplied here; and a little want may overthrow all our design.

I send home the Bachelor, and desire your help for her disposing. I must, of necessity, have her return here, for I may shortly have much use of her; but I desire they may go for shares, and victual themselves, which John Wood and his company are willing to do. I cannot find, that the miscarriage of his voyage was through his default, but contrary winds. Therefore I am desirous he should and that company go still in her, so they will go for shares, and victual themselves. The Blessing I would sell, if any will buy her at £160, or £150 — she cost £145, besides some new sail and rigging, and a new cable, above £20 — the cable is special good; except you should foresee any occasion, that she should rather be kept still; or if there be employment to Sable for her. But, if she continues still to go upon any design, I desire she should go likewise for her share, the men to find themselves; otherwise I would have her laid up at Boston till further occasion. The men I desire should be discharged, as soon as ever they come ashore, and their wages paid them. I thank you for the bread you sent. You write of eight hundred, but there is not above three hundred and an half, at most, delivered, besides one hundred they keep still aboard. The rest I cannot learn what become of it, but that it hath been wastefully spent. They had, besides, half an hogshead of bread of their own, which was likewise spent, and they were but two [torn,] eleven persons, they say, most of that time [much torn;] for they pillaged her the time they had her to Salem pitifully, that she hath neither blocks nor braces, nor running ropes, which the bolt Will saith, that Mr. Holgrave cut them off. He saw him. Therefore I have agreed with John Wood, Frederick and George, to take her to thirds. Thus, with my duty remembered, I rest

Your obedient son,

JOHN WINTHROP.

A. 59.

Son,

Mr. Hooker went hence upon Tuesday the last of May, by whom I wrote to you, and sent all your letters, with one from England, and all such news as came to hand; and with that company, viz. by Tho. Bull and a man of mine own, I sent six cows, four steers and a bull. I left it to James and Thomas Skidmore to send such as might be fittest both for travel and for your use. I now send this by the Rebecca, in which you shall find such provisions as are here expressed on the other side. Mr. Fenwick of Gray's Inn (one of those who employ you) hath written to you by Mr. Hooker, and intends, about a month hence, with my brother P. to be with you. The gentlemen seem to be discouraged in the design here; but you shall know more when they come to you.

I received a very loving letter from my Lord S. wherein he expresseth a great deal of satisfaction in your proceedings; but saith withal, that those up the river have carved largely for themselves, which, he thinks, they will after repent, when they see what helps they have deprived themselves of. The ship, which went to Ireland for sheep, lost all her sheep, being five hundred, and so bare up when she was near this coast. Capt. Mason is dead; and thereupon all their designs against us are (through God's great mercy) fallen asleep. But, of all these things, you shall hear more fully when my other letters come to you. Here are come for you, from my sister Downing, divers chests of commodities, and many firkins of butter and suet, which I have bestowed, till I hear what you will have done with them. There is a great glut of all provisions, so as they are not like to fall[1] in haste.

We had nine pieces of ordnance to the Rebecca her side; but all the means could be used could not get one into her. Sir Math. Boynton hath sent more cattle, and two servants. I intend to send his servants to Ipswich to provide for them against winter; for here is not hay to be had. His letters to you come by Mr. Hooker. Sir A. Hazlerig hath refused my brother P. his bills, which is great damage both to him and Mr. Endecott.

I pray deliver this letter enclosed to John Friend, and if he pay you the money, deliver him his bill, (which is here also enclosed;) if not, I pray return it to me again.

Here was an anvil, with a beak horn at the end of it, which I think was carried to Con. If it be, I pray send it back, for it is challenged.

I paid Mr. Garsford of Salem £5 for a buff coat for Mr. Gardiner, which you must remember to put upon his account. Your wampompeak I put off for £30, to be paid in England for the provisions I send you.

Solling and his wife will come to you by the next, if he hear not to the contrary. I know not what to write more on the sudden. I think your wife writes, but she is now at the Garden with my cousin[2] Mary. The Lord bless and prosper you. Your mother salutes you.

---

[1] Perhaps it should be *fail*. [2] Means niece, daughter of his sister Downing.

Provisions sent in the Rebecca.

A hogshead of oatmeal.
Two hogsheads of meal, ... £8.02
Five casks of peas, ... 10.08
Seven barrels of beef, ... 14.14
A hogshead of pork, which my brother P. puts in, . . . 14.07.7
A frail of figs, which I send to yourself, (in the barrel of raisins).
Two[1] kilderkins of butter, put in by Mr. Peirce for Serjeant Willes.
A barrel of raisins of the sun, (the figs are in the end that hath your mark in black lead,) about two cwt. at 45s. the cwt. which is about four pounds and a half.
Four barrels of meal.
A rundlet of sack, of [blank] gallons.
Biscuit in two great bags, at 30*s*. the cwt.

[1] I have paid for them £7.4.4, which he is to pay you.

This 10 *of the* 4 *mo*. 1636.

To my very loving Son, Mr. JOHN WINTHROP, *Governor of the Plantation upon the mouth of the Conecticot, d'd.*

A. 60.

SON,

I wrote to you by Mr. Hooker, and sent you, withal, the letters out of England, and six cows, four steers, and one bull. I wrote since by Mr. Hodges in the Rebecca, and sent many provisions, as by my letter did appear; since which time the Wren came in, and one brought me your letter, but being very busy with divers friends, I desired him to come to me again at dinner; but I never heard of him since, nor of any other of that vessel, so as I know not what they intend to do with the clay you sent. The potter saith, that you sent formerly is very good. I shall take order with him about your store, etc. I have spoke with Mr. Wilson and Mr. Coddington for money, but can get none. I will send you what I have or can borrow by John Gallop, (£10,) and some wether goats. The Bachelor is to come to you next week with Mr. Peirce's goods, and the lighter, with some ordnance [in] Mr. Peirce his pinnace. Mr. Fenwick, my brother Peter, etc., set forth on horseback on the 27 of this month, and will expect your shallop at the upper towns to carry them down the river, and so will go in Mr. Peirce's pinnace to Long Island, Hudson's River, etc. I would have sent you some ship beer, but Mr. Fleming hath provided a butt brought in John Gallop. Goodwife B. is delivered of a daughter, and abroad again in a week. Your wife grows big, but as lively as any woman in the house, God be praised.

I do not send you George, because they are speaking of putting off servants, etc. I suppose, when they come to you, they will consider of the widow Bushnell and of the other widows at Ten Hills, widow Briskowe, who hath been sick ever since you went abroad, and is a great burden to us.

We hear that Scilla Nova is at the West Indies; but we hear nothing of the Pied Cow.[1]

I must end, with remembrance of mine own and your mother's love and blessing to you and to Stephen. Farewell, my good son.

23 *of the 4th mo.* 1636.

I send you two small sugar loaves by J. Gallop.

Mr. W.'s debt is £310. I showed him his bill, with all the several sums, and of whom he received them. I have laid out, since you went, in provisions, etc., and for seamen's wages, near £200.

John Gallop hath a pair of stockings for Stephen, and shoes and stockings for Hen. Smith.

Serjeant Willes's two kilderkins of B. cost 7.4.4, at 7*d.* the pound. If you have more peas and beef than you need, you may send back some.

If you write into England, send your letters by the first return, and I shall convey them.

I have taken order with Mr. Coggeshall for Mr. Oldham, etc.

To my very loving Son, Mr. WINTHROP, *Governor of the new Plantation upon Connecticut, d'd.*

A 61.

DEAR IN MY THOUGHTS,

I blush to think how much I have neglected the opportunity of presenting my love to you. Sad thoughts possess my spirits, and I cannot repulse

[1] She had come from London the year before, and perhaps was lost in her return.

them; which makes me unfit for any thing, wondering what the Lord means by all these troubles among us. Sure I am, that all shall work to the best to them that love God, or rather are loved of him. I know he will bring light out of obscurity, and make his righteousness shine forth as clear as the noon day. Yet I find in myself an adverse spirit, and a trembling heart, not so willing to submit to the will of God as I desire. There is a time to plant, and a time to pull up that which is planted, which I could desire might not be yet. But the Lord knoweth what is best, and his will be done. But I will write no more. Hoping to see thee to-morrow, my best affections being commended to yourself, the rest of our friends at Newton, I commit thee to God.

Your loving wife,

MARGARET WINTHROP.

Sad BOSTON, 1637.

[Probably May, or other session of the general court, or at the synod.]

To her honored Husband,
these be delivered.

A. 62.

MY GOOD SON,

I received your letter, and heartily rejoice and bless the Lord for his merciful providence towards us all, in delivering your wife from so great a danger. The Lord make us truly thankful. And I hope it will teach my daughter and other women to take heed of putting pins in the mouth, which was never seasonable to be fed with such morsels. I can write you no news, only we had letters from Conectacott, where they were shut up with snow above a month since, and we at Boston were almost ready to break up for want of wood, but that it pleased the Lord to open the bay, (which was so frozen as men went over it in all places,) and mitigate the rigor of the season; blessed be his name. On Friday was fortnight, a pinnace was cast away upon Long Island by Natascott, and Mr. Babbe and others, who were in her, came home upon the ice. We have had one man frozen to death, and some others have lost their fingers and toes. Seven men were carried out to sea in a little, rotten skiff, and kept there twenty-four hours, without food or fire, and at last gat to Pullen Point.

We have appointed the general court the 12 of the 1 month. We shall expect you here before the court of assistants. So, with all hearty salutations from myself and your mother to yourself and wife, and little Betty, and all our good friends with you, I commend you to the blessing of the Lord, and rest

Your loving father,
JO. W.

I send you herein the warrant for Ipswich and Newbury. Commend me to your brother and sister Dudley.

XI*th*, 22, 1637.

To his very loving Son, Mr. JOHN WINTHROP, *at Ipswich, d'd.*

A. 63.

MY DEAR WIFE,

When my brother Stephen went hence, I was not up, nor well, so that I could not write to thee. I thank God I am now much better than I was when he left me. Though I much desire to enjoy thy company, yet I would not have thee cross thy intentions, in staying till that time be past. I hoped to fetch thee home myself, but am yet prevented.

I can get no garden enclosed nor digged; but I hear, that, in new ground, it is best to begin when the weeds are sprung up; for then they will be all killed and grow no more that year. Put my brother Stephen in mind to send me my carbine, as he promised me. So, with my best affections and love to thee, I commend thee to the Lord, and rest

Thine, in my best affections,
J. WINTHROP.

From the Salt House, Monday Morning.

My duty to my mother; my love to my brothers and all friends; forget not. My blessing to Betty and Fitz.

My brother Stephen hath promised to bring thee home, when thou comest.

To my dear Wife, Mrs. ELIZABETH WINTHROP, *at Boston.*

It can hardly be doubted, that it was written in May, 1638 or 1639, before the birth of any other children than Betty and Fitz.

A. 64.

Son,

I received your letter, and do bless the Lord for your recovery and the welfare of your family. You must be very careful of taking cold about the loins; and, when the ground is open, I will send you some pepper-wort roots. For the flux, there is no better medicine than the cup used two or three times, and, in case of sudden torments, a clyster of a quart of water boiled to a pint, which, with the quantity of two or three nutmegs of saltpetre boiled in it, will give present ease.

For the pills, they are made of grated pepper, made up with turpentine, very stiff, and some flour withal; and four or five taken fasting, and fast two hours after. But, if there be any fever with the flux, this must not be used till the fever be removed by the cup. This bearer is in great haste, and so am I. So, with our blessing to you and yours, and salutations to all, etc. I rest

Your loving father,

JO. WINTHROP.

This bearer can tell you all the news, which is come from England by the fishing ships, &c.

To my loving Son, Mr. John Winthrop, *at Ipswich.*
Salutem tibi tuæque plurimam in Christo Jesu.
John Wilson.

No sufficient indication is found of the year in which this letter was written. Of the season the evidence is clear. It was before the opening of spring. From our author's History, II. 21, we might conjecture, that the news from Europe referred to 1640; or guess its date to be near the end of February 1642–3 by the dim light shed on p. 93 of the same volume.

B.

The Accompt of John Winthrop, Esq. late Governour.

Whereas, by order of the last general court, commissioners were appointed, viz. Roger Ludlow, Esq. the deputy governour, and Mr. Israel Stoughton, gent. to receive my accompt of such things as I have received and disbursed for public use in the time of my government; in all due observance and submission to the order of the said court, I do make this declaratory accompt ensuing: —

First, I affirm, that I never received any moneys or other goods committed to me in trust for the commonwealth, otherwise than is hereafter expressed.

Item, I acknowedge I have in my custody certain barrels of common powder, and some match and drumheads, with some things belonging to the ordnance; which powder, being landed at Charlestown, and exposed to the injury of the weather, I took and bestowed first in a tent, which I made of mine own broadcloth, (being then worth eight shillings the yard, but in that service much spoiled). After, I removed it to my storehouse at Boston, where it still remains, save that some of it hath been spent in public service, and five barrels delivered to Dorchester, and four to Roxbury, and three barrels I sold to some ships that needed them, which I will allow powder or money for. The rest I am ready to deliver up to such as shall be appointed to receive them. I received also some meal and peas, from Mr. White of Dorchester in England, and from Mr. Roe[1] of London, which was bestowed upon such as had need thereof in the several towns; as also £10 given by Mr. Thomson. I received also from Mr. Humfrey, some rugs, frieze suits, shoes, and hose, (the certain value whereof I must know from himself,) with letters of direction to make use of the greatest part thereof, as given to help bear out my charge for the public. I paid for the freight of these goods, and disposed of the greatest part of them to others; but how, I cannot set down. I made use, also, of two pair of carriage wheels, which I will allow for: I had not meddled with them, but that they lay useless for want of the carriages, which were left in England. For my disbursements, I have formerly delivered to the now deputy a bill of part of them, amounting to near £300, which I disbursed for public services divers years since, for which I have received in corn, at six shillings the bushel, (and which will not yield me above four shillings,) about £180, or near so much. I disbursed also for the transportation of

[1] Owen Rowe had a share in our Massachusetts company, and thought or talked much of coming to live with us, as appears by his letter to Winthrop, Hutch. Coll. 59. Boston records of 20 June, 1636, prove that "Mr. Owyn Roe of London, having a house and towns lot amongst us, and certain cattle, shall have laid out for him 200 acres of ground at Mount Woollystone." He was, also, a proprietor at New Haven, yet staid in London, became a Colonel in the great civil war, was one of the regicides, and his seal is affixed to the warrant for execution of Charles I. After the restoration, his sorrow for the deed, and rejoicing with all his countrymen at the incoming of Charles II. and submission to accept the mercy of the sovereign, saved him from the infliction of his sentence on conviction of the treason, and he died in the Tower on Christmay day, 1661. See Noble's History of the Regicides, II.

Mr. Phillips his family, which was to be borne by the government till he should be chosen to some particular congregation.

Now, for my other charges, by occasion of my place of government, it is well known I have expended much, and somewhat I have received towards it, which I should have rested satisfied with, but that, being called to accompt, I must mention my disbursements with my receipts, and, in both, shall refer myself to the pleasure of the court.

I was first chosen to be governour without my seeking or expectation, (there being then divers other gent. who, for their abilities every way, were far more fit). Being chosen, I furnished myself with servants and provisions accordingly, in a far greater proportion than I would have done, had I come as a private man, or as an assistant only. In this office I continued four years and near an half, although I earnestly desired, at every election, to have been freed. In this time, I have spent above £500 per annum, of which £200 per annum would have maintained my family in a private condition. So as I may truly say, I have spent, by occasion of my late office, above £1200. Towards this I have received, by way of benevolence, from some towns, about £50, and, by the last year's allowance, £150, and, by some provisions sent by Mr. Humfrey, as is before-mentioned, about £50, or, it may be, somewhat more.

I also disbursed, at our coming away, in England, for powder and great shot, £216, which I did not put into my bill of charges formerly delivered to the now deputy, because I did expect to have paid myself out of that part of Mr. Johnson's estate, which he gave to the public; but, finding that it will fall far short, I must put it to this accompt.

The last thing, which I offer to the consideration of the court, is, that my long continuance in the said office hath put me into such a way of unavoidable charge, as will be still as chargeable to me as the place of governour will be to some others. In all these things, I refer myself to the wisdom and justice of the court, with this protestation, that it repenteth me not of my cost or labor bestowed in the service of this commonwealth; but do heartily bless the Lord our God, that he hath pleased to honor me so far as to call for any thing he hath bestowed upon me for the service of his church and people here, the prosperity whereof, and his gracious acceptance, shall be an abundant recompense to me. I conclude with this one request, (which in justice may not be denied me,) that, as it stands upon record, that, upon the discharge of my office, I was called to accompt, so this my declaration may be recorded also; lest hereafter, when I shall be forgotten, some blemish may lie upon my posterity, when there shall be nothing to clear it, etc.

JOHN WINTHROP.

September 4th, 1634.

[The foregoing was copied for me by direction of Alden Bradford, Esq. then secretary of the commonwealth. It is extremely interesting to observe the diffidence of the author, and his prudence in guarding from imputations, *when he should be forgotten*, against his posterity. No distinct reference can be found, in the text of the History, to the circumstances, by which I could have been justified in denoting the place of this document in the Appendix.]

C. Page 170.

DEAR FRIENDS,

Whereas there is a patent granted to certain persons of quality (friends to New England) of the River of Connecticut, with the places adjoining, together with liberties and prerogatives as in such cases are usual, so that, by virtue thereof, they conceive they have full power, right, and authority to govern and dispose of all persons and affairs that shall fall within the circuit and limits of the said grant; it is therefore conceived requisite, by the agents of the said patentees now present in New England, to lay forth the claims and rights of the said personages to such as here in New England it may concern, to the end, if any thoughts or designs of others have been heretofore, or may be hereafter prejudicial or injurious to the right or possessions of the said patentees, they may so far take notice of the same, as, whatever hath happened in the bypast, or may befall for the future, any way derogating from the former claims, may seasonably meet with a loving and friendly prevention; at least, every one that seems to be interested herein may declare and give reasons of their titles and pretensions thereto, that so, in so weighty an enterprise, the business may be carried an end with order, justice, peace, and joint power and strength for the accomplishing of the same, and fruition of it with blessing and love.

Upon consideration of the premises, we conceive, that the present face of affairs of Connecticut, as it now appears, will admit or require a punctual and plain answer to these necessary queries from the towns, that are lately removed from the Massachusetts Bay to take up plantation within the limits of the foresaid patent.

Imprimis, whether they do acknowledge the rights and claims of the said persons of quality, and in testimony thereof will and do submit to the counsel and direction of their present governour, Mr. John Winthrop the younger, established by commission from them in those parts.

Secondly, under what right and pretence they have lately taken up their plantations within the precincts forementioned, and what government they intend to live under, because the said country is out of the claim of the Massachusetts patent.

Item, what answer and reasons we may return to the said patentees, if the said towns intend to intrench upon their rights and privileges, and justify the same.

These things we tender to you as our truly respected brethren, and do desire you earnestly to take them into your serious and Christian consideration, with as much secrecy as may be, so that we may receive your speedy and loving resolutions, that, by the present opportunities, which now present themselves for returning your answers into England, we discharge our trust, which we have lately been put in mind of. And thus we commend you to the guidance and protection of our good God, and remain

Your loving friends,

H. VANE, Jun.
JOHN WINTHROP.
HUGH PETER.

To our loving and much respected Friends, Mr. LUDLOW, Mr. MAVERICK, Mr. NEWBERRY, Mr. STOUGHTON, *and the rest of our Friends engaged in the business of Connecticut Plantations in the Town of Dorchester, d'd.*

D. Page 235.

SIR,

Yours by Robinson we have received, and careful we shall be (I trust) to observe your instructions, and to hasten home as fast as the cause will permit. We are now in a readiness for Block Island; only we wait for a fair wind. We are informed of many Indians there; so we expect the toughest work we have yet met. But we are assured our cause is good, and so we commend ourselves to God's mercy and power. By reason you sent for Mr. Wilson to come with Mr. Hooker, we being willing to show our loyalty to you, and love to the common cause, we have, without gainsaying, dismissed him, albeit we conceived we had special interest in him, and count ourselves naked without him, and therefore expect supply, if we be required to abide by it. Upon consideration that Mr. Wilson going along in the vessel to Connecticut might the more engage

Mr. Hooker and expedite his journey to you, and for that, being to go to Block Island, we could enjoy him but one Sabbath more, we dismissed him at first view of your letter.

We do thankfully acknowledge your care and tenderness toward us, signified by your writings, and sending my provisions, etc., and desire we may deserve it. *For* the hardship you conceive you put us to, and pity us for, for my part, what I endure is so *little thought of*, that it is not worthy pity, neither doth it trouble me, and therefore I desire it may trouble none of my friends. It is what I have been acquainted with in part before; and if I be never more put to it for God's cause sake, it is much less than I have expected. Whiles we *enjoy* part in what is there to be had, I hope we shall be satisfied.

We hear not of Miantonimo, nor any of the Narrigansets nor Nianticks that were with you, concerning the Pequids they have, or any thing else, albeit we have sent for Miantonimo to come to us. The last day of the week, (being to go to Block Island, and) wanting a guide, we sent Tho. Stanton and twenty men, with Lieut. How, towards the Narragansets to get one, who found divers people in Pequid corn, and desired speech with some of them, but by no means could not obtain it, for they ran all away. Still they endeavored after it, and to know the reason of their running, especially seeing we had formerly expressly told them, they must not use that, for we should then take them for Pequids. At length, they told, that Englishmen had some of them in prison in the bay, and they knew not what Englishmen meant towards them. But we were also told by a squaw, that they were mixt, Pequids and Narragansets together; *and were besides* signs of two rendezvous; she said, one was the Pequids. So, there being twenty *canoes*, ours brought two away, with one kettle and beans, that were at the Pequids' rendezvous, but told them, let them come hither, and, if they were Narragansets, they should have all without any damage.

We conceive you do well, in keeping them to strict, just terms, as also in that you refer them to us in the matters specified; for we conceive, being in the field, with our swords in our hands, we shall do better with them than when the sword is sheathed, and all peace.

Concerning Pequids harbored by them, we have thoughts (after return from Block Island) to require every one of them from those that have them, for these reasons:

1. Their flying to them is no submission to us, but of purpose to avoid it; so that they bear the same good will to us as formerly; that is, they stand enemies, only use the Narragansetts and others as their covering.

2. Standing thus, we can expect no other but that they will do us

mischiefs as opportunity serves; and, besides, be as spurs to the Narragansetts to provoke them to it, and as captains to aid and strengthen them in it, when, etc.

3. Under the vizor of a Narragansett, they will come amongst us, and do us mischiefs.

4. And when a mischief is done, then it will be fathered upon some renegado Pecot, that will have no master to own him; but it will be said, such a one did it, or such a one, etc.

Therefore, if they will not deliver all to us, according to their covenant, we cannot think their intentions to be good toward us, and shall accordingly declare ourselves towards them; though we will not *so* use like faith with them, but first advise with you, unless we be constrained. And if God do harden their hearts, I doubt not but it will be to their perdition. Only I pray for the contrary, if it be the Lord's will.

For Wequash, we fear he is killed; and if he be, 'tis a mere wicked plot, and, seeing he showed faithfulness to us, and for it is so rewarded, it is hard measure to us-ward; and what is meet to be done therein, is difficult to me to conclude; I shall therefore desire your speedy advice.

After return from Block Island, we shall fall upon destroying corn. Near to us it fails much by the weeds, and far from us it will do us little good. The Naragansetts do gather beans in abundance, and we are silent at it; yet, if they should turn enemy, it would be to our great damage. But my opinion is, that they will be twice advised before they will fall out *with us*. Only they will let us bear their injuries as long as we will, and, if they see us in good earnest, I believe they will think upon it, especially whiles the terror of our sword and our God's doings is upon them.

There be many Pequids yet living, and such as will do much mischief. It will be found therefore necessary for one pinnace, one shallop, and some sixty men, to abide here, to take opportunities, partly at Long Island, and elsewhere upon the coasts, (for they lie mostly upon the coast, except such as are under the wing of other Indians). Else I see not many need stay. For, for this place, it is scarce worthy much cost. As for plantation, here is no meadow I see or hear of near; the upland good, but rocky and unfit for ploughs for the most part. Indeed, were there no better, 'twere worthy the best of us, the upland being, as I judge, stronger land than the bay upland.

But if you would enlarge the state, and provide for the poor servants of Christ, that are yet unprovided, (which I esteem a worthy work,) I must speak my conscience. I confess the place and places whither

God's providence carried us, that is, to Quillipeage River, and so beyond to the Dutch, is before this, or the bay either, (so far as I can judge,) abundantly. But unless great necessity, or approved policy, require such undertakings, I would be loath to have a hand in, or that my pen should further them, for I affect not scattering, but would rather part stakes at home; yet, so far as it may tend to public utility, and the enlargement of Christ's kingdom, I hope I should not hinder so good a work, though it be to self's disadvantage. It seems to me, God hath much people to bring hither, and the place is too strait, most think. And if so, then, considering, 1st, the goodness of the land, 2d, the fairness of the title, 3d, the neighborhood of Connecticut, 4th, the good access that may be thereto, wherein it is before Connecticut, even in the three forementioned considerations, (for the land Connecticut men so judge,) and, 5th, that an ill neighbor may possess it, if a good do not,— I should readily give it my good word, if any good souls have a good liking to it.

I am willing, for my own particular, to stay here so long as yourself and the council, or general court, shall see just cause to require me. Yet I also am as willing to be at home so soon as it may be permitted; and, for my part, when some few things more are over, I see nothing against but that I may come home, and therefore shall wait to know your minds therein.

Thus, with my due respect remembered to yourself, *the honored council*, and the rest of the magistrates, desiring your prayers, I humbly *commend* you to God.

Yours, as in duty I am bound,

ISRAEL STOUGHTON.

From PEQUID, *the 2d day of the 6th week of our warfare.*

To his much honored in the Lord, the Governour and Council of the Massachusetts, these present.

[This was probably written 14 August, 1637. They reached home 26th.]

E. Page 245.

[*Remonstrance or Petition by Members of Boston Church, in favor of Wheelwright, March*, 1637. *Copied from the Book of their Antagonist, Thomas Welde, pp.* 23–5.]

We, whose names are underwritten, have diligently observed this honored court's proceedings against our dear and reverend brother in

Christ, Mr. Wheelwright, now under censure of the court for the truth of Christ. We do humbly beseech this honorable court to accept this remonstrance or petition of ours, in all due submission tendered to your worships.

For, first, whereas our beloved brother, Mr. Wheelwright, is censured for contempt by the greater part of this honored court, we desire your worships to consider the sincere intention of our brother to promote your end in the day of fast; for whereas we do perceive your principal intention the day of fast looked chiefly at the public peace of the churches, our reverend brother did, to his best strength, and as the Lord assisted him, labor to promote your end, and therefore endeavored to draw us nearer unto Christ, the head of our union, that so we might be established in peace, which we conceive to be the true way, sanctified of God, to obtain your end, and therefore deserves no such censure, as we conceive.

Secondly, whereas our dear brother is censured of sedition, we beseech your worships to consider, that either the person condemned must be culpable of some seditious fact, or his doctrine must be seditious, or must breed sedition in the hearts of his hearers, or else we know not upon what grounds he should be censured. Now, to the first, we have not heard any that have witnessed against our brother for any seditious fact. Secondly, neither was the doctrine itself, being no other but the very expressions of the Holy Ghost himself, and therefore cannot justly be branded with sedition. Thirdly, if you look at the effects of his doctrine upon the hearers, it hath not stirred up sedition in us, not so much as by accident; we have not drawn the sword, as sometimes Peter did, rashly, neither have we rescued our innocent brother, as sometimes the Israelites did Jonathan, and yet they did not seditiously. The covenant of free grace held forth by our brother hath taught us rather to become humble suppliants to your worships; and, if we should not prevail, we would rather with patience give our cheeks to the smiters. Since, therefore, the teacher, the doctrine and the hearers be most free from sedition, (as we conceive,) we humbly beseech you, in the name of the Lord Jesus Christ, your Judge and ours, and for the honor of this court and the proceedings thereof, that you will be pleased either to make it appear to us, and to all the world, to whom the knowledge of all these things will come, wherein the sedition lies, or else acquit our brother of such a censure.

Farther, we beseech you, remember the old method of Satan, the ancient enemy of free grace, in all ages of the churches, who hath raised up such calumnies against the faithful prophets of God. Elijah was called the troubler of Israel, 1 Kings, 18. 17, 18. Amos was charged for conspiracy, Amos 7. 10. Paul was counted a pestilent fellow, or mover of sedition, and a ringleader of a sect, Acts 24. 5; and Christ himself, as well as Paul, was charged to be a teacher of new doctrine, Mark 1. 27. Acts 17. 19. Now, we beseech you, consider, whether that old Serpent work not after his old method, even in our days.

Farther, we beseech you, consider the danger of meddling against the prophets of God, Psalm 105. 14, 15; for what ye do unto them the Lord Jesus takes as done unto himself. If you hurt any of his members, the head is very sensible of it; for so saith the Lord of Hosts, He that toucheth you toucheth the apple of mine eye, Zech. 2. 8. And better a millstone were hanged about our necks, and that we were cast into the sea, than that we should offend any of these little ones, which believe on him, Matt. 18. 6.

And, lastly, we beseech you consider, how you should stand in relation to us, as nursing fathers, which gives us encouragement to promote our humble requests to you, or else we would say with the prophet, Isa. 22. 4, Look from me, that I may weep bitterly; Labor not to comfort me, etc.; or as Jer. 9. 2, Oh that I had in the wilderness a lodging place of a way-faring man! — And thus have we made known our griefs and desires to your worships, and leave them upon record with the Lord and with you, knowing that, if we should receive repulse from you, with the Lord we shall find grace.

F.

Beloved Brethren,

I met lately with the remonstrance subscribed by yourselves with others. I must confess I saw it once before, but had not then time to read it advisedly, as now I have. I hope soon (by God's assistance) to make it appear, what wrong hath been done to the court, yea, and to the truth itself, by your rash, unwarranted, and seditious delinquency. In the mean time, I thought fit to advertise you of some miscarriages therein; and though your countenancing of others in the like practice leaves me small hope, that you will hearken to my counsel in this, yet, in discharge of my duty and brotherly respect towards you, I have given this attempt, and shall leave the success to God.

1. In this you have broke the ends of your calling, that you did publish such a writing, when you were no members of the court.

2. In that you tax the court with injustice.

3. In that you affirm, that all the acts of that major part of that court are void, whereby you go about to overthrow the foundation of our commonwealth and the peace thereof, by turning all our magistrates out of office, and by nullifying all our laws.

4. In that you invite the body of the people to join with you in your seditious attempt against the court and the authority here established, against the rule of the apostle, who requires every soul to be subject to the higher powers, and every Christian man to study to be quiet and to meddle with his own business.

I earnestly desire you to consider seriously of these things, and if it please the Lord to open your eyes to see your failings, it will be much joy to me, and (I doubt not but) the court will be very ready to pass them by, and accept of your submission, and it may be a means of a further and firm reconciliation; which the Lord grant, and in his good time effect. So I rest

Your loving brother,

J. W.

XI*th*, 15, 1637.

To my worthy Friends and beloved Brethren, Mr. CODDINGTON, Mr. COGGESHALL, *and* Mr. COLBURN.

No reference is made in my notes to this document, because no fit place was afforded by the text. The exasperation of the controversy did not, as usual, turn to gall Winthrop's gentleness of temper, though it seems to me to have had an injurious influence on his judgment.

G. Page 260.

It may please the worthy and much honored governour, deputy, and assistants, and, with them, the present court, to take knowledge, that our desire of staying within this patent was real and strong, if the eye of God's providence (to whom we have committed our ways, especially in so important an enterprise as this, which, we confess, is far above our capacities) had guided us to a place convenient for our families and for our friends. Which, as our words have often expressed, so, we hope, the truth thereof is sufficiently declared by our almost nine months' patient waiting in expectation of some opportunity to be offered us, for that end, to our great charge and hindrance many ways. In all which time we have, in many prayers, commended the guidance of our apprehensions, judgments, spirits, resolutions, and ways into the good hand of the only wise God, whose prerogative it is to determine the bounds of our habitations, according to the ends for which he hath brought us into these countries; and we have considered, as we were able, by his help, whatsoever place hath been propounded to us, being ready to have, with contentment, accepted (if by our stay any public good might be promoved) smaller accommodations, and upon dearer terms (if they might be moderately commodious) than, we believe, most men, in the same case with us, in all respects, would have done. And whereas a place for an inland plantation, beyond Watertown, was propounded to us, and pressed with much importunity by some, whose words have the power of a law with us, in any way of God, we did speedily and seriously deliberate thereupon, it being the subject of the greatest part of a day's discourse. The conclusion was, that, if the upland should answer the meadow ground in goodness and desirableness, (whereof yet there is some ground of doubting,) yet, considering that a boat cannot pass from the bay thither, nearer than eight or ten miles distance, and that it is so remote from the bay, and from any town, we could not see how our dwelling there would be advantageous to these plantations, or compatible with our conditions, or commodious for our families, or for our friends. Nor can we satisfy ourselves, that it is expedient for ourselves, or for our friends, that we choose such a condition, wherein we must be compelled to have our dwelling houses so far distant from our farms as Boston or Charlestown is from that place, few of our friends being able to bear the charge thereof, (whose cases, nevertheless, we are bound to consider,) and some of them, that are able, not being persuaded that it is lawful for them to live continually from the greatest part of their families, as, in this case, they would be necessitated to do. The season of the year, and other weighty considerations, compelled us to hasten to a full and final conclusion, which we are, at last, come unto, by God's appointment and direction, we hope, in mercy, and have sent letters to Connectacutt for a speedy transacting the purchase of the parts about Quillypieck from the natives, which may pretend title thereunto. By which act we are absolutely and irrevocably engaged that way; and we are persuaded, that God will order it for good unto these plantations, whose love so abundantly, above our deserts or expectations, expressed in your desire of our abode in these parts, as we shall ever retain in thankful memory, so we shall account ourselves thereby obliged to be any way instrumental and serviceable for the common good of these plantations as well as of those, which the divine providence hath combined together in as strong a bond of brotherly affection, by the sameness of their condition, as Joab and Abishai were, whose several armies did mutually strengthen them both against several enemies, 2 Sam. 10. 9, 10, 11, or rather they are joined together, as Hippocrates his twins, to stand and fall, to grow and decay, to flourish and wither, to live and die, together. In witness of the premises, we subscribe our names,

JOHN DAVENPORTE.
THEOPH. EATON.

The 12th day of the 1st month, 1638.

To the much honored, the Governour, Deputy, and Assistants, etc.

This letter has, since first published by me, been printed in 3 Mass. Hist. Coll. III. 165, with erroneous date of 1639. Had Winthrop written on the same day, he would have called it 1637. Many years before, I had in my original preface noted the distinction. There can be no mistake. In Sept. 1637 Eaton went, as Winthrop says, from Boston to explore the coast on the Sound, while Davenport was engaged here in the more appropriate function of vindicating the truth against Cotton and Wheelwright; and in April following the date of this letter, they established the beautiful city of New Haven. Holmes, in his Annals, quoting Trumbull's Hist. I. 90, says "1638 on the eighteenth of April they kept their first Sabbath in the place." If the almanac of that year is correct, the day was Wednesday.

H. Page 290.

Authenticity of the Deed *of four Indian Sagamores to Rev. John Wheelwright and others*, 17 *May*, 1629.

Before the 13th June, 1820, I had no more suspicion of the truth of the deed to Wheelwright and four others, of 17 May, 1629, which is the first article of Appendix in Belknap's N. H., I. and may also be seen in Hazard, I. 271 – 274, than of the charter of 4 March, 1628–9, for the colony of Massachusetts Bay, or of any other undisputed document. On that day, casually perusing Gov. Winthrop's History, page 172 of the Hartford edition, after having twice, in former years, collated the whole with the original MS. without perceiving any inconsistency with an instrument, that indeed had no necessary connection with my text, I was struck with the improbability, that Wheelwright and his associates, in 1639, should not have mentioned their *ancient* title, when so severely censured by their former brethren of Massachusetts for *now* "dealing with an Indian there, and buying Winicowet." See page 290 of this volume.

To remove or confirm my doubts, I considered immediately several circumstances, and on the same day wrote for advice to N. A. Haven, jun. Esq. of Portsmouth, competent counsel in such a cause. To aid him in supplying an early answer on some suspicious points, I mentioned, 1. The wretched argument of Cotton Mather, the first article of Appendix in Belknap's N. H., III. 2. The names of the grantees, not generally known, except Wheelwright, who did not probably come over till seven years after, and Wentworth, who was probably too young. 3. The absence of Samuel Sharp, on the ocean, just parted from England, when he is made witness to the signing of the deed. 4. The seven witnesses of delivery of possession, on the same day with execution, not one of whom witnessed the signing; and the doubts raised in 1707, when the handwriting of several, perhaps of all, these seven, could so easily be proved. 5. The argument from History of Winthrop, which seemed irrefragable. I asked, if the original deed were visible, that my own eyes might judge, whether "it has almost as many marks of 1629 as there be years in the number," which was the authoritative declaration of Mather, without seeing the instrument, probably from the overbearing impulses of a celestial vision. My further question was, "When was it last seen? or heard of?" In conclusion, I begged him to inquire of Hon. Jeremiah Mason, or any other competent person, and to answer every particular.

Mr. Haven replied, 20 July, 1820, "I cannot better answer your letter of June 13, than by enclosing a communication from Mr. Nathaniel Adams, to which it gave occasion. Mr. Adams procured for Belknap the copy of Wheelwright's deed, which had been filed among the records of the superior court in 1707, in the case of Allen vs. Waldron. The papers in this case he examined a few years ago, but afterwards mislaid them in the office. They are not now on the regular files. He remembers, that Dr. Belknap inquired in vain for the original deed. If it exist at all, it must be among the heirs of Wheelwright, their executors, administrators, or assigns. —

"Ignari hominumque locorumque,
Erramus."

The communication of Mr. Adams follows:

"PORTSMOUTH, *July 3d*, 1820.

"MY DEAR SIR,

"I have read with some attention Mr. Savage's letter upon the Indian deed to Wheelwright, as well as the deed itself in the Appendix to Belknap's New Hampshire, vol. I. and cannot discover the many suspicious circumstances, with which Mr. Savage thinks it 'pregnant;' and as he is methodical in pointing out his objections, I will pursue the same order in answering them.

"First, with respect to the grantees, three of whom, he says, are unknown in his researches. It appears from the Records of Exeter, that, in the year 1639, soon after the settlement of the town, the brethren of the church there, and the other inhabitants, made a combination, as they called it, or form of government, which was signed by all the inhabitants, and the names of all the grantees in the deed are amongst them. When they came to this country does not appear. William Wentworth was one of the first settlers in Exeter, and continued there as long as their combination lasted, and then removed to Dover. He assisted in defending Heard's garrison in 1689. If he was born 1609, he was twenty years old at the time of executing the deed, eighty at the attack on Heard's, and eighty-eight when he died. His mode of securing the gate at Heard's did not require more muscular strength than many men of that age possess. I see nothing improbable in his being one of the grantees, on account of his age.

"That Wheelwright was not in this country till 1636, is a mistake; for Neal and Wiggin, in a letter to John Mason, Esq. dated August 13th, 1633, say, 'We have treated with a gentleman, who has purchased a trackt of land of the Indians at Squamscott Falls — the gentleman's name being Wheelwright.' Belknap, vol. I. Appendix, No. 6.[1] If Mrs. Pierson's account is correct, that Mr. Wheelwright came over, *with his family*, in the same ship with Samuel Whiting, in 1636, then, as Cotton Mather says, 'he might step over hither to see how the land lay before his transportation of his family.' Belknap, vol. III. Appendix, No. 1.

"2d. Concerning the two English witnesses, Oldham and Sharp. It is acknowledged, that Oldham was in the country at the time, and was not killed till seven years afterwards. But Mr. Savage says, 'that Sharp was, that very day, on the ocean, just parted from England in company with Higginson,' and refers to Prince's N. E. Chronology, I. 185. Prince does not any where assert, that Sharp came over with Higginson. He says that, on the 30th of April, 1629, at a general court of the Massachusetts company in London, it was ordered, 'that thirteen in their plantation shall have the sole ordering of the affairs

[1] By Farmer rejected as a forgery, of which the evidence is palpable, and abundant, and intrinsic.

and government there, by the name of the Governour and Council of London's Plantation in the Massachusetts Bay in New England.' And, at the same court, Sharp was elected a member of this council; but it does not follow, that he was then in England. Endicott was, at the same time, elected governour, although he was in Massachusetts; for he came over in 1628, as appears from Prince's N. E. Chronology, 174; and, as others were sent over with him to begin a plantation, probably Sharp was one of them.

"3d. As to the witnesses to the delivery of possession. This, in my mind, is a corroborative circumstance of the authenticity of the deed. The grantees, desirous of having every thing conducted in the most fair and open manner, procured not only two very respectable witnesses to the execution of the deed, but seven of the first characters in the neighboring plantations to witness the transaction, and to endorse on the deed the delivery of the possession, which they supposed equivalent to the endorsement of livery of seizin in England. Three of these very witnesses, four years afterwards, recognize the deed in question, as appears by Belknap, I., Appendix, No. 6, above referred to; and two of them were directly interested in the suppression of it, if it had been a forgery.

"A copy of the deed, certified by Jos. Hammond, register of deeds for the county of York, was used in the trial of the cause Allen vs. Waldron, in the year 1707, although it was not recorded there until 1713. I cannot say why it was lodged in the register's office for the county of *York*, unless it was, because the heirs of Wheelwright lived in that county. After the record of the deed, his heirs took it into their possession; for, in the year 1720, the people, who settled at Londonderry, then called Nutfield, purchased of Col. Wheelwright of Wells his Indian right. The Rev. Mr. Macgregore, in his letter to Gov. Shute, says, 'His deed, being of ninety years standing, and conveyed from the chief sagamores between the Rivers Merrimack and Pascataqua, with the consent of the whole tribes of the Indian nation, and well executed, is the most authentic we have seen.' Belknap, III. Appendix, No. 4.

"I have not Gov. Winthrop's Journal; but as he did not arrive in this country until 12th June, 1630, it is not surprising, that he did not mention the transaction of Wheelwright's purchase, which took place fifteen months before, and especially as it did not relate to the society, over which he came to preside.

"I shall be gratified if the foregoing observations have any tendency to investigate the truth. If I am mistaken, receive with candour the attempt of "Your friend,

"NATHANIEL ADAMS."

On 1 August, 1820, I replied, with much fuller evidence of the falsity of the deed, but not so full as shall be added to this article. Here the matter rested until 22 November, 1823, when appeared in the Portsmouth Journal an article, under the editor's head, giving several reasons for the opinion, that the deed "is, without doubt, a forgery." In the Historical Collections of New Hampshire, I. 299–304, is a defence of the instrument from the former governour of that state, which is here copied.

"*Remarks on the Authenticity of the Wheelwright Deed.*

"It has been recently affirmed, by a writer in one of our public papers,[1] that this deed 'is, without doubt, a forgery.' The reasons he assigns in support of this opinion are, that Wheelwright was not heard of in this country till 1636, seven years after the date of the deed; that Samuel Sharpe, one of the subscribing witnesses, was then on the ocean; that, of the seven witnesses to the delivery of possession, no one of them witnessed the execution of the deed, though made the same day; as some of these witnesses were officers and agents of Laconia, it is incredible they should have lent their names to an act destructive of their own title; that Wheelwright, in 1634, four years after the purchase from the Indians, claimed only about a mile square at Squamscott Falls; that, when Wheelwright and the other gentlemen at Exeter were censured, in 1639, by Massachusetts, for dealing with an Indian and buying Winnicomett, they made no mention of the grant from the four sagamores; that no trace of Augustine Story, Thomas Wite, and Thomas Levitt is to be found in the history of Massachusetts or New Hampshire; that William Wentworth, one of the supposed grantees, died in 1697; if he was only twenty-one years old when the deed was executed, he must have been eighty-one when he performed the astonishing feat of strength, that Belknap records of him; and that the original deed cannot now be found.

"Though these reasons may merit consideration, they do not, in my opinion, prove that *the deed from the four sagamores is a forgery.* We have no evidence, that Wheelwright did not come to this country till the year 1636. Though he came *with his family* in that year to New England, he might, before that time, have visited and resided in it some time *without* his family, and that appears to be the opinion of one of our early historians, Dr. Cotton Mather, as is expressed in his

---

[1] Portsmouth Journal, November 22, 1823.

letter of 1708 to Vaughan.[1] But we have more conclusive evidence to this point: Neale and Wiggin, who laid out the four first towns in New Hampshire, in their return to John Mason, of August 13, 1633, explicitly state the fact of Wheelwright's having previously purchased of the Indians a tract of land at Squamscott Falls, which, when settled, was to be called *Exeter*.[2]

"The second objection is, that Samuel Sharpe, one of the subscribing witnesses, was on the ocean the very day the deed is dated; and to prove this, the reader is referred to 1 Prince's N. E. Chronology, 185. But, in the passage referred to, there is no evidence that Sharpe was on the ocean that day any more than that John Endicott was, who in fact arrived in Massachusetts the preceding summer, and was then governour of that colony. All that Prince states is, that Endicott, on the 30th of April, 1629,[3] was, by the company in England, appointed governour of Massachusetts, and Sharpe a member of the council in that colony, and not that either of them were then in England, or on the ocean. There is, however, better and more conclusive authority than Prince. I will state the facts, though one of them favors the writer upon the point under consideration. A letter from the council in England, dated April 17–21st, 1629, states, that, previous to its date, they had received a letter from Gov. Endicott, written by him in New England, dated September 13th, 1628; and that they [the council in England] had *re-appointed* him governour, and appointed Samuel Sharpe counsellor, etc., and that they then thought Sharpe, who had embarked for New England, was detained, by bad weather, on the coast of England.[4] But, what is of most importance, neither the letter last mentioned, Prince, or the writer in the Journal, afford any evidence that the Samuel Sharpe to whom they refer was the same man who appears as one of the subscribing witnesses. On the day that deed was executed, Samuel Sharpe, the counsellor, was probably on the ocean; but another man, of the same name, might then be in this country, and in fact subscribe as a witness. The writer appears to admit, that John Oldham, the other English subscribing witness, was then in this country; for he says he was murdered by the Indians in 1636.

"It is not objected to the witnesses of the delivery of possession, that they were not then in this country, but that it was incredible that some of them should be witnesses to a deed that was destructive of their own

---

1 "3 Belknap's N. H. Appendix, No. 1." 2 "Ditto, Appendix, No. 6."

3 "He and Sharpe were appointed at an early day, but probably some time in that month."

4 "Hazard's State Papers, 256–268."

title. I can see nothing incredible or improper in Neale, Vaughan, and Gibbons, who were agents, and perhaps owners, under the Laconia company, subscribing as witnesses to an Indian chief's delivering possession of part of the tract which the company claimed. If they were present when possession was delivered, they must know it, and their certifying it in writing could not operate against them or their employers. Their act neither confirmed Wheelwright's title, or impaired that of the company. Four years after the execution of the deed, two of those witnesses, in their report to Mason, appear to consider Wheelwright's claim to the lands, or some part of them, as good.[1] But the writer, to evade the force of this fact, says, it was only about one mile square; and cites Winthrop's Journal, p. 172, to shew, that, when Massachusetts, in 1639, complained of Wheelwright and his associates for purchasing Winnicomett of the Indians, he did not then state his claim to the large tract conveyed by the deed of 1629. But what necessity was there for his doing it? If a man is required to defend his title to *one* tract of land, is he obliged to assert and vindicate his claim to *two?* According to Winthrop, the complaint of Massachusetts against Wheelwright was not on account of the purchase and settlement of Exeter, but Winnicomett, that is, Hampton. Wheelwright might, within four years from the execution of the first deed, be induced, from motives, which, after the lapse of near two centuries, we are unable to discover, to abandon his right to a great portion of the land described in the deed. We have reason to believe, he had neither the means to settle the whole, or support a controversy with Mason and others.

"Another objection to the authenticity of the deed is, that no trace of three of the grantees named in the deed, to wit, Augustine Story, Thomas Wite, and Thomas Levitt, can be found in the history of Massachusetts or New Hampshire, and that it is remarkable their names should never again occur. Whoever reads the deed must be convinced, that it was obtained by the labor and expense of Wheelwright, and not by those of his associates, and that possession of the premises was delivered to him, and not them. But it is not a fact that we hear no more of the associates; for, in the year 1639, an agreement was made by the settlers at Exeter, for the government of themselves and their concerns. This agreement is signed by thirty-five persons, of whom are John Wheelwright, William Wentworth, and *Thomas Levitt*, three of the five grantees; and, as to the other two, it is highly probable they also settled at Exeter, and signed the contract, but spelled their names different

[1] "1 Belk. N. H. Appendix, No. 6."

from what they were written in the deed, a circumstance that frequently occurs in the old documents relating to this country. In the deed, their names were written Augustine Story and Thomas Wite, but, in signing the agreement, Augustine Starr and Thomas Wright.[1] And the remark respecting William Wentworth, that, if he had been but twenty-one years of age at the time of the purchase in 1629, he must have been eighty-one when he performed the extraordinary feat of strength recorded in Belknap, does not appear to me to impair the authenticity of the Indian deed. In the first place, there is no evidence, that Wentworth, in 1629, was twenty-one years old, for though minors are not capable of giving, they are of receiving deeds. But, admitting he was of that age, the feat of strength, which Belknap states Wentworth performed in 1689, was not greater, if so great, as what he affirms was effected by Waldron, who, he says, was then 'advanced in life to the age of eighty years.'[2] History affords many instances of men, older than either of these, who performed greater feats of strength and activity.

"The last objection is, that the original deed has disappeared. Considering the long period of time that has elapsed since it was given, and the number of generations that have passed away, its preservation would have been more extraordinary than its loss. The deed itself was produced in court in 1707 and 1708, in the case of Allen vs. Waldron; it was on the ancient files in the county of York on the 28th of January, 1713, and was then recorded in the records of deeds in that county.

"There are many other considerations, which support the authenticity of the deed, but it appears unnecessary to state them. I will only add, that, if the deed was forged, Wheelwright must have been privy to it; but the goodness of his character repels the charge: and, if it was forged, it would be incredible, that a man of so much understanding and knowledge as he possessed, should select the names of the officers and agents of the company of Laconia as witnesses, who, of all others, were most interested in detecting and exposing the fraud.

"WILLIAM PLUMER."

My first remarks will be on the internal evidence.

1. No Indian deed, in my knowledge, and I have examined many, was ever drawn so long, formal, and precise. Conveyances between the English were not, for a long space of years, artificially written on our side of the Atlantic. This deed was, it will be said, drawn by one of the grantees. But who could have done it in so clerklike length and

---

[1] "1 Hazard's State Papers, 463." [2] "1 Belknap's N. H. 248, 249."

beauty, more than a year before any lawyer, except Thomas Morton of Merry Mount, came to the country, and half a century before any lawyers here drew such solemn assurances?

2. The names of the sachems are suspicious. Passaconaway was, probably, not sagamore of Penecook alone, but of much more of the country, confined however to the Merrimack, certainly superior lord of Pentucket; yet the deed appears to show an equality with him of Runnaawit, sagamore of Pentucket, and of the two others. There is, in 2 Hist. Coll. IV. 169, a *true* deed of Haverhill, 15 November, 1642, in which Passaquo and Saggahew, "with the consent of Passaconaway," sell Pentucket, and they, without their paramount, affix their marks. I know it may be objected, that, in this very instrument, the grantors describe "Passaconaway our chief sagamore;" but this is one of the strongest marks of fabrication. He was chief sagamore on the Merrimack, and Runnaawit, (whose name is not found, with any territorial jurisdiction, in Drake's Book of the Indians,) sagamore of Pentucket, had therefore done well to express his fealty; but he was not chief of Squamscot, much less of Nuchawanuck, that ever I heard of, nor does it appear from any other paper. The force of this remark must not be evaded, by referring the fact of his superiority, acknowledged apparently by Wahangnonawitt and Rowls, only to the other grantor, because the payment, annually, from each township within the limits, of "one coat of trucking cloth," is reserved to the *chief* alone. Besides this objection, the names of the other three sagamores are hardly known in any other transaction. It may indeed be thought, that Rowls is an easy mistake of transcription for Knowles, who, it is known, was sachem of Nuchawanack, and, in 1643, granted to Humphrey Chadbourne lands still remaining in that family, and, in 1650, to Spencer. See Sullivan's Maine, 143. I have two partial answers to this fact: One, that, in these deeds, he takes no notice of his liege lord, Passaconaway; and the other, that it is probably an English adopted name. But this practice of taking our names was not, in 1629, used by the Indians. Wahangnonawitt was the *real*, and only grantor to Wheelwright and friends, nine years later.

3. In the preamble to the deed, the sachems are made to declare their inclination "to have the English inhabit amongst us, as they are amongst our countrymen in the Massachusetts Bay; by which means we hope, in time, to be strengthened against our enemy, the Tarateens, who yearly doth us damage." This is quite inconsistent with truth, but might readily be suggested to an Englishman of a later age, composing a fictitious document. The shore Indians expressed such fear to Plimouth people in 1621. The Tarrateens did, in 1631, *surprise* the Indians at

Agawam on the sea-side; but what fear could the martial tribes of the upper Merrimack, of Squamscot, and of Nuchawanack, entertain of such *unknown* enemies. The English settlements at Dover and Portsmouth, of six years standing, were their shields, if any could have been needed. Yet this instrument refers to the humble settlement of Massachusetts Bay, i. e. Salem, eight months old, where Higginson *afterwards* found about ten houses and one hundred settlers.

4. The grantees, five in number, "all of the Massachusetts Bay," are each and all unheard of for some years; yet, if the men, women, and children at Salem amounted but to one hundred, and there were not, in which I am confident, half as many more in the bay, some one of these five names should have appeared in the governour and company's letters to Endecott, or in his to them. Especially does this apply to Wheelwright, in the deed called "late of England, a minister of the gospel." We know the ships, in which most of our principal fathers severally came, and the day of arrival of each. Remarkably is this verified of the early ministers, except Blaxton. He, we know, was not accordant with our Puritans; but Wheelwright was of the straitest sect. This reverend gentleman did not visit Plimouth or Salem in their destitute state, May, 1629, wanting the bread of life. Neither of these harbors of refuge had then a minister. Did he leap, with his associates, from the anchoring ground thirty miles into the country, without accepting congratulations of the settlers on the coast? and leap back from Squamscot to England, without a farewell to his friends, coming and going without being seen?

5. These four liberal sagamores "give, grant, bargain, sell, release, ratify, and confirm unto J. W. etc. all that part of the main land bounded by the River of Piscataqua, and the River of Merimack, that is to say, to begin at Nuchawanack Falls in Pascataqua River aforesaid, and so down said river to the sea, and so alongst the sea-shore to Merimack River, and so up along said river to the falls at Pantucket aforesaid, and from said Pantucket Falls, upon a north-west line, twenty English miles into the woods, and from thence to run upon a straight line, north-east and south-west, till [it] meet with the main rivers, that runs down to Pantucket Falls and Nuchawanuck Falls; and the said rivers to be the bounds of the said lands from the thwart line, or head line, to the aforesaid falls, and the main channel of each river, from Pentucket and Nuchawanack Falls to the main sea, to be the side bounds, and the main sea, between Piscataqua River and Merimack River, to be the lower bounds, and the thwart or head line, that runs from river to river, to be the upper bounds; together with all islands within said bounds, as also

the Isles of Shoals, so called by the English, together with all profits, advantages, and appurtenances whatsoever, to the said tract of land belonging, or in any wise appertaining, reserving to ourselves liberty of making use of our old planting land, as also free liberty of hunting, fishing, and fowling." Now it may seem, that, after such a grant in 1629, Passaconaway should not have *consented* to another sale of Pentucket in 1642, in a deed of 22 lines, by sachems, who acknowledged his sovereignty. But a much stronger objection is, that, at the very time, and even above six and seven years before, according to the authentic history of the contemporary Gov. Winslow, settlements were made at Portsmouth and Dover, which both continued without interruption, under the grants to Gorges, the whole of whose pretended rights, and those in actual enjoyment, on the sea between Merimack and Piscataqua, and up the river close to Nuchawanack, must be defeated by this deed. In view of all the foregoing particulars, one can hardly avoid the conclusion, that this deed, which, we may soon see reason to believe, was not made for seventy years after its assumed date, was written with a special reference to the grant of the president and council of New England to John Mason, 7 Nov. 1629, because its lines in the two rivers are the same, and the Indian deed is made to include Isles of Shoals, which were embraced (not indeed by name) in Mason's, and had not been in Gorges's grant. But the including those islands is a very strong objection to the deed. What possible claim of title could these inland Indians have to islands they never saw, or probably heard of? Wheelwright could not, as an *honest* man, which he assuredly was, take their grant of lands of great extent, of which the Hiltons and others at Dover, and the dwellers at Portsmouth, had long been in peaceable enjoyment; but he must have been as *foolish* as dishonest, to take in the isles of the ocean, to which the sagamore of Ipswich, or Squidrayset, beyond Saco, had much more reasonable claims than his supposed grantors.

6. Of the conditions, or provisoes, the bearing of most is to lessen the credibility of the instrument. The first, that "the said John Wheelwright shall, within *ten years* after the date hereof, set down with a company of English, and begin a plantation at Squamsquott Falls," looks more like accommodation of a pre-existent fact to a desired hypothesis, than a real bargain by children of the forest. Savages are not accustomed to postpone enjoyment or revenge. It looks cunning, but it defeats itself. The plantation did begin in ten years, but ought not to have been delayed as many months. — The second is of the same character. It was desirable, less than sixty years after, "that what other inhabitants shall come and live on said tract of land, from time to time,

and at all times, shall have and enjoy the same benefits as the said Wheelwright." But what reason could the grantors have for imposing such a condition? Was not Wheelwright, like any other purchaser, to sell out parcels of his right? — The third is altogether foreign from any imaginable object of the Indians. — The fourth is still more so, and seems borrowed from a habit, that grew a few years after in the Massachusetts court in making grants. It has also a strong likeness to the erection of townships designed in a letter of Neal and Wiggin, more than four years after, which has been hastily thought to confirm this deed, though it proved to be a more clumsy forgery, suggested by this monster fabrication. — The fifth seems utterly destructive of the verity of the transaction. Why should the Indians require, that their grantees, "to avoid contentions amongst them," should be subject to "the government of the colony of the Massachusetts, their neighbours, and to observe their laws and orders until they have a settled government amongst themselves?" What can be more irreconcilable to us, who know the precise circumstances of the colony, then covering only a few acres at Salem? Why should orders by Capt. Endecott, who had not then his commission from the governour and company, extend to regions far beyond the bounds of the company's purchase of the preceding year, and confirmed by the charter a few weeks before this date? Is it not apparent, that the penman of this deed knew the subsequent assertion and exercise of jurisdiction, by Massachusetts, over that region, but had forgotten, or hoped others would forget, that it did not begin till twelve years after? — The sixth is idle repetition of the reservation in the premises. People, who could waste time in the wilderness for such forms, might as well have settled there at once, and would soon have learned better employment. — The seventh is divisible. The first member, providing, that each township should pay to Passaconaway and his successors forever "one coat of trucking cloth a year," "for an acknowledgment," seems indeed to show a reasonable object of the grantors' care, though, as before hinted, under the second head of these remarks, it leaves all but one without any such equivalent. But what should have led to the second member, "and also shall pay to Mr. John Wheelwright aforesaid, his heirs and successors forever, two bushels of Indian corn a year?" Why should the grantors have taken any care to enforce payment to their grantee, by those who purchased of him? It would be no difficult matter, if the deed had been true, to show payment of this yearly "coat of trucking cloth;" for the Indians were quite punctual, and always have been so, in asking for their annuities.

7. After the habendum et tenendum, with warranty, come the seals

and signatures, with two Indian witnesses, whose names are less known than those of the grantors. But the signing is the remarkable point. All the six marks are different, yet not one is an Indian mark. Those, who are conversant with the habits of the aborigines, in this particular, know their pride is exhibited by animal or other devices, on the same principle of human nature, that led civilized men to "the boast of heraldry," to put family or fancy arms and mottoes on their seals. It may be said, that exact copies of the marks should not be expected, because we have only copy, not original of the deed, given by Belknap, and that Hazard has not distinguished the marks. I should not insist much on this circumstance, more than on Hazard's omission of the signature of one of the grantors, but that the copy, in Belknap, which has six different marks, was "corrected by a copy on file, in the superior court of New Hampshire, in the case of Allen vs. Waldron, which copy is attested by the" register of the original deed. Could any one have made for the supreme court a copy, without these *imposing* marks from the original?

Perhaps the strongest circumstance of intrinsic evidence is the attestation, on the *same* "day of May, one thousand six hundred twenty and nine, in the fifth year of our sovereign lord, Charles, king of England, Scotland, France, and Ireland, defender of the faith," etc., by *seven* English gentlemen of reputation, five of whom were afterwards *directly*, and the two others *indirectly*, as agents of Gorges in another plantation, interested against the effect of said deed, that Wahangnonaway, sagamore of Squamsquott, "in behalf of himself and the other sagamores *then present*," did "deliver quiet and peaceable possession of all the lands mentioned in the within-written deed unto the within-named John Wheelwright," and that the deed "was signed, sealed, and delivered in our presence." Yet there are two other English, gentlemen of reputation also, witnesses to signing, sealing, and delivering. Now, why did not the seven, or some of them, sign as witnesses to the first solemnity? Or why did not one or both of the witnesses to the first solemnity sign as witnesses to the last? Where was the deed executed? in the wilderness of Squamscot? or in the English settlements of Dover or Portsmouth? Wherever it was, it was all one transaction. All the nine English are made to say, they saw it signed, sealed, and delivered; yet seven only witness delivery of possession, not one of whom sign in the proper place as witnesses of signing and sealing. All the sachems are said to be present at delivery of possession, as well as at execution of the deed; yet the two English witnesses of signing and sealing say nothing of possession. They were far from home, and might stay out the after ceremony as well as the others. It is usual at Indian treaties for all parties and witnesses to remain to the end of the solemnities, especially if they occupy but one day.

I now turn to the extrinsic evidence.

A deed of 3 April, 1638, (near nine years later than the pretended one,) to Wheelwright, Edward Colcord, and Darby Field of Piscataquack, Samuel Hutchinson, and Augustus, or Augustine, Story of Boston, John Compton of Roxbury, and Nicholas Needham of Mount Wollaston, of all his right, title and interest from Merrimack to the patents of Piscataqua was made by Wehanownowit; and on the same day, and perhaps on the same paper, the same sachem by deed gave to Wheelwright and Story only almost the same exact premises, yet having a careful reservation for Massachusetts rights by the limit, "within three miles on the northern side of the river Merrimack." Colcord and Needham are witnesses, not grantees, of this deed. Both are of admirable brevity, having no idle words, yet granting a decent extent of "thirty miles square." Farmer had these documents inserted, 1824, in Vol. I. 147 of New Hampsh. Hist. Coll. This transaction, an honorable one on Wheelwright's part, furnished some instruction to the projector of the spurious instrument, whose ingenuity was not, probably, called into exercise *before* the death of Robert Mason, heir of the patentee, in 1688.

Mr. Adams says, the grantees were all here 4 October, 1639. This is to him satisfactory proof of the genuineness, to me of the falsity, of the instrument. There can be no doubt, that, if this deed be a forgery, the maker knew of Exeter combination by thirty-five persons at that time, as taken from their records by Hazard, I. 463; for his grantees' names are those of the *four first* signers with the thirty first. But it is beyond credibility, that all five, there in October, 1639, were there, and no others, in May, 1629; for in no other instance, in the whole Atlantic coast of this union, will five men, on any spot at the *first* opening of the country, be found on the same spot ten years after. At Plimouth, *half* died in *three months*. Prince, I. 85, 86. At Salem, we know, there was much mortal sickness in Endecott's little company the first year, and worse the second, after Higginson's fleet of three ships increased the colony. A melancholy tale is told by Winthrop of his companions, in the letters, Appendix, A. 47 and 49. Of our twelve first assistants in the summer of 1630, only five remained next spring, Johnson being dead in less than three months, Rossiter in less than four, Saltonstall, Coddington, Revell, T. Sharp, and Vassall gone to England. Coddington and Vassall did indeed return to America; but the former, within the *fatal* ten years, had left Boston forever, to found a new state at Rhode Island; and Vassall could not even live in Massachusetts. Ludlow and Pynchon, too, were gone within ten years. Though the latter was within the jurisdiction, at Springfield, he was too remote to continue in office. So that nine out of twelve were missing in less than the same period that all our five grantees continue to enjoy life at Exeter.

But Mr. Adams supposes, that all the grantees were here in May, 1629, and that my proof of Wheelwright's coming in 1636, for the *first* time, is a mistake. He refers to Neal and Wiggin's letter to John Mason, 13 August, 1633, Belknap's N. H., I., Appendix, 6: "Because you would have bour towns named as you desired, we have treated with a gentleman, who has purchased a tract of land of the Indians of Squamscut Falls, and your land running up to the said falls on one side of the river from the falls about a mile downward, said gentleman having a mind to said land on your side to a certain creek, and one mile backward from the river, which we agreed on, and the creek is called Wheelwright's, the gentleman's name being Wheelwright, and he was to name said plantation (when settled) Exeter." This letter is verified, seven days *after*, by Vines and Jocelyn.

But that it is a forged letter is clear as can any thing be. On the day of its date at *Northam*, which probably was not the name of Dover for seven years after, and then given in compliment to Rev. Mr. Larkham, who came from Northam in Devonshire, 1640; neither Neal, nor Wiggin, was near that place. Wiggin was in England, and embarked two or three days after in the James, Capt. Grant, and reached Salem from London, 10 Oct. 1633; while Neal embarked at Boston for England on 6 August of that year, after having been here from his government, says Winthrop, "above ten days." See pages 106, and 115 of this vol. "*In the lowest depth a lower deep*," is the exclamation of Satan in his troubles, which much resemble those of the contriver of this deception, whose sole staff was a straw, and every step upon quicksands. Of course the verification of Vines and Jocelyn for this letter, one week after its date, was a shameless falsity; yet certainly signed by neither of the pretended guarantors.

Mrs. Pierson, daughter of Wheelwright, "the more sensible and capable of the two" "very incompetent witnesses to determine the time of their father's *first* coming over into America," told Cotton Mather, "that her father's coming over with his family was in the same ship with Mr. Samuel Whiting the minister of Lynn, and others," and he adds of *them*, "who, we are all sure, came in 1636;" and that she never heard her father speak of visiting America before. Now I leave it to *judges* of probability, not to Mather, who, instead of weighing evidence, had not discretion enough to be trusted to wipe the scales, whether Wheelwright, who lived with his children forty-three years from 1636, can be presumed to have mentioned *particularly* his coming in 1636, when the country was comparatively thriving and well filled, and to have omitted the fact of his coming, in 1628, to a wilderness, which he saw, in his latter days, blossoming as the rose. I say 1628, not 1629, for no vessel in *this* year had yet brought over men to make a treaty with inland Indians. The *minute* information of the daughter was accurate. Whiting left England in April, arrived 26 May, says Mather's Life, in one of the "fifteen great ships," no doubt, mentioned by Winthrop, all in our harbor together. On 12 of June, little more than a fortnight after, our Church Records have "John Wheelwright and Mary his wife" admitted, Nos. 354, 5. In October after, he is mentioned in this History, as "a brother of Mrs. Hutchinson, one Mr. Wheelwright, a silenced minister sometimes in England." I should be pleased with a *probable* explanation of this clergyman's neglect, either to join some of our churches sooner, if he remained a few months after his purchase, or to bring over his family earlier than 1636, if, as the exquisite casuist suggests, "he had stepped over hither to see how the land lay, before his transportation of them." If he had gone back in 1629, why did he not return, if not before, at least, in the ship with his sister, Mrs. Hutchinson, and the Rev. Messieurs Lathrop and Symmes, with other good company, arriving September, 1634? See this History of that date, compared with Symmes's evidence in Hutchinson, II. 493 and 510.

Passing over, for the present, several other remarks of Mr. Adams, which will be amply answered hereafter, in the *trial of the witnesses*, I observe his difficulty about copy and original. "A copy was used in the trial of the cause in 1707," certified by the register, though the original "was not recorded until 1713." Now, when we remember, that this was the cause involving every title in the province, why was not the original brought from the other side of the river, in York? Why should the register, if the original was too precious to be trusted from one town to the next, postpone six years the recording of such a valuable instrument? How he could certify, except from his record, or how he could know the original, never heard of before, to be genuine, are questions of very little concern in that time, when the jury would believe any thing, and distinguish no more between copy and original, than if Mather had been their foreman. The power of the court was, of course, nothing.

The language of Macgregore and others, settlers of Londonderry, proves nothing but their innocence. They were not arrived till some years after the death of Allen, when this or any other forged deed, pretending an age of ninety years, became as good as a true one, nobody appearing to dispute, and every body asserting, its authenticity. The Col. Wheelwright, of whom they purchased, was grandson of our John; but he might believe the deed authentic. His right to grant may have been under the purchase of 1639, or a later one; but, if it were not, it is very clear, it could not be under the deed, of which his father knew no more than he did of my present argument. I am as well satisfied, that he was dead ten or twenty years before that deed was made, as that he lived fifty years after its pretended date.

Mr. Adams wholly avoids or mistakes my argument about Governour Winthrop's silence, which is not, that the governour said nothing about the transaction, "which took place fifteen months before" his arrival; but that Wheelwright and his associates, when, in March, 1638–9, complained of by our court for buying Winicowett of *an* Indian, knowing that we claimed and had taken possession of it, "by building an house there above *two* years since," said nothing about the transaction, did not triumphantly reply, We bought, *ten years* since, all the lands of *four* Indian sachems, from Merrimack to Piscataqua; we bought, last month, of this poor Indian, only his actual enjoyment of Winicowet, but from the sovereigns of the soil more than thirty times Winicowet, before one in seventy of your people came over the ocean. See page 290, and compare it with page 303. Who fabricated this deed, is not known to me. It was heard of first in 1707, but *not in any* of the former numerous trials of the same title. The counsel for defendant were John Pickering and Charles Story. Was Story an heir of the grantee of that name? On their side were court, witnesses, jury, and spectators, with their ears open to hear all the pathetic obtestations of the tenant for his cause and their own, and their eyes closed against any unpleasant view of the adversary's strength, or their own weakness. For the honor of God's people, and their protection against the Egyptians, this imposition of a spurious deed, if known to a few, would seem no worse than perjury, which every lawsuit, involving such interests, furnishes like a hotbed.

In reply to the observations of Gov. Plumer, most of what is said above, in answer to Mr. Adams, will be equally pertinent; and very few remarks are necessary, before the following inquiries about the witnesses. Mr. Plumer's question, "If a man is required to defend his title to *one* tract of land, is he obliged to assert and vindicate his claim to *two*?" is very wide of the point. My complaint is, that he does *not* defend his title to *the one* tract, that is Winicowet, as he would naturally do, if this deed were in existence, by saying, Winicowet is in our great purchase ten years ago. The *elder* title, and the *larger* quantity of land, I say, would have been alleged. Again, Mr. Plumer says, "the deed itself was produced in court in 1707." Now this is contrary to Mr. Adams, who says, "a copy of the deed, certified, etc., was used in the trial." This is probable; for the copy is certified by the *register* of York, not by the *clerk* of New Hampshire tribunal, in which original had been produced at the trial, but was now withdrawn. Mr. Plumer's acquaintance with law processes will satisfy him, that a court does not permit copy of a deed, after original has been used in a suit, to be substituted for original, with the verification of register of a county in a foreign province, instead of its own clerk. But, if it were original, not copy, that was used, I better understand the management, which Mather piously considers "a remarkable display and instance of the Providence of Heaven in the finding of this instrument *just before* the sitting of your last court," so that scrutiny of signatures of men, dead many years, could not be had. For so remarkable a gift of Providence, it would have been respectful to have incurred the expense of recording; but it seemed dangerous, I suppose, for the next five years and a half. Did those, whose title materially depended on it, expect Providence to continue to favor them, by preserving the deed against their own negligence; or did they think the evil of keeping it secret was much less than that of showing it? Mr. Plumer, too, repeats, from C. Mather, the assertion, "if the deed was forged, Wheelwright must have been privy to it; but the goodness of his character repels the charge." I presume the paper was forged ten or twenty years or more after his death; but whether it were earlier or later, there is no privity necessary, probable, presumable, or hardly possible. The character of Wheelwright is valued by me as highly as by Dr. Mather or Gov. Plumer; and I think it is vindicated, by showing, that he was too sensible, as well as too honest, to take or make such a conveyance. But when the pretended deed is shown to be a forgery, and never heard of till it was wanted, and could be in some degree safely produced, a quarter of a century after he was in his grave, how can any stain attach to his character? No doubt there is guilt somewhere, but it may be too late to ascertain, whether it belong to the counsel in the cause, or to the agent of the province, who applied to the ambiguous oracle at Boston, or to some other dealer in such spells and necromancy. Mather had doubts of its forgery, yet encouraged the use of it.

In the No. of the Genealogical Reg. for Oct. 1850, p. 321, the writer of Notes on the Wentworth Family, well known to be Hon. John Wentworth of Chicago, says he was "informed by S. G. Drake, Esq., of Boston, that original documents have been exhibited to him, which conclusively prove the authenticity of this deed." Ten quarterly Nos. of that interesting periodical have appeared since, and the Editor has given his readers not a word of those documents. However, in the Dover Enquirer of 22 Oct. 1850, a writer under the signature of Passaconaway, who may be the same diligent Editor, complains, that the last week's paper had said, that Edward Colcord first came over in 1631; and to his own apparent conviction proves that he was here in 1629, by the deed, I call spurious, made that year to Wheelwright and others. He gives a deposition of Wheelwright, 13 Oct. 1663, that he, "with some others that were set down at Exeter, did employ Edward Colcord to purchase, etc., of the Indians, for which they gave him ten or twelve pounds in money, and had a grant thereof signed by some sagamores with their marks upon it, of which Runawit was one." It may be, that the name of the Indian was Watchanowett, who on the back of Wehanownowit's *great* deed, published by Farmer, as before said, gave confirmation of that grant, 10 April, 1639, and therein specially granted "all the meadows and grounds extending for the space of *one English mile* on the East side of Oyster river." Such a mistake of a strange name, after a lapse of four and twenty years, would not be surprising, especially as the witness refers only to his memory. But it is necessary for the support of this *disputed* deed to make the memory hold almost ten years longer.

Gov. Plumer had ingeniously replied to the argument against the instrument, from the unlikelihood of Wentworth being a grantee, by reason of his youth, that "though minors are not capable of giving, they are of receiving deeds." Still I feel confidence in the objection, for so large a principality would hardly be given to four men, (as this case shows,) of whom he, named the third in order, was only sixteen years old. He died in 1697, and though we know not his precise years, he had *first* of *eight* children, Samuel, born in 1640 or '41, and in 1693 had been, *about eighty years of age*, engaged to preach at Exeter, says his descendant. But if Wentworth might be supposed to partake, though a minor, in the benefit of that deed, what reason could Wheelwright and others have for employing *Edward Colcord* in such very important transaction before 17 May, 1629, when he was younger than Wentworth, indeed a mere stripling? Colcord died, we find, 10 Feb. 1682, aged 67. He was therefore born 1615 or '16; and certainly may be thought hardly fourteen years old, when by the construction, to which Wheelwright's deposition is tortured, he obtained the pretended grant.

Patiently I can wait for the coming of those "original documents," "which conclusively prove the authenticity of this deed," and easily conceive the delight that Mr. Drake must feel in correcting his long cherished error, as in the eighth edition of his Book of the Indians, III. 138, Boston, 1841, he shows, that one of these grantors, Rowls, sachem of Newichawanock "gave no such deed at the time specified."

Before the production of these documents, which may turn out, at last, as several of the accessories of the 1629 deed were, only bold forgeries, I would request him, and all others, that care enough for the truth of this matter to take slight pains to reach it, to inquire of their almanacs, what day of the week was the 17 May, 1629.

In his careful reply to the writer in the Portsmouth Journal of 22 Nov. 1823, who perhaps was my early departed friend, N. A. Haven, Gov. Plumer said, hazardously, "it is not objected to the witnesses of delivery of possession, that they were not then in this country." Let us examine the assertion in its several parts.

Of the nine English witnesses, in whose presence this deed is attested to be signed, sealed, and delivered, 17 May, 1629, I believe we may entertain very strong doubts, whether more than one was then in this country.

1. John Oldham came in the Ann, 1623, to Plimouth, is first mentioned in 1624, by Bradford, in Prince, I. 149, and Morton's Memorial, 74, from which latter Hubbard, 92–94, takes his narrative. In 1625 he lived at Nantasket, (Hubbard, 107,) having, in March, undergone ludicrous and severe punishment for his injurious treatment of Plimouth colony, (Bradford in Prince, I. 153). The next year his character, or at least his conduct, improved, "and we give him liberty," says the Gov. Ib. 158, "to come and converse with us when he pleases." So high did he stand, next year, with the saints he had formerly troubled, that Gov. Bradford, sending to his majesty's council, from Plimouth, 9 June, 1628, the letter about arrest and sending home of Morton, the anarchist, says in it, "this bearer, Mr. John Oldham, who can give your honors further information upon his oath, if need so require, whom we have sent with the prisoner, and to attend your lordships' pleasures," 1 Hist. Coll. III. 63. Morton, we are told, came back next year; but I shall now show, that Oldham, before June, at least, did *not:* 1. It is *highly improbable*, from Sullivan's Maine, 219, reciting the grant in 1629, from the Earl of Warwick, Lord Gorges, Sir Ferd. Gorges, and Thomas Smith, of the territory between Cape Elizabeth and Cape

Porpoise, to John Oldham and Richard Vines, of which livery of seizin was given in 1630, in which grant their undertaking to transport fifty persons thither, must imply their presence in England. 2. It is *impossible;* for, in our venerable Colony Records, then kept in London, at a meeting of the governour and company, 2 March, 1628–9, is this passage: "Touching John Oldham, the governour was ordered to confer with him upon any indifferent course, that might not be prejudicial to the company." Three days after is this record: "5 March. A new proposition being made in the behalf of Mr. Oldham, to be entertained by this company, it was deferred to farther consideration." On 10 of same month, only five days later, the names are given of a large committee "once more to confer with Mr. John Oldham." On "11 May, 1629. This day Mr. Oldham propounded unto Mr. White, that he would have his patent examined, and it's agreed by the court, not to have any treaty with him about it, by reason it's thought, he doth it not out of love but out of some sinister respect." Certainly John Oldham was all this time in London. For these extracts, the New Hampshire gentlemen may rely on my accuracy. But in Hazard, I. 256–268, is the general letter of our governour and company in London to their agent, John Endecott, at Salem, 17 April, 1629, from Gravesend, in which, page 258, may be read, "Mr. John Oldham came from New England not long before your arrival there," [E. arrived September, 1628, and O. had carried the charges, from all our plantations, to his Majesty's council, against Morton, as in Bradford is shown,] "by whom we have had no small distraction in our business, having been cast behind, at the least, two months time in our voyage, through the variety of his vast conceits of extraordinary gain," etc., etc. The voyage was that of the three ships, with Skelton, Higginson, Samuel Sharp, etc., by whom came this letter. They proceed, "Finding him" [Oldham] "a man altogether unfit for us to deal with, we have at last left him to his own way; and, as we are informed, he, with some others, *are providing a vessel and is minded, as soon as he can despatch, to come* for New England," etc., etc., through forty lines it cannot be necessary to transcribe. There is a P. S. to said letter of 21 April, and from the postscript to the P. S. page 268, probably by Gov. Cradock, I am sure every one would infer, that Oldham was still there. Now, what becomes of the confidence, that Oldham *might* have witnessed the deed 17 May of that year? Our ships, that left him in England, arrived in the latter part of June.

2. Samuel Sharp was passenger, with Samuel Skelton, in the George Bonadventure, one of the abovementioned three ships, and she was de-

tained at the Isle of Wight till 4 May, and arrived at Salem 23 June. See in the foregoing letter, in Haz. I. page 262, "We have caused a common seal to be made, which we send you by Mr. Sharpe," and, page 265, "If, at the arrival of *this* ship, Mr. Endecott should be departed this life, (which God forbid,) or should happen to die before the other ships arrive, we authorize you, Mr. Skelton, and Mr. Samuel Sharpe, to take care of our affairs, and to govern the people," etc. The P. S. is of 21 April, page 266, "The aforewritten is, for the most part, the copy of our general letter, sent you, together with our patent, under the broad seal, and the company's seal in silver, by Mr. Samuel Sharpe, passenger in the George, who, we think, is yet riding in the Hope; but, by means of stormy weather, the Talbot and the Lion's Whelp are yet at Blackwall. By these ships, that are to follow, we intend," &c. See, also, the next letter of our governour and company, "London, 28 May, 1629," with P. S. Gravesend, 3 June, Haz. I. 277–285: "Our last unto you was of the 17th and 21st April, sent by the last ships, viz. the George Bonadventure, Thomas Cox master, who set sail from the Isle of Wight the 4th of this month, and seconded by the Talbot, Thomas Beecher master, and the Lion's Whelp, John Gibbs master, who set sail also from the Isle of Wight about the 11th of this month," &c. This letter came by a new expedition of three ships, in one of which, perhaps, John Oldham might have passage, though probably his views, adverse to our company, led him to seek other conveyance, it may be in the vessel he was providing. We have Higginson's own journal in print, kept with the exactness of a log book for each day. It is republished in the invaluable Chronicles of Mass. 213–59, and the rare Collection of Hutchinson, pages 32–44. The sailing of the Talbot, in which he was embarked, and the Lion's Whelp together, on 11 May, from the Isle of Wight, is recorded; and on Tuesday, 30 June, "being come into the harbour" [of Salem,] "we saw the George, to our great comfort, then," [quere *there?*] "being come on Tuesday, which was seven days before us." Now Mr. Plumer, as every body else, must see, that our Samuel Sharp, in the George Bonadventure, coming from the Isle of Wight to Salem, between 4 May and 23 June, could not sign his name to this instrument 17 of the same May. But I am filled with admiration at his suggestion against the identity, that "another man of the same name might then be in this country, and in fact subscribe as a witness." What! *two* Samuel Sharps in New England before the first of July, 1629! I beg the gentlemen of the other side to inquire, how few more on that day than eight hundred English there were on the whole continent, between Newfoundland and Virginia. The computation may take infant Salem, as the most populous, except Plimouth, then eight years and a half old, two hundred; the rest of Massachusetts, one hundred and fifty, (Higginson, in Hutch. Coll. 47, makes "in all, old and new planters, three hundred," and I give in sixteen per cent.;) Plimouth, "near three hundred," is the boast of their friends, Prince, I. 197; and there was less than one hundred and fifty in the rest of one thousand miles of Atlantic coast, counting from five to fifty at Pemaquid, Portsmouth, Dover, Cape Ann, Weymouth, and any other cabin east of Virginia. There are now above two millions and a half of people in New England alone, of whom I crave an enumeration of all that bear the exact name of Samuel Sharp. Will there be four thousand? or four hundred? or forty? It is not, and never was, a common English *sirname*; and the name of baptism is not, probably, united with this sirname more than once in twenty. Of the representatives of New Hampshire in 1824, eleven in two hundred and eleven, are Samuels. Mr. Plumer has no hesitation in proving *John* Wheelwright's purchase in May, 1629, when there were not five hundred English between Virginia and Canada, by a letter of Neal and Wiggin, (by Farmer ascertained to be a forgery, to aid the great one,) about *Mr.* Wheelwright, 13 August, 1633, when there were near five thousand; but he thinks *a* Samuel Sharp might have been a witness on that earlier day, though we prove, that the only one of that name, heard of in our first ten years' history, was then on the ocean. If it were to be regarded, however, as a possibility, that there was a Samuel Sharp at Piscataqua or its neighbourhood 17 May, 1629, how greatly multiplied are the chances against *another* John Oldham, — a name of much rarer occurrence! Yet these are the formal witnesses to signing, sealing, and delivering a deed, when each was some thousands of miles distant. I say each was absent, for the identity of both these, so well known persons, must be presumed. How many hundreds of millions to one against the presumption, is not a matter for my arithmetical powers. Something like such a calculation may be seen in the letters of Herbert Marsh, the late Bishop of Llandaff, and Margaret Professor of Divinity, to Travis, the unhappy archdeacon, whose blunders were the occasion of calling out from Porson the most extraordinary union of perspicacious argument, witty sarcasm, and profound erudition, that our language can exhibit. Can an alibi be better made out? Can a forgery of near two hundred years old be better detected?

3. "Walter Neal, governour," "came in the bark Warwick this summer" [1630] "to Pascataqua, sent as governour there for Sir F. Gorges and others." See page 39 of this History, compared with page 7. It may be guessed, that he had been there before, and went back to

England soon after 17 May, 1629. Might we not presume, he had not before been "governour," the title of the verification? I say, he had never been there, though, unless he were governour, the deed must fall; and quote the language, "humbly presented and submitted by the governour and company of Massachusetts Bay to the king's most excellent majesty," 6 September, 1676, on the solemn subject of our exercise of jurisdiction over New Hampshire adverse to Gorges and Mason, Belknap's N. H., I., Appendix, 14: "Our first exercise of jurisdiction being in the year 1641, eight years after Capt. Neale, agent for Mr. Mason, had wholly deserted the improvement of land and the government of the country, which, indeed, he never used but one year; for in the year 1630 *he first came over*, and in the year 1634 he quitted the place, and in the interim neglected the same, in making a voyage for England," etc.

4. "George Vaughan, factor," seems liable to most of the objection against Neal, governour. I know not when he came first to our country, but presume it was not so early. He left in August, 1634, and there is nothing to be found, but this deed, to render it probable, he had then passed three years here. The very next article to this famous deed, in the Appendix, is a letter from Eyre, of the company of Laconia, to Mr. Gibbons, their *factor*," dated last of May, 1631. Eyre's letter informs Gibbons, that they now "send you a factor to take charge of the trade goods." Was not this factor, coming out in July, 1631, George Vaughan? In the disputed attestation, Gibbons is called trader, as Neal is governour, and Vaughan factor, "for the company of Laconia." Now, if Neal were not sent governour by the company until 1630, it may be presumed, the factor *and* trader had not their appointments sooner. It appears probable, contrary to Belknap, N. H., I. 14, that the company of Laconia was not formed till six months after the date of this deed.

5. "Ambrose Gibbons, trader," came with Neal in the bark Warwick, having written to Eyre, 8 April, 1630, from Plimouth in Old England, 21 July and 14 August, 1630, from Piscataqua. See Eyre's letter in Belknap's N. H., I., Appendix, 2. I conclude, he then came for the *first* time, because his "wife and children" were sent next year; and if he had been here, with appointment from Mason or Gorges, in 1629, then gone to England, and come back, he would, on his *second* voyage, have brought them.

6 and 7. "Richard Vines, governour, and Richard Bonighton, assistant of the plantation at Saco." What a goodly *outside* falsehood hath! But this outside is decorated in such a manner as to lead to detection.

Had the names *alone* been given, some doubt might have remained about these persons. But the offices and the residence are both fatal. Vines was here, as an explorer, many years before any settlement, according to Belknap, Amer. Biog. I. 354–356, and his back might be thought broad enough to carry Bonighton, who is never heard of till long after this deed. But Vines, with Oldham, was, I think, in England, in 1629, taking grant of land here, not possession, till 1630. The appointment of Vines as governour, and of Bonighton, as assistant, of the plantation, which is the important point, was not made till 2 September, 1639. See the commission in Hazard, I., 458–462. Sir Thomas Josselyn, who stands before Vines, did not come over. I know, that that commission from Sir F. Gorges is for the province of Maine "from the entrance of Piscataqua harbor unto the River of Sagadahock;" but I deny, that Vines was governour and Bonighton assistant under any other commission. Further, Saco was not settled till some years after this deed. See 2 Hist. Coll. IV. 187, and Hubbard, 214.

8. "Thomas Wiggin, agent," was not here, probably, for two years after this signing his name. Hubbard, 221, makes him *begin* his plantation in 1631; and when the exact truth is found out by the New Hampshire gentlemen, perhaps, it will show Hubbard's correctness.

9. "Edward Hilton, steward," was, probably, at Piscataqua, and the only one of these nine witnesses, who, we may reasonably believe, was there 17 May, 1629. But we may as reasonably doubt his signature, as that of the others. If the other signatures are disbelieved, in any degree, on account of the description given, by themselves, of themselves, in the attestation, Hilton's is equally suspicious. His is the latest of the subscriptions to witness the delivery of a deed, that destroyed all his title to estate, in the enjoyment of which he had peacefully lived six or seven years; and he must have known that all the preceding eight signatures were fictitious, that the ceremony he was called to verify was a fraud on himself, and on unborn generations. It was false, that such grantors, and grantees, and witnesses were present around him; and his hand could only have been affixed in a *mesmeric* sleep, before mesmerism was invented. These shadowy platoons of Indians and English never were mustered, before he had many years lain in his grave. Our only account of him, for several years, is from Hubbard, 214, and if Wiggin and the others did not come before June, 1629, Hilton was entitled to be called governour, instead of steward; for Mason had not sent over any body superior to him.

As in the question about the date of Roger Williams's Charter, mistaken by Callender, and *twice* misprinted by the Rhode Island

Historical Society, which is stated in full on p. 193 of the next volume, a recurrence to the almanac for the year settled the question; so the aid of chronology decides this dispute. Neither Wheelwright, nor Wentworth, the purchasers, nor Sharp, nor Neal, nor Gibbons, nor Wiggin, nor Hilton, the witnesses, could have partaken in such a transaction on 17 May, 1629, because that day was Sunday. We may almost count this above all the rest of the testimony, certainly instar omnium. On the Lord's day the execution of a deed, or of a criminal, would have been as shocking to the sentiment of our fathers, as I trust it will ever be to their descendants.

The writer, of the Dover Enquirer, "in the name of Passaconaway," deeply regrets that Mr. Farmer "should have so far acquiesced in the mere assertion that the Wheelwright deed was a forgery, as to have bent his otherwise very valuable edition of Dr. Belknap's History down to it;" and to vindicate his phrase of *mere assertion*, he adds, "because there never has been an argument against the validity of that deed, but what was built upon ASSUMED PREMISES." Now these premises are the following facts, which are, severally, independent, and indisputable, any one of them inconsistent with the truth of that document:

1. By the almanac for 1629, the 17th day of May, the date of the spurious deed, was Sunday.

2. John Oldham, the first English witness to signing, sealing, and delivering of said deed, in the wilderness of New Hampshire, was six days before in London, making proposition to our governour and company.

3. Samuel Sharp, the only other English witness to the signing, etc., of said deed, was on board the ship at the Isle of Wight, with Rev. Mr. Skelton, which was there detained, on 4 of the same month of May, and, in the same ship, reached Salem on 23 June after.

4. Walter Neal, governour for Sir F. Gorges, first came over in 1630, according to the declaration, made by our governour and company in Sept. 1676, to the king in council; yet he is called the first witness to delivery of possession on said 17 May, 1629.

5. Richard Vines, governour of the plantation at Saco, another witness, by this designation of governour, etc., to the delivery of possession, was not appointed such governour, until more than ten years had run, scil. 2 Sept. 1639.

6. Richard Bonighton, another witness to the delivery of possession on 17 May, 1629, described as assistant of the plantation at Saco, was not appointed to that office before Sept. 1639.

7. Wheelwright himself, in a deposition 15 April, 1668, printed by

Farmer in Belknap, p. 7, swears to a *totally different* purchase of the Indians, "when I, with others, *first came to* sit down at Exeter;" and Edward Colcord and Samuel Dudley testify to the same, and, moreover and above all, their purchase, so described, quadrates with the deed of 3 April, 1638.

From the foregoing not "ASSUMED PREMISES," but all inherent in the instrument itself, we may justly look further to facts, that, however collateral, are most intimately associated with that deed, being part of the papers in the recorder's office of Rockingham county, published by Dr. Belknap, as justificatory muniments of his work. Perhaps every body would admit, certainly Passaconaway might boast, that the letter, purporting to be by Neal and Wiggin from Northam, 13 Aug. 1633, to their friend and master, John Mason, governour of Portsmouth, Eng., relating to division of lands at Piscataqua, had as intimate relation to the Wheelwright deed of May, 1629, as that of child to its parent. Now, Farmer, in his Ed. of Belknap, p. 13, has, by five independent proofs, demonstrated that the letter "was fabricated for the purpose of supporting the Indian deed." Yet it is a fact, that the New Hampshire adepts in fraud, well knowing the value of this fabricated letter, show a deed under the hands and seals of Richard Vines and Henry Jocelyn, SEVEN DAYS AFTER, to verify by their act, and *at the desire of said Neal and Wiggin*, (so many hundreds and thousands of miles that day distant,) that same *true copy compared with the original*, "to LIE in our files of records." Is there a man, competent to draw an inference, who will doubt, that this deed of Vines and Jocelyn of 20 Aug. 1633, is a palpable forgery? Still, it seemed good to the chief manager to have a little more counterfeiting, and he can and does produce before us "an original letter of G. Vaughan to Mr. Gibbens," of 20 Aug. 1634, just 365 days later than Vines and Jocelyn's hands and seals. It is article X. of appendix to Belkn. I., written from Boston, where he was waiting for a wind to go to England, which did indeed favor the *true* George Vaughan A YEAR LATER; and he incloses to his friend G. "the division of the towns, and the copy of what Neal and Wiggin wrote home." What a splendid fabric of fraud! From the vast Cyclopæan walls that encircle the larger part of New Hampshire, running through the depths of the ocean to include Isles of Shoals, laid with diabolical skill 17 May, 1629, rises the graceful Ionic superstructure of frost work by Neal and Wiggin, of 13 Aug. 1633, decorated, on 20 of the same month, with the airy ornaments of Vines and Jocelyn, and at last the glory of the architect is fixed forever by the halo pinnacle of petty forgery in G. Vaughan 20 Aug. 1634.

If Passaconaway should visit Rome, he might find, among the archives of the Vatican, a letter from Ovid, in his banishment on the Euxine, earnestly imploring clemency of the emperor for a change at least in the place of his exile, and suggesting the benefit of deportation to the milder climate of Cayenne, or a preference for compulsory labors at Norfolk Island, or in the workshops of our Charlestown penitentiary. Perhaps a certificate is filed with it, in which George Psalmanazar and Eleazer Williams assure him of the safe arrival of his two children by the last steamer from Tomi, and that his request for their vaccination should be forthwith obeyed; that the boys had indeed been in great peril at the battle of Lepanto, of which they partook one morning in play hours, and received so many shots between wind and water in their bark, as to cause her to founder, when all their hard gingerbread was lost, but they were taken off by a submarine boat, sent the week before from New England, for this purpose, by Cotton Mather, under command of his coxswain, William Phips. For the land speculation, in which he had employed them, they rejoice to assure him, that one of the towns was named Dauphiny, another Formosa, adjoining Cape Cod, which the general court of Wisconsin had incorporated by the name of Gloucester, out of regard to his uncle the duke, and the fourth town was to be called Shanghæ, from the beauty of its fowl meadows. Here was already established, they say, a noble amphitheatre for gladiatorial shows, with fine gas-light fixtures and anthracite furnaces, the whole to be superintended by William Shakspeare and Dr. Franklin, who had each taken large share in the stock; and they close their advice with promise to send him a kraken and two poulicans to extend his profitable fisheries in the Black Sea. Should a slight suspicion of the authenticity of poor Ovid's epistle break in upon his mind from the water mark of the paper being London, A. D. 1697, he must thereupon conclude that, although the doleful theme belonged to the Tristia, the venerable new-found MS. should rather be transcribed for the next edition of the Metamorphoses.

Degrees in confidence or disbelief ought to be marked by the amount of examination bestowed on the subject of inquiry; yet in the whole round of experience we see, that the quality of the affections, or the state of the mind, does most materially affect, and sometimes wholly pervert, the judgment, after more or less of investigation. Whether my final opinion on the authenticity of the Wheelwright deed be the result of sober research, or inveterate prejudice, its origin is truly stated in the opening sentences of this article; and that it received the concurrence of Mason, Smith, Webster, Atherton, Haven, Cutter, Kelly, and Farmer, men who could not, on such a subject at least, be clouded by interest or passion, was no ways unexpected, though not one nor all of them strengthened my belief. A single opponent appears, but without giving us the benefit of publishing his reasons. It seems to me, that no child-like trust in authority leads him to repose confidence in the integrity of the document, but heroic hardihood of struggle against argument, and manly resistance of conviction. Many people would derive benefit from a moderate dose of skepticism, taken once a quarter; but how vainly may his physician prescribe that course to a hero, whose ostrich stomach can digest a New England gorgon, killed thirty years ago, and then two hundred years old, as was told by the Journal of Portsmouth, where the venomous monster was born and brought up. Still, the right of suspension of judgment is the more to be reverenced, as we find the power of such suspension to be rare; yet to differ from every body else in opinion, on a matter of fact, is but a slender claim to distinction. One gains credit for it from a smaller number than that of those who doubt his sincerity. Even if sincere, such credulousness is not always ludicrous; much more when it is affected, should it be thought pitiable. His intrepidity of belief will, indeed, excite a temporary surprise; still it must not aspire to be preserved in memory of the present or the next generation, with the same wonder as will ever attach to the impudence of the forgery.

I close this examination without other remarks, though very much more presumptive evidence of the fabrication, long after its date, could easily be furnished, and may be imagined. An apology is, perhaps, due to readers for its great length. But two gentlemen, at least, in New Hampshire, could not have complained of the deference shown by me to their opinions, nor slighted the labor bestowed in proving them erroneous. Neither Gov. Plumer, nor Mr. Adams, to my knowledge, made addition to their rejoinders, herein printed, or attempted ever to rebut the facts and arguments they drew from me. Both were probably convinced, if not by this tedious statement, as my former edition gave it, by the brief, yet forcible, exhibition of the matter in Farmer's edition of Belknap, 1831; and lived not long enough to change their belief.

END OF VOL. I.

www.ingramcontent.com/pod-product-compliance
Lightning Source LLC
LaVergne TN
LVHW021303110826
845150LV00003B/461

* 9 7 8 1 4 2 5 5 5 9 6 9 4 *